MW01199227

University of Colorado **Boulder**

U18307 3385869

CICERO, *POST REDITUM* SPEECHES

Cicero,
Post reditum Speeches

Introduction, Text, Translation, and Commentary

GESINE MANUWALD

Great Clarendon Street, Oxford, OX2 6DP,
United Kingdom

Oxford University Press is a department of the University of Oxford.
It furthers the University's objective of excellence in research, scholarship,
and education by publishing worldwide. Oxford is a registered trade mark of
Oxford University Press in the UK and in certain other countries

© Gesine Manuwald 2021

The moral rights of the author have been asserted.

First Edition published in 2021

Impression: 1

All rights reserved. No part of this publication may be reproduced, stored in
a retrieval system, or transmitted, in any form or by any means, without the
prior permission in writing of Oxford University Press, or as expressly permitted
by law, by licence or under terms agreed with the appropriate reprographics
rights organization. Enquiries concerning reproduction outside the scope of the
above should be sent to the Rights Department, Oxford University Press, at the
address above.

You must not circulate this work in any other form
and you must impose this same condition on any acquirer.

Published in the United States of America by Oxford University Press
198 Madison Avenue, New York, NY 10016, United States of America

British Library Cataloguing in Publication Data
Data available

Library of Congress Control Number: 2021932112

ISBN 978–0–19–885075–5

Printed and bound by
CPI Group (UK) Ltd, Croydon, CR0 4YY

Links to third party websites are provided by Oxford in good faith and
for information only. Oxford disclaims any responsibility for the materials
contained in any third party website referenced in this work.

Preface

Cicero's 'exile' was a major event in his biography, but one that he would have preferred to be glossed over in certain contexts or to be considered only from the perspective from which he wanted it to be seen. The speeches composed for his return to Rome (*Post reditum in senatu* and *Post reditum ad Quirites*) are important elements in the campaign for the latter, as they establish Cicero's interpretation of the reasons and circumstances for his departure and return. They are thus telling documents for Cicero's self-portrayal, and, as political speeches of thanks, they are also unique examples of a particular type of oratory at Rome. This volume, providing a general introduction, a reconsidered Latin text, a new English translation, and a full-scale commentary, aims to bring these orations and the issues arising from them back into the discussion, now that these speeches have been confirmed to be genuine. The book also includes the speech *Pridie quam in exilium iret*, doubtless a spurious item, so as to combine all the texts connected with Cicero's departure from and return to Rome in a single volume and enable comparisons between authentic and non-authentic texts from this context.

A number of people have directly or indirectly supported the preparation of this volume. Again I was able to work on this project in the collegial atmosphere of the Department of Greek and Latin at University College London (UCL) and had the opportunity to discuss various aspects of it with colleagues. Beyond London, particular thanks are due to Tom Keeline, who kindly read an earlier version of the entire manuscript and made numerous helpful comments, and to Anthony Corbeill, who generously shared thoughts on the corpus of Cicero's post-exile speeches and the spurious oration. The team at Oxford University Press, particularly Charlotte Loveridge, were enthusiastic about the project from the start and helpful throughout.

London, January 2021   G.M.

Contents

Introduction

1. PREVIOUS SCHOLARSHIP AND THIS COMMENTARY

In the two speeches *Post reditum in senatu* (*RS*) and *Post reditum ad Quirites* (*RQ*) Marcus Tullius Cicero (106–43 BCE) expresses gratitude towards the Senate and the People respectively after his return to Rome in 57 BCE, following his enforced absence ('exile') since spring 58 BCE, and presents his version of the events in those years with a view to re-establishing his position. Cicero's withdrawal from Rome had occurred in the context of a backlash, spearheaded by the Tribune of the People P. Clodius Pulcher, against the treatment of some of the Catilinarian conspirators at the end of Cicero's consular year of 63 BCE.

These two speeches belong to a group of four thematically linked Ciceronian orations (including also *De domo sua* and *De haruspicum responsis*), all of which were regarded as spurious for a long time; when their genuineness was questioned in the eighteenth and nineteenth centuries, these speeches were studied almost exclusively with respect to textual and linguistic issues in the context of this debate on authenticity (see Introduction, section 3.1). While scholars now consider these orations to be genuine (especially after T. Zielinski's studies on prose rhythm, published in 1904), they are still not widely read, perhaps because the authenticity debate has tarnished them and, even when viewed as genuine items, they are thought to be slightly unusual and not to be Cicero's best speeches. Therefore, it has been observed that these speeches have been fairly neglected and that no adequate commentaries exist,[1] while they feature as sources in historical works and biographies of Cicero.

---

[1] See, e.g., Courtney 1960, 95: 'Though no one now accepts the opinion of Markland and Wolf that the speeches *Post Reditum in Senatu, Post Reditum ad Quirites, De Domo, De Haruspicum Responso* are not by Cicero, and the reaction started early, yet the prosecution's case seems to have cast a shadow over them, and with the exception of the *De Domo* they have hardly been treated by Cicero's editors with the same care as the rest of his works.'; Webster 1992 (rev. of Shackleton Bailey 1991): 'The post-reditum speeches are among the most neglected, and most misunderstood, of Cicero's works.'; Berry 1995, 36: 'Until now, virtually nothing has been written on *Sen.* and *Pop.*, except as touching on the question of their genuineness (a matter finally settled only by Zielinski's *Clauselgesetz* in 1904). Unusually for Cicero, there is not even a Victorian school edition.'; Craig 1995, 70–1: 'Yet they have been largely ignored until very recently, in part because of the long-settled debate over their authenticity ... the historical and rhetorical importance of these relatively neglected speeches'; Dyck 2004, 313: 'The speeches Cicero delivered within a year of his return from exile have found little favour with critics.'; 307 n. 38: 'One feels acutely the lack of a modern commentary on this speech [*RQ*], as on its counterpart, *Red. sen.*; ... '; Boll 2019, 3: 'Bei der Rede *cum senatui gratias egit* zeigt sich eine ungerechtfertigte, große Lücke in der modernen Ciceroforschung. Sie wird—besonders im Vergleich zu den meisten anderen Werken in Ciceros Corpus—wohl schon wegen ihrer Kürze und der inhaltlichen Überschneidungen zu späteren, berühmteren

More recently, some researchers have stressed that these speeches are of historical and rhetorical interest as they show Cicero taking steps to regain his position in Rome, displaying his virtuosity in a less common rhetorical genre, operating sophisticated argumentative techniques to present himself as a hero rather than a victim, and adumbrating themes relevant in the following decade.[2] Accordingly, J. Nicholson (1992, 131) concludes: 'For these reasons, the orations *Post reditum* deserve to be rescued from the oblivion to which the old critics mistakenly banished them.'

J. Nicholson's monograph (1992; a revision of a 1991 PhD thesis) on the two speeches *Post reditum in senatu* and *Post reditum ad Quirites* as well as D. R. Shackleton Bailey's translation (1991) of the group of four speeches (plus *Pro Sestio* and *In Vatinium*) represent important attempts to do justice to these speeches and make them more accessible. These works were followed by articles in the 1990s and 2000s, mainly on Cicero's presentation of himself or the themes and motifs used across the group of speeches, and then the monograph by R. Raccanelli (2012). Both books on these orations review the history of scholarship, consider aspects of the speeches' rhetorical genre and argumentative structure, survey the individuals mentioned, and discuss Cicero's relationship to them.

Since the publication of the Teubner edition of the Latin text of the four speeches by T. Maslowski (1981) there had hardly been any work on textual or linguistic issues. The only existing aids to reading the text until recently were Latin commentaries from the nineteenth century and brief Italian commentaries from the middle of the twentieth century, as well as annotated translations into various modern languages also from the twentieth century. In late 2019 a commentary on *Post reditum in senatu* in German by T. Boll (a revision of a PhD thesis) appeared, which includes detailed discussions of textual, rhetorical, and historical issues. The publication of this volume represents a step forward towards fully exploring these speeches, though it only covers one of the orations and does not have sufficient space for in-depth analysis throughout.

Thus, the time seems ripe to bring together textual and linguistic observations from the eighteenth and nineteenth centuries (valuable, even though often made in the context of the authenticity debate) and modern approaches to Ciceronian oratory and thus produce a commentary that will give both these speeches an up-to-date scholarly tool and thus hopefully encourage people interested in Republican oratory and history to engage with them more thoroughly. This commentary focuses on the two speeches *Post reditum in senatu* and *Post reditum ad Quirites*, since these are immediately connected with

---

Reden bisher immer noch stiefmütterlich behandelt. Ein moderner Kommentar liegt zu ihr, wie auch zu der Parallelrede an das Volk, nicht vor.'

[2] See, e.g., Nicholson 1992, 131; Webster 1992 (rev. of Shackleton Bailey 1991); Dyck 2004, 313–14.

Cicero's return and display a specific rhetorical nature as a result of their context of delivery.[3]

The *Oratio pridie quam in exilium iret* also belongs to the thematic complex of Cicero's departure from and return to Rome in 58–57 BCE. This speech is generally taken to be spurious, and its peculiarities in language, style, and content confirm this assessment (see Introduction, section 4). Nevertheless, this text is a valuable complement to the orations *Post reditum in senatu* and *Post reditum ad Quirites*: it enables comparison between what might have been said before leaving (according to someone's imagination) and what was said upon Cicero's return; it allows an insight into how motifs perceived as characteristic of Cicero's presentation of his departure from Rome and its reasons have been adjusted to an earlier point in time within the same sequence of events (supplemented by further material); and the analysis of a truly inauthentic speech from the same context alongside the speeches now accepted as genuine can confirm the validity of this view.

This oration has attracted even less scholarly attention than the genuine *post reditum*-speeches, probably because of its spuriousness.[4] At least there is a separate modern edition by M. De Marco (1991, developing an earlier edition of 1967). After a series of articles by L. Gamberale (1979; 1997; 1998) the speech has recently been discussed in a study by T. J. Keeline (2018) and an article by A. Corbeill (2020). Its resurfacing may be linked to increasing interest in the early reception of Cicero and in issues of authorship.

Therefore, including the speech in this edition should help to open up further avenues of enquiry and assemble all oratorical material immediately connected with Cicero's leaving Rome and returning to the city in a single volume.

2. HISTORICAL BACKGROUND

The speeches *Post reditum in senatu* and *Post reditum ad Quirites* illustrate Cicero's reaction to his return to Rome in September 57 BCE. His departure and subsequent return ultimately were a consequence of events during Cicero's consulship in 63 BCE.[5]

---

[3] Commentaries on *De domo sua* and *De haruspicum responsis* are currently being prepared by other scholars. – This commentary was begun before the work by T. Boll (2019) appeared.

[4] See, e.g., Rouse/Reeve 1983, 58 n. 11: 'Altogether it has aroused remarkably little curiosity'; Nicholson 1992, 7 n. 17 (p. 134): '…, but the *Ante iret in exilium* remains very little noticed'.

[5] For modern biographies of Cicero covering his entire life (including further bibliography and references to ancient sources), see, e.g., Shackleton Bailey 1971; Rawson 1975; Mitchell 1979/1991; Fuhrmann 1992; Lintott 2008; Tempest 2011; for a chronology of events relating to Cicero's life and activities, see Marinone 2004.

The political and social framework, the main events, and the major trials of the 60s and 50s BCE are fairly well documented; yet almost all the evidence derives from the writings of Cicero or later sources based on these. Thus, it is possible to establish most of the historical facts; in terms of identifying reasons, motivations, and characteristics of the main figures involved, Cicero's tendentious interpretation and presentation have to be taken into account. Moreover, Cicero's comments were made over a period of time, with changing political circumstances, and in a variety of contexts with their individual constraints and with different aims. Thus, nuances and emphases vary; nevertheless, one may establish a core version (with some divergences that can be explained) by putting the various pieces of evidence together. Cicero's account of the sequence of events promoted after his return is what R. A. Kaster (2006, 1) has called the 'standard version', to indicate that it is a sketch created by Cicero, and what Kaster (2009) elsewhere describes as a passionate performance, highlighting its choreography designed for maximum impact for pragmatic reasons and for Cicero to present himself as a 'figure of consensus' within Republican ideology. In what follows both what can be regarded as historical facts and Cicero's view and presentation of them will be outlined as far as possible.[6]

When Cicero was elected as one of the consuls for 63 BCE, as a 'new man' (*homo novus*), unanimously, and at the earliest possible opportunity after reaching the required minimum age, as he stresses (Cic. *Leg. agr.* 2.3), he was proud of this achievement. In the febrile political atmosphere of the period, however, the consulship did not proceed as smoothly as he might have wished: at the beginning of the year he had to deal with a bill on land distribution proposed by the Tribune of the People P. Servilius Rullus just before Cicero came into office, which forced Cicero to take a stand on the contentious issue of land assignation in his inaugural speeches as consul (Cic. *Leg. agr.* 1–3); towards the end of the year he was faced with the Catilinarian Conspiracy organized by L. Sergius Catilina (Cic. *Cat.* 1–4; Sall. *Cat.*). On the basis of information conveyed to him, Cicero managed to have some of the Catilinarian conspirators captured and revealed as guilty in a meeting of the Senate on 3 December 63 BCE (Cic. *Cat.* 3). In a further meeting on 5 December 63 BCE, after some controversial discussion, the Senate decreed the death penalty for these men (Cic. *Cat.* 4; Sall. *Cat.* 50.3–53.1); Cicero made arrangements for the executions to happen the same evening (Sall. *Cat.* 55). While this procedure was backed by a *senatus consultum ultimum* passed on 21 October 63 BCE (Sall. *Cat.* 29.2–3; cf. Cic. *Cat.* 1.7) and authorized by the Senate decree of 5 December 63 BCE,

---

[6] For a chronology and summary of events from 63 to 56 or 58–57 BCE relevant to Cicero's situation, see, e.g., De Benedetti 1929; Nicholson 1992, 19–23; Kaster 2006, 1–14; 393–408; Kelly 2006, 110–25; Boll 2019, 6–42; 247–8; for a detailed chronology of events in 58 and 57 BCE (with references to the sources), see Grimal 1967; for an overview of the Senate meetings and their topics in 58–57 BCE, see Stein 1930, 28–37; see also Christopherson 1989.

criticism was soon voiced because Roman citizens were put to death without trial, against *Lex Sempronia de capite civis Romani* of 123 BCE (*LPPR*, pp. 309–10). Already on his final day in office at the end of 63 BCE Cicero was not given the opportunity to deliver the customary resignation speech; instead, he was merely allowed to make the standard oath: Cicero changed the wording of the oath to express the view that he had preserved the Republic by his activities against the Catilinarian Conspiracy (Cic. *Pis.* 6–7; Plut. *Cic.* 23.2–3).

Initiatives against Cicero gathered momentum when P. Clodius Pulcher achieved his goal of being adopted into a plebeian family—with the help of C. Iulius Caesar as *pontifex maximus* and consul in 59 BCE (Cic. *Prov. cons.* 42; Suet. *Caes.* 20.4; Cass. Dio 38.12.2)[7] and while Cn. Pompeius Magnus (Pompey the Great) was one of the augurs (Cic. *Att.* 2.12.1)[8]—and was then elected Tribune of the People for 58 BCE (*MRR* II 195–6). Clodius was opposed to Cicero since the Bona Dea scandal of 62 BCE, when Clodius joined (in disguise) celebrations open only to women, was discovered, and taken to court, with Cicero testifying against him, though Clodius was acquitted as a result of bribery.[9] In 58–57 BCE C. Iulius Caesar and Cn. Pompeius Magnus did not support Clodius openly, yet initially did not intervene to stop him either (Cic. *Sest.* 39–40); thus, it was and is widely thought that Clodius acted with their approval. Later, when Clodius' tactics changed and he interfered with their policies, Cn. Pompeius Magnus in particular contributed to arranging Cicero's recall to Rome (Cic. *RS* 29; *Dom.* 25; 66–7; *Prov. cons.* 43; *Har. resp.* 48–9; *Sest.* 39–41; 67; *Pis.* 76–80; *Att.* 2.9.1; 3.15.1; 3.18; 3.22.2; 3.23.1; *Fam.* 14.1.2; 14.2.2; *Q Fr.* 1.4.4; Vell. Pat. 2.45.3; Cass Dio 38.12–30; Plut. *Cic.* 31.2–3; 33.2–3; App. *B Civ.* 2.14–16; see Cic. *RS* 4 n.). Caesar showed some understanding in that he did not set off for his province in spring 58 BCE until Cicero had left Rome, giving him the option to take up the offer (Cic. *Prov. cons.* 42) to join him as one of his staff.

Early in 58 BCE, among other measures, Clodius promulgated a bill *Lex Clodia de capite civis Romani* (*LPPR*, pp. 394–5), announcing punishment for anyone putting Roman citizens to death without trial, which was to be applied retroactively and prospectively; the bill did not name Cicero, but was seen as being directed against him (Cic. *Dom.* 62; *Att.* 3.15.5; Vell. Pat. 2.45.1; Liv. *Epit.*

---

[7] On C. Iulius Caesar's biography, see, e.g., Gelzer 1960; on the relationship between Cicero and Caesar, see Klass 1939, in relation to the situation in 58–57 BCE, esp. pp. 82–7.

[8] On Cn. Pompeius Magnus' biography, see, e.g., Gelzer 1984; Seager 2002; Christ 2004; on the relationship between Cicero and Cn. Pompeius Magnus, see Johannemann 1935, with regard to the situation in 58–57 BCE, esp. pp. 35–55, see also, e.g., Seager 1965; 2002, 101–9; Spielvogel 1993, 61–77; Tatum 1999, 166–8; Rollinger 2019, 125–7.

[9] On the biography and activities of P. Clodius Pulcher, see Gruen 1966; Lintott 1967; Benner 1987; Tatum 1999; Nippel 2000; Stabryla 2006; Fezzi 2008; on Clodius' activities in 58 BCE, see also Rundell 1979; Fezzi 2001; on the role of the Tribunes of the People in the late Roman Republic, see Bleicken 1981; Thommen 1989; on the social make-up, role, and organization of Clodius' followers, see Nowak 1973, 102–46. – For Cicero's thoughts on the plans of and the relationship between Clodius, Caesar, and Pompeius in 59 BCE, see, e.g., Cic. *Att.* 2.12; 2.15; 2.22.

103; Plut. *Cic.* 30.5–6; Cass. Dio 38.14.4–6). The consuls of 58 BCE, A. Gabinius and L. Calpurnius Piso Caesoninus (*MRR* II 193–4), did not take any action (Cic. *Har. resp.* 47; *Sest.* 30; *Pis.* 30), allegedly because Clodius promulgated another bill arranging advantageous provincial assignments for them (*Lex Clodia de provinciis consularibus*, *Lex Clodia de permutatione provinciarum*: *LPPR*, pp. 393–4): Piso was to receive Macedonia and Gabinius Cilicia, later changed to Syria (e.g. Cic. *RS* 10; 18; 32; *RQ* 11; 13; 21; *Dom.* 23–4; 55; 60; 66; 70; 93; 124; *Sest.* 24–5; 33; 53–4; 55; 69; *Prov. cons.* 2–3; 17; *Har. resp.* 58; *Pis.* 28; 30–1; 37; 49; 56–7; *Att.* 3.1; 3.22.1; Schol. Bob. ad Cic. *Planc.* 86 [p. 168.2–4 Stangl]; *Vir. ill.* 81.4; Plut. *Cic.* 30.2; App. *Syr.* 51).

In reaction to the publication of *Lex Clodia de capite civis Romani*, Cicero changed his attire to mourning dress and tried to provoke pity as if he had been given notice of prosecution; later, he regretted that thereby (and by his subsequent departure), partly on the advice of others, he showed too quickly that he felt affected by the bill, rather than ignoring it (Cic. *Att.* 3.8.4; 3.9.2; 3.14.1; 3.15.4–5; 3.15.7; *Fam.* 14.1.2; 14.3.1; *Q Fr.* 1.3.8; 1.4.1; Plut. *Cic.* 30.6–7; Cass. Dio 38.14.7; App. *B Civ.* 2.15). Senators and knights changed their clothes in sympathy; and the Senate passed a decree on the assumption of mourning dress, against which the consuls then issued edicts (Cic. *RS* 12; 31; *RQ* 8; 13; *Dom.* 26; 99; *Pis.* 17; *Sest.* 26–7; Plut. *Cic.* 31.1). According to later comments, Cicero initially contemplated armed resistance, or it was suggested to him; eventually, he says, he decided to leave Rome, again also on the advice of others, and thus to perform a patriotic deed (in his view) to ensure welfare and peace for the Republic and to avoid an armed confrontation (Cic. *RS* 33–4; *Dom.* 5; 63–4; 88; 91–2; 95–6; *Sest.* 43–9; Plut. *Cic.* 31.4–5; Cass. Dio 38.16.5–6; 38.17.4). Prior to Cicero's departure would have been the time at which an oration like the spurious *Oratio pridie quam in exilium iret* could have been delivered if there was an occasion for such an intervention (see Introduction, section 4).

After having dedicated a statue of Minerva from his house to the goddess on the Capitoline Hill, Cicero left Rome in March 58 BCE, just before the bill proposed by Clodius was voted through and came into effect (Cic. *Sest.* 53; *Leg.* 2.42; Plut. *Cic.* 31.6; *Pomp.* 46.5; Cass. Dio 38.17.4–6; Obs. 68; Cassiod. *Chron.* ad a.u.c. 696 [*MGH*, *AA* XI, p. 133 Mommsen]). Immediately after Cicero's departure his possessions were confiscated, his house on the Palatine Hill was destroyed, and the plot was then partly turned into a shrine (Cic. *RS* 18; *Dom.* 45; 60–2; 100–10; 113; 116; 145–6; *Sest.* 54; *Pis.* 26; *Leg.* 2.42; Ascon. ad Cic. *Pis.* 26 [p. 10.15–19 C.]; Plut. *Cic.* 33.1; Cass. Dio 38.17.6; App. *B Civ.* 2.15). A few days later Clodius promulgated another bill, revised shortly afterwards (*Lex Clodia de exilio Ciceronis*; *LPPR*, pp. 395–6), applying official *aqua et igni interdictio* to Cicero from the day of his departure, for the reason that he had killed Roman citizens without due process and on the basis of a false decree of the Senate; this bill was voted through around 24 April 58 BCE (Cic. *RS* 4; 8; *Dom.* 26; 42–4; 47; 50; 58; 68; 70; 82; *Sest.* 54; 65; 73; *Prov. cons.* 45; *Pis.* 30; *Att.* 3.2; 3.4; 3.12.1; 3.23.2;

Schol. Bob., arg. ad Cic. *Planc.* [p. 153.2-7 Stangl]; Liv. *Epit.* 103; Plut. *Cic.* 32.1; Cass. Dio 38.17.7).[10]

As a result, Cicero was not to be received anywhere or by anyone within 400 or 500 miles of Italy, or the hosts would be equally punished (Cic. *Dom.* 51; 85; *Planc.* 96-7; *Fam.* 14.4.2; *Att.* 3.2; 3.4; 3.7.1; Plut. *Cic.* 32.1; Cass. Dio 38.17.7);[11] his property would be confiscated and sold at auction (Cic. *Dom.* 44; 51; *Sest.* 65; *Pis.* 30); and the matter was not to be taken up again in the Senate or before the People (Cic. *RS* 4; 8; *Dom.* 68-70; *Sest.* 69; *Pis.* 29-30; *Att.* 3.12.1; 3.15.6; 3.23.2-4). Cicero later stresses that there was no law instructing him to leave Rome, and, instead, the second bill just prescribed that he should not be hosted by anyone (Cic. *Dom.* 51).

For Cicero's absence from Rome the term 'exile' has become common in modern scholarship, although Cicero avoids the word and prefers more positive labels (see Introduction, section 3.4). Correspondingly, when he employs technical terms in public utterances, Cicero denies that Clodius' measure against him amounts to a proper *lex* (specifically a *plebiscitum*, voted through in a *concilium plebis* [Cic. *Sest.* 65]) and rather describes it as *privilegium* or *proscriptio* (Cic. *RS* 4 n.); he complains that no trial took place and legally required procedures were not followed (Cic. *RS* 4; 8; 29; *Dom.* 26; 33; 42-51; 57-8; 62; 68-70; 71; 72; 77-9; 83; 86-8; 95; 110; *Sest.* 53; 65; 73; 133; *Prov. cons.* 45; *Pis.* 23; 30; *Mil.* 36; *Att.* 3.15.5; *Leg.* 3.44-5). In fact, the first measure was a general law and the second one a follow-up interdiction after Cicero had left.[12] Since Cicero departed after the promulgation of the first bill, there was no opportunity for a trial.[13]

After leaving Rome, Cicero first travelled south through Italy towards Brundisium (modern Brindisi), then sailed to Dyrrhachium (in modern Albania), and moved on to Thessalonica (in Macedonia), where he arrived in

---

[10] On these laws of Clodius and their context, see Benner 1987, 54-6, 86; Moreau 1987; Venturini [1990] 1996, 268-71; *Roman Statutes*, no. 56, pp. 773-4; Tatum 1999, 151-8; Fezzi 2001, 289-95, 300-7; Stroh 2004, 317-21; Kelly 2006, 225-37. – On the legal circumstances of Cicero's departure, see Bellemore 2008.

[11] On the *correctio* to the bill, which specified the required distance and area, and the differing figures in Cicero vs Plutarch and Cassius Dio, see, e.g., Gurlitt 1900; Sternkopf 1900; 1902; 1909, 41-3 (with different views); Marinone 2004, 105 n. 5 (with an overview of the discussion with references); Kaster 2006, 412-13.

[12] See Sternkopf 1900, 272-7; Gruen 1974, 244-6; on the legal terminology connected with Cicero's 'exile', esp. *privilegium*, see Venturini [1990] 1996. – Modern scholars follow Cicero's assessment to varying degrees: May (1988, 88) regards Clodius' bill as unconstitutional. Guerriero (1964, 33) points out that Cicero presents it as illegal because it violates constitutional conventions. Greenidge (1901, 359-66), providing an overview of the legal measures and their relation to standard procedures, illustrates that features such as banishment without a trial or a date are unusual, but that the entire procedure is not as unconventional as Cicero claims. Claassen (1999, 18 n. 49 [pp. 261-2]) notes that '[t]echnically, Clodius' action against him was later construed as *privilegium*' and (1999, 28 n. 95 [p. 264]) that 'Cicero was not *exiled*, but 'relegated', that is, *banished with retention of his property*, but the terms are used indiscriminately by modern authors.'

[13] See, e.g., Nicholson 1992, 30; Boll 2019, 60.

May 58 BCE and, despite the restrictions in place after the approval of Clodius'
bill, was hosted by Cn. Plancius, quaestor to the provincial governor at the time
(Cic. *RS* 35; *Planc.* 78; 95–102; *Fam.* 14.4.2–3; *Att.* 3.8.1; 3.22.1). In November 58
BCE Cicero returned to Dyrrhachium (Cic. *Att.* 3.22.4; *Fam.* 14.1.6–7) and spent
time there and at Buthrotum (in Epirus). During his absence from Rome Cicero
was regularly informed by letters from friends about efforts for his recall.[14] The
majority of the Senate kept asking for a discussion of Cicero's situation, but the
consuls rejected such a request with reference to Clodius' law, which Cicero
refers to the one on the distribution of the consular provinces rather than to the
one about himself (Cic. *RS* 4 and n.); the Senate even said that they would not
make decisions on anything until the issue concerning Cicero was resolved,
ignoring the law introduced by Clodius that forbade the discussion of Cicero's
situation or regarding it as not valid (e.g. Cic. *Att.* 3.24.2; Plut. *Cic.* 33.3). In view
of Clodius' political agitation, Cn. Pompeius Magnus abandoned his tolerance
and indifference from May 58 BCE and became active in support of Cicero's
recall (Cic. *Dom.* 66; Cass. Dio 38.30.1–3; Plut. *Cic.* 33.2–3; *Pomp.* 48.10–9.3;
see Cic. *RS* 29 n.).

On 1 June 58 BCE the Tribune of the People L. Ninnius Quadratus initiated a
discussion about Cicero's recall in the Senate, but his colleague Aelius Ligus
interceded against a Senate decree (Cic. *RS* 3; *Sest.* 68; Cass. Dio 38.30.3–4). On
29 October 58 BCE eight (out of the ten) Tribunes of the People of the year
promulgated a bill for Cicero's return (*Rogatio VIII tribunorum de reditu
Ciceronis*: *LPPR*, p. 401; *Roman Statutes*, no. 57, pp. 775–6), supported by the
consul designate P. Cornelius Lentulus Spinther; as a result of the intervention
of one of the remaining Tribunes of the People, the measure was not brought to
a vote (Cic. *RS* 4; 8; 29; *Sest.* 69–70; *Att.* 3.23.1–4).

The election of new magistrates for 57 BCE and their entering office at the end
of 58 BCE meant some progress for Cicero's case. The new Tribunes of the
People (coming into office on 10 December 58 BCE) had announced that they
would promulgate bills for Cicero's recall (Cic. *Sest.* 72; cf. *Fam.* 14.3.3); eventually, a measure was proposed in the names of eight of them (after two had
defected). Their endeavours were supported by the initiative of the new consul
P. Cornelius Lentulus Spinther (*MRR* II 199–200) at the Senate's first meeting
on 1 January 57 BCE, when Cicero's situation was discussed:[15] it was decided to
aim for a recall authorized by a meeting of the People rather than by a mere
Senate decree, to remove any potential doubt, though this was not strictly
necessary if Clodius' law was not regarded as valid (Cic. *Dom.* 68–9; *Sest.* 73–4;

---

[14] In addition to the bills and motions reaching discussion stage, several others were drafted;
some of these were conveyed to Cicero and are mentioned in his letters (Williamson 2005, 82–5).
Williamson (2005, 82) counts at least ten proposals.

[15] Strictly speaking, putting forward Cicero's case for debate was a violation of one of Clodius'
laws. Yet this law was ignored or not regarded as valid by some (Cic. *Dom.* 68; 70).

Leg. 3.45; *Att.* 3.15.5). On that day no effective decree was passed because of the intercession of the Tribune of the People Sex. Atilius Serranus (Gavianus) (Cic. *RS* 5; *RQ* 11–12; *Pis.* 34; *Sest.* 72–5; *Fam.* 5.4; *Att.* 3.26).[16] A popular assembly to vote on the bill (*Rogatio Fabricia/VIII tribunorum de reditu Ciceronis: LPPR*, p. 401), proposed in the name of the Tribune of the People Q. Fabricius (Cic. *Sest.* 75), was convened for 23 January 57 BCE (according to the pre-Julian calendar); it was violently disrupted by Clodius' followers (Cic. *RS* 6; 22; *RQ* 14; *Sest.* 75–8; 85; *Mil.* 38; Cass. Dio 39.7.2–3; Plut. *Cic.* 33.4; *Pomp.* 49.3).

After several months of further upheaval, the process ultimately leading to Cicero's recall was set in motion: in May 57 BCE, at a meeting in the Temple of Honos and Virtus, the Senate passed a decree saying that nobody should obstruct the next steps and asking the consuls to send letters to advise provincial governors and allies to support Cicero, to thank communities that had hosted Cicero, and to invite those who wanted the Republic to be safe to assemble in Rome (Cic. *RS* 24; 27–8; *Dom.* 73; 85; *Sest.* 50; 116; 120; 128; *Pis.* 34; *Planc.* 78; *Parad.* 29; Plut. *Cic.* 33.6).[17]

Accordingly, in early July 57 BCE crowds gathered in Rome, while the Senate met in the Temple of Iuppiter Optimus Maximus on the Capitoline Hill and passed a decree (with only Clodius opposing it) acknowledging Cicero as saviour of the country and thus the need for his recall (Cic. *RS* 25–8; *RQ* 10; 15; *Dom.* 14; 30; *Prov. cons.* 22; *Sest.* 129–30; *Pis.* 25; 35; *Mil.* 39; Cass. Dio 39.8.2–3; Cassiod. *Chron.* ad a.u.c. 697 [*MGH, AA* XI, p. 133 Mommsen]).[18] On the following day further decrees were passed at another Senate meeting (held in the *curia*) to arrange for practical matters related to the previous day's decree (Cic. *RS* 27; *Sest.* 129; *Pis.* 35),[19] and the consul Lentulus organized a *contio* to inform the People (Cic. *RS* 16–17; 26; *Sest.* 107–8; 129; *Pis.* 34). The resulting law on Cicero's recall (*Lex Cornelia Caecilia de revocando Cicerone: LPPR*, p. 403) was approved by the centuriate assembly on 4 August 57 BCE (Cic. *RS* 27–8; *RQ* 17; *Dom.* 75; 90; 142; *Sest.* 109; 112; *Pis.* 35–6; *Att.* 4.1.4; *Fam.* 1.9.16; Cass. Dio 39.8.2; Plut. *Cic.* 33.5; *Pomp.* 49.4).[20] Legally, this procedure meant that the laws put forward by Clodius were not repealed and rather that Cicero was exempted

---

[16] On such techniques for delay and obstruction, see De Libero 1992, 25–6.

[17] The temple of Honos and Virtus was built by C. Marius (*MRR* I 570–1; *LTUR* III 33–5), with whose fate Cicero compares his own (Cic. *RS* 38 n.). The choice of this venue evokes parallels between Cicero and Marius and alludes to *virtus* and *honor* as characteristics applying to Cicero (Taylor/Scott 1969, 580; Bonnefond-Coudry 1989, 125–30; *LTUR* III 35; see Cic. *Sest.* 116; *Div.* 1.59).

[18] Taylor/Scott (1969, 582) assume that there was discussion and questioning of senators on that day, but no decree was passed. While Cicero does not mention a formal vote, his descriptions imply that an initial Senate decree was approved.

[19] On the dates, venues, and sequence of these Senate meetings, see Taylor/Scott 1969, 580–2; Bonnefond-Coudry 1989, 63, 74–5; Ryan 1998, 32 n. 137; Kaster 2006, App. n. 26.

[20] Taylor (1949, 60–2) points out that the law for Cicero's banishment was passed by the tribal assembly, dominated by the urban population, and his recall was passed by the centuriate assembly, which was influenced by the Italians, whom the consuls and Cn. Pompeius Magnus had summoned. Cicero later highlights that he was recalled by *cuncta Italia* (Cic. *RS* 24 n.).

from that legislation, which was a workable compromise allowing more people to agree to this measure.[21]

Cicero had been informed of the proceedings and, expecting a positive outcome, had set off from Dyrrhachium on the same day; he arrived in Italy at Brundisium on the following day, on 5 August 57 BCE, and was welcomed by his daughter Tullia (Cic. *Sest.* 131; *Att.* 4.1.4). From Brundisium he travelled in a triumphant procession through Italy to Rome, which he reached on 4 September 57 BCE, the first day of the *Ludi Romani* (Cic. *Dom.* 75–6; *Sest.* 131; *Pis.* 51–2; *Att.* 4.1.4–6; Liv. *Epit.* 104; Vell. Pat. 2.45.3; Plut. *Cic.* 33.7–8; Ps.-Cic. *Inv. in Sall.* 10).

To the period immediately after his return to Rome belong Cicero's two speeches *Post reditum in senatu* and *Post reditum ad Quirites*. These demonstrate gratitude for his recall to all involved, while they are also intended to further the re-establishment of his status as a full member of the community and a respected ex-consul and to present his version of past events (e.g. Cic. *Att.* 4.1.3).[22] Subsequently, Cicero had to address more specific issues connected with his return, such as the restoration of his confiscated fortune and especially of his house on the Palatine Hill (Cic. *De domo sua*; *Att.* 4.2).

A couple of days after the speech of thanks in the Senate Cicero spoke again at another meeting of the Senate in reaction to a shortage and the high price of grain: the proposal presented by Cicero, namely to endow Cn. Pompeius Magnus with a special command to take care of the matter, was approved. Afterwards Cicero addressed the People in a *contio* on this issue (Cic. *Dom.* 3; 5–21; 26–7; *Att.* 4.1.5–7; Cass. Dio 39.9.3; see *RQ*, Introduction).[23]

Although Cicero was delighted at having been recalled and having enjoyed widespread support, he noticed soon after his return that opposition against him resurfaced (Cic. *Dom.* 27; *Att.* 4.1.8; 4.2.5; *Fam.* 1.9.5).

Over the course of his life up to the time of his return to Rome, Cicero had not only composed a large number of letters to family, friends, and colleagues

---

[21] On the procedure followed for Cicero's recall, see Ryan 1998, 29–33.

[22] See, e.g., Fuhrmann 1978, 151; Claassen 1992, 31; Nicholson 1992, 23–4; Webster 1992 (rev. of Shackleton Bailey 1991); Dyck 2004, 313–14; Steel 2007, 106–7; Raccanelli 2012, 12–15, 36, 47; Keeline 2018, 164; Boll 2019, 43–4, 58. – Grasmück (1977, 168, 170) emphasizes the political function of these speeches and singles out Cicero's ambition and eagerness for glory as the main motivation. While the intention to re-establish himself was most likely a motivating factor for Cicero, such an interpretation seems too focused on a single reason.

[23] The date of these speeches can be inferred from the letter to Atticus (Cic. *Att.* 4.1.5–7): a chronological sequence of events is indicated by *postridie…eo biduo* (background: *per eos dies*)…*postridie*. The first *postridie* refers to the day after Cicero's arrival in Rome and is defined as the Nones of September (i.e. 5 Sept.; cf. T 1); *eo biduo* means 'two days later' or 'after those two days', with inclusive reckoning referring to 5 and 6 September (K.-St. I 356–7). Thus, *eo biduo* is calculated from the day identified as the Nones of September and marks 7 September: on that day Cicero spoke in the Senate and to the People. A further Senate meeting took place on the following day (*postridie*). – Cicero highlights that this *contio* was granted by almost all magistrates present to illustrate the general support he is enjoying again. – For Cicero's speeches on the grain supply, see Crawford 1984, 134–5, nos. 40–1.

as well as many forensic and political speeches, but had also tried his hand at a rhetorical treatise in his youth (*De inventione rhetorica*), produced an epic (*De consulatu suo*: F 5–13 *FPL*[4]) and a brief memoir on his consulship in Greek, and contemplated one in Latin (Cic. *Att.* 1.19.10; 2.1.1–3; 2.3.4); he had not yet embarked on the major political, philosophical, and rhetorical treatises of the later 50s and the mid 40s BCE.

The various projects to document his consulship preceding his absence from Rome, exploiting a range of means and literary genres, demonstrate that Cicero was concerned with spreading his version of events and obtaining recognition for his deeds. After Cicero's return, further initiatives followed, such as the famous letter to L. Lucceius written in 55 BCE, asking the addressee to write a historical work on Cicero's consulship (Cic. *Fam.* 5.12). At that stage Cicero says (Cic. *Fam.* 1.9.23; *Q Fr.* 2.7.1; 3.1.24) that he was writing another epic about the period after his consulship, including his absence from Rome; whether this was shared with anyone other than his brother and thus reached any wider circulation is unclear (*De temporibus suis*: F 14–17 *FPL*[4]).[24]

3. CICERO'S *POST REDITUM* SPEECHES

3.1. Definition, title, and authenticity

The term '*Post reditum* speeches', frequently found in scholarship, does not denote a group as clearly defined as Cicero's *Verrines*, *Agrarian Speeches*, *Catilinarians*, or *Philippics*. Thus, in the broadest sense, the label is applied to the fourteen surviving speeches Cicero delivered between his return to Rome in 57 BCE and Caesar's dictatorship and describes an oratorical period rather than a thematic group of speeches.[25] In the narrowest sense the expression refers to the two speeches having *post reditum* in a version of their traditional titles: *Post reditum in senatu* and *Post reditum ad Quirites*. In between these farthest points on the scale, the term can denote the four speeches given soon after Cicero's return and connected with his absence: the two speeches *Post reditum in senatu* and *Post reditum ad Quirites* plus *De domo sua* and *De haruspicum responsis*.[26] This last sense is perhaps the most common, and there are numerous shared motifs occurring in all four orations.

---

[24] On the evidence for *De temporibus suis*, see Harrison 1990. – On Cicero's literary efforts to promote his view of his role in the events of the 60s and 50s BCE, see Kelly 2006, 153–60; on Cicero's 'autobiographical' works and their context, see Tatum 2011, 176–81; on Cicero exploiting writings in a variety of literary genres to create a portrayal of himself and his activities, see Steel 2005, 61; 69.

[25] See, e.g., Riggsby 2002, 159; Grillo 2015, 7.

[26] See, e.g., Watts 1923, 43; MacKendrick 1995, 127.

Here, despite the similarities in this group of four speeches, the term will be employed in the narrow sense, referring to the two speeches bearing *post reditum* in a version of their titles, *Post reditum in senatu* and *Post reditum ad Quirites*, since only these are immediately connected with Cicero's return and display the unique rhetorical character of speeches of thanks upon being recalled, while *De domo sua* and *De haruspicum responsis* respond to specific subsequent developments and deal with aspects of the recovery of Cicero's property.

As for the title of the speech to the Senate, the following headings are found in the manuscripts: *M. Tulli Ciceronis incipit cum senatui gratias egit* (PG), *<Incipit cum> senatui gratias egit* (Schol.), *Incip(it) or(atio) M. T. Cicer(onis) cu(m) de reditu suo senatui gr(ati)as egit* (E), *M. Tullius gratias agit senatui* (H), *M. T. Cic(er)o in senatu(m) post reditu(m)* (X), *Oratio Marci Tulii Cicronis in senatu post reditu* [sic] *ab exilio i(n)c(ipit)* (V), *M. Tullii Ciceronis oratio in senatu post reditum de exilio* (F); these titles identify the speech by defining the occasion of delivery in different ways by the location, the time, and/or the activity.[27] Similar variants exist for the speech before the People: *Inc(ipit) cum populo gratias egit* (PG), *Oratio Marci Tullii Ciceronis cum populo gratias egit* (T), *<Incipit> cum populo <gratias egit>* (Schol.), *Inc(ipit) orat(io) M. T. Cicer(onis) cu(m) de reditu suo p. R. gr(ati)as egit* (EV), *Cicero gratias egit populo* (H).

As there does not seem to be a single and straightforward designation for such a type of speech and the transmission is ambiguous (especially among the different manuscript families for the speech delivered in the Senate), several varieties of the title are in use in scholarship, mainly (*Oratio*) *cum senatui gratias egit*/(*Oratio*) *cum populo gratias egit* and (*Oratio*) *post reditum in senatu* (*habita*)/(*Oratio*) *post reditum ad Quirites* (*habita*). Here, out of the versions suggested by the transmission and common in scholarship, the versions *Post reditum in senatu* and *Post reditum ad Quirites* are preferred (with *oratio…habita* understood) as these are concise and neutral descriptions identifying the occasion, but not defining the contents or Cicero's position.

The inauthenticity of *Post reditum in senatu* and *Post reditum ad Quirites*, along with *De domo sua* and *De haruspicum responsis*,[28] was first proposed by Jeremiah Markland, a Fellow of Peterhouse, Cambridge, in *A Dissertation upon Four Orations Ascribed to M. T. Cicero*, published with other studies on Cicero in 1745: he believed that the speech was probably written by a foreign or provincial author not many years after Cicero's lifetime, using material mostly taken from Cicero's genuine speeches such as *Pro Sestio*, in an overblown style

---

[27] See, e.g., Boll 2019, 94.

[28] For an overview of the authenticity debate, see, e.g., Watts 1923, 46–7; Nisbet 1939, xxix–xxxiv; Guillen 1967, 16–19; Lenaghan 1969, 38–41; Nicholson 1992, 1–18.

and including numerous passages without design or meaning.[29] Immediately, pamphlets asserting the contrary were published in Britain. A more substantial rejoinder soon followed: Johann Matthias Gesner, a professor and librarian at the University of Göttingen and a member of the Göttingen academy, argued against it in two essays entitled *Cicero restitutus* (1753; 1754). Friedrich August Christian Wilhelm Wolf, a professor in Halle and Berlin, a member of the Berlin academy, and a scholar often considered the founder of modern classical philology, revived the discussion in 1801 by publishing a commented edition in which he engaged with the arguments of Markland and Gesner and evaluated the speeches' language and argument in the commentary, confirming Markland's views. Wolf's prestige gave renewed authority to this sceptical position and the general question of authenticity; it influenced the work on these orations and the layout of Cicero editions over the coming century.

   Thus, virtually all scholarship in the nineteenth century focused on confirming or refuting the inauthenticity of these speeches; there were a number of contributions, especially in Germany, on both sides of the debate. In terms of editions, the English classical scholar George Long included these speeches in his commentary on all of Cicero's orations, building on previous discussions and making 'such notes as were necessary for the double purpose of explaining them and proving them to be spurious' (1856, 296–9). Similarly, C. D. Beck (1795–1807) added a critical excursus on the four orations demonstrating their inauthenticity to his edition of Cicero's speeches (vol. IV, pp. 612–27). In the edition of J. C. Orelli (1826–30) the four speeches were printed in the section *M. Tullii Ciceronis scripta dubia et supposititia* (vol. I, 1826, pp. 563–648). In the revised version of J. C. Orelli's edition prepared by I. G. Baiter and C. Halm (1856) the speeches were moved back to their chronological position within the sequence of Cicero's speeches. In addition, the genuineness of the speeches was defended in a series of studies and commentaries over the course of the nineteenth century (e.g. Weiske 1807; Savels 1828, 1830; Lucas 1837; Lahmeyer 1850; Wagner 1857; Lange 1875; Hoffmann 1878; Rück 1881; Müller 1900). Towards the end of the century Theodor Mommsen declared (*StR* III 1037 n. 2 [p. 1038]): 'dass an die Unechtheit der Rede Ciceros für das Haus heutzutage kein Philolog und kein Historiker noch glaubt', and Friedrich Leo (1898, 177) pointed out that a difference in genre necessitates a difference in style. There was a final attack on the speeches' authenticity in 1900 by H. M. Leopold. The question then became regarded as settled after the studies of T. Zielinski (1904) on the rules for *clausulae* in Cicero's speeches, when he showed by significant examples that these

---

[29] One of Markland's arguments is that in *Pro Sestio* Cicero announces a full record and justification of the situation and his behaviour (Cic. *Sest.* 36), which would be odd if this was not the first time. In *Pro Sestio*, however, Cicero is speaking to a different audience, and he has not given a detailed full record in public before.

four speeches follow the same patterns of prose rhythm as the certainly genuine orations (esp. 1904, 218–21).

Moreover, Cicero mentions a speech delivered in the Senate immediately after his return in other writings (Cic. *Att.* 4.1.5 [T 1]; *Planc.* 74 [T 2]) and indicates that he produced a written version of it in advance (Cic. *Planc.* 74 [T 2]). Unless one assumes that the extant speech *Post reditum in senatu* is not a version of the one Cicero delivered on 5 September 57 BCE, there is Ciceronian evidence for its genuineness. Similarly, Cicero mentions the speech *De domo sua* in a letter to Atticus and says that he is sending him a copy (Cic. *Att.* 4.2.2 [Oct. 57 BCE]); again, there is confirmation that Cicero delivered a speech on that occasion and a written version existed. While it cannot be excluded that this speech has been replaced by a later forgery, most straightforwardly this is evidence for the authenticity of the extant speech. In addition, though less decisively, the *post reditum* speeches as they survive were accepted as authentic in antiquity; they were quoted and imitated by a range of ancient authors and were transmitted among Cicero's genuine speeches.

Nowadays the speeches connected with Cicero's return are regarded as genuine. While there are some peculiarities, which can be explained by the unique situation of their delivery (see Introduction, section 3.4), they equally display numerous characteristic features of Ciceronian oratory in style and content.

3.2. Rhetorical genre and structure

The genre and the structure of the speeches *Post reditum in senatu* and *Post reditum ad Quirites* are unique: there are no extant parallels from ancient Rome for such orations of gratitude and repositioning after a politician's return from exile.[30]

These speeches may be defined as political orations in the broadest sense because they were delivered in the Senate and in a *contio* respectively (not in a law court) and address the state of the Republic.[31] Notwithstanding this formal

---

[30] There are not even unambiguous references to speeches given by other Romans upon return from exile. Pina Polo (1996, 103 with n. 35; tentatively followed by van der Blom 2010, 200 n. 95; see also van Ooteghem 1967, 176) assumes, on the basis of a passage quoted in Gellius (Gell. *NA* 13.29.1 [24 F 78 *FRHist*]: *verba sunt Claudii Quadrigarii ex Annalium eius XIII: 'contione dimissa Metellus in Capitolium venit cum mortalibus multis; inde domum proficiscitur, tota civitas eum reduxit.'*), that Q. Caecilius Metellus Numidicus (see Cic. *RS* 25 n.) delivered a speech upon his return. Yet while the statement mentions a *contio*, its occasion cannot be inferred with certainty; the commentary on Claudius Quadrigarius in *FRHist* (III 324–5) doubts the link with the return from exile and rather suggests a connection with the events leading up to it. – An expression of gratitude for recall from exile can be found in a speech by C. Aurelius Cotta as consul to the People, as reported in Sallust (Sall. *Hist.* 2.47.5 M. = 2.43.5 R.: *…, vos, Quirites, rursus mihi patriam deosque penatis cum ingenti dignitate dedistis. pro quibus beneficiis vix satis gratus videar, si singulis animam quam nequeo concesserim;…*).

[31] On ancient definitions of the three rhetorical genres, see, e.g., Cic. *Inv. rhet.* 1.7; *Rhet. Her.* 1.2.

categorization, they are unusual political speeches since they were not given in the context of a debate in the Senate on a particular issue or to inform the People about specific political developments; their avowed purpose is to express gratitude for Cicero's recall (while contributing to Cicero's restoration). The orations are, therefore, more personal in an explicit way than most other Roman public speeches and are to a large extent epideictic in nature (Schol. Bob., arg. ad Cic. *RQ* [p. 110.9–12 Stangl]: T 4). The epideictic character becomes apparent in that they are ostensibly speeches of thanks, praising others for their great deeds on behalf of Cicero and expressing gratitude for their support (combined with criticism of opponents). While voicing thanks, Cicero intends to present himself not as a passive victim who was forced to leave and only able to return as a result of the efforts of others. Therefore, Cicero uses these speeches also to re-establish his position in Rome and to spread his version of events: he describes his departure as a deed of sacrifice on behalf of the Republic and all citizens. Thus, these speeches include self-praise and self-justification, although such a feature, which was not restricted to a particular rhetorical genre, was disapproved of by ancient rhetoricians, including Cicero (e.g. Cic. *Off.* 1.137; Quint. *Inst.* 11.1.15–17).[32] Consequently, the orations display characteristics of political and epideictic speeches as well as features not linked to specific rhetorical genres.[33]

All these elements are closely interwoven, so that it is difficult in most sections to define a dominant genre or to structure the speech into sections of different rhetorical character. What can be identified in the speech given in the Senate is the passage consisting of an invective against the consuls of the previous year (Cic. *RS* 10–18), which does not have a parallel in the speech delivered to the People.[34] Since this section is not only intended to condemn the two men, but also to set off the great efforts of others against them by attributing the departure and the delay in Cicero's recall basically to the consuls in order to remove responsibility from others and himself, it contributes to the positive portrayal of others. Throughout the rest of the speech praise of people

---

[32] Yet in *De domo sua* Cicero claims that what he offers in the *post reditum* speeches is not self-praise but rather a statement in response to allegations (Cic. *Dom.* 93). – Still, the presence of self-glorification must have been an obvious characteristic of Cicero's oratory already in the ancient world, as Quintilian mentions that Cicero boasts of his deeds in his speeches (Quint. *Inst.* 11.1.17).

[33] To what extent this mixture is a transformation of the rhetorical genre (Wuilleumier 1952, 25: 'Ces deux actions de grâces montrent comment Cicéron a transformé le genre en mêlant à l'éloge d'autrui son apologie personnelle.') is difficult to establish in the absence of parallels. – Nicholson (1992, 99–100) and Boll (2019, 6, 43, 58) assign these speeches to the *genus demonstrativum*, though Nicholson (1992, 100–1, 131) qualifies this categorization and acknowledges a combination of elements from different rhetorical genres (see also Condom 1995, 27).

[34] On the invective section, see, e.g., Doblhofer 1987, 216–17. – On Roman invective and its standard elements, see, e.g., Opelt 1965, 128–59; Koster 1980; Corbeill 2002, esp. 200–1; Craig 2004, esp. 190–2; Arena 2007; Powell 2007. – For potential items to be adduced for praise or blame in oratory, see *Rhet. Her.* 3.10–15; Cic. *Inv. rhet.* 1.34–6; 2.177–8.

supporting Cicero and self-justification (as in forensic orations), evidenced by what is presented as great deeds for the Republic (taking up deliberative themes), are combined.

Because of the unique nature of these orations, the structural rules for the arrangement of forensic speeches developed in the schools of rhetoric cannot be applied, apart from the fact that, like almost any speech, each oration has a clearly identifiable effective beginning (*exordium*) and ending (*peroratio*) surrounding a more argumentative main section. Obviously, in composing these texts Cicero will have been influenced by his rhetorical training; yet these speeches are adjusted to such a specific set of circumstances and the particular needs of the moment, combining thanks with self-justification, that they cannot be explained only as a modification of models in the rhetorical tradition; they also demonstrate virtuosity in putting together rhetorical elements to form effective speeches for a unique context.

Both orations start with an expression of thanks (Cic. *RS* 1–2; *RQ* 1–5) and end with Cicero's promises for the Republic (Cic. *RS* 36–9; *RQ* 18–25), surrounding a review of his departure and recall in the middle (Cic. *RS* 3–35; *RQ* 6–17). Beyond that, the two speeches diverge in details of their structure and place the emphasis differently. In addition to the invective section (Cic. *RS* 10–18), the speech in the Senate devotes more space to describing the chaos and unsuccessful activities in 58 BCE (Cic. *RS* 3–7), contrasted with the actions of the supporters who were ultimately successful (Cic. *RS* 8–9; 18–31); it mentions the comparison with previous ex-consuls in the conclusion (Cic. *RS* 36–9), while the fate of these men is treated in a separate section early in the speech to the People, compared and contrasted with Cicero's situation (Cic. *RQ* 6–11).

3.3. Delivery, publication, and audiences

On two occasions Cicero states that he delivered a speech of thanks in the Senate immediately after his return to Rome (Cic. *Att.* 4.1.5 [T 1]; *Planc.* 74 [T 2]), which is confirmed by other sources (T 4–7). There is no further information about the details, for instance whether it was a Senate meeting called for the purpose of welcoming Cicero back or a meeting about another issue in which Cicero was given an opportunity to make a statement or appropriated the space to do so. Only Cassius Dio states that the consuls enabled Cicero to deliver a speech (Cass. Dio 39.9.1 [T 7]).

In *Pro Plancio* Cicero says that, unusually, the speech to the Senate was written out in advance (Cic. *Planc.* 74 [T 2]). Then there might have been little opportunity to adjust it according to the feelings in Rome gauged upon arrival or to audience reactions during delivery. Yet even a written outline ensuring that all important points are mentioned would not have prevented Cicero from deviating from the script. Moreover, it is uncertain whether the written text in existence agrees with what Cicero said on the day. It is often assumed that the speech survives in the form in which it was delivered.[35] Still, later adjustments, as for any speech prepared for circulation after delivery, could have been made if wider distribution was intended.

Since the speech to the Senate was delivered soon after his return, Cicero probably started preparing it prior to his arrival back in Rome. Many scholars assume that it was written during the return journey.[36] Some believe that it was drafted in the latter part of Cicero's stay away from Rome, once he had worked out a version of the events he wanted to spread and under the influence of rhetorical models.[37] The fact that Cicero presents the sequence of events in 58 and 57 BCE with a particular interpretation that remains essentially consistent in all speeches delivered after and connected with his return at least indicates that he had developed a certain version he carried on publicizing. When Cicero formed this view and when exactly he composed a draft of the Senate speech can no longer be determined.

That Cicero decided to deliver the speech on the basis of a written draft has been interpreted as a result of the fact that he suffered from a lack of self-confidence, was afraid of being overcome by emotions, was out of practice after a prolonged absence from Rome,[38] or did not have time to commit the speech to memory.[39] These views have led to the assumption that Cicero not only put together a full written draft, but also delivered the speech from a manuscript in the Senate.[40] Although this view has been challenged, it has been shown that delivering epideictic speeches from written drafts was not entirely unusual and that the wording of Cicero's remark as transmitted suggests that he wrote up a

---

[35] See, e.g., Savels 1828, vi–vii; Rauschen 1886, 10 n. 28 (pp. 34–5); Laurand 1936–8, 4. – For a brief summary and comments on the scholarly discussion on the extent of revisions in the extant published versions of speeches, see Lintott 2008, 15–31.

[36] See, e.g., Nicholson 1992, 15: 'We know from the speech *Pro Plancio* (74) that Cicero composed the *In senatu* in advance, while *en route* to Rome, and that he then read it "de scripto" upon arrival in the city, apparently without having first revised it in order to bring it perfectly into line with actual circumstances. The same is presumably true of the *Ad Quirites*.' – Lange (1875, 18–19, 24, 26) and Rauschen (1886, 10 n. 28 [p. 34]) posit that the speech was finished before Cicero reached Rome and not adapted to the circumstances he encountered there; this scenario is regarded as the reason why he does not mention the enthusiastic reception upon his return and says that he received his possessions back (see Cic. *RQ* 3 n.). For *De domo sua* Shackleton Bailey (1991, 38) still assumes (following Schaum 1889, esp. 8) that Cicero composed the speech in large part before his return and made some additions upon realizing the situation in Rome, but did not update the original text (Cic. *Dom.* 51; 106 vs *Dom.* 128; *Har. resp.* 11; 13). Claassen (1999, 158) talks of 'various speeches after his return, hurriedly composed in the first flush of ebullient victory', which suggests that writing only started after Cicero's recall had been approved.

[37] See Dyck 2004, 302; Kaster 2006, 8 n. 16.

[38] See Nicholson 1992, 125–6; Dyck 2004, 301, with n. 11; Lintott 2008, 9.

[39] See Haury 1955, 143.

[40] See, e.g., MacKendrick 1995, 135; Raccanelli 2012, 8; Boll 2019, 6 (sceptical again Corbeill's review at *BMCR* 2020.10.22).

draft in advance and took it to the Senate meeting.[41] While the considerations mentioned may have played a role, the reason given by Cicero, the significance of the occasion, seems paramount: this oration was the only opportunity to re-establish himself as a respected consular and to render thanks to supporters without offending anyone who might feel that they contributed to his recall; thus it was important to find the right tone and include all relevant details.[42]

The corresponding speech to the People is not mentioned elsewhere by Cicero. It is referred to in the scholia as a complement to the speech in the Senate; they imply that this oration was delivered soon after the speech given in the Senate. Such a presentation could only have taken place at a *contio*, as the scholia state (T 4; 5).[43] In 57 BCE Cicero would not have been in a position to call a *contio*: only magistrates in office could do so and then speak themselves or invite others.[44] Thus, one of the magistrates of the year would have had to call a *contio* for Cicero, perhaps P. Cornelius Lentulus Spinther, one of the consuls of 57 BCE and one of Cicero's supporters (Cic. *RS* 5 n.). This is what Cassius Dio suggests, the only source saying explicitly that the speech was delivered and providing information about the circumstances (T 7). Alternatively, if one doubts the reliability of Cassius Dio's evidence, one might consider the possibility that the speech to the People was never delivered[45] and was only written up and released as a complement to the speech to the Senate so as to demonstrate Cicero's eagerness to engage with both the Senate and the People, treat these two bodies equally, and make similar statements about his position in both venues (see *RQ*, Introduction). Additionally, it has been suggested that the speech to the People was also written out in advance of a potential delivery, on the assumption that, afterwards, it would not make much sense to write up a speech fairly similar to the speech given in the Senate.[46] Since Cicero edited two speeches on other occasions, this does not seem a decisive argument. As fewer names of contemporaries are mentioned in the speech delivered to the People,

---

[41] See Vössing 2008 (in response to a different interpretation and suggestions to change the text at Cic. *Planc.* 74 by Bücher/Walter 2006): see T 2 n.

[42] See also Raccanelli 2012, 8–10. – Soon after the delivery of this speech Cicero says about characteristics of his position in a letter to Atticus (Cic. *Att.* 4.1.3 [Sept. 57 BCE]): *nos adhuc, in nostro statu quod difficillime reciperari posse arbitrati sumus, splendorem nostrum illum forensem et in senatu auctoritatem et apud viros bonos gratiam magis quam optaramus consecuti sumus.*

[43] Cicero delivered speeches to the *contio* as praetor (Cic. *Leg. Man.*) and as consul (Cic. *Leg. Agr.* 2; 3; *Cat.* 2; 3); after his return to Rome the only *contio* speeches are this one and two of the *Philippics* towards the end of his life (Cic. *Phil.* 4; 6). – On the *contio* in Republican Rome, see, e.g., Mouritsen 2001; 2013; Morstein-Marx 2004; Pina Polo 2012; Flaig 2017 (with further references and different views on its political importance as a body and a venue for speeches of politicians).

[44] See, e.g., Kunkel/Wittmann 1995, 249–51.

[45] See, e.g., Lange 1875, 26–7 (assuming publication after Cicero's death); Nicholson 1992, 127–8 (*contra* Fogel 1994, 229–30); Lintott 2008, 13–14, 15. – Lintott (2008, 9) believes that 'Cicero himself may have hesitated to ask a magistrate for the opportunity to deliver it.'

[46] See Nicholson 1992, 126; Lintott 2008, 9, 11. – Paratte (1963, 17) suggests that the speech to the People was written after 5 September 57 BCE because it takes up the main arguments of the speech to the Senate.

it would have been easier to prepare it in the usual way and deliver it without a complete written script.[47]

Written versions of the two speeches composed for delivery upon Cicero's return must have been in circulation from a fairly early period onwards: ancient authors mention, quote, and imitate them. There is no precise evidence on when and how Cicero might have 'published' the texts of the two orations.[48] What is known is that at the time of Cicero's defence of Plancius (54 BCE) a written version of *Post reditum in senatu* was available (Cic. *Planc.* 74 [T 2]) and that a version of *De domo sua* (delivered not much later) was to be sent to Atticus (Cic. *Att.* 4.2.2 [Oct. 57 BCE]). Thus, one can only assume that what survives (now shown to be genuine) is what Cicero saw as appropriate statements to each of the two bodies soon after his return to Rome.

As in other instances in Cicero's oratorical oeuvre, the two speeches *Post reditum in senatu* and *Post reditum ad Quirites* form a pair of speeches on the same issue delivered to the different audiences of the Senate and the People.[49] The situation and the aim are essentially the same for the two speeches (Cicero expressing gratitude for his recall, presenting his departure as a deliberate sacrifice for the community, and re-establishing his position as a senior states-man), and the content is comparable; beyond that, they show some differences in relation to the different audiences.[50]

For instance, the speech to the People is shorter and less detailed, especially as regards the presentation of individuals: there is no separate passage criticiz-ing the consuls of 58 BCE (Cic. *RS* 10–18); the section on individuals supporting Cicero (Cic. *RQ* 11–17; *RS* 18–31) is less elaborate; the expression of gratitude is more general and focused on the People; only important individuals such as

---

[47] Frenzel (1801, 11) believes that the speech in the Senate was delivered before the one to the People, since the repetitions and overlaps would otherwise have been embarrassing; in his view the Senate speech is less elaborately composed, and this matches an earlier point of delivery, as Cicero would have had less time for preparation. This conclusion does not agree with Cicero's statement that he composed a written draft for the speech in the Senate in advance (Cic. *Planc.* 74 [T 2]).

[48] Nicholson (1992, 126), Spielvogel (1993, 74), and Boll (2019, 7) assume prompt publication of the two orations of thanks, which would have been easily possible when both speeches were ready in written form even prior to delivery. Boll also considers that the process of publication might have started before delivery.

[49] On similarities and differences between Cicero's Senate and *contio* speeches within the respective pairs, see, e.g., Mack 1937; Thompson 1978; Fogel 1994; on the stylistic features, see also von Albrecht 1973, 1251–2; 2003, 25–6.

[50] See Guerriero 1955, 10; 1964, 12–13; Caprioli 1966, 69–71; Fuhrmann 1978, 151, 155; Nicholson 1992, 102–6; Spielvogel 1993, 74; Fogel 1994, 230; Claassen 1999, 159; Lintott 2008, 9 n. 17; Boll 2019, 43. – The statement that 'Cicero's speech of thanksgiving to the *Quirites* is for the most part a repetition of his address to the Senate' (Thompson 1978, 60), the description that it is a shortened version of the speech in the Senate (Nicholson 1992, 102; Boll 2019, 43), or the view that some passages were simply transferred from the speech given in the Senate into that given before the People (Spielvogel 1993, 74) illustrate the similarity of the content of the two orations, but require qualification with respect to the structure, tone, and emphasis of each speech.

the consul P. Cornelius Lentulus Spinther and Cicero's relatives are singled out, which thus enhances the personal dimension (Cic. *RQ* 7–8; 11; 15; 18). In the Senate speech Cicero names a large number of supporters[51] and some opponents,[52] with their specific contributions acknowledged individually. Still, Cicero claims that even in the Senate speech he only mentions *causae nostrae duces et quasi signiferi* (Cic. *Planc.* 74 [T 2]); indeed, he focuses on office holders. Details about activities at senatorial level are presumably not deemed of interest to an audience of the People. Vice versa, in the *contio* speech figures likely to be popular with the People such as C. Marius and Cn. Pompeius Magnus are given prominent roles, though not entirely uncritically (Cic. *RQ* 7; 9–11; 16–18); while the focus of the gratitude is on the deeds of the People, activities of the Senate are not ignored (Cic. *RQ* 8; 10; 12; 13; 15–17). There is no separate section on Cicero's departure (Cic. *RS* 32–5): the speech concentrates on Cicero's recall, in which the People were involved and which is relevant to them. The comparison with earlier ex-consuls, given more prominence at the start of the speech (Cic. *RQ* 6–11), stresses that Cicero was recalled because of his own worth and thus reminds the audience that he is a man of the People. In turn, the expression of thanks is effusive and emphatic; Cicero emphasizes his debt to the People and the great joy they have brought to him by their deeds. Moreover, Cicero's position becomes more prominent in the speech to the People: for instance, he begins with his role in the events and only mentions the greatness of benefits, which cannot be matched in a speech, afterwards (Cic. *RQ* 5), while this is the starting point in the speech in the Senate (Cic. *RS* 1).[53] Thus, the entire speech is more triumphant and celebrates Cicero's return and the resumption of his activities for the Republic and the advantages for the People. Gods are mentioned more prominently in the *contio* speech;[54] tone and argumentative style are more emotional, the vocabulary is purer, and there are more repetitions and enumerations (on style, see Introduction, section 3.5).[55]

Such differences are mostly in line with the divergences between Senate and *contio* speeches also observed for other pairs.[56] According to a list of characteristic

---

[51] For an overview, see Nicholson 1992, 45–89 (including those not listed). – On the selection of individuals mentioned, see also Claassen 1999, 159; Raccanelli 2012, 47–9; for reasons why Atticus and Varro are not mentioned and thanked, see Desideri 1963. – On Cicero's 'exile' and his friends in this context, see Citroni Marchetti 2000, 141–212.

[52] For the opponents referred to and their treatment in the speech, see Nicholson 1992, 90–7.

[53] See, e.g., Raccanelli 2012, 33.

[54] See, e.g., Nicholson 1992, 104–5; Boll 2019, 50.

[55] In light of the categories investigated, Cipriani (1975, 337) notes 'una perfetta coerenza stilistica' between the two speeches, though he states later (1975, 344) that 'per quanto le due orazioni obbediscano ad un identico gusto oratorio, quella rivolta al senato è senz'altro più ricca di figure retoriche'.

[56] For comparisons of the two speeches, see, e.g., Weiske 1807, 230–1; Mack 1937, 18–48; Claassen 1992, 32, 34; 1999, 159; Fogel 1994, 230–8; Boll 2019, 43–57. – Some characteristics of Senate and *contio* speeches and differences between them were already noted in the ancient

features,[57] most of the typical elements of Cicero's *contio* speeches can be found here: rendering thanks for *beneficia* received from the People (Cic. *RQ* 2; 5–6; 22; 24); highlighting the self-sacrifice on behalf of the Republic and a promise to work hard for the community (Cic. *RQ* 1; 24); claims to be a true *popularis* and allusions to popular figures such as C. Marius or Cn. Pompeius Magnus (Cic. *RQ* 10–11; 16; 18; 19–20); references to divine support and protection (Cic. *RQ* 1); emotional mentions of family and homes (Cic. *RQ* 1–3; 8).

3.4. Argumentative and rhetorical strategies

In contrast to Cicero's more obviously political speeches, the speeches *Post reditum in senatu* and *Post reditum ad Quirites* are not intended to prompt the respective audiences to take a particular course of action. Instead, they aim at persuading them of a certain attitude and view, namely a specific version of what happened in 58 and 57 BCE as well as a positive assessment of Cicero's role in these events and his relationship to the Republic.[58] Spreading his view of the events is a step towards re-establishing Cicero's position in Rome. Cicero works towards this goal by employing a number of related and frequently repeated themes and motifs. While in his first reflections in hindsight he regarded his reaction to P. Clodius Pulcher's bills as a mistake (see Introduction, section 2), Cicero here reinterprets his departure as a heroic deed coinciding with the absence of the *res publica* and avoiding civil war.

That this portrayal is adapted to the occasion upon Cicero's return emerges from the fact that his presentation of himself and other people in the letters written during his absence from Rome differs from that in these speeches: Cicero's letters include criticism for the lack of activity on his behalf, complaints about his fate, regrets about his absence from Rome, and grief at the situation (e.g. Cic. *Att.* 3.1–27; *Fam.* 14.1; 14.2; 14.3; 14.4; *Q Fr.* 1.3; 1.4).[59] That being in Rome was important to Cicero is confirmed by letters sent from Cilicia during his provincial governorship in 51–50 BCE, when he expresses his longing to be

---

rhetorical tradition, including adaptation to the respective audiences or the need for more rhetorical flourish before the People (e.g. Cic. *De or.* 2.333–4; 3.195; Quint. *Inst.* 11.1.45).

[57] See Fantham 2000, 104–5, 111.

[58] Already noted by the scholiast (Schol. Bob. on Cic. *RQ* 1 [p. 110.21–3 Stangl]): *vigilanter medellam pudori suo adhibuit dicendo tristem magis profectionem quam ignominiosum illud exilium fuisse, ut non sit infame, quod solam habuerit iniuriam.*

[59] See, e.g., Grasmück 1977, 170; 1978, 115, 118; Rundell 1979, 318; Spielvogel 1993, 75; Claassen 1999, esp. 158–63. – On aspects of Cicero's letters from 'exile', see Degl'Innocenti Pierini 1996; Citroni Marchetti 2000; Garcea 2005; on 'Cicero's letters of appeal', see Claassen 1999, 105–10. – On Cicero's attitudes to and presentation of his 'exile', see, e.g., Grasmück 1978, 110–27; May 1988, 88–127 (with reference to other speeches delivered after the return to Rome); Narducci 1997; Claassen 1999, 158–63; Kelly 2006, 154; Cohen 2007 (more generally on the concept); La Farina 2008; Rampulla 2008; on Cicero's presentation of himself after his return, see Degl'Innocenti Pierini 2006.

in the city of Rome (e.g. Cic. *Att.* 5.15.1 [3 Aug. 51 BCE]; *Fam.* 2.12.2–3 [June 50 BCE]; 2.13.3 [May 50 BCE]).

The most prominent of the strategies of positive presentation in the speeches after Cicero's return is the shaping of his departure and absence. Obviously, one function of the speeches is to express gratitude to the audiences and selected individuals for their contribution to his recall and the assistance provided during his absence; the need to convey elaborate thanks suggests that Cicero was in a position requiring support. At the same time it is implied that the term 'exile' does not apply to Cicero's circumstances, and Cicero's departure from Rome is presented as a positive action he was in control of: he decided to leave, along with the Republic, when there was no opportunity for political intervention, and thereby prevented civil unrest (Cic. *Dom.* 72–6; *Parad.* 4.27–32).

Such nuancing is clear from the terminology: to refer to the situation of being away from Rome and related feelings in the *post reditum* speeches or later texts, Cicero never employs the term 'exile' (unless to say that it does not apply; e.g. Cic. *Parad.* 30: *nescis exilium scelerum esse poenam, meum illud iter ob praeclarissimas res a me gestas esse susceptum?* – 'Don't you know that exile is a penalty for crimes, but that this journey of mine was undertaken because of the outstanding actions done by me?'),[60] but rather expressions (sometimes also covering the situation of family members)[61] indicating the fact of departure and withdrawal or the emotions associated with that move, such as *discessus*,[62] *digressus*,[63] *profectio*,[64] *excedo*,[65] *me absente*,[66] *cedo*,[67] *calamitas*,[68] *aerumna*,[69] *pernicies*,[70] *miseriae*,[71] and *dolor*.[72] Correspondingly, Cicero does not refer to his recall as a 'rescue', 'liberation', or 'removal of a banishment clause', but more

---

[60] See, e.g., Nicholson 1992, 30–1; Robinson 1994; Pina Polo 1996, 103 n. 38; Dyck 2004, 309; La Farina 2008, esp. 330–2; Raccanelli 2012, 37 n. 18; Grillo 2015, 5–6; Boll 2019, 61.

[61] In the letters some of these characterizations are not just euphemisms for 'exile', but also convey feelings in line with the nuances of these terms (e.g. *aerumna, miseriae*). See also Schol. Bob. ad Cic. *De aere alieno Milonis* (p. 172.10–12 Stangl): *bene elocutus est de exilio suo, quod maluit discessionem vocare quam poenam. et aliis orationibus similiter coloravit neque metu neque ulla conscientia criminum se maluisse discedere, sed praecavisse potius ne ad arma per seditionem veniretur.*

[62] E.g. Cic. *RS* 3; 19; *Dom.* 15; 17; 59; 60; 85; 95; 115; *Prov. cons.* 45; *Sest.* 49; 60; 128; 133; *Pis.* 21; 31; 32; *Vat.* 6; 7; *Planc.* 73; 86; *Mil.* 103. – *discessus* can denote Cicero's leaving or his staying abroad (Nisbet 1939, ad Cic. *Dom.* 15).

[63] E.g. Cic. *Pis.* 63.   [64] E.g. Cic. *RS* 23; *RQ* 1; cf. *profectus* at Cic. *Dom.* 86; 87.

[65] E.g. Cic. *RS* 7.   [66] E.g. Cic. *RQ* 8; *Dom.* 3; 57; *Sest.* 50; 69.

[67] E.g. Cic. *RS* 4; *Dom.* 5; 56; 58; 68; 99; *Pis.* 19.

[68] E.g. Cic. *RS* 20; 24; 36; *RQ* 6; 9; *Dom.* 30; 65; 72; 76; *Sest.* 32; *Fam.* 14.3.1; 15.4.13; *Att.* 3.7.2; 3.8.4; 3.10.2; 3.14.2; 3.25.1; *Q Fr.* 1.3.1; 1.3.3; 1.3.4; 1.3.8; 1.4.5; cf. *Dom.* 72–6.

[69] E.g. Cic. *RS* 34; *Sest.* 49; *Att.* 3.8.2; 3.11.2; 3.14.1. – See Schol. Bob. ad Cic. *Sest.* 49 (p. 131.29–30 Stangl): *notabiliter singulari numero, non plurativo, aerumnam dixit, referens ad exilium scilicet, cuius patientiam inter glorias suas conputat.*

[70] E.g. Cic. *Sest.* 25; 42; 53; *Pis.* 19; *Att.* 3.4; 3.10.2.   [71] E.g. Cic. *Att.* 3.4; *Fam.* 14.3.1.

[72] E.g. Cic. *RS* 35; *Dom.* 100; 103; *Sest.* 52.

neutrally to concerns for or restoration of his *dignitas*[73] and *salus/salvus esse*,[74] and generally to *reditus/redire*,[75] *adventus*,[76] or the situation of *restitutio/restitutus*[77] and *conservare*.[78] Cicero even stresses that the recall did not state that he was now permitted to return (since this had been the case all along if Clodius' law was regarded as not valid), but that he was summoned back (Cic. *Dom.* 71: *quod idem tu, Lentule, vidisti in ea lege quam de me tulisti. nam non est ita latum ut mihi Romam venire liceret, sed ut venirem; non enim voluisti id quod licebat ferre ut liceret, sed me ita esse in re publica magis ut arcessitus imperio populi Romani viderer quam ad administrandam civitatem restitutus.* – 'And in the bill you carried concerning me, Publius Lentulus, you had the same point in mind. It provided, not that I should be free to return to Rome, but simply that I should return. You did not wish to propose that I should be free to do what I was free to do, but that I should resume my place in public life as one summoned by command of the Roman People rather than as one restored.' [trans. D. R. Shackleton Bailey]). If the report on what Q. Caecilius Metellus Numidicus (see Cic. *RS* 25 n.) says in a letter while in 'exile' from Rome is correct, his presentation of himself provides a precedent for ignoring that the condition of 'exile' formally comes into effect by removal from Rome and for the view that one's behaviour and attitude are more important (Gell. *NA* 17.2.7: *Q. Metellus Numidicus, qui caste pureque lingua usus Latina videtur, in epistula, quam exul ad Domitios misit, ita scripsit: 'illi vero omni iure atque honestate interdicti, ego neque aqua neque igni careo et summa gloria fruniscor.'* – 'Q. Metellus Numidicus, who seems to have used the Latin language in a faultless and pure way, wrote in a letter, which he, as an exile, sent to the Domitii, as follows: "They have been debarred from every right and honour; I lack neither water nor fire, and I enjoy the greatest glory." ').[79] In *De domo sua* Cicero admits that he felt grief at leaving Rome (in an un-Stoic way): again, he does not present this as a sign of weakness but instead as an indication of the extent of his sacrifice; for if one left something behind one did not care about, it would not be a sacrifice (Cic. *Dom.* 97–8).

Moreover, Cicero presents his departure as a voluntary self-sacrifice for the sake of the community: while he claims that he could have offered resistance, he decided not to do so, since this might have led to civil war, and the welfare of the community was more important.[80] In his view, he thus saved Rome a

---

[73] E.g. Cic. *RS* 26; 31; *RQ* 6; 15; *Dom.* 7; 9; 14; 57; 74; *Har. resp.* 6.

[74] E.g. Cic. *RS* 3; 4; 5; 7; 8; 22; 24; 26; 28; 29; 34; *RQ* 13; 15; *Dom.* 7; 27; 30; 54; 74; 99; 147; *Sest.* 130; 147; *Prov. cons.* 43; *Har. resp.* 6; 46; 50; *Vat.* 10. – On the use and nuances of *salus* in these speeches, see MacKendrick 1995, 129, 131–2, 141, 142–3.

[75] E.g. Cic. *RS* 6; 23; *Dom.* 17; 64; 87; 99; 100; 143; 147; *Fam.* 14.4.3.

[76] E.g. Cic. *Dom.* 17.   [77] E.g. Cic. *Dom.* 27; 29; 100; 143.

[78] E.g. Cic. *RS* 8; 9; *RQ* 16; *Dom.* 9; 57.   [79] See Cohen 2007, 112 n. 9.

[80] E.g. Cic. *RS* 6; 32–4; 36; *RQ* 1; 13–14; *Dom.* 5; 30; 63–4; 68; 76; 88; 91–2; 95–6; 145; *Sest.* 35–6; 39; 42–9; 53; *Planc.* 86–90; *Mil.* 36; *Leg.* 3.25; comparing himself to the precedent of Metellus at *Sest.* 36–9; *Planc.* 89; cf. *Inv. in Sall.* 10.

second time; his recall acknowledged his role as a saviour of the Republic.[81] This presentation of Cicero's actions was already noted by a scholiast;[82] modern scholars have remarked that Cicero creates a 'myth' about himself.[83] Such a construct enables Cicero to assume a more self-confident position than beneficiaries usually do and to imply that the recall was a deserved response to what he did for the community.[84] In Cassius Dio Cicero's departure is not described heroically: he reports that Cicero had decided to let the issue be resolved by armed conflict with Clodius' adherents and was dissuaded from this course of action by Cato and Hortensius (Cass. Dio 38.17.4).[85]

At some points in the speeches delivered after his return Cicero characterizes himself as a civilian general, taking up his descriptions in the *Catilinarian Orations* (*dux togatus*: Cic. *Cat.* 2.28; 3.23), stresses how he saved the Republic through non-violent action in agreement with the Senate, and highlights that he is undergoing a *devotio* for the community, adjusting to his situation the vow of Roman generals to sacrifice their own lives to obtain victory for the army and their country (e.g. Cic. *RS* 32–4; *RQ* 1). He thus transfers such actions carried out on the battlefield to the civil realm (see Cic. *RQ* 1 n.).[86] In a speech to the People included in Sallust's *Histories* the consul C. Aurelius Cotta willingly offers devotion for the sake of the Republic, which consists in death, just as in the military paradigm (Sall. *Hist.* 2.47.9–12 M. = 2.43.9–12 R.). Only in Cicero's case is a deed already committed (and not entirely voluntarily) redefined as a sacrifice, and it consists in leaving to avoid civil war.

A related aspect is that Cicero claims that he did not abandon the Republic. Instead, according to him, the Republic went away with him (there was no functioning political system), and they returned together.[87] In a slight variation

---

[81] E.g. Cic. *RS* 33–4; 36; *RQ* 1; 16; 17; *Dom.* 63–4; 76; 96–9; 122; 132; 145; *Sest.* 43–9; 73; *Prov. cons.* 23; 45; *Pis.* 23; 78 (ironic statement of Piso); *Leg.* 3.25. – See, e.g., Grasmück 1977, 168; 1978, 116; Fuhrmann 1978, 157; Pina Polo 1996, 103–4, 109–10; Grillo 2015, 5–6; Boll 2019, 61–2.

[82] Schol. Bob. ad Cic. *Sest.* 45 (p. 130.25–8 Stangl): *etiam ex hoc laudem discessui suo et gloriam veluti denuo conservatae rei p. temptat adsciscere, quod maluerit urbe decedere quam dimicationis obire fortunam. quanta haec igitur vis oratoria est, ut exilium quoque magis virtutis eius quam poenae fuerit!*; ad *Planc.* 89 (p. 168.20–2 Stangl): *verum sibi, ut coeperam dicere, ipse Tullius maximam laudem praestruxit, qui ad tutelam salutis publicae patientiam discessus illius, quamvis non mediocri cum dolore, susceperit, ut multo sit laudabilior Metello, . . .* – Velleius Paterculus follows Cicero's portrayal of events when he says that Cicero suffered exile as a reward for having saved the Republic (as consul) (Vell. Pat. 2.45.2: *ita vir optime meritus de re publica conservatae patriae pretium calamitatem exili tulit.*).

[83] See Fuhrmann 1978, 157; MacKendrick 1995, 135.

[84] See also Raccanelli 2012, 34–5. – On the role of *beneficium* and associated connotations in Roman culture, see Lentano 2005. – Presenting his departure as a service to the community is in line with the requirements set out later in *De officiis* (44 BCE) that, if one is capable, one should be active for the state, preferably by aiming for peace and in the interests of everyone's welfare neglecting one's own (e.g. Cic. *Off.* 1.70–2; 1.79; 1.85–6).

[85] See Kelly 2006, 111.   [86] See Nicolet 1960; Dyck 2004.

[87] E.g. Cic. *RS* 34; 36; *RQ* 14; 18; *Dom.* 87; 141; *Parad.* 4.27–30. – See, e.g., Fantham 1972, 123; Doblhofer 1987, 243–7; Narducci 1997, 66–7; Cohen 2007, 111, 112.

of this motif, Cicero sometimes even claims that he was recalled by the Republic (Cic. *Sest.* 52: *videtis me tamen in meam pristinam dignitatem brevi tempore doloris interiecto rei publicae voce esse revocatum* – 'you see that the commonwealth has nonetheless called me back, after a brief interval of grief, to the worthy standing that I previously enjoyed' [trans. R. A. Kaster]).[88] Thus, Cicero essentially identifies himself with the Republic[89] and establishes a close link between its welfare and his activities,[90] while, in a different context, he acknowledges that the *res publica* is everyone's business and he just took the lead as consul, followed by others (Cic. *Sull.* 9).[91]

Accordingly, somewhat paradoxically, Cicero is both an advocate of the Republic, having saved her, and a client receiving protection from the Republic.[92] The underlying argument seems to be that political exile only exists by separation from a functioning political system; since this was not the case during Cicero's absence, he was not in 'exile', and those who forced him to leave were even responsible for creating this situation of non-exile because of their destruction of the political system at Rome.[93] When Cicero says that the Republic had also left and that leaving was the more beneficial deed for the Republic, his conduct is justified and given a positive interpretation.[94]

At the same time Cicero introduces himself as a victim or martyr,[95] because he was forced to leave Rome as a result of him having saved the Republic for the first time (i.e. by combating the Catilinarian Conspiracy: e.g. Cic. *Cat.* 3.15; 3.25–6; *RS* 36; *Sest.* 49; *Pis.* 6), and he notes that he left without having been taken to court or found guilty (Cic. *Dom.* 26; 33; 43; 47; 83; 88; 110; *Sest.* 53). Cicero even calls the bill on his 'exile' a *proscriptio* (Cic. *RS* 4; 8; *Dom.* 48; 50; 58; *Sest.* 133; *Prov. cons.* 45; *Pis.* 30); this makes it seem arbitrary, harsh, and unlawful and alludes to the procedures under L. Cornelius Sulla, when Roman citizens were declared outlaws and could be killed and have their property

---

[88] The image of Cicero recalled by the Republic or the country (Cic. *RQ* 10) recurs with reference to his movements in 44 BCE (Cic. *Off.* 3.121; *Fam.* 10.1.1). Glucker (1988) suggests that this motif might have been used in Cicero's *De temporibus suis* as an element of his self-presentation.

[89] E.g. Cic. *RS* 4; 10; 16; 17–18; 25; 29; 34; 36; *RQ* 14; 16; *Dom.* 17; 42; 63; 73; 96; 99; 141; 146; *Sest.* 15; 24; 26; 31; 54; *Prov. cons.* 45; *Har. resp.* 3; 15; 45; *Pis.* 77; *Sest.* 83; *Vat.* 7–8; *Balb.* 58. – See Grasmück 1977, 168; 1978, 116; May 1981; Nicholson 1992, 32, 35–7; MacKendrick 1995, 129, 134, 139–40, 141, 145; Pina Polo 1996, 104; La Farina 2008, 336–7; Boll 2019, 62–3. – A certain parallelization between the fate of the speaking politician and the Republic also occurs in the speech by consul C. Aurelius Cotta in Sallust's *Histories* (Sall. *Hist.* 2.47.4 M. = 2.43.4 R.).

[90] In *Pro Milone* Cicero associates the *salus* of the defendant T. Annius Milo with the *salus* of the *res publica* (e.g. Cic. *Mil.* 1; 63).

[91] See Hodgson 2017, 143–4. – On Cicero's argument based on his interpretation and presentation of his relationship to the *res publica*, see Hodgson 2017, 141–62.

[92] See May 1981, 310.   [93] See Cohen 2007, 116, 126.

[94] See Dyck 2004, 303. – As Cicero departed before the second law, naming him, was passed, there was no legal requirement to leave at the time; therefore, in theory, his departure contradicted the obligations of a senator to be present in Rome and attend Senate meetings (on this duty, see Cic. *Dom.* 8; *Leg.* 3.11; 3.40; Gell. *NA* 14.7.10; see also, e.g., Bonnefond-Coudry 1989, 357–8).

[95] See Nicholson 1992, 37–9; Robinson 1994, 479; Pina Polo 1996, 103.

confiscated (Cic. *Dom.* 43).[96] Cicero also describes the bill as a *privilegium*, arguing that this, rather than *lex*, is the correct term for a measure directed against a named individual according to Roman law, going back to the Twelve Tables (Cic. *Dom.* 43; 58). Thereby, he takes up a term from the early days of the Roman Republic which had hardly been used since and presents an interpretation of it as a ban on specific laws against individuals, a reading not supported by the word's original use, but taken up by later Roman jurists.[97] Such a strategy avoids an emphasis on the lack of a trial, as this was the point of criticism concerning the treatment of the captured Catilinarian conspirators he was responsible for. Still, Cicero may have felt that the two situations were not comparable when in 63 BCE a *senatus consultum ultimum* was in place and the Catilinarian conspirators were convicted by the Senate after the presentation of unequivocal evidence at a meeting convened to decide their fate (Cass. Dio 37.38). Moreover, Cicero highlights his particular status by comparisons with historical examples: in contrast to others, he was called back without much family support, only because of his own worth and by a decree of the Senate and the People, and without any bloodshed and tumult (Cic. *RS* 37–8; *RQ* 6–11; *Dom.* 87).[98]

In order to emphasize the significance of his recall, Cicero stresses throughout that he has been recalled unanimously by all orders and formal bodies of the Roman Republic and by the whole of Italy (e.g. Cic. *RS* 25; 26; 29; 39; *RQ* 1; 10; 12; 16; 18; *Dom.* 30; 57; 87; *Sest.* 128).[99] He also presents his return like a 'rebirth' (e.g. Cic. *Att.* 3.20.1; 4.1.8; *Sest.* 131): this second birth surpasses the first, natural birth; for, according to Cicero, one can appreciate everything more after having lived without it and because everything is now received back fully developed and simultaneously (Cic. *RS* 1; 27; *RQ* 2–5).[100] The notion that a recall from exile can be like a rebirth appears briefly in the speech of the consul C. Aurelius Cotta in Sallust's *Histories* (Sall. *Hist.* 2.47.3 M. = 2.43.3 R.): Cotta went into exile in 90 BCE in anticipation of a vote of condemnation under the *Lex Varia* and returned in 82 BCE (App. *B Civ.* 1.37).

Because the focus in these two speeches is on expressing gratitude and re-establishing Cicero's position, there is no specific reference to obtaining the remainder of his property. This matter is dealt with separately later (Cic. *Dom.*); at the time of composing the initial speeches Cicero might not have foreseen the extent of the argument required to regain his property.

---

[96] See, e.g., Claassen 1999, 160.   [97] See Bleicken 1975, 196–217.

[98] See, e.g., Riggsby 2002, 161–3.

[99] The emphasis on the agreement of various groups was already noted as a rhetorical strategy by C. Iulius Victor (*RLM*, pp. 402.33–403.4: *utimur autem iudicatu tum omnium, tum plurimorum, tum optimorum, praeterea eorum, qui in unaquaque arte peritissimi sunt. omnium iudicatu utitur Marcus Tullius cum dicit, nullum ordinem in civitate fuisse, quibus non libentibus ab exilio rediret: plurimorum autem iudicatu, cum ex senatus consulto sibi domum restitutam: optimorum iudicatu, cum Pompeium et ceteros auctores reditus sui nominat: scientium iudicatu, cum domum suam dicit a religione pontificum sententia liberatam.*).

[100] See Raccanelli 2012, 54–5; Cole 2013, 63–5.

Cicero's presentation of himself is complemented by corresponding ones of his opponents and supporters, especially in the speech in the Senate. He puts the activities against him down to individuals, particularly the Tribune of the People P. Clodius Pulcher and the consuls of 58 BCE; by contrast, he singles out supportive actions of the Senate, the knights, and other magistrates, even if not all of these had a concrete result. This strategy allows Cicero to identify people responsible for his predicament and to acknowledge enmity towards men who are his known enemies and no longer in a powerful office, while he can claim unanimity with others and thus resume his role as a respected ex-consul within the Senate. Despite the opposition, in these speeches Cicero never mentions P. Clodius Pulcher by name (he is referred to either indirectly or as *inimicus*) and only refers to the consuls of 58 BCE by name once in the speech to the Senate (Cic. *RS* 16).[101] The speech before the Senate underlines the contrast between Cicero's behaviour as a consul and consular and that of the consuls of 58 BCE. In the *contio* speech the criticism is more subdued: there is no extended section of invective against the consuls, and Clodius, a former Tribune of the People, is not described equally critically or marked as an enemy and criminal.[102]

The voicing of profuse thanks in a carefully calibrated way to groups and a selection of individuals, contrasted with invective against others, ensures that the respective audiences can feel that they have contributed to the resolution of the conflict and the deeds beneficial for the Republic and that they are aligned with the 'right' side. Thus, not all expressions of gratitude might be heartfelt; some may have been included for political reasons.[103] By presenting his fate and his activities not just as a personal matter, but as affecting the Republic, Cicero makes the conflict relevant to both types of audiences and can enlist them as supporters of his policies for the future.

Cicero's self-justification, the assessment of friends and enemies, and the presentation of his role with regard to the *res publica* and his political ideals in the speeches *Post reditum in senatu* and *Post reditum ad Quirites* adumbrate themes recurring in speeches of the subsequent decade.[104] When Cicero stresses that he was recalled by all orders and all parts of Italy (e.g. Cic. *RS* 38–9; *RQ* 1; 9–10; 16; 18; *Sest.* 107–8; *Pis.* 34–6), this can be regarded as a version of the ideal of *concordia omnium* and *consensus Italiae*. He also emphasizes the restoration of *otium* in connection with his return (e.g. Cic. *RQ* 1; 16), a concept here combined with *dignitas* for the first time in Cicero's works.[105]

---

[101] See Nicholson 1992, 95–6; Morstein-Marx 2004, 216; Steel 2007; Lintott 2008, 9. – On the use of names, see esp. Steel 2007.

[102] On the criticism of P. Clodius Pulcher in the speeches delivered after Cicero's return, see Seager 2014.

[103] See MacKendrick 1995, 135.   [104] See Nicholson 1992, 131.

[105] On the motifs of *concordia ordinum* and *otium cum dignitate* in Cicero's post-exile speeches, see Nicholson 1992, 32, 39–45. – Hodgson's (2017, 149) point that Cicero's oratory aims to conceal his weakness seems unspecific; more precisely, Cicero uses oratory to argue away any weaknesses and to present himself as being in a strong position.

The nature of exile had been discussed in the Greek tradition, for instance in the work Περὶ φυγῆς by the Hellenistic Cynic philosopher Teles (transmitted at Stob. 3.40.8). As emerges from later writings, Cicero was aware of this topic as an element of philosophical discussions (Cic. *Tusc.* 3.81 [45 BCE]). He adds further philosophical considerations on exile in *Paradoxa Stoicorum* (46 BCE); its fourth paradox is dedicated to exile (Cic. *Parad.* 4.27–32): attitude and circumstances are placed above location, so that one might be in exile while being in one's native country and not in exile while being abroad.[106] Cicero outlines that a *civitas* exists only where law and order are maintained and political institutions operate properly. Accordingly, he concludes that he was not expelled from a *civitas*, which did not exist at the time. On the contrary, he acted as an exemplary citizen, while Clodius was in exile, since not place, but attitude defines exile. The basis of such an argument can already be found in the speeches delivered upon his return, when Cicero denies that he was ever in 'exile' and brings his absence from Rome into parallelism with that of the Republic.

3.5. Language, style, and prose rhythm

The speeches *Post reditum in senatu* and *Post reditum ad Quirites* belong to the larger group of orations delivered after Cicero's return to Rome throughout the 50s BCE (see Introduction, section 3.1). The following features have been identified for speeches of this period: they exhibit well-crafted regular periods and a rich, varied, and expressive syntax, with mutual influence among the works in different literary genres produced by Cicero; they display a greater variety of styles within single orations; they often include both sarcastic, ironic, and critical passages about opponents and more elevated passages about Cicero's achievements; they are marked by a large number of antitheses, historical examples, and particular constructions of indirect questions, participial phrases, and negated expressions.[107] The average sentence length in the two orations connected directly with Cicero's return (based on the analysis of a sample) is not unusual for speeches of this period.[108]

In addition, the two speeches exhibit stylistic characteristics prompted by the specific circumstances and their generic peculiarity (see Introduction, section 3.2). The shared situation and content result in some similarities in expression, while the different audiences addressed lead to divergences in emphasis, tone, and style (see Introduction, section 3.3).[109]

---

[106] On this concept, see Herescu 1961.
[107] See, e.g., von Albrecht 1973, 1305–8; 2003, 103–5.   [108] See Johnson 1971.
[109] On the style of these two speeches and differences between them, see, e.g., Wuilleumier 1952, 24, 25; Paratte 1963, 20–2; Bellardi 1975, 9–11; Nicholson 1992, 121–5; MacKendrick 1995, 129–35, 139–46.

According to Cicero's description in the later treatise *Orator* (46 BCE), the style in epideictic speeches is different from that in forensic speeches (Cic. *Orat.* 207–11): in epideictic speeches almost the whole text should be periodic and rhythmic, whereas in forensic speeches such a style should only be used in selected passages. The two *post reditum* speeches belong to neither category exclusively, but the awareness of such stylistic differences and of their potential effect suggests that Cicero will have thought about the appropriate style to apply, especially when he prepared at least one of the speeches in writing in advance (Cic. *Planc.* 74 [T 2]).

In spite of some differences the tone and style of both speeches is mostly solemn and impressive, approximating the medium, temperate style, though it varies according to the content of particular passages.[110] For instance, the invective section on Cicero's opponents in the speech to the Senate (Cic. *RS* 10–18) includes terms of abuse, foreign and colloquial words, and a high number of metaphors and comparisons not occurring in other parts of the oration to the same extent.[111] Thus, the speech in the Senate displays a more varied style, changing between the opening, the invective, the more narrative parts, and the concluding sections. In contrast, the speech to the People is rhetorically more coherent; there is only one diminutive (Cic. *RQ* 20), and it does not contain colloquial expressions or sustained irony. The tone of that speech is also more restrained in terms of criticism and more rhetorically elaborate and emotional; this is achieved, for instance, by more details about Cicero's family, more appeals to the gods, and more repetitions and sequences.[112]

While both speeches contain metaphors, those in the Senate speech tend to be more varied and allusive.[113] One of the more striking and meaningful rhetorical features—generally more developed in the speech to the Senate—is the partial personification of the *res publica*, described as affected by the activities of opponents, in need of help, and even driven out (e.g. Cic. *RS* 3; 6; 17; 18; 34; 36; 39; *RQ* 11; 18).

As the speeches are intended to present the *beneficium* Cicero received from the Senate and the People as something extraordinary and to render effusive thanks in return, they include numerous hyperbolic expressions. For instance, the deeds of support for Cicero, the underlying attitude, and the appropriate reaction in response are described as *divinus* (Cic. *RS* 1; 28; 30; *RQ* 1; 2; 5; 15; 25),

---

[110] See Laurand 1936–8, 310–11; Paratte 1963, 18 (on Cic. *RQ*); von Albrecht 1973, 1293; 2003, 20–5.

[111] On the syntactical structures and rhetorical figures in both speeches, see Cipriani 1975, 157–66, 175–9.

[112] See, e.g., von Albrecht 1973, 1251–2; 2003, 25–6; MacKendrick 1995, 136, 146.

[113] On metaphors in both speeches and differences between them, see Fantham 1972, 121–5. – According to (slightly questionable) figures compiled by MacKendrick (1995, 131, 142), the speech in the Senate includes 278 metaphors (i.e. about seven per paragraph), and the speech before the People has 265 metaphors (i.e. about eleven per paragraph); both figures are well above average in comparison with other Ciceronian speeches analysed according to the same method.

incredibilis (Cic. *RS* 1; 26; *RQ* 2; 5), *inauditus* (Cic. *RQ* 7), or *immortalis* (Cic. *RS* 1; *RQ* 1); some of the most emphatic expressions are qualified by words such as *paene* or forms of *quidam*, toning down the bold transfer. There are frequent two-part expressions, as parallels or contrasts, perhaps to balance and lend more weight to these points (often marked by the structure *non modo/solum...sed etiam* and its variations). Numerous mentions of and addresses to *di immortales* intensify the impact of these orations, especially in the speech to the People (Cic. *RS* 2 [3x]; 9; 30; *RQ* 1 [2x]; 4; 5 [3x]; 14; 18 [3x]; 25). While some of these references to the gods are conventional, satisfying the assumed religious feelings of the audience, others present the positive developments affecting Cicero and the audience as being willed by the gods (e.g. Cic. *RS* 9; *RQ* 1; 18).[114]

In both speeches Cicero uses historical *exempla* to illustrate his situation in relation to other ex-consuls who had to leave Rome and later came back.[115] The presentation is selective and ignores the wider context so that Cicero can make points conducive to his argument. The comparison is more prominent and occurs at an earlier stage in the speech to the People (Cic. *RS* 37–8; *RQ* 6–11). Such an organization suggests that the *exempla* are not simply introduced as ornaments but rather with a specific intention; for the emphasis of the juxtaposition is not so much on the peaceful return, endorsed by everyone, but on the fact that Cicero was basically on his own and had no relatives to lobby for him, being a 'new man' aligned with the People (as he outlines in the introduction of his inaugural speech as consul to the People: Cic. *Leg. agr.* 2.1–10).

Some statistics suggest that the frequency of *clausulae* and rhetorical figures is low in both *Post reditum in senatu* and *Post reditum ad Quirites*, that there are more 'Attic *clausulae*' than 'Asianic *clausulae*', and that the number of subordinate clauses is high.[116] These characteristics might have been seen as an argument for inauthenticity in earlier scholarship; now they are best interpreted as an indication of the nature of these speeches and the development of Cicero's oratory in this period.

T. Zielinski's studies on *clausulae* in Cicero's speeches (1904) demonstrated that the patterns found in these orations do not substantially differ from those typical of his other speeches, while certain characteristics set off Cicero's speeches from other Latin prose texts. The presentation of this evidence and the resulting conclusions were generally accepted and put the discussion of the authenticity of the *post reditum* speeches to rest.

Zielinski's book still presents a lot of useful data on the identifiable types of *clausulae* and their relative distribution.[117] Not much work on a similar scale

---

[114] On the role of religion in Cicero's speeches, see Heibges 1969, esp. 847–8.

[115] For a list of historical *exempla* in both speeches, see Bücher 2006, 244.

[116] See Cipriani 1975, esp. 15.

[117] See Zielinski 1904; for further studies on the prose rhythm of Cicero's speeches, see, e.g., Bornecque 1909; Primmer 1968; Nisbet 1990 (on *clausulae* in *cola*); Hutchinson 1995; for the role of prose rhythm for considering questions of authenticity, see Berry 1996. – For a recent

had been done until recently, when T. Keeline and T. Kirby (2019) looked at prose rhythm in Latin literature again from a global perspective, this time with the help of digital methods. Although they are cautious and aware of the possible drawbacks of a computerized approach, which should be supplemented by other methods, their statistics demonstrate that there are broad tendencies of prose rhythm in Cicero's speeches distinguishing them from his writings in other literary genres and from the prose texts of other Latin writers, while there is also variation within the corpus of Ciceronian speeches, probably due to developments over time or the character of individual orations.

Within the framework of what can be observed for Cicero's speeches, the statistical analysis by Keeline and Kirby shows that the pattern of *clausulae* in the two speeches *Post reditum in senatu* and *Post reditum ad Quirites* is not unusual.[118] For instance, with respect to the most frequent types of *clausulae* (cretic plus trochee, double cretic, and ditrochee), *RS* and *RQ* have 39.41 per cent and 37.62 per cent cretic-trochee *clausulae*, 12.94 per cent and 10.89 per cent double cretic *clausulae*, and 32.94 per cent and 37.62 per cent double trochee *clausulae*, respectively. This compares with the following figures for all of Cicero's speeches: 28.70 per cent, 23.78 per cent, and 26.24 per cent. While these percentages differ, other Ciceronian speeches close in time to *RS* and *RQ* show distributions of *clausulae* similar to those of *RS* and *RQ* (e.g. *Arch.*: 34.85 per cent, 18.18 per cent, 36.36 per cent; *Sest.*: 33.22 per cent, 16.09 per cent, 28.97 per cent; *Scaur.*: 33.53 per cent, 14.45 per cent, 31.21 per cent). In light of the fact that the *clausulae* in these speeches cannot be regarded as particularly unusual, *clausulae* will be identified in the commentary only where they are relevant for the constitution of the text or have given rise to scholarly discussions.

In the spurious *Oratio pridie quam in exilium iret* (see Introduction, section 4) the clausulae are significantly different. In this speech the figures for the most frequent types of *clausulae* compiled in the same way are: 19.84 per cent cretic-trochee *clausulae*, 9.16 per cent double cretic *clausulae*, 36.64 per cent double trochee *clausulae*, showing a marked difference in the first group. More obviously, the percentages of spondaic clausulae are 10.58 per cent in *RS*, 4.95 per cent in *RQ*, and 17.55 per cent in the spurious speech, and the percentages for 'artistic' *clausulae* are 86.47 per cent in *RS*, 89.10 per cent in *RQ*, and 67.17 per cent in the spurious speech. Thus, if *Oratio pridie quam in exilium iret* was genuine, it would be Cicero's least rhythmic speech in terms of *clausulae*, except for the deliberately different *Pro Q. Roscio comoedo*; rather than being comparable to Cicero's speeches, this oration's rhythmic profile is closer to the (equally spurious) invective *In Sallustium*. Thus, renewed rhythmic analysis confirms

---

discussion of prose rhythm with respect to Greek prose literature, see Hutchinson 2018. – For an overview of *clausulae* in Cic. *RS* and *RQ*, see Cipriani 1975, 167–72, 181–4; for a discussion of *clausulae* in Cic. *RS*, see Novotný 1925.

[118] See Keeline/Kirby 2019.

that *RS* and *RQ* can be regarded as Ciceronian, while it provides another reason for the inauthenticity of *Oratio pridie quam in exilium iret*.[119]

4. THE SPURIOUS *ORATIO PRIDIE QUAM IN EXILIUM IRET*

The *Oratio pridie quam in exilium iret* has been transmitted with the speeches delivered by the historical Cicero after his return to Rome, presumably because of its content and the purported date of delivery (see Introduction, section 5.1). Yet the oddity of the presupposed situation, the inconsistencies in the speech, and the deviations from Cicero's typical style led to doubts about its authenticity from an early stage. The oration was first identified as spurious by Dionysius Lambinus (1520–72).[120] As a result of its acknowledged inauthenticity, the speech received hardly any attention for a long time. More recently, in line with renewed attention to the concepts of fake, forgery, pseudepigraphy, and the textual examples of such cases, interest in this speech has revived (see Introduction, section 1).

Beyond the fact that the speech is not by Cicero and is a product of the first few centuries CE, there are no agreed views on its precise date of composition or the author. Cicero's lifetime is the obvious *terminus post quem*, and the earliest extant manuscript (P, ninth century) provides the *terminus ante quem*.[121] Several options for the date of composition within that range have been put forward: the text's most recent editor has suggested a date in the second century CE.[122] Other scholars have favoured a later date, but still within late antiquity, such as the third or fourth centuries CE.[123] An earlier date, possibly the first or the early second century CE, within the context of rhetorical education and declamation, has now also been considered, while it has been noted that any date between the first and the fourth centuries CE has to be regarded as possible.[124] Parallels with expressions in datable authors from the first few centuries CE are too unspecific or too small in number to enable a narrowing down of the chronological range. The fact that there are no traces of the movement of

---

[119] Many thanks to T. Keeline and T. Kirby, who, in addition to the data compiled for their article, have kindly provided the figures for *Oratio pridie quam in exilium iret* and suggested ways of analysis. – On the different patterns of prose rhythm in *Oratio pridie quam in exilium iret*, see also Corbeill 2020, 19–20.

[120] See De Marco 1991, 5.

[121] For a brief overview of the reception of Cicero's oratorical and rhetorical works (with further references), as the context in which this speech must be seen, see Kennedy 2002.

[122] See De Marco 1967, 37; 1991, 5.

[123] See Gamberale 1997, 331; 1998, 54, 55, 70, 74; La Bua 2019, 83.

[124] See Keeline 2018, 150–1; Corbeill 2020, 20–1, with n. 12. – Wiseman (2004, 180, with n. 58) regards the text as 'undatable', while he is open to considering an early date.

archaism popular in the second century CE might suggest that the text was composed before rather than after this period. Irrespective of the precise date, it is plausibly assumed that the speech is not an intentional fake and rather originated in the context of declamations in the schools of rhetoric as a piece composed for a particular historical occasion (and then became attached to Cicero's genuine orations);[125] in its recourse to an abundance of rhetorical figures the speech is line with the declamatory tradition.[126] As scholars have noted,[127] in parts the speech almost appears as a cento of Ciceronian phrases and motifs, as was common in the declamatory tradition. At the same time there are subtle differences from their use in genuine orations by Cicero, the speech draws on a wide range of sources, and also includes unique and rare phrases or expressions that do not occur elsewhere or are otherwise first attested in authors writing after Cicero's lifetime.

In view of the author's familiarity with classical history it has been proposed that *Oratio pridie quam in exilium iret* was inspired by information such as that given in a passage in Plutarch, describing how in response to Clodius' law-making activity Cicero put on mourning clothes and made suppliant entreaties to the People and how a large number of knights also changed their dress, escorted him, and joined his supplications (Plut. *Cic.* 30.6–31.1).[128] This narrative suggests a series of informal supplications to groups or individuals among the People, while the oration's text presupposes an occasion for the delivery of a one-off set-piece oration and mentions a *contio* (*Exil.* 19).[129] There is no evidence that Cicero delivered a proper speech before he left Rome in 58 BCE. Since in that year Cicero was not in a position to call a *contio*, one of the magistrates in office would have had to do this; in view of their hostility as described by the historical Cicero, it is unlikely that they would have created such an opportunity for him. Moreover, it is doubtful whether he would have delivered such a speech to mark his yielding. Cicero could have produced a pamphlet in the shape of a speech intended for written circulation and not for oral delivery, in order to create a more rounded record of his journey away from Rome and back.[130] If such a piece was not merely intended to gather support for Cicero at the time of his departure, but to have a longer life and spread Cicero's views, one might expect a version putting more emphasis on Cicero's achievements making a departure from Rome seem unjust and less emphasis on appeals for help.

---

[125] See, e.g., Gamberale 1998, 74; La Bua 2019, 83. – On early pseudepigraphic material on Cicero, see Keeline 2018, 147–95, esp. 164–77 on the role of the 'exile' in this tradition. – On the concept of the 'Roman fake', see Peirano 2012.

[126] See Keeline 2018, 168.

[127] See esp. De Marco 1991; Gamberale 1997; 1998; Keeline 2018, 167–71 (with examples); also Corbeill 2020, 24–7.

[128] See, e.g., De Marco 1967, 37; 1991, 5 (link to Plutarch doubted by Gamberale 1998, 54; esp. Keeline 2018, 151).

[129] See Keeline 2018, 151 and n. 17.

[130] Corbeill (2020, 17 n. 3) notes that this possibility has to be considered.

Still, as the speech fills a potential perceived gap in the texts documenting Cicero's departure from and return to Rome, it could be regarded as a 'creative supplement' to the genuine texts.[131]

In the speeches delivered after his return to Rome the historical Cicero presents his exile as a heroic deed and a sacrifice for the community, putting all the blame on P. Clodius Pulcher; this version is generally picked up by later authors.[132] The reactions to *suasoria* themes connected with Cicero and reported by Seneca the Elder indicate that some declaimers were critical, for instance, of Cicero's dealing with adversity, but generally a positive presentation of Cicero was predominant (Sen. *Suas.* 6.14; 6.22; 6.24). The speech set at the point of Cicero's departure stands out by presenting Cicero at a point in his life when he does not address the challenge entirely heroically or at least does not create the impression that he is in charge. The speech thus is linked to a particular moment in Cicero's life, but in its vagueness as to what is required would perhaps not have been the most effective in this particular historical situation; at the same time the speech appears as a combination of elements taken from Cicero's writings composed in different literary genres and at different times combined with some historical facts and thus may be seen as a psychological description of his changing mood. This might be quite an accurate description of Cicero's feelings at the time, but is probably not what Cicero would have liked to have seen published.

Such a portrayal might be a deliberate variation illustrating another facet of Cicero's biography and personality. In addition, it has been observed that in style, language, and conventions the text of the speech displays features that are idiosyncratic, un-Ciceronian, and unusual in the declamatory tradition, and thus it has been suggested that the author might have included those on purpose 'to demonstrate that he knows how *not* to write like Cicero'.[133] While this is a potential explanation for the oration's characteristics, they or at least some of them could also be the result of someone making use of a variety of elements taken from the rhetorical tradition without being overly concerned about or fully aware of how these combine to create a portrayal the historical Cicero might have intended or relate to the motifs and stylistic conventions found in Cicero's genuine works.

In any case the author clearly engages with a wide range of classical and particularly Ciceronian sources and rehearses motifs common in the works of the historical Cicero (e.g. Cicero not guilty of any crime or having preserved the Republic), giving them a particular twist in that they are employed to request help from the audience and adding some moralistic reasoning as to why this is required and appropriate. At the same time the composition of the audience remains vague, and it is not clearly defined what they are meant to do.

---

[131] For the terminology, see Peirano 2012, 10.   [132] See Keeline 2018, 164, 171.
[133] See Corbeill 2020.

Further, the position of the speaker varies over the course of the speech: while he initially appears to hope for an arrangement allowing him to stay in Rome, there seems to be a tendency to become resigned to having to leave Rome towards the end. Still, he calls on the audience, asking that his memory be kept and praised, so that he emerges superior to his enemies. Such a tenor would agree with the assumption that the speech was written in hindsight by someone familiar with Cicero's writings and the history of the period, while not fully recreating Cicero's own style (on the content and argument of this speech, see *Exil.*, Introduction).

This speech is not the only spurious speech presented as an additional oration by Cicero elaborating on a historical and political situation he encountered. There is also, for instance, a *Quinta Catilinaria*, along with a *Responsio Catilinae*.[134] In contrast to *Oratio pridie quam in exilium iret* these texts are usually dated to the medieval period on the basis of a linguistic analysis revealing non-classical features. They might be declamation speeches produced in France in the context of a revival of classical oratory and rhetoric. The earliest manuscript in which these texts have survived (Biblioteca Apostolica Vaticana, MS Reg. Lat. 84, fol. 26r–29v) contains, besides the *Etymologies* of Isidore of Seville, also a discussion of *modus loquendi*. Thus, these speeches are documents of the long-running impact Cicero's genuine speeches have had not only on practical oratory, but also on the rhetorical tradition. Unlike *Quinta Catilinaria* and *Responsio Catilinae*, *Oratio pridie quam in exilium iret* is transmitted within the context of Cicero's genuine speeches and a significantly earlier document of the reactions they created.

5. NOTE ON TEXT AND TRANSLATION

5.1. Transmission

Cicero's speeches from the years after his return to Rome seem to have been transmitted as a unit since late antiquity (*Post reditum in senatu, Post reditum ad Quirites, De domo sua, De haruspicum responsis, Pro Sestio, In Vatinium, Pro Caelio, De provinciis consularibus*, and *Pro Balbo*, along with Ps.-Cicero, *Oratio pridie quam in exilium iret*).[135]

---

[134] For the text of *Quinta Catilinaria*, see De Marco 1991, 29–49; for an analysis, see Haye 1999, 226–31.
[135] On aspects of the transmission history and textual issues of *RS* and *RQ*, see Stock 1888, Peterson 1910; Klotz 1912; 1913; Wuilleumier 1952, 28–37; Guillen 1967, 21–8; Lenaghan 1969, 42–5; Maslowski 1980; 1981, praef.; 1982; Maslowski/Rouse 1984; Boll 2019, 72–88; for a description of the manuscripts, see Rouse/Reeve 1983, 57–61, 83–5; on an additional manuscript, see F. De Marco 1957. – For some considerations on the origin of the corpus, see La Bua 2019, 82–4.

The three speeches *Post reditum in senatu*, *Post reditum ad Quirites*, and *Oratio pridie quam in exilium iret* in the main share the same transmission. The major sources for the text of all of them are the four manuscripts P (cod. Parisinus 7794), G (cod. Bruxellensis 5345, olim Gemblacensis), E (cod. Berolinensis 252, olim Erfurtensis), and H (cod. Harleianus 4927), which go back, directly or via intermediaries, to a common source (now lost), which T. Maslowski (1981) calls A (for *RS* and *RQ*) and De Marco marks as Ω (for *Exil*.).[136] In details, however, the manuscript evidence differs. The most extensive transmission exists for *Post reditum in senatu*, since, in addition to the manuscripts deriving from A, called the Paris family (because of manuscript P), there is another group, the so-called z-family.

The relationships between the various manuscripts can be summarized for *Post reditum in senatu* as follows: P descends from A and was revised by a corrector at an early stage (P²) and again later (P³, influenced also by H²). G and E form a second branch: they are descended from A via a common exemplar (m) and an intermediate source (y). In addition to G and E, the later manuscripts ε (cod. Erlangensis 847), V (cod. Vaticanus 1525, olim Palatinus), and F (lectiones codicis Pithoeani) also belong to this branch; they are probably descended from m via a shared exemplar n. H represents a third branch of this family. This manuscript shares readings with P and GE (via y) and also includes readings from P²; because of omissions, rearrangements, and emendations (some of them probably owing to deliberate interventions in the text), it is regarded as a problematic source.[137] P² consulted y (an ancestor of m); moreover, P² has had an influence on G's corrector G² and E's corrector E² and on the intermediate source n, which is dependent on m. Thus, there are various interrelations between the different manuscripts of this group. The z-family can be discerned from E², ε, V, F, and X (fragmenta Parisina 18104); there is contamination between the A-family and the z-family, since ε, V, and F also depend on A via intermediate stages and the influence of P² is discernible in X.[138]

The situation for *Post reditum ad Quirites* is basically similar, but different in so far as the z-family does not exist for this speech and E omits a large part of the text (and E² does not exist). For this section the second branch of the Paris

---

[136] The overview of the transmission situation is based on the editions of Maslowski (1981) and of De Marco (1991). – For a full explanation of textual sigla, see the lists just before the Latin text of each speech.

[137] See Maslowski 1981, xxvi–xxviii.

[138] See Maslowski 1981, xii–xiii: 'Horum omnium ratione habita persuasum mihi est duos quasi rivulos memoriae orationis *cum sen. gr. egit* ex antiquis temporibus ad nos deductos esse per codices duos, i.e. per (A) et archetypum familiae z. uterque codex non solum sua vitia sed etiam quandam recensionem exhibuit, i.e. quibusdam locis varias lectiones quae aetate Romana legentibus notae fuerint, atque suam inscriptionem. quae sententia per se spectata nullam dubitationem movere debet. ceterum non infitias eo olim unam editionem exstitisse ad quam utraque familia ultimo gradu redierit. sed ut hodie se res habent, duo archetypa in hac oratione sumenda mihi videntur, quorum ex uno PGEH, altero XE²εVF profluxerint.'

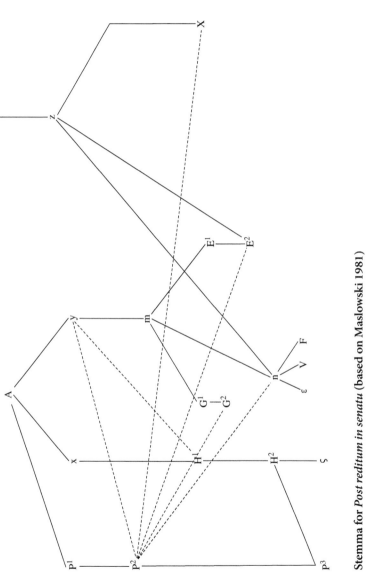

Stemma for *Post reditum in senatu* (based on Maslowski 1981)

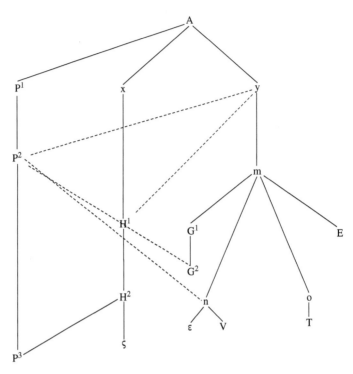

Stemma for *Post reditum ad Quirites* (based on Maslowski 1981)

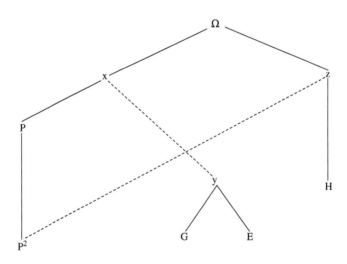

Stemma for *Oratio pridie quam in exilium iret* (based on De Marco 1991)

family is made up only of G, ϵ, V (F does not include this speech), and additionally T (cod. Trecensis 552), which derives from m via an intermediary o.

The Teubner edition of *Post reditum in senatu*, *Post reditum ad Quirites*, *De domo sua*, and *De haruspicum responsis* by T. Maslowski (1981) is based on the examination and collation of all relevant manuscripts and provides a full critical apparatus; on balance it often gives preference to the A-family, but also acknowledges that a number of important readings have been preserved in the z-family (codd. rec. are not fully documented).

The edition of the *Oratio pridie quam in exilium iret* relies only on the manuscripts deriving from A, namely P, G, E, and H, following the most recent editor of this speech, M. De Marco (1991), who disregards ϵ (p. 6: 'minoris momenti'), but takes account of H in contrast to I. G. Baiter (1856). M. De Marco (1991) agrees with T. Maslowski (1981), the editor of the genuine *post reditum* speeches, in the assessment of the relative status of the manuscripts, the descent of the extant manuscripts ultimately from a common ancestor, and the close relationship of G and E. The two editors vary slightly in their dating of these manuscripts and differ in details of the stemmatic analysis: according to De Marco, the exemplar of G and E depends on an intermediary source between Ω (~A) and P, and P^2 is not influenced by H^2, but rather by an intermediate source, via which H goes back to Ω.

Two *editiones principes* of all of Cicero's speeches were published in 1471, one in Rome and one in Venice.[139]

The stemmata given here illustrate the relationship between all the manuscripts adduced by the respective editors for the various speeches.

5.2. The text and translation in this edition

The Latin text of the speeches *Post reditum in senatu* and *Post reditum ad Quirites* in this edition has been developed from that of the Teubner edition by T. Maslowski (1981);[140] the Latin text of the *Oratio pridie quam in exilium iret* has been derived from the edition by M. De Marco (1991);[141] information on the manuscripts and their readings has been taken from the *praefatio* and apparatus criticus of the respective edition (and occasionally earlier editions and studies

---

[139] Rome: ISTC ic00541000 (https://data.cerl.org/istc/ic00541000); Venice: ISTC ic00542000 (https://data.cerl.org/istc/ic00542000). – For a list of early editions, see Guillen 1967, 29.

[140] On his principles of orthography, see Maslowski 1981, xxxiv–xxxv. – See Nicholson 1992, 17: 'The latest and best edition is T. Maslowski's 1981 Teubner which provides a carefully updated recension with very full apparatus, based on an exhaustive reexamination of all the mss and a cautious sifting of generations of emendations.'

[141] Previously, the speech *Pridie quam in exilium iret* was edited by Baiter (1856) and Müller (1890).

on the text).[142] As discussed in the commentary and noted in the apparatus, the transmission is problematic in places; in some cases, therefore, readings or conjectures different from those printed in the reference editions have been adopted. A list of the major departures from the reference editions (not including minor differences in punctuation, spelling, paragraphing etc.) is provided at the end of this volume.

The sigla used in the critical apparatus (see lists just before the Latin text of each oration) have been taken from T. Maslowski's (1981) edition for the genuine speeches and from M. De Marco's (1991) edition for the spurious *Oratio pridie quam in exilium iret*. For all speeches the critical apparatus has the format of a positive apparatus, in the interests of clarity.

In terms of spelling conventions, this text follows the principles of T. Maslowski's edition, for instance by only capitalizing proper names and writing *v* for consonantal *u*.

The English translation is meant to be a guide to understanding the Latin text. Therefore, it is intended to be fairly literal and to capture the style and structure of the Latin as far as possible (with the usual adjustments due to the requirements of the English language). This version might, therefore, read less fluently than a free-standing, self-contained English translation, but seems appropriate as a means to elucidate the Latin in the context of a commentary.

---

[142] For the testimonia (printed before the text of the speeches) only a limited apparatus criticus is provided.

Text and translation

Text

Testimonia

(1) Cic. *Att.* 4.1.5 (Sept. 57 BCE): postridie in senatu, qui fuit dies Non. Sept., senatui gratias egimus.

(2) Cic. *Planc.* 74 (54 BCE): nihil autem me novi, nihil temporis causa dicere, nonne etiam est illa testis oratio quae est a me prima habita in senatu? in qua cum perpaucis nominatim egissem gratias, quod omnes enumerari nullo modo possent, scelus autem esset quemquam praeteriri, statuissemque eos solum nominare qui causae nostrae duces et quasi signiferi fuissent, in his Plancio gratias egi. recitetur oratio, quae propter rei magnitudinem dicta de scripto[1] est; in qua ego homo astutus ei me debebam cui nihil magno opere deberem, et huius offici tanti servitutem astringebam testimonio sempiterno. nolo cetera quae a me mandata sunt litteris recitare; praetermitto, ne aut proferre videar ad tempus aut eo genere uti litterarum quod meis studiis aptius quam consuetudini iudiciorum esse videatur.

(3) Cic. *Fam.* 1.9.4 (Dec. 54 BCE, to Lentulus): ego me, Lentule, initio <beneficio>[2] rerum atque actionum tuarum non solum meis sed etiam rei publicae restitutum putabam et, quoniam tibi incredibilem quendam amorem et omnia in te ipsum summa ac singularia studia deberem, rei publicae, quae te in me restituendo multum adiuvisset, eum certe me animum merito ipsius debere arbitrabar quem antea tantum modo communi officio civium, non aliquo erga me singulari beneficio debitum praestitissem. hac me mente fuisse et senatus ex me te consule audivit et tu in nostris sermonibus conlocutionibusque vidisti[3].

(4) Schol. Bob., arg. ad Cic. *RQ* (p. 110.3–12 Stangl): <...>[4] superiore commune est. restitutus enim M. Tullius, quod eandem causam beneficii videbat in suam

---

[1] de scripto *vel* descripta *codd.*

[2] initio <beneficio> (*vel* beneficio) *Sternkopf*: initio *codd.*

[3] vidisti *vel* ipse vidisti *vel* audisti *codd.*

[4] <argumentum huius orationis Tullianae prorsus cum> *ed. Romana Angeli Mai 1828* : <huic orationi ad populum principium et argumentum prorsus cum> *Luterbacher*

Translation

Testimonia

(1) In the Senate, on the following day, which was the day of the Nones of September [5 Sept. 57 BCE], we expressed our thanks to the Senate.

(2) But of the fact that I say nothing new, nothing for the sake of this situation, isn't that speech also a witness that was the first to be delivered by me in the Senate? In that one, although I had expressed thanks by name to very few, since all could in no way be enumerated, but it would be a crime to pass over anyone, and I had decided to mention by name only those who had been the leaders and standard-bearers, as it were, of our cause, among these I expressed thanks to Plancius. The speech shall be read out; because of the importance of the matter it was delivered from a written text. In that [speech] I, a clever man, put myself under obligation to a person to whom I owed nothing much, and I confirmed the servitude arising from that great deed of his by a perpetual testimonial. I do not wish to have read out other things that have been set down by me in writing; I pass over those, so that I do not seem either to bring them up for the occasion or to employ that kind of writing that seems to be more suited to my literary endeavours than to the conventions of the courts.

(3) I believed, Lentulus, that initially through <the favour> realized by your doings and actions I was restored not only to my family, but also to the Republic, and, since I owed you some incredible love and all kinds of the greatest and special devotion towards you, I thought that towards the Republic, which had assisted you a lot in restoring me, I should definitely show that attitude, as it deserves, that previously I had only shown as owed to the common duty of citizens, not to some special favour towards me. That I had been of this mind both the Senate heard from me in your consulship and you saw in our talks and conversations.

(4) <…> is shared with the previous [speech]. For M. Tullius, having been restored, since he saw the same reason for the favour conferred upon his standing by the goodwill of almost all, when he had expressed gratitude to the Senate,

dignitatem prope omnium favore conlati, cum gratias egisset senatui, etiam populo consequenter agendas arbitratus in contionem processit et eadem paene quae aput patres conscriptos dixerat nunc etiam populo audiente percenset, magis, ut opinor, gloriae suae consulens, ut existimetur omnium ordinum consensu restitutus nec ulla populi <pars>[5] ab sua dignitate dissenserit: quo videlicet honestius gloriatur necessarium se tuendae patriae iudicatum. et hic igitur demonstrativae qualitatis implet exsecutionem, simul et beneficia commemorans et vim querellae in invidiam conferens inimicorum, quia sive auctores fuerant exolandi sive quia diu facultatem non permiserant revertendi.

(5) Schol. Bob., arg. ad Cic. *Planc.* (p. 153.7–9 Stangl): dein postea restitutus inter ceteros et ipsi gratias egit iis orationibus quarum alteram in contione, alteram vero habuit in senatu.

(6) Schol. Bob. ad Cic. *Planc.* 74 (p. 165.5 Stangl): suffecerat enim de ea oratione dixisse qua vel senatui vel populo gratias egit.

(7) Cass. Dio 39.9.1: κατῆλθέ τε οὖν ὁ Κικέρων, καὶ χάριν τῇ τε βουλῇ καὶ τῷ δήμῳ, παρασχόντων αὐτῷ τῶν ὑπάτων καὶ {κατὰ}[6] τὸ συνέδριον καὶ τὴν ἐκκλησίαν, ἔγνω.

M. Tulli Ciceronis post reditum
in senatu oratio

Sigla (Maslowski 1981, 1)

P = cod. Parisinus 7794, saec. IX med.

   P^1 = prima manus

   P^2 = correcturae eiusdem fere aetatis

   P^3 = correcturae multo recentiores

G = cod. Bruxellensis 5345 (olim Gemblacensis), saec. XI in.

   G^1 = prima manus

   G^2 = correcturae paulo recentiores

---

[5] populi <pars> *Stangl* : <pars> populi *edd. vet.* : populi ab sua dignitate dissensio fuisse *Luterbacher*

[6] *del.* Boissevain ('*Inde a Roberto Stephano haec ita eduntur* : παρασχόντων αὐτῷ τῶν ὑπάτων, καὶ κατὰ τὸ συνέδριον καὶ <κατὰ> τὴν ἐκκλησίαν ἔγνω, *quae non uno nomine displicent, maxime vero eo quod futile est dicere Ciceronem senatui in curia et populo in contione populi gratias egisse. (non ita Cic. ad Att. 4.1.5 ex.)*').

believing that consequently it should also be expressed to the People, proceeded to a meeting of the People and now goes through almost the same as what he had said among the senators also with the People listening, more, as I believe, concerned about his own glory, so that he would be believed to have been restored by the consensus of all classes and that no <part> of the People had disagreed with his standing: thus, obviously, he boasted more creditably that he was regarded as necessary for defending the country. And here, then, he fulfils the execution of the demonstrative quality, as, at the same time, he both recalls the favours and turns the force of complaint against the ill will of the enemies, either because they had been authors of banishing him or because, for a long time, they had not granted the opportunity to return.

(5) Then, after having been restored, he [Cicero] expressed thanks, among others, also to him [Plancius] in those orations of which he delivered one at a popular meeting and the other in the Senate.

(6) For it had been sufficient to have talked about that speech by which he [Cicero] expressed thanks, be it to the Senate, be it to the People.

(7) Then Cicero returned, and he expressed gratitude to the Senate and to the People, when the consuls granted him [the chance to address] both the council and the assembly of the People.

M. Tullius Cicero's oration in the Senate after his return

E = cod. Berolinensis 252 (olim Erfurtensis), saec. XII in.

    E^1 = prima manus

    E^2 = correcturae eiusdem aetatis

H = cod. Harleianus 4927, saec. XII ex.

    H^1 = prima manus

    H^2 = correcturae recentiores

X = fragmenta Parisina 18104, saec. XII ex.

ϵ = cod. Erlangensis 847, anno 1466 exaratus

V = cod. Vaticanus 1525 (olim Palatinus), anno 1467 exaratus

F = lectiones codicis Pithoeani in margine exemplaris Lambiniani (Argentorati 1581) quod Heidelbergae adservatur adscriptae

ω = superiores illi codices omnes praeter X et F

s = codices recentiores non nulli

Schol. = Scholiasta Bobiensis

[1 1] si, patres conscripti, pro vestris immortalibus in me fratremque meum liberosque nostros meritis parum vobis cumulate gratias egero, quaeso obtestorque ne meae naturae potius quam magnitudini vestrorum beneficiorum id tribuendum[7] putetis. quae tanta enim potest exsistere ubertas ingeni, quae tanta dicendi copia, quod tam divinum atque incredibile genus orationis, quo quisquam possit vestra in nos universa promerita non dicam complecti orando[8], sed percensere numerando[9]? qui mihi fratrem optatissimum, me fratri amantissimo, liberis nostris parentes, nobis liberos, qui dignitatem, qui ordinem, qui fortunas, qui amplissimam rem publicam, qui patriam, qua nihil potest esse iucundius, qui denique nosmet ipsos nobis reddidistis. [2] quod si parentes carissimos habere debemus, quod ab iis nobis vita, patrimonium, libertas, civitas tradita est, si deos immortalis, quorum beneficio et haec tenuimus et ceteris rebus aucti sumus, si populum Romanum, cuius honoribus in amplissimo consilio et in altissimo gradu dignitatis atque in hac omnium terrarum arce conlocati sumus, si hunc ipsum ordinem, a quo saepe magnificentissimis decretis sumus honestati, immensum quiddam et infinitum est quod vobis debeamus[10], qui vestro singulari studio atque consensu parentum beneficia, deorum immortalium munera, populi Romani honores, vestra de me multa iudicia nobis uno tempore omnia reddidistis, ut, cum multa vobis, magna populo Romano, innumerabilia parentibus, omnia dis immortalibus debeamus, haec antea singula per illos habuerimus, nunc universa per vos reciperarimus[11].

[2 3] itaque, patres conscripti, quod ne optandum quidem est homini, immortalitatem quandam per vos esse adepti videmur. quod enim tempus erit umquam cum[12] vestrorum in nos beneficiorum memoria ac fama moriatur? qui illo ipso tempore, cum vi, ferro, metu, minis obsessi teneremini, non multo post discessum meum me universi revocavistis referente L. Ninnio, fortissimo atque optimo viro, quem habuit ille pestifer annus et maxime fidelem et minime timidum, si dimicare placuisset, defensorem salutis meae. postea quam vobis decernendi potestas facta non est[13] per eum tribunum plebis qui, cum per se rem publicam lacerare non posset, sub alieno scelere delituit[14], numquam de me siluistis, numquam meam salutem non ab iis consulibus qui[15] vendiderant flagitavistis. [4] itaque

---

[7] id tribuendum *GEH* : adtribuendum *P* : attribuendum *ϵVF*

[8] orando *PGEH* : ornando *ϵVF*

[9] numerando ω : enumerando *ς*

[10] debeamus ω *praeter H* : debemus *ς, Lambinus* : habeamus *H*

[11] reciperarimus *P¹* : recuperarimus *P²G* : recuperaverimus *Eϵ* : recuperavimus *HV*

[12] cum *PGE* : quo *HϵV*

[13] facta non est *ϵVF* : non est *P¹GEH¹* : non est permissa *H²P³*

[14] delituit *E²ϵVF* : deluit *P¹* : delevit *P²GE¹* : diruit *Hς*

[15] qui *PGEH* : qui rem p. *ϵVF* : qui publicam *Klotz*

[**1** 1] If, Members of the Senate, in return for your immortal services towards me, my brother, and our children, I will have expressed my gratitude to you not sufficiently copiously, I ask and plead with you not to believe that this is to be attributed to the abilities given to me by nature rather than to the magnitude of your favours. For can there exist such great abundance of talent, such comprehensive command of oratory, such a divine and unbelievable kind of speech by which anyone could, I do not say, cover fully in eloquent presentation, but in an enumeration survey your services towards us in their entirety? You have restored to me the most desired brother, me to the most loving brother, to our children the parents, to us the children, you have restored standing, status, property, the greatest Republic, the country, compared to which nothing can be more delightful, finally ourselves to us. [2] And if we ought to consider our parents as dearest, since from them life, possessions, freedom, and citizenship have been transmitted to us, if the immortal gods, by whose favour we have both retained these items and been advanced with regard to other things, if the Roman People, by whose marks of esteem we have been placed in the most distinguished council and in the highest position of rank and indeed in this stronghold of the entire world, if this order itself, by which we have often been honoured with the most magnificent decrees, it is something immense and infinite that we owe to you, who, by your singular support and unanimity, have returned the favours of our parents, the gifts of the immortal gods, the honours of the Roman People, your many decisions about me, all this to us at a single point in time, so that, while we owe much to you, a great deal to the Roman People, innumerable things to our parents, everything to the immortal gods, we previously had all this one by one through those, have now regained it all in its entirety through you.

[**2** 3] Accordingly, Members of the Senate, what a human being cannot even wish for, we seem to have obtained some kind of immortality through you. For will there ever be such a time when the glorious memory of your favours towards us dies? You, who at that very time when you were held besieged by force, swords, fear, and threats, not long after my departure, altogether called me back on the motion of L. Ninnius, a very courageous and excellent man, whom that pestilent year had both as the most loyal and as the least fearful protector of my well-being, if it had been decided to fight. After you had not been given the opportunity to pass a decree through that Tribune of the People who, since he could not wound the Republic by himself, hid beneath someone else's villainous character, you were never silent about me, you never did not demand my well-being from those consuls who had sold it. [4] Thus, it has been achieved by your support and leadership that this very year, which I had

vestro studio atque auctoritate perfectum est ut[16] ipse ille annus[17], quem ego
mihi quam patriae malueram esse fatalem, octo[18] tribunos haberet qui et promulgarent de salute mea et ad vos saepe numero referrent. nam consules modesti
legumque metuentes impediebantur lege (non ea quae de me, sed ea quae de
ipsis lata erat), quam meus inimicus promulgavit[19] ut, si revixissent ii qui haec
paene delerunt, tum ego redirem; quo facto utrumque confessus est, et se illorum vitam desiderare et magno in periculo rem publicam futuram si, cum[20]
hostes atque interfectores rei publicae revixissent, ego non revertissem. atque[21]
illo ipso tamen[22] anno cum ego cessissem, princeps autem civitatis non legum
praesidio sed parietum vitam suam tueretur, res publica sine consulibus esset
neque solum parentibus perpetuis verum etiam tutoribus annuis esset orbata,
sententias dicere prohiberemini, caput meae proscriptionis recitaretur, numquam dubitastis meam salutem cum communi salute coniungere.

[3 5] postea vero quam singulari et praestantissima virtute P. Lentuli consulis
ex superioris anni caligine et tenebris lucem in re publica Kalendis Ianuariis
dispicere[23] coepistis, cum Q. Metelli, nobilissimi hominis atque optimi viri,
summa dignitas, cum praetorum, tribunorum plebis paene omnium virtus et
fides rei publicae subvenisset, cum virtute, gloria, rebus gestis Cn. Pompeius
omnium gentium, omnium saeculorum, omnis memoriae facile princeps tuto
se venire in senatum arbitraretur, tantus vester consensus de salute mea fuit ut
corpus abesset meum, dignitas iam in patriam revertisset.

[6] quo quidem mense quid inter me et meos inimicos interesset existimare
potuistis. ego meam salutem deserui, ne propter me civium vulneribus res
publica cruentaretur; illi meum reditum non populi Romani suffragiis sed
flumine sanguinis intercludendum putaverunt. itaque postea nihil vos civibus,
nihil sociis, nihil regibus respondistis; nihil iudices sententiis, nihil populus
suffragiis, nihil hic ordo auctoritate declaravit; mutum forum, elinguem curiam,
tacitam et fractam civitatem videbatis. [7] quo quidem tempore, cum is excessisset, qui caedi et flammae vobis auctoribus[24] restiterat, cum ferro et facibus

---

[16] ut *EϵV* : *om. PGH*
[17] annus *EϵV* : anno *H* : minus *PG*
[18] octo *ϵV* : hoc *P* : hos *GE* : cum *H*
[19] quam...promulgavit *Lambinus* : cum...promulgavit *codd.* : cum...promulgavi<sse>t *Ernesti*
[20] si cum *ϵV* : si eum *F* : sicut *P¹* : si aut *P²GE*
[21] atque *ϵVF* : itaque *PGEH* : idemque *Peterson*
[22] tamen *ω praeter H* : *om. H*
[23] dispicere *P¹* : despicere *ω* : respicere *s*
[24] vobis auctoribus *GEϵV* : vobis auctoritatibus *P* : vestris auctoritatibus *H*

preferred to be fatal to me rather than to the country, had eight Tribunes, who both put forward a bill about my well-being and frequently raised it for debate with you. For the consuls, restrained and observing the laws, were hindered by a law (not by that one about me, but by that one that had been put forward about them), which my enemy had proposed, that, if those had come back to life who almost destroyed these things here, then I could return; by this deed he admitted both that he longed for the life of those men and that the Republic would be in great danger if, when the enemies and murderers of the Republic had come back to life, I had not returned. And yet in that very year when I had left and the leading man in the community guarded his life not by the protection of the laws, but of the walls [of his house], when the Republic was without consuls and deprived not only of permanent parents, but also of annual guardians, when you were prevented from making statements, when the section on my proscription was read out, you never hesitated to link my well-being with the common well-being.

[**3** 5] But when, as a result of the outstanding and most excellent virtue of the consul P. Lentulus, you had begun to discern, out of the dark shadows of the preceding year, some light in the Republic on the Kalends of January, when the supreme prestige of Q. Metellus, a most high-born person and an excellent man, when the virtue and loyalty of almost all praetors and Tribunes of the People had come to the support of the Republic, when Cn. Pompeius, with regard to virtue, glory, and achievements easily the leading man throughout all nations, all future ages, and all memory, believed that he came into the Senate safely, so great was your consensus about my well-being that my person was still absent, but my standing had already returned to the country.

[6] In this month indeed you were able to judge what the difference was between me and my enemies. I abandoned my well-being, so that the Republic would not be stained with blood by wounds of citizens because of me; those believed that my return should be cut off, not by the votes of the Roman People, but by a river of blood. Therefore, later, you gave no replies to citizens, none to allies, none to kings; judges announced nothing by verdicts, the People nothing by votes, this order nothing by their authority; you saw a silent Forum, a voiceless Senate house, a mute and broken community. [7] At that time, after that man who had withstood carnage and fire on your authority had departed, you saw people with swords and torches move swiftly through the entire city, the houses

homines tota urbe volitantis, magistratuum tecta impugnata, deorum templa
inflammata, summi viri et clarissimi consulis fasces fractos, fortissimi atque
optimi tribuni plebis sanctissimum corpus non tactum ac violatum manu, sed
vulneratum ferro confectumque vidistis. qua strage non nulli permoti magistratus partim metu mortis, partim desperatione rei publicae paululum a mea
causa recesserunt; reliqui fuerunt quos neque terror nec vis, nec spes nec metus,
nec promissa nec minae, nec tela nec faces a vestra auctoritate, a populi Romani
dignitate, a mea salute depellerent.

[4 8] princeps P. Lentulus, parens ac deus nostrae vitae, fortunae, memoriae,
nominis, hoc specimen virtutis, hoc indicium[25] animi, hoc lumen consulatus
sui fore putavit, si me mihi, si meis, si vobis, si rei publicae reddidisset. qui ut est
designatus, numquam dubitavit sententiam de salute mea se et re publica dignam dicere. cum a tribuno plebis vetaretur, cum praeclarum caput recitaretur,
ne quis ad vos referret, ne quis decerneret, ne disputaret, ne loqueretur, ne pedibus iret, ne scribendo adesset, totam illam, ut ante dixi, proscriptionem[26] non
legem putavit, qua[27] civis optime de re publica meritus nominatim sine iudicio
una cum senatu rei publicae esset ereptus. ut vero iniit magistratum, non dicam:
quid egit prius, sed quid omnino egit aliud nisi ut me conservato vestram in
posterum dignitatem auctoritatemque sanciret? [9] di immortales, quantum
mihi beneficium dedisse videmini, quod hoc anno P. Lentulus consul est[28]!
quanto maius dedissetis si superiore anno fuisset! nec enim eguissem medicina
consulari, nisi consulari vulnere concidissem. audieram ex sapientissimo homine
atque optimo cive et viro, Q. Catulo, non saepe unum consulem improbum,
duo[29] vero numquam post Romam conditam[30] excepto illo Cinnano[31] tempore
fuisse. qua re meam causam semper fore firmissimam dicere solebat, dum
vel unus e[32] re publica consul esset. quod vere dixerat si illud {de duobus
consulibus}[33] quod ante in re publica {non}[34] fuerat perenne ac proprium
manere potuisset. quod si Q. Metellus illo tempore consul fuisset {inimicus}[35],
dubitatis quo animo fuerit in me conservando futurus, cum in restituendo
auctorem fuisse adscriptoremque videatis?

---

[25] indicium *s* : iudicium *ω*
[26] proscriptionem <vim> *Shackleton Bailey*
[27] qua *P²HϵV* : quia *PGE*
[28] consul *ω praeter H* : *om. H* | est *EϵV* : *om. P¹GH¹* : praefuit *H²P³* : fuit *Manutius* : populi
Romani fuit *Peterson*
[29] duo *P¹GE¹H* : duos *P²E²ϵV*
[30] post Romam conditam *E²ϵVF* : *om. PGE¹H*
[31] Cinnano *edd.* : cynnano *ϵV* : germane *P¹* : cesonino *GEP³* : cesonini *H* : *om. P²*
[32] e *Shackleton Bailey* : in *ω*
[33] *del. Karsten, Shackleton Bailey*
[34] *om. ϵV, Wolf*
[35] *del. Halm* : non inimicus *HP³s* : <etsi> inimicus (?) *Peterson*

of magistrates attacked, the temples of gods set on fire, the fasces of a supreme man and illustrious consul broken, the most sacred body of the most courageous and best Tribune of the People, not touched and hurt by hand, but wounded and dispatched by the sword. Moved by this carnage, some magistrates, partly out of fear of death, partly in despair about the Republic, withdrew a little from my cause; the others were those whom neither terror nor force, neither hope nor fear, neither promises nor threats, neither weapons nor torches could turn away from your authority, from the dignity of the Roman People and from my well-being.

[4 8] P. Lentulus, the father and god of our life, destiny, reputation, esteem, was at the forefront; he believed that this was going to be a specimen of his virtue, an indication of his character, a shining light of his consulship, if he had given me back to me, to my family, to you, to the Republic. As soon as he had become designate, he never hesitated to make a statement about my well-being, worthy of him and the Republic. When he was prohibited by a Tribune of the People, when the glorious section was read out that nobody opened a debate among you, that nobody made a decision, that nobody argued their point of view, that nobody spoke, that nobody voted, that nobody was there at the recording, he regarded all this, as I said earlier, as a proscription, not as a law, by which a citizen who had done excellent service for the Republic had been snatched away from the Republic by name without trial, along with the Senate. To be sure, as soon as he had entered office, I am not saying: what did he do first, but what else did he do at all, other than that he confirmed your dignity and authority for the future with me having been saved? [9] Immortal gods, what a great favour are you seen to have conferred upon me in that P. Lentulus is consul this year! A how much greater one would you have conferred if he had been [consul] the previous year! For I would not have needed consular medicine if I had not fallen by a consular wound. I had heard from a very wise person and an excellent citizen and man, Q. Catulus, that there had not often been a single wicked consul, but never two since the foundation of Rome except in that time of Cinna. For this reason he was accustomed to say that my cause would always be very strong as long as there was indeed one consul acting in the interest of the Republic. He would have said this truly if that situation {concerning the two consuls}, which had {not} been the case in the Republic before, could have remained uninterrupted and as a defining feature. And if Q. Metellus had been consul at that time {my enemy}, do you doubt what attitude he would have had in preserving me when you see that he was a supporter and seconder in restoring me?

[10] sed fuerunt ii consules[36], quorum mentes angustae, humiles, parvae[37], oppletae tenebris ac sordibus nomen ipsum consulatus, splendorem illius honoris, magnitudinem tanti imperi nec intueri nec sustinere nec capere potuerunt, non consules, sed mercatores provinciarum ac venditores vestrae dignitatis. quorum alter a[38] me Catilinam, amatorem suum, multis audientibus, alter Cethegum consobrinum reposcebat; qui me duo sceleratissimi post hominum memoriam non consules sed latrones non modo deseruerunt in causa praesertim publica et consulari, sed prodiderunt, oppugnarunt, omni auxilio non solum suo sed etiam vestro ceterorumque ordinum spoliatum esse voluerunt.

[5 11] quorum alter tamen neque me neque quemquam fefellit. quis enim ullam ullius boni spem haberet in eo cuius primum tempus aetatis palam fuisset ad omnium[39] libidines divulgatum, qui ne a sanctissima quidem parte corporis potuisset hominum impuram intemperantiam propulsare? qui cum suam rem non minus strenue quam postea publicam confecisset, egestatem et luxuriem domestico lenocinio sustentavit, qui nisi in aram tribunatus confugisset, neque vim praetoris nec multitudinem creditorum nec bonorum proscriptionem effugere potuisset—quo[40] in magistratu nisi rogationem de piratico bello tulisset, profecto egestate et improbitate coactus piraticam ipse fecisset, ac minore quidem cum rei publicae detrimento quam quo{d}[41] intra moenia nefarius hostis praedoque versatus est—, quo inspectante ac sedente legem tribunus plebis tulit ne auspiciis obtemperaretur, ne obnuntiare concilio aut comitiis, ne legi intercedere liceret, ut lex Aelia et Fufia ne valeret, quae nostri maiores certissima subsidia rei publicae contra tribunicios furores esse voluerunt. [12] idemque postea, cum innumerabilis multitudo bonorum de Capitolio supplex ad eum sordidata venisset, cumque adulescentes nobilissimi cunctique equites Romani se ad lenonis impudicissimi pedes abiecissent, quo vultu cincinnatus ganeo non solum civium lacrimas verum etiam patriae preces repudiavit! neque eo contentus fuit, sed etiam in contionem escendit[42] eaque dixit quae, si eius vir Catilina revixisset, dicere non esset ausus, se Nonarum Decembrium, quae me consule fuissent, clivique Capitolini poenas ab equitibus Romanis esse repetiturum. neque solum id dixit, sed quos ei commodum fuit compellavit, Lucium vero Lamiam, equitem Romanum, praestanti dignitate hominem et saluti meae pro familiaritate, rei publicae pro fortunis suis amicissimum, consul imperiosus exire ex[43] urbe iussit. et cum vos vestem mutandam censuissetis

[36] ii consules $P^2G\epsilon V$: hii consules P^1 : consules hii X : duo consules EH
[37] parv(a)e $G\epsilon$: parvous (?) V : prav(a)e $PEHX$
[38] a ω : om. P^1
[39] omnium $XE^2\epsilon V$: omnes PGE^1H
[40] quo $E^2\epsilon V$: qui PGE^1H
[41] quo{d} *Garatoni* : quod ω
[42] escendit P : ascendit $GEH^2\epsilon V$: ascedit H^1
[43] ex ϵV : om. $PGEH$

[10] But such men were consuls whose minds—mean, ignoble, petty, filled completely with ignorance and meanness—were able neither to have regard for nor to sustain nor to carry out the very name of consulship, the splendour of that office, and the greatness of such an important magistracy, not consuls, but merchants of provinces and sellers of your dignity. Of whom one demanded back from me Catilina, his lover, in the hearing of many, the other Cethegus, his cousin; those men, the two most criminal in the memory of men, not consuls, but plunderers, not only deserted me, especially in a public and consular cause, but betrayed me, attacked me, wished me deprived not only of all their help, but also of yours and the other orders.

[5 11] Yet, one of these two deceived neither me nor anyone. For who would have had any hope of anything good with regard to him whose first period of life had been openly put to common use for the desires of all, who had not been able to push back the impure licentiousness of men not even from the most august part of the body? Who, when he had squandered his own fortune no less strenuously than later the public one, supported need and indulgence by domestic brothel-keeping, who, if he had not taken refuge at the altar of the tribunate, would not have been able to escape the force of the praetor or the large number of creditors or the announcement of the sale of his possessions—in that office, if he had not put forward a bill about the war against the pirates, indeed, forced by poverty and shamelessness, he would have done piracy himself, and certainly with less damage to the Republic than with what he created as he remained inside the city walls as a wicked public enemy and brigand—, who was looking on and sitting there while a Tribune of the People put forward a law that one should not obey the auspices, that it should not be allowed to announce unfavourable omens to a public meeting or a voting assembly, not to veto a law, that *Lex Aelia et Fufia* should not be valid, which our ancestors wanted to be the surest supports of the Republic against tribunician fury. [12] And later, when an uncountable multitude of good men dressed in mourning had come to him as suppliants from the Capitol and when the most distinguished young men and all Roman knights had thrown themselves at the feet of the most immoral pimp, with what a face did the same man, the glutton with curled hair, reject not only the tears of citizens, but also the entreaties of the country! And he was not only not content with that, but even mounted the platform at a popular meeting and said what his husband Catilina, if he had come back to life, would not have dared to say, that he would demand penalties from the Roman knights for [their behaviour at] the Nones of December, those in my consulship, and [on] the ascent to the Capitol. And he did not only say that, but he accused those who it was convenient for him; indeed, the dictatorial consul ordered Lucius Lamia, a Roman knight, a man of outstanding distinction and most supportive of my well-being in accordance with our friendship and of the Republic in accordance with his social position, to leave the city. And when you

cunctique mutassetis atque idem omnes boni iam ante fecissent, ille unguentis oblitus cum toga praetexta, quam omnes praetores aedilesque tum abiecerant, inrisit squalorem vestrum et luctum gratissimae civitatis fecitque, quod nemo umquam tyrannus, ut quo minus occulte vestrum malum gemeretis nihil in<ter>cederet[44], ne aperte incommoda patriae lugeretis ediceret. [6 13] cum vero in circo Flaminio non a tribuno plebis consul in contionem, sed a latrone archipirata productus esset, primum processit qua auctoritate vir! vini, somni, stupri plenus, madenti coma, composito capillo, gravibus oculis, fluentibus buccis, pressa voce et temulenta, quod in civis indemnatos esset animadversum, id sibi dixit gravis auctor vehementissime displicere. ubi nobis haec auctoritas tam diu tanta latuit? cur in lustris et helluationibus[45] huius calamistrati saltatoris tam eximia virtus tam diu cessavit?

nam ille alter, Caesoninus Calventius[46], ab adulescentia versatus est in foro, cum eum praeter simulatam fictamque[47] tristitiam nulla res commendaret, non iuris <scientia>[48] {studium}[49], non dicendi vi<s, non peri>tia rei militaris[50], non cognoscendorum hominum <studium>[51], non liberalitas. quem praeteriens cum incultum, horridum maestumque vidisses, etiam si agrestem et inhumanum existimares, tamen libidinosum et perditum non putares[52]. [14] cum hoc homine an cum stipite[53] in foro constitisses nihil crederes interesse: sine sensu, sine sapore, elinguem[54], tardum, inhumanum negotium, Cappadocem modo abreptum de grege venalium diceres. idem domi quam libidinosus, quam impurus, quam intemperans, non ianua receptis sed pseudothyro[55] intromissis voluptatibus! cum vero etiam litteras[56] studere incipit et beluus[57] immanis cum Graeculis philosophari, tum est Epicureus, non penitus illi disciplinae, quaecumque est, deditus, sed captus uno verbo voluptatis. habet autem magistros non ex istis ineptis qui dies totos de officio ac de virtute

---

[44] in<ter>cederet *Maslowski* : indiceret ϵ*V* : diceret *PGEH* : in<ter>diceret *Busche* : impediret *Müller (in app.)* : diceret <impedire> *Peterson* : <se intercedere e>diceret *Madvig*

[45] et helluationibus *PGE¹HX* : etiam helluoni (-nis *F*) *E²*ϵ*VF*

[46] c(a)esoninus *PG²E²*ϵ*V* : cessoninus *E¹* : cers- *vel* censoninus *G¹* : cessonius *H* | calventius *ω* praeter ϵ*V* : calventicius ϵ*V*

[47] fictamque *E²F* : victamque ϵ*V* : versutamque *PG²* : irritamque *G¹EH*

[48] iuris <scientia> *Madvig* : iuris *E²*ϵ*VF* : inconsulta *P¹* : ĉôŝ *P²* : cos. *G* : *om. E¹* : iuris <notitia> *Klotz* : consilium *Peterson*

[49] *del. Lambinus*

[50] vi<s, non peri>tia rei militaris *Madvig* : vitia rei (viciari *E¹*) militaris *PGE¹* : non (*sil. F*) rei militaris *E²*ϵ*VF* : vi<s, non scien>tia rei militaris *Geertz* : <non scien>tia rei militaris *Lambinus*

[51] <studium> *Lambinus, Madvig*

[52] putares *E²* ϵ*VF* : putasti *PH* : putastis *E¹* : dubitasti *G*

[53] stipite *E²*ϵ*VF* : stipe *P¹* : etiope *P²* : stipe vel ethiope *G* : vel aethiope stipe *E¹* : esope *H*

[54] elingue{m} *Ernesti*

[55] pseudothyro *P²* : pseudotiro *X* : psedothyro *P¹* : pseudothyra *E²* (falsa ianua pseudothyra *mg.*) : pseudotyra ϵ*V* : *om. GE¹* : porro *H*

[56] litteras *PG¹H* : litteris *EG²*ϵ*V*

[57] beluus *edd. Augustino nitentes* : veluus *P¹* : heluus *P²* : belluus *G* : helluus *E¹* : belua *E²*ϵ*V* : *om. H*

had decreed that clothing should be changed and all of you had changed it and all good men had previously already done the same, he, smeared with unguents, with a purple-bordered toga, which all praetors and aediles had then discarded, mocked your mourning dress and the grief of the most grateful community, and he did what no tyrant ever did, that he did not interfere in any way against you lamenting your misfortune secretly, but ordered that you should not lament the troubles of the country openly. [**6** 13] But when in the Circus Flaminius, not a consul had been brought before a public meeting by a Tribune of the People, but a pirate chief by a bandit, in the first place, with what authoritativeness did the man step forward! Full of wine, sleep, and lewdness, with hair dripping with unguents, well-dressed locks, heavy eyes, drooping cheeks, a low and drunken voice, he, the serious authority figure, said that what was taken as punitive action against unconvicted citizens displeased him very strongly. Where was such great authority so long in hiding for us? Why did such outstanding virtue of this dancer with artificially curled hair remain inactive in brothels and debauches for so long?

Further, that other one, Caesoninus Calventius, was busy in the Forum from his youth, when, besides his feigned and made-up austerity, no matter recommended him, not <knowledge> {aim} of the law, not the force of speaking, <not experience> of military matters, not <the aim> to get to know men, not generosity; when, in passing by, you had seen him squalid, unkempt, and gloomy, even if you might have believed him to be uncivilized and uncultured, still, you would not have thought him to be licentious and depraved. [14] Whether you had stood together with this man or with a tree trunk in the Forum, you would believe that there was no difference: you would call him a thing without sensibility, without refinement, voiceless, dull, without human feeling, a Cappadocian just now snatched away from a flock of newly imported slaves for sale. The same man at home, how libidinous, how morally foul, how licentious, with pleasures not received through the front door, but admitted through a concealed door! Indeed, when he begins to study even literature and, as a savage brute, to philosophize with the Greeklings, then he is an Epicurean, not fully dedicated to that school, whatever it is, but captured by the single word 'pleasure'. And in fact he has teachers not from those foolish men who talk

disserunt, qui ad laborem, ad industriam, ad pericula pro patria subeunda
adhortantur, sed eos qui disputent horam nullam vacuam voluptate esse debere,
in omni parte corporis semper oportere aliquod gaudium delectationemque
versari. [15] his utitur quasi praefectis libidinum suarum, hi voluptates omnes
vestigant atque odorantur, hi sunt conditores instructoresque convivi, idem
expendunt atque aestimant voluptates sententiamque dicunt et iudicant quantum cuique libidini tribuendum esse videatur. horum ille artibus eruditus ita
contempsit hanc prudentissimam[58] civitatem ut omnis suas libidines, omnia
flagitia latere posse arbitraretur, si modo vultum importunum in forum detulisset. [7] is nequaquam me quidem {non}[59]—cognoram enim propter Pisonum
adfinitatem quam longe hunc ab hoc genere cognatio materna Transalpini
sanguinis abstulisset—, sed vos populumque Romanum non consilio neque
eloquentia, quod in multis saepe accidit, sed rugis supercilioque decepit. [16]
Luci Piso, tune ausus es isto oculo, non dicam isto animo, ista fronte, non vita,
tanto supercilio, non enim possum dicere tantis rebus gestis, cum A. Gabinio
consociare consilia pestis meae? non te illius unguentorum odor, non vini
anhelitus, non frons calamistri notata vestigiis in eam cogitationem adducebat
ut, cum illius re similis fuisses, frontis tibi integumento ad occultanda tanta
flagitia diutius uti non liceret? cum hoc tu[60] coire ausus es, ut consularem dignitatem, ut rei publicae statum, ut senatus auctoritatem, ut civis optime meriti
fortunas provinciarum foedere addiceres? te consule, tuis edictis et imperiis
senatui populi Romani[61] non est licitum non modo sententiis atque auctoritate
sua, sed ne luctu quidem ac vestitu rei publicae subvenire? [17] Capuaene te[62]
putabas, in qua urbe domicilium quondam superbiae fuit, consulem esse, sicut
eras eo tempore[63], an Romae, in qua civitate omnes ante vos consules senatui
paruerunt? tu es ausus in circo Flaminio productus cum tuo illo pari dicere te
semper[64] misericordem fuisse? quo verbo senatum atque omnis bonos tum
cum a patria pestem depulissem[65] crudelis demonstrabas fuisse. tu misericors
me, adfinem tuum, quem comitiis tuis[66] praerogativae primum custodem
feceras[67], quem Kalendis Ianuariis tertio loco sententiam rogaras, constrictum
inimicis rei publicae tradidisti, tu meum generum, propinquum tuum, tu

---

[58] prudentissimam *ω praeter* ε : pudentissimam ε
[59] is nequaquam me quidem {non} *Müller* : is me quamquam me quidem non *P*¹ : is me quamquam (quandam *G*) equidem non *P*²*GE*¹*H* : se me quamquam quidem minime (minime quidem
F, aut hoc aut illud *E*²) non *E*²ε*VF* : is quamquam me quidem minime *Klotz*
[60] tu *X*ε*VF* : *om. PGEH*
[61] populi r. *P*ε*V* : populo r. *GH* : populoque r. *E*
[62] te *post* consulem *habet* ε*V*
[63] sicut eras eo tempore *del. Garatoni, Halm*
[64] te semper *PGEH* : semper te ε*V* : te *Schol.*
[65] depulissem *E*²ε*V* : depullissem *ex* depell- *V* : *om. PGE*¹ : expellerent *ed. Rom.* : depellerent
edd. | tum…depulissem *om. H* : quo verbo ceteros demonstrabas crudeles fuisse *Schol. Bob. ad loc.*
(p. 109.14–15 St.)
[66] tuis *E*²ε*VF* : *om. PGE*¹*H*
[67] feceras *E*²ε*V* : praeferas *PG*¹*E*¹ : praefeceras *HG*²

about duty and virtue for entire days, who exhort to take on toil, diligence, and dangers on behalf of the country, but those who argue that no hour ought to be free from pleasure, that in every part of the body there should always be present some pleasure and delight. [15] He uses these as commanders of his lusts, as it were, these track down all kinds of pleasures and smell them out, they are organizers and arrangers of dinner parties, the same people weigh and estimate pleasures and pronounce opinions and decide how much seems to be appropriate to be given to each lust. Educated in the arts of these men, he looked down on this very sagacious community so much so that he believed that all his lusts, all his shameful acts could be hidden if only he had brought a grim face down to the Forum. [7] By no means did this man deceive me at any rate {not}—for because of the relationship with the Pisos I had come to know how far the maternal kinship with Transalpine blood had carried him away from this family—, but he deceived you and the Roman People, not by counsel or eloquence, which often happens in the case of many, but by frowning and a haughty look. [16] Lucius Piso, have you dared with that look (not to say with that mind), with that brow (not with life), with such haughtiness (for I cannot say with such great deeds) to join in plans for my ruin with A. Gabinius? Did not the smell of that man's perfumes, not the breath reeking of wine, not the forehead marked by the traces of curling tongs bring you to that consideration that, when you had been similar to him in deed, it would no longer be possible for you to use the concealment provided by your countenance to hide the great extent of your shameful acts? Did you dare to conspire together with him, so that you handed over the consular dignity, the status of the Republic, the authority of the Senate, the fortunes of a particularly well-deserving citizen by a pact for provinces? In your consulship, because of your edicts and orders, it was not allowed to the Senate of the Roman People, not only not by decrees and its authority, but not even by grief and clothing, to come to the support of the Republic? [17] Did you believe that you were a consul in Capua, a city in which there once was the home of arrogance, as you were at that time, or in Rome, a community in which all consuls before you obeyed the Senate? You have dared, brought forward in the Circus Flaminius, with your like-minded mate, to say that you had always been pitiful? With that word you pointed out that the Senate and all good men had been cruel then, when I had thrust off destruction from the country. You, the pitiful person, handed over me, your relation, whom, at your election assembly, you had made first teller of the first century to vote, whom you had asked for his view in third place on the Kalends of January, me, restrained, to the enemies of the Republic, you pushed away my son-in-law, your close relative, and your relative by marriage, my daughter, with extremely arrogant and extremely cruel

adfinem tuam, filiam meam, superbissimis et crudelissimis verbis a genibus tuis reppulisti; idemque tu clementia ac misericordia singulari, cum ego una cum re publica non tribunicio sed consulari ictu concidissem, tanto scelere tantaque intemperantia fuisti ut ne unam quidem horam interesse paterere inter meam pestem et tuam praedam, saltem dum conticisceret illa lamentatio et gemitus urbis! [18] nondum palam factum erat occidisse rem publicam, cum tibi arbitria funeris solvebantur—uno eodemque tempore domus mea diripiebatur, ardebat, bona ad vicinum consulem de[68] Palatio, de Tusculano ad item vicinum alterum consulem deferebantur—, cum isdem operis suffragium ferentibus, eodem gladiatore latore, vacuo non modo a bonis sed etiam a liberis atque inani foro, ignaro populo Romano quid ageretur, senatu vero oppresso et adflicto duobus impiis nefariisque consulibus aerarium, provinciae, legiones, imperia donabantur.

[8] horum consulum ruinas vos consules vestra virtute fulsistis, summa tribunorum plebis praetorumque fide et diligentia sublevati[69].

[19] quid ego de praestantissimo viro, T. Annio, dicam, aut quis de tali cive satis digne umquam loquetur[70]? qui cum videret sceleratum civem aut domesticum potius hostem, si legibus uti liceret, iudicio esse frangendum, sin ipsa iudicia vis impediret ac tolleret, audaciam virtute, furorem fortitudine, temeritatem consilio, manum copiis, vim vi esse superandam, primo de vi postulavit; postea quam ab eodem iudicia sublata esse vidit, ne ille omnia vi posset efficere curavit; qui docuit neque tecta neque templa neque forum nec curiam sine summa virtute ac maximis opibus et copiis ab intestino latrocinio posse defendi; qui primus post meum discessum metum bonis[71], spem audacibus, timorem huic ordini, servitutem depulit civitati.

[20] quam rationem pari virtute, animo, fide P. Sestius secutus pro mea salute, pro vestra auctoritate, pro statu civitatis nullas sibi inimicitias, nullam vim, nullos impetus, nullum vitae discrimen vitandum umquam putavit; qui causam senatus exagitatam contionibus improborum sic sua diligentia multitudini commendavit ut nihil tam populare quam vestrum nomen, nihil tam omnibus carum aliquando quam vestra auctoritas videretur; qui me cum omnibus rebus quibus tribunus plebis potuit defendit, tum reliquis officiis iuxta ac si meus frater esset sustentavit;

---

[68] in *Shackleton Bailey*
[69] sublevati *PGE*[1]*H* : sublevastis *E*[2]ϵ*V*
[70] loquetur *ω praeter E* : loquitur *E*
[71] metum bonis *PGH* : cum bonis *E*[1] : bonis metum *E*[2]ϵ*VF*

words, from your knees; and equally, you with your outstanding clemency and pity, when I had fallen together with the Republic not by a tribunician, but by a consular blow, displayed such a villainous disposition and such licentiousness that you did not permit there to be even a single hour between my ruin and your booty, at least until that lamentation and groaning of the city became silent! [18] It had not yet been made public that the Republic had passed away, when the expenses of the funeral were paid to you—at one and the same time my house was looted, it was on fire, the goods were brought to my neighbour, the consul, from the Palatine, from the estate at Tusculum likewise to my neighbour, the other consul—, when, with the same hired rowdies voting, with the same scoundrel as proposer, in a Forum not only empty of good men, but also of free men and deserted, while the Roman People did not know what was going on and the Senate was oppressed and crushed, the treasury, provinces, legions, commands were presented to two impious and wicked consuls.

[8] The ruins created by these consuls have been strengthened by you, consuls, by means of your virtue, supported by the greatest loyalty and assiduity of the Tribunes of the People and the praetors.

[19] What shall I say about the most outstanding man, T. Annius, or who will ever be able to talk about such a citizen in a sufficiently worthy manner? When he saw that a criminal citizen or rather an internal enemy, if it was possible to use laws, must be crushed by a trial, but that, if force hindered and abolished the law courts themselves, audacity must be conquered by virtue, fury by courage, recklessness by counsel, a gang by troops, violence by violence, he first prosecuted him on account of violence; after he had seen that the law courts had been abolished by this very person, he took care that this man could not achieve everything by force; he demonstrated that neither houses nor temples nor the Forum nor the Senate house could be protected from this internal band of robbers without the greatest virtue and the greatest resources and troops; he was the first after my departure to drive off anxiety from the good men, hope from the audacious, fear from this order, slavery from the community.

[20] Following that pattern with equal virtue, disposition, and loyalty, P. Sestius believed that for the benefit of my well-being, of your authority, of the political order of the community no enmities, no violence, no attacks, no danger to life ought ever be avoided by him; he recommended the cause of the Senate, attacked by public speeches of rascals, to the masses with his assiduity in such a way that nothing appeared so popular as your name, nothing so dear to all ever as your authority; he defended me with all matters by which a Tribune of the People could and also supported me with further beneficial acts, as if he was my brother; through his clients, freedmen, household slaves, resources, and

cuius ego clientibus, libertis, familia, copiis, litteris ita sum sustentatus ut meae calamitatis non adiutor solum, verum etiam socius videretur.

[21] iam ceterorum officia <ac>[72] studia vidistis: quam cupidus mei C. Cestilius, quam studiosus vestri, quam non varius fuerit in causa. quid M. Cispius? cui ego ipsi, parenti fratrique eius sentio quantum debeam; qui, cum a me voluntas eorum in privato iudicio esset offensa, publici mei benefici memoria privatam offensionem oblitteraverunt. iam T. Fadius, qui mihi quaestor fuit, M. Curtius, cuius ego patri quaestor[73] fui, studio, amore, animo huic necessitudini non defuerunt. multa de me C. Messius et amicitiae et rei publicae causa dixit, legem separatim[74] initio de salute mea promulgavit. [22] Q. Fabricius si, quae de me agere conatus est, ea contra vim et ferrum perficere potuisset, mense Ianuario nostrum[75] statum reciperassemus[76]; quem ad salutem meam voluntas impulit, vis retardavit, auctoritas vestra[77] revocavit.

[9] iam vero praetores quo animo in me fuerint vos existimare potuistis, cum L. Caecilius privatim me suis omnibus copiis studuerit sustentare, publice promulgarit de mea salute cum collegis paene omnibus, direptoribus autem bonorum meorum in ius adeundi potestatem non fecerit. M. autem Calidius statim designatus sententia sua quam esset cara sibi mea salus declaravit. [23] omnia officia C. Septimi, Q. Valeri, P. Crassi, Sex. Quintili, C. Cornuti summa et in me et in rem publicam constiterunt.

quae cum libenter commemoro, tum non invitus non nullorum in me nefarie commissa praetereo. non est mei temporis iniurias meminisse, quas ego etiam si ulcisci possem, tamen oblivisci mallem. alio transferenda mea tota vita est, ut bene de me meritis referam gratiam, amicitias igni perspectas tuear, cum apertis hostibus bellum geram, timidis amicis ignoscam, proditores non indicem[78], dolorem profectionis meae reditus dignitate consoler. [24] quod si mihi nullum aliud esset officium in omni vita reliquum nisi ut erga duces ipsos et principes atque auctores salutis meae satis gratus iudicarer, tamen exiguum reliquae vitae tempus non modo ad referendam verum etiam ad commemorandam gratiam mihi relictum putarem.

---

[72] *add. Halm* | studiaque *s, ed. Rom.* : {studia} *Kayser*

[73] patri questor *EHG*² : p. quaest*or *P* : p. testor *G*¹ : questor pari *εVF*

[74] separatim *edd.* : separatam *ε* : sepatam *V* : speratim *P* : speciatim *GE*

[75] nostrum *PGEH* : vestrum *εVF*

[76] reciperassemus *edd.* : recipirassemus *P* : recuperassemus *GE* : reciperassem *H*¹ : recuperassem *H*² : recuperasset *E*² : recuperasset si *εV* : recuperasse si *F*

[77] vestra *PEH* : nostra *GεV*

[78] non indicem *ω* : indicem *s, Peterson* : convincam *Müller* : vindicem *Madvig* : non vindicem *Hotman*

letters I was supported in such a way that he seemed to be not only a helper, but even a comrade of my calamity.

[21] Further, you have seen the services <and> devotion of others: how well-disposed towards me C. Cestilius was, how devoted to you, how not wavering in the cause. What about M. Cispius? I know myself how much I owe to him, his father, and his brother; when their sentiments had been offended by me in a private law suit, they consigned to oblivion the private resentment by the memory of my services for the public. Further, T. Fadius, who was my quaestor, M. Curtius, for whose father I was quaestor, did not fail in their duty to this bond by their effort, love, and spirit. C. Messius said a lot about me for the sake of friendship and the Republic; at an early stage he separately promulgated a law about my well-being. [22] If Q. Fabricius had been able to achieve what he tried to arrange about me against violence and the sword, we would have recovered our standing in the month of January; goodwill urged him towards my well-being, violence slowed him down, your authority revived him.

[9] And further, you could have judged of what mind towards me the praetors were, when L. Caecilius privately made an effort to sustain me with all his resources and publicly promulgated a bill concerning my well-being with almost all colleagues and did not give the plunderers of my property the right to come to court. And M. Calidius, as soon as he was designate, declared by his statement how dear my well-being was to him. [23] All services of C. Septimius, Q. Valerius, P. Crassus, Sex. Quinctilius, and C. Cornutus were obvious as outstanding both towards me and towards the Republic.

I mention these things gladly, and I also, not unwillingly, pass over the wicked deeds of some against me. It is not suitable for my current situation to call to mind injustices that I, even if I could avenge them, still would prefer to forget. My entire life has to be transferred elsewhere, so that I pay thanks to those who have conferred services upon me, preserve the friendships tested in fire, wage war with open enemies, pardon fearful friends, do not reveal traitors, and assuage the pain of my departure with the dignity of my return. [24] If no other duty was left for me in my entire life other than that I was regarded as sufficiently grateful towards only the leaders and foremost men and the authors of my well-being, still I would believe that too brief a period, consisting in the rest of my life, was left to me, not only to show my gratitude, but even to mention it.

quando enim ego huic homini ac liberis eius, quando omnes mei gratiam referent? quae memoria, quae vis ingeni, quae magnitudo observantiae tot tantisque beneficiis respondere poterit? qui mihi primus adflicto et iacenti consularem fidem dextramque porrexit, qui me a morte ad vitam, a desperatione ad spem, ab exitio ad salutem vocavit[79], qui tanto amore in me, studio in rem publicam fuit ut excogitaret quem ad modum calamitatem meam non modo levaret sed etiam honestaret. quid enim magnificentius, quid praeclarius mihi accidere potuit quam quod illo referente[80] vos decrevistis ut cuncti ex omni Italia qui rem publicam salvam vellent ad me unum hominem fractum et prope dissipatum, restituendum et defendendum venirent, ut, qua voce ter omnino[81] post Romam conditam consul usus esset pro universa re publica apud eos solum qui eius vocem exaudire possent, eadem voce senatus omnis ex omnibus agris atque oppidis civis totamque Italiam ad unius salutem defendendam excitaret? [10 25] quid ego gloriosius meis posteris potui relinquere quam hoc, senatum iudicasse qui civis me non defendisset eum rem publicam salvam noluisse? itaque tantum vestra auctoritas, tantum eximia consulis dignitas valuit ut dedecus et flagitium se committere putaret, si qui non veniret.

idemque consul, cum illa incredibilis multitudo Romam et paene Italia ipsa venisset, vos frequentissimos in Capitolium convocavit. quo tempore quantam vim naturae bonitas haberet et vera nobilitas intellegere potuistis. nam Q. Metellus, et inimicus et frater inimici, perspecta vestra voluntate omnia privata odia deposuit; quem P. Servilius, vir cum clarissimus tum vero optimus mihique amicissimus, et auctoritatis et orationis suae divina quadam gravitate ad sui generis communisque sanguinis facta virtutesque revocavit, ut haberet in consilio et fratrem {ab inferis}[82], socium rerum mearum, et omnis Metellos, praestantissimos civis, paene ex Acherunte excitatos, in quibus Numidicum illum Metellum[83], cuius quondam de patria discessus honestus omnibus sane, luctuosus tamen visus est[84]. [26] itaque exstitit[85] non modo salutis defensor, qui ante hoc suum[86] beneficium fuerat inimicus, verum etiam adscriptor dignitatis

---

[79] vocavit *PG¹EH* : revocavit *G²ϵV*

[80] referente *ϵVF* : rente *P* : petente *GEH*

[81] ter omnino *E²ϵVF* : teromanino *PG* : om. *E¹* : re romule *H*

[82] *del. Lambinus, Madvig*

[83] Metellum *del. Manutius*

[84] honestus *E¹* : honestis *PGH* : molestus *E²ϵVF* : honestus ⟨bonis⟩ *Halm (in app.)* : honestissimus *Madvig 1873, 213* | sane *GE¹* : ne *P¹* : in *P²* : ipsi ne *E²ϵVF* : om. *H* : sed *Halm (in app.), Madvig* | tamen *Halm (in app.), Madvig 1873, 213* : tandem *PGE¹H* : quidem *E²ϵVF* | visus est *PGEH* : est visus *ϵVF*

[85] extitit *E²ϵV* : dimittit *PGE¹H* : divinitus extitit *Müller* : idem extitit *Klotz* : dimit⟨tens iram suam rei p. exti⟩tit *Sydow*

[86] suum *E²ϵVF* : unum *PGE¹H* : su⟨mm⟩um *Klotz* : unicum *Halm* : divinum *Koch* : novum *Müller*

For when will I, when will all my family show gratitude to this man and his children? What memory, what force of intellect, what extent of deferential regard will be able to measure up to so many and such great favours? He was the first to stretch out to me, afflicted and lying low, his consular assurance and right hand, he called me from death to life, from desperation to hope, from destruction to well-being; he showed so much love towards me, devotion towards the Republic that he considered in what way he might not only lighten, but also give honour to my calamity. For what more magnificent, what more splendid thing could happen to me than what you decreed upon his motion, that all from the whole of Italy who wanted the Republic [to be] safe should come to restore and protect me, a single individual, broken and almost destroyed, that by those words that three times altogether since the foundation of Rome a consul had used on behalf of the entire Republic among those only who could hear his voice, by the same words the Senate aroused all citizens from all the fields and all towns as well as the whole of Italy to protect the well-being of a single person? [**10** 25] What more glorious thing could I leave behind for my descendants than this, that the Senate had been of the opinion that a citizen who had not protected me did not wish the Republic safe? Therefore, your authority and the outstanding dignity of the consul had so much power that, if anyone did not come, they thought that they committed a disgraceful and shameful act.

And the same consul, when that incredible multitude and almost Italy itself had come to Rome, summoned you to the Capitol in very large numbers. At that time you were able to understand how much power goodness of nature and true nobility have. For, after he had perceived your inclination, Q. Metellus, both an enemy and a cousin of an enemy, gave up all private hatred; P. Servilius, a most distinguished man and, moreover, an outstanding individual and a great friend to me, by a certain divine dignity of both his authority and his speech, directed him back to the deeds and virtues of his family and the common blood, so that he had in his counsel both the brother {from the underworld}, the partner of my exploits, and all Metelli, outstanding citizens, almost called up from Acheron, among them that Metellus Numidicus, whose departure from the country in the past certainly seemed honourable to all, though grievous. [26] Thus, there emerged not only a defender of my well-being who, before that favour of his, had been an enemy, but even an official supporter of my

meae. quo quidem die cum vos[87] quadringenti decem septem[88] essetis, magistratus autem omnes adessent, dissensit unus, is qui sua lege coniuratos etiam ab
inferis excitandos putarat. atque illo die cum rem publicam meis consiliis conservatam gravissimis verbis et plurimis iudicassetis, idem consul curavit ut
eadem a principibus civitatis in contione postero die dicerentur, cum quidem
ipse egit ornatissime meam causam perfecitque astante atque audiente Italia
tota ut nemo cuiusquam conducti aut perditi vocem acerbam atque inimicam
bonis posset audire.

[11 27] ad haec non modo adiumenta salutis sed etiam ornamenta dignitatis
meae reliqua vos idem addidistis: decrevistis ne quis ulla ratione rem impediret; qui[89] impedisset, vos[90] graviter molesteque laturos; illum contra rem publicam salutemque bonorum concordiamque civium facturum, et ut ad vos de eo
statim referretur; meque, etiam si diutius calumniarentur, redire iussistis. quid?
ut agerentur gratiae qui e municipiis venissent. quid? ut ad illam diem, res cum
redissent, rogarentur ut pari studio convenirent. quid denique ille dies[91], quem
P. Lentulus mihi fratrique meo liberisque nostris natalem constituit non modo
ad nostram verum etiam ad sempiterni memoriam temporis? quo die nos
comitiis centuriatis, quae maxime maiores comitia iusta dici haberique voluerunt, arcessivit in patriam, ut eaedem centuriae quae me consulem fecerant
consulatum meum comprobarent; [28] quo die[92] quis civis fuit qui fas esse
putaret, quacumque aut aetate aut valetudine esset, non se[93] de salute mea sententiam ferre? quando tantam frequentiam in campo, tantum splendorem
Italiae totius ordinumque omnium, quando illa dignitate rogatores, diribitores[94] custodesque vidistis? itaque P. Lentuli beneficio excellenti atque divino
non reducti sumus in patriam sicut non nulli clarissimi cives, sed equis insignibus et curru aurato reportati.

[29] possum ego satis in Cn. Pompeium umquam gratus videri? qui non solum
apud vos, qui omnes idem sentiebatis, sed etiam apud universum populum
salutem populi Romani et conservatam per me et coniunctam esse cum mea

---

[87] vos $E^2 \epsilon VF$: *om. PGE^1*

[88] quadrigenti decem septem P^2 : quadrigenti XVII E^2 : CCCCXVII ϵVF : quadrigenti decem
matem P^1 : quadrigenti · X · S · (r. senatores *sscr.* G^2) G : quadrigenti ex senatu E^1

[89] qui P^2F : quid P^1 : qui id GE : *om.* ϵV

[90] vos $E^2 \epsilon VF$: *om. PGE^1*

[91] ille dies ϵVF : ille die^s (s *fort. sscr.* E^2) E : illo die PG : <de> illo die *Wuilleumier*

[92] {quo die} *vel* eo die *Madvig*

[93] se ω *praeter* ϵV : *om.* ϵV

[94] diribitores *edd.* : dirivitores P^1 : dirivictores P^2 : dirivatores GE^1 : direptores $E^2 \epsilon VF$: *om.* H

dignity. On that day indeed, when you were 417 and all magistrates were present, a single person was of a different opinion, he who had thought that by his law the conspirators should be roused up even from the underworld. And on that day, when, by very solemn and very many words, you had judged the Republic saved by my counsels, the same consul saw to it that the same was said by the foremost men in the community at a public meeting on the following day, when he himself certainly argued my case in very ornate style and achieved, while the whole of Italy was standing by and listening, that nobody could hear the voice of anyone hired or reckless, a voice harsh and hostile to the good men.

[**11** 27] It was also you who, to these [that are] not only supports of my well-being, but also ornaments of my dignity, added what remained: you decreed that nobody should in any way hinder the matter; that you would be grieved and annoyed if anyone had hindered; that this man would act against the Republic, the well-being of the good men, and the unity of the citizens, and that reference should be made about him to you immediately; and you ordered that I, even if they brought false accusations for longer, should return. What of? That thanks should be rendered to those who had come from the municipal towns. What of? That they should be asked for that day, when the matters had been resumed, to come together with equal zeal. What, in short, of that day that P. Lentulus constituted for me and my brother and our children as a birthday not only for our recollection, but also for that of everlasting time? On that day he called me back into the country by the *comitia curiata*, the *comitia* that in particular the ancestors wanted to be called and regarded as lawful, so that the same centuries that had made me consul would approve of my consulship. [28] On that day, what citizen was there who believed that it was proper for him, of whatever age or health he was, not to cast a vote for my well-being? When did you see such a large body of people in the Campus, such splendour from the whole of Italy and from all classes, when polling-clerks, distributors, and tellers of such dignity? Therefore, by the outstanding and divine favour of P. Lentulus we have not been brought back into the country like some very respected citizens, but rather have been carried back on shining horses and a gilded chariot.

[29] Can I ever be seen sufficiently grateful towards Cn. Pompeius? He who not only among you, who all felt the same, but also among the entire People said that the well-being of the Roman People had both been preserved by me and

dixerit[95], qui causam meam prudentibus commendarit, imperitos edocuerit eodemque tempore improbos auctoritate sua compresserit, bonos excitarit, qui populum Romanum pro me tamquam pro fratre aut pro parente non solum hortatus sit, verum etiam obsecrarit, qui cum[96] ipse propter metum dimicationis et sanguinis domo se teneret, iam[97] a superioribus tribunis petierit ut de salute mea et promulgarent et referrent, qui in colonia nuper constituta cum ipse gereret magistratum, in qua nemo erat emptus intercessor, vim et crudelitatem privilegi auctoritate honestissimorum hominum et publicis litteris consignavit[98] princepsque Italiae totius praesidium ad meam salutem implorandum putavit[99], qui cum ipse mihi semper amicissimus fuisset, etiam ut suos necessarios mihi amicos redderet elaboravit[100].

[**12** 30] quibus autem officiis T. Anni beneficia remunerabor? cuius omnis ratio, cogitatio, totus denique tribunatus nihil aliud fuit nisi constans, perpetua, fortis, invicta defensio salutis meae. quid de P. Sestio loquar? qui suam erga me benivolentiam et fidem non solum animi dolore sed etiam corporis vulneribus ostendit.

vobis vero, patres conscripti, singulis et egi et agam gratias; universis egi initio[101], quantum potui, satis ornate agere nullo modo possum. et quamquam sunt in me praecipua merita multorum, quae sileri nullo modo possunt, tamen huius temporis ac timoris mei non est conari commemorare beneficia in me singulorum; nam difficile est non aliquem, nefas quemquam praeterire. ego vos universos, patres conscripti, deorum <in> numero[102] colere debeo. sed ut in ipsis dis immortalibus non semper eosdem atque alias alios solemus et venerari et precari, sic in hominibus de me divinitus meritis omnis erit aetas mihi ad eorum erga me merita praedicanda atque recolenda. [31] hodierno autem die nominatim a me magistratibus statui gratias esse agendas et de privatis uni qui pro salute mea municipia coloniasque adisset, populum Romanum supplex obsecrasset, sententiam dixisset eam quam vos secuti mihi dignitatem meam reddidistis. vos me florentem semper ornastis, laborantem mutatione vestis et prope luctu vestro, quoad licuit, defendistis. nostra memoria senatores ne in suis quidem periculis mutare vestem solebant; in meo periculo senatus veste

---

[95] cum mea dixerit *H* : cum me adixerit *F* : cum me addixerit *E²εV* : dixerit cum mea dixerit *P* : dixerit cum mea (ea *E¹*) *GE¹*

[96] cum *E²εV* : *om. PGE¹*

[97] iam *PG* : etiam *EεV*

[98] consignavit *ω* : consignarit *Lambinus*

[99] putavit *ω* : putarit *Lambinus*

[100] elaboravit *ω* : elaborarit *Lambinus*

[101] initio *PGE¹H¹* : ab initio *E²εVF*

[102] deorum <in> numero *Kayser*

been linked with mine, who recommended my cause to the sagacious, instruct-
ed the inexperienced, and at the same time reined in the rascals with his
authority and encouraged the good men, who not only urged the Roman
People on my behalf as if on behalf of a brother or of a parent, but also entreated
them, who, when he kept himself at home because of fear of fighting and blood,
requested already from the previous Tribunes that they put forward a bill about
my well-being and present it in the Senate, who, in the recently founded colony,
in which nobody was a bought proposer of vetoes, when he was in office himself, placed the force and cruelty of the special law on record by a resolution of
the most respected men and by public documents and was the first to be of the
opinion that the protection of the whole of Italy had to be invoked for my well-
being, who, while he himself had always been the greatest friend to me, also
made an effort that he turned those closely associated with him into my friends.

[12 30] But by what friendly offices will I pay back the favours of T. Annius? All
his reasoning, thinking, in short, his entire tribunate was nothing other than a
firm, constant, strong, undefeated defence of my well-being. What shall I say
about P. Sestius? He demonstrated his goodwill and loyalty towards me not
only by distress of mind, but even by wounds of the body.

As regards you indeed, Members of the Senate, to you individually I both have
rendered and will render thanks; to all of you I rendered thanks at the beginning, as much as I could; in no way can I render them in a sufficiently ornate
style. And even though there are outstanding great services conferred upon me
by many which cannot be passed over in silence in any way, still it is not appropriate for this occasion and my anxiety to try to recall the benefactions towards
me by individuals; for it is difficult not to omit someone, an offence to omit
anyone. I must venerate all of you, Members of the Senate, like gods. But as with
respect to the immortal gods themselves we are accustomed both to honour
and to pray to not always the same and rather different ones on different occasions, thus with respect to the men who have conferred services upon me in a
godlike manner, my entire life will be there for me to praise their services
towards me and renew my worship for them. [31] On the present day, however,
I have decided that thanks should be rendered by me by name to the magistrates and, out of the private people, to a single individual, who had approached
municipal towns and colonies on behalf of my well-being, beseeched the
Roman People as a suppliant, put forward that motion that you followed, and
thus returned my dignity to me. You have always honoured me, while I was
flourishing, defended me, while I was suffering, through a change of dress and
almost by your mourning, as far as it was allowed. Within our memory senators
were not accustomed to change their dress even in danger to themselves; in
danger to me the Senate appeared in changed dress, as far as it was allowed

mutata fuit, quoad licuit per eorum edicta qui mea pericula non modo suo praesidio sed etiam vestra deprecatione nudarunt.

[32] quibus ego rebus obiectis, cum mihi privato confligendum viderem cum eodem exercitu quem consul non armis sed vestra auctoritate superaram, multa mecum ipse reputavi. [13] dixerat in contione consul se clivi Capitolini poenas ab equitibus Romanis repetiturum; nominatim alii compellabantur, alii citabantur, alii relegabantur; aditus templorum erant non solum praesidiis et manu verum etiam demolitione sublati. alter consul, ut me et rem publicam non modo desereret, sed etiam hostibus rei publicae proderet, pactionibus se[103] suorum praemiorum obligarat. erat alius ad portas cum imperio in multos annos magnoque exercitu, quem ego inimicum mihi fuisse non dico, tacuisse, cum diceretur esse inimicus, scio. [33] duae partes esse in re publica cum putarentur, altera me deposcere propter inimicitias, altera timide defendere propter suspicionem caedis putabatur. qui autem me deposcere videbantur ii[104] hoc auxerunt dimicationis metum quod numquam infitiando suspicionem hominum curamque minuerunt.

qua re cum viderem senatum ducibus orbatum, me a magistratibus partim oppugnatum, partim proditum, partim derelictum, servos simulatione collegiorum nominatim esse conscriptos, copias omnis Catilinae paene isdem ducibus ad spem caedis et incendiorum esse revocatas, equites Romanos proscriptionis, municipia vastitatis, omnis caedis metu esse permotos, potui, potui[105], patres conscripti, multis auctoribus fortissimis viris me vi armisque defendere, nec mihi ipsi[106] ille animus idem meus vobis non incognitus defuit. sed videbam, si vicissem praesentem adversarium, nimium multos mihi alios esse vincendos; si victus essem, multis bonis et pro me et mecum, etiam post me, esse pereundum; tribuniciique sanguinis ultores esse praesentis, meae mortis poenas iudicio et[107] posteritati reservari. [14 34] nolui, cum consul communem salutem sine ferro defendissem, meam privatus armis defendere, bonosque viros lugere malui meas fortunas quam suis desperare. ac[108] si solus essem interfectus, mihi turpe, si cum multis, rei publicae funestum fore videbatur. quod si mihi aeternam esse aerumnam propositam arbitrarer, morte me ipse potius quam sempiterno dolore multassem. sed cum viderem me non diutius quam ipsam rem publicam ex hac urbe afuturum, neque ego illa exterminata mihi remanendum[109] putavi, et illa simul atque revocata est me secum pariter reportavit. mecum leges, mecum quaestiones, mecum iura

---

[103] se *Halm* : eos ω
[104] ii *Halm (in app.)* : in *PGE* : *om.* εV
[105] potui, potui *P* : potui *codd. rel.*
[106] ipsi *Heumann* : ipse ω
[107] aut *Shackleton Bailey*
[108] ac *P*εV : at *GEH*
[109] remanendum *PGE¹H* : remanendum esse amplius *E²*εV : remanendum amplius *F*

through the edicts of those who stripped my dangerous circumstances not only of their protection, but also of your entreaties.

[32] With those matters in the way, when I saw that I, as a private person, would have to fight with the same army that I, as consul, had conquered not with arms, but with your authority, I pondered many things with myself. [13] A consul had said in a public meeting that he would seek penalties for the ascent to the Capitol from the Roman knights; some were accused by name, others were summoned to trial, others again were relegated; access to temples was removed, not only by guards and force, but also by demolition. The other consul, so that he not only deserted me and the Republic, but even betrayed them to the enemies of the Republic, had placed himself under obligation by agreements concerning rewards for him. There was another person at the gates with command for many years and a large army, of whom I do not say that he was an enemy of mine, but I know that he was silent when he was said to be an enemy. [33] When two factions were believed to be in the Republic, one was believed to demand me for punishment because of enmity, the other to defend me timidly because of a presentiment of slaughter. But those who seemed to demand me increased the fear of fighting by the fact that they never reduced the presentiment and concern of people by denying.

Therefore, when I saw the Senate bereft of leaders, me partly opposed, partly betrayed, partly abandoned by the magistrates, slaves recruited by name under the pretence of clubs, all troops of Catilina almost with the same leaders recalled towards hope of slaughter and burning, the Roman knights moved by fear of proscription, the municipal towns by that of devastation, all by that of slaughter, I could, I could, Members of the Senate, have defended myself with force and arms, with many very courageous men suggesting this, and that same spirit of mine, well known to you, would not have been lacking to me. But I saw that, if I had conquered the present opponent, there would be too many others for me to conquer; that, if I had been conquered, many good men would have to perish both on my behalf and with me, even after me; and that avengers of the tribunician blood were present, but the penalty for my death was reserved for judgement by posterity. [14 34] I did not wish, since, as a consul, I had defended the common well-being without the sword, to defend mine by arms as a private citizen, and I preferred good men to be sad about my fortune rather than to despair of their own. And if I alone had been killed, it seemed that it would be disgraceful for me, if [I had been killed] with many, grievous for the Republic. If I believed that eternal distress was placed before me, I, of my own account, would have punished myself by death rather than by perpetual grief. But when I saw that I would not be away from this city for longer than the Republic itself, I did not believe that I should remain when it had been banished, and it, as soon as it had been recalled, brought me back together with it. With me laws, with me judicial commissions, with me rights of magistrates, with me the authority

magistratuum, mecum senatus auctoritas, mecum libertas, mecum etiam frugum ubertas, mecum deorum et hominum sanctitates omnes et religiones
afuerunt. quae si semper abessent, magis vestras fortunas lugerem quam
desiderarem meas; sin aliquando revocarentur, intellegebam mihi cum illis una
esse redeundum. [35] cuius mei sensus certissimus testis est hic idem qui custos capitis fuit, Cn. Plancius, qui omnibus provincialibus ornamentis commodisque depositis totam suam quaesturam in me sustentando et conservando
conlocavit. qui si mihi quaestor imperatori fuisset, in fili loco fuisset; nunc
certe erit in parentis, cum fuerit quaestor[110] non imperi sed doloris mei.

[36] quapropter, patres conscripti, quoniam in rem publicam sum pariter cum
re publica restitutus, non modo in ea defendenda nihil imminuam[111] de libertate
mea pristina, sed etiam adaugebo. [15] etenim si eam tum defendebam cum
mihi aliquid illa debebat, quid nunc me facere oportet cum ego illi plurimum
debeo? nam quid est quod animum meum frangere aut debilitare possit, cuius
ipsam calamitatem non modo nullius delicti, sed etiam duorum[112] in rem
publicam beneficiorum testem esse videatis? nam et[113] importata[114] est quia
defenderam civitatem, et mea voluntate suscepta est, ne a me defensa res publica
per eundem me extremum in discrimen vocaretur.

[37] pro me non, ut pro Publio Popilio, nobilissimo homine, adulescentes filii,
non propinquorum multitudo populum Romanum est deprecata, non ut pro
Q. Metello, summo et clarissimo viro, spectata iam adulescentia filius, non L. et
C. Metelli consulares, non eorum liberi, non Q. Metellus Nepos, qui tum consulatum petebat, non Luculli, Servilii, Scipiones, Metellarum[115] filii, flentes ac
sordidati populo Romano supplicaverunt, sed unus frater, qui in me pietate
filius, consiliis parens, amore, ut erat, frater inventus est, squalore et lacrimis et
cotidianis precibus desiderium mei nominis renovari et rerum gestarum
memoriam usurpari coegit. qui cum statuisset, nisi me per vos[116] reciperasset,
eandem subire fortunam atque idem sibi domicilium et vitae et mortis
deposcere{t}[117], tamen[118] numquam nec magnitudinem negoti nec solitudinem
suam nec vim inimicorum ac tela pertimuit. [38] alter fuit propugnator mearum

---

[110] quaestor ω : particeps *Wolf* : consors *Peterson*
[111] imminuam $E^2\epsilon VF$: minuam PGE^1H
[112] duorum $E^2\epsilon VF$: divinorum PGE^1H : binorum *Madvig 1873*
[113] nam et $E^2\epsilon V$: nam PGE^1H
[114] importata PGE^1H : imputata $E^2\epsilon VF$
[115] Metellarum *Manilius* : metellorum ω
[116] me per vos $E^2\epsilon VF$: per vos me H_S : per vos PGE^1
[117] deposcere{t} *Madvig* : deposceret ω
[118] tamen *del. Lambinus*

of the Senate, with me liberty, with me even the abundance of produce, with me all kinds of observation of duties and scrupulous behaviour towards gods and men have been away. If they were away forever, I would grieve more at your fortune than I would long for mine; but if they were recalled at some point, it was my understanding that I would have to return together with them. [35] Of this view of mine the surest witness is this very same person who was the guardian of my life, Cn. Plancius, who, having abandoned all insignia and rewards of provincial administration, devoted his entire quaestorship to maintaining and preserving me. If he had been a quaestor to me as general, he would have been in the place of a son; now he will certainly be in the place of a parent, when he was a quaestor not of my supreme power, but of my grief.

[36] Therefore, Members of the Senate, since I have been restored to the Republic together with the Republic, I will not only, in protecting it, not take anything away from my previous outspokenness, but even increase it. [15] For, if in the past I protected it when it owed me something, what should I do now when I owe it a great deal? For what is there that could break or weaken the spirit of myself, whose very misfortune you see as testimony not only of no crime, but even of two favours conferred upon the Republic? For it [i.e. the misfortune] was inflicted because I had protected the community, and it was embraced voluntarily by me, so that the Republic, protected by me, would not be brought to extreme danger again by me.

[37] For me there were not, as for Publius Popilius, a very noble man, sons in early manhood, not a large mass of relatives entreating the Roman People, not, as for Q. Metellus, an outstanding and famous man, a son in early manhood of already proven worth, not L. and C. Metellus, ex-consuls, not their children, not Q. Metellus Nepos, who was then standing for the consulship, not men like Lucullus, Servilius, Scipio, sons of Metellae, in tears and in mourning clothes, imploring the Roman People, but only my brother, who was found to be for me, through his dutiful respect, a son, through advice, a parent, through love, as he was, a brother, who, by mourning dress, tears, and daily entreaties, caused the desire for my person to be revived and the memory of my deeds to be spoken of frequently. Although he had decided, if he had not recovered me through you, to endure the same fortune and to demand the same place for life and death for himself, still, he never feared either the magnitude of the task or his own loneliness or the force and the weapons of the enemies. [38] A second champion and constant supporter of my fate was [a man] of greatest virtue and

fortunarum et defensor adsiduus summa virtute et pietate C. Piso gener, qui minas inimicorum meorum, qui inimicitias adfinis mei, propinqui sui, consulis, qui Pontum et Bithyniam quaestor prae mea salute neglexit. nihil umquam senatus de P. Popilio decrevit, numquam in hoc ordine de[119] Q. Metello mentio facta est; tribuniciis sunt illi rogationibus interfectis inimicis denique restituti, cum alter eorum senatui paruisset, alter vim caedemque fugisset. nam C. quidem Marius, qui hac hominum memoria tertius ante me consularis tempestate civili expulsus est, non modo a senatu non est restitutus, sed reditu suo senatum cunctum paene delevit. nulla de illis magistratuum consensio, nulla ad rem publicam defendendam populi Romani convocatio, nullus Italiae motus, nulla decreta municipiorum et coloniarum exstiterunt.

[39] qua re, cum me vestra auctoritas arcessierit, populus Romanus vocarit, res publica implorarit, Italia cuncta paene suis umeris reportarit, non committam, patres conscripti, ut, cum ea mihi sint restituta quae in potestate mea non fuerunt, ea non habeam quae ipse praestare possim, praesertim cum illa amissa reciperarim, virtutem et fidem numquam amiserim.

M. Tulli Ciceronis post reditum ad Quirites oratio

Sigla (Maslowski 1981, 20)

P = codex Parisinus 7794, saec. IX med.

P[1] = prima manus

P[2] = correcturae eiusdem fere aetatis

G = cod. Bruxellensis 5345 (olim Gemblacensis), saec. XI in.

G[1] = prima manus

G[2] = correcturae paulo recentiores

E = cod. Berolinensis 252 (olim Erfurtensis), saec. XII in., deficit post § 6 *Romanum*

---

[119] de *E²G²ϵVF* : *om. PG¹E¹H*

dutiful respect, C. Piso, my son-in-law, who disregarded the threats of my enemies, the enmity of my distant relative, his kinsman, the consul, and who, in his role as quaestor, left aside Pontus and Bithynia in view of my well-being. The Senate never decreed anything about P. Popilius, never in this body was mention made of Q. Metellus; through tribunician bills, after the death of their enemies, they were eventually restored, because one of them had obeyed the Senate, the other had fled force and slaughter. C. Marius, then, who, within living memory, was expelled as the third consular before me in civil disturbance, was not only not restored by the Senate, but almost wiped out the entire Senate by his return. No consensus about those men among the magistrates, no calling together of the Roman People to defend the Republic, no demonstration of feeling in Italy, no decrees of municipal towns and colonies existed.

[39] Therefore, since your authority summoned me, the Roman People called me, the Republic implored me, the whole of Italy almost carried me back on its shoulders, I will not let it happen, Members of the Senate, that, when that has been restored to me which was not in my power, I will not have what I can offer myself, especially since I recovered those things after I lost them, but never lost virtue and loyalty.

M. Tullius Cicero's oration to the Roman People after his return

H = codex Harleianus 4927, saec. XII ex.

   H¹ = prima manus

   H² = correcturae recentiores

T = cod. Trecensis 552, saec. XIV med., deficit post § 23 *etiam*

ε = cod. Erlangensis 847, anno 1466 exaratus

V = cod. Vaticanus 1525 (olim Palatinus), anno 1467 exaratus

ω = superiores illi codices omnes praeter E et T inde a locis adlatis

ς = codices recentiores non nulli

Schol. = Scholiasta Bobiensis

[1 1] quod precatus a Iove Optimo Maximo ceterisque dis immortalibus sum, Quirites, eo tempore cum me fortunasque meas pro vestra incolumitate otio concordiaque devovi, ut, si meas rationes umquam vestrae saluti anteposuissem, sempiternam poenam sustinerem mea voluntate susceptam, sin et ea quae ante gesseram conservandae civitatis causa gessissem et illam miseram profectionem vestrae salutis gratia suscepissem, ut, quod odium scelerati homines et audaces in rem publicam et in omnes bonos conceptum iam diu continerent, id in me uno potius quam in optimo quoque et universa civitate defigeretur[120]—hoc si animo in vos liberosque vestros fuissem, ut aliquando vos patresque conscriptos Italiamque universam memoria mei misericordiaque desideriumque[121] teneret, eius devotionis me esse convictum iudicio deorum immortalium, testimonio senatus, consensu Italiae, confessione inimicorum, beneficio divino immortalique vestro maxime laetor. [2] <namque,> Quirites[122], etsi nihil est homini magis optandum quam prospera, aequabilis perpetuaque fortuna secundo vitae sine ulla offensione cursu, tamen, si mihi tranquilla et placata omnia fuissent, incredibili quadam et paene divina, qua nunc vestro beneficio fruor, laetitiae voluptate caruissem. quid dulcius hominum generi ab natura datum est quam sui cuique liberi? mihi vero et propter indulgentiam meam et propter excellens eorum ingenium vita sunt mea cariores; tamen non tanta voluptate erant suscepti quanta[123] nunc sunt restituti. [3] nihil cuiquam fuit umquam iucundius quam mihi meus frater; non tam id sentiebam cum fruebar quam tum cum carebam et postea quam vos me illi et mihi eum reddidistis. res familiaris sua quemque delectat; reliquae meae fortunae reciperatae plus mihi nunc voluptatis adferunt quam tum incolumes[124] adferebant. amicitiae, consuetudines, vicinitates, clientelae, ludi denique et dies festi quid haberent voluptatis carendo magis intellexi quam fruendo. [4] iam vero honos, dignitas, locus, ordo, beneficia vestra quamquam mihi semper clarissima visa sunt, tamen ea nunc renovata inlustriora videntur quam si obscurata non essent. ipsa autem patria, di immortales, dici vix potest quid caritatis, quid voluptatis habe<a>t[125]: quae species Italiae, quae celebritas oppidorum, quae forma regionum, qui agri, quae fruges, quae pulchritudo urbis, quae humanitas civium, quae rei publicae dignitas, quae vestra maiestas! quibus ego omnibus antea rebus sic fruebar ut nemo magis; sed tamquam bona

---

[120] defigeretur *Wimmel* : deficeret ω : defigerent *Lambinus* : desaeviret *Gesner* : *num* expleretur *aut* defervesceret? *Peterson (in app.)*

[121] misericordiaque ω *praeter* G^1 : misericordia G^1 | desideriumque εV : desiderium *PGET* : *del. Halm* | <ac> desiderium *Klotz* : <et> desiderium *Wuilleumier*

[122] <namque,> Quirites *Peterson* : quirites *EHT* : qui r. *P* : q. r. *G*εV : Quirites *cum praecedentibus coniunxit ed. Rom.* ita: laetor, Quirites. et si (et si <enim> *Hotman*) : qua re *Madvig* : quia *Courtney* : etenim *Shackleton Bailey*

[123] tanta (*om.* εV) voluptate…quanta ω : tantae voluptati…quantae *Schol.*

[124] incolumes *ς* : incolumitate P^1 : incolumitatis P^2GTεV : incolo- *EH* : incolumi *Markland* : <in> incolumitate *Halm* : incolumitate <adfectae> *Sydow*

[125] habe<a>t *Lambinus* : habet ω

[**1** 1] As for the fact that I prayed to Iuppiter Optimus Maximus and other immortal gods, Romans, at that time when I offered up myself and my property on behalf of your safety, tranquillity, and concord, that, if I had ever put considerations for myself before your well-being, I would sustain everlasting punishment, accepted voluntarily, but that, if I both had done what I had done in the past for the sake of preserving the community and had undertaken that wretched journey in the interest of your well-being, the hatred that criminal and reckless men held conceived against the Republic and against all good men already for a long time was focused on me alone rather than on all best men and the entire community—if I had been of such an attitude towards you and your children that at some point recollection of me, pity, and desire would hold under their sway you, the senators, and the whole of Italy: I am extremely happy that I have been approved in respect of this sacrifice by the judgement of the immortal gods, the testimony of the Senate, the consensus of Italy, the confession of my enemies as well as your divine and immortal favour. [2] <For certainly,> Romans, even though nothing is more to be desired by a human being than prosperous, steady, and perpetual good fortune in a favourable course of life without any mishap, still, if everything had been tranquil and calm for me, I had lacked some incredible and almost divine pleasure of happiness, which I now enjoy because of your favour. What sweeter item has been given to the race of humans by nature than their children to everyone? But to me, both because of my fondness and because of their excellent talent, they are dearer than my own life; still, they have not been accepted into the family with as much pleasure as they have now been restored. [3] Nothing was ever more delightful to anyone than my brother to me; I did not feel this so when I enjoyed [him] than at the time when I lacked [him] and after you had returned me to him and him to me. Their personal property delights everyone; my property recovered (what remains of it) now provides more enjoyment to me than it used to provide in the past being intact. Friendships, close connections, neighbourly relations, clientships, finally, games and festive days, what they have in pleasure I have understood more through lacking than through enjoying them. [4] Further, office, status, rank, standing, and your favours, although they have always seemed outstanding to me, still, now that they have been renewed, seem shining more brightly than if they had not been dimmed. Moreover, the country itself, immortal gods, it can hardly be said what affection, what pleasure it entails: what attractiveness of Italy, what busy life in towns, what characteristic appearance of the regions, what fields, what produce, what beauty of the city, what humane character of the citizens, what standing of the Republic, what majesty of you! All these things I was enjoying previously in such a way that nobody did more. But just as good health is more pleasant to those who have

valetudo iucundior est iis qui e gravi morbo recreati sunt quam qui numquam
aegro corpore fuerunt, sic haec omnia desiderata magis quam adsidue percepta
delectant.

[2 5] quorsum igitur haec disputo? quorsum? ut intellegere possitis neminem
umquam tanta eloquentia fuisse neque tam divino atque incredibili genere
dicendi qui vestram[126] magnitudinem multitudinemque beneficiorum, quam[127]
in me fratremque meum et liberos nostros contulistis, non modo augere aut
ornare oratione, sed enumerare aut consequi possit. a parentibus, id quod
necesse erat, parvus sum procreatus, a vobis natus sum consularis. illi mihi
fratrem incognitum qualis futurus esset dederunt, vos spectatum et incredibili
pietate cognitum reddidistis. rem publicam illis accepi temporibus eam quae
paene amissa est[128], a vobis eam reciperavi quam aliquando omnes unius opera
servatam iudicaverunt. di immortales mihi liberos dederunt, vos reddidistis.
multa praeterea a dis immortalibus optata consecuti sumus; nisi vestra voluntas fuisset, omnibus divinis muneribus careremus[129]. vestros denique honores,
quos eramus gradatim singulos adsecuti, nunc a vobis universos habemus, ut
quantum antea parentibus, quantum dis immortalibus, quantum vobismet
ipsis, tantum hoc tempore universum cuncto populo Romano debeamus[130].

[6] nam cum in ipso beneficio vestro tanta magnitudo est ut eam[131] complecti
oratione non possim, tum in studiis vestris tanta animorum declarata est
voluntas ut non solum calamitatem mihi detraxisse, sed etiam dignitatem auxisse
videamini. [3] non enim pro meo reditu ut pro P. Popili, nobilissimi hominis,
adulescentes filii et multi praeterea cognati atque adfines deprecati sunt, non ut
pro Q. Metello, clarissimo viro, iam spectata aetate filius, non Lucius Diadematus
consularis, summa auctoritate vir, non C. Metellus censorius, non eorum liberi,
non Q. Metellus Nepos, qui tum consulatum petebat, non sororum filii, Luculli,
Servilii, Scipiones; permulti enim tum, Metelli aut Metellarum[132] liberi, pro
Q. Metelli reditu vobis ac patribus vestris supplicaverunt. quod si ipsius summa
dignitas maximaeque res gestae non satis valerent[133], tamen fili[134] pietas, propinquorum preces, adulescentium squalor, maiorum natu lacrimae populum

---

[126]   vestram *ω praeter εV* : nostram *εV* : vestrorum *Orelli* : *del. Shackleton Bailey*
[127]   quam *P²GETεV* : qua *P¹* : quae *ς* : *om. H¹* : que *inter* in *et* me *scr. H²*
[128]   est *ω* : esset *Ernesti*
[129]   careremus *ς* : caruerimus *PG¹EHεV* : caruissemus *T* : carerimus *G¹*
[130]   debeamus *H* : debemus *ω*
[131]   eam *ω praeter P* : iam *P*
[132]   metellarum *P²G* : metellorum *ETεV*
[133]   valerent *ς* : valent *ω* : valebant *Halm*
[134]   fili *edd.* : filii *Naugerius* : illi *ω*

recovered from a serious illness than to those who have never had a bodily illness, so all these things delight more after having been missed than when constantly taken in.

[2 5] To what end then am I saying this? To what end? So that you might understand that nobody ever was in command of such great eloquence or such a divine and unbelievable form of speaking that, with respect to the magnitude and multitude of your favours that you have conferred upon me, my brother and our children, they might be able, not to enhance and embellish them by an oration, but simply to enumerate and cover them. By my parents, as was necessary, I was brought into the world as an insignificant child; by you I was born as a consular. They gave me a brother as someone unknown as to what he was going to be like; you have given him back as someone of observed merit and known for unbelievable dutiful respect. In those times I received the Republic as such a one that was almost lost; from you I have regained it as such a one that, as all have eventually determined, was saved by the efforts of one man. The immortal gods gave me children; you have given them back. Many things besides wished for from the immortal gods did we obtain; if there had not been your goodwill, we would lack all divine gifts. Finally, the honours from you, which we had attained gradually one by one, we now have altogether from you, so that how much we previously owed to the parents, to the immortal gods, and to yourselves, so much altogether we owe to the entire Roman People at this time.

[6] For there is such magnitude in the very favour from you that I cannot cover that in a speech; moreover, so much goodwill of minds has been demonstrated in your devotion [to my cause] that you evidently have not only removed the misfortune from me, but have even enhanced my standing. [3] For my return there were not, to be sure, as for that of P. Popilius, a most noble man, sons in early manhood and besides many blood relations and in-laws entreating, not, as for Q. Metellus, an eminent man, a son of an age with already proven worth, not the consular L. Diadematus, a man of greatest authority, not the ex-censor C. Metellus, not their children, not Q. Metellus Nepos, who was then standing for the consulship, not the sons of sisters, men like Lucullus, Servilius, Scipio; for very many, Metelli or children of Metellae, at that time petitioned you and your fathers on behalf of Q. Metellus' return. If, then, the outstanding dignity and the greatest achievements of the man himself were not of sufficient value, still, the dutifulness of the son, the entreaties of the relatives, the mourning clothes of the young men, the tears of the older man were able to move the

Romanum movere potuerunt. [7] nam C. Mari, qui post illos veteres clarissimos consulares hac vestra patrumque memoria tertius ante me consularis subiit
indignissimam fortunam praestantissima sua gloria, dissimilis fuit ratio; non enim
ille deprecatione rediit, sed in discessu civium exercitu se armisque revocavit.

at me nudum a propinquis, nulla cognatione munitum, nullo armorum ac
tumultus metu, C. Pisonis, generi mei, divina quaedam et inaudita pietas
atque[135] virtus fratrisque miserrimi atque optimi cotidianae lacrimae sordesque
lugubres a vobis deprecatae sunt. [8] frater erat unus qui suo squalore vestros
oculos inflecteret, qui suo fletu desiderium mei memoriamque renovaret; qui
statuerat, Quirites, si vos me sibi non reddidissetis, eandem subire fortunam[136]:
tanto in me amore exstitit ut negaret fas esse non modo domicilio, sed ne sepulcro
quidem se a me esse seiunctum. pro me praesente senatus hominumque
praeterea viginti milia vestem mutaverunt, pro eodem absente unius squalorem sordesque vidistis. unus hic qui quidem[137] in foro posset esse mihi pietate
filius inventus est, beneficio parens, amore idem qui semper fuit frater. nam
coniugis miserae squalor et luctus atque optimae filiae maeror adsiduus filique
parvi desiderium mei lacrimaeque pueriles aut itineribus necessariis aut magnam partem tectis[138] ac tenebris continebantur. [4] qua re hoc maius est vestrum in nos promeritum quod non multitudini propinquorum sed nobismet
ipsis nos reddidistis. [9] sed quem ad modum propinqui, quos ego parare non
potui, mihi ad deprecandam calamitatem meam non fuerunt, sic illud quod
mea virtus praestare debuit, adiutores, auctores hortatoresque ad me restituendum ita multi fuerunt ut longe superiores omnes hac dignitate copiaque supe-
rarem. numquam de P. Popilio, clarissimo ac fortissimo viro, numquam de
Q. Metello, nobilissimo et constantissimo cive, numquam de C. Mario, custode
civitatis atque imperi vestri, in senatu mentio facta est. [10] tribuniciis superiores illi rogationibus nulla auctoritate senatus sunt restituti, Marius vero non
modo non a senatu sed etiam oppresso senatu est restitutus, nec rerum gestarum memoria in reditu C. Mari sed exercitus atque arma valuerunt; at de me ut
valeret[139] semper senatus flagitavit, ut aliquando proficeret[140], cum primum
licuit, frequentia atque auctoritate perfecit. nullus[141] in eorum reditu motus
municipiorum et coloniarum factus est, at me in patriam ter suis decretis Italia
cuncta revocavit. illi inimicis interfectis, magna civium caede facta reducti

[135] pietas atque *Ernesti* : satque *P* : auctoritas atque *codd. rel.* : alacritas atque *Sydow*
[136] fortunam ω : fortunam <nam> *Halm*
[137] qui quidem ς : quidem ω | hic quidem *bis G*[1]
[138] tectis *edd.* : lectis ω
[139] valeret ς : valerent *G*[1]*TεV* : valerem *G*[2] : valuerunt *P*
[140] proficeret ς : perficet *P*[1] : perficeretur *P*[2]*GTεV* : pervinceret *Madvig*
[141] nullus ς : nullius ω

Roman People. [7] For, as regards C. Marius, who, after those illustrious ex-consuls of the past, within the memory of yourselves and your fathers, was the third consular before me to undergo a most unworthy fate despite his most outstanding glory, the method was different; for that man did not return through entreaty, but amid divisions among the citizens he recalled himself with an army and arms.

But as for me, bereft of relatives, protected by no kinsfolk, with no threat from arms and tumult, some divine and unheard-of dutiful respect and virtue of C. Piso, my son-in-law, and the daily tears and sorrowful mourning clothes of my most miserable and best brother have entreated you. [8] My brother was the only one who turned your eyes by his squalor, who revived your longing and recollection of me through his weeping; he had decided, Romans, that, if you had not returned me to him, he would undergo the same fortune: he proved himself of such a great love for me that he denied that it was right for him to be separated from me not only as regards the dwelling, but not even as regards the grave. For me, when present, the senate and twenty thousand men besides changed dress; for the same man, when absent, you saw the filth and mourning clothes of a single person. A single person who at any rate was able to be in the Forum was discovered to be for me, because of dutifulness, a son, because of kindness, a parent, because of love, just as he has always been, a brother. For the mourning dress and grief of my miserable wife and the incessant sadness of the best daughter and the longing for me and the boyish tears of my little son were confined to necessary journeys or, in large part, to obscurity inside the house. [4] Therefore, your service conferred upon me is greater for the reason that you did not give us back to a multitude of relatives, but to ourselves. [9] But while there were no relatives, whom I could not supply, to plead for me to avert my misfortune, yet what my virtue ought to provide, namely helpers, supporters, and encouragers to restore me, there were so many that I surpassed by far all the earlier men by such high rank and great number. Never was there any mention in the Senate of P. Popilius, a most respectable and most courageous man, never of Q. Metellus, a most noble and most steadfast citizen, never of C. Marius, the guardian of the community and your empire. [10] Those earlier men were restored by tribunician bills with no resolution of the Senate; yet Marius was not only not restored by the Senate, but even after the Senate had been oppressed, and not the memory of achievements, but rather an army and weap-ons were of importance as regards the return of C. Marius. But, concerning me, that it [i.e. the memory of achievements] should be of importance, the Senate always demanded; that it [i.e. the Senate] was successful eventually, as soon as it was possible, it achieved by its large numbers and authority. No demonstra-tion of the feelings of municipal towns and colonies happened in connection with the return of those men, but in my case the whole of Italy recalled me to the country with its decrees three times. Those were brought back after their

sunt, ego iis a quibus eiectus sum provincias obtinentibus, inimico autem, optimo viro et mitissimo, altero <cum> consule[142] referente reductus sum, cum is inimicus qui ad meam perniciem vocem suam communibus hostibus prae- buisset spiritu[143] dumtaxat viveret, re quidem infra omnes mortuos amandatus esset. [5 11] numquam de <P.>[144] Popilio L. Opimius, fortissimus consul, num- quam de Q. Metello non modo C. Marius qui erat inimicus, sed ne is quidem qui secutus est, M. Antonius, homo eloquentissimus, cum A. Albino[145] collega senatum aut populum est cohortatus.

at pro me superiores consules semper ut referrent flagitati sunt; sed veriti sunt ne gratiae causa facere viderentur, quod alter mihi adfinis erat, alterius causam capitis receperam; qui provinciarum foedere inretiti[146] totum illum annum querelas senatus, luctum bonorum, Italiae gemitum pertulerunt. Kalendis vero Ianuariis postea quam orba res publica consulis fidem tamquam legitimi tutoris imploravit, P. Lentulus consul, parens, deus, salus[147] nostrae vitae, fortunae, memoriae, nominis, simul ac de sollemni deorum religione[148] rettulit[149], nihil humanarum rerum sibi prius quam de me agendum iudicavit. [12] atque eo die confecta res esset, nisi is tribunus plebis quem ego maximis beneficiis quaestorem consul ornaram, cum et cunctus ordo et multi eum summi viri orarent et Cn. Oppius socer, optimus vir, ad pedes flens iaceret, noctem[150] sibi ad deliberandum postulasset; quae {deliberatio}[151] non in red- denda, quem ad modum non nulli arbitra<ba>ntur[152], sed, ut patefactum est, in augenda mercede consumpta est. postea res acta est in senatu alia nulla, cum variis rationibus impediretur; <s>ed[153] voluntate tamen perspecta[154] senatus causa ad[155] vos mense Ianuario deferebatur.

---

[142] <consule cum> altero consule *Luterbacher* : <consule> ante altero *add. Madvig, ante* refe- rente *Mommsen apud Orellium*

[143] spiritu *s* : siritu *P* : si ritu *GTεV*

[144] *add. edd.* : *om. ω*

[145] <neque solus neque> cum A. Albino *Shackleton Bailey*

[146] inretiti *edd.* : irretiti *Cratander* : irinati *P* : irritaqui *G* : irritaque *T* : irritatus *εV* : inligati *Halm (in app.)* : infrenati *Koch* : frenati *Luterbacher*

[147] salus *ω praeter HG²* : salutis *HG²*

[148] de sollemni deorum religione *Halm* : solempni de *s* : solem de *P* : sole de *GTε* : sole *V* : *om. H*

[149] rettulit *edd.* : retulit *ω*

[150] noctem *H* : noctemque *PGTεV* : *ante* noctemque *lac. statuit Klotz (explevit <respondere* dubitasset>)

[151] *del. Shackleton Bailey*

[152] arbitra<ba>ntur *Cratander* : arbitrantur *ω*

[153] <s>ed *Halm (in app.)* : et *ω* : *om. s* : ex *Mommsen*

[154] perspecta *Angelius* : perfecta *ω*

[155] ad *s* : apud *ω*

enemies had been killed, after a mass slaughter of citizens had taken place; I was brought back while those by whom I was driven away were in possession of provinces and while an enemy, a very good and very mild person, <along with> the other consul, put forward the issue, when that enemy, who, for my destruction, had provided his voice to the foes of the community, was only just alive by breathing, but in fact had been relegated [to a place] below all the dead. [5 11] Never, as regards <P.> Popilius, did L. Opimius, a most valiant consul, never, as regards Q. Metellus, did not only C. Marius, who was his enemy, but not even he who succeeded him, M. Antonius, a very eloquent man, along with the colleague A. Albinus, rouse the Senate or the People.

But for me the previous consuls were always pressed that they should bring the matter to the Senate; yet they feared that they seemed to do this for the sake of partiality because one of them was related to me, and for the other I had undertaken a case with a capital charge; they, entangled in a pact concerning the provinces, endured the complaints of the Senate, the grief of the good men, the groans of Italy for that entire year. But on the Kalends of January, after the orphaned Republic had implored the tutelage of the consul like that of a legal guardian, P. Lentulus, consul, parent, god, saviour of our life, fortune, memory, and name, as soon as he had put forward matters concerning the solemn veneration of the gods, decided that no mortal matters should be dealt with by him earlier than my case. [12] And on that day the matter would have been concluded if not that Tribune of the People (whom, when quaestor, I, as consul, had decorated with the greatest favours), when both the entire body and many distinguished men beseeched him and Cn. Oppius, his father-in-law, an outstanding man, lay at his feet in tears, had requested the night for him to think it over; this {thinking} was not spent, as some believed, on returning, but, as became clear, on increasing the reward. Afterwards no other matter was dealt with in the Senate, while it was hindered by various means; but, after the inclination of the Senate had been perceived all the same, the matter was referred to you in the month of January.

[13] hic tantum interfuit inter me et inimicos meos. ego, cum homines in tribunali Aurelio palam conscribi centuriarique vidissem, cum intellegerem veteres ad spem caedis Catilinae copias esse revocatas, cum viderem ex ea parte homines cuius partis nos vel principes numerabamur, partim quod mihi inviderent, partim quod sibi timerent, aut proditores esse aut desertores salutis meae, cum duo consules empti pactione provinciarum auctores se inimicis rei publicae tradidissent, cum egestatem, avaritiam, libidines suas viderent expleri non posse nisi <me>[156] constrictum domesticis hostibus dedidissent[157], cum senatus equitesque[158] Romani flere pro me ac mutata veste vobis supplicare edictis atque imperiis vetarentur, cum omnium provinciarum pactiones, cum omnia cum omnibus foedera <ac> reconciliationes[159] gratiarum sanguine meo sancirentur[160], cum omnes boni non recusarent quin vel pro me vel mecum perirent, armis decertare pro mea salute nolui, quod et vincere et vinci luctuosum rei publicae fore putavi. [14] at inimici mei, mense Ianuario cum de me ageretur, corporibus civium trucidatis[161] flumine sanguinis meum reditum intercludendum putaverunt. [6] itaque, dum[162] ego absum, eam rem publicam habuistis ut aeque me atque illam restituendam putaretis. ego autem in qua civitate nihil valeret senatus, omnis esset impunitas, nulla iudicia, vis et ferrum in foro versaretur, cum privati parietum <se>[163] praesidio non legum tuerentur, tribuni plebis vobis inspectantibus vulnerarentur, ad magistratuum domos cum ferro et facibus iretur, consulis fasces frangerentur, deorum immortalium templa incenderentur, rem publicam esse nullam putavi. itaque neque re publica exterminata mihi locum in hac urbe esse duxi, nec, si illa restitueretur, dubitavi quin me secum ipsa reduceret.

[15] an ego, cum mihi esset exploratissimum P. Lentulum proximo anno consulem futurum, qui illis ipsis rei publicae periculosissimis temporibus aedilis curulis me consule omnium meorum consiliorum particeps periculorumque

[156] *add. Naugerius*
[157] dedidissent *ς* : dedissent *ω*
[158] equitesque *T* : equites *ω*
[159] <ac> reconciliationes *R. Klotz, Madvig* : reconciliatione *PGTεV* : reconciliationes *Hς* : <de> reconciliatione *Mommsen* : reconciliationes<que> *Koch* : <in> reconciliatione *Maslowski*
[160] sancirentur *P¹* : sarcirentur *ω*
[161] trucidatis <et> *Shackleton Bailey*
[162] dum *Halm (in app.)* : cum *ω*
[163] se *hic add. Halm, ante* privati *ς, ante* parietum *Orelli*

[13] Here there was such a difference between me and my enemies: I, when I had seen individuals at the Aurelian tribunal openly being enrolled and arranged in centuries, when I understood that Catilina's old troops were recalled to the prospect of slaughter, when I saw that men from that party of which we were reckoned even as the foremost, partly because they envied me, partly because they feared for themselves, were either betrayers or deserters of my well-being, when the two consuls, bought by a pact concerning the provinces, had surrendered themselves as supporters to the enemies of the Republic, when they saw that their poverty, avarice, and lusts could not be filled unless they had given <me>, held in check, to internal enemies, when the Senate and the Roman knights were forbidden by edicts and commands to shed tears for me and to plead with you with changed dress, when pacts concerning all provinces, when all treaties with all <and> restorations of goodwill were sanctioned by my blood, when all good men did not refuse to perish, be it for me, be it with me, I did not wish to fight with arms for my well-being, since I believed that both conquering and being conquered would be grievous for the Republic. [14] But my enemies, when in the month of January there was discussion about me, believed that my return had to be cut off, after the slaughter of the bodies of citizens, by a river of blood. [6] Consequently, while I was absent, you considered the Republic to be such that you believed that I and it equally had to be restored. I, however, believed that, in a community in which the Senate was of no value, there was complete impunity and no courts, while force and steel reigned in the Forum, when private individuals guarded <themselves> by the protection of the walls [of their houses], not of the laws, Tribunes of the People were wounded while you were looking on, people went to the houses of magistrates with sword and torches, the fasces of consuls were broken, the temples of the immortal gods were set on fire, there was no Republic at all. Therefore, neither did I think that, once the Republic had been expelled, there was a place for me in this city, nor did I doubt that it would lead me back with itself if it was restored.

[15] Or could I doubt, since it had become very certain to me that P. Lentulus would be consul in the following year, he who, during those most hazardous times of the Republic, as curule aedile, while I was consul, had been a sharer in

socius fuisset, dubitarem quin is me confectum consularibus vulneribus consulari medicina ad salutem reduceret? hoc duce, collega autem eius, clementissimo atque optimo viro, primo non adversante, post etiam adiuvante, reliqui magistratus paene omnes fuerunt defensores salutis meae. ex quibus excellenti animo, virtute, auctoritate, praesidio, copiis T. Annius et P. Sestius praestanti in me benivolentia et divino studio exstiterunt; eodemque P. Lentulo auctore et pariter referente collega frequentissimus senatus uno dissentiente, nullo intercedente dignitatem meam quibus potuit verbis amplissimis ornavit, salutem vobis, municipiis, coloniis omnibus commendavit. [16] ita me nudum a propinquis, nulla cognatione munitum consules, praetores, tribuni plebis, senatus, Italia cuncta semper a vobis deprecata est, denique omnes qui vestris maximis beneficiis honoribusque sunt ornati, producti ad vos ab eodem[164] non solum ad me conservandum vos cohortati sunt, sed etiam rerum mearum gestarum auctores, testes, laudatores fuerunt. [7] quorum princeps ad cohortandos vos et ad rogandos fuit Cn. Pompeius, vir omnium qui sunt, fuerunt, erunt virtute, sapientia, gloria princeps. qui mihi unus uni privato amico eadem omnia dedit quae universae rei publicae, salutem, otium, dignitatem. cuius oratio fuit, quem ad modum accepi, tripertita: primum vos docuit meis consiliis rem publicam esse servatam causamque meam cum communi salute coniunxit hortatusque est ut auctoritatem senatus, statum civitatis, fortunas civis bene meriti defenderetis; tum {me}[165] in perorando posuit vos[166] rogari a senatu, rogari ab equitibus Romanis, rogari ab Italia cuncta, deinde ipse ad extremum pro mea vos salute non rogavit solum verum etiam obsecravit. [17] huic ego homini, Quirites, tantum debeo quantum hominem homini debere vix fas est. huius consilia, P. Lentuli sententiam, senatus auctoritatem vos secuti in eo <me>[167] loco in quo vestris beneficiis fueram, isdem centuriis quibus conlocaratis reposuistis. eodem tempore audistis eodem ex loco summos viros, ornatissimos atque amplissimos homines, principes civitatis, omnes consularis, omnes praetorios eadem dicere, ut omnium testimonio per me unum[168] rem publicam conservatam esse constaret. itaque cum P. Servilius, gravissimus vir et ornatissimus civis, dixisset opera mea rem publicam incolumem magistratibus deinceps traditam, dixerunt in eandem sententiam ceteri. sed audistis eo tempore clarissimi viri non solum auctoritatem, sed etiam testimonium, L. Gelli; qui quia suam classem adtemptatam magno cum suo periculo paene sensit, dixit in contione vestrum[169], si ego consul cum fui non fuissem, rem publicam funditus interituram fuisse.

---

[164]   ab eodem ς : ab eadem *PGT∈V* : *om. Hς*
[165]   *del. edd. vet.* : <optu>me *Walter* : <pro> me *Sydow*
[166]   vos *del. Halm*
[167]   in eo <me> *ed. Rom.* : secuti <me> *Halm (in app.)*
[168]   unum *P* : *om.* ω
[169]   contione: 'vestrum si …' *interpunxit Halm* : contione vestra *Cratander*

all my plans and a companion in dangers, that he would lead me, worn away by consular wounds, back to safety by consular medicine? With him as the leader and with his colleague, a very mild and outstanding man, initially not adverse, later even supportive, the other magistrates, almost all, were defenders of my well-being. Out of those, as a result of an excellent mind, virtue, authority, protection, and resources, T. Annius and P. Sestius were conspicuous for their outstanding goodwill towards me and godlike zeal; and with P. Lentulus again as the initiator and the colleague proposing with him, a very well-attended Senate, with a single person dissenting and nobody vetoing, adorned my dignity with the most ample words that it could and entrusted my well-being to you and all municipal towns and colonies. [16] In the same way consuls, praetors, Tribunes of the People, the Senate and the whole of Italy constantly entreated you for me, bereft of relatives, protected by no kinsfolk; eventually all who had been decorated with the greatest favours and honours from you, brought before you by the same person, not only exhorted you to preserve me, but were also advocates, witnesses, and eulogizers of my achievements. [7] Of those the foremost to exhort and urge you was Cn. Pompeius, the foremost man of all those who are, were, and will be in virtue, wisdom, and glory. He, a single person, gave to me, a single private friend, all the same things that [he gave] to the entire Republic: well-being, tranquillity, dignity. His speech was, as I have learned, divided into three parts: first he told you that the Republic had been saved by my plans and linked my cause with the common well-being and exhorted you to defend the authority of the Senate, the condition of the community, and the fortunes of a well-deserved citizen; then {me}, in concluding, he stated that you were urged by the Senate, urged by the Roman knights, urged by the whole of Italy; then, at the very end, he not only urged you for my well-being, but even pleaded with you. [17] To this human being, Romans, I owe so much as is hardly right for a human being to owe to a human being. Following his advice, P. Lentulus' statement and the Senate's authority, you put <me> back into that place in which I had been through your favours, by the same centuries by which you had placed me there. At the same time you heard from the same place outstanding men, much adorned and very distinguished individuals, the foremost men in the community, all former consuls, all former praetors say the same thing, so that it was evident by the testimony of all that through me alone the Republic had been preserved. Accordingly, when P. Servilius, a much-respected man and a well-decorated citizen, had said that through my efforts the Republic had been handed over unharmed to the next magistrates, others spoke to the same effect. Moreover, you heard at that time not only the authoritative opinion, but also the testimony of an outstanding man, L. Gellius: since he almost experienced amid great danger to himself that his fleet had been seduced, he said at your public meeting that, if I had not been consul when I was, the Republic would have perished entirely.

[8 18] en ego tot[170] testimoniis, Quirites[171], hac auctoritate senatus, tanta consensione Italiae, tanto studio bonorum omnium, causam[172] agente P. Lentulo,
consentientibus ceteris magistratibus, deprecante Cn. Pompeio, omnibus
hominibus faventibus, dis denique immortalibus frugum ubertate, copia, vilitate reditum meum comprobantibus {se} mihi[173], meis, rei publicae restitutus
tantum vobis quantum facere possum, Quirites, pollicebor: primum, qua sanctissimi homines pietate erga deos immortalis esse soleant, eadem me[174] erga
populum Romanum semper fore numenque vestrum aeque mihi grave et
sanctum ac deorum immortalium in omni vita futurum; deinde, quoniam me
in civitatem res publica ipsa reduxit, nullo me loco rei publicae defuturum. [19]
quod si quis existimat me aut voluntate esse mutata aut debilitata virtute aut
animo fracto, vehementer errat. mihi quod potuit vis et iniuria et sceleratorum
hominum furor detrahere, eripuit, abstulit, dissipavit; quod viro forti adimi
non potest, id et[175] manet et permanebit.

vidi ego fortissimum virum, municipem meum, C. Marium—quoniam
nobis quasi aliqua fatali necessitate non solum cum iis[176] qui haec delere voluissent, sed etiam cum fortuna belligerandum fuit—eum tamen vidi, cum esset
summa senectute, non modo non infracto animo propter magnitudinem
calamitatis, sed confirmato atque renovato. [20] quem egomet dicere audivi
tum se fuisse[177] miserum cum[178] careret patria quam obsidione liberavisset,
cum sua bona possideri ab inimicis ac diripi audiret, cum adulescentem filium
videret eiusdem socium calamitatis, cum in paludibus demersus concursu ac
misericordia Minturnensium corpus ac vitam suam conservaret, cum parva
navicula pervectus in Africam, quibus regna ipse dederat, ad eos inops supplexque venisset; reciperata vero sua dignitate se non commissurum ut, cum ea
quae amiserat sibi restituta essent, virtutem animi non haberet, quam numquam perdidisset. sed hoc inter me atque illum interest quod ille qua re plurimum potuit ea ipsa re inimicos suos ultus est, armis, ego qua consuevi utar,
<verbis>[179], quoniam illi arti in bello ac seditione locus est, huic in pace atque

[170] tot *Hς* : *om.* ω
[171] quirites *Hς* : qui r. (rem *P*) p. ω
[172] causam *Halm (in app.)* : cum *PGTεV* : *om. Hς* : consule *Klotz* : coram *Walter* : <vobis>cum
Luterbacher
[173] mihi *H* : se mihi (*ex* mini *P¹*) ω
[174] me ς : *om. PGTεV* : *ante* semper *hab.* H
[175] id et *G²* : ideo *PG¹TεV* : id mihi *H* : id ς : id ei *Kasten* : id vero *Halm (in app.)* : id omne
Peterson : id adeo *Busche* : id <est> et *Sydow*
[176] iis *edd.* : is *G¹* : his *PHG²T* : hys εV
[177] <non> tum se fuisse *Shackleton Bailey* : tum se <non> fuisse *Hotman, Markland*
[178] cum *Hς* : si *P²GTεV* : *om. P¹*
[179] utar <verbis> *Maslowski* : <verbis> utar *Sydow* : utar ω : pietate utar *H* : utar pietate ς : utar
<lenitate> *Lambinus* : utar <oratione> *Peterson* : utar <aequitate> *Busche* : utar <facultate> *Klotz* :
<arte> utar *Wolf, Kayser* : <vi> utar *Mommsen* : ego <venia>, qua consuevi, utar *Luterbacher*

[8 18] Look, in view of so many testimonies, Romans, of such a resolution of the Senate, of such a great unanimity of Italy, of such support of all good men, of P. Lentulus arguing the case, of other magistrates agreeing, of Cn. Pompeius entreating, of all individuals favourably inclined, finally of the immortal gods approving my return by abundance, plentiful supply, and cheapness of grain {themselves}, I, restored to me, my family, and the Republic, will promise to you, Romans, as much as I can do: first, the piety that the most upright individuals are accustomed to display towards the gods, the same I will always display towards the Roman People, and your divine will shall be equally venerable and sacrosanct to me as that of the immortal gods in all my life; secondly, since the Republic itself has brought me back into the community, I will not fail the Republic under any circumstances. [19] If anyone believes that I have a changed inclination or weakened valour or a worn-out spirit, they err strongly. What violence and injustice and the frenzy of criminal men could remove from me, they have seized, taken away, and shattered; what cannot be taken away from a courageous man, that both lasts and will persist.

I saw a very courageous man, my townsman, C. Marius—since by some fated inevitability, as it were, we had to fight a war not only with those who had wished to destroy these matters, but also with fortune—, I saw him, when he was in extreme old age, yet not only not with weakened spirit because of the greatness of his misfortune, but with a strengthened and renewed one. [20] I heard him say that he had been wretched at the time when he lacked his country, which he had freed from siege, when he heard that his property was being appropriated and looted by enemies, when he saw his son, a young man, sharing the same misfortune, when, submerged in marshes, he preserved his body and life by the sympathetic gathering of the people of Minturnae, when, having travelled on a small ship to Africa, he had come to those to whom he himself had given kingdoms, being destitute and suppliant; but that, after he had recovered his standing, he would not let it happen that, when what he had lost had been restored to him, he would not have the excellence of mind that he had never lost. But there is this difference between me and him, that he took vengeance on his enemies by that very means by which he was most powerful, by arms, and I will use what I have been accustomed to, <words>, since for the former art there is a place in war and political discord, for the latter in peace otio. [21] quamquam ille animo irato nihil nisi de inimicis ulciscendis agebat; ego de ipsis inimicis[180] tantum quantum mihi res publica permittit[181] cogitabo.

[9] denique, Quirites, quoniam me quattuor omnino hominum genera violarunt—unum eorum qui odio rei publicae, quod eam ipsis invitis[182] conservaram, inimicissimi mihi fuerunt, alterum, qui per simulationem amicitiae nefarie me[183] prodiderunt, tertium, qui cum propter inertiam suam eadem adsequi non possent, inviderunt[184] laudi et dignitati meae, quartum, qui cum custodes rei publicae esse deb{u}erent[185], salutem meam, statum civitatis, dignitatem eius imperi quod erat penes ipsos vendiderunt—, sic ulciscar facinora <eor>um singula[186] quem ad modum a quibusque sum provocatus, malos civis rem publicam bene gerendo[187], perfidos amicos nihil credendo atque omnia cavendo, invidos virtuti et gloriae serviendo, mercatores provinciarum revocando domum atque ab iis[188] provinciarum ratione repetenda.

[22] quamquam mihi, Quirites[189], maiori curae est quem ad modum vobis, qui de me estis optime meriti, gratiam referam quam quem ad modum inimicorum iniurias crudelitatemque persequar. etenim ulciscendae iniuriae facilior ratio est quam benefici remunerandi, propterea quod superiorem esse contra improbos minus est negoti quam bonis exaequari. tum etiam ne tam necessarium quidem est male meritis quam optime meritis referre quod debeas. [23] odium vel precibus mitigari potest vel[190] temporibus rei publicae communique utilitate deponi vel difficultate ulciscendi teneri vel vetustate sedari; bene meritos ne[191] colas nec exorari fas est neque id rei publicae remittere[192] utcumque[193] necesse est; neque est excusatio difficultatis, neque aequum est tempore et die memoriam benefici definire. postremo qui in ulciscendo remissior fuit bono

---

[180] inimicis *PGT* : *om. ϵV* : amicis *Zielinski*

[181] permittit ω : permittet *Shackleton Bailey*

[182] invitis ς : convitis *P¹* : convictis ω

[183] me *H* : *om.* ω

[184] inviderunt *G²* : inviderent ω

[185] deb{u}erent *Ernesti* : debuerunt ω : debuerint *Heumann*

[186] facinora <eor>um singula *Halm* : facinorum singula *P* : facinora singula ω : facinora singulo<rum> *Halm (in app.)* : facinorum <genera> singula *Sydow*

[187] gerendo *T* : regendo ω

[188] iis ς : his *PGHT* : hys ϵV

[189] quirites *Gulielmius* : quin *P* : quam *GTϵV* : *om. H* : quidem *Lambinus*

[190] vel *H* : *om.* ω

[191] ne ς : *om. PGTϵV* : quin *H* : ut *Jeep*

[192] remittere *Garatoni* : repetere ω : rependere *Jeep*

[193] utcumque ς : utrū|cumque *P¹* : utrumque *P²GϵV* : † utrumcumque † *Maslowski* : utique *Lambinus* : verum neque *Jeep* : utcumque <se res habent> *e.g. Courtney* : <nisi> utique *Shackleton Bailey*

and tranquillity. [21] He, however, with an angry mind, was busy with nothing other than taking revenge on enemies; I will think about these very enemies as much as the Republic allows me to.

[9] Further, Romans, since altogether four types of people have hurt me—one of them consisting of those who out of hatred of the Republic, because I had preserved it against their will, were most inimical to me, the second those who, under the pretence of friendship, betrayed me wickedly, the third those who, since they could not achieve the same because of their own laziness, were envious of my renown and standing, the fourth those who, when they ought to have been guardians of the Republic, sold my well-being, the condition of the community, and the dignity of that supreme power that was under their control—, I will take revenge for the individual deeds of each of them in the same way in which I was challenged by each of them: on bad citizens by conducting public affairs well, on treacherous friends by not believing anything and guarding against everything, on the envious by being a servant to virtue and glory, on traders of provinces by calling them home and demanding an account of the provinces from them.

[22] And yet, Romans, it is of greater concern to me how I offer thanks to you, who have conferred such great services upon me, than how I seek requital for the injuries and cruelty of the enemies. For the procedure of avenging an injury is easier than repaying a favour, particularly because it is a smaller task to be superior in relation to rascals than to be on a par with good men. Moreover, it is not even so necessary to give back what you owe to those who have done a bad service than to those who have done a great service. [23] Hatred can be soothed by entreaties or dropped because of the situation of the Republic and the common good or repressed due to the difficulty of avenging or allayed by a long period of time; that you do not cherish in your mind those who have done good services it is neither right to be persuaded, nor is it necessary in any event to drop that for the sake of the Republic; neither is there the excuse of difficulty, nor is it appropriate to limit the memory of a favour by time and a date. Finally, he who was more relaxed in avenging certainly benefits from good rumour; but

rumore certe utitur[194]; at gravissime vituperatur qui in tantis beneficiis quanta vos in me contulistis remunerandis est tardior, neque solum ingratus, quod ipsum grave est, verum etiam impius appelletur necesse est. {atque in officio persolvendo dissimilis est ratio et pecunia debita[195], propterea quod pecuniam qui retinet non dissolvit, qui reddidit non habet; gratiam et qui rettulit habet, et qui habet dissolvit.}[196]

[**10** 24] quapropter memoriam vestri benefici colam benivolentia sempiterna, <nec eam>[197] cum anima exspirabo mea, sed etiam, cum me vita <defecerit>, monumenta[198] vestri in me benefici permanebunt. in referenda autem gratia hoc vobis repromitto semperque praestabo, mihi neque in consiliis de re publica capiendis diligentiam neque in periculis a re publica propulsandis animum neque in sententia simpliciter ferenda[199] fidem neque in hominum voluntatibus pro re publica laedendis libertatem nec in perferendo labore industriam nec in vestris commodis augendis grati[200] animi benivolentiam defuturam. [25] atque haec cura, Quirites, erit infixa animo meo sempiterna, ut cum vobis, qui apud me deorum immortalium vim et numen tenetis, tum posteris vestris cunctisque gentibus dignissimus ea civitate videar quae suam dignitatem non posse se tenere, nisi me reciperasset, cunctis suffragiis iudicavit.

[M. Tulli Ciceronis] Oratio pridie
quam in exilium iret

Sigla (De Marco 1991, 10)

    P = cod. Paris. Bibl. Nat. 7794, saec. IX²

      P¹ = librarius se ipse corrigens

---

[194] bono rumore certe utitur *Maslowski* : in eorum (meorum *εV*) aperte (apperte *P¹*) utitur (utetur *T*) *PGTεV* : in os (mox plerique *ς*) aperte laudatur *Hς* : non fere reprehenditur *Madvig* : in eo rumore certe utitur *Jeep* : secundo rumore aperte utitur *Wuilleumier* : in eo rum<or populi summis laudibus> aperte utitur *Sydow* : in eo suo iure aperte utitur *Mommsen* : in eo vix reprehenditur *Klotz (alii sim.)* : in ea re venia certe utitur *Koch* : iure suo aperte utitur *Klotz (in app.)* : in eo consilium aperte laudatur *Peterson* : laudatur *Fuhrmann* : is fere semper laudatur *Shackleton Bailey*

[195] pecunia debita *ω* : pecuniae debitae *ς*

[196] atque … dissolvit *om. Hς*

[197] <nec eam> *Klotz* : <nec ea> cum anima <exspirabit> mea, sed etiam *Madvig* : sempiterna <neque solum me vivo>, sed etiam *Halm* : nec tantum dum *Peterson*

[198] me vita *Madvig* : anima *Halm* : me ulla *P* : nulla *GεV* : mortuo *H* | <defecerit> *Madvig* : <defecerit mea> *Halm* | <multa> monumenta *Madvig, Halm* : <illa> monumenta *Peterson*

[199] ferenda *PG²εV* : feranda *G¹* : referenda *H* : e re p. ferenda *Jeep*

[200] grati *edd.* : gratam *ω*

he is most severely censured who in repaying such great favours as you have conferred upon me is somewhat slow, and it is necessary that he is not only called ungrateful, which is serious in itself, but also undutiful. {And regarding paying in full for an obligation the principle is different from that regarding money owed, particularly since he who retains the money has not repaid it, he who has returned it does not have it; as regards gratitude, both he who has returned it retains it and he who retains it has paid it.}

[**10** 24] Therefore, I will cherish the memory of your favour with everlasting goodwill, <and> I will <not> breathe <it> out with my life-giving spirit, but even, when life <has left> me, memorials of your favour conferred upon me will remain. And in returning thanks I promise this to you and will always fulfil it, that neither in taking thought for the Republic carefulness nor in warding off dangers from the Republic courage nor in putting forward my views in the Senate openly honesty nor in harming the wishes of individuals on behalf of the Republic outspokenness nor in enduring toil industry nor in enhancing your benefits the goodwill of a grateful mind will be lacking for me. [25] And this concern, Romans, will be fixed in my mind as everlasting, that I seem most worthy of this community to you who hold the sway and divinity of immortal gods in my judgement, and also to your descendants and all nations, of the community who decided by all votes that it could not maintain its dignity if it had not regained me.

[M. Tullius Cicero's] Oration on the day before he went into exile

P^2 = corrector saec. XIV

G = cod. Gemblacensis (Bruxell. 5345), saec. XI

   G^1 = librarius se ipse corrigens

E = cod. Erfurtensis (Berolin. 252), saec. XII

H = cod. Londin. Harl. 4927, saec. XII

   H^1 = corrector eiusdem aetatis

Ω = consensus omnium codicum

[1 1] si quando inimicorum impetum propulsare ac propellere cupistis, defendite nunc universi unum, qui, ne omnes ardore flammae occideretis, mei capitis periculo non dubitavi providere. nam quem virtutis gloria cum summa laude ad caelum extulit, eundem inimicorum invidia indignissime oppressum deprimit ad supplicium. si liberum conceptam dulcedinem animo inclusam continetis, nolite eo velle carere, qui carissimam vestram procreationem sibi esse duxit[201]. [2] est enim liberale officium serere beneficium, ut metere possis fructum; fidei conducit in loco debitum retribuere. illic enim animi voluntas propensa comprobatur, hic memoria conlaudatur. itaque, si omnibus grave iugum servitutis esse debet in libertate educatis, sit is vestris animis acceptissimus, qui a vestro corpore iugum acerbissimum reppulit servitutis. [3] et, si maiores vestri eos imperatores, qui militum virtute hostium fregerunt furorem, iucundissimo fructu libertatis reconciliato non solum statuis dignos putarunt, sed etiam aeterna triumphi laude decorarunt, tum vos eum consulem, qui non militum praesenti fortitudine, sed sua eximia animi virtute hostilem civium mentem senatus auctoritate vindicavit, existimate vobis retinendum esse in civitate. [2 4] si quae beneficia singulis civibus privatimque dantur, ea solent iis esse fructuosa, a quibus sunt profecta, iure[202] et merito possum ego vos ad defensionem meae salutis adhortari, quos conservavi universos. nam neque maius est defendere unum quam populum, neque verius ab singulis quam ab omnibus repetere offici praemium et fructum[203], propterea quod in unius periculo saepe contentio parva est, ut levis sit labor defensori sustinendus, in rei publicae insidiis, quo firmius est quod oppugnatur, eo[204] paratiores sunt inimici, ut iis nisi magna sollicitudine, industria, virtute non queat resisti. [5] et singulorum opes saepe sunt tenues et infirmae ad gratiam referendam, ut opitulari bene merentibus nequeant, si maxime cupiant; universorum auxilium eo plurimum prodest quo<d> firmioribus opibus est nixum. iure igitur, quoniam et maior impensa in patriam officii facta est, quam in privata fit[205] defensione, et plus a vobis praesidii quam a ceteris opis ad salutem potest adferri, vos optestor, quos mihi et debere et posse intelligo opitulari. [6] non convenit enim, cum ego ad proferendum[206] officium tam fuerim expeditus, vos ad gratiam referendam esse tardiores: ne[207], cuius amplitudinem et gloriam laude atque honoribus amplificare debeatis, eius incolumitatem et salutem deserendam existimetis.

---

[201] duxit P^2 : dixit Ω
[202] iure *edd.* : tute Ω
[203] praemium et fructum P : fructum et praemium *GEH*
[204] eo *GEH* : *om.* P, *edd.*
[205] fit P^2 : fuit Ω
[206] proferendum *De Marco* : promerendum Ω
[207] tardiores, ne *edd.* : tardiones ne Ω

[**1** 1] If you have ever wished to drive off and repel an attack of enemies, now, all of you, defend the single person who, under threat to my own life, have not hesitated to see to it that all of you were not killed by the intensity of the flare-up. For the same person whom the glory of virtue has extolled to the sky with greatest praise the ill-will of the enemies has crushed most unworthily and now reduces to punishment. If you have perceived the sweetness of children and stored it in your mind, do not wish to lack the person who regarded your offspring as of the greatest value to him. [2] For it is a noble task to sow a favour so that you can reap the fruit; it is proper to hand back duly what is owed to loyalty at the right moment. For there the well-disposed intention of the mind is approved; here the memory is praised. Therefore, if for all who have been educated in liberty the yoke of servitude must be grievous, he shall be most welcome to your minds who has thrust back the harshest yoke of servitude from your body. [3] And if your ancestors regarded those generals who crushed the fury of the enemy by the virtue of the soldiers, after the very pleasant and enjoyable possession of liberty had been restored, not only worthy of statues, but ordained them even with the eternal praise of a triumph, then be of the opinion that you must retain in the community that consul who punished, not by the ready courage of soldiers, but by his own outstanding virtue of mind, the hostile attitude of citizens on the authority of the Senate. [**2** 4] If those favours that are given to individual citizens privately tend to be fruitful for those from whom they have originated, I can encourage you with good reason and deservedly to the defence of my well-being, you, all of whom I have preserved. For neither is it greater to protect a single person than a people nor more just to demand back from single individuals than from all the reward and profit from a duty rendered, especially since in the dangerous situation of a single person the effort is often small, so that the trouble the protector has to bear is light, while in an ambush against the Republic, by as much as what is opposed is stronger, by so much the enemies are readier, so that they cannot be opposed unless by great painstakingness, diligent activity, and valour. [5] And the means of individuals are often small and weak for rendering thanks, so that they cannot be of service to those who deserve well, even if they desire it greatly; the support of all is of most use inasmuch as it is based on stronger means. Rightfully, then, since a greater outlay has been spent on a duty towards the country than happens in the defence of private people, and more protection can be contributed by you than help by others towards [my] well-being, I beseech you, of whom I know that you both ought to and are able to give help to me. [6] For it does not befit, since I have been so ready to display my duty, that you are rather slow at rendering gratitude: do not believe that the safety and well-being of that person whose eminence and glory you ought to extol by praise and honours should be abandoned.

[3] etenim errat si qui arbitratur M. Tullium idcirco in periculum capitis vocari quod deliquerit aliquid, quod patriam laeserit, quod improbe vixerit; non citatur reus audaciae, virtutis reus citatur; non accusatur quod rem publicam oppugnarit[208], sed quod homo novus perniciosum nobilium restinxerit furorem; non obest mihi nocens et turpis, sed honestissime lautissimeque[209] acta vita; non odio bonorum, sed invidia premor malorum. [7] intelligunt homines tot et tam praeclaris testimoniis monimentisque virtutis comparatis M. Tullio[210], dum sit incolumis, fore voluptati: idcirco vitam eripere cupiunt, uti cum spiritu sensum quoque adimant iucunditatis. nonne igitur indignum est eos praemiis meis invidere, qui virtute certare noluerunt, eos in contentionem venire honoris, qui officiis se superari animo aequissimo tulerunt? si dulcis est gloria, consequere virtutem; noli abicere labores, perdere[211] honorem: honorem dico? immo vero famam, fortunam, familiam, liberos, caput, corpus, ipsum denique sanguinem atque animam. cedo invitus de re publica, cedo oppressus de fortuna, de dignitate, discedo ab re publica victus audacia malorum. [8] liceat manere, si non illum M. Tullium custodem urbis, defensorem omnium, patrem patriae, at certe reliquias Tulli; liceat in conspectu civium, in hac urbe, quam ex parricidarum faucibus eripuit, remanere, tecta hominum[212], fana deorum, universam videre periculi <expertem>[213] civitatem; liceat ex hac flamma evolare, praesertim qui illud impium incendium perditorum hominum lacrimis potius meis quam vestro sanguine restingui malui. neque enim ego peto ut mihi detis vitam, sed datam repeto ut reddatis. si meministis quod dedi, non debetis {istis}[214] oblivisci retribuere quod debuistis.

[4 9] vos, vos optestor, di immortales, qui meae menti lumina praetulistis, cum consensum extinxi coniurationis arcemque urbis incendio[215] ac flamma liberavi[216] liberosque vestros a gremio et complexu matrum ad caedem et cruorem non sum passus abstrahi. non[217] igitur potest fieri a clientibus ut recipiar, cum, a

---

[208] vi oppugnarit *Orelli*

[209] lautissimeque *Ω, Müller* : laudatissimeque *edd., Orelli* : sanctissimeque *Gamberale*

[210] M. Tullio *edd.* : m. tullium *Ω*

[211] perdere *Orelli* : petere *Ω* : † petere *Baiter* : *fort.* proterere *aut* opterere *Müller (in app.)*

[212] hominum *Gamberale* : omnium *Ω*

[213] <expertem> *Halm* : * * *Baiter* : periculo liberatam suo *Orelli*

[214] *del. Orelli, Baiter* : istorum *H*

[215] incendio *P* : ab incendio *GEH*

[216] liberavi <...> *lac. coni. De Marco*

[217] non *Ω* : num *edd.*

[3] And indeed they are in error, if anyone believes that M. Tullius is brought into danger of his life for the reason that he has committed any offence, that he has harmed the country, that he has lived with a lack of morals; not as someone accused of audacity is he summoned: as someone accused of virtue is he summoned; he is not accused because he attacked the Republic, but because, as a 'new man', he suppressed the pernicious fury of noblemen; what is against me is not a guilty and disgraceful life, but a life lived most honestly and splendidly; not by the hatred of the good men, but by the envy of the bad men am I oppressed. [7] [These] people realize that, after so many and so great testimonies and memorials of virtue have been obtained, these will be a pleasure for M. Tullius, as long as he is safe. Therefore, they wish to snatch away his life, so that, along with the soul, they also take away the consciousness of pleasantness. Isn't it unworthy, then, that those who did not wish to contend in virtue are envious of my rewards, that those who bore very patiently that they were surpassed in offices come into contention for honour? If glory is sweet, seek after virtue; do not abandon toils, do not lose honour: honour, I say? In fact, good reputation, fortune, family, children, free status, the body, even blood and the soul themselves. Against my will I go away from the Republic; I, oppressed, go away from prosperity and from standing; I leave the Republic, overwhelmed by the audacity of bad men. [8] Let it be allowed to stay, if not for that M. Tullius, the guardian of the city, the protector of all, the father of the fatherland, but at least for the remains of Tullius; let it be allowed to stay in the sight of citizens, in this city, which he has snatched from the throats of parricides, to see the houses of people, the shrines of gods, the entire community <free> from danger; let it be allowed to escape from this flame, especially since I preferred that impious fire caused by bad men to be extinguished by my tears rather than your blood. For I do not ask that you give me life, but I ask back for the life that was given, that you give it back. If you remember what I gave, you ought not to forget {to those} to pay back what you owe.

[4 9] You, you I beseech, immortal gods, who have carried the lights before my mind, when I extinguished the collusion manifesting itself in the conspiracy and freed the citadel of the city from fire and flare-up and did not permit your children to be snatched away from the lap and embrace of mothers to death and bloodshed. Therefore, it cannot happen that I am received by clients while those

quibus debeam retineri, reicere instituant. socii quo fugient[218], cum aditus custodi[219] praeclusus sit? quo modo[220] spes salutis reliquis residebit, cum civibus
praeclusa sit expectatio incolumitatis? pax et concordia extraneis gignetur,
cum domesticis non insideat, sed publice providenti[221] eripiatur[222]? [10] nam quid
ego improborum facta renovem oratione, ut redintegratione[223] illius coniurationis animos vulnerem[224] vestros? auxilium ab alienis efflagitabitis, cum[225]
cives deseratis? sociorum invocem subsidium, cum a civibus interclusum sit
praesidium? quam colere gentem non institui? utrum custos accipiar an ut
proditor excludar? si ut conservator, vestra erit ignominia; si ut oppugnator,
praecisa[226] erunt omnia. itaque, quod putavi fore gaudium, id exstitit exitio.

[11] si, Quirites, eundem in ceterorum periculis haberemus animum, quem in
nostris difficultatibus, et pro innocentissimo quoque propugnare et nocentis-
simum quemque oppugnare nobis utilissimum esse arbitraremur, et, si cum
optimi cuiusque rebus adversis nostram salutem, cum deterrimorum autem
secundis nostra pericula putemus coniuncta, frequentes profecto talibus cona-
tis obviam ire nitamur, neque partim innocentia freti, partim nobilitate nixi,
partim potentia ac multitudine amicorum fulti, cum perfacile existimemus
adversariorum vim ac factionem a nobis repelli posse, subito ipsi simili periculo
circumventi, in nostro eventu aliorum reminiscentes casus, iure id nobis
accidere nequiquam queramur[227]. [5 12] quis est[228] enim, Quirites, qui, cum
inimicorum nostrorum vim ac violentiam perspiciat cumque nostrum periculosissimum casum recognoscat, qui non sibi ac suis diffidat fortunis? quo enim
se satis tutum arbitrabitur[229] praesidio? virtutis gloria? at ea nos[230] ipsa hoc
tempore oppugnat. multitudine amicorum? at parum est fortes esse amicos[231],
si in eorum potestate nostra sita salus[232] non est. paucitate inimicorum? at id
non in ipsius, sed in aliorum voluntate positum est. nam non satis est, ne cui
iniuriam facias, providere, si tamen sunt voluntarii inimici, qui tuis praemiis te
oppugnent.

---

[218] fugient *H* : fugiant *PGE*
[219] custodi *PGEH* : custodi patrie *P²* : custodi patriae *Orelli*
[220] quo modo *G* : comodorum *P* : vel commodorum quomodo *E* : quo *H*
[221] providenti *GEH* : providendi *P*
[222] eripiatur *GE* : reperiatur *PH*
[223] redintegratione *HP²* : redintegratio *PGE*
[224] vulnerem *HP²* : vulneret *PGE*
[225] cum <iam> *edd.* | cives <vestros> *Orelli*
[226] praecisa *P²* : praetiosa *PG* : praeciosa *E*
[227] queramur *Ω* : quereremur *Orelli* : queremur *Kayser*
[228] est *suppl. P²H¹*
[229] arbitrabitur *E* : arbitratur *P²GH* : ante annos *P*
[230] at ea nos *PGE* : at ea vos *P²* : at *om. H*
[231] at parum est fortes esse amicos *Baiter (in app.)* : apparuere fortasse amicos *P* : aperuerunt
non fortes esse se amicos *P²* : apparuere fortes se esse amicos *GE* : aspernere fortasse amicos *H* :
† apparuere fortasse amicos *Baiter* : aperuerunt non fortes esse se amicos *Orelli*
[232] salus *PGE* : sit vis *H*

by whom I ought to be retained start to reject me. Where will the allies flee while approach has been closed for the guardian? How will hope for well-being reside with the rest, while the expectation of safety is closed for citizens? Peace and concord will be created for foreigners, while it is not present for locals, but is snatched away from him who takes care in the public interest? [10] Now, why shall I revisit the deeds of rascals in my speech, so that by the renewal of that conspiracy I wound your minds? Will you demand help from foreigners, while you desert citizens? Shall I call for help from allies, while assistance has been cut off by citizens? Which nation have I not set about to pay respect to? Will I be accepted as a guardian or be excluded like a traitor? If like a preserver, it will be your ignominy; if like an opponent, everything will be cut off. Accordingly, what I thought would be joy, that has turned out to be a disaster.

[11] If, Romans, we had the same opinion in dangerous situations of others as in our difficulties, and we thought that it was most useful for us to fight in defence of every most innocent man and to fight against every most guilty man, and, if we should believe that our well-being is connected with the bad fortune of the very best men, our dangers, however, with the good fortune of the worst men, let us indeed make an effort in great numbers to oppose such attempts and let us not, partly trusting [our] innocence, partly relying on [our] nobility, partly propped up by the power and great number of friends, as we believe that the force and faction of opponents can be thrust back very easily by us, be surrounded suddenly ourselves by a similar danger and, remembering the fortunes of others in our circumstances, complain fruitlessly that this is happening to us justly. [5 12] For who is there, Romans, who, when they notice the force and violence of our enemies and when they recognize our very dangerous situation, do not have any confidence in themselves and their fate? For by what protection will they believe themselves sufficiently safe? By glory of virtue? But this itself opposes us at this time. By the number of friends? But it is not enough that friends are courageous if our well-being does not rest in their power. By the small number of enemies? But this rests not on the will of oneself, but on that of others. For it is not sufficient to make sure that you do not do any injustice to anybody if there are still enemies of their own accord who attack you because of your rewards.

[13] atque adeo cum haec omnia omnibus sunt gravia et acerba, tum vero nobis misera atque intoleranda, quorum et officia in rem publicam recentissima et incommoda ob rem publicam frequentissima in familia versantur. nunc, si eadem condicio disceptationis proponetur, aequi auditores adhibebuntur, aures non obtunsae criminatione, sed vacuae praebebuntur, qui sunt assecuti summum gradum honoris non despoliabuntur honore, qui sperant facilius et proclivius ad laudem nobilitatis pervenient. quam ob rem nolo me duce supplicii vos ad fraudem deduci, ut ego ad pristinum statum recidam casus. nunc igitur, si lingua est concertandum, innocentiae virtute fretus supero, si facta compensanda sunt, conferamus aequitatem, si violentiae impetu opprimimur, decedam pro omnibus unus tribunicio furori, quoniam laborem pro cunctis perferre consuevi. [6 14] si igitur aliquo tempore iis hominibus consuluistis, quorum animus religione[233] pietatis defunctus est[234], debetis mihi quoque prospicere, qui numen[235] deorum consecratum sartum ac tectum ab omni periculo[236] conservavi et vos ut tutam ac tranquillam fortunam traheretis mea perfeci vigilantia. nam me, quem paulo ante fortuna erexerat ad gloriam, <cui>[237] virtus contulit[238] laudem, populus tribuit honorem, eundem tribuni furor exagitatus depellit[239] ad calamitatem. quoniam animadvertistis illam conspirationem conflatam ita esse restinctam ut nulla scintilla compareat incendii, vos quoque tribuniciam sedate temeritatem—qui nunc se mihi inimicum[240] ostendit, se prius esse vestrum[241] professus est inimicum—; ne rei crudelitas, experta in me, in vos convalescat et calamitas, remorata longius, serpat ac progrediatur, praecavete. [15] nunc vel solus delectus[242] ad calamitatem vel primus ad tale evocatus periculum, omnium animos iure debeo commovere. omnia sunt immutata: manus religantur ad demonstrandam iniuriam; lingua inciditur ad deplorandam calamitatem; animus praecluditur ad exponendam rei indignitatem[243]. humilitatem generis obiciunt nobis, qui novam rationem suscitant, veteres[244] maiorum obterunt[245] laudes. sed quid ego plura de illorum aut in me maledictis aut in vos scelerate loquar factis? quorum cognita improbitas, me tacente, coarguitur turpitudine[246] vitae, ut de his non sit necesse inimicos praedicare, de quorum scelere ne amici quidem aut ipsi possint negare. [7 16] vos ego appello, quorum de me maxima

---

[233] religione P^2 : religioni Ω
[234] est *suppl.* P^2 | est religionis pietate defunctus *Orelli*
[235] numen *PH* : numini P^2GE
[236] periculo *PGH* : piaculo *E*
[237] *suppl. Baiter*
[238] contulit *PGE* : retulit P^2 : extulit ad *H*
[239] depellit *H* : depulit *PGE*
[240] inimicum *PGE* : iniquum *H*
[241] se prius esse vestrum *PGE* : sed vestrum prius esse *H*
[242] delectus *edd.* : defectus Ω
[243] indignitatem *PEH* : indignationem *G*
[244] veteres *PH* : *om. GE*
[245] obterunt P^1 : obterant Ω
[246] turpitudine *PGE* : turpitudoque P^2H

[13] And, in fact, while all this is grievous and harsh for all, it is indeed particularly miserable and intolerable for us, whose very recent duties for the Republic and very frequent disadvantages because of the Republic affect our family. Now, if the same condition for a dispute will be proposed, fair listeners will be adduced and ears not dimmed by the charge, but open will be provided, then those who have reached the highest stage of public office will not be despoiled of the honourable position, those who are hopeful will more easily and more effortlessly reach the reputation of distinction. For that reason, I do not want you to be drawn, under my leadership, to a deceitful punishment, so that I lapse back into the former state of my misfortune. Now then, if one must contend with the tongue, I am superior, relying on the virtue of innocence; if deeds are to be balanced, we might have recourse to parity; if we are oppressed by the onslaught of violence, I will give way to tribunician madness, one person for all, since I have become used to enduring hardship on behalf of all. [**6** 14] If, then, at some point you took thought for those men whose mind has carried out a scrupulous regard for dutiful respect, you ought to look after me too who have preserved the hallowed divinity of the gods in good condition and safe from every danger and have achieved by my vigilance that you spend the life destined to you in safety and quiet. For, me, whom a little earlier fortune had raised to glory, <upon whom> virtue has conferred renown, the People bestowed honour, me, the same person, the aroused fury of a Tribune thrusts into calamity. Since you have noticed that this stirred-up conspiracy was extinguished in such a way that no spark of a fire appeared, you too should restrain the temerity of the Tribune—who now shows himself as my enemy and earlier professed himself to be your enemy—; take precautions, so that the cruelty of the situation, having been experienced against me, does not strengthen against you and the calamity, having lingered for a rather long time, creeps on and progresses. [15] Now, be it that I am the only person selected for calamity, be it that I am the first person called forward to such a danger, I justly ought to move the minds of all. Everything has changed: hands to demonstrate injury are bound; speech to deplore calamity is cut off; the will to set forth the indignity of the situation is stifled. They reproach us with humility of descent, they who call forth a novel method and treat the old-time praiseworthy deeds of the ancestors with the utmost contempt. But what shall I say more about either the abusive words of those men against me or their criminal deeds against you? Their well-known outrageous behaviour is made manifest, even with me being silent, by the disgracefulness of their life, so that it is not necessary for enemies to shout out about these people of whose wicked disposition not even their friends or they themselves could make a denial. [**7** 16] I call upon you, whose power over me is

est potestas; apud vos loquor de mea calamitate, quos habui semper innocentiae et virtutis meae testes. igitur ex civitate bene meritus de re publica civis
exturbatur, innocens expellitur, consularis homo, non minimis facultatibus
usus quondam amicorum[247], nunc partim ab invidis, partim ab inimicis circumventus indigne[248]. huic si opem non tuleritis in periculo capitis, vos, credo,
retinebitis[249] vestram libertatem, qui neque tanta[250] valetis auctoritate neque
tantorum officiorum inpensam fecistis[251] in patriam! mihi credite, hoc in uno
incommodum confirmatum multorum infirmabit incolumitatem et, si initio
non erit refutatum, impune ad omnium perniciem convalescet. proinde, aut in
meo periculo salutem integram praestate communem aut in vestris hoc idem
expectate incommodum fortunis.

[17] nemo tam perdita auctoritate, tam facinerosa inventus est vita, qui, cum de
scelere fateretur, non tamen sententiis prius iudicum convinceretur quam supplicio addiceretur. ego, repente vi tribunicia correptus, non modo loquendi
libere in iudicio, sed ne consistendi quidem in civitate habeo potestatem. eicior
non solum sine teste, sine iudice, sine crimine[252], sine accusatore, sed[253] sine
etiam scelere. [18] hostibus, in bello, qui dissident voluntate, dimicant armis,
vitam cotidie oppugnant, in ipsa acie cum proeliantur, licet loqui, licet disputare: mihi in pace, civi, qui perditorum hominum fregi furorem, pro fortunis
meis apud vos loqui non licebit? servi, qui ad supplicium verberibus caesi tra-
huntur, apud eos saepe disputant, quos necare voluerunt: ego, consularis, apud
eos non loquar quos conservavi? tacebo, si necesse est, tacebo, inquam, animo
aequo, quoniam virtus mea, me tacente, agit meam causam. [8 19] itaque, ut ego
in contione[254] mea nihil ponam de meis rebus gestis, tamen in animis et[255]
memoria vestra[256] largiter relinquam; isti modo videant qua ratione hanc meam
mutam fugam ferre possint. etenim si a me, ut isti existimant, Lentuli mortui
sordes, si Catilinae notissimus furor, si amentia Cethegi, si luxuries ac stupra
Cassi poenas repetunt, profecto istis hora nulla, eiecto Tullio[257], vacua a[258]
periculo aut expectatione periculi relinquetur. ita in dies non meis insidiis,
quae nullae a me parantur, sed suorum conscientia scelerum cruciati mihi
absenti et populo Romano dabunt poenas.

---

[247] amicorum <multorum praesidio munitus> *Orelli*
[248] indigne *PGE* : eget *add. P²* : eget igne *H* : <eget> indigne *Orelli*
[249] <non> retinebitis *Gamberale*
[250] tanta *P²GEH* : tantum *P*
[251] fecistis *Baiter* : e istis *P* : egistis *P²GEH*
[252] <sed> sine crimine *Baiter* : sine crimine, <sed> sine accusatore *Orelli*
[253] sed *H* : *om. PGE*
[254] contione *PGE* : contentione *H*
[255] et *GEH* : *om. P*
[256] memoria *PGEH* : memoriam *P²* | vestra *PH* : vestris *GE*
[257] <M.> Tullio *Orelli*
[258] vacua a *Ω* : *add.* deest a *P²*

very great; I talk about my calamity to you, whom I have always had as witnesses of my innocence and virtue. Well then, a citizen who has done good services for the Republic is thrust out of the community, an innocent person is expelled, a man who is an ex-consul, having availed himself of what is not very slight support of friends in the past, is now prosecuted unworthily, partly by jealous people, partly by enemies. If you will not have offered help to him in a situation of danger for life, you, I believe, will retain your liberty, you who neither are powerful with such great authority nor have made the effort of such great beneficial acts for the country! Believe me, this misfortune in the case of a single person, when confirmed, will weaken the safety of many and, if it will not be suppressed at the beginning, will gain strength for the detriment of all without punishment. Thus, either keep the common well-being unimpaired in this dangerous situation affecting me or expect this same misfortune in your destinies.

[17] Nobody has been found of such a depraved worthiness, of such a wicked life, who, even if he admits a crime, still, is not first condemned by the votes of judges before he is doomed to punishment. I, suddenly caught by tribunician force, not only do not have the opportunity of speaking freely in a trial, but not even of coming forward in the community. I am thrown out, not only without a witness, without a judge, without a charge, without an accuser, but without even a crime. [18] In war it is possible for enemies who disagree in their inclination, decide with arms, and attack life daily, when they are fighting in the very battle line, to speak, it is possible to argue; for me, in peace, as a citizen who have crushed the madness of wicked individuals, on behalf of my fate, it shall not be possible to speak before you? Slaves who, flogged by rods, are being dragged to execution often argue before those whom they wanted to kill; I, an ex-consul, shall not speak before those whom I kept unharmed? I will be silent, if it is necessary; I will be silent, I say, with a calm mind, since my virtue pleads my case while I am silent. [8 19] Accordingly, while I do not state anything concerning my deeds in my speech before the People, I will still leave them in your minds and memory plentifully; those men shall only see in what way they can bear this silent flight of mine. If, indeed, as those men believe, the baseness of the dead Lentulus, if the very well-known madness of Catilina, if the madness of Cethegus, if the indulgence and sexual misbehaviour of Cassius demand satisfaction from me, undoubtedly, after Tullius has been thrust out, no hour will be free from danger or expectation of danger for them. So, they, tortured daily, not by an ambush of mine, which is not at all prepared by me, but by their awareness of their own crimes, will pay penalties to me in my absence and to the Roman People.

[20] quas ob res ego amentiae cupiditatique paucorum omnium salutis causa decedam, neque in eum[259] locum[260] <rem>[261] deducam[262] aut[263] progredi patiar ut opera mea manus inter vos conseratis caedesque civium inter se fiat, multoque potius ipse patria liberisque meis carebo quam propter unum me vos de fortunis vestris reique publicae dimicetis. sic enim ab initio fui animatus, ut non magis mea causa putarem me esse natum quam rei publicae procreatum. [21] sed illud queror, quod non iam ad unius perniciem, sed ad universorum struitur calamitatem[264], conqueri, commiserari, dicere, expurgare, suspicionem demovere, crimen diluere non licere, ore oppresso cervices esse praebendas; quae tamen omnia non tam sunt calamitosa quod mihi sunt subeunda, quam perniciosa quod in rem publicam sunt introducta. quam ob rem statutum est atque decretum in his temporibus civitatis omnia perpeti quae volet furor libidinosus. [9] vim volunt afferre: praesto sum; eicere volunt: exeo; indicta causa volunt abire[265]: causam non dico. aliud quippiam conantur: agant; nihil duri, nihil acerbi[266] mihi erit quod rem publicam tutabitur; non enim victus illis cedo[267], sed incolumibus vobis me condono. [22] neque enim mors miseranda est, quae ob rem publicam capitur, neque exilium[268] turpe est, quod virtute suscipitur, cum praesertim non nullam hae poenae habeant in se consolationem. nam vitam si eripiunt, non adiment gloriam <im>mortalem[269]; si exilio multabunt, corpus non animum a re publica removebunt. nam, ubicumque ero, hoc cogitabo, haec semper futura mea[270], meque vobis ereptum, non a vobis repudiatum existimabo[271].

[23] illud ab vobis universis[272] peto postuloque, si, dum in civitate manere licitum est, nemini iniuste periculum creavi, nemini innocenti fui calamitati, si omnibus auxilio paesidioque esse consuevi, plurimosque in hac civitate sum

---

[259] in eum *PH* : in eo *P²* : eo *GE*

[260] locum *P¹* : *om. Ω*

[261] <rem> *Halm* : <eo> *Orelli* : * * *Baiter*

[262] deducam *PH* : deducar *P¹P²GE*

[263] aut *PH* : ut *GE*

[264] calamitatem *P²H* : honestatem *PGE*

[265] abire *P* : adire *H* : audire *P²GEH¹*

[266] duri…acerbi *Ω* : durum…acerbum *Müller*

[267] cedo *PH* : concedo *GE*

[268] exilium *edd.* : exitium *Ω*

[269] <im>mortalem *edd.* : mortalem *P* (*add.* deest mortalem *P²*) : mortale *GEH*

[270] futura *G¹* : funera *G* : cura mea erit *H, Orelli* : futura mea <mens> *Gamberale*

[271] *post* existimabo *add.* insidiae nullae…dabunt poenas [*cf. Exil. 19*] *P* (*add.* deest tota hec sententia *P²*) *GE*

[272] vobis universis *edd.* : vobis *GE* : universis *PH*

[20] For these reasons I will give way to the madness and greed of a few for the sake of everyone's well-being, and I will neither bring <things> to that point nor allow them to advance so that through my activity you fight among yourselves and that slaughter of citizens occurs among themselves; and much rather I will do without the country and my children than that because of me alone you fight about your fortunes and that of the Republic. For thus I have been minded from the beginning that I did not believe that I was born more for my sake than begotten for that of the Republic. [21] But I complain about this, which is devised no longer for the destruction of a single individual, but for the calamity of all, that it is not permitted to lament, to commiserate, to speak, to justify, to remove a suspicion, to dissolve a charge, that, with the mouth shut, the neck must be offered; yet all this is not so calamitous, because I have to undergo it, as pernicious, because it has been introduced into the Republic. For that reason, it has been decided and decreed in these conditions of the community to endure everything that capricious frenzy will wish. [9] They want to use force: I am ready; they want to throw [me] out: I leave; they want [me] to go away with the case not pleaded: I do not plead my case. They try whatever else: let them do it; nothing hard, nothing harsh will there be for me, as it will protect the Republic; for I am not yielding to them as someone defeated, but I sacrifice myself to you while you are unharmed. [22] For neither is death that is taken because of the Republic miserable, nor is exile that is taken up with virtue disgraceful, especially since these penalties have some consolation in them. For if they snatch away life, they will not take away <ever>lasting glory; if they punish by exile, they will remove the body, not the mind from the Republic. For, wherever I will be, I will think this, that this will be my future, and I will believe that I have been snatched from you, not repudiated by you.

[23] That I ask and demand from all of you that, if, while it was permitted to remain in the community, I have not created danger for anyone unjustly, have not been a disaster for anyone innocent, if I was accustomed to be of help and

tutatus, uti vos liberos meos in vestram fidem[273] recipiatis eosque defendatis neve inimicos meos longius in familiam nostram progredi patiamini, utique, sive hinc abiero sive hic ero oppressus, ea maneat opinio et existimatio, quae virtute parta, non quae infelicitate inlata est.

[**10** 24] nunc ego te, Iuppiter Optime Maxime, cuius nutu ac dicione sola terrarum gubernantur, teque, particeps conubii, socia regni, Regina Iuno, teque, Tritonia, armipotens Gorgophona[274] Pallas Minerva, ceterique di deaeque immortales, qui <in>[275] excellenti tumulo civitatis sedem Capitoli in saxo incolitis constitutam, ut non solum cunctam[276] intueri[277], sed etiam tueri possitis civitatem; a quorum ego quondam altariis[278] impiam civium manum removi, a quorum templis meo periculo funestam flammam[279] reppuli, ne inlustrissimum orbis terrarum monumentum cum principe omnium terrarum occideret civitate; teque, Iuppiter Stator, quem vere huius imperii statorem maiores nostri nominaverunt, cuius in[280] templo hostilem impetum Catilinae reppuli a muris, cuius templum a Romulo, victis Sabinis, in Palati radice cum[281] Victoriae[282] est conlocatum, oro atque opsecro: ferte opem pariter rei publicae cunctaeque civitati meisque fortunis, resistite tribunicio furori, favete innocentiae, subvenite solitudini, miseremini senectutis, nolite eum supplicem a vobis absterrere et excludere, qui in suo magistratu funestam facem a vestris reppulit templis. [25] si C. Mario auxilio fuistis, quod in clivo[283] Capitolino improborum civium fecerat caedem, si P. Scipioni, quod Hannibalis furibundam mentem a vestris reppulit templis, si denique Cn. Pompeio, quod terra marique hostes reddidit pacatos, sic nunc in meis calamitatibus aliquam ferte opem divinam; ut saepe multorum in periculis fecistis, sic nunc in meis miseriis divinum aliquod auxilium et numen ostendite.

[**11** 26] deinde vos, quorum potestas proxime ad deorum immortalium numen accedit, oro atque opsecro, quibus singillatim saepe supplex ad pedes iacui, ut eum, quem singuli stratum atque abiectum sublevastis, nunc universi conservatum velitis: si neminem umquam vestrum laesi, si nemini innocenti obfui,

[273]　fidem *GE* : sedem *PH*
[274]　gorgophona *PH* : gorgona *P²GE*
[275]　*suppl. Baiter (in app.)*
[276]　cunctam *PGEH* : cuncta *PG¹*
[277]　intueri *P²* : intui *PGH* : tui *E*
[278]　altariis *PGEH* : altaribus *P²*
[279]　flammam *H* : facem *suppl. P²*
[280]　in *PGEH* : a *P²*
[281]　cum *P²* : tum *PGE*
[282]　Victoriae *GE* : Victoria *PH*
[283]　in clivo *PG* : in clito *E* : divo *H*

support to all and have protected very many in this community, you receive my children into your tutelage and defend them and do not let my enemies proceed in a farther-reaching way against our family and that, whether I will have gone away from here or whether I will have been oppressed here, such an opinion and assessment remains that has been produced by virtue, not such a one that has been brought on by misfortune.

[**10** 24] Now you, Iuppiter Optimus Maximus, by whose nod and power the lands of the world are governed, and you, sharer of the marriage, partner in ruling the realm, Queen Iuno, and you, Tritonia, weapon-bearing Gorgon-slayer Pallas Minerva, and the other immortal gods and goddesses, who, <on> the lofty hill of the city, inhabit the dwelling set upon the rock of the Capitol, so that you are able not only to watch the entire community, but also to protect it; from whose altars I once removed the impious hand of citizens, from whose temples, with danger to myself, I thrust back the deadly torch, so that the most illustrious monument in the world would not fall down with the foremost community of the entire world, and you, Iuppiter Stator, whom our ancestors rightly named the stayer of this empire, in whose temple I thrust back the hostile approach of Catilina from the city walls, whose temple was built by Romulus after the victory over the Sabines at the foot of the Palatine with that of Victoria, I plead and beseech you: bring help equally to the Republic and the whole community and to my destiny, offer resistance to tribunician madness, favour innocence, bring relief to loneliness, have pity on old age, do not wish him, as a suppliant, to be driven off from you and shut out, who, in his magistracy, thrust back the deadly firebrand from your temples. [25] If you helped C. Marius, because he had made a bloodbath of rascal citizens on the Capitoline Hill, if P. Scipio, since he thrust back the frenzied mind of Hannibal from your temples, if eventually Cn. Pompeius, since he rendered the enemy peaceful on land and on sea, thus now bring some divine help in my calamity; as you have often done in the dangers of many men, so now show some divine help and divinity in my misery.

[**11** 26] Then you, whose power comes very close to the divinity of the immortal gods, I plead and beseech you, at whose feet I have often lain suppliant individually, that all of you now wish him, whom you have individually lifted up when he was prostrate and humble, to be preserved; if I have never hurt any of you, if I have never been an obstacle to anyone innocent, but even, on the contrary, have not hesitated to bring help whenever anyone desired my assistance, if,

sed etiam e contrario, ut quisque meum auxilium desideravit, opem ferre non dubitavi, si denique, quaecumque administravi, ex vestra auctoritate et patrum conscriptorum voluntate feci, si malui inimicorum cupiditati quam rei publicae et legitimae auctoritati poenas sufferre, uti existimetis ex illo[284] crudelissimo inimicorum impetu ereptum in antiquum statum dignitatis restitui convenire. [27] sed quoniam neque mihi libere loquendi neque vobis clementer iudicandi[285] neque omnino iudicandi paucorum furore et audacia facta est potestas, sed oppressa est res publica armis, metu debilitata servili, uti liberum spiritum ducendi nullam habeat potestatem, cedam inermus armatis, innocens nocentibus, privatus furibundo magistratui. neque enim Q. Metellus quicquam de sua virtute detraxit, quod cessit L. Saturnino furenti, neque C. Cotta, quod Q. Vario tribuno plebis, inferiore genere orto, cedendum putavit, neque C. Marius, qui quantas res gesserit, vestra vobis libertas indicio esse poterit, neque M. Tullius suum animum a vestra abalienavit potestate, cum praecipuum[286] vobis obsidem sui animi vestram reliquerit libertatem. [28] quam ob rem testor deos deasque immortales vestrasque maxime mentes me non vitae turpitudine, non prae[287] magnitudine scelerum, non propter reliquae aetatis infamiam poenas iure et lege persolvere, sed propter virtutis invidiam, propter iucundissimam ingenii laudem, propter magnitudinem rerum gestarum crudelissime civitate privari. quodsi idem accidit Q. Caepioni, si Mancino, si Rutilio, mihi hoc accidisse non magnopere erit mirandum, cum praesertim non generis antiquitate, sed virtutis ornamentis summam laudem sim consecutus.

[**12** 29] nunc vos, equites Romani, optestor, quorum virtute nomen Romanum victoriam cum laude possidet coniunctam, quorum factis gloriantur cives, laetantur socii, gemunt hostes, ut, si erga vos omni tempore optime fui animatus, si mea pericula neglexi, dum timorem a patria propulsarem, si aeque liberis vestris prospexi ac vos parentes[288] consuestis[289], ut nunc me velitis, vestris opibus defensum[290], incolumem in hac civitate retinere—quae civitas, cum a scelerata coniuratione esset incensa, meo luctu[291] ac labore restincta est—nec patiamini me a meis liberis abstractum, a coniuge abreptum, ab aris focisque

---

284 ex illo *PH* : exilio *G* : auxilio *E*
285 iudicandi *Ω* : audiendi *P²* : vindicandi *Halm*
286 praecipuum *P* : pretium *GEH*
287 prae *P* : pro *GEH*
288 parentes *Gamberale* : parentibus *Ω*
289 consuestis *PH* : consuletis *G* : consulitis *G¹E*
290 defensum *P²GH* : *om. PE*
291 luctu *Ω* : ductu *edd.*

finally, whatever I have administered, I have done with your authority and the agreement of the senators, if I have preferred to pay penalties to the greed of enemies rather than to the Republic and legitimate authority, that you believe that it is fitting that I am snatched away from this most cruel attack of the enemies and restored to the former position of distinction. [27] But since the opportunity has not been given either to speak freely to me or to judge mildly or to judge at all to you, because of the madness and audacity of a few, but the Republic has been oppressed by arms, weakened by fear of slavery, so that it does not have the chance of drawing in the breath of a free individual, I will yield, an unarmed person to armed men, an innocent person to guilty men, a private man to a mad magistrate. For neither did Q. Metellus take anything away from his virtue, because he yielded to the mad L. Saturninus, nor C. Cotta, because he believed that he should yield to Q. Varius, a Tribune of the People, born from a rather humble family, nor C. Marius, who has done great deeds, of which your liberty will be able to be a sign for you, nor did M. Tullius turn away his mind from your power when he left your liberty to you as foremost pledge of his frame of mind. [28] For that reason I call the immortal gods and goddesses as witnesses and your minds in particular that I do not pay penalties justly and legally as a result of a disgraceful life, not for the magnitude of crimes, not because of the infamy of the rest of my life, but because of envy of my virtue, because of the most pleasant reputation of my talent, because of the magnitude of my deeds I am deprived of the community in the most cruel fashion. If the same happened to Q. Caepio, if to Mancinus, if to Rutilius, it will not be such a big surprise that this happened to me, especially since I have achieved greatest renown not through the age of my family, but through the ornaments of virtue.

[**12** 29] Now, I implore you, Roman knights, by whose virtue the Roman name possesses victory connected with renown, by whose deeds the citizens pride themselves, the allies are happy, the enemies groan, that, if I was of the best mind towards you at all times, if I neglected the dangers to myself while I thrust off fear from the country, if I looked after your children in the same way as you are used to as parents, that you now wish to retain me, protected by your resources, unharmed in this community—a community that, when it had been inflamed by a criminal conspiracy, was quenched by my grief and labour—and do not let me be separated from my children, snatched away from my wife, driven out from hearth and home as an innocent man, to spend life in exile, to

innocentem proiectum, vitam degere in exilio, miserrimi[292] mortalis casum
subire. [30] proicitur Tullius in exilium, itaque nimirum[293] innocens ab inimico,
religiosus a scelerato, benivolus huic civitati ab hoste. o misera vitae ratio, quae
tam diu resides in voluptate, quam diu fortunae poscit libido! egone inimicus
huic civitati? quam ob rem? quia inimicos necavi. egone hostis? quid ita? quia
hostes interfeci. heu condicionem huius temporis! antea gloria ac laude dignis-
simi ducebantur, qui haec perfecerunt, nunc scelerati ac parricidae esse dicun-
tur, qui haec administrarunt.

sint sane scelerati, superet istorum victoria, si modo victoria appellanda
est, in qua civitatis inest luctus; habeant hanc palmam ex innocentis cruore.
tantum illud[294] a vobis, equites Romani, peto et rogo, ut, quem saepenumero
vestra laude cohonestastis, eundem in dubiis vitae periculis vestra virtute
conservetis.

---

[292] miserrimi *P²* : miseremini *Ω*
[293] itaque : nimirum *Baiter* : in exilium † itaque nimirum *Müller* : in exilium. at a quo? nimirum
Orelli [*cf. Cic. Att. 9.9.3* : itaque nimirum hoc illud est ...]
[294] illud *PEH* : *om. G*

endure the situation of the most wretched mortal. [30] Tullius is driven out into exile, thus, surely, an innocent person by a foe, a scrupulous one by a criminal, a well-meaning supporter of this community by an enemy. Oh, you distressing pattern of life, which remain in pleasure for as long as the will of fortune demands! I hostile to this community? For what reason? Because I have killed hostile men. I an enemy? Why so? Because I have killed enemies. Oh, the condition of this time! Previously those who accomplished these things were regarded as very worthy of glory and praise; now those who have carried out these things are said to be criminals and parricides.

Let them be criminals, let the victory of these men be superior, if only that has to be called victory in which there is grief for the community; let them have this victory palm from the blood of an innocent man. That much only I ask and request from you, Roman knights, that you preserve that same person, whom you have often honoured by your praise, in precarious dangers to his life by your virtue.

Commentary

Testimonia

Introduction

In three later works of different literary genres (T 1–3) Cicero mentions that he delivered a speech of thanks to the Senate after his return to Rome; he notes that it included thanks to Cn. Plancius (T 2), quaestor of the governor of Macedonia in 58 BCE (Cic. *RS* 35 n.), and P. Cornelius Lentulus Spinther (T 3), one of the consuls of 57 BCE (Cic. *RS* 5 n.).

The Scholia Bobiensia on Cicero's speeches remark that Cicero delivered two speeches, one in the Senate and one to the People (T 4–6). In the most detailed comment the scholiast suggests that these two orations were determined not just by Cicero's desire to express his thanks to everybody, but also by his intention to re-establish his standing in the community (T 4). The later Greek historian Cassius Dio records that Cicero delivered speeches of thanks to the Senate and to the People when the consuls gave him the opportunity to do so (T 7).

Notes

(1) This remark in a letter from Cicero to Atticus, written shortly afterwards, provides the date of Cicero's speech of thanks to the Senate (5 Sept. 57 BCE), namely the day after Cicero's return to Rome, and confirms that a version of the speech (*RS*) was delivered (see Introduction, section 2; *RS*, Introduction).

(2) This passage in Cicero's *Pro Plancio* provides a comment on the content of the speech of thanks to the Senate and on its mode of composition and delivery. In the context of the later trial (54 BCE) Cicero notes that the earlier speech is available as a piece of evidence, since it was delivered on the basis of a written text (see Introduction, section 3.3).

The remark indicates that, unusually, the speech of thanks to the Senate was written up before delivery, rather than afterwards (for the standard practice, see, e.g., Cic. *Off.* 2.3; *Rosc. Am.* 3; *Att.* 1.13.5; 15.1a.2); typically, only key sections, openings, or formal elements would be prepared in writing (e.g. Cic. *Phil.* 1.3; Quint. *Inst.* 10.7.30). Here it is also implied that the text composed in advance is still available at the time of Plancius' trial and not substantially different from the delivered speech. The reason for creating a written draft, according to Cicero, was the importance of the occasion and the need to render adequate thanks to everyone who deserved it. Accordingly, Cicero states that he expressed gratitude generally (cf. Cic. *Sest.* 108) and thanked by name a few people who stood out in their support for him, including the defendant Plancius (Cic. *RS* 35).

The unusual scenario has given rise to scholarly discussion. Bücher/Walter (2006; also Bücher 2006, 243 n. 70) comment that Cicero would not have gone into the Senate with a manuscript on such an occasion; they argue that the transmitted text *dicta de scripto* is without parallels in Cicero and should be changed to *edita de scripta* or, more likely, *diligenter descripta* (Bücher 2006, 243 n. 70 considers *dicta descripta*): in this scenario Cicero could have written the speech in advance, but he would not claim to have delivered it from a written text. Thus, depending on the choice of readings, the text of the speech would have been edited on the basis of a written draft or of minutes taken during delivery; it would be implied that this version is close to what was said on the day and could thus be adduced as evidence. In response, Vössing (2008) collects parallels for *de scripto dicere* (Cic. *Sest.* 129; *Phil.* 10.5; *Fam.* 10.13.1; *Att.* 4.3.3) and points out that it was not entirely unusual to read out epideictic speeches (that one might occasionally bring a written script is envisaged at Cic. *De or.* 1.152). Therefore, in the absence of further evidence about what happened in 57 BCE, there is no sufficient reason to change the text and posit another scenario that is not attested elsewhere and transfers the motif of the importance of the occasion from the composition to the recording and transmission of the speech.

The first speech to be delivered by Cicero in the Senate in this context is 'the first after his return to Rome'.

(3) In this letter to P. Cornelius Lentulus Spinther, one of the consuls in 57 BCE (Cic. *RS* 5 n.), written a few years later (54 BCE), Cicero says that the Senate could hear Cicero's attitude during Lentulus' consulship, i.e. as outlined in a speech given by Cicero in the Senate in 57 BCE. Since this attitude consists of a debt of gratitude to Lentulus and the Republic for restoring Cicero and of his resulting willingness to show himself to be a dutiful citizen, this must refer to Cicero's speech of thanks delivered in the Senate, in which he comments on Lentulus' support (Cic. *RS* 8–9). In the speeches given after his return Cicero claims a number of times that he and the Republic had been away together and returned together (see Introduction, section 3.4), but they do not include the strong version of this motif, namely that the Republic assisted Lentulus in recalling Cicero; this might be a variant developed here for the conversation with Lentulus.

(4) In the introduction to the commentary on the speech of thanks delivered to the People (*RQ*) the scholiast notes that its substance is similar to that of the speech given in the Senate: indeed, while the content is not exactly the same, many points and motifs occur in both speeches (see Introduction, section 3.3). The reason for this procedure, according to the scholiast, is that Cicero wished to demonstrate that he was recalled unanimously by all parts of the population.

The scholiast does not feel that the main purpose of these speeches is to express genuine thanks; he rather sees these speeches as part of a publicity campaign to re-establish Cicero's status.

In passing, the scholiast mentions that Cicero delivered the speech to the People at a *contio* (also in T 5), the usual venue for such speeches. In 57 BCE Cicero was not in a position to call a *contio*; thus, magistrates in office would have had to do this for him (see T 7; Introduction, section 3.3).

The scholiast goes on to note that Cicero fulfils the requirements of the *genus demonstrativum* (e.g. Lausberg 1998, §§ 239–54) by voicing praise of his supporters and blame for his enemies (e.g. Quint. *Inst.* 3.7.1). In fact, criticism of Cicero's enemies is less extensive and less strong in the speech to the People (Cic. *RQ* 13–14) than in the speech given in the Senate (esp. Cic. *RS* 10–18). Generally, epideictic speeches do not often include examples of both praise and blame.

(5) In the introduction to Cicero's speech *Pro Plancio* the scholiast comments that, after his return to Rome, Cicero delivered a pair of orations in the Senate and at a *contio* in which he expressed thanks (see T 4): thus, both speeches are described as having been delivered and having similar content. In the context of *Pro Plancio*, the scholiast highlights that Cicero expressed thanks to Plancius. Read literally, the statement means that Cicero thanked Plancius in both speeches; yet he does so only in the speech given in the Senate (Cic. *RS* 35). The scholiast may regard the pair of speeches as one unit and just indicate that it includes an expression of thanks to Plancius.

(6) Commenting on the passage in *Pro Plancio* (Cic. *Planc.* 74) in which Cicero mentions the speech of thanks to the Senate (T 2), the scholiast explains that it was sufficient for Cicero to refer to the speech by which he expressed thanks, be it to the Senate, be it to the People (without the need for further evidence or argument). A speech of thanks in which gratitude for Plancius is expressed identifies Cicero's oration given in the Senate. Therefore, it is odd that the text provides the alternative *vel senatui vel populo* with reference to a single speech, while in T 5 the scholiast identifies two speeches and distinguishes between them (*alteram . . . alteram*). Maybe the two options are given for the sake of completeness (although the phrasing is grammatically problematic), or what was originally an explanary gloss has entered the text.

(7) The only testimonium not deriving from the writings of Cicero or Cicero's commentators is part of a description of the historical events of the period by the Greek historian and Roman senator Cassius Dio. He notes that, after his return to Rome, Cicero delivered speeches of thanks to the Senate and the People when given the opportunity by the consuls. This remark provides the detail that the consuls arranged for Cicero to speak to the Senate and to the People. It is uncertain whether the statement is based on specific evidence or inferred from common practice or from what is known about the attitude of that year's consuls towards Cicero. Since a reference to this circumstantial point is added,

Cassius Dio might have had access to sources including this information; then this remark would confirm that both speeches were delivered and that Cicero's appearances before both bodies were arranged by his supporters (see Introduction, section 3.3).

M. Tulli Ciceronis post reditum in senatu oratio

Introduction

Cicero's speech of thanks to the Senate (Cic. *RS*) was given on 5 September 57 BCE, the day after his arrival back in Rome (Cic. *Att.* 4.1.5 [T 1]; see Introduction, section 2). In the later speech *Pro Plancio* (54 BCE) Cicero says that, because of the importance of the matter, this speech was delivered on the basis of a written text (Cic. *Planc.* 74 [T 2]; see n.). The argument in *Pro Plancio* (according to the transmitted text) implies that the version of the Senate speech available at the time of the delivery of *Pro Plancio* was at least substantially the same as the one written out in advance. The preparation of this speech would presumably have started prior to Cicero's arrival back in Rome (see Introduction, section 3.3).

In this speech Cicero expresses thanks to a variety of groups of people who supported him during his absence from Rome and singles out a few individuals, including the consuls of 57 BCE and Cn. Plancius. In *Pro Plancio* he states that it would not have been appropriate to omit anybody deserving thanks, while it was impossible to refer to everyone; therefore, he decided to focus on thanking by name only the most important figures (Cic. *Planc.* 74 [T 2]). His friend T. Pomponius Atticus, for instance, who was not present on that occasion, is not mentioned, while Cicero privately acknowledges that he owes a great deal to him (Cic. *Att.* 4.1.1–2). Moreover, Cicero does not refer to any consuls designate; therefore, it is possible that the elections of the consuls for the coming year had been postponed until after Cicero's restoration (Brunt 1981, 230–1). Since Cicero contrasts the activities on his behalf with the measures directed against him by P. Clodius Pulcher and his followers and with the lack of support from the consuls of 58 BCE (Cic. *RS* 10–18), the speech includes both praise of his supporters and criticism of his opponents.

While this oration is presented as a speech of thanks and Cicero as being in debt to those who were loyal to him and worked for his recall, he uses the occasion also to reaffirm his role in the Republic and to re-establish himself as an influential politician (as the scholiast observes: T 4). Accordingly, Cicero emphasizes that he left Rome and did not attempt to defend himself by force in order to avoid bloodshed, in line with the attitude shown during his consulship, and thus saved the Republic a second time (e.g. Cic. *RS* 33–4). He claims that his own fate and that of the Republic are closely linked and that he and the

Republic have been away and returned together (e.g. Cic. *RS* 34; 36). Consequently, he interprets his recall as a confirmation of his previous policy. On this basis Cicero can proclaim that he will resume his unceasing work for the welfare of the Republic (e.g. Cic. *RS* 36; 39). This theme recurs in other speeches delivered by Cicero soon after his return (Haury 1955, 143–4; see Introduction, section 3.4).

Outline of structure and contents

1. Introduction (1–2): Cicero's expression of thanks
2. Main section (3–35): Review of Cicero's departure and recall
   2.1. Cicero's recall (3–7)
      2.1.1. Unsuccessful senatorial activity in 58 BCE (3–4)
      2.1.2. Renewed senatorial attempts in 57 BCE (5)
      2.1.3. Political chaos caused by 'enemies' in 57 BCE (6–7)
   2.2. Activities of Cicero's supporters and opponents (8–31)
      2.2.1. Supporters: consuls of 57 BCE (8–9)
      2.2.2. Opponents: consuls of 58 BCE (10–18)
      2.2.3. Supporters: magistrates and senators (18–31)
   2.3. Cicero's departure (32–5)
3. Conclusion (36–9): Cicero's promise to the Republic

Because of its particular nature (see Introduction, section 3.2), this speech, like the corresponding speech to the People, does not follow any of the standard structures of orations outlined in rhetorical handbooks. Still, various sections in a logical sequence can be distinguished, and the oration is in line with rhetorical advice to the extent that an emphatic introduction and conclusion frame the body, providing a detailed presentation (on the oration's structure, see Weiske 1807, 248–9 [assuming lacunae and interpolations]; Mack 1937, 19–20; Wuilleumier 1952, 23–4, 43; Guillen 1967, 20; Thompson 1978, 121; Fuhrmann 1988, 155; Shackleton Bailey 1991, 5; Nicholson 1992, 114–21; Condom 1995, 27–8; MacKendrick 1995, 124–7; Boll 2019, 68–71).

The speech starts with an effusive expression of thanks because the Senate has returned everything Cicero ever received all at once; therefore, it is claimed, essentially no form of oratory is fully adequate to render appropriate thanks (Cic. *RS* 1–2). In the main section Cicero goes on to look at the reasons for his departure and recall and at the people involved (Cic. *RS* 3–35). This flashback is organized in reverse order, so that the recall is discussed first (Cic. *RS* 3–7) and the departure at the end of the section (Cic. *RS* 32–5). Such an arrangement places the decision to leave for the benefit of the Republic immediately before the promise about what he will do after his return in the conclusion (Cic. *RS* 36–9), so that the speech can end with a sustained expression of Cicero's commitment to the Republic. In the middle of the main section Cicero talks about his supporters and opponents (Cic. *RS* 8–31): supporters are discussed at the beginning and the end, first the consuls of 57 BCE and then other magistrates and senators (Cic. *RS* 8–9; 18–31), with the opponents, the consuls of 58 BCE, in the middle (Cic. *RS* 10–18). Thus, again, the impression of continuous support for Cicero is overwhelming; still, he does not forgo the opportunity to voice criticism, which sets off the supportive activities and also addresses fundamental issues of the role of magistrates.

There are no obvious structural remarks, which would presumably be inappropriate in a speech of this kind, which is not meant to have a foregrounded logical argument; the transitions are clear through fronted names or themes at the moves to new aspects.

Notes

1. Introduction (1–2): Cicero's expression of thanks

The introduction of this speech (Cic. *RS* 1–2) consists of an emphatic and elaborate expression of thanks. Cicero does not indicate the occasion or the circumstances (obvious to contemporaries) or the oration's aim and structure: the start with an expression of thanks, indicating the theme, is more effective.

In this initial expression of thanks Cicero does not name any individuals or define precisely what the Senate did beyond recalling him and enabling him to return to his accustomed position in Rome; instead, he emphasizes the greatness of the Senate's services as they have given back to him at once everything he had previously obtained from different sources (such as parents, gods, People, and Senate) at different stages of his life (e.g. Bortone 1938, 14). Cicero thus starts with an extended *captatio benevolentiae* (cf. Quint. *Inst.* 3.7.24).

By claiming that the Senate's services are so extensive that it is almost impossible to render thanks adequately, Cicero expresses his gratitude elaborately and forestalls any possible criticism (*prolepsis*) in case he should be seen as not being sufficiently grateful or not expressing his gratitude appropriately (Loutsch 1994, 494). When Cicero effectively claims that no oratorical genre exists to match the services rendered, this is a ploy to enhance their greatness and the corresponding inadequacy of his thanks (in mock modesty, as the speech then renders thanks effusively). On another level, such a claim might allude to the particular rhetorical character of this speech. The conceit that the greatness of the subject matter and/or the inadequacy of the speaker prevents the deserved and required praise of the subject is found in Greek encomiastic speeches and is outlined as a tactic in rhetorical manuals (Men. Rhet. Περὶ ἐπιδεικτικῶν [III 368.1–9.17 *RhG*]).

In view of the rules for an *exordium* (in a forensic speech) given in Cicero's *De inventione* (Cic. *Inv. rhet.* 1.22), this *exordium* includes elements of the start *ab nostra persona*, as Cicero talks of his restoration out of a desperate situation, *ab auditorum persona*, as he praises the audience's efforts for him, and *ab rebus*, as he talks positively about his case (Loutsch [1994, 494] defines the opening as an example of an *exordium ab rebus ipsis* in an epideictic speech). Such a start is a way of making the audience *benivolus*, *attentus*, and *docilis* (Cic. *Inv. rhet.* 1.20); this is supported by Cicero stressing the greatness of the cause and its universal relevance (Cic. *Inv. rhet.* 1.23; similar points at *Rhet. Her.* 1.6–8).

The structure and style of the opening are designed for maximum effect; feelings are expressed, but in a calculated, not a spontaneous way (Mack 1937, 20–2, 99–106). Such a beginning provides the framework for singling out a selection of specific acts provoking gratitude. While Cicero starts by thanking the senators profusely for their *beneficium* and thus puts himself in the position of debtor towards them, he makes it clear that he deserves such a *beneficium*, thus recalls his merits in Rome, and starts working towards his restoration as a senior statesman (Raccanelli 2012, 24–9). Still, the speech to the People (Cic. *RQ*) opens in a more obviously self-confident way, highlighting Cicero's successful sacrifice on behalf of the community (e.g. Boll 2019, 95).

1 si…putetis: the speech begins with an indirect announcement of its theme, namely the expression of gratitude to the Senate. By using the initial sentence to indicate that he might not be able to render adequate thanks in view of the enormous favours received, Cicero asserts the Senate's great contribution at the start, forestalls any possible objections and indicates (in mock modesty) that he is approaching the difficult task all the same (Cic. *RS* 30). – Opening a speech with a *si*-clause is a frequent structure in Cicero's speeches. Such a clause often comments on the potential reactions of the audience or an unnamed generic person (Kaster 2006, 107–8, on Cic. *Sest.* 1). There are also parallels for such a *si*-clause referring to Cicero's abilities and attitude, followed by a causal clause (with *nam* or *enim*) explaining the conditions or reservations adumbrated in the first sentence (Cic. *Rab. perd.* 1; *Arch.* 1; *Mil.* 1).

patres conscripti: the usual address to the audience in Senate speeches (Dickey 2002, 284–5; on its possible origin, see Liv. 2.1.11). Its use in the first sentence establishes a rapport with the audience from the beginning. Such addresses are a feature of polite Latin speech and can be used for emphasis, while they are not needed for identifying the interlocutor (Dickey 2002, 250). There are seven addresss to *patres conscripti* in this speech (Cic. *RS* 1; 3; 30 [2x]; 33; 36; 39), clustered at its beginning and its end.

pro vestris immortalibus…meritis: before Cicero expresses gratitude explicitly, the extraordinary nature of the Senate's interventions on his behalf (and thus the amount of gratitude required) is highlighted by elevating their actions and hyperbolically assigning 'divine' status to them, which would have to be matched by a 'divine' oration (Cic. *RS* 30; on the presentation of mortal deeds as immortal, see Cole 2013, 69). – The expression frames (in hyperbaton) the enumeration of people who have benefited from these services. – A similar comment occurs in the speech to the People, where the services are attributed to that audience and are described less hyperbolically (Cic. *RQ* 5).

in me fratremque meum liberosque nostros: primarily, the Senate's support affected Cicero as he was called back to Rome; on a secondary level, his brother and the children benefited from Cicero's return (Cic. *RS* 27; *RQ* 2–3; 5; *Att.* 3.15.4). That Cicero includes his relatives among the beneficiaries of the Senate's services makes these appear greater, since they affect a larger number of people, and it presents Cicero's recall as an issue involving the entire family rather than just an individual. – Cicero's wife is not mentioned, presumably because the focus is on blood relatives and the continuation of the family. Treggiari (2007, 73) notes that 'the emphasis on male members of the family is in accordance with etiquette, for it was not proper to name women in a public speech'; yet there are examples of his wife being mentioned elsewhere in Cicero's speeches (e.g. Cic. *Cat.* 4.3; *Dom.* 96; *Sest.* 145). – The enumeration is construed as a list of three items, with the second and the third each added by -*que*; this structure occurs again later in this speech (Cic. *RS* 27), while it is generally rare (K.-St. II 29–30). These three items are listed with a slightly different construction in the speech before the People (Cic. *RQ* 5: *in me fratremque meum et liberos nostros*), which might suggest that *me* and *fratrem meum* are presented as closely connected (K.-St. II 30–1).

fratremque meum: Cicero's younger brother Quintus Tullius Cicero (*c.* 102–43 BCE; *RE* Tullius 31; aedile in 65, praetor in 62 [*MRR* II 173], provincial governor in Asia in 61–58 BCE [MRR II 181, 185, 191, 198]; see Nicholson 1992, 75–6; Goldmann 2012, 209–17; Raccanelli 2012, 84–90; Boll 2019, 37–8). Quintus returned to Rome from his province in April 58 BCE; afterwards, Cicero claims, he worked tirelessly for his brother's return (Cic. *RS* 37 n.). – The aspects that Cicero's separation from his brother during his absence from Rome caused grief and that they rejoiced at being reunited are mentioned frequently in the speeches given after Cicero's return (e.g. Cic. *RS* 27; 37; *RQ* 3; 8; *Dom.* 59; 96; *Sest.* 49; 145; cf. *Att.* 3.10.2; 3.15.4).

liberosque nostros: *nostros* could be a reference just to Cicero (as he frequently speaks of himself in the first person plural; K.-St. I 87–8) or encompass Cicero and his brother. As the expression follows on from *fratremque meum* (similarly in comparable enumerations), the difference in the number of the personal pronoun makes a reference to the children of Cicero and of his brother likely. – Cicero's children are Tullia and Marcus (see Nicholson 1992, 76–7; Treggiari 2007, 73): Tullia (79–45 BCE; *RE* Tullius 60) first married C. Calpurnius Piso Frugi (from *c.* 63 BCE), who died in 57 BCE (Cic. *RS* 15 n.), then (56–51 BCE) Furius Crassipes (*RE* Furius 54), and finally (50–46 BCE) P. Cornelius Dolabella (cos. suff. 44 BCE; *RE* Cornelius 141); the last two marriages ended in divorce.

Tullia died in childbirth in 45 BCE, which was a cause of great grief for Cicero. Marcus (b. 65 BCE [Cic. *Att.* 1.2.1]; *RE* Tullius 30), still a young child at the time of this speech (Cic. *RQ* 8), survived the proscriptions and became suffect consul in 30 BCE. Cicero's brother Quintus had a son also called Quintus (*RE* Tullius 32). – The speeches given after Cicero's return and letters written during his absence contain frequent references to his sadness at the separation from his children and the joy at being reunited upon his return (e.g. Cic. *RQ* 2; 8; *Sest.* 49; 145; *Dom.* 59; 96; cf. *Att.* 3.10.2; 3.15.4; 3.19.2).

cumulate: *cumulate gratias agere* is not attested elsewhere in classical Latin, but *cumulatissime gratiam referre* is (Cic. *Fam.* 5.11.1). The adverb stresses how hard it is to express thanks adequately to match the services received (*OLD* s.v. *cumulate* 'Abundantly, copiously, liberally'). It is common in Cicero and otherwise rare (almost all of the attested occurences in classical Latin [just over twenty] occur in Cicero's works).

quaeso obtestorque ne...tribuendum putetis: a similar phrase is found in a panegyrical expression of gratitude by Claudius Mamertinus in the fourth century CE (Mamertinus, *Pan. Lat.* 3(11).31.3: *nunc, si tibi, imperator, parum ampla nec respondere meritis tuis oratione usus videbor, quaeso obtestorque te <ne> meae id naturae potius quam magnitudini beneficiorum tuorum putes esse tribuendum.*; see Cic. *RQ* 24 n.). The wording in Mamertinus points to the reading *id tribuendum* in Cicero's text as in some manuscripts (*id* picking up the *si*-clause) rather than *attribuendum* as in others (Maslowski 1981, in app.; Boll 2019, 96; *contra* Luterbacher 1912, 346). – Phrases such as *quaeso obtestorque* are typically linked with an accusative object identifying the people appealed to (e.g. Cic. *Dom.* 147). Occasionally, they appear without an object when it can be supplied from the context (e.g. Liv. 30.12.16; Plin. *Pan.* 94.5).

meae naturae potius quam magnitudini vestrorum beneficiorum: indicates again the greatness of the Senate's favours (cf. *pro vestris immortalibus... meritis*). From the start Cicero takes care to combat the impression that he might not be sufficiently grateful: it is not his lack of will or ability (*OLD* s.v. *natura* 12 'Abilities, natural endowments'), but the extent of the favours that might make it impossible to express thanks appropriately.

beneficiorum: a frequent term in this pair of speeches to designate the favour consisting in Cicero's recall (e.g. Cic. *RS* 3; 24; 26; 28; 30; *RQ* 2; 5; 6; 23; 24).

quae tanta..., quae tanta..., quod tam...orationis: the reason (*enim*) why it is almost impossible to thank the Senate adequately is that an appropriately grand and divine type of oratory matching the Senate's divine services does not exist (expressed by a rhetorical question amounting to a negative statement). In the speech before the People the same concept is expressed in a less abstract, more personalized, and more straightforward format (Cic. *RQ* 5; see also Boll 2019, 97); a similar rhetorical tricolon occurs in a later speech (Cic. *Marc.* 4: *nullius tantum flumen est ingeni, nullius dicendi aut scribendi tanta vis, tanta* *copia, quae non dicam exornare, sed enarrare, C. Caesar, res tuas gestas possit.*). – The attribution of 'divine' qualities to human beings and entities in Cicero's post-exile speeches is an element of hyperbolic rhetoric. According to MacKendrick (1995, 143) *divinus* has eroded to mean little more than 'extraordinary'. While *divinus* came to be applied to a variety of items, it is often qualified (e.g. by *paene* or *quidam* or by a combination with another adjective) when connected with non-divine items; thus, the original meaning still seems to be recognized.

tanta...ubertas ingeni: *OLD* lists this passage as an example of *ubertas* meaning 'Fertility of language or style' (*OLD* s.v. *ubertas* 3). While the entire sequence refers to oratory, this term is concerned with the rich supply of talent enabling a speaker to deploy oratory in its full range; therefore, a general transferred meaning is more likely (*OLD* s.v. *ubertas* 1b '(transf.) abundance'; for the phrase, see Quint. *Inst.* 10.1.109).

enim: is usually the second word in a sentence in classical Latin, but can take a later position if, for instance, the first two words are closely connected or *enim* is preceded by a pronoun (K.-St. II 133–4).

tanta dicendi copia: indicates a developed ability to employ all the resources of oratory (*OLD* s.v. *copia* 6; Cic. *Leg. Man.* 42; *De or.* 1.170; 1.215; *Brut.* 138; *Inv. Rhet.* 1.1; *Rhet. Her.* 1.1).

tam divinum atque incredibile genus orationis: suggests comprehensively, as the final item in the series, that the standard oratorical formats are insufficient to honour the Senate's great favours appropriately (cf. Cic. *RQ* 5) and a 'divine' type of style would be needed to match the Senate's 'divine' deeds. – For *genus orationis/dicendi* with reference to style, see, e.g., Cic. *Orat.* 42; 180.

in nos: could take up *in me fratremque meum liberosque nostros* in shortened form or refer to Cicero only. Both might be implied; with the following sentence concerned with Cicero (while other family members are mentioned), a focus on him is predominant.

universa: highlights the all-encompassing nature of the Senate's services to Cicero (as again at the end of the paragraph).

promerita: less frequent that the simplex *merita*, perhaps chosen for the sake of variation and euphony. This participle used as a noun occurs again in the speech before the People (Cic. *RQ* 8) and perhaps in *De inventione* (Cic. *Inv. rhet.* 2.83: *postea levius demonstrando se poenitum quam sit illius promeritum* [*promeritum Kayser* : *promeritus vel pro meritis codd.*]).

non dicam complecti orando, sed percensere numerando: two contrasting expressions with parallel constructions: the two infinitives, each complemented by a gerund, highlight the difficulty of providing adequate oratory: even to list all the favours would be challenging, not to speak of presenting them in a rhetorically developed format (*OLD* s.v. *complector* 8; *percenseo* 4; *numero*[1] 5). – The alternative reading *ornando* (for *orando*) might seem to express the idea of embellishment better, but a verb making explicit the act of speaking is preferable to qualify *complecti*, and *orare* provides a sufficient contrast to *enu-merare*. While most editors print *numerando* of the main tradition, Boll (2019, 97) argues for *enumerando*, as found in two late manuscripts, because of its appearance in the comparable statement in the speech before the People (Cic. *RQ* 5) and the respective frequency of the two verbs with the appropriate sense in Cicero. This reading, however, has the sentence end in a heroic clausula, which should be avoided. – A phrase with similar wording is again (see note above) found in a later panegyrical speech (*Pan. Lat.* 8(5).1.3: *quaevis* [Mynors : *quamvis* codd.] *enim prima tunc in renascentem rem publicam patris ac patrui tui merita, licet dicendo aequare non possem, possem tamen vel censere numer-ando.*): there, a rhetorically embellished presentation is defined as impossible, while listing the achievements is deemed manageable. – The phrase *non dicam* also appears later in the speech to emphasize the choice of a particular expres-sion rather than another (Cic. *RS* 8; 16).

qui . . . reddidistis: a list of items restored to Cicero (and vice versa) by his recall (cf. Cic. *Fam.* 3.10.10 [April 50 BCE]; *Att.* 3.15.4 [17 Aug. 58 BCE]), illustrat-ing the great favours received from the senators (cf. Cic. *RS* 3): the sequence (punctuated by anaphoric *qui*) starts with two pairs of reciprocal phrases refer-ring to family members; this is followed by a group of three items indicating the standing in the community and then by two extended phrases denoting the Republic and the country described with expressions of praise; it is concluded by a final item (marked by *denique*) referring to Cicero, demonstrating that he regained his personality (cf. Cic. *RS* 8). – The relative clause standing on its own depends on an implied *vos* (extrapolated from *vestris . . . meritis* and *vestra . . . promerita* in the preceding sentence; see K.-St. I 30–1). – The speech to the People (Cic. *RQ* 2–5) has a similar list, albeit having a more emotive tone and providing more detail.

fratrem optatissimum: *optatus* means 'desired', but is also attested '(*as a term of endearment*)' (*OLD* s.v. *optatus*; see, e.g., Cic. *Q Fr.* 2.6.2: *vale, mi optime et optatissime frater, et advola*); thus, it covers the nuances of both 'most beloved' and 'most missed'. For the reverse expression of the brothers' relationship, where the focus is on affection, the unambiguous term *amantissimo* is used.

amantissimo: for similar public expressions of Cicero's affection for his brother (including this term), see Cic. *Cat.* 4.3; *Dom.* 96; *Sest.* 76.

parentes: Shackleton Bailey (1987, 271) suggests reading *parentem*, arguing that the phrase only applies to Cicero and his son and not also to Cicero's brother and his son. Even though the comment indeed refers to Cicero and his children, a change of the unambiguously transmitted text is not required: while Cicero first refers to himself in the first person singular in relation to his brother, he switches to the plural when he talks about the relationship to his children. Therefore, in this phrase, where the plural (*nostris, nobis*) denotes a single per-son (K.-St. I 87–8; Pinkster 2015, 1119–20), *parentes* is an appropriate comple-ment, especially as terms for relationships often occur in the plural even with reference to one person (K.-St. I 87). The change to the plural creates a balanced expression in juxtaposition with the plural *liberi*.

dignitatem: Cicero frequently states that his *dignitas*, 'standing' (*OLD* s.v. *dignitas* 4), was re-established by his recall to Rome (e.g. Cic. *RS* 5; 26; 27; 31; *Dom.* 9; *Sest.* 52; 129).

ordinem: denotes the status in the community (*OLD* s.v. *ordo* 5), perhaps with emphasis on the position as a senator, as *ordo* may refer particularly to the Senate (*OLD* s.v. *ordo* 4).

fortunas: after Cicero's departure, his property (*OLD* s.v. *fortuna* 12) was seized and his house destroyed; after a struggle during which he delivered the speech *De domo sua*, his possessions were returned (Cic. *RS* 18; *RQ* 3 nn.; Introduction, section 2). At this stage Cicero might not yet have realized that the restoration of his property would not be straightforward (see Introduction, section 3.3).

amplissimam: indicates a position of great distinction and power for the Roman Republic.

patriam: refers to Rome and Italy or, as the abstract version, the Republic (Cic. *RQ* 4) rather than Cicero's birthplace Arpinum (on the distinction between these two *patriae*, see Cic. *Leg.* 2.5). – In the speeches delivered after Cicero's return, *patria* is used to enhance the emotional dimenson (here besides *res publica*) in connection with the joy at returning or to identify the entity that feels for Cicero's predicament and has been supported previously (on *patria* in these speeches, see Peck 2016, 120–3).

qua nihil potest esse iucundius: a relative clause introduced by a comparative ablative (K.-St. II 467–8). *iucundius* expresses the notion of pleasure without a connotation of affection (*OLD* s.v. *iucundus* 1). – In *De officiis* Cicero describes the close and important relationship with *res publica* and *patria*, for which sacrifices might have to be made; accordingly, those aiming to destroy *patria* are regarded as detestable individuals (Cic. *Off.* 1.57). If a comparable view forms the background here, such a statement is not merely an expression of gratitude and joy, but could also be an implicit political declaration of Cicero's values in contrast to those of his opponents.

denique nosmet ipsos nobis: the climax of the sequence, namely that Cicero's personality has been restored by the Senate's efforts, implying that he was not able to be his true self while away. A similar thought appears in a slightly different argumentative context in the speech before the People (Cic. *RQ* 8).

2 quod si parentes... reciperarimus: Johnson (1971, 49–50) notes the length of this sentence, regarding it as inelegant; in his view it is structured as a paratactic sequence, while containing unnecessarily elaborate words. This long sentence, however, can be regarded as carefully structured: it opens with four *si*-clauses referring to parents, gods, the Roman People, and the Senate respectively; these are followed by another emphatic expression of thanks, explained by the fact that the Senate has returned simultaneously all the favours previously received individually (listing the four groups again); finally, the list of bodies Cicero is indebted to is repeated (in the order Senate, People parents, gods), only to be topped by the activities of the Senate (referred to another time), which returned everything to Cicero in one go. While Cicero expresses appreciation to all important groups, the role of the Senate is thereby highlighted.

quod si parentes: may seem to start a generic statement; yet the continuation makes it clear that this sentence still refers to Cicero's situation. – Cicero's father M. Tullius Cicero was a member of the equestrian order but did not reach higher political offices in Rome (*RE* Tullius 28); Cicero's mother was a Helvia (*RE* Helvius 19; on the parents, see Plut. *Cic.* 1.1–2). Cicero inherited (Plut. *Cic.* 8.3) the estate of his family at Arpinum (Cic. *Leg.* 2.5; *Leg. agr.* 3.8) on his father's death in 68 BCE (Cic. *Att.* 1.6.2 [end of November 68 BCE]) or 64 BCE (Ascon. ad Cic. *Tog. cand.*, arg., p. 82 C.).

carissimos habere debemus: to be supplied also to the following items listed anaphorically in incomplete *si*-clauses (with the form *carissimos* adjusted as necessary).

vita, patrimonium, libertas, civitas: the series of items received from one's parents starts with two obvious, concrete ones; these are then complemented by two characteristics of an individual's position in the community: if the parents are freeborn Roman citizens, freedom and citizenship along with the concomitant rights are passed on to their children. These gifts from parents are not explicitly defined as *beneficia*, but in the context amount to such (Kranz 1965, 15).

et haec tenuimus et ceteris rebus aucti sumus: divine support enables people like Cicero to retain what they have received (*haec*) from their parents (the perfect tense expressing a situation created by the completed action; K.-St. I 125; Pinkster 2015, 446–7) and to enhance their standing beyond that. The vague *ceteris rebus* removes the need to specify what further gifts and favours have been received and to what extent they are owed to the gods.

cuius honoribus: a paraphrase for election to office, highlighting the Roman People's esteem expressed thereby (*OLD* s.v. *honor*[1] 2); *cuius* is a *gen. subiectivus* referring to *populum Romanum*. In this context *honor* does not denote 'office' (*OLD* s.v. *honor*[1] 5; thus Boll 2019, 100–1), as carrying out an office is only the result of the process described. – In a senatorial context the word *honor* is preferred, while in speeches before the People their involvement is highlighted by the term *beneficium* (Cic. *RQ* 4 n.; Kranz 1964, 61).

in amplissimo consilio: i.e. the Senate (*OLD* s.v. *consilium* 3b; *amplus* 8; for the phrase, see Cic. *Phil.* 3.34). Cicero became a member of the Senate when he completed his quaestorship in 75 BCE. – In this period election to office typically led to membership of the Senate (Kunkel/Wittmann 1995, 440–3), so that this status could be described as an (indirect) honour or favour received from the People (e.g. Cic. *Verr.* 2.4.25; Kranz 1964, 51–2).

et…atque: while the sequence of *et…atque* in a series of three equally weighted items is rare and often doubtful (K.-St. II 37), different copulative conjunctions are used in case of different kinds of relationships between the items. Here the last phrase includes a deictic element (*hac*), is a further strengthening, and has a broader application, which may explain the choice of *atque* with its connotations of emphasis (K.-St. II 16).

in altissimo gradu dignitatis: i.e. the consulship, which Cicero held in 63 BCE (*OLD* s.v. *gradus* 8; *dignitas* 3; for the phrase, see Cic. *Dom.* 98; *Sest.* 20; *Mur.* 30; *Phil.* 1.14).

in hac omnium terrarum arce: the term can denote metaphorically (on the metaphor, see Fantham 1972, 124) Rome's dominant position in the world by virtue of its Senate (*OLD* s.v. *arx* 3; cf. Cic. *Cat.* 4.11; *Sull.* 33) and concretely the 'Roman citadel on the Capitoline Hill' symbolizing this position (*OLD* s.v. *arx* 1; cf. Cic. *Leg. agr.* 1.18; *Verr.* 2.5.184; on the two potential meanings, see also Boll 2019, 101). The addition of the demonstrative *hac* indicates a deictic dimension, with Cicero pointing towards the Capitol while he speaks; the phrase then has a concrete meaning, but still implies a position as the centre of power. One could even venture the conclusion that this meeting of the Senate was held on the Capitol, like the meeting two days later for which the venue is attested (Cic. *Dom.* 5–7; Cass. Dio 39.9.2–3; Bonnefond-Coudry 1989, 41).

hunc ipsum ordinem: i.e. the Senate (*OLD* s.v. *ordo* 4; Cic. *RS* 6; *Cat.* 1.20). – The term refers to the same people, i.e. the senators, who are addressed in the second person in the next part of the sentence (Watts 1923, 51 n. a): in the sequence of *si*-clauses the Senate is mentioned as an entity, in parallel with the parents, the Roman People, and the gods; in the subsequent praise of the Senate and the gratitude required of Cicero, the senators are addressed directly.

magnificentissimis decretis: might refer to decrees passed after the suppression of the Catilinarian Conspiracy, calling for a festival of thanksgiving and awarding Cicero the title of *pater patriae* (Cic. *Cat.* 3.15; *Pis.* 6; *Sest.* 121; Plut. *Cic.* 23.6; thus Boll 2019, 101), and/or to those passed during Cicero's absence, especially the one agreed at the meeting of the Senate in the Temple of Honos and Virtus in spring 57 BCE, asking the consuls to send letters to enjoin foreign kings, allies, Roman governors, and their staff to ensure Cicero's safety, to thank civil communities that had sheltered Cicero, and to call together all who desired the Republic's safety (Cic. *RS* 24–7; *Sest.* 50; 116; 128–9; *Dom.* 85; *Planc.* 78; *Pis.* 34–5; Plut. *Cic.* 33.6; App. *B Civ.* 2.15; for the phrase, see Cic. *Div.* 1.59). *saepe* is probably an oratorical exaggeration: it insinuates that there was more than one occasion and thus that the view expressed by such decrees was a constant assessment of Cicero by the Senate.

immensum quiddam et infinitum: the services of the Senate towards Cicero go beyond what is ordinarily received from parents, gods, and countrymen because they have returned to Cicero all at once any individual favours received over a period of time (for the phrase in a different context, see Cic. *Nat. D.* 1.26).

debeamus: Boll (2019, 101) argues for the indicative *debemus* found in some more recent manuscripts, as he regards the subjunctive as unusual. Yet the subjunctive can be justified by the consecutive connotation of the relative clause (K.-St. II 303).

singulari studio atque consensu: the decree for Cicero's recall was passed almost unanimously, with only P. Clodius Pulcher opposing it (Cic. *RS* 26 n.; see Introduction, section 2).

parentum...iudicia: summarizes in abbreviated form the benefits received from others and in the past, as described in the first part of this sentence.

vestra de me multa iudicia: decrees of the Senate in favour of Cicero (*magnificentissimis decretis*) amount to 'judgements' or 'pronouncements' about him (*OLD* s.v. *iudicium* 7). – *multa* picks up what is implied in *saepe* (see note above).

uno tempore omnia...antea singula...nunc universa: an emphatic expression explaining why the services of the Senate are so outstanding by an effective contrast: Cicero's recall means that all the benefits received separately from different parties in the past are given back to him altogether at a single point in time. – The simultaneous return of everything is also stressed in the speech to the People; there, it is attributed to that audience rather than to the Senate (Cic. *RQ* 5). Here, the People are listed, among others, as an entity that gave something to Cicero in the past (as the electorate and to achieve comprehensiveness, they could not be omitted); in the speech to the People, the Senate is not mentioned, as it is not essential for the framework there (Boll 2019, 46).

multa...magna...innumerabilia...omnia: the third reiteration of the list, now in a different order with the Senate fronted. The adjectives qualify the benefits and create a climactic sequence with gradual distinctions; they do not match exactly what was said earlier in the paragraph: there, for instance, four items owed to parents are identified (not *innumerabilia*). Here, Cicero makes sure that he shows the appropriate respect to each group while highlighting the Senate's contribution.

per illos: the entities listed in what precedes, i.e. the Senate, the Roman People, parents, and the gods. – The summary uses the masculine plural, the standard form for references to different groups (K.-St. I 57; Pinkster 2015, 1256–7).

2. Main section (3–35): Review of Cicero's departure and recall

The main section (Cic. *RS* 3–35) gives an overview of the events leading up to Cicero's departure from Rome in 58 BCE, the attitudes of a number of people in key roles, and the series of initially unsuccessful and later successful initiatives to recall Cicero in 57 BCE. What is provided is not a straightforward narrative in chronological sequence, but rather a sketch of important moments in reverse order. The section starts with the result, a survey of the activities leading to his recall, as this is most important to Cicero and the basis for the expression of thanks (Cic. *RS* 3–7). This is followed by a detailed discussion of the roles of various individuals (Cic. *RS* 8–31). Taking up the theme of Cicero's return in 57 BCE, after new consuls had come into office, the passage starts with praise for these consuls (Cic. *RS* 8–9); this contrasts with a derogatory presentation of the consuls of the preceding year (Cic. *RS* 10–18); in ring composition, the conclusion highlights the efforts of other magistrates supporting Cicero (Cic. *RS* 18–31). At the end of the main section, in a flashback, Cicero returns to the situation in Rome at the time of his departure and asserts that he left to avoid bloodshed and for the sake of the Republic (Cic. *RS* 32–5).

This arrangement puts the essential statements about Cicero emphatically at either end, with the positive feature of the recall placed at the beginning; the criticisim of his opponents is sandwiched in between. Such a sequence leads to a smoother, less objectionable, and more varied structure than a chronological narrative (on creating an effective sequence in line with the requirements of the case rather than following standard rules, see *Rhet. Her.* 3.17–18).

The section thus provides a description of the events and individuals involved in Cicero's departure and return from his point of view; it combines praise for and gratitude to the people loyal to him and instrumental in arranging his recall (along with criticism of opponents) with confident statements of his service for the Republic. Cicero thereby fulfils his duty of rendering thanks, but also marks his re-entry into the political arena as a successful, respected, and dedicated politician (see also May 1988, 89).

2.1. Cicero's recall (3–7)

In the first part (Cic. *RS* 3–7) of the main section (Cic. *RS* 3–35) Cicero thanks the senators for recalling him and praises their loyalty in adverse circumstances, thus enhancing a good rapport with the audience. By highlighting both the attempts at supporting him and the obstacles created by his opponents, he establishes a clear division from the start, with himself and the senators on one side and the few 'enemies' on the other. By emphasizing the senators' attitude rather than concrete results, he creates the impression that he and the senators have always been united and that support for him has never faltered.

2.1.1. Unsuccessful senatorial activity in 58 BCE (3–4)

Cicero starts the discussion of the events leading to his recall (Cic. *RS* 3–4) in the first part (Cic. *RS* 3–7) of the main section (Cic. *RS* 3–35) by extending the praise of the senators when he highlights that they showed support for him and tried to arrange his return already in 58 BCE despite obstructing activity from two Tribunes of the People (P. Clodius Pulcher and Aelius Ligus) and lack of support from the consuls (L. Calpurnius Piso Caesoninus and A. Gabinius), who are identified by their political functions, but not named. Although the initiatives of the Senate did not have an immediate effect, mentioning them enables Cicero to flatter the audience and create the impression of continuous support.

3 patres conscripti: the main section starts with another address to the audience (Cic. *RS* 1 n.). The opening emphatic statement on the effect of the Senate's intervention thereby receives greater weight, and interaction with the audience is maintained.

immortalitatem: to show the greatness of the Senate's favour, Cicero compares it to conferring immortality (Cole 2013, 64). The statement is qualified (on this use of *quidam*, see Pinkster 2015, 1109–10); otherwise, the claim would be inappropriate for a human being, especially since it is phrased with reference to what Cicero has obtained (rather than what the Senate has given). – In another speech Cicero similarly describes the effect of the People's reaction (though with less qualification) when he stepped down from his consulship (Cic. *Pis.* 7: *mihi populus Romanus universus illa in contione non unius diei gratulationem sed aeternitatem immortalitatemque donavit, cum meum ius iurandum tale atque tantum iuratus ipse una voce et consensu approbavit.*). In *De domo sua* it is suggested that immortal fame can be acquired by the reactions to enforced absence (Cic. *Dom.* 86: *nam etsi optabilius est cursum vitae conficere sine dolore et sine iniuria, tamen ad immortalitatem gloriae plus adfert desideratum esse a suis civibus quam omnino numquam esse violatum.*).

quod...moriatur: this rhetorical question clarifies the notion of 'immortality': it is not that Cicero will be 'immortal', but rather that the memory of the Senate's great services for him will be 'immortal'.

quod...tempus erit...cum: *cum* is the reading of some manuscripts; others have *quo* (relative clause with consecutive sense: K.-St. II 296). A temporal *cum* with the present subjunctive (K.-St. II 332) appropriately describes the nature of the time (see also Boll 2019, 103).

memoria ac fama: a hendiadys amounting to 'glorious memory' (*OLD* s.v. *memoria* 5; *fama* 7).

qui: an independent relative clause referring to *vos* (*revocavistis*), implied in *vestrorum* in the previous sentence (for a similar construction, see Cic. *RS* 1).

illo ipso tempore, cum...: a paraphrastic indication of the time after Cicero's departure (58 BCE) described from his perspective: the Tribune of the People P. Clodius Pulcher was dominant in the Republic, armed gangs were present in Rome, the consuls L. Calpurnius Piso Caesoninus and A. Gabinius (Cic. *RS* 4 n.) did not carry out their office responsibly, and the Republic was not able to function properly (e.g. Cic. *Pis.* 26; 32; see Introduction, section 2). – In addition to indicating a climate of violence, threats, and fear, the sketch might allude to the Senate being prevented from expressing its views when the consuls neglected the pleas for discussion of Cicero's case and forbade the wearing of mourning clothes in his support (Cic. *RS* 4; 12 [and n.]; *Sest.* 25; 32).

vi, ferro, metu, minis: a sequence of four items (in asyndeton) affecting the Senate physically and psychologically: the first two items are symbols of concrete violent action, the last two refer to the emotional situation characterized by frightenting threats.

obsessi teneremini: *teneo* with a past participle emphasizes a lasting situation (K.-St. I 763–4; Pinkster 2015, 478–81).

non multo post discessum meum: after the indication of a period at the start of the sentence (*illo ipso tempore, cum*), this phrase identifies a particular point in time during Cicero's absence (for the construction of the temporal expression, see K.-St. I 403–4; Pinkster 2015, 842). As the continuation of the sentence reveals, the reference is to the meeting of the Senate on 1 June 58 BCE. Since Cicero left Rome in March (see Introduction, section 2), the intervening time could be described as *non multo* in relation to the length of Cicero's absence as a whole. – *discessus* is one of the euphemistic terms for Cicero's departure and absence that are preferred in the speeches given after his return (see Introduction, section 3.4).

universi: stresses the Senate's unanimity in their support for Cicero (cf. Cic. *Sest.* 68: *decrevit senatus frequens... dissentiente nullo*).

revocavistis: does not refer to the actual recall (in 57 BCE), but rather to a Senate decree calling for it, though it was not ratified at the time. Describing the Senate's intervention as a fact rather than as an intention emphasizes that the Senate supported Cicero throughout. – The initiative is highlighted as praiseworthy and a demonstration of the Senate's support for Cicero, since it happened at a time when the Senate's activity was suppressed.

referente L. Ninnio: L. Ninnius Quadratus (*RE* Ninnius 3), a Tribune of the People in 58 BCE (*MRR* II 196; see Wiseman 1964, 127; Nicholson 1992, 66), opposed his colleague P. Clodius Pulcher and supported Cicero. Soon after Cicero's departure Ninnius proposed a motion, which was approved as a Senate decree, that mourning dress should be assumed (Cic. *Sest.* 26; Cass. Dio 38.16.3–4). At a Senate meeting on 1 June 58 BCE Ninnius put forward a motion for Cicero's recall which was endorsed by the Senate, but not ratified as a decree because of the intercession by another Tribune of the People, Aelius Ligus (Cic. *Dom.* 49: *ille novicius Ligus, venalis adscriptor et subscriptor tuus*; *Sest.* 68: *decrevit senatus frequens de meo reditu Kalendis Iuniis, dissentiente nullo, referente L. Ninnio, ... intercessit Ligus iste nescio qui, additamentum inimicorum meorum.*; Cass. Dio 38.30.3–4; see Introduction, section 2; on this case, see De Libero 1992, 34; on tribunician intercession against bills and Senate decrees, see Mommsen, *StR* I 266–92; De Libero 1992, 29–49; Kunkel/Wittmann 1995, 594–607). – *referre* is the technical term for raising a matter in the Senate and putting forward a proposal (*OLD* s.v. *refero* 7).

ille pestifer annus: Cicero's assessment of the year 58 BCE (Cic. *RS* 4; 5). – The expression *pestifer annus* occurs once elsewhere in the classical period (Ps.-Quint. *Decl.* 12.5); the adjective *pestifer* only appears in Cicero's writings from his return to Rome onwards (Boll 2019, 104–5).

placuisset: Cicero stresses (more implicitly than in the speech to the People: Cic. *RQ* 13) that his party, in contrast to his opponents, preferred not to decide the issue by fighting, but would have been able and ready to do so. – With no agent named, it is left open who made the decision: Cicero, his supporters, or both.

defensorem: in addition to the generic laudatory description attached to the mention of his name (*fortissimo atque optimo viro*) indicating Ninnius' attitude and fighting prowess, the relative clause adds praise in relation to Cicero's fate in this year (Cic. *Sest.* 68: *referente L. Ninnio, cuius in mea causa numquam fides virtusque contremuit*). The noun and the adjective governed by it are separated by an inserted clause that concedes that the qualification is somewhat hypothetical, as the course of action in which this characteristic could have been demonstrated was not taken. It is implied that the activities in the Senate are a sufficient indication of what Ninnius would have done if fighting had occurred. – The term *defensor* makes Cicero's case appear the justified one, to be defended against attacks.

salutis meae: *salus* is the preferred word in the speeches delivered after Cicero's return to describe his well-being, safety, rescue, and concern for his situation, as well as the safe and secure state of a functioning Republic: it is sufficiently general to encompass all these notions and conveys positive connotations (see Introduction, section 3.4).

decernendi potestas: the decree of the Senate could not be passed formally because of the veto of a Tribune of the People. The point is not that the power or willingness of the Senate was lacking, but rather the opportunity for it to carry out its standard role (*OLD* s.v. *potestas* 5).

per eum tribunum plebis: Cicero does not name 'that Tribune of the People' and instead describes the individual in a derogatory fashion by his position and an added relative clause: the Tribune is introduced particularly negatively when it is suggested that he is not even able to carry out his criminal designs against the Republic by himself. Suppressing the name, assumed to be known to the audience, enables the orator to provide a characterization from his perspective (Uría 2006, 18–19). The only Tribune of the People who could be identified by such a negative description is P. Clodius Pulcher: he is 'hiding' by not intervening in public himself. – P. Clodius Pulcher (*RE* Clodius 48; see also Boll 2019, 38–42; see Introduction, section 2) is not mentioned by name in this speech (Steel 2007, esp. 116; Boll 2019, 105–6; see Introduction, section 3.4). Nicholson (1992, 95) counts five, perhaps six passing allusions to Clodius in *RS* (Cic. *RS* 4: *meus inimicus*; 11: *tribunus plebis*; 19: *sceleratum civem aut domesticum potius hostem*; 25: *inimici*; 26: *unus*; perhaps 18: *eodem gladiatore*) and potentially two in *RQ* (Cic. *RQ* 10: *inimicus*: 15: *uno dissentiente*), not including oblique references. Nicholson further observes that Clodius assumes a more prominent role in the slightly later speeches on similar issues, *De domo sua, De haruspicum responsis*, and *Pro Sestio*, assuming that Cicero preferred to gauge the situation first. – When the blocking of a Senate's decree for Cicero's recall is seen as an instance of *rem publicam lacerare* (see, with the stronger compound, Cic. *Mil.* 24: *annum integrum ad dilacerandam rem publicam quaereret*), Cicero's fate is identified with that of the Republic (see Introduction, section 3.4).

sub alieno scelere: the person behind whose *scelus* the Tribune of the People (i.e. P. Clodius Pulcher) was hiding is not identified either. This individual must be Aelius Ligus (*RE* Aelius 83), another Tribune of the People in 58 BCE (*MRR* II 195). Cicero had originally regarded him as a supporter (Cic. *Sest.* 69). Aelius Ligus then joined P. Clodius Pulcher (Cic. *RS* 4 and n.); he interceded against the passing of the motion proposed by Ninnius on 1 June 58 BCE (Cic. *Sest.* 68) and perhaps against another proposed by the other Tribunes of the People on 29 October 58 BCE (see Cic. *RS* 8 n.; Introduction, section 2). *scelus* provides a characterization of Aelius Ligus' disposition (*OLD* s.v. *scelus* 2e; cf. Cic. *RS* 17) from Cicero's point of view (for further negative descriptions of Aelius Ligus, see Cic. *Dom.* 49; *Har. resp.* 5; *Sest.* 94).

delituit: a vivid description of the Tribune of the People hiding behind someone else's activities (*OLD* s.v. *delitisco* 1; cf. Liv. 4.42.5).

numquam...numquam: the repetition of this word with the double description of basically the same activity (positively and negatively, by an emphatic expression with litotes in the second part) highlights the Senate's ongoing support for Cicero: the Senate continually demanded Cicero's recall as an item for discussion, although a law by P. Clodius Pulcher forbade this (Cic. *RS* 8 and n.) and there was no support from the consuls.

non...flagitavistis: Cicero frequently employs *flagitare* for the senators requesting a discussion of his situation from the consuls (Cic. *RQ* 10; 11; *Dom.* 70; *Sest.* 25; 69). The verb does not reveal in what way the request is made. Mommsen (*StR* III 949) seems to suggest that the measures include anonymous shouts from the crowd.

ab iis consulibus qui vendiderant: the consuls (i.e. of 58 BCE, L. Calpurnius Piso Caesoninus and A. Gabinius) are described as those 'who had sold': the absolute use of the verb leaves the allegation vague. The statement in the next paragraph distinguishing between a law about Cicero and one about the consuls provides a more obvious allusion: as a result of P. Clodius Pulcher's law assigning lucrative provinces to them, the consuls did nothing to stop his activities (see Cic. *RS* 4 n.; Introduction, section 2). Since they thereby put their personal advantage above the welfare of the Republic, one could consider supplying *rem publicam* as the object of *vendiderant* (as in some manuscripts). The contrast is more forceful if *meam salutem* from the preceding clause is supplied and the attitude of the senators and of the consuls to Cicero's well-being is juxtaposed; the consuls can be said to have 'sold' Cicero's well-being by their 'pact' with P. Clodius Pulcher. That the consuls 'sold' Cicero's well-being as well as the *res publica* (or elements of it) is also claimed elsewhere by Cicero (Cic. *RQ* 21; *Pis.* 15; 56).

4 itaque: the paragraph illustrates the circumstances under which the activity on Cicero's behalf manifested itself. Ninnius' intervention (Cic. *RS* 3 and n.) was followed by further supportive initiatives for Cicero (Cic. *Sest.* 68).

vestro studio atque auctoritate: highlights the Senate's support for Cicero as well as its influence on political activity in Rome (*OLD* s.v. *studium* 5; *auctoritas* 7). In connection with *studio*, *auctoritate* is likely to refer to the position of the Senate rather than to an informal decree (on the meanings of *auctoritas*, see Heinze 1925; on *auctoritas senatus* in the Republican political system, see Bleicken 1975, 294–324).

perfectum est ut: Cicero presents the fact that the majority of the Tribunes of the People took action in his favour as a result of the Senate's attitude, which assigns a share in this positive action to the audience.

ipse ille annus, quem…fatalem: i.e. the year 58 BCE. – The description emphasizes that activities for Cicero's recall took place in the very year in which he left Rome and in which some of the magistrates acted in an obstructive way.

malueram: by claiming that he had preferred himself, rather than the country, to be negatively affected, Cicero displays a patriotic and selfless attitude.

fatalem: the year was 'deadly' for neither Cicero nor the country in a literal sense, but the strong term (*OLD* s.v. *fatalis* 4b) conveys vividly how Cicero would like the effects of his opponents' actions (on himself and thus, in his view, the Republic) to be seen (for similar descriptions of that year, see, e.g., Cic. *RS* 3; 5; *Sest.* 15).

octo tribunos: in this period there were usually ten Tribunes of the People per year (Kunkel/Wittmann 1995, 558–9). Cicero claims that eight of the Tribunes of the People of 58 BCE (i.e. all except P. Clodius Pulcher and Aelius Ligus) supported him (Cic. *Sest.* 69). Six of these Tribunes of the People are known by name (*MRR* II 195–7).

promulgarent de salute mea: on 29 October 58 BCE eight Tribunes of the People promulgated a law on Cicero's return (*Rogatio VIII tribunorum de reditu Ciceronis: LPPR*, p. 401; *Roman Statutes*, no. 57, pp. 775–6; on the bill, see Moreau 1989a; Cic. *Att.* 3.23.1–4 [29 Nov. 58 BCE]; *Sest.* 69–70; see Cic. *RS* 8 n.; Introduction, section 2). – On Cn. Pompeius Magnus' potential involvement, see Cic. *RS* 29 n. – On *salus* in this context, see Cic. *RS* 3 n.; Introduction, section 3.4.

ad vos…referrent: suggests that, beyond submitting a bill for a law to be voted on by the People, the Tribunes brought up Cicero's case for discussion in the Senate on numerous occasions in spite of P. Clodius Pulcher's law forbidding this (Cic. *RS* 8 and n.).

nam…quam…promulgavit ut: Maslowski (1981) keeps transmitted *cum… promulgavit* (supported by Boll 2019, 108), but a mere chronological statement lacks the required logical connection. Courtney (1989, 47–8) reads *promulgavi<sse>t* with Ernesti and regards *nam…lata erat* as a parenthesis; then further changes to the text as suggested by Shackleton Bailey (1987, 271–2:

promulgavit. (*sed in illa lege ita scriptum erat*) *ut*) become unnecessary. The long parenthesis remains difficult. Adjusting the punctuation reduces the length of the parenthesis, and changing *cum* to *quam* (Lambinus, adopted, e.g., by Peterson 1911) makes the reference point clearer. The *quam*-clause (with subordinate *ut*-clause) contrasts P. Clodius Pulcher's activities against Cicero with the initiatives of the other Tribunes of the People described in the preceding *qui*-clause. The comment on the type of law is a statement outside the main construction explaining why the consuls do not take action on Cicero's behalf.

consules: the consuls of 58 BCE, L. Calpurnius Piso Caesoninus (*RE* Calpurnius 90; quaest. *c.*70, aed. 64?, praet. by 61, cos. 58, censor 50 BCE [*MRR* II 162, 179, 193–4, 247–8, 541–2]; see, e.g., Englisch 1979, esp. 22–36; Goldmann 2012, 154–62; Grilli 2015, 23–7; Boll 2019, 26–31) and A. Gabinius (*RE* Gabinius 11; tr. pl. 67, praet. by 61, cos. 58 BCE [*MRR* II 144–5, 179, 193–4]; see, e.g., Sanford 1939; Badian 1959; Goldmann 2012, 21–74; Grilli 2015, 27–9; Boll 2019, 26–31).

modesti legumque metuentes: ironic: such an attitude would be expected from consuls, but these consuls are said to act accordingly only when the law concerned is in their interest (cf. Cic. *Dom.* 70 [also on these consuls]: *homines legum iudiciorumque metuentes*). Cicero's actual view of these consuls is implied in the claim that they sold his well-being (Cic. *RS* 3 and n.). – *metuentes* functions as an adjective and is therefore construed with a genitive; this construction expresses a permanent quality (K.-St. I 450; Pinkster 2015, 222–3).

impediebantur lege (non…lata erat): continuing the irony, Cicero claims that the consuls were not inhibited by P. Clodius Pulcher's law forbidding anyone to raise Cicero's case (*Lex Clodia de exilio Ciceronis: LPRR*, pp. 395–6; *Roman Statutes*, no. 56, pp. 773–4; see Moreau 1987; see Introduction, section 2; Cic. *RS* 8; *Att.* 3.15.6 [17 Aug. 58 BCE]: *quid enim vides agi posse aut quo modo? per senatumne? at tute scripsisti ad me quoddam caput legis Clodium in curiae poste fixisse, NE REFERRI NEVE DICI LICERET. quo modo igitur Domitius se dixit relaturum? quo modo autem iis quos tu scribis et de re dicentibus et ut referretur postulantibus Clodius tacuit? ac si per populum, poteritne nisi de omnium tribunorum pl. sententia?*; *Dom.* 69–70; *Sest.* 69; *Pis.* 29–30; *Att.* 3.12.1; 3.23.2–4), but rather by another one assigning the provinces of Macedonia and Syria (originally Cilicia: on this exchange, see Goldmann 2012, 32–3) to the consuls Piso and Gabinius respectively, put forward at the same time as the one against Cicero, often described by him as an instance of mercantile negotiation (*Lex Clodia de provinciis consularibus, Lex Clodia de permutatione provinciarum: LPPR*, pp. 393–4; Cic. *RS* 3; 10; 16; 18; *RQ* 10; 11; 13; 21; *Dom.* 23–4; 55; 60; 70; 124; *Har. resp.* 3; 58; *Sest.* 24–5; 33; 44; 53–4; 55; 69; 71; 93; 94; *Prov. cons.* 2; 3; 13; *Pis.* 28; 29–31; 37; 49; 56; 57; 95; *Planc.* 86; *Att.* 3.1 [c. 22 March (?) 58 BCE]; *Fam.* 1.9.13 [Dec. 54 BCE]; Schol. Bob. ad Cic. *Planc.* 86 [p. 168.2–9 Stangl]; *Vir. ill.* 81.4; Plut. *Cic.* 30.2; on this procedure in relation to standard practice, see, e.g., Kaster 2006, 172–3, on Cic. *Sest.* 24). Cicero's insinuation that the consuls do not take action because of the deal concerning the provinces presents them as irresponsible magistrates abusing their position and the conventions of the Republic for their own advantage; in the speech to the People potential personal considerations for their reluctance to support Cicero are also mentioned (Cic. *RQ* 11; Mack 1937, 33–4).

meus inimicus: i.e. P. Clodius Pulcher, frequently referred to as *inimicus* in the speeches after Cicero's return (e.g. Cic. *RS* 25; *RQ* 10; *Dom.* 100; 101) and never mentioned by name (Cic. *RS* 3 n.).

promulgavit: when the standard verb for proposing a bill is used, although the law had been approved, the ideas and wording chosen by the proposer receive particular emphasis. – *promulgavit* is an example of a perfect employed with the force of a pluperfect (K.-St. I 129–30; Lebreton (1901, 220).

si...tum: *tum* marks the conclusion after the conditional subordinate clause (K.-St. II 387).

si revixissent: Cicero claims that P. Clodius Pulcher's law on Cicero's banishment said that Cicero could return when the Catilinarian conspirators condemned to death by the Senate and executed during Cicero's consulship on 5 December 63 BCE had come back to life (Cic. *RS* 26). Such a proposition is not something that could be realized and implies that Cicero could never return. It is unlikely that the law included a section with this wording (thus not indicated as a potential element in *LPPR* or *Roman Statutes*): this statement is rather Cicero's exaggerated description of the law's impact and intention in his view.

ii qui haec paene delerunt: is Cicero's indirect identification and characterization of the Catilinarian conspirators. By recalling their destructive plans, which he interprets as being directed against the Republic (*hostes atque interfectores rei publicae*), and noting that these plans have not come to fruition (*paene*), Cicero makes the audience remember the threat to themselves and their livelihoods as well as the fact that he saved them and the Republic. – The demonstrative pronoun *haec* does not have an antecedent; it has a deictic function and refers to Rome and its political institutions in front of the audience (for *haec* denoting the political system at Rome, see, e.g., Cic. *Prov. cons.* 24; *Cat.* 4.16; 4.23; *Flacc.* 104; *Mil.* 63). Boll (2019, 109) considers that the pronoun might indicate the Senate; but when Cicero refers to the Senate in speeches given to that body, he typically speaks of *hic ordo* or *vos*, and the perspective here is broader, not limited to the Senate.

utrumque: introduces two subsequent accusative and infinitive constructions linked by *et...et*.

confessus: for the sake of the argument Cicero ignores that the premise, namely that the dead Catilinarians might come back to life, cannot be realized and interprets the assertion as an acknowledgement by P. Clodius Pulcher that he sides with these men and that Cicero effectively opposed them and is the only one able to combat threats to the Republic emanating from such people (see also Nicholson 1992, 27).

desiderare: probably 'To long for, desire often an absent or dead person or a lost thing' (*OLD* s.v. *desidero* 1), while the connotation 'To feel or notice the absence of, miss, find lacking' (*OLD* s.v. *desidero* 4) is also present.

magno in periculo … revertissem: another aspect of the relationship between himself and the Republic as Cicero sets it up in these two speeches (see Introduction, section 3.4) is that his presence is necessary to preserve the Republic, as it would otherwise be in danger from people not supporting it.

interfectores rei publicae: seems to be the only instance in the classical period for *interfector* or *interficere* with an abstract entity in a metaphorical sense as the object. Markland (1745, 244) criticizes it as a 'harsh … Metaphor'; yet it expresses vividly these men's hostility to the Republic (for similar phrases, see Cic. *Pis.* 15: *voluit ille senatum interficere*; *Sest.* 24: *rem publicam contrucidarunt*).

atque: the transmission is split between *itaque* and *atque*; most editors choose *itaque* (see Schönberger 1913, 1381–2; Boll 2019, 110), while Peterson (1911) conjectures *idemque* (questioned by Luterbacher 1912, 346; Schönberger 1913, 1381; Busche 1917, 1356), and Shackleton Bailey (1991, 227) prefers *atque* (already supported by Busche 1917, 1356). Both long sentences in this paragraph beginning with *itaque* would be awkward, although Schönberger (1913, 1381) interprets it as a deliberate anaphora (see also Boll 2019, 119). This sentence is more likely to add (*atque*) the third manifestation of the Senate's attitude in favour of Cicero in the face of opposition (Cic. *RS* 3–4: *qui illo ipso tempore…*; *postea quam vobis…*; *atque illo ipso tamen anno…*): general support and acknowledgement of its importance despite the lack of leaders.

illo ipso … anno cum ego cessissem: i.e. 58 BCE, when Cicero left Rome in the spring (cf. *ipse ille annus, quem ego mihi quam patriae malueram esse fatalem*). – *cedere* is one of the terms by which Cicero describes his departure from Rome (see Introduction, section 3.4).

illo ipso tamen anno: *tamen* indicates that, despite the hostile atmosphere and all the obstacles in that year, the senators did not reduce their support for Cicero and the Republic (*OLD* s.v. *tamen* 3; for the word order, cf., e.g., Tac. *Ann.* 6.27.4: *qui eadem familia corruptis moribus, inlustri tamen fortuna egere*).

princeps … civitatis: i.e. Cn. Pompeius Magnus (106–48 BCE; *RE* Pompeius 31; cos. 70, 55, 52 BCE [*MRR* II 126, 214–15, 233–4]; see, e.g., Johannemann 1935; Seager 2002; Hodgson 2017, 150–1; Boll 2019, 16–21). – Pompey is described as *princeps civitatis* also in *De domo sua* (Cic. *Dom.* 66), subsumed among *principes civitatis* later in this speech (Cic. *RS* 26), and referred to as *princeps* elsewhere (Cic. *RS* 5; *RQ* 16). The wording does not reflect an official title but rather expresses appreciation of Pompey's standing. In the speech to the People Pompey's initiatives are singled out even more, presumably in view of his popularity among that audience (Mack 1937, 41–2; Klass 1939, 87–8; Boll 2019, 47). – After his return to Rome Cicero ignores any recent difficulties and instead highlights the good relationship between the two of them, praises Pompey's qualities, achievements, and activities in connection with his absence, and expresses his gratitude (Cic. *RS* 5; 29; *RQ* 16–18; *Dom.* 19; 27–30; 66; 69; *Har. resp.* 46; *Sest.* 15; 39–41; 107; 129; *Pis.* 34–5; 76–7; *Planc.* 93; see Nicholson 1992, 51–6). The positive presentation in the speeches delivered after Cicero's return is an element of a strategy to align Pompey with the position of Cicero and the Senate (Grasmück 1977, 172). In this speech Cicero presents Pompey as the greatest private benefactor (Cic. *RS* 29), matching the consul P. Cornelius Lentulus Spinther (cos. 57 BCE; Cic. *RS* 5 n.), the greatest public benefactor (Cic. *RS* 8; 27–8), and highlights his interventions (Raccanelli 2012, 69–84). Elsewhere close collaboration between these two men is indicated (Cic. *Dom.* 30; *Att.* 3.22.2 [27 Nov. 58 BCE]; Cass. Dio 39.6.2). At the end of 58 BCE Cicero was expecting future support from Pompey (Cic. *Fam.* 14.1.2 [28. Nov. 58 BCE]; 14.2.2 [5 Oct. 58 BCE]). Pompey initially did not intervene, but later supported Cicero when P. Clodius Pulcher's actions had become more irritating and problematic for him (see Introduction, section 2).

parietum vitam suam tueretur: after a slave of P. Clodius Pulcher allegedly sent to kill Cn. Pompeius Magnus with a dagger was discovered in the vestibule of the Temple of Castor used for a meeting of the Senate in August 58 BCE, Pompey stayed in his house for the rest of the year and avoided public appearances for fear of further violence (Cic. *RS* 29; *RQ* 14; *Dom.* 66–7; 110; 129; *Har. resp.* 48–9; 58; *Sest.* 69; *Pis.* 16; 28–9; *Mil.* 18–19; 37; 73; Ascon. ad Cic. *Mil.* 37 [p. 46.25–6 C.]; Schol. Bob. ad Cic. *De aere alieno Milonis* [pp. 171.2–4; 172.2 St.]; Plut. *Pomp.* 49.2; cf. Nowak 1973, 128–9). The incident serves to illustrate how Clodius' actions affect even the greatest men in the community and the functioning of the Republic, where laws should be providing protection. While such an allusion could be read as criticism of Pompey's cowardice, it may be seen as implying that, when even Pompey withdraws to avoid violence, Cicero's departure is justified (Riggsby 2002, 176–7).

sine consulibus: in Cicero's view the consuls of 58 BCE, L. Calpurnius Piso Caesoninus and A. Gabinius, did not behave as consuls should. Cicero, therefore, feels that they do not deserve the name of consuls and does not regard them as such (Cic. *RS* 10–18; *Sest.* 17–25; 32; 33; *Dom.* 24; 91; *Pis.* 9; 19; 23; 30–1; *Planc.* 87; *Vat.* 18; *Fam.* 1.9.13 [Dec. 54 BCE). – Before they came into office, Cicero thought that these consuls would be favourable to him (Cic. *Q Fr.* 1.2.16 [between 25 Oct. and 10 Dec. 59 BCE]; Cass. Dio 38.15.6).

parentibus perpetuis: a metaphorical description of the Senate and the ex-consuls, who remain in the position of caring for the Republic for more than a year. – The relationship between the Republic and the senators is described like that between children and parents to illustrate their position of responsibility and the lack of guidance if they fail.

tutoribus annuis: a metaphorical term for the annual magistrates and the consuls in particular, who are meant to look after the *res publica* like guardians. In Cicero's view the consuls of 58 BCE could not be regarded as proper consuls.

Thus, the orphaned *res publica* can be said to be only able to implore a *tutor* again after 1 January 57 BCE (Cic. *RQ* 11).

orbata: while, according to what Cicero has said so far, it is not the case that all senior senators and office holders failed to support him, he here implies that none of them was able to carry out their role properly. As this notion is expressed from the point of view of the Republic, it probably means that they were not able to fulfil all their political duties appropriately; since the fates of Cicero and the Republic are linked, this situation also affects their efforts on Cicero's behalf. – *orbata* is construed with a simple ablative (K.-St. I 374; cf. Cic. *RS* 33). *orbo* literally denotes the loss of relatives and can then be applied to the loss of anything valuable (*OLD* s.v. *orbo* 2); the basic sense is alluded to in the collocation with *parentibus* and *tutoribus* (the consul Lentulus later described as a parent: Cic. *RS* 8; *RQ* 11; for the metaphorical application of *orbo*/*orbus*, see Cic. *De or.* 3.3; *Fam.* 3.11.3). – Fantham (1972, 122) notes that a simpler version of the metaphor occurs in the speech to the People, assuming that the double and stylistically refined expression would be too formal for a *contio* (Cic. *RQ* 11). Not only is the metaphor presented more straightforwardly in that speech; additionally, the focus is different and the emotional tension is heightened: in the *contio* speech the emphasis is on the positive change under new consuls and on the personified Republic seeking help from them as from parents or guardians.

sententias dicere prohiberemini: Cicero alleges that the senators were prevented from voicing their views. In light of the next phrase this must allude to the section in P. Clodius Pulcher's law determining that Cicero's case should not be discussed (Cic. *RS* 8 and n.) and does not imply that any discussion in the Senate was prohibited. – Boll (2019, 112) favours Lehmann's (1880, 354) conjecture <*vos*> in front of *sententias* because all other elements of this sequence specify the agent (Lehmann also considered adding *vos* in front of *dicere* or reading *senatus* [*senatores*] *vos sententias dicere*). Naming the agent is grammatically necessary in the other elements of the *cum*-clause except the first one on Cicero, where it is added for emphasis (*ego cessissem*), and this item on the Senate (which has a verb in the passive voice expressing restriction). The emphasis is on the main clause *numquam dubitastis*: it would be weakened if *vos* was added to the preceding clause.

caput meae proscriptionis recitaretur: a section of of P. Clodius Pulcher's law on Cicero. The law is not referred to neutrally, but tendentiously by identifying its effect on Cicero and implying its unlawfulness.

caput: denotes individual provisions ('clauses' or 'sections') of a bill or law (*OLD* s.v. *caput* 18).

proscriptionis: Cicero frequently claims that the decision concerning him initiated by P. Clodius Pulcher was not a *lex*, but rather a *privilegium* or *proscriptio* (see Introduction, sections 2 and 3.4). *proscriptio* can refer to the sale of property or to the publication of lists (particularly in the time of Sulla and the second triumvirate) of names of individuals who were declared outlaws and could thus be killed and have their goods confiscated (*OLD* s.v. *proscriptio* 1, 2). Cicero's choice of words assimilates the measures against him arranged by Clodius to the procedure of the historical proscriptions (Cic. *Dom.* 43) and thus makes them appear harsh, unjustified, and unlawful.

meam salutem cum communi salute coniungere: Cicero ascribes to the Senate what he does throughout: creating a parallel between his own fortune and that of the community (Introduction, section 3.4). As Cicero's argument in this paragraph implies that his presence in Rome is essential for the welfare of the Republic, this statement amounts to a claim that the senators, continuing with efforts for his recall despite all obstacles, supported both Cicero and the Republic.

2.1.2. Renewed senatorial attempts in 57 BCE (5)

In this paragraph (Cic. *RS* 5) within the first part (Cic. *RS* 3–7) of the main section (Cic. *RS* 3–35) Cicero moves to the change and positive effect caused by the assumption of office by new magistrates at the start of 57 BCE (cf. Cic. *RQ* 11–12). Although even then it was not possible to arrange his recall immediately, he describes the positive atmosphere as a step forward, so that he can conclude the paragraph with the hyperbolic statement that his *dignitas* had then already returned to Rome, even if not his body.

5 P. Lentuli consulis: P. Cornelius Lentulus Spinther (*RE* Cornelius 238; aed. cur. 63, praet. 60 BCE), one of the consuls of 57 BCE (*MRR* II 199–200; see, e.g., Nicholson 1992, 56–60; Goldmann 2012, 75–90; Raccanelli 2012, 51–60; Boll 2019, 31–4). – In contrast to the consuls of the preceding year Lentulus is introduced by name and with an overwhelmingly positive characterization. Cicero frequently praises Lentulus and expresses his gratitude to him for having worked for his recall (e.g. Cic. *RS* 8–9 [and n.]; 24–8; *RQ* 11; 15; 17–18; *Dom.* 7; 30; 70–1; *Sest.* 70; 72; 144; *Pis.* 34; 80; *Mil.* 39; *Fam.* 1.1.1; 1.9.4; *Att.* 3.22.2; *Brut.* 268; see also Cic. *RS* 4 n.).

ex superioris anni caligine et tenebris: another metaphorical description of the pitiful character of the year 58 BCE (Cic. *RS* 3; 4); this mood was about to change with the arrival of the new consuls (*OLD* s.v. *ex* 13). – For the collocation (hendiadys), see Cic. *Verr.* 2.3.177; *Leg. agr.* 2.44; for similar metaphors of light, see Cic. *Prov. cons.* 43; *Dom.* 24; *Pis.* 34; *Planc.* 96 (on such metaphors, see Fantham 1972, 125).

lucem: in a continuation of the metaphor, the start of a new year and the assumption of office by new consuls are presented as bringing 'light' after the previous year's darkness, marking a fresh beginning.

Kalendis Ianuariis: i.e. 1 January 57 BCE, when the new consuls enter office. – Since 153 BCE consuls in Republican Rome started their term of office on 1 January (Kunkel/Wittmann 1995, 86–7).

dispicere: the appropriate verb for the metaphor (in one manuscript, while the others have *despicere*; yet *di-* and *de-* are often confused in the transmission): the new 'light' and thus the change could be seen (*OLD* s.v. *dispicio* 3).

coepistis: the verb in the second person plural describes the change in atmosphere at the turn of the year from the perspective of the senators in the audience. The verb's meaning does not imply that the turn for the better was not completed during Lentulus' consulship, but rather that the process started with his entering office on 1 January.

Q. Metelli: Q. Caecilius Metellus Nepos (*RE* Caecilius 96; see, e.g., van Ooteghem 1967, 280–94; Epstein 1987, 44; Nicholson 1992, 60–2; Goldmann 2012, 121–32; Boll 2019, 31–4), the other consul of 57 BCE (*MRR* II 199–200) and a cousin of P. Clodius Pulcher (Cic. *Dom.* 70), was an opponent of Cicero prior to 57 BCE (Cic. *RS* 25; 26; *Dom.* 7; *Sest.* 72; Cic. *Att.* 3.12.1; Cass. Dio 39.6.3), but, upon entering his consulship, he stopped the opposition (Cic. *RS* 9; 25–6; *RQ* 10; 15; *Dom.* 7; 70; *Prov. cons.* 22; *Sest.* 72; 87; 130; *Pis.* 35; *Fam.* 5.4; *Att.* 3.24.2; Cass Dio 39.8.2). As a Tribune of the People for 62 BCE (*MRR* II 174), Nepos prevented Cicero from delivering the final speech at the end of his consulship in December 63 BCE, when Cicero swore an elaborate oath confirming his support for the Republic instead (Cic. *Fam.* 5.2.6–8; *Pis.* 6; 35; *Sull.* 33–4; Plut. *Cic.* 23.1–2; Cass. Dio 37.38.1–2). – While Cicero mentions the previous enmity of Nepos later in the speech, here his current support is highlighted, and past events are ignored, so as to create a contrast to the behaviour of the consuls of the preceding year (see also Boll 2019, 113).

nobilissimi hominis atque optimi viri: in this collocation *nobilissimi* refers to noble descent (*OLD* s.v. *nobilis* 5) and *optimi* to character (cf. Cic. *RS* 25, on P. Servilius). In connection with *summa dignitas* the expression emphasizes the standing and the positive characteristics of Nepos.

praetorum, tribunorum plebis paene omnium: Cicero makes a similar claim in the speech to the People (Cic. *RQ* 15; see also Cic. *RS* 18). The statement here is vague and ambiguous: factually, *paene omnium* qualifies both *praetorum* and *tribunorum*. Yet *paene omnium* could be read as describing *tribunorum* only: the support for Cicero would appear even greater if opponents are only found among the Tribunes of the People. – On the supportive praetors and Tribunes of the People in 57 BCE, see Cic. *RS* 19–23 and nn. – The magistrates not supportive of Cicero (Cic. *Sest.* 69–70; 72; 74; 82; 94; 126; *Pis.* 35; *Mil.* 39; Ascon. ad Cic. *Pis.* 35 [p. 11.15–18 C.]; Schol. Bob. ad Cic. *Mil.* 39 [p. 122.29–30 Stangl]) were the praetor (one out of eight) Ap. Claudius Pulcher (*RE* Claudius 297; praet. 57 BCE [*MRR* II 200]; see, e.g., Constans 1921; Goldmann 2012, 163–8), brother of P. Clodius Pulcher (Brennan 2000, 474; on his support for his brother, see Cic. *RS* 22 n.), and the Tribunes of the People (two out of ten) Sex. Atilius Serranus (Gavianus) (*RE* Atilius 70; quaest. 63, tr. pl. 57 BCE [*MRR* II 168, 201–2]; see Cic. *RQ* 12 n.) and Q. Numerius Rufus (*RE* Numerius 5; tr. pl. 57 BCE [*MRR* II 202]). These three men were also against giving Cicero the opportunity to speak at a *contio* in September 57 BCE (Cic. *Att.* 4.1.6; see *RQ*, Introduction). Ap. Claudius Pulcher contributed to preventing an attempted prosecution of P. Clodius Pulcher under the *Lex Plautia de vi* (*TLLR* 261; Brennan 2000, 458).

subvenisset: abstract nouns expressing characteristics of the men as subjects, combined with their names or functions in the genitive, rather than personal constructions (K.-St. I 242), put more emphasis on these accomplishments; thus, the construction enhances the positive description of Cicero's supporters.

virtute, gloria, rebus gestis: in this tricolon of positive features by which Pompey excels (on the construction, see K.-St. I 398) *virtus* is the personal characteristic on which the other two are based: it enables *res gestae* leading to *gloria* (arranged as *hysteron proteron*). – For a similar description of a different person, see Cic. *Div. Caec.* 69.

Cn. Pompeius: Cn. Pompeius Magnus (Cic. *RS* 4 n.).

omnium gentium, omnium saeculorum, omnis memoriae facile princeps: beyond the first mention as *princeps...civitatis* (Cic. *RS* 4), Pompey is described as *princeps* in all space and time (Cic. *Fam.* 3.11.3: *alterum, quod Pompei et Bruti fidem benevolentiamque mirifice laudas. laetor virtute et officio cum tuorum necessariorum, meorum amicissimorum, tum alterius omnium saeculorum et gentium principis, alterius iam pridem iuventutis, celeriter, ut spero, civitatis*). The notion of 'time' is expressed by two phrases, of which the first probably looks to the future (*OLD* s.v. *saeculum* 8) and the second to the past (*OLD* s.v. *memoria* 7), indicating that Pompey is oustanding in the entire period yet to come and the phase people can remember.

tuto: with the new consuls in office, Pompey no longer had to fear for his safety and could again leave his house and come into the Senate (Cic. *RS* 4 and n.).

tantus vester consensus de salute mea: while Cicero's recall was not officially decreed until the middle of 57 BCE, attempts were made from the beginning of the year (see Introduction, section 2). To continue the presentation of the Senate's positive view of him and their support for his case, Cicero focuses on the attitude rather than the effect; and he highlights the overall consensus and ignores any opponents just alluded to.

corpus...dignitas: the contrast between Cicero's physical presence in Rome and his appreciation there stresses the impact of the Senate's position and presents it as almost more important than the actual return.

2.1.3. Political chaos caused by 'enemies' in 57 BCE (6–7)

In the final paragraphs (Cic. *RS* 6–7) of the first part (Cic. *RS* 3–7) of the main section (Cic. *RS* 3–35) Cicero describes the mayhem caused by his 'enemies' in the first half of 57 BCE following the violent disruption of the voting on a bill to recall Cicero in January (cf. Cic. *RQ* 13–14). When Cicero ends by saying that only few were prompted thereby to abandon his case and the rest stood steadfastly and courageously by him, he again highlights the loyalty and support of the senators. He thereby implicitly displays his gratitude and demonstrates that he and his audience are united in their political attitude.

6 quo ... mense: i.e. in January 57 BCE. – This is the first chronological marker after the mention of the new consuls coming into office (Cic. *RS* 5); it is followed by *postea* and *quo quidem tempore* (Cic. *RS* 6–7).

inimicos: presumably P. Clodius Pulcher and his followers, also called *inimici* elsewhere (e.g. Cic. *Sest.* 68; 72; 75; *Pis.* 18). Again, Cicero's opponents are not identified by name (Cic. *RS* 3 n.), and the size of the group is not defined; the vagueness, on the one hand, has the allegations appear less directly offensive; on the other hand, it makes claims not supported by evidence sound more plausible. Seager (2014, 227) interprets the description as referring to Clodius, Piso, and Gabinius; but it is doubtful whether the consuls of 58 BCE are the main target when Cicero talks about early 57 BCE and these two men will be discussed in detail later (Cic. *RS* 10–18).

interesset: Cicero goes on to outline the difference in attitude between himself and his enemies (cf. Cic. *RQ* 13) by a vivid contrast between his efforts to avoid bloodshed and their readiness to shed blood to obtain their goals. The instances refer to different points in time: Cicero's decision to leave in spring 58 BCE and his enemies' attempts to prevent his return subsequently. The sketch of the opponents' activities leads to a description of the political situation resulting from their interventions in Cicero's absence, in line with the chronological exposition.

potuistis: Cicero does not directly assert a difference between himself and his enemies but rather describes it as something the audience could assess. Thus, the audience becomes a participant in the argument, and the issue appears as an item for which there is accessible evidence.

ego ... illi: the contrast is highlighted by the sentence structure: *ego* and *illi* (i.e. *mei inimici*) are placed emphatically at the start of their respective clauses.

deserui: Cicero asserts that he did not stay and fight to preserve his position and thus prevented violence and a bloodbath for the sake of the Republic (Cic. *RS* 34; *Dom.* 63–4; *Sest.* 45–6), whereas his enemies believe that they could achieve their goals by a bloodbath. This argument avoids the impression that Cicero acted like a coward by leaving Rome before the banishment had been officially confirmed (see Riggsby 2002, 170). – The phrase 'abandon one's *salus*' (i.e. 'abandon concern for one's *salus*'; cf. Cic. *RQ* 13) only becomes a virtuous deed in this context: it implies that offering resistance might have been better for Cicero personally, but that he decided to sacrifice his well-being for the communal welfare (Cic. *RS* 33–4; see Introduction, section 3.4).

flumine sanguinis: Cicero alleges that his enemies did not use standard legal means (voting by the People) to prevent his return but rather resorted to violence (cf. Cic. *RQ* 14). – On 23 January 57 BCE the Tribune of the People

Q. Fabricius, together with colleagues, was about to propose Cicero's recall to a meeting of the People for approval (see Cic. *RS* 21; 22 nn.; Introduction, section 2). The attempt was obstructed by P. Clodius Pulcher's gangs with violence; they attacked magistrates and Cicero's brother (Cic. *RS* 1 n.); there was bloody fighting against Cicero's supporters (e.g. Nowak 1973, 129–31). Cicero talks vaguely of a group of disreputable and violent opponents; only Cassius Dio and Plutarch imply that Clodius was present (Cic. *RS* 22; *RQ* 14; *Sest.* 75–8; 85; *Mil.* 38; Cass. Dio 39.7.1–3; Plut. *Pomp.* 49.3).

intercludendum: this metaphorical expression describes Cicero's return as being cut off by a river of blood (*OLD* s.v. *intercludo* 1b), illustrating vividly that arranging measures for Cicero's recall was prevented by violence rather than any constitutional means (on these metaphors, see Fantham 1972, 122).

itaque . . . videbatis: Cicero claims that all political and juridical business was suspended as a result of the violence (for the disastrous situation during his absence in Cicero's view, see Cic. *RS* 19; *RQ* 14; *Sest.* 5; 15; 31; 53; 85–90; *Pis.* 26; 32; *Vat.* 8). – Different explanations of how such a situation (even if somewhat exaggerated by Cicero) might have come about have been proposed: some scholars have suggested that a suspension of public business due to a formal *iustitium* (on *iustitium*, see Kunkel/Wittmann 1995, 225–8) was in place in early 57 BCE (Maslowski 1976, 30; Brunt 1981; Kaster 2006, 275, on Cic. *Sest.* 71–92; see Cic. *RS* 19 n.). Other scholars believe that the suspension of business occurred as a result of the violence without any further arrangements (Stein 1930, 32, with n. 178) or of the suppression of the courts, but was not caused by a formal *iustitium* authorized by the Senate (Tatum 1999, 179 n. 25 [p. 307]), or that it happened because 'Nepos, Appius, and a tribune issued a decree suspending judicial proceedings' applying only to the courts (Mitchell 1991, 153 and n. 29; *contra* Kaster 2006, 305–6, on Cic. *Sest.* 89). Boll (2019, 116) notes that there was a Senate decree from summer 58 BCE to the effect that no other matter should be arranged before Cicero's case had been resolved, but that this did not lead to a complete standstill of public life, and that from late 58 BCE onwards some Senate decrees were passed (Cic. *Att.* 3.24.2). However, while this section of the speech focuses on the Senate, it encompasses other aspects of public life, not regulated by such a Senate decree.

postea: i.e. after the violent disruption of the meeting of the People in January 57 BCE. – Brunt (1981, 229) refers this description to the situation after Cicero's departure in March 58 BCE, but the context suggests an exposition in chronological sequence.

nihil . . . civibus, nihil sociis, nihil regibus: an anaphoric and asyndetic tricolon, stressing that the Senate (*vos*) was not in a position to deal properly with any of the domestic or foreign parties it usually interacted with. Since the enforced inactivity of the Senate is again mentioned in general at the end of the next sentence (next to that of other political bodies), the effect on the Senate is highlighted, as appropriate in front of this audience.

sociis: *socii* were initially Rome's allies in Italy, providing military service, though after the Social War many received Roman citizenship. Later the term referred to allies inhabiting provinces outside Italy (*OLD* s.v. *socius*² 4b). – Originally, the consuls and the Senate seem to have had meetings with foreign delegates early in each year, before the consuls left Rome on military business. This practice continued even after the consuls had begun to spend most of the year in Rome; it was enshrined in law (*Lex Gabinia de senatu legatis dando* of 67 BCE: *LPPR*, p. 373) in the first century BCE (Mommsen, *StR* III 1155–6; Cic. *Q Fr.* 2.11.3; *Fam.* 1.4.1).

regibus: i.e. kings of foreign countries allied to Rome (for an overview of the status of kingdoms allied to Rome and perceptions in the Republican and early imperial periods, see Cimma 1976), though the precise status and the terminology applied could vary; there was some overlap with *socii* (Lintott 1993, 32–6).

respondistis: denotes official responses by the Senate (*OLD* s.v. *respondeo* 4).

nihil iudices…, nihil populus…, nihil hic ordo: another anaphoric and asyndetic tricolon lists the three main bodies in the Roman Republic and indicates that none of them was able to make and publicize decisions in their characteristic ways. The three functions correspond roughly to what is recognized as the three branches of government in modern political systems (judicial, legislative, executive). That the judges are added to the common collocation of the Senate and the People illustrates the complete suspension of political and juridical business.

sententiis: i.e. judicial pronouncements or verdicts (*OLD* s.v. *sententia* 5), rather than opinions expressed in the Senate (*OLD* s.v. *sententia* 3).

nihil populus suffragiis: the People usually declare their views by voting in elections or in decisions about laws and other policy matters (*OLD* s.v. *suffragium* 1).

hic ordo: has a deictic force in a speech delivered in the Senate (on *ordo* for Senate, see *OLD* s.v. *ordo* 4; Cic. *RS* 1; 2 and nn.), while in this series of public bodies an impersonal description is preferred to an address to the senators forming the audience.

auctoritate: alludes to the Senate's authority and authoritative pronouncements as well as informal decrees (*OLD* s.v. *auctoritas* 4, 6). The term is taken in the latter sense by Shackleton Bailey (1991, 8) and MacKendrick (1995, 130): if this was the primary meaning, a plural form might be expected to indicate a series of instances; and one might wonder why the impact is not described with respect to proper Senate decrees.

declaravit: is suitable for all three groups listed, since this verb is not a technical term for a particular body but rather a general expression for making an announcement (*OLD* s.v. *declaro* 1; for its use with reference to the Senate, see Cic. *Pis.* 35: *eisque verbis ea de me senatus auctoritas declarata est*).

forum . . . curiam . . . civitatem: this tricolon again lists the three bodies mentioned in the previous phrase, now with different descriptions and with the
order of the last two items reversed. The three entities are described by three
different adjectives with similar meanings; the last (referring to the institution
rather than the location of the activity) is defined by a double expression, as
another adjective with a different sense is added. These variations and the final
position make *civitas* appear particularly affected; as it is the most comprehensive, it has a generalizing and concluding force.

7 quo . . . tempore, cum: the time is defined by the absence of Cicero, who is
not named but rather identified by a description of his achievements in the
third person (*is . . . qui*); this form of expression creates a contrast between the
quiet situation created by Cicero's efforts when he was in a position to do so (i.e.
in 63 BCE) and the violence and limitation of political procedures in his absence
(i.e. in the first half of 57 BCE). – The pluperfect subjunctive in the temporal
cum-clause implies a characterization of the nature of the time (K.-St. II 331–2;
Pinkster 2015, 641–3), while the indicative in the inserted relative clause presents Cicero's past success as a fact (K.-St. II 291).

quo quidem tempore: continues the chronological sequence (Cic. *RS* 6 n.). –
The phrase appears a number of times in Cicero's writings (e.g. Cic. *Cat.* 3.19;
Phil. 2.37; 2.49), but not in other Republican authors.

is: i.e. Cicero (for this way of talking about himself, see also Cic. *RS* 8; 16; *RQ*
16; *Sest.* 53: *civis erat expulsus is qui rem publicam ex senatus auctoritate cum
omnibus bonis defenderat*; *Pis.* 23: *cum civis is, quem hic ordo adsentiente Italia
cunctisque gentibus conservatorem patriae iudicarat*).

excessisset: another of the paraphrases Cicero employs for his departure
from Rome (see Introduction, section 3.4). The verb emphasizes the departure
and denotes a stronger sense of withdrawing than *abire* (cf. Cic. *Cat.* 2.1: *abiit,
excessit, evasit, erupit*).

caedi et flammae vobis auctoribus restiterat: describes Cicero's activities
against the Catilinarians in 63 BCE. When what was resisted is identified as
murder and arson rather than as a politically motivated intervention, and the
role of the Senate in prompting the interventions is highlighted (Cic. *RS* 32;
Sest. 53; 63; 145; Cass. Dio 38.14.4–5), it is implied that Cicero's actions were
justified and thus not a reason for the activities leading to his leaving Rome
(Nicholson 1992, 26–7). – *vobis auctoribus* (*OLD* s.v. *auctor* 12) may refer to the
senatus consultum ultimum passed in October 63 BCE (Cic. *Cat.* 1.3; Sall. *Cat.*
29; Cass. Dio 37.31.2; Plut. *Cic.* 15.5) and/or to the decree on the death penalty
for the captured conspirators agreed on 5 December 63 BCE (Cic. *Cat.* 4; Sall.
Cat. 50.3–5.6).

cum . . . vidistis: Cicero sketches the situation by reference to what the audience could see at the time, again to keep them involved and to indicate that they
have first-hand evidence of the situation during his absence (Cic. *RQ* 14). The

list starts with an indication of overall disorder and danger, then mentions attacks on magistrates and gods generally, and finishes with examples of a consul and a Tribune of the People. The generic format means that it is not entirely clear throughout what is alluded to. Kaster (2006, 275, 292–3, on Cic. *Sest.* 71–92, 79) identifies a list of five items in which items one and two refer to P. Clodius Pulcher's attack on T. Annius Milo's house, item five to P. Sestius, and items three and four probably to the same riot at the Temple of Castor (see below).

cum ferro et facibus homines tota urbe volitantis: the first item describes unrest and threatening conditions affecting the entire city of Rome. *ferro et facibus* correspond as concrete items to the preceding abstract *caedi et flammae*: this connection implies that, after Cicero's departure, there was nobody to resist such attacks; the verb (*OLD* s.v. *uolito* 3; cf. Cic. *Leg. agr.* 2.99) insinuates that these people move around quickly and penetrate all areas. – *homines* are not defined: they are probably supporters of P. Clodius Pulcher. – On the preposition *cum* with the ablative expressing concomitant circumstances, see K.-St. I 408; Pinkster 2015, 901–2.

magistratuum tecta impugnata: elsewhere Cicero mentions that the house of the urban praetor of 57 BCE, L. Caecilius Rufus (*MRR* II 200; listed as a supporter at Cic. *RS* 22), was attacked (Cic. *Mil.* 38: *potuitne L. Caecili, iustissimi fortissimique praetoris, oppugnata domo?*; cf. Nowak 1973, 131–2); the reason might have been that Caecilius Rufus 'refused access in court to those who had taken possession of the property of Cicero, now in exile' (Brennan 2000, 453). According to Asconius there are no other references to this incident (Ascon. ad Cic. *Mil.* 38 [p. 48.22–3 C.]). In other contexts Cicero says that the house of the Tribune T. Annius Milo (Cic. *RS* 19 n.) was attacked in 57 BCE (Maslowski 1976), apparently twice, early in the year and again in November (Cic. *Sest.* 85; 88; 90; *Att.* 4.3.3; *Mil.* 38). Kaster (2006, 275, 301, 307, on Cic. *Sest.* 71–92, 86, 90) refers the comments in *RS* and *RQ* to the first attack on Milo's house, not regarding the plural as relevant and pointing to the similarity in the description of the circumstances (Cic. *RS* 7: *ferro et facibus*; *RQ* 14: *cum ferro et facibus*; *Sest.* 85: *ferro, facibus*; 90: *ferrum flammamque*), but such a feature might be a generic element of a vivid sketch, and here this detail is not explicitly linked to the attack on the house. – The plural in *RS* and *RQ* (Cic. *RQ* 14) could be an emphatic intensification or indicate that the houses of more than one magistrate were targeted. – The verb *impugnata* has the confrontation appear like a military attack (*OLD* s.v. *impugno* 1).

deorum templa inflammata: in this unspecific comment the plural might again be chosen for emphasis. The remark has been seen (Wolf 1801, 22; Condom 1995, 33 n. 20; MacKendrick 1995, 124) as an allusion to P. Clodius Pulcher, through his henchman Sex. Cloelius, setting fire to the Temple of the Nymphae in the Campus Martius (*LTUR* III 350–1); this incident seems to have taken place in late February or early March 56 BCE (Cic. *Cael.* 78; *Mil.* 73; *Har.*

resp. 57; *Parad.* 4.30–1). Therefore, the comment has been referred (Kaster 2006, 292–3, 298, on Cic. *Sest.* 79, 84; also Guerriero 1955, 24) to the tumult in the Temple of Castor in early 57 BCE (Cic. *Sest.* 79), though fire is not mentioned in the accounts clearly describing this incident. Setting temples on fire (without specific details) appears as an item in a list of disturbances caused by P. Clodius Pulcher (Cic. *Sest.* 84).

consulis fasces fractos: apparently, in a tumult in 58 BCE the *fasces* of one of the consuls (Gabinius) were broken (Cic. *Pis.* 28; Cass. Dio 38.30.2). In 57 BCE P. Sestius announced to a consul of that year an unfavourable omen at an assembly at the Temple of Castor (Cic. *Dom.* 13; *Sest.* 79; 83); thereupon P. Clodius Pulcher's troops confronted Sestius: it is likely that the *fasces* of the consul Q. Caecilius Metellus Nepos were broken on this occasion (inferred from the context and the assumed chronology in *RS* and *RQ*). Tatum (1999, 170–1, 179–80) describes the two occasions on which a consul's *fasces* were shattered, in 58 and 57 BCE respectively, and refers this passage to the latter incident (so also Kaster 2006, 275, 293, on Cic. *Sest.* 71–92, 79). – Of the two consuls of 57 BCE, the positive characterization (*summi viri et clarissimi consulis*) may suggest an allusion to the consul P. Cornelius Lentulus Spinther, whose support of Cicero is singled out (thus Bortone 1983, 17; Bellardi 1975, 96 [cautiously]; MacKendrick 1995, 124; Shackleton Bailey 1992, 39 [tentatively]; Boll 2019, 118 [considering either consul]). But, as Gelzer (1939, 924) indicates, the reference to this incident in *De domo sua* (Cic. *Dom.* 13) implies that the consul Q. Caecilius Metellus Nepos was involved (so also Goldmann 2012, 128). In this speech Nepos has been characterized as *nobilissimi hominis atque optimi viri* (Cic. *RS* 5). The positive epithets here balance *fortissimi atque optimi tribuni plebis* in the subsequent phrase and highlight the position of the victim to make the deed appear more outrageous (no attributes in Cic. *RQ* 14). – Breaking the insignia of magisterial power is a vivid illustration of political upheaval (for breaking the *fasces* on other occasions, see Ascon. ad Cic. *Corn.* [p. 58.20–3 C.]; Cass. Dio 36.39.3; 38.6.3).

tribuni plebis: P. Sestius, a Tribune of the People in 57 BCE (*RE* Sestius 6; quaest. 63, tr. pl. 57 BCE [*MRR* II 168, 202]; on his family, see Cic. *Sest.* 6–7; see, e.g., Nicholson 1992, 68–70; Raccanelli 2012, 60–5; Boll 2019, 34–7), was a supporter of Cicero (Cic. *RQ* 15; *Sest.* 3–5); in 56 BCE Sestius was charged under the *Lex Plautia de vi* and successfully defended by Cicero with the speech *Pro Sestio* (*TLRR* 271). – In early 57 BCE, when Sestius announced to the consul an unfavourable omen at an assembly at the Temple of Castor, thus trying to stop proceedings (Nowak 1973, 132–3; Kaster 2006, 293–4, on Cic. *Sest.* 79), he was attacked, wounded, and left for dead by supporters of P. Clodius Pulcher (Cic. *RS* 20; 30; *RQ* 14; *Sest.* 79; 81; 85; 90; *Mil.* 38; *Q Fr.* 2.3.6; Plut. *Cic.* 33.4).

sanctissimum corpus: Tribunes of the People had a sacrosanct status (Bleicken 1981, 93; Kunkel/Wittmann 1995, 555–7, 572–3; Cic. *Leg.* 3.9; Liv. 3.55.6–10). The superlative may indicate that this characteristic applies particularly to this Tribune, who was of such good character; the collocation with *corpus* highlights the item affected by the violation.

non tactum...confectumque: the violation of the Tribune's sacrosanct status is presented as particularly serious because he was even subjected to a serious physical injury with a sword. This notion is emphasized by the choice of verbs and the word order, whereby the phrase emphatically ends with *confectum*, indicating the result of the action (*OLD* s.v. *conficio* 16). On that occasion Sestius was not killed, merely thought to be dead; the wording illustrates the impact of the assault and may imply that the attackers believed that they had killed Sestius.

qua strage...recesserunt: Cicero acknowledges that the outbreak of violence and the attacks on individuals made some magistrates abandon his cause (Cic. *RS* 33). When he implies that these magistrates initially supported him, gives valid reasons for their behaviour, and claims that they withdrew just a little (*paululum*), their conduct is explained, and it is implied that their change of mind hardly detracted from the general support for Cicero. – In 57 BCE one praetor and two Tribunes of the People were not on Cicero's side (Cic. *RS* 5 n.; cf. Cic. *Pis.* 35), though their attitude does not seem to have been determined by the events in January. The phrasing rather suggests a reference to *timidi amici* (Cic. *RS* 23), people favourable to Cicero, but without the courage to take action.

partim metu mortis, partim desperatione rei publicae: these reasons why some magistrates wavered show that their change of mind was determined by their assessment of the general situation (as a personal risk and a threat to the political system) rather than a lack of confidence in Cicero.

reliqui fuerunt: as a complement to *non nulli*, Cicero suggests that the others, i.e. the majority, remained his supporters. Cicero gives a list of eight items (linked by *neque/nec* and arranged as four pairs of two) that could not deter this group: the first and the last pair sketch the climate of violence (first in the abstract and then with reference to concrete items), the two pairs in the middle describe the men's emotional reactions to initiatives of the opponents in a *hysteron proteron*. – The relative clause has consecutive sense and therefore takes the subjunctive (Lebreton 1901, 319–20; K.-St. II 296).

a vestra auctoritate, a populi Romani dignitate, a mea salute: Cicero again puts his own fate and that of the community in parallel (see Introduction, section 3.4). Here the point of comparison is not the *res publica*, but rather the Senate and the Roman People (with an appropriate noun for each entity): thus, the presentation focused on individuals and the influential entitites in the Republic is continued. The judiciary is no longer included; the emphasis is on politics and the institutions that might enable Cicero's return.

2. Activities of Cicero's supporters and opponents (8–31)

In the middle part (Cic. *RS* 8–31) of the main section (Cic. *RS* 3–35) Cicero details the activities of his supporters and opponents. In reverse chronological

order and leading on from the discussion of attempts at his recall in the preceding part (Cic. *RS* 3–7), he starts with the assistance received from the consuls of
57 BCE (Cic. *RS* 8–9); this theme is continued at the end of the section with the
mention of support from other magistrates and senators (Cic. *RS* 18–31). In
between, in a flashback, criticism of the consuls of 58 BCE is inserted (Cic. *RS*
10–18). This jutxtaposition sets off the support Cicero received: that he was
helped by politicians at all levels (with only few exceptions) emerges as the
overwhelming impression.

In describing their interventions, Cicero characterizes the supporters as
aligned with the Republic and its values (*boni*); he thus again insinuates a close
connection between his situation and the welfare of the Republic (Thompson
1978, 55–62; see Introduction, section 3.4). In the Senate Cicero highlights the
achievemens of people as individuals while in the speech in the *contio* there is
emphasis on their function in the sequence of events and their influence on
activities of the People (Mack 1937, 27–30 on Cic. *RS* 8–30 vs *RQ* 9–17).

2.2.1. Supporters: consuls of 57 BCE (8–9)

This subsection (Cic. *RS* 8–9), which opens the part on Cicero's supporters and
opponents (Cic. *RS* 8–31), offers elaborate praise of the consul P. Cornelius
Lentulus Spinther, one of the consuls of 57 BCE (Cic. *RS* 5 n.). It contrasts his
initiatives with those of the consuls of the previous year and highlights how he
worked tirelessly for Cicero's recall from the point of his election in the face of
obstacles. Since the other consul of 57 BCE, Q. Caecilius Metellus Nepos, was
Cicero's enemy in the past (Cic. *RS* 25 n.), he is mentioned more briefly, but his
support is acknowledged.

In the Senate Cicero probably feels obliged to start with the consuls and to
underline their activities, as they enabled the Senate decree eventually leading
to Cicero's return. Accordingly, the praise is emphatic and personal, whereas
in the speech to the People the procedures initiated by the consuls and the
consequences for the People are prominent (Mack 1937, 34–5 on Cic. *RS* 4; 8 vs.
RQ 11).

8 princeps: among those who did not waver in their support for Cicero (Cic.
RS 7), the consul Lentulus is singled out: *princeps* (*OLD* s.v. *princeps*[1] 2) is
emphatically fronted. The notion that Lentulus led the activities for Cicero's
recall (Cic. *RS* 24) is combined (in a somewhat condensed construction) with
the concept that Lentulus regarded having Cicero recalled as an ornament of
his consulship (Cic. *Sest.* 70).

parens ac deus…nominis: the consul Lentulus is described similarly in the
speech before the People (Cic. *RQ* 11: *Lentulus consul, parens, deus, salus nostrae
vitae, fortunae, memoriae, nominis*; cf. *Sest.* 144: *P. Lentulum, cuius ego patrem
deum ac parentem statuo fortunae ac nominis mei, fratris liberorumque nostrorum*). In the latter the genitives depend on *salus* (*OLD* s.v. *salus* 6); here they are

linked to *parens ac deus* (*OLD* s.v. *deus* 2a), which intensifies the expression (on Cicero's gratitude to Lentulus, see Cic. *RS* 24). – The characterization of Lentulus as a parent (Raccanelli 2012, 51–60) and god (Cole 2013, 70–1) is a strong metaphorical description of his intervention's greatness and impact; similarly, later Lentulus' initiatives are said to have created a second 'day of birth' for Cicero, when he almost recalled him from death to life (Cic. *RS* 27; see Introduction, section 3.4), and his *beneficium* is defined as 'divine' (Cic. *RS* 28).

nostrae vitae, fortunae, memoriae, nominis: a list of aspects of Cicero's existence rescued by Lentulus ranging from Cicero's life as the physical basis via his fate, which includes circumstances, to his recognition as a respected and esteemed person (*OLD* s.v. *fortuna* 8; *memoria* 5; *nomen* 12).

hoc: anaphorically repeated three times, looks forward to the *si*-clause and is the subject of *fore*.

specimen virtutis…indicium animi…lumen consulatus sui: Cicero alleges that the consul felt that support for Cicero would reflect well on him, thereby presenting it as a praiseworthy course of action and a significant deed: it would not only be an example of his virtuous character (*OLD* s.v. *animus* 14), but even a highlight of his consulship.

si…reddidisset: a shortened version of the items returned to each other as listed earlier (Cic. *RS* 1), with an effective fourfold repetition of *si*. The list consists of two 'personal' and two 'public' items, including the benefits of the recall for the audience and the community. The series of datives places the emphasis on who receives Cicero back. The sequence starts with Cicero, last in the earlier instance, and ends with *res publica*; thus, the two items important for Cicero and frequently put in parallel (see Introduction, section 3.4) frame the list.

meis: i.e. Cicero's family (on his brother, children, and wife, see Cic. *RS* 1; *RQ* 8 nn.).

designatus: Lentulus was consul designate in the second half of 58 BCE (for Lentulus' interventions on Cicero's behalf as consul designate, see Cic. *Dom.* 70; *Sest.* 70; *Att.* 3.22.2). – Elections for the consulship (and other magistracies) of 57 BCE took place in July 58 BCE (Ramsey 2019, 218 and n. i), as can be inferred from mentions in Cicero's letters (Cic. *Att.* 3.12.1 [17 July 58 BCE]; 3.13.1 [5 Aug. 58 BCE]; 3.14.1 [21 July 58 BCE]; *Q Fr.* 1.4.3 [Aug. 58 BCE]).

sententiam…dicere: a technical term for making a statement in the Senate (*OLD* s.v. *sententia* 3). Since *consules designati* were asked for their views early in a debate (e.g. Sall. *Cat.* 50.4) and senators were able to comment on any issue in their *sententia* (Mommsen, *StR* III 939; cf. Gell. *NA* 4.10.8), Lentulus would have been able to make comments on Cicero's situation at various meetings of the Senate from a position of authority. Such interventions presuppose that Clodius' law forbidding discussion of Cicero's case is ignored and not regarded as valid (see Introduction, section 2).

se et re publica dignam: if a statement on Cicero's *salus* can show that the consul is worthy of himself and the Republic, this implies that support for

Cicero is justified and agrees with the values of the Republic and the duties of a consul.

cum a tribuno plebis vetaretur: while the preceding sentence describes the activities of Lentulus as consul designate in general, this clause seems to allude to a particular incident. The occasion is probably (Gelzer 1939, 921; Kunkel/ Wittmann 1995, 605; Boll 2019, 122) the motion of eight Tribunes of the People on 29 October 58 BCE (Cic. *RS* 4 n.) supported by the consul designate Lentulus in a *sententia*. It was apparently blocked by one of the remaining two Tribunes of the People, P. Clodius Pulcher or Aelius Ligus (Cic. *RS* 3 n.): the wording suggests that, by bringing up the relevant sections of P. Clodius Pulcher's law on Cicero (see Introduction, section 2), the Tribune stopped the discussion of the motion and prevented a subsequent vote (though this did not change Lentulus' view of this law).

praeclarum caput: the law on Cicero included a section forbidding anyone to raise Cicero's recall in the Senate or before the People (see Cic. *RS* 4 n.; Introduction, section 2). – *praeclarum* has ironic force (Weiske 1807, 255; MacKendrick 1995, 131; *OLD* s.v. *praeclarus* 3; cf. Sall. *Iug.* 14.21).

ne quis … adesset: this list is not a direct quotation from the law; the instructions are reported in indirect speech and have been adapted to an address to the Senate (e.g. *ad vos* instead of *ad senatum*); yet the text of the law could have inspired some of the wording. – The sequence of anaphoric short clauses provides an overview of the major stages in the production of a Senate decree, partly based on standard terminology. No object for the various senatorial activities is given; that they refer to Cicero's situation is clear from the context and the historical circumstances (on the phrasing of the law and its implications, see Moreau 1987, 481–2). The technical words follow the sequence from initiating a discussion via voting (including discussion) to recording. Inserted between making a decision and voting are non-technical words indicating discussion (*disputaret*; *loqueretur*), presumably understood as an element of the decision-making process (Mommsen [*StR* III 942 n. 5] refers them to the right of magistrates to speak, for which no technical term existed), although they would precede *decerneret* in a strict chronological sequence (for *disputare* for statements in the Senate, see, e.g., Cic. *Fam.* 5.2.1). The first verb *referret* applies mainly to the consuls as the chairs of meetings who bring matters to the Senate for discussion and eventually decrees (e.g. Cic. *Fam.* 8.8.5). The law affects consuls (Cic. *RS* 4; *Dom.* 68; 70; *Sest.* 69; *Pis.* 29–30), consuls designate (Cic. *Dom.* 70), praetors (Cic. *Att.* 3.15.6), and all senators (Cic. *Dom.* 68; *Sest.* 69), threatening punishment for disobedience. Nevertheless, the provisions seem to have been ignored by some, and senators and magistrates still spoke on Cicero's behalf (Cic. *Dom.* 68; 70; *Sest.* 69). Overall, the wording is less formal than in some of the letters in which Cicero refers to elements of this law (Cic. *Att.* 3.12.1; 3.15.6; 3.23.2–4). – Markland (1745, 244–5) remarked that some elements of the law mentioned here were not given in Cicero's letters, that the wording was different in some cases (e.g. *ne loqueretur* vs *neve dici liceret*), and that *ne pedibus iret* without the addition of *in sententiam* was ridiculous (also Wolf 1801, 23). While Cicero seems to reproduce parts of the law fairly literally in the letters, in the speech he summarizes the effect in less formal and less technical language and rather gives a brief list of forbidden actions, highlighting that any standard activity was prohibited. Long (1856, 304) observed that *decerneret* is 'a false expression', since it is the Senate who decides. Indeed, while *decernere* can describe the activity of individuals (Cic. *Fam.* 1.1.3), if it refers to Senate decrees, it is generally applied to the Senate. Here, just as in what seems to be the phrasing of the law, the matter is described in an individualistic, distributive way: all activities are given in the singular applied to individual senators, while they concern the entire Senate.

ne pedibus iret: a paraphrase for voting: for a vote on a proposed decree, senators would move to designated different areas of the venue (Mommsen, *StR* III 991–2). – The phrase usually includes *in sententiam* or something similar (*OLD* s.v. *pes* 6b), though this is most frequently the case with reference to a specific *sententia* (e.g. Liv. 5.9.2: *in quam sententiam cum pedibus iretur*; but cf. Liv. 27.34.7: *sed tum quoque aut verbo adsentiebatur aut pedibus in sententiam ibat*). Here, the meaning is clear from the context even without the addition, and the sequence does not employ the full official terminology.

ne scribendo adesset: after a decree was passed by the Senate, it was recorded and witnessed as correct by a number of senators in attendance (Mommsen, *StR* III 1005, 1008). – For the phrase, see, e.g., Cic. *Prov. cons.* 28; *Har. resp.* 13; *Fam.* 8.8.5; 8.8.6; 12.29.2; 15.6.2 (K.-St. I 747; Lebreton 1901, 385).

ut ante dixi: as this phrase is sandwiched between *totam illam* and *proscriptionem*, it is not just a reminder that the issue has been mentioned (Cic. *RS* 4), but rather emphasizes that the correct word *proscriptio* has been introduced previously.

proscriptionem non legem: Cicero ascribes his assessment of P. Clodius Pulcher's law on him (see Cic. *RS* 4 n.; Introduction, sections 2 and 3.4) to the consul Lentulus to motivate the latter's initiative (Cic. *Dom.* 70; cf. also the view of L. Aurelius Cotta, as reported by Cicero, Cic. *Sest.* 73). This view of Lentulus is not mentioned in the speech to the People (Mack 1937, 35).

proscriptionem: Shackleton Bailey (1987, 272) argues that a supplement is necessary and suggests reading *proscriptionem <vim>* ('he considered that entire proscription, as I have called it, an act of violence, not a law'), but the contrast is between regarding P. Clodius Pulcher's measures as a *proscriptio* or as a *lex*. *totam illam* summarizes the content of the law as outlined in the preceding subordinate clauses; its gender and number are determined by the following complements (K.-St. I 34).

civis optime de re publica meritus: i.e. Cicero. – In referring to himself by his status of *civis* (rather than by his name or in the first person), Cicero can make the action against him seem more outrageous, since it attacks a well-deserving Roman citizen. – For the claim *optime de re publica meritus*, see Cic. *RS* 16; *Dom.* 9.

nominatim: P. Clodius Pulcher's second *lex* on the matter pronounced the *interdictio* of fire and water against Cicero after he had left Rome (*Lex Clodia de exilio Ciceronis*). Clodius' first *lex* did not mention Cicero's name (*Lex Clodia de capite civis Romani*; see Introduction, section 2). – By focusing on a citizen individually, the measure disqualifies as a law in Cicero's presentation: in his interpretation, according to ancient Roman statutes, laws directed against particular individuals were not permitted; such directives would be *privilegia* (see Introduction, section 3.4).

sine iudicio: Cicero frequently criticizes that he, as a Roman citizen, was effectively condemned and sent away without even having been charged, without trial, and without due process (Cic. *Dom.* 43; 47; 88; *Sest.* 53), which goes against Roman laws and conventions according to him (Cic. *Dom.* 33; *Sest.* 73; see Introduction, section 3.4). Cicero conveniently passes over the fact that he was regarded as having allowed Roman citizens, the captured Catilinarian conspirators, to be killed without trial and this was a reason for the opposition against him and that he left Rome before the implications of the first law could be enforced.

una cum senatu: here Cicero does not state a parallel between himself and the Republic (see Introduction, section 3.4); instead, he juxtaposes himself and the Senate when he claims that the law directed against him equalled the abolishment of the powers of the Senate in the Republic. That the Senate's options for action were reduced due to the activities of his opponents during Cicero's absence is mentioned elsewhere (Cic. *RS* 18; *RQ* 14; *Sest.* 34), but this is the result of the dominance of P. Clodius Pulcher and his followers in the city and not of the stipulations in the law.

ut … iniit magistratum: i.e. when consul Lentulus entered office on 1 January 57 BCE. – From that point onwards, Cicero claims, Lentulus was even more (than as consul designate) focused on arranging Cicero's return (Cic. *RQ* 11; *Pis.* 34), emphasized by *vero* (*OLD* s.v. *uero*[1] 5).

quid omnino egit aliud nisi: the collocation seems to be only attested here: it (along with the emphasis on this phrase by *non dicam*; see Cic. *RS* 1 n.) highlights strongly that, after entering office, Lentulus' sole focus was on working towards Cicero's return.

ut … sanciret: a hyperbolic description of the importance of Cicero's rescue. By stating that the consul's actions were focused on restoring the Senate's standing, based on Cicero's salvation, Cicero makes the description appear less self-centred, in line with the previous claim that the Senate's role was affected by the activities against him. Apart from an attempt to involve the audience, these comments could be based on the view that, since in confronting the Catilinarian conspirators Cicero followed the Senate's authority, the repercussions also affect the Senate, and his return justifies the Senate's decision. – In this context

the verb has a less technical meaning (*OLD* s.v. *sancio* 4). – On the characterization of Lentulus' role in prompting the Senate decree for Cicero's return and
putting forward the proposal, see Cic. *RS* 26 n.

me conservato: Cicero applies the same verb (*servare*/*conservare*) to himself
that he uses elsewhere for his efforts with respect to the Republic and his fellow
citizens (e.g. Cic. *RS* 26; *RQ* 1; 17; 21; *Cat.* 2.14; 3.1; 3.15; 3.29; 4.18; 4.20; 4.23;
Dom. 5; 26; 72; 93–4; *Har. resp.* 58; *Mil.* 36; *Phil.* 2.2; 2.51).

9 di immortales: the only address to the gods in this speech: it highlights the
outstanding benefit of Lentulus' consulship for Cicero. The phrase is not used
as an inserted exclamation (Cic. *RQ* 4), but rather functions as a direct address
to the gods followed by verbs in the second person. Such a combination is relatively rare and only appears in Cicero's speeches from the post-exile period
onwards (Cic. *Dom.* 104; *Har. resp.* 25; *Sest.* 93; *Cael.* 59; *Phil.* 4.9; see Corbeill
2020, 28 n. 29).

beneficium: Cicero praises Lentulus' consulship by characterizing it as a
beneficium given by the gods, although the People elect the consuls and are
credited with that role (also called *beneficium*) elsewhere in Cicero's speeches
(e.g. Cic. *Leg. agr.* 2.1–7). Here the emphasis is not on the process, but rather on
the outstanding good fortune for Cicero that Lentulus is consul in that year.

videmini: 'you are seen', rather than 'you seem'.

quod: introduces a clause providing further explanation of a noun (*beneficium*) in the main clause (K.-St. II 270–1).

hoc anno: i.e. 57 BCE.

consul est: the declaration of Lentulus' being consul in the current year follows on from the steps leading up to it (activities as consul designate and entering office), described in the past tense. – Busche (1917, 1356; also Boll 2019, 124)
defends *est*, found in some manuscripts, against Peterson's conjecture (1911)
populi Romani fuit (developed from *praefuit* in other manuscripts), because the
perfect tense is not appropriate in combination with *hoc anno*, the current year.

quanto maius dedissetis: continues the address to the gods. The exclamation is not meant as criticism (i.e. because they made Lentulus consul one year
late), but rather a reflection of how Cicero's fate would have been different if
Lentulus had been consul in the preceding year and a transition to outlining the
contrast between the consuls of the current and those of the past year.

superiore anno: i.e. in 58 BCE.

medicina consulari…consulari vulnere: an explanation of the previous
exclamations, by means of a medical metaphor: if the consuls of the previous
year had not inflicted a wound on Cicero (i.e. had not permitted or contributed
to his leaving Rome), he would not have needed the medicine of this year's
consuls to heal the wound (i.e. by being recalled) (Cic. *RQ* 15). In order to put
blame on the consuls of the preceding year and to make the consuls of the
current year stand out, Cicero implies that other consuls in post in the past year

would not have colluded with P. Clodius Pulcher and thus have been able to prevent Cicero's leaving Rome. – An attributive adjective is used instead of a (subjective) genitive (K.-St. I 211; see, e.g., Cic. *RS* 17; 24).

sapientissimo homine atque optimo cive et viro: emphasizes Catulus' outstanding characteristics both as a human being and as a citizen.

Q. Catulo: Q. Lutatius Catulus (*RE* Lutatius 8; cos. 78, censor 65 BCE [*MRR* II 85, 157]; see, e.g., Nicholson 1992, 63–4; Kaster 2006, 326, on Cic. *Sest.* 101) was defeated by C. Iulius Caesar in the elections for *pontifex maximus* in 63 BCE (*MRR* II 171) and declared Cicero 'father of the fatherland' after the suppression of the Catilinarian Conspiracy in that year (Cic. *Pis.* 6; *Sest.* 121; cf. Cic. *Att.* 9.10.3; Plin. *HN* 7.117; Plut. *Cic.* 23.6). The portico built by Catulus' homonymous father (cos. 102 BCE) on the Palatine was destroyed by Clodius, like Cicero's house (Cic. *Dom.* 102; 114; 137; *Cael.* 78). In 87 BCE Catulus had followed his father's opposition against L. Cornelius Cinna and C. Marius; thus, after Cinna's victory their lives were in danger: Catulus survived, while his father did not (Schol. Bob. ad Cic. *Arch.* 6 [p. 176.24 Stangl]).

non saepe . . . fuisse: Catulus' alleged statement praises the quality of Roman consuls, asserting that it is very rare that even one of them is *improbus* and that only once both of them were. A different version of this statement is given in *De domo sua* (Cic. *Dom.* 113: *o Q. Catule! . . . tantumne te fefellit, cum mihi summa et cotidie maiora praemia in re publica fore putabas? negabas fas esse duo consules esse in hac civitate inimicos rei publicae; sunt inventi qui senatum tribuno furenti constrictum traderent, qui pro me patres conscriptos deprecari et populo supplices esse edictis atque imperio vetarent, quibus inspectantibus domus mea disturbaretur, diriperetur, qui denique ambustas fortunarum mearum reliquias suas domos comportari iuberent.*). – *improbus* is originally a moral term; it is widely used in Cicero as a description of opponents of the *res publica* and thus can be a characterization of an irresponsible consul (Opelt 1965, 159–60; Hellegouarc'h 1972, 528–30; Achard 1981, 197–8 *et al.*).

post Romam conditam: this phrase only appears in some manuscripts and is not required for the sense. It could thus be regarded as an explanatory addition that entered the text. But Cicero employs such an emphatic way of speaking elsewhere in speeches of this period (Cic. *RS* 24; *Har. resp.* 12; *Sest.* 128); therefore, the fuller version is to be preferred (Klotz 1913, 494; Boll 2019, 126).

excepto illo Cinnano tempore: an allusion to events of the 80s BCE: in 87 BCE, because of his neglect of L. Cornelius Sulla's reforms and his support of C. Marius' recall (*c.* 157–86 BCE; *RE* Marius 14 [Suppl. 6]; cos. 107, 104, 103, 102, 101, 100, 86 BCE [*MRR* I 550, 558, 562, 567, 570, 574; II 53]), the consul L. Cornelius Cinna (*RE* Cornelius 106; cos. 87, 86, 85, 84 BCE [*MRR* II 45–6, 53, 57, 60]) was expelled from Rome by his colleague Cn. Octavius (*RE* Octavius 20; cos. 87 BCE [*MRR* II 45–6]). Subsequently, when Cinna had gained Marius' support and seized control of the city, Octavius was killed in office, and Cinna and Marius took vengeance on their enemies (on Cinna, see Lovano 2002; for a brief summary of the evidence, see *MRR* II 45–6). Cicero often expresses the view that Cinna and Octavius, as well as Sulla and Marius, brought strife and bloodshed to the Republic (Cic. *Cat.* 3.24; *Har. resp.* 54; *Sest.* 77; *Vat.* 23; *Phil.* 13.1–2; 14.23; *Att.* 7.7.7; *Nat. D.* 3.81; *Tusc.* 5.54–6; *De or.* 3.8; on Cicero's views of Cinna, see Lovano 2002, 145–7). – L. Cornelius Cinna was consul in 87 BCE with Octavius, in 86 with Marius, and in 85 and 84 with Cn. Papirius Carbo (*RE* Papirius 38; cos. 85, 84 BCE [*MRR* II 57, 60]). While Marius is mentioned positively or neutrally in the speech to the People (Cic. *RQ* 9–11), the reference to him in this speech is equivocal (Cic. *RS* 38; see Cic. *RS* 38; *RQ* 7 nn.). Thus, the assessment that there were two bad consuls in Cinna's time could apply to all the years in which Cinna was consul, although 87 BCE seems to have been the most violent (Bortone 1938, 18, apparently refers the remark to the consulship of Cinna and Carbo). – As an indication of time *Cinnanum tempus* (Cic. *Dom.* 83; *Har. resp.* 18) is neutral in its phraseology, while *regnum* and *regnare* (Cic. *Har. resp.* 54; *Cat.* 3.9; *Phil.* 5.17; *Nat. D.* 3.81) as well as *dominatio* (Cic. *Att.* 8.3.6) and *dominatus* (Cic. *Phil.* 1.34) would be more obviously negative. Carney (1960, 115) notes that the frequency of such phrases indicating the time by reference to Cinna (rather than Marius) presents Cinna as the dominant force. This tendency is in line with Cicero's nuanced depiction of Marius, who may be given a positive portrayal depending on audience and context.

meam causam semper fore firmissimam: an encouraging, but vague statement attributed to Catulus: *mea causa* probably denotes Cicero's position as a result of his response to the Catilinarian Conspiracy; these actions, it is implied, would be approved by sensible consuls, so that there would not be any fear of retaliation. Boll (2019, 126) interprets the statement as an allusion to Catulus' support of Cicero's activities against the Catilinarian Conspiracy, but the phrasing is open and impersonal.

dum vel unus e re publica consul esset: Shackleton Bailey (1979, 262; 1991, 227) proposed changing the transmitted *in re publica* to *e re publica*, understood as the opposite of *improbus* (cf. Cic. *Phil.* 8.13: *bonos et utilis et e re publica civis*). Such a modification is needed if *consul* is interpreted in a neutral sense; the meaning of the clause must be that Cicero will be safe as long as there is at least one proper consul. If *consul* is taken in a qualified sense of 'a consul who is worthy of this title', as Cicero uses the term elsewhere or, rather, denies that consuls behaving inappropriately deserve that name (Cic. *RS* 4 and n.), the text makes sense as it stands (as, e.g., in Kasten's [1977, 17] translation; see Boll 2019, 126–7). Then, however, the phrase *in re publica* becomes superfluous; the transmission could have been affected by interference with the expression *in re publica* in the folllowing sentence. Thus, reading *e re publica* looks like an elegant solution.

dixerat si ... manere potuisset: the mixture of indicative and subjunctive in the counterfactual conditional construction could indicate that the verb in the fronted main clause presents a non-completed action as completed (K.-St. II 403–4;

also Pinkster 2015, 660–1): the speaking has obviously been completed, but the demonstration of the validity of the statement has not. – The current situation, when, as Cicero implies, there are two consuls who are *improbi*, is presented as unusual and as a major cause of Cicero's needing to leave Rome.

illud: is the subject of the *si*-clause and the antecedent of the *quod*-clause. Construction and context indicate that the complement is not 'that statement', but rather 'that situation'.

{de duobus consulibus}: Karsten (1879, 409) and Shackleton Bailey (1991, 227) suggest deleting this phrase, which Karsten sees as an unnecessary and weak addition. Such prepositional phrases are not unusual with noun phrases (K.-St. I 215; Pinkster 2015, 1044–5; e.g. Cic. *Verr.* 2.5.94: *illud Uticense exemplum de Hadriano*). Still, in connection with a pronoun, the construction is clumsy, and the phrase looks like an inserted explanatory gloss.

quod ante in re publica {non} fuerat: what should have continued is the earlier situation in the Republic, namely that there has always been at least one good consul. Thus, a negation, as found in most manuscripts (retained e.g. by Peterson 1911; Maslowski 1981; supported by Boll 2019, 127), would give the opposite sense. Therefore, leaving it out, as some manuscripts do (followed by Shackleton Bailey 1991, 227), is preferable. The insertion of the negation looks like an attempt to emphasize that the situation in 58 BCE is unlike anything that existed before without considering the logical sequence.

perenne ac proprium manere potuisset: two alliterative adjectives indicate the uninterrupted continuation and the defining quality of the traditional situation in the Republic (*OLD* s.v. *perennis* 2; *proprius* 3; cf. Cic. *Leg. Man.* 48). – The phrasing implies that the nature of the consuls in the preceding year has led to the interruption of the sequence of good consuls at Rome.

Q. Metellus: Q. Caecilius Metellus Nepos, one of the consuls in 57 BCE (Cic. *RS* 5 n.).

illo tempore: i.e. in the previous year, 58 BCE.

{inimicus}: is deleted by most editors, as first suggested by Halm (1856; supported by Boll 2019, 128), since the word is regarded as a gloss that entered the text, namely a comment explaining Nepos' previous attitude mentioned later (Cic. *RS* 25). Guillen (1967, 38) and Shackleton Bailey (1991, 227) retain the transmitted text. Bellardi (1975, 47) suggests adopting the reading *non inimicus* found in some manuscripts, emphasizing that, as consul, Nepos is no longer *inimicus*. Frenzel (1801, 30) mentions the text *unicus* or *unicus inimicus* in some editions (e.g. that by Ernesti, who suggests *unus* instead); he believes that *inimicus* should be deleted as a gloss and that some scribes regarded it as suspicious and hence changed it to *unicus*. If the word is kept, the reading *<etsi> inimicus* (Peterson 1911 in app.) seems most plausible: it would emphasize that even Nepos, though an enemy of Cicero, would have supported Cicero in contrast to what the actual consuls of the preceding year did. Still, such an allusion would detract from the force of the later statement about Nepos' change of mind and his development into a supporter of Cicero (Cic. *RS* 25–6), and he is introduced positively at his first mention in this speech (Cic. *RS* 5). Thus, deletion seems to be the best option.

fuerit…futurus: in a dependent counterfactual conditional construction this form fulfils the function of a pluperfect subjunctive (K.-St. I 408; also Lebreton 1901, 397–9; Pinkster 2015, 433).

me conservando: although the same phrase is applied to the initiatives of Lentulus in recalling Cicero (Cic. *RS* 8 and n.), here it refers to potential activities to prevent Cicero from being exiled (if Nepos had been consul in the preceding year) rather than to those to restore him (contrasting with *restituendo*).

auctorem…adscriptoremque: indicates Nepos' recent support for Cicero's recall, similarly stressed again later (Cic. *RS* 26 [and n.]). – The word *a(d)scriptor* is only found in Cicero (Cic. *RS* 9; 26; *Dom.* 49; *Leg. agr.* 2.22) and is likely to have been a *terminus technicus* in connection with bills (Ferrary 1996, 219–22): this is obvious in *De lege agraria*, where the word denotes the further supporters of a bill beyond the main proposer, after whom the law would be named (Cic. *Leg. agr.* 2.22: *collegas suos, ascriptores legis agrariae*). In the other instances it has sometimes been interpreted in a transferred sense, denoting a strong supporter. Ferrary argues that it should be taken in its literal sense in all cases. Here, such an interpretation would mean that the bill was proposed by Lentulus and supported by Nepos (*Lex Cornelia Caecilia de revocando Cicerone*; *LPPR*, p. 403; cf. Cass. Dio 39.8.2). Yet a more general expression of support is also possible.

videatis: again an appeal to evidence available to the audience, to corroborate Cicero's description (e.g. Cic. *RS* 6; 7).

2.2.2. Opponents: consuls of 58 BCE (10–18)

After some preparatory allusions to their predecessors, the praise of the consuls of 57 BCE in the preceding subsection (Cic. *RS* 8–9) is juxtaposed with criticism of the consuls of 58 BCE in this subsection (Cic. *RS* 10–18), an element without an equivalent in the speech before the People. Here Cicero follows Roman conventions of invective (see Introduction, section 3.2) in that he does not merely describe how L. Calpurnius Piso Caesoninus and A. Gabinius interfered with initiatives on Cicero's behalf and showed lack of support in their consular year, but also mentions details from previous periods of their lives and other characteristics, such as their physical appearance, intellectual ability, social position, way of life, or morally objectionable behaviour in their youth, to paint an overall negative portrait (e.g. Cic. *Prov. cons.* 6–16; *Sest.* 18–26; *Pis. passim*) contrasting with that of the consuls for the current year (Mack 1937, 32–4). Accordingly, the style tends to be affective, emotional, and personal, while still in line with the conventional tone of speeches in the Senate (Mack 1937, 114–23).

Cicero provides a fundamental critique of the men's ability as consuls, even denying that they could be regarded as such (Cic. *RS* 4 [and n.]; 10): he claims that they did not respect the Senate as appropriate, put their own advantage above the welfare of the Republic, and did not behave in a responsible manner (on this invective section, see Thompson 1978, 55–7; Koster 1980, 120–3; Boll 2019, 64–7). Thus, Cicero's criticism appears less like a personal vendetta and more like concern for the Republic. Such a portrait makes the activities of the successors in 57 BCE stand out as glorious examples. Moreover, the focus on the consuls' inappropriate behaviour colluding with P. Clodius Pulcher reduces the role of Cicero's questionable activity as a reason and rather presents his absence from Rome as the result of a cabal of inferior men.

Since most of the alleged misdemeanours are only known from Cicero's invective passages in this and other speeches, it is difficult to establish to what extent they might have some historical basis. References to events or appearances in public presumably have a grain of truth; specific insights Cicero claims for himself only are more likely to be inaccurate or at least exaggerated. While Piso is also ridiculed in two poems by Catullus (Catull. 28; 47), it is generally assumed that he was a responsible politician (cf. App. *B Civ.* 3.54); he became censor in 50 BCE (*MRR* II 247–8).

10 sed fuerunt ii consules: in contrast to the thought experiment of what the situation would have been like if P. Cornelius Lentulus Spinther and Q. Caecilius Metellus Nepos had been consuls a year earlier, the actual consuls of 58 BCE are presented, though they do not deserve the name of consul according to Cicero (Cic. *RS* 4 n.). This introductory statement concerning both men first illustrates their character by indicating their mental capacity and then exemplifies it by describing their inability to carry out their role as consuls and alluding to the arrangement concerning the provinces, before each of them is presented individually. – The reading *ii* (or variants) in most manuscripts stresses the character of these consuls while *duo*, found in a couple of manuscripts (favoured by Boll 2019, 129), highlights that in that year there were two bad consuls with the bad consequences implied in Q. Catulus' statement just reported (Cic. *RS* 9). The variant *ii* puts more emphasis on the 'unconsular' character of these men, which is an appropriate introduction to the invective section (for the indicative in the subsequent relative clause, see K.-St. II 298). The numeral *duo* later in the paragraph has the function of indicating that the statement refers to both men; that sentence could have influenced the text in some manuscripts here.

parvae: preferred to the alternative reading *pravae* (adopted by Peterson 1911) as it is a more appropriate element in the tricolon (Schönberger 1913, 1382; 1914, 645–6; Busche 1917, 1355; Boll 2019, 129). All three adjectives illustrate the consuls' ignobility and pusillanimousness (*OLD* s.v. *angustus* 8; *humilis* 7; *paruus* 6). – *angusta mens* and *parva mens* are not attested elsewhere in the classical period; *humilis mens* appears in the superlative form in Seneca (Sen. *Ep.* 92.26).

tenebris: *OLD* lists this passage as an example of the meaning '(fig.) Mental darkness, lack of knowledge or understanding, ignorance' (*OLD* s.v. *tenebrae* 3), with the note '(*cf.* sense 1c)', thus indicating the metaphorical quality. Boll (2019, 130) considers that *tenebrae* might refer to the consuls' moral baseness: yet a reference to character does not seem to be a common meaning of *tenebrae*. Only if *tenebris ac sordibus* is understood as a hendiadys would it be possible to see the entire expression as a description of negative character, with *tenebris* emphasizing *sordibus*. But indicating the consuls' 'mental darkness', i.e. 'ignorance', separately emphasizes their negative characteristics and balances the preceding triad of adjectives.

sordibus: indicates meanness of character and, in view of what follows, might imply greed specifically (*OLD* s.v. *sordes* 4, 5).

nec intueri nec sustinere nec capere: because of their limited intellectual and moral capacities, these consuls are said not to be able to grasp the implications of the office of consul and to display the corresponding behaviour. This is expressed by a threefold description of the consulship, in a climactic sequence from the name via the appearance to the importance of the magistracy, and a series of three matching verbs (*OLD* s.v. *intueor* 7; *sustineo* 5; *capio*[1] 15; cf. Cic. *Pis.* 24; *Phil.* 7.5).

non consules, sed: after the description of the consuls' character it is revealed in conclusion that they are not actually consuls, in the sense of having the appropriate qualifications and carrying out the office as required. This assessment is contrasted (*sed*) with what Cicero regards as their true characterization on the basis of their recent behaviour (for this structure, see Cic. *RS* 10; 13).

mercatores provinciarum: refers to the assignment of provinces to the consuls on Clodius' initiative (see Cic. *RS* 4 n.; Introduction, section 2). Cicero frequently criticizes the arrangement as a 'sale' or 'deal' in which the consuls give away elements of a functioning Republic and features of worthy citizens for their personal advantage. The metaphorical use of *mercatores* (Cic. *RQ* 21; *Fam.* 1.9.13 [Dec. 54 BCE]) vividly expresses this criticism (on the metaphor, see Opelt 1965, 146; Fantham 1972, 120, 122–3, who describes it as an abusive metaphor deriving from comedy).

venditores vestrae dignitatis: engaging the audience, Cicero presents their position as affected by the consuls' machinations (cf. Cic. *Sest.* 17). As the consular provinces were distributed according to a law proposed by P. Clodius Pulcher as Tribune of the People, the Senate was debarred from its right to assign them according to the *Lex Sempronia de provinciis consularibus* (*LPRR*, p. 311 [i.e. Senate assigns provinces before election of consuls, with no intercession allowed]; cf. Cic. *Dom.* 24; *Vat.* 36), though this law was not observed on other occasions in the late Republic either (Balsdon 1939, 182, with n. 82).

quorum alter...alter: A. Gabinius and L. Calpurnius Piso respectively (Cic. *Dom.* 62).

a me Catilinam...reposcebat: one manuscript omits the preposition *a*, which results in a grammatically equally possible, but potentially ambiguous double accusative (K.-St. I 300 [noting the variant readings]; Pinkster 2015, 164–7 [on the double accusative]). Therefore, the reading *a me*, transmitted in the other sources, is preferable (Maslowski 1980, 406–7; Boll 2019, 130).

Catilinam, amatorem suum: L. Sergius Catilina (*RE* Sergius 23; praet. 68, propraet. in Africa 67 BCE [*MRR* II 138, 147]), after an early military career, was praetor in 68 BCE and afterwards propraetor in Africa. Upon return from the province he intended to stand in the second elections for the consulship of 65 BCE, but his candidacy was not approved. He was not able to stand for the consulship of 64 BCE because of an impending trial for misconduct as provincial governor (*TLLR* 212), but competed in the elections for 63 BCE, when Cicero and C. Antonius Hybrida were elected. In Cicero's consular year Catiline stood again unsuccessfully for the consulship of 62 BCE. He then launched the so-called Catilinarian Conspiracy, which was confronted by activities led by Cicero; some conspirators were captured and put to death; Catiline was killed in battle in early 62 BCE. – Cicero repeatedly alludes to and alleges an amorous relationship between Catiline and Gabinius (Cic. *RS* 12; *Pis.* 20; *Dom.* 62; *Planc.* 87; on Gabinius' sexual activities in his youth, see Cic. *RS* 11 and n.).

multis audientibus: the vague reference to witnesses of the requests by these men is meant to give the allegations force and reliability. That these witnesses are not identified and there is no direct link to the experiences of the audience might suggest that there is no easily demonstrable evidence.

Cethegum consobrinum: C. Cornelius Cethegus (*RE* Cornelius 89; *MRR* II 489), a cousin of the consul L. Calpurnius Piso Caesoninus (Cic. *Dom.* 62), was a senator in 63 BCE and one of the Catilinarian conspirators (Sall. *Cat.* 17.4). He was among those who were captured and put to death by the consul Cicero after the Senate had decreed the death penalty for these men (Sall. *Cat.* 55.6; 57.1). Initially, Cethegus had urged the conspirators to take action and not to delay their plans (Sall. *Cat.* 43.3), in line with his character (Sall. *Cat.* 43.4).

duo: resumes the discussion of both men in parallel, after the distributive *quorum alter...alter.*

sceleratissimi: alludes to the potential simultaneous existence of two consuls who are *improbi*, with reference to Catulus' statement (Cic. *RS* 9), although the comment is immediately qualified by the assertion that these men are not really consuls, which gives the statement an even wider application. As a political term of abuse, *sceleratus* denotes an opponent of the *res publica*; in line with the original meaning, the word's connotations suggest a criminal (Opelt 1965, 160). This characteristic is applied to these consuls elsewhere (Cic. *Dom.* 58; 122) as well as to each of them individually (Cic. *Pis.* 28; 74; 89).

post hominum memoriam: generic *hominum* indicates that this phrase denotes all human memory or history. Elsewhere in these speeches complements limit the period to 'living memory' (Cic. *RS* 31: *nostra memoria*; 38: *hac hominum memoria*; *RQ* 7: *hac vestra patrumque memoria*).

non consules sed latrones: repeats in stronger form the preceding juxtaposition *non consules, sed mercatores provinciarum ac venditores vestrae dignitatis*, building on the claim that these men do not deserve the name of consul (Cic. *RS* 4 and n.). While *latro* is a term of abuse for political opponents (Cic. *RS* 13 n.), here (in connection with *mercatores*) the connotation of 'robber, plunderer' is also active (*OLD* s.v. *latro²* 2).

deseruerunt...prodiderunt, oppugnarunt: a climactic tricolon indicating increasingly active opposition to Cicero's case on the part of the consuls; the object (*me*) is fronted, separated from the verbs, for emphasis (cf. Cic. *RS* 32; *Har. resp.* 3). – The notion that people desert and/or oppose Cicero, not linked to these consuls (Cic. *RQ* 13; *Dom.* 2), and with reference to magistrates more widely (Cic. *RS* 33), appears elsewhere in speeches connected with Cicero's return.

in causa praesertim publica et consulari: implies that it would have been the consuls' duty to take care of Cicero's case in the public interest (Cic. *Pis.* 19: *cum enim esset omnis causa illa mea consularis et senatoria, auxilio mihi opus fuerat et consulis et senatus*). By presenting his situation as an issue of general political significance (i.e. because of his initiatives for the Republic, especially during his consulship), Cicero can claim that the consuls (like the Senate) would have been obliged to support him.

omni auxilio non solum suo sed etiam vestro ceterorumque ordinum: apart from the fact that the consuls were not supportive, they were keen to see the activities of others prevented. The consuls did not enable a discussion and resolution in the Senate. Therefore, no positive decree of the Senate was presented to the rest of the population, and no bill on which the public could have voted was proposed. The law including the ban on formal discussions of Cicero's case was put forward by P. Clodius Pulcher, not by the consuls (Cic. *RS* 8 n.), but the consuls claimed to adhere to it and thus rejected calls by Senate to raise this issue (Cic. *RS* 4). – By this phrasing Cicero presupposes that the other groups, given the chance, would have supported him.

11 quorum alter: i.e. A. Gabinius. – The initial comment on each of the consuls (Cic. *RS* 10: *quorum alter...alter*) is a brief negative remark on their relationships, followed by another statement on the behaviour of both of them (*duo*) in Cicero's case (Cic. *RS* 10). The individual presentation is now resumed with more detailed portrayals (another *alter* follows at Cic. *RS* 13).

tamen...fefellit: Cicero claims that the consuls' lack of support was not a surprise in the case of Gabinius, because in view of his behaviour up to this point it was obvious to everyone that nothing good (i.e. activities supporting the Republic in Cicero's sense) could be expected of him (Cic. *Sest.* 20: *atque eorum alter fefellit neminem. quis enim clavum tanti imperi tenere et gubernacula* *rei publicae tractare in maximo cursu ac fluctibus posse arbitraretur hominem emersum subito ex diuturnis tenebris lustrorum ac stuprorum, vino, ganeis, lenociniis adulteriisque confectum? cum is praeter spem in altissimo gradu alienis opibus positus esset, qui non modo tempestatem impendentem intueri temulentus, sed ne lucem quidem insolitam aspicere posset.*). As for Piso, only Cicero claims to have realized his true character at an early stage (Cic. *RS* 15). – Although Cicero here conveys the view that Gabinius could never be expected to do anything good, in 67 BCE Cicero approved of the bill Gabinius put forward as Tribune of the People granting Cn. Pompeius Magnus a special command to fight the pirates (Boll 2019, 133).

ullam ullius boni spem haberet: for *bonum* as a noun (*OLD* s.v. *bonum* 2) in a political context, see, e.g., Cic. *Sest.* 24: *statuebam sic, boni nihil ab illis nugis exspectandum, mali quidem certe nihil pertimescendum.* – The collocation *ullam ullius* emphasizes that there was no hope at all. – The question is expressed by a potential subjunctive referring to the past (K.-St. I 179; Pinkster 2015, 487–8).

cuius … qui … qui … qui … quo: an effective series of anaphoric and asyndetic clauses describing aspects of Gabinius' immoral and irresponsible behaviour. The sequence provides a brief overview of Gabinius' life by highlighting selectively details from his youth, his tribunate, and his consulship (typical of invective).

primum tempus aetatis … divulgatum: Cicero repeatedly raises the allegation of promiscuous sexual behaviour in Gabinius' youth (Cic. *Dom.* 126; *Sest.* 18; cf. Schol. Bob. ad Cic. *Sest.* 18 [p. 128.4–5 Stangl]). In addition, he highlights a particular relationship with Catiline (Cic. *RS* 10; 12 and nn.). – *primum tempus aetatis* does not denote the first few years of one's life, but rather the initial period of pursuing specific activities in one's youth (Boll 2019, 133). Still, the emphasis is on engaging in such behaviour at a young age (Cic. *Dom.* 126: *Gabinio…, cuius impudicitiam pueritiae, libidines adulescentiae…*).

ne a sanctissima quidem parte corporis: a paraphrase for the mouth with reference to oral sex acts (Adams 1982, 211–12 with n. 1), which makes the behaviour appear even more horrendous (for the phrase, see Lactant. *Div. inst.* 5.9.17: *qui denique inmemores quid nati sint, cum feminis patientia certent, qui sanctissimam quoque corporis sui partem contra fas omne pollutant ac profanent, qui virilia sua ferro metant et, quod est sceleratius, ut sint religionis antistites, …*).

confecisset: describes Gabinius as irresponsibly wasteful with regard to both private and public funds, after reaching political offices (Cic. *Sest.* 26; *OLD* s.v. *conficio* 15).

domestico lenocinio: insinuates that, after having squandered his fortune, Gabinius was only able to earn enough money for his way of life by keeping a brothel in his house (Cic. *RS* 12; for the phrase, see Cic. *Verr.* 2.3.6). – According to Cicero's comments in *Pro Sestio*, Gabinius had a lascivious sex life in his youth, was later bankrupt (Cic. *Sest*. 18), and went bankrupt while or although he was active as a prostitute (Cic. *Sest*. 26, depending on the constitution of the Latin text). – The slightly paradoxical collocation *egestatem et luxuriem* (see *egestate et improbitate coactus* below), denoting the simultaneous presence of two contrasting features, indicates that, after having lost his fortune, Gabinius remained poor while he earned money in a disreputable way to be spent immediately on a decadent lifestyle. Since *luxuria/luxuries* can mean not only 'luxury' (*OLD* s.v. *luxuria* 3), but also 'unruly or wilful behaviour', including 'disregard for moral restraint, licentiousness' (*OLD* s.v. *luxuria* 2), the phrasing implies that the money is required to satisfy Gabinius' lascivious and extravagant way of life. It is not necessary to assume two different meanings for *sustentare* and understand *sustentare egestatem* as 'to delay poverty' (thus Boll 2019, 135); in both collocations the notion of 'support' is appropriate (*OLD* s.v. *sustento* 3).

in aram tribunatus: Gabinius was Tribune of the People in 67 BCE (*MRR* II 144–5) and thus benefited from the sacrosanctity of Tribunes of the People during their year of office (Kunkel/Wittmann 1995, 572–3). To indicate Gabinius' desperate situation, Cicero describes Gabinius starting the tenure of the tribunate by a metaphor typically applied to suppliants taking refuge at altars (with a different metaphor at *Sest*. 18: *in tribunatus portum perfugerat*; see also Fantham 1972, 124; for similar metaphors, see Cic. *Q Rosc*. 30; *Verr*. 2.2.8; 2.5.126).

confugisset … effugere potuisset: the phrasing (with different compounds of the same simple verb) highlights that for Gabinius assuming the tribunate was a flight from pressing debt (Cic. *Sest*. 28).

neque … potuisset: the three-part polysyndetic list indicates different aspects of threats faced by debtors, thus emphasizing Gabinius' destitute situation and the salvation provided by the tribunate.

vim praetoris: the remit of praetors covered juridical functions (Kunkel/Wittmann 1995, 326–9), including the chairing of disputes between parties in civil cases and decisions on the transfer of property. Prodigals could be assigned a *curator* by a praetor to look after their property (Kaser 1955, 315).

multitudinem creditorum: the assertion of the existence of a large number of creditors (without any evidence) suggests a huge amount of debt and the near-impossibilty of avoiding these obligations without the respite provided by the tribunate.

bonorum proscriptionem: an announcement of the (enforced) sale of the possessions of a person in debt (*OLD* s.v. *proscriptio* 1; cf. Cic. *Quinct*. 56; for details of the procedure, see Gai. *Inst*. 3.79).

quo in magistratu: as Tribune of the People in 67 BCE, Gabinius put forward a bill (*rogatio*) for an extraordinary command for Cn. Pompeius Magnus (Cic. *RS* 4 n.) to fight the pirates (*Lex Gabinia de bello piratico*: *LPPR*, pp. 371–2), which was passed despite initial opposition from the Senate (Cass. Dio 36.23–37; Plut. *Pomp*. 25–6). While Cicero praises Gabinius' initiative in the earlier speech on Cn. Pompeius Magnus in the context of its argument (Cic. *Leg. Man.* 57–8), here he does not acknowledge that Gabinius' law meant that the situation created by the pirates could eventually be addressed effectively; instead, he exploits the initiative to assimilate Gabinius to the pirates with respect to his character and behaviour. – Peterson (1911), Bellardi (1975, 48), and Boll (2019, 135–6) prefer the reading *qui* of the main manuscripts, which Bellardi and Boll see in line with the anaphoric repetition of *qui* in this sentence. Yet the relative clause provides further information about Gabinius' activities as Tribune of the People (the sequence continues with *quo inspectante* afterwards); and defining the magistracy clarifies that Gabinius' role as Tribune of the People is discussed, while *in magistratu* on its own would lack a point of reference.

piratico bello: before Cn. Pompeius Magnus intervened successfully, the Romans had been fighting against pirates for some time (e.g. Cic. *Leg. Man.* 54–5; on the pirates' activities and Roman responses, see, e.g., *CAH* IX² 243, 244, 248–50; Pohl 1993).

egestate et improbitate coactus: emphasizes again that Gabinius was bankrupt and would not have had any scruples about earning money even by dishonourable means like piracy (see *egestatem et luxuriem domestico lenocinio sustentavit* above; Cic. *Pis.* 12). The phrase is a slight zeugma: Gabinius might be forced by poverty to look for disreputable ways of earning money, while he would be prompted, rather than literally forced, by his shamelessness to consider such ways of making money.

piraticam ipse fecisset: an unfounded and illogical conclusion, to increase the criticism of Gabinius' character and deflect from a potentially useful measure: if Gabinius had not been instrumental in organizing the fight against the pirates, he would have had to become a pirate out of financial necessity. – The phrase presents piracy as a kind of occupation (*OLD* s.v. *facio* 23). Because of the similarity to phrases in comedy (e.g. Plaut. *Curc.* 160: *viden ut anus tremula medicinam facit?*; *Epid.* 581: *ego lenocinium facio…?*), Fantham (1972, 124) detects a comic flavour; indeed, the chosen wording might enhance the ridiculous dimension of envisaging Gabinius engaged in such an occupation.

quam quo{d}: Garatoni's conjecture (adopted e.g. by Maslowski 1981) provides a smooth continuation of the comparison *minore…cum…detrimento*, with a phrase short for *quam cum eo detrimento quo*: Gabinius would have caused less damage to the Republic as a pirate than he caused as a magistrate in Rome. Boll (2019, 136–7) argues for keeping the transmitted text (as Peterson 1911), which results in a complex construction.

intra moenia…versatus est: Gabinius is defined as a *hostis*, a public enemy, inside the city walls (while not officially classified as such) and a brigand (on Cicero's use of *praedo* for political opponents, see Opelt 1965, 133–4; Achard 1981, 329; for the collocation *hostis praedoque*, see Cic. *Verr.* 2.2.17; 2.4.75; see also Opelt 1965, 130). This description characterizes Gabinius as a kind of 'domestic pirate' causing even more damage by directly affecting the city of

Rome. While *praedo* can serve as a term of abuse against political opponents, its primary meaning agrees with the context in which Gabinius is described as being in need of money and willing to acquire funds by any means. Opelt (1965, 130) refers the description *nefarius hostis praedoque* to Gabinius' plundering of the province, but the context indicates activities within the city.

quo...voluerunt: after the description of Gabinius' behaviour as Tribune of the People, this clause continues the sequence with a switch to the consulship. The transition is not made explicit; it can be inferred from the fact that Gabinius now watches someone else as Tribune of the People push through a bill, and the summary of the bill's content identifies the situation for a contemporary audience. The first item mentioned concerning the consulship is an incident when Gabinius did not behave as he should have according to Cicero by letting the Tribune of the People carry on; this is followed by situations in which he is said to have actively done something damaging (Cic. *RS* 12).

inspectante ac sedente: may sound like a neutral description, but implies strong criticism of the fact that Gabinius, as consul, remained passive and did not intervene to stop the activities of the Tribune of the People P. Clodius Pulcher; if they happen in his presence and under his eyes, this passivity amounts to approval (Cic. *Sest.* 33; *Pis.* 9; *Vat.* 18; more active collaboration at Cic. *Sest.* 55: *nam latae quidem sunt consulibus illis—tacentibus dicam? immo vero etiam adprobantibus*).

legem tribunus plebis tulit: one of the bills put forward by P. Clodius Pulcher, Tribune of the People in 58 BCE (again not named: Cic. *RS* 3 n.), was *Lex Clodia de iure et tempore legum rogandarum* (*LPPR*, p. 397): it was put up for voting on 4 January 58 BCE (Cic. *Pis.* 9–10) and seems to have covered rules for holding *comitia* and the role of *obnuntatio* and *intercessio.* – The corresponding speech to the People does not have a detailed discussion of these laws: Driediger-Murphy (2019, 33–4) notes that augury is mainly mentioned in Cicero's senatorial speeches and thus before an audience familiar with it. In addition, procedural details of the lawmaking process might be deemed not of interest to the People.

ne...ne...ne...ut...ne valeret: the series of *ne*/*ut*-clauses mentions aspects of the law- and decision-making process, which, according to Cicero, Clodius' law intended to abolish, while they had been guaranteed by *Lex Aelia et Fufia* (for a similar list, see Cic. *Sest.* 33: *isdemque consulibus sedentibus atque inspectantibus lata lex est, ne auspicia valerent, ne quis obnuntiaret, ne quis legi intercederet, ut omnibus fastis diebus legem ferri liceret, ut lex Aelia, lex Fufia ne valeret: qua una rogatione quis est qui non intellegat universam rem publicam esse deletam?*).

auspiciis: *auspicia* (*OLD* s.v. *auspicium* 1 'Augury from the behaviour of birds, auspices') were required, for instance, at the appointment of magistrates or decisions of the assembly of the People; thus, negative auspices could invalidate or delay political decisions (on definition, types, and the role of *auspicia*, see Mommsen, *StR* I 76–116; Wissowa 1912, 527–34; on types of 'sky-watching' [with references], see Driediger-Murphy 2019, 133–7).

obnuntiare: *obnuntiatio* is the right of magistrates to block legislative or electoral action in assemblies by announcing that they would observe the heavens, as this could potentially result in adverse omens; if the assembly was still held as planned, the outcome of the observations had to be reported at the start. *obnuntiatio* could, therefore, be used as a political tool to stop or vitiate ongoing decision-making processes (see, e.g., De Libero 1992, 56–68; Tatum 1999, 125–33).

concilio aut comitiis: occasions at which proceedings might be blocked by *obnuntiatio*: *concilium* is a broader and more general term, also used outside the political sphere; it denotes a public meeting at which deliberation and in addition voting may take place (*OLD* s.v. *concilium* 1; cf. Gell. *NA* 15.27.4). *comitia* encompasses different types of formal voting assemblies (see, e.g., Mommsen, *StR* III 149, with n. 1; Botsford 1909, 119–38; Cic. *RS* 17; 27 nn.). – The words are datives dependent on *obnuntiare* (*OLD* s.v. *obnuntio* 2b; cf. Cic. *Sest.* 79: *obnuntiavit consuli*), indicating the the entities affected by the announcement.

legi intercedere: on the right of intercession, including opposition to bills, see Cic. *RS* 3 n.

ut…ne: this negation (in contrast to simple *ne* in the preceding clauses) occurs particularly in solemn phrases and laws in Cicero's writings (K.-St. II 209). This tendency may be the reason why it is chosen in connection with the mention of specific laws.

lex Aelia et Fufia: probably two different laws (esp. Cic. *Har. resp.* 58), though mostly mentioned together (Cic. *Har. resp.* 58; *Sest.* 33; 56; 114; *Vat.* 5; 18; 23; 37; *Prov. cons.* 46; *Pis.* 9–10; Cic. *Att.* 1.16.13; 2.9.1; 4.16.5; Schol. Bob. ad Cic. *Vat.* 23 [p. 148.10–12 Stangl]; Ascon. ad Cic. *Pis.* 9 [p. 8.17–22 C.]; Cass. Dio 38.13.3–6). These laws were apparently introduced in the second century BCE, though the exact date is uncertain; their authors are also unknown (*Lex Aelia* and *Lex Fufia de modo legum ferendarum*: *LPPR*, pp. 288–9; dated to *c.* 158 BCE; cf. Cic. *Pis.* 10; *Vat.* 23). The precise nature of these laws (dealing with *obnuntiatio* and the timing of assemblies) and of P. Clodius Pulcher's legislative intervention in relation to them is not clear, as the character of the evidence, mostly references in Cicero's speeches and their commentators, makes unequivocal conclusions difficult (see *MRR* I 452–3; Mommsen, *StR* I 111–12, with n. 4; Balsdon 1957, 15–16; Sumner 1963; Astin 1964; Weinrib 1970; Mitchell 1986; Benner 1987, 52; De Libero 1992, 65–8; Fezzi 1995 [with bibliography and overview of the primary sources]; Tatum 1999, 125–33; Kunkel/Wittmann 1995, 622–3; Riggsby 2002, 187; Elster 2003, 401–5 [with further references]; Kaster 2006, 194–6, on Cic. *Sest.* 33; Boll 2019, 138–9). – Cicero criticizes the fact that one of Clodius' bills intended the abolishment of *Lex Aelia et Fufia*; he regards this as a violation of tradition and the fundamentals of the Republic. Some of the elements of

Lex Aelia et Fufia were still in force later. Thus, if it was not simply ignored, Clodius' bill probably aimed at a (potentially sensible) modification of procedures regulated by these laws (perhaps including the introduction of the requirement to carry out *obnuntiatio* by an announcement of the observations in person: Mitchell 1986; Tatum 1999, 131–2) rather than an abolishment, while Cicero presents any modification of these traditional laws as an 'abolishment' in line with the exaggerated depiction of Clodius' actions.

quae: refers to *lex Aelia et Fufia* and grammatically agrees with the complement *subsidia* (K.-St. I 37). In references to these laws the noun *lex* is usually given once, in the singular, and governs both *Aelia et Fufia*; in *Pro Sestio* (*Sest.* 33), where Cicero aims to imitate formal legalistic language, the phrase is *lex Aelia, lex Fufia* (Pinkster 2015, 1277). *Lex Aelia et Fufia*, covering more than one regulation, can be taken up by words in the plural (Cic. *Pis.* 10; *Vat.* 18; Ascon. ad Cic. *Pis.* 9 [p. 8.19 C.]).

nostri maiores: reminders of wise measures introduced by the ancestors, which should, therefore, not be changed, constitute a frequent type of argument in Cicero's speeches, capitalizing on the Roman system of values (Roloff 1938).

contra tribunicios furores: P. Clodius Pulcher's measures are presented as outrageous because they are said to abolish regulations introduced to safeguard the Republic against interventions of Tribunes of the People (described from the perspective of the Senate). Such a comment (cf. Cic. *Vat.* 18: *lex Aelia et Fufia, quae leges saepe numero tribunicios furores debilitarunt et represserunt*) implies that there might be good reasons why Clodius, as Tribune of the People, intended to abolish or modify these laws. While Clodius' measures might have limited tribunician activity, they would also curb the opportunities of other magistrates to block tribunician plans and of Tribunes to act against each other. – Kunkel/Wittmann (1995, 625–6) assume that *Lex Aelia et Fufia* gave the Tribunes of the People control over *obnuntiatio*, at least over the decision whether any observations were sufficient grounds for *obnuntiatio*: then Cicero's characterization of these laws would be odd. Weinrib (1970, esp. 404–5) argues that the laws enabled Tribunes of the People to exercise *obnuntiatio* against each other and were, therefore, seen as a way of curbing tribunician activity; accordingly, Weinrib (1970, 405–6) believes: 'By repealing the *leges Aelia et Fufia* Clodius was safeguarding himself against the possibility of interference by his colleagues. In so doing he was subverting a long-standing weapon against demagogic activity.'

12 idemque postea: introduces the second item to be criticized from A. Gabinius' consulship (response to reactions to the publication of the bill on punishment of Roman citizens in spring 58 BCE). It suggests a vague chronological sequence after the first item mentioned, dating to a point early in Gabinius' consulship (Cic. *RS* 11: inaction in relation to bills promulgated by

P. Clodius Pulcher at the start of his term of office). Subsequent points have no further chronological markers; they are all connected with Cicero's situation, which develops from the bill underlying the description here (Cic. *RS* 12–13).

idemque: still the consul A. Gabinius. – The word is the fronted subject of the exclamation forming the main clause after the two inserted *cum*-clauses (in which he is referred to by *ad eum* and *ad lenonis impudicissimi pedes*).

cum ... venisset: a large number of people (Cic. *RQ* 8; Plut. *Cic.* 31.1: 20,000), including the senators, changed into mourning clothes (*OLD* s.v. *sordidatus* b; cf. Cic. *RS* 37), in support of Cicero (who had done the same), apparently soon after the first bill (indirectly) targeting Cicero was published in spring 58 BCE (Cic. *RS* 16; *Dom.* 55; 99; *Sest.* 26–7; 32; 53; *Pis.* 17–18; *Planc.* 87; Cass. Dio 38.16.3; see Introduction, section 2).

bonorum: as often in Cicero, the term has a political sense and denotes responsible citizens supporting the Republic in his view (e.g. Hellegouarc'h 1972, 484–95; Achard 1981, 60–1; on the word in contrast to *audaces*, see Wirszubski 1961; on *boni*, see also MacKendrick 1995, 130, 143). In the speeches given after his return the term denotes people supporting Cicero and sharing his views of the Republic (Cic. *RS* 12; 33; 34; *RQ* 11; 13; *Dom.* 99; *Sest.* 26; 27).

de Capitolio: the description of what must be the same situation in *Pro Sestio* suggests that people came down from the Capitol to the Temple of Concord at the foot of the Capitoline Hill, where a meeting of the Senate was taking place (Cic. *Sest.* 26: *hic subito cum incredibilis in Capitolium multitudo ex tota urbe cunctaque Italia convenisset, vestem mutandam omnes meque iam omni ratione, privato consilio, quoniam publicis ducibus res publica careret, defendendum putarunt. erat eodem tempore senatus in aede Concordiae, quod ipsum templum repraesentabat memoriam consulatus mei, cum flens universus ordo cincinnatum consulem orabat; nam alter ille horridus et severus consulto se domi continebat.*).

supplex ... sordidata: these adjectives agree with *multitudo* and refer to the people forming the *multitudo*.

ad eum: the same passage in *Pro Sestio* (Cic. *Sest.* 26) reveals that, of the two consuls, only A. Gabinius was visible in public at the time (Cic. *Sest.* 26).

adulescentes nobilissimi cunctique equites Romani: singled out to increase the contrast between the *leno impudicissimus* and the people throwing themselves at his feet. – To increase the weight of these (presumably two distinct) groups, in the case of the young men their social status (members of the nobility) is highlighted, and in that of the knights their large number (literally 'all' is probably an exaggeration).

cunctique equites Romani: in *Pro Sestio* it is implied that the pleading took place in the Senate (Cic. *Sest.* 26), though Cassius Dio says that the consuls did not grant the knights access to the Senate to make an appeal (Cass. Dio 38.16.2–4).

lenonis impudicissimi: i.e. the consul A. Gabinius, described in abusive terms rather than by his function (on this allegation, see Cic. *RS* 10; 11 and nn.).

abiecissent: while the description of Gabinius is similar to that in *Pro Sestio* (Cic. *Sest.* 26: *ad pedes lenonis impurissimi*), the verb there is *proiecistis* (*OLD* s.v. *proicio* 5b '(refl. or pass.) to prostrate oneself (in submission, etc.)'). *abiecissent* (*OLD* s.v. *abicio* 3b '(w. *ad pedes* and sim.) to throw oneself at the feet of') is frequent in combination with *pedes* (e.g. Cic. *Sest.* 74) and expresses a notion of even greater submissiveness.

cincinnatus ganeo: *ganeo* (*OLD* s.v. *ganeo* 'A glutton, debauchee') is another term of abuse suggesting immoderation and wastefulness (Opelt 1965, 157; see, e.g., Naev. *Com.* 118 R.$^{2-3}$; Ter. *Haut.* 1033–4; Varro, *Men.* 315 B.; Cic. *Cat.* 2.7; *Sest.* 111; *Pis.* F 18; Sall. *Cat.* 14.2). *cincinnatus* (*OLD* s.v. *cincinnatus* 1 'Having the hair curled or in ringlets (esp. by artificial means)') insinuates an effeminate appearance (e.g. Cic. *Sest.* 26; *Pis.* 25; Plaut. *Mil.* 923–4; *Truc.* 609–11, Quint. *Inst.* 1.5.61). – On the characteristics of what was regarded and presented as effeminate appearance and behaviour, the implications and consequences in Republican Roman society, and the uses in invective, see, e.g., H. Herter, s.v. Effeminatus, *RAC* 4, 1959, 618–50; Edwards 1993, 63–97; Corbeill 1996, 128–73; 1997; 2002, 209.

civium lacrimas…patriae preces: when Cicero equates the citizens' concerns and interventions on his behalf with the wishes of the *patria*, he gives his case broader relevance: such a status justifies the large-scale participation and makes Gabinius' ignoring the entreaties appear even more unacceptable. – *patria* is semi-personified; this term (rather than, e.g., *res publica*) gives the statement a more emotional flavour (Cic. *RS* 1 n.).

neque…sed etiam: in the sequence *non* (here *neque*)…*sed etiam* the negation logically has the force of *non modo non* (K.-St. II 66).

eo: i.e. Gabinius' actions described in the previous sentence.

in contionem escendit: both *OLD* (s.v. *escendo* 1b) and *TLL* (V.2.857.24–37, s.v. *escendo*) list *escendo in rostra, tribunal vel sim.* as an idiom, but in almost all cases given in *TLL* the textual transmission is divided in a similar way as it is here (between *escendere* and *ascendere*). Most modern editors opt for *escendit*, though Klotz (1915, ed.; 1919) and Wuilleumier (1952, 50) print *ascendit*, and Busche (1917, 1355) and Boll (2019, 142) support this version. *escendere* probably has the added connotation of 'come forward' (and not only describes 'climb'), which is appropriate for the preparations for a public speech (in contrast to climbing the tribunal). Here the verb is applied in a transferred sense, as it is not combined with scaling a physical structure. The collocation *in contionem e-/ascendere* occurs elsewhere in Cicero, also with divided transmission (Cic. *Att.* 4.2.3; *Q Fr.* 1.2.15; *Fin.* 2.74).

contionem: the consul A. Gabinius not only rejected pleas of knights and senators, but also delivered a *contio* (Pina Polo 1989, 298, App. A, no. 293; Hiebel 2009, 449) in which he threatened punishments for the knights (Cic. *RS*

32; *Sest.* 28; *Dom.* 55; *Planc.* 87). Lintott (2008, 177) seems to refer this threat to the other consul, L. Calpurnius Piso Caesoninus, but the context indicates its attribution to A. Gabinius.

eaque: looks forward to the *quae*-clause and the subsequent accusative and infinitive construction.

dixit quae…dicere non esset ausus: Cicero defines what Gabinius said as something that Catiline would not have dared to say if he had come back to life (Cic. *Sest.* 28). With Catiline presented as the arch-villain and the enemy of the Republic par excellence, this comparison expresses vividly that what Gabinius said was extremely appalling. The content reproduced here matches what Cicero states about the speech elsewhere (Cic. *RS* 32; *Sest.* 28; *Dom.* 55). Whether Gabinius actually said this cannot be confirmed from other sources (Boll 2019, 219); while Cicero is likely to have sharpened what Gabinius allegedly said, it is unlikely that he completely invented such a comment, talking about it in a public speech given not long after the incident mentioned.

eius vir Catilina: the illustration of the outrageous nature of Gabinius' comment is combined with another element of invective. The (unnecessary) description of Catiline as Gabinius' *vir* does not imply a kind of 'marriage' between the two men but rather indicates their alleged homosexual relationship (Cic. *RS* 10 n.).

Nonarum Decembrium, quae me consule fuissent, clivique Capitolini: the genitives are dependent on *poenas* and indicate the issue for which punishment is sought, identified by the time and the location of the activity (Cic. *RS* 32; *Sest.* 28). The date is the Nones of December in Cicero's consulship, i.e. 5 December 63 BCE, the day on which the fate of the captured Catilinarian conspirators was decreed at a meeting of the Senate in the Temple of Concordia (Cic. *Cat.* 4; Sall. *Cat.* 50.3–53.1) and their execution was then organized by Cicero (Sall. *Cat.* 55). Elsewhere Cicero presents it as a great day (e.g. Cic. *Flacc.* 102: *o Nonae illae Decembres quae me consule fuistis! quem ego diem vere natalem huius urbis aut certe salutarem appellare possum.*). On that day knights in arms were positioned on the slope leading up to the Capitol (Cic. *Att.* 2.1.7; *Phil.* 2.16; 2.19; Sall. *Cat.* 49.4; 50.3; Suet. *Iul.* 14.2; Cass. Dio 37.35.3).

neque solum id dixit, sed: adds another item Gabinius mentioned at that *contio* (on the collocation *non solum…sed*, see K.-St. II 60): the general threat is followed by the announcement of actions against individual knights (Cic. *RS* 32).

quos ei commodum fuit: the infinitive *compellare* (*OLD* s.v. *compello*² 3b) has to be supplied from the main clause. – Such a criterion for launching accusations presents the measure as arbitrary.

Lucium…Lamiam: the knight L. Aelius Lamia (*RE* Aelius 75; aed. 45 [*MRR* II 307], praet. 42 BCE? [*MRR* II 359]; see Nicholson 1992, 77–8) was relegated from Rome in 58 BCE (Cic. *RS* 32; *Sest.* 29; *Pis.* 23; 64; *Fam.* 11.16.2; 12.29.1; Ascon. ad Cic. *Pis.* 23 [p. 9 C.]; Schol. Bob. ad Cic. *Planc.* 87 [p. 168.13–14

Stangl]; Cass. Dio 38.16.4; on actions against knights, see Cic. *RS* 32 n.). Lamia was back in Rome by February 54 BCE (Cic. *Q Fr.* 2.12(11).2). – Relegation of Roman citizens without a link to criminal trials was unprecedented (Cic. *Fam.* 11.16.2: *a Gabinio consule relegatus est, quod ante id tempus civi Romano Romae contigit nemini.*; Mommsen, *StR* I 155 with n. 6).

equitem Romanum . . . amicissimum: Cicero highlights Lamia's social standing and his good character, demonstrated by his support for Cicero and the Republic. Elsewhere Lamia is described as the leader of the equestrian order (Cic. *Fam.* 11.16.2: *nam Clodianis temporibus, cum equestris ordinis principes esset proque mea salute acerrime propugnaret*), which might be alluded to in *praestanti dignitate*. – *amicissimum* has different nuances with respect to Cicero and to the Republic (*OLD* s.v. *amicus*[1] 2a), which are again put in parallel (see Introduction, section 3.4).

pro familiaritate: for friendly relations between Cicero's and Lamia's families, see Cic. *Q Fr.* 2.3.7; *Att.* 5.8.2–3; 11.7.2.

rei publicae pro fortunis suis amicissimum: the qualification *pro fortunis suis* (balancing *pro familiaritate* in relation to Cicero) indicates that Lamia provides as much support as can be expected in relation to his social status (*OLD* s.v. *fortuna* 11b; *pro*[1] 16b). The collocation *pro fortunis suis* does not seem to be attested elsewhere in classical Latin.

consul imperiosus: the attribute (*OLD* s.v. *imperiosus* 2), in combination with *iussit*, asserts that this consul acts like a dictator and thus ignores the politial conventions of the Roman Republic.

exire ex urbe: *ex*, omitted in some manuscripts, is usually accepted into the text; *exire* with preposition is the standard construction, and *exire* with mere ablative is rare (K.-St. I 370).

vos vestem mutandam censuissetis cunctique mutassetis: after the publication of P. Clodius Pulcher's first bill affecting Cicero, the Senate decreed that mourning clothes should be put on to mark Cicero's treatment (see Cic. *RS* 3 n.; Introduction, section 2). Cicero frequently claims that such a move as a matter of public policy for the sake of a single person was unprecedented and thus signalled a particular honour as well as the importance of his fortune for the Republic (Cic. *RS* 16; 31; *RQ* 8; 13; *Dom.* 26; 99; *Sest.* 26–7; 32–3; 53; 145; *Pis.* 17–18; *Planc.* 87; Plut. *Cic.* 31.1; *Comp. Dem. et Cic.* 4.2; Cass. Dio 38.16.3). In contrast to private changes of dress, a general *mutatio vestis* as a result of a Senate decree amounts to a political declaration indicating that the entire community is affected by difficult circumstances (Heskel 1994, 142; Edmondson 2008, 30–1; Kaster 2009, 313; Starbatty 2010, 71–6; Dighton 2017). While Kaster (2009, 313) accepts that the demonstration 'that a threat against the civic status of a single man was tantamount to a threat against them all, against the public interest—the commonwealth, *res publica*—as a whole' had indeed not happened previously, changes of dress by the Senate to indicate political protest are attested a number of times in the late Republic (overview in Dighton 2017).

cunctique...omnes boni: other mentions of this process indicate that the Senate passed a decree to change into mourning clothes; whether or not this was then done by all senators (*cuncti*) cannot be ascertained (the consul, at any rate, did not change his dress). When Cicero says that all good men (*boni*) had changed their clothes previously, this probably means that they (including senators) did so individually before the Senate decree and not that all *boni* (not including senators) did so before the senators. The vague phrasing avoids potentially offending members of the audience when their support is to be highlighted. Elsewhere Cicero says that the Senate passed the decree after the other orders had changed their dress (Cic. *Pis.* 18).

ille: i.e. the consul A. Gabinius, who stands out from the others, as he still appears in his ordinary dress. This feature can function as an invective reproach, since specific attire was regarded as appropriate to particular occasions, and people who did not conform could be seen as not sharing the sentiments or awareness of the situation expressed by a particular type of clothing (Heskel 1994, 142–3). The context clarifies that the comment refers to the consul A. Gabinius and not to P. Clodius Pulcher, who was putting on a *toga praetexta*, which he was not even entitled to wear (thus Edmondson 2008, 31).

oblitus: a derogatory description of Gabinius using unguents (Cic. *RS* 13 [and n.]; 16; *Sest.* 18; *Pis.* 25) marked as inappropriate in the circumstances, in addition to being regarded as effeminate and extravagant. Romans who wished to appear serious did not apply unguents and criticized their use as degenerate and lascivious (e.g. Gell. *NA* 6.12.5; Sen. *Ep.* 86.11; 86.13; 108.16; 122.3; *Dial.* 7.7.3; on the use of unguents by men in Rome, see Colin 1955). – The recourse to unguents (esp. for the hair) is highlighted elsewhere in Cicero with reference to other individuals as a sign of effeminate and then irresponsible and politically unreliable behaviour (Cic. *Rosc. Am.* 135; *Verr.* 2.3.31; *Cat.* 2.5; 2.10; 2.22; *Phil.* 13.31).

cum toga praetexta: according to Cicero the consul still wore the magistrate's uniform while other office holders had exchanged theirs for mourning clothes. – The *toga praetexta* was a purple-bordered toga worn by curule magistrates (Mommsen, *StR* I 418–19).

omnes praetores aedilesque: Cicero stops short of saying that 'all other magistrates' put on mourning clothes, which would be an implausible exaggeration in view of the attitude of some of the Tribunes of the People; yet this comment still makes the consul appear isolated among the magistrates. The aim of avoiding commenting on the Tribunes of the People might be the reason why Cicero highlights the *toga praetexta*, which was commonly worn by curule magistrates, of whom the main representatives were consuls, praetors, and curule aediles (e.g. Cic. *Verr.* 2.5.36; *Vat.* 16; Vell. Pat. 2.65.3; Dion. Hal. *Ant.* 5.47.3;). Thus, the statement about everyone changing their clothing is supplemented by a comment on the magistrates with distinctive dress. This explains the structure of the sentence, which Markland (1745, 246–7) criticized: he felt that mentioning praetors and aediles separately was unnecessary, as they are included in *cuncti* (*contra* Savels 1828, xxii).

abiecerant: while this verb means 'to cease to wear, take off' (*OLD* s.v. *abicio* 6c), it has the connotation of 'to throw away as useless or unwanted, discard' (*OLD* s.v. *abicio* 6a); it therefore is a strong expression of the fact that the bright magistrates' toga has been discarded, as it has become unwanted and inappropriate in view of Cicero's predicament.

inrisit: according to Cicero, Gabinius not only did not put on mourning clothes himself, but even mocked the others for doing so.

squalorem vestrum et luctum gratissimae civitatis: *squalor* describes the appearance and *luctus* the underlying feeling demonstrated by wearing mourning dress. The first item refers to the addressed senators, the second to the populace as a whole. – When *civitas* is defined as *gratissima*, it implies presumably that people are grateful to Cicero for his previous initiatives on behalf of the common welfare and are sad to see his current predicament, as they demonstrate by their clothing.

fecitque ... tyrannus ... ediceret: in Cicero's presentation the consul is said to act in a dictatorial manner when preventing the Senate from observing its own decrees by issuing an edict ordering the Senate to take off their mourning clothes and by ignoring their concerns for the public welfare (Cic. *RS* 16; 17; 31; *RQ* 13; *Dom.* 55; 113; *Sest.* 32–3; 44; 52; *Pis.* 17–18; 23; *Planc.* 87; Schol. Bob. ad Cic. *RS* 16 [p. 109.5–9 Stangl]; Plut. *Cic.* 31.1; *Comp. Dem. et Cic.* 4.2; Cass. Dio 38.16.3). The intervention is presented in a forceful way when it is contrasted with the explicit mention that there was no official prohibition on private mourning, which the consul could not control. Therefore, the contrast is probably introduced by Cicero; the report about what is and is not affected by the edict is given from his perspective (Gabinius would not have called the situation *incommoda patriae*). – According to Cicero such behaviour surpasses even what tyrants have done (see *consul imperiosus*). In such a political context the negative term *tyrannus* reinforces the idea of suppression and unjustified dictatorial government (on *tyrannus* as a political term of abuse, see Opelt 1965, 129–30). – All Roman magistrates had the right to make announcements by edicts; these were particularly used to permit or forbid certain actions (Mommsen, *StR* I 202–9; Kunkel/Wittmann 1995, 178–81), while the cancellation of Senate decrees in that way is unusual (Kaster 2006, 190–1, on Cic. *Sest.* 32).

fecitque, quod nemo umquam tyrannus, ut: *facio ut* is a frequent paraphrase emphasizing the action described by the verb in the subordinate clause (K.-St. II 235). Here it enables the parenthetic comment on tyrants (supply *fecit* in the *quod*-clause).

ut quo minus ... nihil in<ter>cederet, ne ... ediceret: the text is corrupt and has been reconstructed in different ways. In any case the *ut*-clause consists of two parts in adversative asyndeton; the verbs in each part (*in<ter>cederet*; *ediceret*) govern another subordinate clause each, introduced by *quo minus* and *ne* respectively. To enable *ut* to serve as an introduction for the entire clause, the first part is negated by *nihil* linked to the verb.

gemeretis: usually intransitive, but also sometimes used transitively as here (Cic. *Sest.* 78; *Att.* 2.18.1; K.-St. I 260–2; Lebreton 1901, 176).

in<ter>cederet: Maslowski's (1981) conjecture of transmitted (*in*)*diceret* (Maslowski 1980, 407–9; cf. Busche 1917, 1356–7: *in<ter>diceret*) gives a possible idiom (*OLD* s.v. *intercedo* 5 'To intervene against, obstruct, hinder, oppose'; cf. Liv. 8.2.1–3: *nihil intercedi quo minus Samniti populo pacis bellique liberum arbitrium sit*), while *indicere quominus* and *interdicere quominus* do not seem to be attested. Bellardi (1975, 48) and Boll (2019, 145; supported in Corbeill's review at *BMCR* 2020.10.22) defend transmitted *diceret*, which is not impossible, but results in an unusual and complex construction.

incommoda patriae: the general phrasing (also *vestrum malum*) focuses on the dire situation of the country (Cicero's fortune can be seen as exemplifying these circumstances or affecting the country as a whole: see Introduction, section 3.4); thus, the contrast between the Senate and the consul becomes a constitutional issue.

ediceret: for another description of the same measure with similar wording and content, see Cic. *Pis.* 18: *edicere est ausus cum illo suo pari, quem tamen omnibus vitiis superare cupiebat, ut senatus contra quam ipse censuisset ad vestitum rediret. quis hoc fecit ulla in Scythia tyrannus ut eos quos luctu adficeret lugere non sineret? maerorem relinquis, maeroris aufers insignia: eripis lacrimas non consolando sed minando. quod si vestem non publico consilio, patres conscripti, sed privato officio aut misericordia mutavissent, tamen id his non licere per interdicta potestatis tuae crudelitatis erat non ferendae; cum vero id senatus frequens censuisset et omnes ordines reliqui iam ante fecissent, tu ex tenebricosa popina consul extractus cum illa saltatrice tonsa senatum populi Romani occasum atque interitum rei publicae lugere vetuisti.*

13 in circo Flaminio: the Circus Flaminius (*LTUR* I 269–72) was a large area created by C. Flaminius Nepos (cos. 223, 217, cens. 220 BCE) near the Tiber at the southern end of the Campus Martius just outside the city's sacred boundary (*pomerium*: *LTUR* IV 96–105) and served various functions. It was sometimes used as a venue for meetings of the People (*contiones*); commanders could then be invited to participate, as they would not lose their *imperium* when remaining outside the city boundary (Morstein-Marx 2004, 59–60). Thus, in the case of this *contio* (Pina Polo 1989, 299, App. A, no. 296), within the context of reactions to the bill on punishment for Roman citizens, P. Clodius Pulcher could call on not only the consuls of 58 BCE, but also C. Iulius Caesar (cos. 59 BCE), who was about to depart for his province, before the meeting. By involving these men, Clodius seems to have intended to gain public support for his measure and initiate public denunciation of Cicero (Cic. *RS* 17; *Sest.* 33; *Pis.* 14; Cass. Dio 38.16.5–17.3).

a tribuno plebis consul: i.e. P. Clodius Pulcher and A. Gabinius. Cicero's view of these men is expressed in the next phrase: he denies them the identification by their offices, as they do not present the required attitude (Cic. *RS* 4 and n.), and instead describes them as *latro* and *archipirata*, indicating their use of violence and neglect of rules (see Opelt 1965, 132–3; Achard 1981, 328–9 [on *latro*]; Opelt 1965, 134 [on *archipirata*]). Elsewhere Cicero applies the terms *latro* and *latrocinium* to Clodius and his followers (Cic. *RS* 19; *Sest.* 34; 76; *Pis.* 11), but also *archipirata*, in a developed metaphorical application of the term (Cic. *Dom.* 24; cf. *RS* 11).

in contionem... productus: a *terminus technicus* for bringing magistrates before a *contio* (*OLD* s.v. *produco* 2; e.g. Cic. *RQ* 16; *Dom.* 40; *Vat.* 24; *Phil.* 2.78; *Att.* 1.14.1; *Fam.* 12.7.1; Val. Max. 3.7.3).

qua auctoritate vir: full of irony (see *haec auctoritas* and *gravis auctor* later in the paragraph): this introduction contributes to denigrating the individual, who appears in a sorry state while pronouncing high-brow moral statements.

vini... temulenta: by means of standard topics of invective (see Introduction, section 3.2; Cic. *RS* 10–18 n.) Gabinius is again characterized as an effeminate and debauched drunkard and thus not as someone whose views and actions as a consul could be taken seriously (for similar descriptions of Gabinius, see Cic. *Sest.* 18; 20; *Pis.* 25; for similar descriptions of other opponents, see Cic. *Har. resp.* 55; *Verr.* 2.5.94).

vini: on being a drunkard as an element of invective, see, e.g., Opelt 1965, 158.

stupri: on the allegation of illicit sexual intercourse, see Cic. *RS* 11 n.

madenti coma, composito capillo: for this feature of Gabinius, see Cic. *Pis.* 25 (see Opelt 1965, 153). – *coma* as a collective singular and *capillus* also in the singular are the standard forms in Cicero and in the classical period (K.-St. I 70; for the phrase, see Cic. *Rosc. Am.* 135: *composito et dilibuto capillo*). – For dripping hair, which implies that it is full of perfume, see, e.g., Verg. *Aen.* 4.215–17; Tib. 1.7.51; Ov. *Am.* 1.6.37–8; *Her.* 21.161; Mart. 10.20.20; for shiny hair (because of perfume), see also Mart. 10.65.6–7.

gravibus oculis: vividly and visibly illustrates the effect of being *vini, somni, stupri plenus* (*OLD* s.v. *grauis* 7).

fluentibus buccis: a further element of a negative description of an inappropriate appearance in public (see Cic. *Pis.* 25: *fluentes purpurissataeque buccae*; *OLD* s.v. *fluo* 13b '(of the body or its parts) to be limp, languid, or torpid, droop, etc.'). The phrase reappears elsewhere in Cicero in the description of an unattractive Gaul depicted on a shield, mentioned for humorous effect (Cic. *De or.* 2.266: *demonstravi digito pictum Gallum in Mariano scuto Cimbrico sub Novis distortum, eiecta lingua, buccis fluentibus*). Because of the word's appearance in this sketch, because *fluentes* and *purpurissatae* in *In Pisonem* must denote different aspects, and because the presentation here has moved from over-elaborate hairstyle to unattractive facial complexion, *fluens* in this context is more likely to mean 'drooping' or 'flabby' (Nisbet 1961, 88, on Cic. *Pis.* 25) than 'dripping with cosmetics' (considered by Boll 2019, 147–8).

pressa voce et temulenta: implies that Gabinius' lifestyle has affected the clarity of his voice.

quod in civis indemnatos esset animadversum: i.e. the decision to apply the death penalty to the captured Catilinarian conspirators, who had not been subject to a proper trial (*OLD* s.v. *animaduerto* 8b). This aspect, which became the key criticism of the procedures in 63 BCE (see Introduction, section 2), is highlighted from the perspective of Cicero's opponents in this report of what Gabinius said. The impersonal phrasing avoids explicitly assigning responsibility.

id: takes up the preceding *quod*-clause.

sibi: belongs to *displicere* and refers to Gabinius, the subject of the sentence.

gravis auctor: ironic (*OLD* s.v. *auctor* 4), linked to equally ironic preceding and subsequent *auctoritas* (*OLD* s.v. *auctoritas* 6c): the phrase indicates the expected authoritative role of a consul and contrasts with the derogatory description of this man's appearance (for the same phrase applied to the other consul of that year, see Cic. *Pis.* 14).

ubi ... cessavit: two questions continue the ironic comment: now that Gabinius has displayed an attitude looking like *auctoritas* and *virtus*, Cicero expresses wonder why these features have been hidden for such a long time. By reminding the audience, in the second question, of how they have been obscured, he makes it appear implausible that, after such a past, Gabinius' current apparent display could be true and taken seriously (and thus that, in fact, there are no *auctoritas* and *virtus* that were hidden).

nobis ... latuit: this is not an example of a normally transitive verb (with accusative) used intransively with dative, which is possible for *latere* (K.-St. I 258–9), but *nobis* rather functions as a *dativus ethicus* (K.-St. I 323–4; Pinkster 2015, 931–2). – The interwoven word order (*haec auctoritas ... tanta* and *tam diu ... latuit*) and the emphasis on the extent (*tanta* and *tam diu*; also *tam eximia ... tam diu* in the following question) highlight the contrast between the allegedly great authority and virtue and their long obscurity and thus increase the ironic force of the question (see also Boll 2019, 148).

lustris et helluationibus: Gabinius is characterized as *helluo* elsewhere in Cicero (Cic. *Sest.* 26; 55; *Prov. cons.* 11; *Pis.* 41). The form *helluatio* (as transmitted in a number of manuscripts) is attested only here in classical Latin (*OLD* s.v. *helluatio* 'A debauch'). Elements of this word family, especially when used as terms of abuse, imply squandering in private and political life mostly for the sake of luxury and pleasure (Opelt 1965, 157; Achard 1981, 330–1). – For emphasis, *lustrum* (cf. Cic. *RS* 11) adds a location for the debauchery (*OLD* s.v. *lustrum*[1] 3; cf. Cic. *Sest.* 20: *ex diuturnis tenebris lustrorum ac stuprorum*), rather than indicating the activities carried out there or a characteristic of them (thus Boll 2019, 148).

calamistrati: ridicules Gabinius' (sophisticated and effeminate) hairstyle (*OLD* s.v. *calamistratus* 'Having the hair artificially curled, effeminately adorned'); elsewhere Cicero refers to Gabinius' *frons calamistri notata vestigiis* (Cic. *RS* 16 [and n.]) and describes him by *calamistrata coma* (Cic. *Sest.* 18; see also Cic. *Pis.* 25: *erant illi compti capilli et madentes cincinnorum fimbriae*).

saltatoris: similar critical descriptions of Gabinius as a 'dancer' occur elsewhere in Cicero (Cic. *Dom.* 60; *Pis.* 18; 22; *Planc.* 87); that Cicero characterized Gabinius thus is confirmed by Macrobius (Macrob. *Sat.* 3.14.15). Nisbet (1961, 78–9, on Cic. *Pis.* 18) notes that reproaches of appearing as a dancer were conventional in Rome (e.g. Cic. *Cat.* 2.23; *Mur.* 13; *Deiot.* 26) and that this allegation may have been developed from a single incident. Dance was seen as an indecent and effeminate activity worthy of criticism (Corbeill 1996, 135–9; 1997, 104–7).

virtus: ironically applied to Gabinius, when he appears to be law-abiding and thus rejecting unjustified action against Roman citizens.

nam ille alter: from Gabinius (Cic. *RS* 11–13) Cicero's discussion turns to the other consul of 58 BCE (Cic. *RS* 13–18), L. Calpurnius Piso Caesoninus (Cic. *RS* 4 n.), whom he also attacks in *In Pisonem* (55 BCE). In this case Cicero focuses on the facade Piso is creating, hiding his true nature, his non-noble background, and his philosophical aspirations (Corbeill 1996, 169–73).

nam: used rhetorically, marking the transition to a new subject, added in response to a potential, unexpressed objection (K.-St. II 117–18; *OLD* s.v. *nam* 4; cf. Cic. *RS* 38).

Caesoninus Calventius: the consul Piso's father was another L. Calpurnius Piso Caesoninus (*RE* Calpurnius 89), and Piso's maternal grandfather was Calventius. According to what Cicero says elsewhere, Calventius worked as a merchant and auctioneer and was an Insubrian Gaul who settled at Placentia (in northern Italy, about 60 km from Milan) and later came to Rome (Cic. *RS* 15; *Prov. cons.* 7; *Pis.* 14; 53; 62; 67; F 9; F 11; F 14; F 15; *Q Fr* 3.1.11; Schol. Bob. ad Cic. *RS* 15 [p. 108.27–8 Stangl]). Cicero thus taunts Piso with his non-noble and foreign background, a frequent item of invective (see, e.g., Opelt 1965, 149–51; Corbeill 1996, 170–1; Introduction, section 3.2).

versatus est in foro: in contrast to Gabinius (allegedly concerned with satisfying his private indulgences, at least until becoming Tribune of the People) Piso is said to have been active and visible in public from an early age. From Cicero's remarks elsewhere (Cic. *Pis.* 2) it can be inferred that Piso went smoothly through the full *cursus honorum*, even though the precise dates for the various offices are uncertain (Cic. *RS* 4 n.). – According to Cicero, although Piso was more visible in public than Gabinius, it was more difficult to see his true character (Corbeill 1996, 169–70): Cicero claims that Piso's appearance was deceptive, his true bad character was hidden, and he aimed to keep his real interests secret, and that this tactic of Piso's was successful with the majority of people, while Cicero saw through it (Cic. *RS* 15; contrast

RS 11). Such a presentation highlights Cicero's discernment and his concern for the Republic; it also enables Cicero to reproach Piso for details not generally known or even untrue. – In what follows Piso's outward appearance is contrasted with his true nature, and his appearance *in foro* with what happens *domi* (Cic. *RS* 14).

cum: introduces a temporal clause giving concomitant details of the action described in the main clause (K.-St. II 345–56).

simulatam fictamque tristitiam: in the context of the description of Piso and in connection with the allegation that it is feigned, *tristitia* cannot refer to feelings and must have a more neutral meaning (*OLD* s.v. *tristitia* 3 'Sternness, severity, austerity'). – *simulatam fictamque* is a rhetorically effective doublet, emphasizing the false hollowness (for variations of this collocation in Cicero's writings, see Cic. *Pis.* F 17; *Flacc.* 93; *Caecin.* 14; *Clu.* 72; *Q Fr.* 1.1.13). Therefore, this reading is to be preferred (Klotz 1913, 494–5; adopted by Maslowski 1981) to *versutamque* (also transmitted), defended by Bellardi (1975, 48) and kept by Peterson (1911) and Guillen (1967, 41; but see Boll 2019, 150–1). Jeep (1860, 615) suggests *personatamque* instead of *versutamque*: as one of the transmitted variants make sense, there is no need to change the text.

nulla res commendaret: *nulla res* is illustrated by the subsequent list of items encompassing the characteristics and skills typically expected of a respected Roman in public life (juridical and military knowledge, rhetorical ability, activities in political competition). – On Piso's lack of accomplishments and the deceit operated, see Cic. *Sest.* 21–2; *Pis.* 1; F 17.

non iuris <scientia> {studium}, non dicendi vi<s, non peri>tia rei militaris, non cognoscendorum hominum <studium>, non liberalitas: the corrupt transmitted text indicates a series of five anaphorically and asyndetically linked nouns, with the first four each further described by a dependent genitive. There should be different nouns in the nominative for each item as well as suitable combinations of nominative and dependent noun. Madvig's (1873, 212) reconstruction adopted here fulfils these criteria and also gives common collocations (followed by Bellardi [1975, 102] and Fuhrmann [1978, 522]). Maslowski (1981; adopted by Shackleton Bailey 1991, 227) prints a reconstruction of the corrupt transmitted text suggested by Klotz (1913, 495–7) partly based on earlier proposals (approved by Busche 1917, 1357). Yet *iuris <notitia>* in this version is a rare collocation, in classical Latin attested only once in Tacitus (Tac. *Dial.* 31.8); another passage in Cicero (Cic. *Cato* 12) mentioned by Klotz is not an actual parallel. Boll (2019, 149, 151) suggests *non iuris studium, non dicendi vi<s, non peri>tia rei militaris, non † cognoscendorum hominum, non liberalitas*, which does not fully resolve all the textual problems (for discussion of the text, see Boll 2019, 151–2). – All these items should be developed characteristics; thus *studium* ('aim/effort to acquire something') is less appropriate in connection with 'law', but possible with 'getting to know men', as the process is crucial for this activity and a feature of Roman politics.

non dicendi vi<s>: oratorical ability was a key feature in Roman Republican politics. Piso's alleged lack of it, another element of invective (see Introduction, section 3.2), recurs as a point of criticism in this speech and in *In Pisonem* (Cic. *RS* 14; *Pis.* 1; F 3; F 8).

cognoscendorum hominum <studium>: in a society based on networking and personal support public figures need to aim at getting to know people; it is important to be familiar with a large number of potential voters and influential individuals and to be able to address them by name (sometimes with the help of a *nomenclator*, reminding the master of names), especially during election campaigns (Cic. *Mur.* 77; Cicero, *Comment. Pet.* 31–2; 41; Hor. *Epist.* 1.6.49–55). – As potential alternatives to <*studium*>, Boll (2019, 152) suggests *vis, potestas,* or *facultas*. In this reconstruction of the text *studium* is preferable, as it is based on the transposition of a transmitted word, avoids repetition, and emphasizes the individual's activity (for *studium cognoscendi*, without reference to *homines*, see Cic. *De or.* 2.74; *Lael.* 104).

liberalitas: a certain amount of generosity, for instance in sponsoring public projects such as games or buildings, would be expected from politicians in the Republican period (e.g. Cic. *Mur.* 37).

incultum, horridum maestumque: the first two words describe a rough and uncultured appearance as regards dress and hair, while the third item refers to facial expression visualizing a state of mind (*OLD* s.v. *incultus*[1] 2; *horridus* 3; *maestus* 3; for the collocation applied to another politician characterized negatively, see Cic. *Leg. agr.* 2.13: *corpore inculto et horrido*). Cicero frequently mentions the uncultured appearance of Piso (e.g. Cic. *Sest.* 19; 21; 26; see Opelt 1965, 153).

vidisses . . . existimares . . . putares: a generic second person singular (continued in Cic. *RS* 14; see K.-St. I 653–4).

libidinosum et perditum: a climax in relation to the preceding adjectives and highlighting the deceit: Piso looks unkempt and uncultured, so that one might assume that he is rustic and uncivilized; in fact, however, he has a depraved moral character.

14 cum hoc homine . . . diceres: following on from the preceding claim that Piso might appear uncultured (Cic. *RS* 13), this sentence goes on to elaborate on his lack of mental faculties and civilized education.

stipite: is the most plausible reading of the transmitted text: it indicates that Piso is like a tree trunk rather than a human being, because of his limited intellectual capabilities and lack of empathy. For the term applied to people, see, e.g., Cic. *Har. resp.* 5; *Pis.* 19 (*OLD* s.v. *stipes* 2d; Otto 1890, 332, s.v. *stipes*; Laurand 1936–8, 310).

in foro constitisses: the construction of this verb with *in* + ablative indicates both the movement to a place and the subsequent position there, with emphasis

on the position as the result (K.-St. I 588–91; Pinkster 2015, 124). – *in foro* takes up *versatus est in foro* (Cic. *RS* 13) and contrasts with *domi* in what follows.

constitisses ... crederes: continues the address in the generic second person (Cic. *RS* 13; see n.). – *crederes* governs the infinitive *interesse*, which in turn governs the preceding double indirect question without an introductory conjunction.

sine sensu: indicates that, as appropriate to a tree trunk, there is a lack of sensation, sensibility, and emotions in Piso, in contrast to what is assumed for a human being (*OLD* s.v. *sensus* 6b).

sine sapore: *sapor* is explained as '(of persons) distinctive character' by *OLD* (*OLD* s.v. *sapor* 2b, with this passage as the only example). Similarly, Shackleton Bailey (1991, 12) translates the phrase as 'colorless' and explains it as 'lit. flavorless' (1991, 12 and n. 37). In the context of illustrating the human accomplishments Piso lacks, however, the phrase must be a derogatory description of a person 'without refinement' (Lewis & Short, s.v. *sapor*).

elinguem: Ernesti suggested a change to *elingue{m}* (supported by Wolf 1801, 33; Courtney 1960, 95) to create a grammatically accurate form agreeing with *negotium*. There are, however, instances of abstract nouns metaphorically applied to people combined with complements displaying a personal gender (K.-St. I 27; e.g. Cic. *Off.* 3.91; *Fam.* 1.9.15; *Mil.* 84; *Verr.* 2.4.9). – For the allegation that Piso is unable to speak well, see Cic. *RS* 13 n.

tardum: for the meaning, see *OLD* s.v. *tardus* 5 'Slow-witted, dull, stupid'.

inhumanum negotium: continues the notion that Piso is not a proper civilized human being. – *negotium* referring to a human being (*OLD* s.v. *negotium* 12), apparently on the model of similar Greek expressions, appears a few times in Cicero's letters (Cic. *Q Fr.* 2.11.4; *Att.* 5.18.4; 6.1.13), but not in Cicero's treatises or elsewhere in the speeches (Lebreton 1901, 70; Laurand 1936–8, 310). – *inhumanum* takes up the alternative *cum hoc homine an cum stipite* and implies that the latter is the case (*OLD* s.v. *inhumanus* 2).

Cappadocem: a term of abuse because of the large number of slaves from Cappadocia (part of present-day Turkey) in Rome, who were often regarded as physically strong, yet stupid, lazy, and making money by disreputable means (e.g. Petron. *Sat.* 63.5; Pers. 6.77; Mart. 10.76.3; *Anth. Pal.* 11.238). A further application of the term with abusive connotations occurs in another Ciceronian speech (Cic. *Flacc.* 61: *unum atque idem erat tempus cum L. Flacco consuli portas tota Asia claudebat, Cappadocem autem illum non modo recipiebat suis urbibus verum etiam ultro vocabat.*). Both passages are listed in *TLL* (s.v. *Cappadoces*) under the rubric 'imprimis de servis' (*Onomasticon* II, p. 169.41). Piso is compared to a Syrian slave in *In Pisonem* (Cic. *Pis.* 1: *iamne vides, belua, iamne sentis quae sit hominum querela frontis tuae? nemo queritur Syrum nescio quem de grege noviciorum factum esse consulem. non enim nos color iste servilis, non pilosae genae, non dentes putridi deceperunt; oculi, supercilia, frons, voltus*

denique totus, qui sermo quidam tacitus mentis est, hic in fraudem homines impulit, hic eos quibus erat ignotus decepit, fefellit, induxit.), with reference to the physical appearance of his face and its contrast with his hypocritical and deceptive expression (MacDowell 1964).

modo abreptum de grege venalium: similar to the abuse at the beginning of *In Pisonem*, where Piso is described as a Syrian slave *de grege noviciorum* (Cic. *Pis.* 1). For, as Quintilian outlines, *venalis* is used in the sense of *novicius* with reference to slaves (Quint. *Inst.* 8.2.8: *item quod commune est et aliis nomen intellectu alicui rei peculiariter tribuitur, ut 'urbem' Romam accipimus et 'venales' novicios et 'Corinthia' aera, cum sint urbes aliae quoque et venalia multa et tam aurum et argentum quam aes Corinthium.*; *OLD* s.v. *nouicius* 1 '(of slaves) Newly imported or purchased; (m. as noun) a newly imported slave'; *uenalis* 1b '(of a person) that is for sale as a slave; (as noun) a slave put up for sale in the market (spec. one newly imported, cf. Quint. *Inst.* 8.2.8)'). One of a group of newly imported slaves for sale would be ordinary and unattractive as well as untrained and unfamiliar with life in Rome.

idem domi: introduces an exclamation without a finite verb. The exclamation words are postponed so as to give prominence to fronted *idem domi*: this structure indicates that the characterization of Piso continues and marks the transition to the description of what happens *domi*, in contrast to the preceding *in foro* (Cic. *RS* 13–14).

domi: as in the case of Gabinius (Cic. *RS* 11), Cicero alleges that Piso has a lascivious sexual life (Cic. *Pis.* 42; 70; F 18), a standard item of invective (e.g. Corbeill 2002, 201). – When Cicero says elsewhere that he will not dwell upon what happened in the house, as it can be denied (Cic *Pis.* 11: *mitto enim domestica, quae negari possunt, haec commemoro quae sunt palam*), this shows that he is aware that such claims cannot be proved; at the same time this situation can be exploited to put forward unfounded allegations. Here there is an indirect justification for talking about domestic matters when Cicero states that he knows Piso, a distant relation of his, well and is able to see through his public facade (Cic. *RS* 15 [and n.]). – At home, it is claimed, Piso is not quite so inactive, dull, and senseless as he appears in public, but he only acts to satisfy his unchaste desires.

quam libidinosus, quam impurus, quam intemperans: the adjectives in this anaphoric and asyndetic tricolon combine to illustrate Piso's unbridled (sexual) desires and foul character (*OLD* s.v. *libidinosus* 2; *impurus* 2; *intemperans* 2).

non ianua ... voluptatibus: alleges a debauched life in secret, where *voluptates* are not received through the front door, but are admitted through 'a concealed door' (*OLD* s.v. *pseudothyrum*). If *voluptates* move into a house by a particular path, the word must function as an *abstractum pro concreto* and refer to people and the pleasures they bring (*OLD* s.v. *uoluptas* 2). – In classical Latin the transliterated Greek word *pseudothyrum* occurs only here and in Cicero's *Verrines* (Cic. *Verr.* 2.2.50: *ea quem ad modum ad istum postea per pseudothyrum* *revertantur, tabulis vobis testibusque, iudices, planum faciam.*), also in a context of criticism (Laurand 1936–8, 310); it appears again twice in the late antique writer Orosius (Oros. *Hist.* 7.6.17; 7.29.3). The term is not attested in Greek texts; the Septuagint just has the forms ψευδοθυρίς and ψευδοθύριον. The word could have been coined for derogatory purposes, here alluding to Piso's sympathies with Greek philosophers, his limited education, and his morally dubious behaviour.

cum vero etiam: introduces emphatically the next point after the comment on Piso's lascivious life at home: his attempts at philosophy. The claim that he indulges in *voluptates* at home provides a transition.

litteras studere: *studere* with accusative (if not a neuter pronoun) is rare (cf. Plaut. *Mil.* 1437; *Truc.* 337; Titin. *Tog.* 85 R.²⁻³) and might be a colloquial construction.

beluus: this form is attested for Cicero by Augustinus (*GL* V, p. 520.26–30: *nam ubi geminata u littera in nominativo est, nomen est, non participium, ut fatuus ingenuus arduus carduus exiguus beluus, ut Cicero dixit, et talia. contra regulam participiorum mortuus putatur esse participium, sed in vim regulamque nominis conversum est.*); accordingly, it is a plausible restoration of the transmitted text, since the unusual word might have led to corruption, although the term (instead of *belua*; e.g. Cic. *Pis.* 1; 8; *Prov. cons.* 15) is not found elsewhere other than in a few glossaries. Klotz (1913, 483–4) originally is cautious to accept this form and later (1915, 212–14) suggests that its choice and the colloquial construction of *studere* might be elements of the ridicule and criticism of Piso, indicating and imitating his low level of education. – On the charge of defining an opponent as a 'beast' and its nuances in Cicero, see May 1996.

cum Graeculis philosophari: Cicero mockingly notes that Piso engages with literature and philosophy. Before saying anything about the nature of the philosophy favoured by Piso, Cicero insinuates that this endeavour is not very sophisticated because of Piso's limitations (*beluus immanis*). Then, by using a derogatory diminutive for the Greeks, Cicero goes on to suggest that Piso is not doing what a Roman consul should, when he spends time with Greek philosophy and pursues a less serious activity (cf. Cic. *Sest.* 110; *Pis.* 70; on Cicero's attitude to Greek language, literature, and customs, see, e.g., Swain 2002, 136–8). – Obviously, Cicero is well acquainted with Greek philosophy and interacts with it in his treatises; yet he stresses in their introductions that he only does so in his spare time and writes these treatises as a service for his countrymen (e.g. Cic. *Div.* 2.1–7; *Tusc.* 1.1). In his public speeches Cicero often feigns less familiarity with Greek art and culture to comply with the assumed views of Roman audiences.

Epicureus … voluptatis: Cicero claims that Piso sympathizes with the philosophy of Epicurus (on Epicureanism in late Republican Rome, see, e.g., MacGillivray 2012), for which there is a potential basis: the Epicurean philosopher Philodemus dedicated the treatise *On the Good King According to Homer* to Piso (*P. Herc.* 1507), and the Villa dei Papiri in Herculaneum, where writings of Epicurus and Philodemus have been found, is thought to have belonged to Piso (e.g. E. Badian, *OCD*, s.v. Calpurnius [*RE* 90] Piso Caesoninus, Lucius; on Piso, Philodemus, and the Villa dei Papiri, see also Englisch 1979, 81–95). – Cicero ridicules Piso's engagement with the Greek philosophy of Epicurus, as he does so, not because he understands its underlying principles, but rather because he is attracted by the importance of the term *voluptas*, which he interprets as *libido* (Cic. *Sest.* 23; *Pis.* 20; 37; 42; 65; 68–72; 92; Ascon. ad Cic. *Pis.* 68 [p. 16.12–13 C.]). In Epicurean philosophy the Greek term *hēdonē* denotes a pleasant feeling free from pain and is not linked to lusts or excessively lascivious behaviour; the importance of *hēdonē* in Epicurean doctrine was often misinterpreted or turned into the allegation of a lustful life (e.g. Erler/ Schofield 1999, 642–3). Thus, in his criticism Cicero turns standard elements of anti-Epicurean polemic against Piso (DeLacy 1941). Therein Cicero cleverly only offers allusions: the phrase *quaecumque est* leaves details of the tenets of Epicurean philosophy open; it creates the appearance that Cicero is not too familiar with it and that it is not worth investigating, while this enables him to make unsubstantiated and inaccurate claims.

autem: adds a further detail (*OLD* s.v. *autem* 4).

magistros non ex istis ineptis qui…, sed eos qui: defines Piso's 'philosophical teachers' by contrasting them with the representatives of another philosophical school.

ex istis ineptis qui…adhortantur: denotes another philosophical school, the Stoics, who discussed *virtus* and *officium* and were not averse to involvement in public life (e.g. Sellars 2006, 129–33; on Roman Stoicism, see, e.g., Verbeke 1973, 35–40; on Stoicism, see, e.g., Sellars 2006). The negative characterization *ineptis* is ironic and represents the perspective attributed to Piso, who prefers a philosophical school that (in his view) advocates pleasure rather than discussing and taking on public duties (Cic. *Sest.* 23). The sketch of the Stoics' views in the relative clause is neutral or even positive (though *dies totos* might represent the view of Piso, who regards it as excessive) and thus shows that they are not *inepti* in the context of Roman ideology, while Piso could be described as such by his choice of philosophy and his irresponsible behaviour as a magistrate.

qui…, qui…adhortantur, sed…qui disputent: of the two relative clauses, each describing the representatives of one philosophical school, the first (with two asyndetically and anaphorically linked parts) has the indicative and the second the subjunctive: this distribution of moods presents the characterization of the Stoics as a fact and that of the Epicureans as a consequence of their nature (K.-St. II 296–8; Lebreton 1901, 310–11).

qui…versari: an exaggerated (and thus mocking) description of the Epicureans, claiming that according to their doctrine no point in time and no part of the body should ever be free from pleasure. – In ridicule, the Epicurean doctrine of the ideal of experiencing measured pleasure and being free of pain (Cic. *RS* 15 n.) is turned into the availability of constant bodily pleasures.

15 his…hi…hi…idem: the repeated pronouns refer to Piso's Epicurean *magistri* (Cic. *RS* 14). The list of their activities is meant to show that their role is to identify and assess pleasures for Piso (Corbeill 1996, 135).

quasi praefectis libidinum suarum: the paradoxical collocation (softened by *quasi*) combines a term for official political and military roles with *libidines* as the area of activity: such an expression indicates the absurd values relevant for Piso and his *magistri*, who approach pleasure like an issue of public business (for a similar transfer, see Gell. *NA* 15.8.2: *praefecti popinae atque luxuriae*). – The term *voluptas* (Cic. *RS* 14) has been replaced by *libido*, which triggers even more negative connotations. *voluptas* again appears in the next phrase, so that the proper philosophical term can be exploited to ridicule the Epicurean principle of weighing up pleasures.

hi…iudicant: after the emphatic introductory phrase defining the position of these men, subsequent clauses illustrate the activities of these 'commanders of lusts/pleasures'. The roles are each described by a double expression of two words with similar meaning and transferred from different spheres. As Fantham (1972, 124) notes, the series of metaphors is taken from the areas of hunting, catering, finance, consulting, and law: this list thus demonstrates vividly that these men pursue standard activities that are not, however, applied to the usual objects but rather all spent on catching and judging pleasure.

vestigant atque odorantur: a neutral term is followed by an illustrative metaphor (*OLD* s.v. *odoror* 2), indicating that these men will discover pleasures everywhere. – The metaphor recalling hunting dogs might suggest that these men, like Piso (Cic. *RS* 14), do not behave like proper humans (Boll 2019, 158).

conditores instructoresque convivi: this passage is given in *OLD* at the entry for *conditor*[1]; but, as *OLD* implies (also Laurand 1936–8, 311), as regards figurative uses, there may be a pun on *conditor*[2] (*OLD* s.v. *conditor*[1] 4 'An organizer'; *condītor*[2] 'A person who seasons; (in quot. fig.; in pun on *conditor* CONDITOR[1])'). In connection with *convivium* this is likely to be the case. The noun *instructor* (*OLD* s.v. *instructor* 'A person who equips or arranges') occurs only here and then again in late antiquity (Laurand 1936–8, 311). *convivi* must be a collective singular referring to the type of activity. – For the allegation that Piso held excessive dinner parties, see Cic. *Pis.* 22; 66–7. – In some Greek comedies Epicurus and Epicurean philosophy were apparently presented as teaching culinary pleasures and supporting wastrels (e.g. Alexis, *Asotodidaskalos* [F 25 K.-A.]; Bato, *Synexapaton* [F 5 K.-A.]; Damoxenus, *Syntrophoi* [F 2 K.-A.]; Hegesippus, *Philetairoi* [F 2 K.-A.]). Thus, these might be potential inspiration for these elements of Cicero's portrayal of Piso (DeLacy 1941, 51).

expendunt atque aestimant voluptates: a mocking allusion to a principle of Epicurean ethics advising 'weighing up' the relative pleasure and pain of each activity with a view to their effects: it is not necessary or possibile to satisfy all desires; this is only required for necessary and natural ones; one may sometimes experience greater pleasure by avoiding a smaller pleasure or undergoing a temporary displeasure (on these Epicurean doctrines, see, e.g., Erler 1994, 154–9; Erler/Schofield 1999, 648–57).

sententiamque dicunt: the technical term for voicing an opinion in the Senate is transferred to the sphere of judging *voluptates/libidines*; this phrasing highlights again Piso's preferences in contrast to the duties of a responsible politician.

quantum cuique libidini tribuendum: the previous phrase appropriating Epicurean vocabulary has *voluptas*; here, where the wording deviates from Epicurean terminology and mockingly adopts Roman technical terms, Cicero reverts to *libido* (cf. *praefectis libidinum*), so as to make what these people assess seem outrageous and inappropriate in relation to what is expected of a Roman politician and a true Epicurean philosopher.

horum ille artibus eruditus: i.e. Piso skilled in the arts of the Epicureans. – Although the wording sounds positive, the statement is ironic; in view of how these 'arts' have just been described, being an expert in them is not a praiseworthy feature.

hanc prudentissimam civitatem: although Cicero goes on to claim that, in contrast to himself, the Roman populace was deceived, he starts by flattering it (including the senators in the audience), which also makes Piso's aim appear more ridiculous. The importance of the quality of *prudentia* for a community is acknowledged and attributed to the Romans among others elsewhere in Cicero's speeches (Cic. *S. Rosc.* 69–70). The alternative reading *pudentissimam* looks like a spelling mistake or an error influenced by the surrounding discussion about *libidines* and *flagitia*. The point is that Piso is well aware of what he is doing and so naive as to assume that he could deceive the alert Roman populace by veiling his abject behaviour.

latere: Cicero repeatedly claims that Piso tried to hide his true characer and activities: such behaviour makes his bad characteristics even worse, since it implies that he is aware of their inappropriateness.

importunum: this alleged characteristic is linked to the facial expression, since only there does it appear as it is feigned to hide a lascivious lifestyle. The collocation *importunus vultus* does not seem to be attested elsewhere. *OLD* gives a separate meaning for this passage '(ref. to appearance) grim, threatening' (*OLD* s.v. *importunus* 2d), while *TLL* subsumes it under the general sense with regard to people (*TLL* VII.1.663.35–71, s.v. *importunus*), which equals the superordinate meaning in *OLD* (*OLD* s.v. *importunus* 2 '(of persons) Regardless of others in the pursuit of one's objectives, unaccommodating, troublesome, oppressive, relentless, demanding, etc.').

detulisset: that the face is 'carried down' to the Forum shows that it only serves to create a certain outward appearance in public and may imply that it is put on like a mask. – *de-ferre* is probably used in analogy to *in forum descendere* (e.g. Cic. *De or.* 2.267), as people move there from their living quarters on the hills.

is nequaquam me quidem {non}: Müller's (1885, 435) restoration of the corrupt text (adopted, e.g., by Peterson 1911; Maslowski 1981) stays close to the transmission and gives the required sense in a straightforward phrase. Jeep (1862, 3) suggested changing the punctuation with only minor adjustments to the transmitted letters and thus reading *isne quemquam, me quidem non (cognoram enim... abstulisset) sed vos populumque Romanum,... decepit?*: this reconstruction results in a convoluted and less effective sentence. Boll (2019, 159–60) retains the text of one manuscript (*is me, quamquam me quidem non*), understood as Cicero correcting himself: for such a structure one would expect a comprehensive expression, including Cicero and others, as the first object. – That Piso's intentions to deceive were not successful in his case highlights Cicero's own discernment. Cicero has to stress his ability to see through Piso's deceptive appearance (Cic. *Sest.* 21; *Pis.* 1) when he insists on a discrepancy between appearance and character, contrary to Roman beliefs, usually adduced by Cicero, of a match between external characteristics and internal character (Corbeill 1996, 171). Asserting that Piso's negative features are not immediately visible and can only be noticed by people who have closer knowledge of his character allows Cicero to allege manifestations of negative behaviour for which there is no obvious evidence (Schol. Bob. ad Cic. *RS* 15 [p. 108.24–9 Stangl]:...*non esse deceptum hac simulatione Pisonis, quem penitus cognitum habuerit, propter generum suum scilicet C. Pisonem qui erat ex eadem familia; sed populum vel maxime deceptum, qui vultui magis eius quam rebus crediderit, ut consulem designaret....non vult ergo iudicio populi consulem factum videri, sed errore.*).

cognoram: Cicero explains that, because of his familiarity with the family of the Pisones, he was not deceived by Piso's outward appearance.

propter Pisonum adfinitatem: Cicero's daughter Tullia (Cic. *RS* 1 n.) was married to C. Calpurnius Piso Frugi (*RE* Calpurnius 93; quaest. 58 BCE [*MRR* II 197]; see Nicholson 1992, 74–5) from *c.* 63 BCE until his death in 57 BCE. This Piso, Cicero's son-in-law, belonged to a different branch of the Calpurnii Pisones, but Cicero still notes this Piso's kinship (and, by extension, his own) with the consul Piso (Cic. *RS* 17; 38; *RQ* 11; *Sest.* 20; *Pis.* 12; cf. Schol. Bob. ad Cic. *RS* 15 [p. 108.25 Stangl]; on the relationship expressed by *affinis*, see Cic. *RS* 17 n.; on Piso Frugi, see Cic. *RS* 38 n.).

cognatio materna Transalpini sanguinis: Cicero insinuates that the addition of Transalpine blood via the maternal line (which his son-in-law did not share) affected the respected Roman traditions in the Piso family (Cic. *Sest.* 21): by this construction Cicero's opponent can be set off from other members of the Piso family; thus, Cicero can exploit the kinship to claim familiarity, but avoids his son-in-law being affected by the negative presentation of the consul Piso. To emphasize the detrimental effect of the addition of foreign blood, Cicero locates Piso's maternal family in Transalpine Gaul, although he says elsewhere that Piso's grandfather was an Insubrian Gaul (a people who had Transalpine roots, but lived in the region of Cisalpine Gaul in historical times) and had settled at Placentia, where he received citizenship (on the consul Piso's family background, see Cic. *RS* 13 n.).

abstulisset: employed in an unusual metaphorical transfer of its basic meaning 'to carry away' (*OLD* s.v. *aufero* 1).

non consilio neque eloquentia: Piso would not be able to deceive with these qualities, since, according to Cicero, he is lacking them (Cic. *RS* 13–14). – Interestingly, Cicero admits that one can deceive by *eloquentia*, though he might not classify his own tendentious speeches as 'deceit'.

in multis: could be either masculine (referring to people) or neuter (referring to instances): in a reference to deceit by characteristics of individuals the former is more likely.

rugis supercilioque: used in both a literal and a transferred sense of the attitude expressed by these facial features.

decepit: Cicero asserts that Piso's true character is hidden behind an allegedly serious and respectable facade created especially by his forehead and eyebrows (Cic. *Sest.* 19–20; *Prov. cons.* 8; *Pis.* 1; 12; 14; 20; 68; 70). – According to Quintilian appropriate movement and positioning of the eyebrows are important features of a good orator (Quint. *Inst.* 1.11.9–10; 11.3.78–9). The description is also reminiscent of typical theatre masks as sketched by Quintilian (Quint. *Inst.* 11.3.74), which might enhance the impression of faking an appearance. – On this description of Piso, its function, and the possible link to theatre masks, see Hughes 1992; Renda 2002; Klodt 2003, 49–50; Tondo 2003, 146–7; Meister 2009, 76 with n. 39; for an overview of different interpretations of such an appearance of Piso, see Grillo 2015, 125–6, on Cic. *Prov. cons.* 8; on the role of physical appearance, its meaning, and exploitation in Republican discourse, see Corbeill 1996; 2006 (on appearance as representing character and feelings, see Cic. *Leg.* 1.26–7); Tondo 2003; Meister 2009.

16 Luci Piso…A. Gabinio: the only mention of L. Calpurnius Piso Caesoninus and A. Gabinius by their proper names in this speech, in which Cicero avoids naming his opponents (Steel 2007, 112). A direct address (highlighted by the emphatic position of the vocative at the start of the sentence: K.-St. I 256) enables an immediate reproach and increases the impact of the invective (Uría 2006, 15, 19). As Piso was a provincial governor in Macedonia in 57–55 BCE (*MRR* II 202–3, 210, 218), he must have been away at the time of the delivery of this speech (Steel 2007, 112). He can still be addressed in a particular passage to make the invective more effective and more vivid. – *Pro Sestio* includes apostrophes to Piso, while the speech as a whole is not addressed to him (Cic. *Sest.* 32; 33; for addresses to absent people, see, e.g., Cic. *Mil.* 102).

tune ausus es: the first of a series of questions addressed to Piso. The surprised question expresses amazement at the fact that Piso, with his assumed serious appearance, collaborated with the openly debauched Gabinius, since this would affect the impression of him and suggest that he might be more similar to Gabinius than people (who do not have Cicero's insight) may think (Corbeill 1996, 172).

isto oculo...rebus gestis: a list of ablatives of manner (K.-St. I 408–12; Pinkster 2015, 862–4).

oculo...fronte...supercilio: these features combine to make up Piso's feigned *vultus importunus* (Cic. *RS* 15; cf. Schol. Bob. ad Cic. *RS* 16 [p. 109.2–4 Stangl]:...*insectatur non tantum mores eius, sed etiam liniamenta voltus et omnem habitum, quo gravitatem non praeferat, sed mentiatur. oratio cum acerbitate stomachi concepta, ut ipsis verborum qualitatibus animus irascentis appareat.*).

non dicam...non...non enim possum dicere: each of the three items attributed to Piso is coupled with another item that cannot be applied to him. The contrast is expressed in varying forms with different degrees of emphasis (Cic. *RS* 1 n.). The juxtaposition of features that can and cannot be applied to Piso according to Cicero highlights that there is no reliable character and no substance (in terms of mindset, way of life, or deeds) behind the facade.

cum A. Gabinio consociare: since the verbs *consociare* and *coire* (later in this paragraph) can have a negative connotation of conspiring (*OLD* s.v. *consocio* 2; *coeo* 9), the phrasing contributes to having the consulship of these men appear as a kind of irresponsible conspiracy.

pestis: describes the effect of the consuls' plans against Cicero from his point of view.

te illius: the address to Piso continues; *illius* refers to Gabinius.

unguentorum odor...vestigiis: for these negative characteristics attributed to Gabinius, see Cic. *RS* 13 and nn.

vini anhelitus: for the phrase, see Cic. *Phil.* 13.4.

frons calamistri notata vestigiis: *calamistrum* is a Roman version of curling tongs (Mannsperger 1998, 16–25): this instrument apparently consists of a solid cylinder around which the the hair is wound and which is then inserted into another, heated and hollow metal cylinder (for mentions of *calamistrum*, see Varro, *Ling.* 5.129; Petron. *Sat.* 102; Non., p. 546.12 M. = 876 L.). Because of the application of heated metal near the head, the hair could be burnt or injuries could happen. The comment alleges that Gabinius has his hair curled and on one occasion an accident left a mark on his forehead. Such a remark criticizes Gabinius for having recourse to this feminine way of styling his hair (Cic. *RS* 13) and the inept way in which it was done. Highlighting this feature might also assimilate Gabinius to a slave marked by a branding iron (for marks on the forehead of slaves from a branding iron and attempts to cover them, see Mart. 2.29.9–10).

adducebat: the tense implies that Gabinius' appearance and behaviour were visible for some time and that this still did not prompt Piso to be cautious in avoiding collaboration to maintain his seemingly respectable appearance.

re: Cicero argues that, once a deed demonstrating the true character has been done showing that Piso is similar to Gabinius despite his different outward appearance, concealment will no longer work. – On *similis* with the genitive, see K.-St. I 448–9.

fuisses: indicates the completion of the joint deed as a precondition for the deceit no longer working.

frontis...integumento: takes up the preceding *fronte*, while the paraphrase stresses the aspect of concealment (*OLD* s.v. *integumentum* 2; cf. Cic. *Pis.* 12: *vereor ne qui sit qui istius insignem nequitiam frontis involutam integumentis nondum cernat*).

liceret: does not indicate 'permission' in a strong sense but rather suggests that it would no longer be possible for Piso in the eyes of the public to hide his true character when the association with Gabinius would have revealed it as similar to the latter's.

cum hoc tu: *tu* only appears in some of the manuscripts: retaining it makes the question more emphatic, highlights the collaboration of the two men by the juxtaposition with *cum hoc*, and is in line with the frequently repeated personal pronoun for emphasis in this section (see also Boll 2019, 163).

provinciarum foedere: refers to the bill that P. Clodius Pulcher put forward concerning the assignment of provinces to the consuls of 58 BCE and Cicero's claim that this was a deal in return for the consuls not interfering with Clodius' activities (see Cic. *RS* 4 n.; Introduction, section 2).

addiceres: a technical term indicating that important assets have been handed over in an irregular way (*OLD* s.v. *addico* 2). *OLD* marks this use of the verb as '*ellipt.*' (cf. Cic. *Phil.* 7.15: *regna addixit pecunia*). From the context it is clear that the indirect object must be P. Clodius Pulcher; in the speeches of thanks after his return Cicero does not mention him directly (Cic. *Pis.* 56: *addicebas tribuno pl. consulatum tuum*). The objects of the verb are presented as an anaphoric and asyndetic list, while they denote items on different levels: *consularem dignitatem* refers to Piso's and Gabinius' reputation, as they compromise their status as consuls by entering into such a pact, and thus also the reputation of the office of consul; *rei publicae statum* denotes the implications for the political system (similar to *status civitatis*; Cic. *RS* 20 n.); *senatus auctoritatem* indicates that the arrangement ignores the role of the Senate and the relevance of its decrees (*OLD* s.v. *auctoritas* 11); *civis optime meriti fortunas* (in emphatic final position) means that the fate of Cicero (whose achievements are again highlighted) is put under Clodius' control. In response to a situation characterized by these features, Cn. Pompeius Magnus is said to have encouraged the People to stand up for precisely these values (Cic. *RQ* 16). – Highlighting that these consuls did not value the role of the Senate creates an implicit contrast with Cicero's behaviour as consul in 63 BCE, when he consulted the Senate on what to do about Catiline and the Catilinarian conspirators (Weiske 1807, 263), and also with what he is doing currently when he recognizes the Senate's efforts for his recall.

te consule...subvenire: exemplifies the consuls' irresponsible political behaviour outlined in the previous sentences by an instance concerning the Senate.

te consule, tuis edictis et imperiis: the two ablatives are not parallel: *te consule* is an ablative absolute indicating the time, and *tuis edictis et imperiis* is an *ablativus causae* qualifying the main verb: here Piso alone is made responsible for interference with decrees of the Senate. – While *edictum* is a technical term for a decree of a magistrate, *imperium* is a general expression for a command. The collocation thus may emphasize the arbitrary nature of the orders issued by the consuls (cf. Cic. *RQ* 13).

senatui populi Romani: more commonly the Senate and the Roman People are mentioned in parallel (*SPQR*), while here the Senate is described as that of the Roman People: this phrase (see also Sall. *Cat.* 34.1; Liv. 39.39.9) indicates the Senate's importance and authority in the Republic and thus makes the behaviour of the consuls towards the Senate appear even more appalling.

non modo sententiis atque auctoritate sua, sed ne luctu quidem ac vestitu: the measures are highlighted as particularly outrageous: they prevent the Senate not only from demonstrating a position by the standard elements of debates and statements, but also from showing feelings through a change of dress. While it could be argued that the law on Cicero initiated by P. Clodius Pulcher forbade discussions of his fate in the Senate (see Cic. *RS* 4 n.; Introduction, section 2), the point here is that the consul goes further and even stops any displays of sympathy by a separate edict. – *sententia* refers to statements made by senators in discussions in the Senate; as indicated by *sua*, *auctoritas* denotes the authority of the Senate (*OLD* s.v. *auctoritas* 6c), presumably referring to the impact of its pronouncements. – For the structure *non...non modo...sed ne...quidem*, see K.-St. II 61–2.

ne luctu quidem ac vestitu: in support of Cicero, the Senate decreed a change of dress, and the senators put on mourning clothes (Cic. *RS* 12 and nn.; see also Schol. Bob. ad Cic. *RS* 16 [p. 109.6–9 Stangl]: *cum decrevisset enim senatus vestis mutationem, videlicet adiuturus causam Ciceronis, ab iisdem consulibus coactus est habitum suum pristinum, laetiorem scilicet, recuperare. et se igitur amplificat qui tantum dolorem omnium meruit, et hunc quasi tyrannum insectatur qui senatui nec lugere permiserit.*). The double expression indicates that *vestitus* demonstrates *luctus* (Cic. *Sest.* 32: *erat igitur in luctu senatus*); the emphasis is on *luctus* (*ne...quidem*), as banning particular emotions can be seen as especially appalling.

rei publicae: if putting on mourning clothes is defined as support for the Republic, Cicero's fate is again implicitly identified with that of the Republic (see Introduction, section 3.4).

17 Capuaene: Piso was *duumvir* (a chief magistrate of a colony) at Capua in the same year (58 BCE) in which he was consul at Rome (Cic. *Sest.* 19; cf. *Pis.* 25); Cicero, therefore, mockingly calls him *Campanus consul* elsewhere (Cic. *Dom.* 60; *Pis.* 24). The colony at Capua was established in the preceding year (59 BCE) under the consul C. Iulius Caesar as a result of his agrarian legislation (Vell. Pat. 2.44.4; see also Cic. *RS* 29 n.). – When the scholion claims that Piso was a Campanian, there seems to be a misinterpretation of Cicero's statement (Schol. Bob. ad Cic. *RS* 17 [p. 109.11 Stangl]: *fuit enim Piso natione Campanus.*). – The comment alludes to the fact that in the Second Punic War the Capuans were said to have demanded that one of the Roman consuls should be from Capua, which was rejected by the Roman Senate (Liv. 23.6.6–8). In a speech of 63 BCE Cicero mockingly claims that the *duumviri* in Capua preferred themselves to be called *praetores* and might soon demand the title of *consules* (Cic. *Leg. agr.* 2.92–3).

domicilium…superbiae: *superbia* was a proverbial characteristic of Capuans that was said to stem from good living conditions (Otto 1890, s.v. *Campanus* 2; e.g. Cic. *Leg. agr.* 1.18; 1.20; 2.91; 2.92; 2.95; 2.97; Liv. 7.31.6; 9.6.5; 9.40.17; Gell. *NA* 1.24.2; Auson. *Ordo urb. nobil.* 8.13–15 [Capua]; Amm. Marc. 14.6.25). – On Cicero's application of this feature, see Schol. Bob. ad Cic. *RS* 17 [p. 109.11–13 Stangl]: βαρέως *itaque Capuensibus adscribit vitium superbiae: quod ipsum et in ea oratione facit quam habuit contra legem agrariam, copiosius multo et effusius* (on Cicero's presentation of Capua in the speeches on the agrarian law of 63 BCE, see Cic. *Leg. agr.* 1.18–22; 2.76–97). – Mentioning this (irrelevant) detail contributes to tainting Piso: it is suggested that he was a magistrate in a town with characteristics similar to his own.

consulem: Cicero describes Piso's role in both Capua and Rome as 'consul' to create a straightforward comparison, although the terminology is not accurate for Capua. – The rhetorical aim invalidates Markland's criticism (1745, 145–6; 247–8) that the author of this speech misunderstood Cicero's abuse and wrongly called Piso 'consul' also with respect to Capua (*contra* Savels 1828, xxiii).

sicut eras eo tempore: the parenthetical remark is not just an indication of the time. Affirming that Piso had the role of 'consul' in Capua in that year (58 BCE) emphasizes the inaccurate terminology applied; this highlights Piso's claim to power and his way of carrying out these offices, which is only appropriate to Capua in Cicero's view. – The phrase is deleted by Garatoni, followed by Halm (1856). Jeep (1863, 2–3) suggests *sicubi eras eo tempore* ('if you were consul at this time anywhere'), arguing that Cicero says several times that Piso and Gabinius cannot be regarded as consuls (Cic. *RS* 4 n.); here, however, the focus is on the interpretation and realization of the role in different places.

Romae, in qua civitate: the term on which the relative clause depends is repeated within the relative clause, substituted by a word of similar meaning (K.-St. II 283–4).

in qua civitate…paruerunt: in Rome, Cicero claims, all consuls so far have complied with the wishes of the Senate. Such a situation, however, was not always the case: in another speech Cicero says without criticism that consuls did not do what the Senate had decreed (Cic. *Leg. agr.* 2.36). In Cicero's view, presumably, in such cases there were good reasons for deviation, and the consuls merely did not do what they were asked to do, but did not actively forbid the Senate to follow its own decrees (as the consuls of 58 BCE did according to Cicero: see Cic. *RS* 12 n.).

ante vos: although the sentence is still addressed to Piso (second person singular), deviating from the Senate's wishes is attributed to both consuls of 58 BCE. – The word order identifies this expression as a qualification of *omnes…consules.*

in circo Flaminio productus: on this incident, see Cic. *RS* 13 (with reference to Gabinius) and *RS* 13 n.

cum tuo illo pari: when Piso's colleague is identified by *par* (*OLD* s.v. *par²* 1), in light of the previous description, this suggests an association in unprecedented behaviour rather than their jointly holding a major office responsibly (see also Cic. *Pis.* 18: *edicere est ausus cum illo suo pari, quem tamen omnibus vitiis superare cupiebat, ut senatus contra quam ipse censuisset ad vestitum rediret.*).

semper misericordem fuisse: Cicero mocks Piso's alleged *misericordia* in *In Pisonem* by contrasting it with his decision to prevent the Senate from mourning openly (Cic. *Pis.* 17–18). At this *contio* Piso seems to have condemned and criticized Cicero's actions as consul in confronting the Catilinarian Conspiray as *crudelitas* (Cic. *Pis.* 14; Cass. Dio 38.16.5–6); Cicero mockingly claims that Piso implies that he, by contrast, is *misericors.*

quo verbo: i.e. *misericors.*

senatum atque omnis bonos: *atque* does not link two separate groups (*boni* may be among the senators); rather, the second item enhances the first in that it denotes a larger group, including people outside the Senate (K.-St. II 16–17).

cum a patria pestem depulissem: Cicero's description of the suppression of the Catilinarian Conspiracy in 63 BCE presents it as an act of rescuing the country (see Introduction, section 3.4). – Here *pestis* denotes primarily the destruction planned by the conspirators (*OLD* s.v. *pestis* 1, 4) rather than the person responsible (*OLD* s.v. *pestis* 5). – Primmer (1968, 248) and Boll (2019, 165) argue for the conjecture *depellerent* (adopted by Peterson 1911), the former mainly for rhythmical reasons and the latter to remove the pluperfect. This change would shift the responsibility for removing the *pestis* from Cicero to the Senate and the *boni*. While in speeches after his consulship, when justifying his behaviour, Cicero has a tendency to assign responsibility also to the Senate, here he describes a precondition for their action (in the pluperfect): Cicero removed the *pestis*; thereupon, the Senate acted with a decree against the captured conspirators.

crudelis: Cicero argues that, by characterizing himself as *misericors*, Piso defines those who opposed the conspirators as *crudelis* (on this rhetorical feature, see Schol. Bob. ad Cic. *RS* 17 [p. 109.16–17 Stangl]: ἐκ τοῦ ἐναντίου. *syllogismo usus est breviter a contrario: ut, qui se misericordem dixerit, crudelitatem senatui exprobraverit.*). Describing the action against the conspirators as *a patria pestem depellere* presents it as a right and justified intervention. The object *senatum atque omnis bonos* suggests a large group of right-minded people agreeing with Cicero in contrast to Piso's opinion.

tu...tu...tu: three anaphoric and asyndetic phrases describe Piso's treatment of three relatives.

misericors: Cicero mocks Piso's claim of being *misericors* in contrast to the *crudelitas* of others, recalling that he does not even treat his relatives well; in particular he contributes to handing Cicero over to the *inimici* and profits from his downfall (Schol. Bob. ad Cic. *RS* 17 [p. 109.19–21 Stangl]: ... μένον εἰς εἰπόντα. *in eundem Pisonem retorsit invidiam crudelitatis, qui nec sibi contemplatione adfinitatis opem tulerit, magis consentiens actionibus Clodianis*).

adfinem tuum: Cicero and the consul Piso were related via Cicero's son-in-law C. Calpurnius Piso Frugi (Cic. *RS* 15 n.); Cicero thus was 'a relation by marriage' for the consul Piso (see on *meum generum...filiam meam*).

quem...feceras, quem...rogaras: Cicero highlights that the political and public distinctions awarded to him by the consul Piso initially (Cic. *Pis.* 11) contrast with Piso's later behaviour.

comitiis tuis praerogativae primum custodem feceras: at voting assemblies (*comitia*) the *centuria praerogativa* was the *centuria* selected by lot to vote first, out of the *centuriae* making up the first class (Cic. *Div.* 1.103; *Phil.* 2.82); the vote of the *centuria praerogativa* could influence subsequent stages of the voting and thus the outcome (Cic. *Planc.* 49; *Mur.* 38; on the *praerogativa*, see, e.g., Taylor 1949, 56–7; 1966, 91–6). – A *custos* took charge of the voting tablets and the counting, so as to prevent the tablets being tampered with; candidates were permitted to nominate *custodes* for each ballot box (Mommsen, *StR* III 406–8; *Lex Flavia Malacitana*, *CIL* II 1964, c.55; Varro, *Rust.* 3.5.8). It was a mark of honour to be asked by a candidate to serve as a *custos*. Candidates not able to nominate anyone could be regarded as not enjoying proper support (Cicero, *Comment. Pet.* 8). – *comitiis tuis* (possessive pronoun instead of a *gen. obiectivus*: see, e.g., Cic. *Leg. agr.* 2.4) indicates that Piso asked Cicero to fulfil this role for the voting assembly at which he was elected consul (Cic. *Pis.* 11: *cui* [i.e. Ciceroni] *primam comitiis tuis dederas tabulam praerogativae*). The addition of *primum* (*primam* in Cic. *Pis.* 11) suggests that each candidate was able to nominate several *custodes* and Piso gave Cicero the leading role (Mommsen, *StR* III 406 n. 4). – Boll (2019, 166) argues for the reading *praefeceras* (following

Peterson 1911). While assuming this verb as the original text might explain the versions found in other manuscripts (*feceras; praeferas*), putting it into the text changes the sense: it then says that Cicero was put in charge of the elections or the *centuria praerogativa*, while the role rather is to monitor the voting process. The prefix *prae-* should be disregarded; it may have entered the text as a result of confusion with *praerogativa*.

Kalendis Ianuariis tertio loco sententiam rogaras: in Cicero's time, at the Senate's first meeting of the year (on 1 January), the presiding consul determined the order in which senators in each category, especially among the ex-consuls who were consulted first, would be asked to speak (Gell. *NA* 14.7.9). It was an honour to be asked for one's opinion early in the debate; this position increased one's influence on the discussion (on the speakers in the Senate, their order, and influence, see Mommsen, *StR* III 974–5; Bonnefond-Coudry 1989, 620–54; Ryan 1998, 259–76). – If Cicero rightly says that Piso made the decision about the order in which to ask senators for their opinion, Piso must have been the leading consul in January 58 BCE. – If Cicero was the third to be called upon (Cic. *Pis.* 11: *eum,…, quem in senatu sententiam rogabas tertium*), other ex-consuls must have been asked before him (Grimal 1967, 26; Ryan 1998, 259). These are often thought to have been Cn. Pompeius Magnus (cos. 70 BCE) and M. Licinius Crassus (cos. 70 BCE), but there is no evidence to establish that. Englisch (1979, 28) assumes that Cicero was called to speak straight after the two consuls; yet, according to the conventions, he would be the third person to be asked for their opinion.

constrictum: not literally 'put in bounds' but rather metaphorically 'restrained' (*OLD* s.v. *constringo* 4; for the word in political contexts, see, e.g., Cic. *Dom.* 23; 113; *Sest.* 24), perhaps as a result of the laws passed against Cicero (cf. Liv. 4.13.11: *constricti legibus de provocatione*). – In the speech before the People the same action is attributed to both consuls (Cic. *RQ* 13); here the emphasis in on how Piso treated his kinsman.

inimicis rei publicae: by this definition of his opponents (i.e. P. Clodius Pulcher and his followers) Cicero again elevates the conflict from a personal to a general one, equating himself with the Republic (see Introduction, section 3.4; Seager 2014, 227).

tradidisti: implies that Piso lets the *inimici* carry out their plans against Cicero without any attempts at intervention.

meum generum…filiam meam: Cicero's son-in-law C. Calpurnius Piso Frugi (Cic. *RS* 15 n.) and Cicero's daughter Tullia (Cic. *RS* 1 n.). The two of them are described by their kinship with Cicero and with consul Piso in chiastic order. – The different words to express the relationship take account of the different types of kinship (*OLD* s.v. *propinquus* 4 'Near (in kinship), closely related', b '(as noun) a relative, kinsman'; *affinis*² 2 'A relation by marriage').

verbis…reppulisti: in *In Pisonem* Cicero reports an encounter between himself, his son-in-law, and the consul Piso and what the consul said on this

occasion (Cic. *Pis.* 12–13); this meeting, however, seems to be an incident different from the one envisaged here. The rejection, with reference only to Piso
Frugi, is mentioned briefly in *Pro Sestio* (Cic. *Sest.* 54: *et Piso gener, a Pisonis
consulis pedibus supplex reiciebatur*); this speech also refers to Piso Frugi's
efforts to intercede with his kinsman on Cicero's behalf (Cic. *Sest.* 68). – Piso's
words are described by the feature he ascribes to Cicero in contrast to himself
(*crudelitas*) and the quality (*superbia*) assigned to the place (Capua) where Piso
held a position as a magistrate in office. – Falling at the feet or clasping the knees
of the person addressed were common suppliant gestures in antiquity, with the
former more frequently attested in Rome and the latter in Greece (Naiden
2006, 44–51; 130; see, e.g., Liv. 8.35.3; 8.37.9; 25.7.1). Here the description could
indicate metaphorically that Cicero and his relatives approached the consul
Piso as suppliants; then it does not mean literally that he pushed them away, as
they were at his knees. This presentation makes the rejection appear more dras-
tic and unfriendly. – On the rough treatment of Cicero's family in connection
with his absence from Rome, see, e.g., Cic. *Dom.* 59–60; *Sest.* 54.

   clementia ... singulari ... tanto ... intemperantia: both descriptions *clementia ac misericordia singulari* (picking up and elaborating on the preceding
misericors) and *tanto scelere tantaque intemperantia* seem to be ablatives of
quality (K.-St. I 454–6; Pinkster 2015, 782–3), the first attributive with *tu* and
the second predicative with *fuisti*; such ablatives are more usually joined with
verbs, but are occasionally found dependent on noun phrases (e.g. Cic. *Tusc.*
1.85). The two expressions are in ironic tension: the first gives Piso's alleged
attitude; the second characterizes Piso's true nature according to Cicero.

   ego una cum re publica: again an identification of Cicero and the Republic
(see Introduction, section 3.4; for the phrasing, see Cic. *Dom.* 63: *una cum re
publica*).

   non tribunicio sed consulari ictu: although the initiative to remove Cicero
in 58 BCE came from the Tribune of the People P. Clodius Pulcher (see
Introduction, section 2), in the course of the criticism of the consuls of that
year, the blame is put on the latter (Cic. *RS* 9; *RQ* 15). While one could claim
that the consuls did not hinder the activities of the Tribune of the People (for
whatever reason: see Cic. *RS* 4 n.), the contrast here presents them as the main
drivers.

   tanto scelere: denotes a character trait rather than a particular deed (*OLD*
s.v. *scelus* 2e; see Cic. *RS* 3 n.).

   inter meam pestem et tuam praedam: in view of the continuation of the
argument (Cic. *RS* 18 n.), *praeda* must mean the plundering of Cicero's house
(though Bellardi [1975, 106 n. 12] refers it to the provinces for the consuls):
according to *Pro Sestio* the law on the assignment of the consular provinces was
approved at the same time as that on Cicero's *pernicies*, namely at the time of his
departure from Rome (Cic. *Sest.* 53: cf. *Sest.* 25; 44); immediately after the
passing of these laws, Cicero's house was plundered (Cic. *Sest.* 54: *hac tanta*

perturbatione civitatis ne noctem quidem consules inter meum <interitum> et suam praedam interesse passi sunt). In comparison to the description in *Pro Sestio* this sketch is more intense: it is not a night, not even an hour (*ne unam quidem horam interesse paterere*) that the consuls let pass before taking hold of the 'booty'. – *pestis* takes up *consilia pestis meae* (Cic. *RS* 16) and has Cicero's departure appear like destruction or death, increasing the contrast with the gain drawn from the situation by others.

saltem dum…urbis: the consuls are said to have not even waited to seize Cicero's possessions until the first wave of grief had subsided, presumably envisaged as having been provoked by the decisions affecting Cicero and his departure (Cic. *RS* 12). *urbs* refers to the people in the city of Rome; the phrasing insinuates that the entire city (with a few notorious exceptions) lamented for Cicero.

18 nondum: stresses the haste of Piso and his colleague and alleges that they took action for their own advantage before anything had been made official. What was to be announced is defined as *occidisse rem publicam*. This is obviously not an announcement that would be made: Cicero again emphatically identifies his absence and the law confirming his status with the death of the Republic (see Introduction, section 3.4). The statement must mean that the law on Cicero's exiled status had not yet come into force. Not all factual details are included in this metaphorical presentation; the focus is on the rapid actions and greed of the consuls and the 'death' of the Republic as a result of the activities of P. Clodius Pulcher and the consuls.

palam factum: while this expression can indicate any public announcement, it was used particularly with reference to announcing someone's death and thus fits into the metaphorical context (Schol. Bob. ad Cic. *RS* 18 [p. 109.23–4 Stangl]: *haec etiam μεταφορὰ est ab hominibus iam demortuis et deploratis, de quibus dicitur 'palam factum', cum mors eorum nuntiatur.*).

cum…solvebantur…cum…donabantur: the complex construction is best explained as a sequence of two *cum*-clauses following the initial main clause in the pluperfect (*nondum…rem publicam*); the first *cum*-clause includes a parenthesis detailing how *arbitria funeris solvebantur* takes place (*uno eodemque tempore…deferebantur*). The two *cum*-clauses illustrate how the consuls immediately profit from the situation in two ways: by receiving Cicero's property and by being assigned lucrative provinces.

tibi: i.e. the consul L. Calpurnius Piso Caesoninus, who is still the focus; later in the sentence the perspective is broadened to include both consuls.

arbitria funeris solvebantur: Cicero continues with the metaphor that his removal from Rome means death for him and the Republic. As with any death, funeral expenses (*OLD* s.v. *arbitrium* 6b; Schol. Bob. ad Cic. *RS* 18 [p. 109.24–6 Stangl]: *'arbitria' vero 'funeris' sumtus dicit illos qui ad exhibitionem funeris inpenduntur per eos qui expediendae sepulturae curam sustinent.*) are to be paid:

typically, these are fees for the undertaker. Here, metaphorically, it is the gain the consuls obtain: thus, they are presented as undertakers (making a profit) in relation to the death of Cicero and the Republic (Cic. *Dom.* 98; *Pis.* 21).

uno eodemque tempore: Cicero emphasizes how quickly, when nothing was yet official, the consuls destroyed and plundered his property (for the collocation, cf., e.g., Cic. *Off.* 3.27: *una continemur omnes et eadem lege naturae*).

domus mea diripiebatur, ardebat, ... deferebantur: Cicero's house in Rome was plundered and set on fire: the first two verbs describe these activities sequentially; the third verb adds further detail to the action indicated by the first verb and extends it to another property.

diripiebatur: for the verb applied to property, see, e.g., Cic. *Dom.* 113; *Fam.* 16.12.1 (*OLD* s.v. *diripio* 4).

ardebat: for Cicero's house on fire, see Cic. *Dom.* 62; *Sest.* 54; *Pis.* 26; *Planc.* 95; *Mil.* 87.

bona ... deferebantur: the goods from Cicero's house on the Palatine were appropriated by Piso, who received them into the house of his mother-in-law nearby; the items from Cicero's house in Tusculum came to Gabinius, who owned a villa at Tusculum near to Cicero's, which was later rebuilt on a grand scale (Cic. *Dom.* 124; *Sest.* 93; *Pis.* 48). – Cicero frequently mentions the seizing and destruction of his property and its appropriation by the consuls (Cic. *Dom.* 60; 62; 98; 113; *Sest.* 54; 65; 145–6; *Pis.* 26; *Mil.* 87; *Planc.* 95; *Att.* 4.1.3; see also Ascon. ad Cic. *Pis.* 26 [p. 10.15–19 C.]: *post profectionem ex urbe Ciceronis bona eius P. Clodius publicavit; postquam direpta sunt omnia quae aut in domo aut in villis fuerunt, et ex eis ad ipsos consules lata complura, domus direpta primum, deinde inflammata ac diruta est.*; Cass. Dio 38.17.6).

de Palatio: Shackleton Bailey (1985, 141) argues that *de Palatio* cannot mean 'from my Palatine house' and therefore suggests reading *in Palatio*. The indication of a place rather than of movement, however, would not agree well with *deferebantur*, and the change would remove the parallel with *de Tusculano* (in chiastic order: *ad ... de ..., de ... ad ...*). Further, from mentions of his houses in other speeches it can be inferred that Cicero saw both *Palatium* and *Tusculanum* as indicating the areas in which the houses are situated (*domus in Palatio, villa in Tusculano*: Cic. *Dom.* 62; *domus ardebat in Palatio*: Cic. *Dom.* 62; *Sest.* 54; *in Palatio mea domus*: Cic. *Pis.* 26). *de Palatio* then means 'from the Palatine'; the house is mentioned in an earlier phrase in the sentence.

isdem ... eodem: indicate that the voters and the proposer act in the same roles on more than one occasion. While no other occasion is explicitly identified in this sentence, because of the chronological parallelism between the law on the provinces for the consuls and the laws affecting Cicero, the latter must be the reference points.

operis: refers to the accomplices of the consuls and of P. Clodius Pulcher (*OLD* s.v. *opera* 9b '(in politics) a hired rowdy'). – For other mentions of Clodius' *operae*, see, e.g., Cic. *Har. resp.* 28; *Dom.* 14; 79; *Sest.* 38; 57; 59; 65; *Vat.*

40; *Att.* 1.14.5; on their membership and role, see Nowak 1973, 108–17; Tatum 1999, 142–7.

gladiatore latore: i.e. P. Clodius Pulcher as the proposer (*OLD* s.v. *lator* 1) of these laws: he is not identified by name (Cic. *RS* 3 n.) and instead by a derogatory term (*OLD* s.v. *gladiator* 2 'A cut-throat, assassin, ruffian'). Cicero also calls Clodius *gladiator* elsewhere (Cic. *Har. resp.* 1; 15; *Sest.* 55; 88; 106; *Vat.* 37; *Pis.* 19; on this term applied by Cicero in a political context, see Opelt 1965, 135–6). In the context of voting, *lator* indicates the role of the person who puts forward a bill to be voted on (rather than initially promulgating it).

vacuo...adflicto: Cicero asserts that key entities of the Roman Republic were sidelined and not involved in the political process: the Forum, where political activity takes place, was empty of respectable people, and the two main bodies, the People and the Senate, were not informed or involved (see also Cic. *RS* 6). In *Pro Sestio* the situation at the passing of these laws is described similarly (Cic. *Sest.* 53: *lex erat lata vastato ac relicto foro et sicariis servisque tradito, et ea lex quae ut ne ferretur senatus fuerat veste mutata*). – As the laws were voted through, people must have been present and participated in the lawmaking. The presentation suggests that these individuals were Clodius' followers and that *boni* and *liberi* were not involved (although people who are not technically *liberi* would not be entitled to vote: Nowak 1973, 126). Such a description gives a reason why the laws were passed despite the alleged support of Cicero in Rome and removes any responsibility from the senators in the audience.

vacuo...foro: Cicero suggests that, because of the threats of violence and the limited opportunities for political involvement, *boni* and *liberi* are no longer around in the Forum (Cic. *Pis.* 23: *viri boni lapidibus e foro pellerentur*). The distinction between *boni* and *liberi* implies that *liberi* are a larger group than *boni*, the supporters of the Republic (on *liberi* in 58–57 BCE, see Achard 1981, 63–4; on *boni*, see Cic. *RS* 12 n.). The description insinuates that all Roman citizens are on Cicero's side and prevented from exercising their citizen rights (cf. Cic. *Leg.* 3.25: *quis enim non modo liber, sed etiam servus libertate dignus fuit, cui nostra salus cara non esset?*). – *vacuo...atque inani foro* describes the appearance of the Forum by a hendiadys; the first item is further specified by a two-part expression (*non modo...sed etiam*).

ignaro...ageretur: Cicero claims that the Roman People are not kept informed of political developments, presumably because in this scenario the citizens are no longer visiting the Forum and there are no *contiones* (for Cicero telling the People about recent meetings of the Senate at *contiones*, see, e.g., Cic. *Cat.* 3; *Phil.* 4; 6). Such a situation could be regarded as a particular insult, since it not merely restricts activities, but even ignores the role of the Roman People within the political system.

senatu...oppresso et adflicto: Cicero does not specify in what way the Senate was oppressed and crushed; he merely claims that the Senate is not able to operate in its accustomed way. The strong wording illustrates the complete elimination of the usual functioning of the Senate (for these verbs in political contexts, see, e.g., Cic. *Sest.* 52; *Dom.* 26; *Phil.* 2.55; 8.5). There may be an implicit reference to the consuls ignoring the Senate's decree on putting on mourning dress (Cic. *RS* 12 n.) and to the ban on discussing Cicero's case (Cic. *RS* 4 n.).

duobus impiis nefariisque consulibus: a concise statement of Cicero's assessment of the consuls of 58 BCE. For them at least their political function is given, while for P. Clodius Pulcher even his office is suppressed.

aerarium, provinciae, legiones, imperia: refers to the arrangements for the consular provinces along with the associated funding and military command (see Cic. *RS* 4 n.; Introduction, section 2). – On the public *ornatio* of provinces regulating the provision of staff, finance, and military forces, see Kunkel/ Wittmann 1995, 382; Rafferty 2019, 87–100. – On Piso's proconsulship, his activities, the equipment granted, and Cicero's depiction of his tenure, see, e.g., Nisbet 1961, 172–80; Englisch 1979, 37–53; Goldmann 2012, 157–62.

aerarium: public funding awarded to the consuls for administering their provinces. While this was a standard element of the procedure, Cicero suggests critically that in this case a large sum was awarded, appropriated illegally, and abused (Cic. *Dom.* 23; 55; *Pis.* 28; 37–8; 57).

imperia: on the assignment of proconcular command, see Cic. *Dom.* 23; 55.

donabantur: the entire sentence presents the way in which political decisions are made (through the collusion of P. Clodius Pulcher and the consuls, ignoring standard procedures) as unconstitutional and outrageous; the presentation culminates in this final word, indicating that important political and military functions are given to the consuls like a gift.

2.2.3. Supporters: Magistrates and senators (18–31)

This subsection (Cic. *RS* 18–31) of the second part (Cic. *RS* 8–31) of the main section (Cic. *RS* 3–35) returns (cf. Cic. *RS* 3–5; 8–9) to offering thanks to individuals and groups who supported Cicero (cf. Cic. *RQ* 15–17). To avoid causing offence, Cicero stresses that on this occasion he is unable to thank everyone separately and that the gratitude for named people focuses on the magistrates and one private individual (Cic. *RS* 31; see Cic. *Planc.* 74 [T 2]); in addition, Cicero makes sure to include the entire audience in generic expressions of thanks.

The following men are mentioned: the Tribunes of the People T. Annius Milo (Cic. *RS* 19; 30), P. Sestius (Cic. *RS* 20; 30), C. Cestilius, M. Cispius, T. Fadius, M. Curtius Peducaeanus, C. Messius (Cic. *RS* 21), Q. Fabricius, the praetor urbanus L. Caecilius Rufus, the praetors M. Calidius (Cic. *RS* 22), C. Septimius, Q. Valerius Orca, P. (Licinius) Crassus (Dives), Sex. Quinctilius (Varus), C. Caecilius Cornutus (Cic. *RS* 23), the consuls again (Cic. *RS* 24–5, including a reference to the ex-consul P. Servilius Vatia Isauricus, Cic. *RS* 25), senators (Cic. *RS* 26–8), and Cn. Pompeius Magnus (Cic. *RS* 29). Thus the individuals are arranged in groups according to rank in ascending order: first the Tribunes of the People, then the praetors, then the consuls complemented by the private individual Cn. Pompeius Magnus. T. Annius Milo and P. Sestius are the only magistrates (apart from the consuls and the senators generally) who are mentioned again, briefly towards the end (Cic. *RS* 30), to highlight their particular efforts, just as their activities are described in detail at the start of the section (Cic. *RS* 19; 20), separated from those of others (Cic. *RS* 21), and they open the list of Tribunes; they are also the only officials (apart from the consuls) to reappear in the speech to the People (Cic. *RQ* 15). Cn. Plancius (Cic. *RS* 35), who supported Cicero in his absence outside Rome, and Cicero's relatives (Cic. *RS* 37–8) are mentioned in different contexts outside this sequence, since they do not belong to the public figures in Rome in that year; this distribution illustrates the specific roles of all involved.

By introducing and presenting each one in a different manner Cicero sustains variety and prevents the list from becoming monotonous, in addition to subtle nuances in the way in which each person's contributions are acknowledged. For each individual the area in which they have been active is indicated, while the amount of detail is limited; this section is not meant to be a full account of what everyone did, but rather a summative record of their positions and key actions. What is emphasized in all cases is that these people showed unswerving loyalty to Cicero, made interventions to restore him, and at the same time did so for the sake of the Republic, as they are all good citizens upholding the traditional Republic in Cicero's sense. Thus, again, the section is not simply a private vote of thanks, but rather a demonstration of how the majority of influential magistrates work for the benefit of the Republic, which includes enabling Cicero to return to Rome. Presumably because the focus is on rendering his thanks, Cicero reports activities for his recall that happened in his absence to an audience who were in Rome at the time, without any apologies for doing so, as they are appended in other speeches (Cic. *Sest.* 72; *Pis.* 36).

The section concludes with the statement that Cicero is unable to thank everyone individually (Cic. *RS* 30–1); expressing the fear that one is unsure whom to praise and afraid of passing over someone is a rhetorical conceit (e.g. *Rhet. Her.* 3.12). Adducing it here singles out the men discussed and ensures that nobody will be offended by not having been mentioned. The entire audience is included in generic thanks to the group of senators (Cic. *RS* 26–8); the gratitude to the community is emphasized at the end. In contrast to the speech to the People, where the different supporters are recapitulated in a list, such an ending puts the emphasis on the community and, by recalling Cicero's dire state, provides a transition to the next section on his circumstances (Mack 1937, 42–3, on *RS* 30–1 vs *RQ* 18).

18 horum consulum ruinas: i.e. the ruinous condition to which the consuls L. Calpurnius Piso Caesoninus and A. Gabinius (cos. 58 BCE) brought the

Republic (*gen. subiectivus*: K.-St. I 415). – The concrete meaning of *ruina* applied in a transferred sense to the Republic (for the metaphorical application to the political situation, see, e.g., Cic. *Prov. cons.* 43; *Sest.* 5; *Vat.* 21) introduces the architectural metaphor continued in *fulsistis* and *sublevati*.

vos consules: the consuls of the current year, P. Cornelius Lentulus Spinther and Q. Caecilius Metellus Nepos (cos. 57 BCE), contrasted with their predecessors (cf. Cic. *RS* 5; 8–9). The direct address to these consuls, who must have been in the audience, endows the praise with greater weight.

vestra virtute: from the beginning these consuls are endowed with positive characteristics, and they are said to use these for the benefit of the Republic.

fulsistis: a metaphorical expression (derived from architecture: Fantham 1972, 125): the new consuls have 'strengthened the ruins' caused by their predecessors by rebuilding the Republic (for the phrase, see Cic. *Har. resp.* 60; *Phil.* 2.51).

summa ... sublevati: the praise is extended to the Tribunes of the People and the praetors of 57 BCE, who will be mentioned individually in what follows; the unanimity of the office holders in the current year is stressed (Cic. *RS* 5). – The concrete meaning of *sublevare* (*OLD* s.v. *subleuo* 1) continues the metaphor from architecture; the verb here has the sense of 'support' (*OLD* s.v. *subleuo* 2).

19 praestantissimo viro: even before the mention of his name, T. Annius Milo, the first of Cicero's supporters to be presented, is introduced by a positive description.

T. Annio: T. Annius Milo (Papianus) (*RE* Annius 67; tr. pl. 57, praet. 55 BCE [*MRR* II 201, 215]; see, e.g., Nicholson 1992, 66–8; Boll 2019, 34–7) was a natural son of a Papius and an Annia and was later adopted by T. Annius, his maternal grandfather (Ascon. ad Cic. *Mil.* 95 [p. 53 C.]). In 52 BCE Milo was charged with the murder of P. Clodius Pulcher, who had been killed in a scuffle between his bands and those of Milo (*TLRR* 309). Milo, defended by Cicero (Crawford 1984, 210–18, no. 72), was found guilty and went into exile in Massilia (modern Marseilles). Cicero then wrote and published a different version of the speech as *Pro Milone*: Milo is said to have commented that 'he should not be eating such mullets in Massilia...., if any such defence had been made' (Cass. Dio 40.54.2–4 [trans. E. Cary]). – Cicero often refers to Milo by *praenomen* and *nomen* (e.g. Cic. *RS* 30; *RQ* 15; *Har.* 6; *Sest.* 87; *Vat.* 41; *Mil.* 1; 6; 77; 83; 100).

aut quis...loquetur: this second, generically phrased rhetorical question clarifies that the first question as to what Cicero should say about Milo is not prompted by a lack of material or ability, but rather by Milo's worthiness: it would be difficult for anyone to honour him adequately in a speech. Thus, the conceit of the potential inadequacy of expressions of gratitude introduced with regard to the Senate as a whole at the start (Cic. *RS* 1) is applied to an individual.

satis digne: the adverb *digne* appears in Cicero only three times and is connected with *satis* in all instances (Cic. *Verr.* 2.1.82; *Sen.* 2).

qui...: a long sentence with repeated *qui* (referring to Milo) describing his activities against P. Clodius Pulcher and in support of the Republic in Cicero's view.

sceleratum civem aut domesticum potius hostem: P. Clodius Pulcher is again identified by his role in Cicero's view rather than by his position (and not named: Cic. *RS* 3 n.): when he is defined as a *sceleratus civis*, his citizen status is acknowledged even if his character is described in a derogatory way; when he is called a *hostis*, he is associated with external enemies; the tension from this enemy being inside the community (and the resulting greater threat) is indicated by the attribute *domesticus* (Cic. *RQ* 13). The correction (*aut...potius*; K.-St. II 101) highlights the appropriate description in Cicero's view (for a similar expression, see Cic. *Sest.* 39: *perditorum civium vel potius domesticorum hostium mortem*).

sin...tolleret: Cicero stresses that Milo used violence as a last resort and when provoked by Clodius (Cic. *Sest.* 86; 92; 95; *Mil.* 35; 38; 40; *Att.* 4.3.5): according to Cicero, Milo was clear that one should take action against a *sceleratum civem aut domesticum potius hostem* by legal proceedings if possible; when the normal workings of the courts were interrupted by *vis*, Milo decided to confront *vis* by *vis*: then he first (*primo*) took Clodius to court *de vi* (*Lex Plautia de vi*: LPPR, pp. 377–8), but the trials did not come to pass (*TLRR* 261; 262); later (*postea quam*), when he saw that his opponent had suspended the courts, he curbed his violence otherwise (with details conveniently left vague and a stress on protection). Thus, the armed bands set up by Milo and their violent actions (on Milo's troops, see Nowak 1973, 147–58) are mentioned positively as a measure of defending the Republic (Grasmück 1977, 172 with n. 79). – The absence of law courts is first described in an abstract and impersonal way, caused by *vis*; only the second phrase, motivating Milo's moving away from court action against Clodius, attributes the absence of law courts to Clodius (*eodem*), which serves as a justification for Milo. – One attempted trial in early 57 BCE (*TLLR* 261) did not come to pass when magistrates supporting Clodius obstructed it (see also Cic. *RS* 6 n.); another attempt later in the year (*TLLR* 262) had to be dropped because the selection of a jury was blocked before the elections of magistrates, and then Clodius was elected and assumed the aedileship for 56 BCE (Cic. *Sest.* 89; 95; *Har.* 50; Cass. Dio 39.7.3–4).

audaciam...vi: a sequence of five contrasting pairs, opposing positive and negative features (attributed to Milo and Clodius respectively). – *audax/audacia* often has a political connotation in Cicero and is applied to opponents of the *res publica*; thus, Cicero can claim that Milo uses *virtus* to oppose *audacia* (Wirszubski 1961, 14–15; on the political use of *audax*, see also Achard 1981, 247–8).

neque tecta…curiam: a polysyndetic list of four items arranged as two pairs: the first two items refer to individual and sacred buildings, the last two to venues representing the activities of the main political bodies, the People and the Senate. Such a sequence implies that Milo's activities (by *virtus* paired with [justified] force) were necessary to safeguard the basic functions of the Republic endangered by Clodius.

intestino latrocinio: develops the introduction of Clodius as *sceleratum civem aut domesticum potius hostem*. Like *latro* (Cic. *RS* 13 n.), *latrocinium* here is a term of abuse for the group of Clodius and his followers (*OLD* s.v. *latrocinium* 3 '(meton.) A band of robbers; (also pl.) robbers') rather than denoting an act of robbery (for the comparable expression *domesticum latrocinium*, see Cic. *Sest.* 1; 144).

primus: presenting Milo as the first to take effective action ignores any other initiatives in support of Cicero (see Introduction, section 2), thus singles out Milo's intervention (strengthened by the emphasis on its effect), and almost presents him as a trailblazer.

post meum discessum: one of Cicero's frequent paraphrases for his leaving Rome (see Introduction, section 3.4).

metum…civitati: a list of four items illustrating the impact of Milo's activities; in this sequence determined by *depulit* positive effects are described by removing negative features. The first two items juxtapose the contrasting political groups of *boni* (Cic. *RS* 12 n.) and *audaces*; the last two items describe the positive effects for the community divided up between the Senate (*huic ordini*) and the citizenry as a whole (*civitati*). – Illustrating the political usage of the terms *boni* and *audaces*, Wirszubski (1961, 13–14) comments on the contrast between them (see also Cic. *RQ* 1): from the point of view of the *boni*, the *audaces* are seen as reckless people endangering the established system. Thus, the contrast between them is connected with that between *metus* and *spes*: the *boni* fear impactful attacks against the system by the *audaces*, and the *audaces* hope that their actions will be sucessful. – The *civitas* was not literally in *servitus* when Milo intervened: according to this presentation Milo removed the first attempts at creating such a situation emanating from the activities of the consuls and Clodius in 57 BCE.

depulit: the combination of *depellere* with the dative (indicating the person from whom something is removed) seems to be a less common construction, but it is attested elsewhere in Cicero (Cic. *Fam.* 5.20.4: *nam et Volusi liberandi meum fuit consilium et ut multa tam gravis Valerianis praedibus ipsique T. Mario depelleretur a me inita ratio est.*; *Tusc.* 3.77: *ut sibi virtutem traderet turpitudinemque depelleret*; cf. Liv. 35.44.6: *depulso cervicibus eorum imperio Romano*; *OLD* s.v. *depello* 7).

20 quam rationem pari virtute, animo, fide: serves as a transition from T. Annius Milo (Cic. *RS* 19 n.) to P. Sestius: both men pursue a similar plan of activities and display similar characteristics.

P. Sestius: P. Sestius, a Tribune of the People in 57 BCE (Cic. *RS* 7 n.). – Cicero regarded Sestius as a supporter from his election to the tribunate onwards (Cic. *Q Fr.* 1.4.3), and he is presented as having worked tirelessly in his support (Cic. *Sest.* 124; also *RQ* 15). Sestius drafted a bill about Cicero's recall (which Cicero did not like) in autumn 58 BCE before entering office (Cic. *Att.* 3.20.3; 3.23.4). Like Milo, Sestius put together an armed band when nothing else seemed promising (Cic. *Sest.* 78–80; 84; 90; 92).

pro mea salute, pro vestra auctoritate, pro statu civitatis: in describing Sestius' intervention as designed to benefit Cicero, the senators in the audience, and the situation of the community, Cicero makes the praise of Sestius look less self-centred and more justified and again presents his fate as relevant for the Republic as a whole (see Introduction, section 3.4). – The same three items (in different order) recur in the speech before the People as features that this audience had been asked to defend by supporting Cicero's recall (Cic. *RQ* 16) and have been mentioned before as items put at risk by the consuls (Cic. *RS* 16). – The collocation *status civitatis* expresses an abstract concept of 'political organization' and thus refers to basic principles that need to be ensured and can be threatened (e.g. Cic. *Rep.* 1.33–4; 1.70–1; 2.2; *Leg.* 3.4; *Q Fr.* 3.5.1; *Phil.* 7.4; *Flacc.* 3; *Har. resp.* 41; 45; on the terminology of *res publica* vs other phrases, see Schofield 1995, 68).

nullas … discrimen: the four-part asyndetic and anaphoric sequence highlights Sestius' determination in that he did not avoid any dangers and even the risk to his own life. – Sestius was attacked by Clodius' men in early 57 BCE and sustained wounds in the assault (Cic. *RS* 7 and n.).

vitae discrimen: this collocation is rare in Cicero's writings (cf. Cic. *Verr.* 2.76; 5.157; *Sest.* 45; *Balb.* 25).

qui … videretur: picks up and elaborates on the notion that Sestius' activities were to the benefit of the Senate.

causam senatus exagitatam … commendavit: Sestius counters attacks on the Senate, by continuous confrontation, as *sua diligentia* suggests. – *causa senatus* (not *senatus*) as the object of the original opposition (*exagitatam*) suggests a fundamental attack.

contionibus improborum: speeches by Clodius and his supporters at meetings of the People. Their identification as *improbi* disqualifies them morally and declares them to be unfit to be serious and responsible politicians; in Cicero's terminology this expression forms a contrast to *boni* (Cic. *RS* 12 n.), the supporters of the Republic (Cic. *RS* 9 n.).

multitudini: when Cicero defines the People as *multitudo*, rather than as *populus*, the wording may imply a negative connotation (*OLD* s.v. *multitudo* 5; cf., e.g., Cic. *Dom.* 4: *quod in imperita multitudine est vitiosissimum, varietas et inconstantia et crebra tamquam tempestatum sic sententiarum commutatio*) and be triggered by the preceding allegation of demagogy. Cicero immediately stresses that, under Sestius' influence, the People became extremely well disposed towards the Senate.

populare: in the two speeches of thanks the term *popularis* occurs only here. Here Cicero highlights that Sestius managed to have the Senate appear *popularis* to the People; in line with Cicero's statements elsewhere, the underlying assumption is that *popularis* is what is good for the People, and this can be provided by the Senate upholding the Republic rather than by a demagogic Tribune of the People (MacKendrick 1995, 130: 'In a perhaps unconscious paradox, Sestius is said to have made the Senate "popular" (20).'). Similarly, in *Pro Sestio* Cicero says about a speech by consul Lentulus on his behalf that nothing so *popularis* had ever been heard (Cic. *Sest.* 107). Complementing such a description, in other speeches Cicero asserts that Clodius is not *popularis* (Cic. *Dom.* 77; on Cicero's views on *popularis* in this period, see Cic. *Sest.* 96–135). – Generally, *popularis* is an important term in the political struggle of the late Republic (see, e.g., C. Meier, s.v. Populares, *RE Suppl.* X, 1965, 549–615; Hellegouarc'h 1972, 518–41; Seager 1972; Achard 1981, 193–7; Mackie 1992; Robb 2010). Cicero tends to define a true *popularis* as someone working in the interests of the populace as understood by him; this version of *popularis* can include key features of an ideology typically connected with *optimates* (Gelzer 1939, 868; 1969, 73–4 = 2014, 69–70; Seager 1972, 336). Moreover, Cicero frequently provides his own definitions of *popularis* and sometimes distinguishes them from other uses of the term (e.g. Cic. *Sest.* 96; *Phil.* 7.4; *Rab. perd.* 11–15; *Dom.* 77–81; *Fam.* 12.4.1; *Off.* 2.78).

nihil tam … carum: *carum* (parallel to *nihil tam populare*) is neuter, determined by *nihil* rather than by what follows after *quam* (cf. Cic. *Leg. agr.* 1.23: *nihil tam populare quam pacem, quam concordiam, quam otium reperiemus*; 2.8: *quid enim est tam populare quam pax? … quid tam populare quam libertas? … quid tam populare quam otium?*; 2.102: *potest nihil esse tam populare quam id, quod ego vobis in hunc annum consul popularis adfero, pacem, tranquillitatem, otium*). The adjective insinuates emotional alignment and thus support on this basis.

cum … tum: Cicero stresses that in his support Sestius went beyond what he could do as a Tribune of the People and also offered personal assistance like a family member (exemplified in what follows). In line with his position, Sestius is compared to a 'brother', rather than to a 'parent' (Cic. *RS* 8) like the consul (Raccanelli 2012, 61–2).

iuxta ac si: this collocation appears only here in Cicero and only once elsewhere in classical Latin (Sall. *Iug.* 45.2: *praeterea transvorsis itineribus cottidie castra movere iuxta ac si hostes adessent vallo atque fossa munire, vigilias crebras ponere et eas ipse cum legatis circumire*). It expresses a comparison with something that is assumed, yet not actually the case (K.-St. II 453–5). For a similar expression, cf. Cic. *Mur.* 10: *qua re quod dandum est amicitiae, large dabitur a me, ut tecum agam, Servi, non secus ac si meus esset frater, qui mihi est carissimus, isto in loco.*

sustentavit … sum sustentatus: repeating the same verb, first in the active voice referring to Sestius and then in the passive voice referring to Cicero, enhances the interrelatedness and illustrates the immediate effect of Sestius' activities on Cicero.

clientibus … litteris: this sequence of five elements illustrating Sestius' support consists of three groups of people dependent on Sestius in different ways and two physical items. – All these elements are presented as having an instrumental function; therefore, for both things and people the mere ablative without a preposition is used (K.-St. I 380; Lebreton 1901, 406–7; Pinkster 2015, 875).

clientibus: free men for whom Sestius was *patronus*.

familia: in combination with *clientibus* and *libertis, familia* probably refers to the slaves in Sestius' control rather than the 'family' in the modern sense (*OLD* s.v. *familia* 2). – Cicero indicates that Sestius roused all sorts of people dependent on him to become active in assisting him, while he does not provide details on how this support manifested itself.

copiis: (unspecified) 'resources' provided to Cicero (cf. Cic. *RS* 22, on L. Caecilius).

litteris: Sestius sent encouraging letters to Cicero while the latter was away from Rome (e.g. Cic. *Att.* 3.17.1; *Q Fr.* 1.4.2). – As an alternative possibility, Boll (2019, 178) considers that *copiis* could refer to 'troops' and *litteris* to the legal attempts at recall. In this enumeration more general meanings referring to personal initiatives of an individual are more likely (as preferred by translators).

calamitatis non adiutor solum, verum etiam socius: concludes the description of Sestius' assistance with a concise and emphatic description of his role and activities: by his personal involvement Sestius almost became a *socius* in Cicero's predicament (as he acted like a 'brother').

calamitatis: a general term that may refer to political misfortune, frequently applied to Cicero's absence from Rome (see Introduction, section 3.4).

21 iam ceterorum officia \<ac\> studia vidistis: this transition expresses appreciation for the activities of others (listed in what follows), while it sets off the actions (presented in greater detail) by Milo (Cic. *RS* 19) and Sestius (Cic. *RS* 20) as particularly impressive (see Cic. *RS* 18–31 n.).

iam: marks the transition to the next item (*OLD* s.v. *iam* 8; see Cic. *RS* 4 n.), followed by *iam T. Fadius* (Cic. *RS* 21) and *iam vero praetores* (Cic. *RS* 22).

\<ac\>: Halm's (1856) addition of a coordinating conjunction (widely accepted by editors) is in line with the style of this speech as regards collocations of two items, and this conjunction could easily have been lost in the transmission (by haplography). The combination of the two nouns linked with *et* is attested elsewhere in Cicero (Cic. *Mur.* 45; *Att.* 3.15.4; *Fam.* 13.50.2; *Flacc.* 52). Boll (2019, 179) suggests maintaining the two-part asyndetic expression; while this is not impossible, such a construction makes the statement less weighty.

vidistis: engages the audience and points to evidence they have witnessed; it has Cicero's praise of individuals appear as based on known facts and also saves him from listing details (cf. Cic. *RS* 22: *vos existimare potuistis*). – The verb is regarded as a *perfectum praesens* and thus triggers a present sequence of tenses (K.-St. I 124–6; II 178–9; Lebreton 1901, 256; Pinkster 2015, 443, 559).

quam...quam...quam: the anaphoric and asyndetic tricolon emphasizes C. Cestilius' support: again Cicero highlights the loyalty to both himself and the Senate (Cic. *RS* 20); *causa* in the third item seems to encompass the cause of both (*OLD* s.v. *cupidus* 2; *studiosus* 3; for the combination of *cupidus* and *studiosus* expressing support, see Cic. *Sest.* 41: *virum studiosum mei, cupidissimum rei publicae conservandae*).

C. Cestilius: one of the Tribunes of the People in 57 BCE supporting activities for Cicero's recall (*RE* Cestilius; *MRR* II 202; see Nicholson 1992, 70).

M. Cispius: a Tribune of the People in 57 BCE (*RE* Cispius 4; *MRR* II 202, 463; see Nicholson 1992, 70), attacked in the tumult of 23 January 57 BCE (Cic. *Sest.* 76). Shortly afterwards Cispius was taken to court (*TLLR* 279); he was defended by Cicero (Crawford 1984, 170–2, no. 57), yet found guilty (Cic. *Planc.* 75–7; Schol. Bob. ad Cic. *Planc.* 75–6 [p. 165.10–26 Stangl]).

parenti fratrique eius: the father and the brother of M. Cispius (brother: perhaps *RE* Cispius 3; father: unknown). – For this magistrate the relatives are also mentioned, since their support for Cicero's side is particularly remarkable in view of an earlier conflict.

qui...oblitteraverunt: Cicero stresses that even those who had been offended by him in a private matter (*in privato iudicio*) regarded his services for the public good as important (*publici mei benefici memoria*) and thus no longer pursued their private resentment (*privatam offensionem*): such a reaction highlights the outstanding nature of Cicero's services and the breadth of his support (cf. Cic. *RS* 25).

voluntas eorum... offensa: the people offended are M. Cispius and his relatives (Tatum 1999, 177 n. 5 [p. 305]); details about the private lawsuit (prior to Cicero's absence from Rome) are not given and not known (*TLLR* 259). – On the meaning of *voluntas*, see *OLD* s.v. *uoluntas* 8; Cic. *Flacc.* 6; *Mur.* 47; *Att.* 2.21.5.

publici mei benefici: while throughout this speech Cicero expresses gratitude for *beneficia* received (Cic. *RS* 1; 3; 24; 26; 30), here he highlights a *beneficium* conferred on the public (Cic. *RS* 36; *Dom.* 74; 88; *Sull.* 26; 27). This *beneficium* is not identified; Cicero presumably thinks of his 'saving' of the Republic when it was attacked by Catiline (see Introduction, section 3.4). In Cicero's view his second *beneficium* for the public, departing from Rome in the face of Clodius' activities, allowed the populace to continue enjoying the positive effects of his first *beneficium* (Cic. *RS* 36 n.; on this meaning and use of *beneficium*, see Kranz 1964, 121–3).

T. Fadius: T. Fadius (Gallus?) was a Tribune of the People in 57 BCE (*RE* Fadius 9; *MRR* II 202) and had been quaestor in Cicero's consular year of 63 BCE (*MRR* II 168; on Fadius, see Nicholson 1992, 71; on his name, see Shackleton Bailey 1962; *MRR* III 89). Cicero was hopeful of Fadius' support soon after his election (Cic. *Q Fr.* 1.4.3). As Tribune designate, in November 58 BCE, Fadius had a bill on Cicero's return drafted by C. Visellius (Cic. *Att.* 3.23.4 [29 Nov. 58 BCE]). In 52 BCE Fadius was taken to court, found guilty, and went into exile (Cic. *Fam.* 5.18; *TLLR* 318).

M. Curtius: M. Curtius Peducaeanus was a Tribune of the People in 57 BCE (*RE* Curtius 23; *MRR* II 202; praet. 50 BCE [*MRR* II 248]; see Nicholson 1992, 70–1; cf. Cic. *Q Fr.* 1.4.3) and presumably an adopted son of Sex. Peducaeus.

cuius ego patri quaestor fui: Cicero was quaestor of Sex. Peducaeus, governor of Sicily, in 75 BCE (*MRR* II 98). – Sex. Peducaeus was probably the adoptive father of M. Curtius Peducaeanus. The term *pater* can be applied to an adoptive father (e.g. Cic. *Rep.* 2.1).

huic necessitudini: a close relationship through commonality in holding office, especially regarding the quaestorship (cf. Cic. *Div. Caec.* 46; 61; *Fam.* 13.10.1; 13.26.1); *huic* refers to the connections created by the magistracies described earlier in the sentence (Cic. *RS* 35 n.).

C. Messius: a Tribune of the People in 57 BCE (*RE* Messius 2; *MRR* II 202; aed. 55 BCE [*MRR* II 216]; see Nicholson 1992, 72). Apparently, in advance of the initiative of the group of Tribunes of the People led by Q. Fabricius (Cic. *RS* 22 and n.), Messius put forward a bill on his own (*Rogatio Messia de reditu Ciceronis*: *LPPR*, p. 401). It is not clear how the content of this bill relates to the one that Q. Fabricius (as *princeps rogationis*) tried to put to a vote in January 57 BCE (Cic. *Sest.* 75; see Introduction, section 2). Boll (2019, 182) believes that Messius' bill was supported by eight Tribunes of the People led by Q. Fabricius. But the sources imply a separate promulgation of the bill initiated by a group of Tribunes of the People. Thus, the second bill was probably similar in content, but promulgated afresh (Tatum 1999, 177, with n. 6 [pp. 305–6]; Williamson 2005, 82; Kaster 2006, 277–8, on Cic. *Sest.* 72). Ferrary (1996, 220) suggests that Messius withdrew his bill and gave his support to that of Fabricius. – *initio* emphasizes that Messius initially put forward a bill on his own and later collaborated with other Tribunes of the People; at the same time the initiative must have taken place at the beginning of the tribunate. Boll (2019, 181–2) finds the expression suspiciously brief (with *tribunatus* to be supplied): the necessary contextual information, however, can be inferred. – Later in 57 BCE Messius put forward a bill to give Cn. Pompeius Magnus charge of the grain supply (*Rogatio Messia de cura annonae Cn. Pompeio mandanda*: *LPPR*, p. 402), going beyond the consuls' proposal (Cic. *Att.* 4.1.7). In 54 BCE Messius was taken to court, perhaps in connection with the campaign for the aedileship in 55 BCE, and defended by Cicero, apparently successfully (*TLRR* 289; Cic. *Att.* 4.15.9; Crawford 1984, 180–1, no. 61).

et amicitiae et rei publicae causa: again Cicero creates a parallel between the personal relationship and the consequences for the Republic (Cic. *RS* 20; 21).

separatim: Boll (2019, 181) feels that *separatim* seems to prepare a contrast that does not follow, namely that Messius was involved in other proposals of laws in the course of this tribunate, and therefore considers the conjecture *statim*. It is true that a contrast balancing *separatim* (plausibly restored from the transmitted corrupt readings) is not expressed explicitly; but it is implied by the subsequent sentence referring to another bill put forward by a group of Tribunes of the People led by Q. Fabricius.

22 Q. Fabricius: a Tribune of the People in 57 BCE (*RE* Fabricius 7; *MRR* II 202; see Nicholson 1992, 72–3). He took the lead in putting forward a bill for Cicero's recall on 23 January 57 BCE (Cic. *RS* 21 n.) and was then attacked violently by armed bands (Cic. *Mil.* 38; *Sest.* 75; 78; Cass. Dio 39.7.1–3). While this bill was supported by the majority of the Tribunes of the People, Fabricius must have been the first mentioned in the draft, so that the bill would be named after him and he would chair the meeting at which it was voted on (Ferrary 1996, 220).

si…potuisset: to underline both Fabricius' efforts for him and the widespread support for his return, Cicero claims that, if Fabricius' initiative had not been hindered by violence (from Clodius and his supporters), he would have been restored in January 57 BCE.

quae de me agere conatus est: while the phrase *agere de* suggests an official procedure (*OLD* s.v. *ago* 41b), the expression is generic and the object *quae* (taken up after the relative clause by *ea*) is vague: such a description saves Cicero from having to define what Fabricius' initiative consisted in: this would have meant mentioning support for him in a negative context of lack of success (even if it was not the initiator's fault).

nostrum statum reciperassemus: while the transmission for the verb is partly corrupt, this generally accepted restoration is fairly certain. Elsewhere too (e.g. Cic. *RS* 3; 8) Cicero changes between first person singular (*de me*) and plural when talking about himself. When Cicero describes his return as regaining his *status* (*OLD* s.v. *status*[2] 9), the emphasis is not on the return as such, but on recovering his social and political position.

impulit…retardavit…revocavit: this asyndetic tricolon with three verbs in homoioteleuton mirrors the sequence of initiative, interruption, and renewed activity. With Fabricius and the Senate active in the positive framing parts, a connection is established, and the senators in the audience are given a share in the efforts to support Cicero in the face of opposition. Therefore, *revocare* is most likely to have the sense of 'to recall to health or vigour, restore, revive' (*OLD* s.v. *reuoco* 11) and to indicate that the Senate's backing prompted Fabricius to carry on working for Cicero's recall despite the opposition experienced (by *vis* applied by Clodius' supporters).

iam vero praetores: the subject of the subordinate clause at the start of the sentence (preceding the conjunction) identifies the new topic: the praetors of 57 BCE (Cic. *RS* 22–3), after the discussion of the Tribunes of the People (Cic. *RS* 19–22). – *iam vero* marks the transition to the next item (Cic. *RS* 4; 21 nn.). – This introduction initially insinuates that all praetors were supportive of Cicero; only later in the sentence is a qualification made (*paene omnibus*); the focus is on highlighting the supporters rather than singling out opponents.

vos existimare potuistis: Cicero highlights that the audience could witness the attitude and behaviour of the praetors: such a statement makes the description plausible and engages the audience in a discussion of Cicero's personal situation (see Cic. *RS* 21: *vidistis*; on the sequence of tenses, see Cic. *RS* 21 n.).

L. Caecilius: L. Caecilius Rufus, praetor urbanus in 57 BCE (*RE* Caecilius 110; *MRR* II 200; see Nicholson 1992, 64–5) and Tribune of the People in 63 BCE (*MRR* II 167; cf. Cic. *Sull.* 62–6), a half-brother of P. Cornelius Sulla. – In the year of his praetorship L. Caecilius Rufus' house was attacked (see Cic. *RS* 7 n.).

privatim . . . publice: for Caecilius Cicero highlights that he supported him as a private individual and in his official role as praetor, thus implying that he was keen to support Cicero in every way.

suis omnibus copiis: the nature of these private resources is not specified; they might be of a financial kind (cf. Cic. *RS* 20, on P. Sestius).

promulgarit: Caecilius used his position as a magistrate to propose a bill concerning Cicero. – The passage implies that the (seven) praetors put forward a bill on Cicero's recall under the leadership of L. Caecilius Rufus (*Rogatio Caecilia*: *LPPR*, p. 402).

cum collegis paene omnibus: out of the eight praetors of the year, one, Ap. Claudius Pulcher (*RE* Claudius 297; praet. 57, cos. 54 BCE [*MRR* II 200, 221]), brother of P. Clodius Pulcher, did not support Cicero, like two Tribunes of the People (Cic. *RS* 5 n.). – On Appius' assistance for his brother, see Cic. *Sest.* 87; Cass. Dio 39.6.3 (vs Cic. *Dom.* 87).

direptoribus . . . bonorum meorum: the designation of those who took Cicero's property in his absence (Cic. *RS* 18 and n.) as 'plunderers' reflects his assessment (see also Ascon. ad Cic. *Pis.* 26 [p. 10.15–19 C.]).

in ius adeundi: the second way in which Caecilius, as city praetor, used his position to support Cicero was by not permitting those who took Cicero's property to appear in court (*OLD* s.v. *adeo*[1] 8; *potestas* 5), to confirm their possession of it (as praetors had juridical functions: see Cic. *RS* 11 n.).

M. . . . Calidius: a praetor in 57 BCE (*RE* Calidius 4); on him as an orator (*ORF*[4] 140), see Cic. *Brut.* 274–8; Quint. *Inst.* 10.1.23; Hieron. *Ab Abr.* 1960 = 57 BCE (pp. 154–5k Helm).

statim designatus: the adverb specifies the chronological position of the participial construction (K.-St. I 789). It stresses that Calidius became active on Cicero's behalf as soon as it was possible by having obtained a prominent position as a magistrate designate straight after the election before entering office. – Elections for the consulship of 57 BCE were held in mid-July 58 BCE (Cic. *RS* 8 n.), immediately after which praetors were presumably elected.

sententia sua: apparently Calidius demonstrated his support for Cicero by a statement in the Senate; as praetor-elect he would have been asked to speak at a relatively early stage in the debate (Cic. *RS* 17 n.).

cara sibi mea salus: the phrasing implies a personal concern for Cicero's well-being (Cic. *RS* 20 and n.).

23 omnia officia…constiterunt: Cicero lists the five remaining praetors more briefly than the two just discussed (Cic. *RS* 22), while he still highlights their endeavours for him. He thus implicitly distinguishes all the others from the remaining praetor, Ap. Claudius Pulcher, the only one in opposition, while he obscures the fact that one is missing in the list (Cic. *RS* 22 n.). Without providing details, Cicero states that the *officia* of these men are excellent and obvious (*OLD* s.v. *consto* 9a; cf. Cic. *Planc.* 24: *quod huius ipsius in illum ordinem summa officia quaesturae tribunatusque constabant*; *Att.* 11.12.2: *quo minus mea in te officia constarent*).

C. Septimi: C. Septimius, a praetor in 57 BCE (*RE* Septimius 7; *MRR* II 201; see Nicholson 1992, 65; Goldmann 2012, 198).

Q. Valeri: Q. Valerius Orca, a praetor in 57 BCE (*RE* Valerius 280; *MRR* II 201; see Nicholson 1992, 65; Goldmann 2012, 218).

P. Crassi: P. Licinius Crassus Dives, a praetor in 57 BCE (*RE* Licinius 71; *MRR* II 200–1; see Nicholson 1992, 65).

Sex. Quintili: Sex. Quinctilius (Varus), a praetor in 57 BCE (*RE* Quinctilius 4; *MRR* II 201; see Nicholson 1992, 65; Goldmann 2012, 197–8).

C. Cornuti: C. Caecilius Cornutus, a praetor in 57 BCE (*RE* Caecilius 43; *MRR* II 200; see Nicholson 1992, 65; Goldmann 2012, 120–1).

et in me et in rem publicam: again creates a parallel between the fate of Cicero and the Republic, applying also to the activities in support.

quae: refers to the supportive actions outlined in the preceding sections, contrasting with *nefarie commissa*.

cum libenter…, tum non invitus: both phrases express a similar idea, while the second is stronger as a result of the litotes: it requires more effort and it is a greater achievement to pass over injuries suffered.

praetereo: Cicero presents himself as generous in passing over deeds committed against him. When he qualifies such actions as *nefarie*, he implicitly utters criticism while claiming not to do so (*praeteritio*). At the same time, by defining the group responsible for such actions as *non nulli*, Cicero creates the impression that it is a negligible entity; thus, one can afford to ignore them, and their existence does not invalidate the impression of overwhelming support for Cicero. – The statement not to go into actions against him contrasts with the preceding invective section against the consuls of the previous year (Cic. *RS*

10–18); what Cicero probably means is that he is omitting a list of individuals who have not supported him, to match the list of supporters just given. The role of the consuls of 58 BCE is a separate issue because of their leading position. – Mack (1937, 44–8) notes that the envisaged confrontation of the opponents and the threat of punishment are more severe in the speech to the Senate than in that to the People (reading *vindicem* [Madvig 1873, 212] or *indicem* without *non*). The wording may be stronger; still, in both speeches Cicero expresses his focus on showing gratitude and on carrying out revenge indirectly by being an exemplary citizen and confronting open enemies (Cic. *RQ* 21–3).

mei temporis: when Cicero claims that it is not suitable (with emphatic negation) to his present circumstances to remember the wrongs done to him (*OLD* s.v. *tempus*[1] 11; on *esse* with genitive, see K.-St. I 452–3), he emphasizes his willingness not to be resentful and to focus on good deeds.

quas…mallem: Cicero's ostentatious generosity in forgoing revenge might be a way of obscuring the fact that he would not be able to (Grasmück 1977, 167). – The construction is a present counterfactual conditional expressed by the imperfect subjunctive (K.-St. II 398–9); the relative pronoun is the object both in the superordinate relative clause and in the subordinate concessive clause.

alio transferenda mea tota vita est: this announcement of a change of direction in an impersonal and metaphorical phrase explains what Cicero will do instead of pursuing revenge: his entire life will be devoted to thanking his supporters, pardoning those who did not support him, and confronting open enemies. These intentions are presentend in generic terms without any identification of individuals, which avoids becoming too personal or causing offence.

bene de me meritis referam gratiam: as Cicero does in the current speech and will do in future.

amicitias igni perspectas: the term 'fire' metaphorically indicates the severity of Cicero's enforced absence and the test of friendships (of those who continued to assist Cicero) occasioned thereby. – The comment is based on the idea that the strength of friendships becomes apparent in difficult situations (see the line of Ennius [*Trag.* 166 *TrRF*] *amicus certus in re incerta cernitur*, quoted at Cic. *Amic.* 64; cf. Cic. *Fam.* 9.16.2: *ut quasi aurum igni sic benevolentia fidelis periculo aliquo perspici possit*). – The metaphor of testing by fire (Cic. *Off.* 2.38; Catull. 100.5–6; see Fantham 1972, 125; on the proverbial saying, see Otto 1890, 170, s.v. *ignis* 2) is inspired by the belief that gold, the most precious metal, is the only one to be incombustible so that its quality can be measured by fire (Plin. *HN* 33.59).

apertis hostibus: people openly confronting Cicero in contrast to those who merely did not take action to support him. These *hostes* probably include men like P. Clodius Pulcher and the consuls of 58 BCE (for the expression, see Cic. *Dom.* 29; *Sest.* 35). – By applying terms such as *hostes* and *proditores* to his opponents Cicero has his case appear as a fundamental political issue.

bellum geram: presumably again with words and civil means and not with arms and violence, in line with Cicero's practices (see Cic. *RS* 6; 33–4 nn.; Introduction, section 3.4; for the thought and the metaphor, see Cic. *Sull.* 28; *Sest.* 4; *Fam.* 12.22.1).

timidis amicis: Cicero shows himself conciliatory in announcing that he will pardon these friends and in defining fear (rather than, e.g., political opportunism) as the reason for their inactivity (Cic. *RS* 7). – Boll (2019, 186) suggests that Pompey, Caesar, Metellus Nepos, and perhaps Gabinius could be meant; but Cicero is unlikely to describe these men as *timidi amici* in this context.

proditores: in speeches and letters Cicero talks about people who betrayed and/or deserted him (Cic. *RQ* 13; 21; *Att.* 3.8.4 [29 May 58 bce]; 3.13.2 [5 Aug. 58 bce]; 3.19.3 [15 Sept. 58 bce]; *Fam.* 1.9.13 [Oct. 54 bce]; 14.1.1–2 [Nov. 58 bce]; *Q Fr.* 1.3.5; 1.3.8 [13 June 58 bce]). Such men might include (Courtney 1960, 96; Spielvogel 1993, 68–73; Shackleton Bailey on Cic. *Att.* 3.8.4; 1979, 262; Boll 2019, 187) Q. Hortensius Hortalus, who was among those who advised Cicero to leave Rome, and perhaps Q. Arrius (Cic. *Att.* 3.9.2 [13 June 58 bce]; *Q Fr.* 1.3.8 [13 June 58 bce]; Cass. Dio 38.17.4), and Cn. Pompeius Magnus, who avoided Cicero, torn between allegiance to C. Iulius Caesar and long-standing familiarity with Cicero (Plut. *Cic.* 31.2–3), as well as the consuls of 58 bce, L. Calpurnius Piso Caesoninus and A. Gabinius, who, especially Piso, had initially seemed well disposed (Cic. *RS* 10; *Har. resp.* 3; Cass. Dio 38.16.5–6; Plut. *Cic.* 31.4–5).

non indicem: the manuscript reading, which has often been changed, can stand: the meaning fits the argument that Cicero will forget rather than reveal offences against him (Luterbacher 1912, 346; Courtney 1960, 95–6; Shackleton Bailey 1979, 262; Lebek 1984, 7; Boll 2019, 187). On the basis of his reading of the context, Mack (1937, 46–7; see above on *praetereo*) argues for deleting *non* (also deleted by Peterson 1911).

dolorem profectionis meae reditus dignitate: in this chiastic expression (*meae* in the middle grammatically belongs to *profectionis*, but conceptually goes with the two genitives on either side) Cicero balances his departure (again *profectio*: see Introduction, section 3.4; though *dolor* is admitted) with his return and presents the return as superior by assigning it *dignitas*, probably referring to its honourable nature marked by the official decision to recall him and the welcome he received (cf. Riggsby 2002, 171). This phrase, operating on a more comprehensive level than the preceding items in this sequence, concludes it on a climactic, positive note turned towards the present and the future.

24 officium ... ut ... iudicarer: Cicero again stresses his duty to spend time and effort on rendering thanks and the need to be seen to be sufficiently grateful, but concedes that, in view of the enormous services provided, there will not be enough time during the rest of his life to do so (for other expressions of the difficulty of rendering thanks adequately, see Cic. *RS* 1; 19; 29; 30).

reliquum … relictum: there is little difference in meaning between the two expressions; in the context it is appropriate that the first seems to express neutrally what is left, whereas the second implies the connotation that it is left for a purpose (*OLD* s.v. *reliquus* 2; *relinquo* 12b).

duces ipsos et principes atque auctores salutis meae: the collocation *et … atque* in a sequence of three items is rare (K.-St. II 37). Thus, the sequence might rather be a juxtaposition of two items, one of which is expressed by two elements (K.-St. II 30–1): *duces* and *principes* are likely to go together and denote a leadership role (MacKendrick 1995, 132: 'At §24, *principes* are 'originators', who are also 'chief men': a pun.'), while *atque* makes an emphatic addition (K.-St. II 16–17), demonstrating that they initiated activities for Cicero's welfare. – The phrase characterizes the key players in arranging Cicero's return; it does not reveal any identities or indicate which of the individuals mentioned in the speech might belong to this category. – *ipsos* (K.-St. I 628–9) emphasizes that even if Cicero focused on giving thanks just to the leaders, there would not be sufficient time to do so adequately over the rest of his life.

exiguum reliquae vitae tempus: *reliquae vitae* seems to be a kind of *gen. appositivus*, describing what *exiguum … tempus* consists in (K.-St. I 418–19).

referendam … commemorandam gratiam: contrasts actively showing one's gratitude (*OLD* s.v. *refero* 13b) and mentioning it (*OLD* s.v. *commemoro* 2).

quando enim: Cicero proceeds to explain with an example (*OLD* s.v. *enim* 3d) that there will not be sufficient time to show gratitude appropriately (again *gratiam referent*). – In this two-part anaphoric and asyndetic structure *gratiam referam* has to be supplied to the first part and *huic homini ac liberis eius* to the second part.

huic homini: *hic homo* without attributes may be used to refer to a male individual who is present or has been mentioned before (e.g. Cic. *Verr.* 2.1.10; *Leg. Man.* 28; 39; 47; *Balb.* 8–9) Here it does not refer not to the speaker, as *hic homo* can in comedy, and no specific individual has been mentioned in what precedes. Thus, in view of the subsequent description, *huic* is most likely to have a deictic function and refer to the consul P. Cornelius Lentulus Spinther (on Lentulus' support for Cicero, see Cic. *RS* 8 n.), who, according to the alternation of leading consuls, would have chaired this Senate meeting in September (Cic. *RS* 26; *RQ* 11 nn.).

liberis eius: a son, P. Cornelius Lentulus Spinther (*RE* Cornelius 239), received the *toga virilis* and was elected augur (*MRR* II 207) in 57 BCE, when his father was consul (Cic. *Sest.* 144; Schol. Bob. ad Cic. *Sest.* 144 [pp. 143.29–4.2 Stangl]). – Further details on children of Lentulus are not known.

omnes mei: in order to emphasize his gratitude and the impossibility of rendering it appropriately, Cicero posits that not only he, but also all his family will want to show their appreciation to Lentulus and might not be able to do so appropriately. This addition balances the extension to Lentulus' family in this relationship of gratitude.

vis ingeni: while this phrase as part of a tricolon is similar to *ubertas ingeni* in a tricolon at the beginning of the speech also considering the faculties needed for an appropriate rendering of thanks (Cic. *RS* 1), *ingenium* here refers to the power of the mind to note and remember good deeds rather than the ability to create an adequate speech about them.

magnitudo observantiae: the third item of the tricolon indicates the required appreciative attitude in view of the great favours received (*OLD* s.v. *obseruantia* 2).

respondere: expresses the correspondence between favours received and the action and abilities required in return (*OLD* s.v. *respondeo* 13).

qui … qui … qui: refers to *huic homini*, i.e. the consul P. Cornelius Lentulus Spinther (anaphoric and asyndetic tricolon).

primus: Lentulus, who had already demonstrated his sympathy as consul designate (Cic. *RS* 8 n.), was not the first to take action on Cicero's behalf (see Introduction, section 2). Yet, after having come into office, he was the first person of consular rank to show support for Cicero; the consuls of the previous year were opposed to such measures, and Lentulus' consular colleague Q. Caecilius Metellus Nepos was not the leading consul in January (Cic. *RS* 26; *RQ* 11 nn.) and was less forthcoming due to his previous enmity towards Cicero (Cic. *RS* 5 n.).

consularem fidem dextramque: a zeugmatic expression: only a hand can literally be stretched out to someone lying low; the combination with *fidem* indicates the metaphorical value of the 'right hand' and identifies the kind of support (for similar expressions, see Cic. *Verr.* 2.5.153; Liv. 1.58.7; Verg. *Aen.* 4.597).

a morte … ad salutem: an anaphoric and asyndetic tricolon of three pairs of contrasts emphatically illustrates the effect of Lentulus' intervention on Cicero's situation and state of mind.

tanto amore in me, studio in rem publicam: once again Cicero creates a parallel between himself and the Republic (Cic. *RS* 20; 21; see Introduction, section 3.4) and thus presents activities on his behalf (and gratitude for them) as being of general relevance. – The two descriptive nouns denote different levels of emotional involvement as appropriate for people vs abstract items.

calamitatem meam non modo levaret sed etiam honestaret: explained in the following sentence (*enim*): honour and renown are obtained by the manner of Cicero's recall (on *calamitas*, see Cic. *RS* 20 n.; Introduction, section 3.4).

quid praeclarius mihi accidere potuit: for the phrase, see Cic. *Vat.* 8: *quid ergo, homo imperitissime solidae laudis ac verae dignitatis, praestantius mihi potuit accidere?*

illo referente vos decrevistis: on the initiative of the consul Lentulus, the Senate passed a decree at a meeting held in the Temple of Honos and Virtus (*LTUR* III 33–5) in May 57 BCE (Cic. *Dom.* 73; 85; *Sest.* 50; 116; 120; 128; *Pis.* 34; *Planc.* 78; Plut. *Cic.* 33.6; see Introduction, section 2): the consuls should send

letters to advise provincial governors and allies to support Cicero, thank communities that had hosted Cicero, commend him to their care, and invite those
who wished the Republic to be safe to assemble in Rome (for ratification of the
bill on Cicero's return).

decrevistis ut…, ut…: two long *ut*-clauses provide elements of the contents
of this Senate decree. The report cannot be fully verbatim; at least, it is adapted
to the current speaking situation by changes in pronouns. Still, the decree is
likely to have included a version of the phrase *qui rem publicam salvam vellent*:
Cicero would probably not emphasize such a detail if it was not in the recent
Senate decree. The emphatic expression *ad me unum hominem fractum et prope
dissipatum* could be Cicero's exaggeration. – Where Cicero mentions this
Senate decree in other speeches (Cic. *Dom.* 73; *Sest.* 128; *Pis.* 34), he also stresses
the extraordinary nature of such a decree on behalf of a single individual, and
he notes the public importance and the respect shown thereby. – Boll (2019,
190, 191) assumes that Cicero quotes from the Senate decree and suggests that
the identification of Cicero's well-being with that of the Republic in the decree
explains Cicero's frequent use of this motif. In Cicero's report, however, there is
no straightforward identification, and Cicero's parallelization of himself and
the Republic in the speeches goes beyond what he says about the Senate decree.
It is more plausible that Cicero adjusted the presentation of the Senate decree
to his overall description of the situation.

cuncti…ad unius salutem: the repetition of numerals highlights that an
appeal was made to the whole of Italy to show its support for the Republic by
the restitution of a single individual (for emphasis on the involvement of the
whole of Italy, see, e.g., Cic. *RS* 25; 26; 39; *RQ* 1; 10; 16; 18; *Dom.* 30; 57; 87; *Sest.*
128). – Cicero interprets this call and the response as evidence of his importance, recognized throughout the country. The invitation to people from outside
Rome to participate in the voting might have had a more practical reason and
been intended to offset the dominance of the urban populace, probably including a larger number of P. Clodius Pulcher's followers.

qui rem publicam salvam vellent: elsewhere too Cicero uses the expression
'who wanted the Republic safe' with respect to this Senate decree calling people
together (Cic. *Dom.* 73; *Sest.* 128; *Pis.* 34). The phrase is a formula typically used
in connection with recruiting troops in a state of emergency (Serv. ad Verg.
Aen. 7.614; 8.1). By recalling the standard context for this formula Cicero
assimilates his recall to a moment of national crisis and its resolution (see also
Bellardi 1975, 112 n. 6).

fractum et prope dissipatum: an illustration of Cicero's desperate situation:
dissipatus is unusual in this sense with reference to a single individual (*OLD* s.v.
dissipo 3 'To disintegrate and reduce to fragments, destroy completely, shatter');
it is, therefore, qualified by *prope* and added as an intensification of *fractum*.
The combination of these terms appears elsewhere in Cicero with reference to
res familiaris (Cic. *Att.* 4.1.3: *in re autem familiari, quae quem ad modum fracta,*

dissipata, direpta sit non ignoras, valde laboramus). – Boll (2019, 191) sees an allusion to Cicero's destroyed property, but the expression focuses on the person.

restituendum et defendendum: this collocation (*defendendum* taken up in *ad unius salutem defendendam* and *qui civis me non defendisset*, Cic. *RS* 24–5) suggests that the support for Cicero is to extend beyond restoration and include protection.

ter: Cicero elsewhere mentions three other occasions when the formula was used (although in the first instance not by a consul): (1) in 133 BCE P. Scipio Nasica Serapio employed it, as if he was consul (regarding the actual consul as inactive), to provoke initiatives against Ti. Sempronius Gracchus (Cic. *Tusc.* 4.51: *iratus videtur fuisse Ti. Graccho tum, cum consulem languentem reliquit atque ipse privatus, ut si consul esset, qui rem publicam salvam esse vellent, se sequi iussit.*; cf. Vell. 2.3.1; Val. Max. 3.2.17); (2) in 100 BCE, towards the end of the year, the consuls C. Marius et L. Valerius Flaccus called people to action against the praetor C. Servilius Glaucia and the Tribune of the People L. Appuleius Saturninus (Cic. *Rab. perd.* 20: *fit senatus consultum ut C. Marius L. Valerius consules adhiberent tribunos pl. et praetores, quos eis videretur, operamque darent ut imperium populi Romani maiestasque conservaretur. adhibent omnis tribunos pl. praeter Saturninum, <praetores> praeter Glauciam; qui rem publicam salvam esse vellent, arma capere et se sequi iubent.*); (3) in 67 BCE the consul C. Calpurnius Piso used the phrase to rally support against activities of the Tribune of the People C. Cornelius (Cic. *Corn.* I 46 Puccioni = I 45 Crawford = Ascon. ad Cic. *Corn.* [p. 75.20–3 C.]: *at enim extremi ac difficillimi temporis vocem illam, C. Corneli, consulem mittere coegisti: qui rem p. salvam esse vellent, ut ad legem accipiendam adessent.*). – Livy adds another occasion when a *decurio equitum* employed the formula in 423 BCE (Liv. 4.38.1–3).

qui eius vocem exaudire possent: after the passing of the Senate decree the consuls sent letters to communities in Italy (esp. Cic. *Pis.* 34: *consulis voce et litteris*), while on past occasions the consuls uttered the formula in Rome. Though in earlier instances too the spoken words of the consuls would have reached people beyond those in the audience, Cicero emphasizes the planned wider reach in his case. – Thus, in Cicero's presentation, the difference between his case and past instances is that the words were uttered by the Senate, were delivered to a wider audience, and called for support of an individual in the interests of the Republic (Boll 2019, 191). – *vox*, combined with *exaudire*, has the primary meaning of 'the human voice' (*OLD* s.v. *uox* 1); it includes the sense of 'a spoken utterance, word' (*OLD* s.v. *uox* 7), which becomes dominant in the repetition *eadem voce*.

omnis ex omnibus agris atque oppidis civis totamque Italiam: in *totam Italiam* the geographical term metonymically represents the people living in Italy (see also, e.g., Cic. *RS* 25; 26; 29; 39; *RQ* 1; 10; 11; 16; 18), a frequent feature in Cicero's works (Lebreton 1901, 75–6). The expression emphasizes the totality by focusing on the geographical extension and complements the first item. Thus, *totamque Italiam* does not add another group, but rather another definition: the first item denotes all individuals, whether living in the countryside or in towns; the second specifies the area covered as Italy. – The choice of the specific term *civis* might imply that all these inhabitants of Italy have become Roman citzens (at the end of the Social War) and therefore have an interest in the *res publica* and are entitled to decisions about its condition.

25 meis posteris: Cicero not only expresses gratitude for having been recalled in such an honourable fashion, but also states (by means of a rhetorical question) that he could not leave anything more glorious behind for his descendants. This extolling of the manner of his return (Cic. *Sest.* 128) has the potential disgrace incurred by the removal from Rome appear overshadowed by the glory of the return (on this tactic, see Riggsby 2002, 167–72). – The possessive limits the statement to Cicero's descendants rather than it being a reference to posterity in general; this gives Cicero's recall importance for the entire family (also Cic. *RS* 1; 24; 27) and makes the Senate's activities more significant, without claiming an impact on all posterity (but cf. Cic. *RS* 3; 27).

hoc: looks forward to the accusative and infinitive construction *senatum iudicasse*. This in turn governs an accusative and infinitive construction in which the agent is expressed by a relative clause whose antecedent (*civis*) is included in the relative clause and taken up by *eum*.

qui civis ... noluisse: develops a negative version of the formula mentioned as part of the Senate decree (Cic. *RS* 24) and applies it to individuals: any citizen not supporting Cicero would show their lack of concern for the Republic. This is not exactly what the Senate apparently decreed (see also Boll 2019, 192), and Cicero qualifies this statement as a view of the Senate (*iudicasse*) rather than a decree (Cic. *RS* 24: *decrevistis*). Such an inference with the reversed perspective and the stronger wording enables Cicero to criticize those not demonstrating any support (by presenting it as the Senate's opinion) and to highlight again the close relationship between his situation and that of the Republic (see Introduction, section 3.4).

vestra auctoritas ... eximia consulis dignitas: while the formula was issued by the consul, Cicero attributes its effect to the authority of both the Senate (the audience) and the consul (P. Cornelius Lentulus Spinther), as it resulted from a Senate decree.

ut ... veniret: repeats the conclusion, yet with reference to individual behaviour: not turning up as requested would ignore the authority of the Senate and the consul and thus be an act of *dedecus et flagitium*. Such a claim emphasizes the resounding effect of the consul's announcement (Cic. *Pis.* 36: *ex vobis audio nemini civi ullam quo minus adesset satis iustam excusationem esse visam*). – *venire* is used absolutely without an indication of purpose as before (Cic. *RS* 24) or of venue as afterwards (Cic. *RS* 25), since these can be inferred. The purpose is identified before the venue: the former is more important, and the location would have been obvious for the contemporary audience (the place for public meetings and voting in Rome).

dedecus et flagitium: for the collocation, see, e.g., Cic. *Mur.* 12; *Off.* 3.86.

idemque consul: i.e. the consul P. Cornelius Lentulus Spinther.

illa incredibilis multitudo...et paene Italia ipsa: according to Cicero a large number of people followed the consuls' request and came to Rome, 'almost Italy itself' (Cic. *Pis.* 34). Although this claim is repeated elsewhere (Cic. *RS* 24 n.), it is an exaggeration designed to illustrate the level of support for Cicero. At least qualifying *Italia ipsa* by *paene* makes it less hyperbolic, while Cicero says that *tota Italia* was asked to come (Cic. *RS* 24) and *Italia tota* was in attendance at the subsequent *contio* (Cic. *RS* 26). – The particle *et* has explicative function and illustrates what the *incredibilis multitudo* consists in (K.-St. II 25–6).

vos frequentissimos: the phrase *frequentissimus senatus* appears sixteen times in Cicero (Cic. *RQ* 15; *Dom.* 14; 70; *Har. resp.* 13; 14; 15; *Sest.* 129; *Pis.* 6; 34; *Leg. agr.* 1.26; *Mil.* 12; 66; *Phil.* 2.12; 2.99; *Leg.* 3.18; *Att.* 1.17.9) and nowhere else. According to Ryan (1998, 38–9) *frequentissimus senatus* is a non-technical term denoting a well-attended meeting; as all recorded instances refer to the period after Sulla, it might indicate 'crowded' in relation to the previous total of 300 senators. At the same time, *frequens senatus* is a technical term and means 'quorate', indicating an attendance of more than 200 senators (on the terms and numerical value of *frequens* and *frequentissimus senatus*, see Ryan 1998, 27–45). By contrast, Bonnefond-Coudry (1989, 425–35 [with a list of occurrences]) argues that *senatus frequens* is not a technical term but rather denotes a well-attended meeting of the Senate or a majority of senators voting for something, apparently without distinguishing between different forms of *frequens*. – In Cicero's address to the senators *vos* replaces *senatus*; the phrase thus is equivalent to *frequentissimus senatus* (at Cic. *RQ* 15, *Dom.* 14 and *Sest.* 129 about this meeting): not only did a large number of members of the public from all over Italy assemble in Rome; in addition, many senators attended the corresponding Senate meeting. Later in this speech Cicero claims that 417 senators and all magistrates were present (Cic. *RS* 26 and n.). Such a high turnout (irrespective of the quorum required) indicates the Senate's support for Cicero; for, despite the requirement to attend Senate meetings (Cic. *Leg.* 3.11), senators often chose not to attend so as to show opposition or avoid discussions of difficult issues (Bonnefond-Coudry 1989, 357–435). – *frequentissimos* has a predicative function and indicates the result of the summoning rather than being part of the consul's order (K.-St. I 679). The calling of a *senatus frequens* in connection with an appropriate technical verb such as *edicere* can represent the order of the organizing magistrate (Cic. *Att.* 9.17.1; *Phil.* 3.19; Liv. 28.9.5; see Bonnefond-Coudry 1989, 358–61).

in Capitolium convocavit: the first of two Senate meetings in early July 57 BCE was held in the Temple of Iuppiter Optimus Maximus on the Capitol (Cic. *Dom.* 14; *Prov. cons.* 22; *Sest.* 129; see Introduction, section 2; on the possible practical arrangements for hosting a large meeting of the Senate in this temple, see Taylor/Scott 1969, 559–68). – Weigel (1986, 337–8, 340) argues that there were no religious grounds for selecting this meeting space (as suggested for sessions in this temple by Taylor/Scott 1969, 560) and assumes that the reason for choosing this venue in all known cases was 'the combination of a critical or very important situation with special needs for the dramatic setting, ample space, audibility, and security which the Capitoline could provide' (340).

quo tempore: i.e., at the time of this meeting of the Senate. – Since the next sentence starts with *nam* and thus explains this comment, it must refer to what follows, rather than to what precedes, and thus apply to Nepos, who is thereby introduced favourably before details are discussed or his name is given.

Q. Metellus: Q. Caecilius Metellus Nepos, cos. 57 BCE (Cic. *RS* 5 n.).

frater inimici: *frater* (of P. Clodius Pulcher) denotes 'cousin' (*OLD* s.v. *frater* 2) or 'half-brother'. Elsewhere too Cicero talks of Nepos or his brother and P. Clodius Pulcher as *fratres* (Cic. *Dom.* 7; 13; 70; *Har. resp.* 45; *Cael.* 60; *Att.* 4.3.4). The familial relationships are not entirely certain (for an overview of reconstructions proposed, see Tatum 1999, 34–6, with references). – Clodius is again identified as *inimicus* (Cic. *RS* 4 n.) and not named (Cic. *RS* 3 n.). Here this leads to a double mention of *inimicus* referring to two individuals; this phrasing enhances the contrast between Nepos' initial opposition and his later support for Cicero.

perspecta…deposuit: Cicero highlights that Nepos was previously hostile to him and dropped his opposition during his consulship, placing the common welfare above personal dissensions (Cic. *RS* 5 n.; similarly on M. Cispius and his relatives at Cic. *RS* 21). Describing Nepos' letting go of his enmity as a sign of *naturae bonitas* and *vera nobilitas* has Nepos' earlier enmity appear as a temporary aberration and presents forgetting his personal grudge for the sake of the public good as a sign of his true noble nature (Cic. *RQ* 10; 15; *Pis.* 35). At the same time Cicero implies that Nepos was prompted by the views of the majority (*perspecta vestra voluntate*); thus, the change of attitude may have been a case of expediency (Goldmann 2012, 128–9; Boll 2019, 194–5). Cassius Dio mentions fear as a motive (Cass. Dio 39.8.2). Ryan (1998, 32) suggests that a bargain was struck on the terms of the Senate decree, which enabled Nepos to drop his resistance at the last minute; there is no clear evidence to confirm such a suggestion.

omnia privata odia: that Cicero defines the previous position as *privata odia* may allude to the opposition between Cicero and Nepos' relative Clodius because of the familial dimension. When Nepos, as Tribune of the People, prevented Cicero from speaking to the People on the last day of his consulship in

December 63 BCE (Cic. *RS* 5 n.), this intervention was probably of a political nature. Introducing the nuance of a private conflict enables Cicero to present a plausible development of Nepos' attitude and to highlight again the political importance of Cicero's case for the Republic.

P. Servilius: P. Servilius Vatia Isauricus (*RE* Servilius 93; cos. 79, censor 55–54 BCE [*MRR* II 82, 215]; see Nicholson 1992, 62–3), also mentioned in the speech before the People (Cic. *RQ* 17), was a respected ex-consul. He served as provincial governor in Cilicia after his consulship and fought against the pirates and the Isauri, and he supported the punishment of the captured Catilinarian conspirators in Cicero's consular year of 63 BCE (Cic. *Dom.* 132; *Phil.* 2.12; *Att.* 12.21.1).

vir cum clarissimus tum vero optimus mihique amicissimus: in this collocation (Cic. *RS* 5 n.), the first phrase indicates rank (*OLD* s.v. *clarus* 7), and the second denotes character and personal relationship (cf. Cic. *Sest.* 39: *Cn. Pompeio, clarissimo viro mihique et nunc et quoad licuit amicissimo*). – Cicero typically endows P. Servilius Vatia Isauricus with honorific epithets (Cic. *RQ* 17 and n.; *clarissimus* also at Cic. *Verr.* 2.1.56; *Leg. agr.* 2.50; *Dom.* 43; *Prov. cons.* 1; *Fam.* 13.68.3). A similar combination of general praise and appreciation of support for Cicero occurs in a later speech (Cic. *Prov. cons.* 1: *P. Servilium, qui ante me sententiam dixit, virum clarissimum et cum <in> universam rem publicam tum etiam erga meam salutem fide ac benevolentia singulari*). – *vero* added to the *tum… cum* construction puts particular emphasis on the second part (*OLD* s.v. *uero*[1] 5c).

auctoritatis et orationis suae divina quadam gravitate: Servilius has an effect on Nepos both by his position of authority and by his speech (Cic. *Dom.* 132; *Prov. cons.* 22; *Sest.* 130). The term *oratio* points to a formal speech rather than a private conversation; another reference to the incident suggests that Servilius spoke at a Senate meeting in the Temple of Jupiter (*Prov. cons.* 22). – Servilius' *gravitas* (*OLD* s.v. *grauitas* 6) is defined (with qualification) as 'divine'; still, this assimiliation to the divine sphere is more subdued than Lentulus' description as *parens ac deus* (Cic. *RS* 8) (Cole 2013, 71).

ad sui generis communisque sanguinis facta virtutesque revocavit, ut… visus est: Servilius exerted an influence upon Nepos by recalling the great deeds of his ancestors and the family tradition and by encouraging him to take advice from his forefathers as counsellors, as it were. In addition to a general reference to the ancestors, Servilius apparently went on to name individual examples, including Metellus Numidicus, who also had to leave Rome; his personality and fate are given more prominence in the report of the incident in *Pro Sestio* (Cic. *Sest.* 130). – P. Servilius Vatia Isauricus was a grandson and Q. Caecilius Metellus Nepos was a great-grandson of Q. Caecilius Metellus Macedonicus (Cic. *Dom.* 123). The grandfather of Q. Caecilius Metellus Macedonicus was L. Caecilius Metellus (cos. 251, 247 BCE), who won a decisive victory in the First Punic War which gave Rome control over Sicily. – *revocavit*

(*OLD* s.v. *reuoco* 13) governs a direct object (*quem*), a prepositional phrase headed by *ad* indicating direction, and then an *ut*-clause.

ut haberet...excitatos: that Servilius reminded Nepos of his family tradition and encouraged him to act in this virtuous spirit is illustrated by the scenario that, in order to decide on the best course of action, he should be taking advice at a council meeting with his dead relatives.

haberet in consilio: a *consilium* was an informal council private individuals or magistrates could consult for non-binding advice in matters such as court proceedings, religious questions, issues of property, or the conduct of a war. The advisers were called as a group by the person seeking advice, informed of the matter, and asked for their opinions (Mommsen, *StR* I 307–19; W. Liebenam, s.v. Consilium, *RE* IV 1, 1901, 915–22; for the phrase, see Liv. 36.8.6; 40.8.4).

fratrem: Nepos' brother is Q. Caecilius Metellus Celer (*RE* Caecilius 86; cos. 60 BCE; [*MRR* II 182–3]; see van Ooteghem 1967, 245–79), a praetor during Cicero's consulship in 63 BCE (*MRR* II 166), and afterwards a provincial governor in Gallia Cisalpina (*MRR* II 176), who died in 59 BCE (Cic. *Sest.* 131; *Cael.* 59).

{ab inferis}: while Celer was dead by the time of this speech and *ab inferis* appears in a comparable passage in *Pro Sestio* (Cic. *Sest.* 130), the phrase does not fit into this sentence without a governing verb and awkwardly doubles *paene ex Acherunte excitatos*, which refers to all men mentioned and expresses the same idea more vividly. This phrase is, therefore, best deleted with Lambinus (followed by Madvig 1873, 212; Maslowski 1981; supported by Boll 2019, 195–6; yet kept by Peterson 1911). It may be a gloss that entered the text, added to indicate that Cicero is talking about Nepos' dead brother (rather than Clodius, also called *frater*).

socium rerum mearum: as praetor in Cicero's consular year of 63 BCE, Celer supported Cicero by raising and leading an army (Cic. *Cat.* 2.5; 2.12; Sall. *Cat.* 30.5; cf. Cic. *Cat.* 1.19); he is described similarly in a comparable context in another speech (Cic. *Sest.* 131). After Cicero's consulship Celer was temporarily annoyed at Cicero because of his treatment of Celer's brother (Cic. *Fam.* 5.1–2).

paene ex Acherunte excitatos: a metaphorical expression for 'consulting' with and thus adopting the spirits of one's dead ancestors, as if they were called up from the Underworld (indicated by Acheron as *pars pro toto*) to sit on one's council. – In *Orator* Cicero advises against calling the dead up again from the underworld in a speech (Cic. *Orat.* 85). Here, it is not Cicero's own speech and not a rhetorical ploy, but rather a way of indicating the benefit of advice from deceased ancestors, i.e. by considering how they have acted and would have acted in the current situation.

Numidicum illum Metellum: Q. Caecilius Metellus Numidicus (*RE* Caecilius 97; cos. 109, censor 102 BCE [*MRR* I 545, 567]; *ORF*[4] 58; see, e.g., van Ooteghem 1967, 124–77; Kelly 2006, 84–8, 178–9) acquired his cognomen (and celebrated a triumph) after waging war against Jugurtha in Numidia (Sall. *Iug.* 43–88); he had some rhetorical and philosophical education (Cic. *De or.* 1.215; 3.68; *Brut.* 135). In 100 BCE, when the Tribune of the People L. Appuleius Saturninus (*RE* Appuleius 29; tr. pl. 103, 100, 99 BCE [*MRR* I 563, 575–6; II 1]), supported by C. Marius, put forward a land law (assigning land to Roman veterans) on which all senators were required to take an oath or accept a penalty, Numidicus refused to swear the oath and may have been taken to court as a result (*TLRR* 77; Gruen 1965b; 1968, 181–3). Numidicus then left Rome for voluntary exile on Rhodes (Liv. *Epit.* 69; Plut. *Mar.* 29.8) and later in Asia (Val. Max. 4.1.13; *Vir. ill.* 62.2), followed by a formal *aqua et igni interdictio*. After the defeat of Saturninus and his accomplices, Numidicus was recalled, thanks to the efforts of his relatives, and returned to Rome (Cic. *RS* 37; 38; *RQ* 9–11; *Dom.* 82; 87; 123; *Sest.* 37; 101; 130; *Pis.* 20; *Planc.* 69; 89; *Clu.* 95; *Balb.* 11; *Fam.* 1.9.16; Liv. *Epit.* 69; Plut. *Cato min.* 32.3; *Mar.* 31.1; Cass. Dio 38.7.1; App. *B Civ.* 1.29–33). – Numidicus frequently appears as a paradigm for Cicero (e.g. Nicholson 1992, 32–4; Pina Polo 1996, 108; Degl'Innocenti Pierini 2000, 250–3; Kelly 2006, 143–5, 153–4 [esp. 153 n. 64: 'There are thirty-one passages in the extant Ciceronian corpus that mention Metellus Numidicus, twenty-two of which deal with his exile. Cicero seems to have seen Metellus as a kindred spirit, since their political careers had several parallels. Both men had resisted the actions of radical tribunes of the plebs, withdrew into voluntary exile due to the machinations of their enemies, but in the end managed a triumphant return to Rome.']; van der Blom 2010, 130–2; see Cic. *RS* 37–8 nn.). When Cicero notes in *In Pisonem* that Numidicus left Rome to avoid an armed conflict (Cic. *Pis.* 20), he implicitly establishes a parallel between his own 'exile' in his interpretation and that of Numidicus. – As a famous member of the family (K.-St. I 622), Numidicus is referred to as *Numidicus ille Metellus* (Cic. *Sest.* 130; *Arch.* 6). In view of these parallels, there is no reason to delete *Metellum* as suggested by Manutius and adopted, for instance, by Peterson (1911).

de patria discessus: Numidicus' 'exile' is described in a positive paraphrase similar to those Cicero adduces for his own absence fom Rome (see Introduction, section 3.4). – The prepositional phrase functions as an attribute of the noun (K.-St. I 213–14; Pinkster 2015, 1045).

honestus omnibus sane, luctuosus tamen: the transmission here is divided, and the text can be restored in various ways. This version (adopted by Maslowski 1981) creates a plausible sense with little change to what is transmitted in some manuscripts (for the dual aspect of Metellus' fate, see Cic. *Sest.* 130: *Numidici illius Metelli casum vel gloriosum vel gravem*). *omnibus* is Cicero's exaggeration and gives the statement greater force than a reduction to *omnibus bonis* (according to Halm's conjecture). A contrast between everybody's view and that of Metellus (*molestus omnibus, ipsi ne luctuosus quidem*), as suggested by the readings of other manuscripts, is not required and would highlight the negative aspects of the situation when the emphasis is on Metellus as a model (on the text, see Courtney 1963, 15–16; Maslowski 1980, 409–11; Boll 2019, 196–7).

26 exstitit: is basically the reading of one group of manuscripts (*extitit*), while others have *dimittit*. Earlier editors have been reluctant to put just *exstitit* in the text, suspecting that something must have got lost (e.g. Müller 1885, 440: *divinitus extitit*; Peterson 1911: *divinitus exstitit*; Klotz 1913, 488: *idem extitit*; Sydow 1941, 168: *itaque dimit<tens iram suam rei p. exti>tit non modo salutis defensor*). Yet the concise phrase *itaque exstitit non modo salutis defensor* (preferred by recent editors) is effective in illustrating Nepos' change of mind as a result of Servilius' intervention (*itaque*; see Cic. *RS* 25) and his immediate activity on behalf of Cicero (on the text, see also Boll 2019, 197–8).

qui ... fuerat inimicus: Cicero highlights Nepos' switch from being an enemy (Cic. *RS* 25 n.) to conferring a *beneficium* upon him, i.e. contributing to Cicero's honourable recall.

ante hoc suum beneficium: for *suum* Klotz' (1913, 488) conjecture *su<mm>um* is often adopted (supported by Busche 1917, 1357; on the text, see also Boll 2019, 198). Such an emphasis on the greatness of Metellus Nepos' *beneficium* sounds inappropriate, especially in relation to the qualification of Lentulus' activities (Cic. *RS* 28). Instead, *suum* clarifies whose *beneficium* it is and stresses that this *inimicus* turned to providing a *beneficium*. The other transmitted version (*unum*) would emphasize that there is only one *beneficium* from Nepos, which might invalidate the praise. – The combination of a possessive and a demonstrative pronoun is attested elsewhere in Cicero (Cic. *Dom.* 8; *Sest.* 32).

adscriptor: a technical term for a supporter of a law or a Senate decree (Cic. *RS* 9 n.). The complement is *dignitatis meae*, which is not the procedural item supported; this probably is a shortened expression and rather indicates the result of the measure, the restoration of Cicero's standing: this is what is to be highlighted rather than legal technicalities. – While in this speech Nepos is described as an *adscriptor* of the measure to restore Cicero (Cic. *RS* 9; 26), in *Pro Sestio* he is presented as initiating the debate in the Senate (Cic. *Sest.* 130); in the speech to the People and in *De domo sua* both consuls are said to be acting together (Cic. *RQ* 10; 15; *Dom.* 70). Elsewhere, putting forward the bill is attributed to Lentulus (Cic. *RQ* 17; *Dom.* 71; 75). The consuls apparently acted jointly in front of the People (Cic. *Pis.* 35; Cass. Dio 39.8.2). The measure, therefore, seems to have been a joint initiative by the consuls in the Senate and before the People, with Lentulus taking the lead (e.g. Stein 1930, 33). As Lentulus chaired the first Senate meeting of the year in January (Cic. *RQ* 11 and n.), and the consuls took the lead in alternate months, he would have been the leading consul in July. Highlighting Lentulus' role is convenient for Cicero, since he was his unequivocal and stronger advocate. Here Cicero stresses that Nepos not only became a supporter in principle, but also engaged in concrete action on his behalf. – In most cases Cicero describes the consuls' activity as *referre*, the appropriate term for consuls raising a topic in the Senate for discussion and for the expected activity of consuls chairing a session. Here *adscriptor* implies support of a motion put forward. Occasionally, most prominently in the speech before the People, Cicero calls the consuls *auctores* and thus implies an even more active role (for such a position of a consul, see Val. Max. 7.6.1).

quo...die: in July 57 BCE, probably 8 July, referring to the earlier of two subsequent Senate meetings concerning Cicero in that month (on the chronology, see Kaster 2006, App. 1).

cum: partly with a temporal sense, providing details on the circumstances on that day, and partly with a concessive sense, contrasting the number of people present with the single dissenting voice.

vos quadringenti decem septem essetis: the only evidence for the precise number of senators attending that meeting. While senators were obliged to attend Senate meetings, they did not always do so: for instance, a Senate meeting a few days after the one at which this speech was delivered was attended by almost no ex-consuls, while they attended again on the following day (Cic. *Att.* 4.1.6). Although Cicero highlights the large number of senators supporting him for the purposes of the argument, that Senate meeting about Cicero apparently indeed had a particularly good turnout (Cic. *RS* 25 n.). Of the six examples of Senate meetings for which attendance figures are attested, this is the highest (Mommsen, *StR* III 851; Taylor/Scott 1969, 532; Weigel 1986, 337), closely followed by another meeting in 61 BCE attended by about 415 men (Cic. *Att.* 1.14.5). Elsewhere Cicero regards a meeting attended by almost 200 senators as well attended considering its timing just before the holidays (Cic. *Q Fr.* 2.1.1). – *vos* (omitted in some manuscripts) is needed (see also Boll 2019, 199) for a contrast with *magistratus*.

magistratus autem omnes adessent: *autem* contrasts the senators with the magistrates as the senators attended in large numbers, but not everyone came, while all the magistrates were present. The emphasis on numbers prepares the contrast with what follows: while so many people were in the Senate, only one person was of a divergent opinion. – The wording does not make it clear whether the magistrates are seen as included in the 417 senators or as present in addition. With most senior magistrates being senators (Kunkel/Wittmann 1995, 440–3: in Cicero's time magistrates essentially became senators after their term of office in their first magistracy, if not before, with the official *lectio* being a formality), it could be the former (Kaster 2006, 365, on Cic. *Sest.* 129: '417 members attended, including all magistrates'); then the magistrates are mentioned separately because none of them is missing and their conduct is particularly influential and telling. De Benedetti (1929, 776) also opts for the former interpretation (though allowing for a few junior magistrates not yet senators), while apparently assumming 416 as the overall figure ('Erano presenti 416 senatori, fra cui quasi tutti i magistrati; si oppose soltanto Clodio e nessuno osò intercedere.'). Mitchell (1991, 155: 'It was attended by 417 senators....The motion was approved by everyone present with the single exception of Clodius.') similarly seems to subsume the magistrates among the senators, but equally to assume that the magistrates participated in the voting. Yet magistrates were not eligible to vote while in office and were not counted among the voting members (Mommsen, *StR* III 851, 944–6; Taylor/Scott 1969, 532). Taylor/Scott (1969, 532–3), therefore, regard the senators and the magistrates as two separate groups, with the magistrates in office not technically senators, and assume that about 450 people were present. This is more plausible in light of the conventions in the Senate and enhances the argument that among such a large number only a single individual disagreed. – Weiske (1807, 270) suggests that *magistratus* refers to *tribuni plebis*, since, although they had rights of senators, they were always considered as a distinct group: this is a specific interpretation not supported by the usual meaning of the term and the overall structure of the sentence.

dissensit unus: i.e. P. Clodius Pulcher (for Clodius as the single person with a different view, see Cic. *RQ* 15; *Dom.* 14; *Har. resp.* 14; *Sest.* 129; 130). – The verbs describing Clodius' position (*dissentire*; in one case *dissidere*) denote a difference in opinion, but do not indicate how it manifested itself. It is usually inferred that Clodius voted against the motion (e.g. Stein 1930, 33; Wuilleumier 1952, 20).

is qui...putarat: identifies Clodius (again not named) by a reference to Clodius' bill on Cicero's banishment in Cicero's presentation (Cic. *RS* 3; 4 nn.). The summary here is even more ironically pointed and derisive than the earlier one: it is not only a tendentious reproduction of the content, but also implies that Clodius is so stupid or arrogant that he believed that the law could even reverse death.

atque illo die: refers to *quo...die* and adds the preparation for the interaction with the People to the activities in the Senate.

rem publicam meis consiliis conservatam: in the speeches of this period Cicero describes both his fighting the Catilinarian Conspiracy and his recent absence from Rome as acts on behalf of the Republic (Cic. *Dom.* 99; *Pis.* 78; *Sest.* 49; 73; see Introduction, section 3.4). On occasion he goes so far as to claim that he was recalled to preserve the Republic (Cic. *Dom.* 5). Cicero's definition of his leaving Rome is unlikely to be assigned to the Senate at this stage. Thus, Cicero's claim that the Senate was of the opinion that the Republic had been saved by his initiative must be his interpretation with reference to the Catilinarian Conspiracy (thus Boll 2019, 200); when Cicero's actions against the Catilinarians are seen as justified in the public interest, the Senate is presented as implicitly declaring the reason for the accusations leading to Cicero leaving Rome as invalid. Cicero gives this interpretation of his intervention not only as his own view, but also as the assessment of others (Senate: *Har. resp.* 58; various senators: Cic. *RQ* 17; Pompey: Cic. *RS* 29; *RQ* 16; everyone: Cic. *RQ* 5; *Mil.* 73). Attributing such an opinion to the Senate shows that Cicero was recalled because his importance for the Republic was recognized: clarifying this enables Cicero to regain his standing. – The phrasing implies that the assessment of Cicero's activities was stated emphatically as the Senate's opinion (*gravissimis verbis et plurimis*), but the verb *iudicare* does not make it clear whether it was included in the Senate decree. A reference to the same Senate meeting in *Pro Sestio* says that such a motion was put forward by Cn. Pompeius Magnus and accepted by the Senate (Cic. *Sest.* 129: *vel quod in templo Iovis optimi maximi factum est, cum vir is qui tripertitas orbis terrarum oras atque regiones tribus triumphis adiunctas huic imperio notavit, de scripto sententia dicta, mihi uni testimonium patriae conservatae dedit; cuius sententiam ita frequentissimus senatus secutus est ut unus dissentiret hostis, idque ipsum tabulis publicis mandaretur ad memoriam posteri temporis sempiternam: . . .*).

idem consul: one might expect this consul to be Nepos, who is mentioned in what immediately precedes; but on the basis of what Cicero narrates elsewhere (Cic. *Sest.* 107–8; *Dom.* 75; *Pis.* 34) it must be the other consul, Lentulus, taking up the preceding *idemque consul* (Cic. *RS* 25). Perhaps *idem* means that the same consul organized the *contio* and put forward the motion in the Senate; the initiative is not applied to Metellus, who is characterized as an *adscriptor*.

eadem: i.e. *verba*, supplied from the preceding clause.

a principibus civitatis: besides the consul, *principes civitatis* (Cic. *RQ* 17; *Pis.* 34) spoke at this *contio* in support of Cicero, including Cn. Pompeius Magnus, P. Servilius Vatia Isauricus, L. Gellius, and senior senators such as ex-consuls and ex-praetors (Cic. *RQ* 16–17; *Dom.* 30; *Sest.* 107–8; *Pis.* 34; *Mil.* 39; on this *contio*, see Hiebel 2009, 450). – Officials organizing a *contio* could ask others, including private individuals, priests, and other magistrates, to speak (e.g. Thommen 1989, 172–9, including a list of all who are known to have been asked to speak at *contiones* organized by someone else).

in contione: this *contio* at which Cicero's case was made and the approval of the proposed bill was recommended is different from the later *comitia centuriata* at which the vote on the bill took place (Cic. *RS* 27–8).

postero die: on the day after the Senate meeting just described, probably on 9 July 57 BCE.

ipse: again the consul Lentulus. – *cum* introduces a temporal clause with explicative function (K.-St. II 330–1; Lebreton 1901, 338); the conjunction is emphasized by *quidem*. The clause stresses that, while several *principes civitatis* spoke, the consul made a particularly impressive appearance in support of Cicero.

egit . . . meam causam: the consul not only arranged the *contio*, but also delivered an effective speech. – *causam agere* originally has a legal meaning (*OLD* s.v. *causa* A3). While the phrase came to be used in a non-legal transferred sense, the connotations of this choice of phrasing (also at Cic. *Sest.* 107: *egit causam summa cum gravitate copiaque dicendi tanto silentio*) create the impression that the consul defends Cicero like an advocate in court and thus indicate strong support. – *ornatissime* describes the style of the speech (*OLD* s.v. *ornatus*[1] 2).

astante atque audiente Italia tota: obviously, the whole of Italy was not in attendance in a literal sense: Cicero rhetorically highlights the great number and regional diversity of the people at the *contio* (Cic. *Sest.* 107: *tota in illa contione Italia constitit*), in line with the earlier statements that people from all over Italy were called to Rome and many came (Cic. *RS* 24–5).

cuiusquam conducti aut perditi: an allusion to Clodius' supporters, who, according to Cicero, were morally depraved (*perditi*) and hired with bribes to voice (dis)approval and interrupt opponents at meetings (*conducti*). Cicero presents these men as a class of people opposed to the supporters of his recall and the Republic (*bonis*). – *aut* does not connect mutually exclusive alternatives; instead, after a negation, *aut* adds another item qualifying the first one (K.-St. II 103): a description of these people is followed by a characterization.

vocem acerbam atque inimicam bonis: indicates the noise (by means of disruptive exclamations) these people would make at such a *contio* characterized from the point of view of the speakers presented as supporting Cicero and the Republic. – According to what Cicero says elsewhere, the speeches at this *contio* were listened to in silence without any disruptive shouts from opponents such as Clodius' followers (Cic. *Sest.* 107–8). Cicero does not indicate how this silence was achieved; his narrative implies that the lack of disruption was a result of the consul's effective speech and the unanimous agreement of the assembly. Mouritsen apparently assumes that there were measures in place to prevent Clodius' followers from attending (Mouritsen 2001, 47: 'In 57 the senate made the consul call a *contio*, which explicitly excluded the followers of Clodius,...', apparently referring the passage in *Pro Sestio* to a different *contio* [2001, 48]); there is no evidence for such actions.

bonis: again in political sense (Cic. *RS* 12 n.).

27 ad haec...reliqua...addidistis: returns to activities of the Senate and refers to further Senate decrees about Cicero passed on the day after the meeting of the Senate just described, i.e. on the same day as a *contio* (see Cic. *RS* 26 n.; Introduction, section 2). These decrees go beyond recalling Cicero and specify details concerning the circumstances (Cic. *Sest.* 129; *Pis.* 35), including measures in cases of obstruction (for the typical phrasing, see Cic. *Fam.* 8.8.6: *senatum existimare neminem eorum, qui potestatem habent intercedendi, impediendi, moram adferre oportere quo minus de r. p. p. R. q. p. ad senatum referri senatique consultum fieri possit; qui impedierit, prohibuerit, eum senatum existimare contra rem publicam fecisse. si quis huic s. c. intercesserit, senatui placere auctoritatem perscribi et de ea re ad senatum p. q. t. referri.*).

ad haec non modo adiumenta salutis sed etiam ornamenta dignitatis meae: it is more likely that *non modo adiumenta salutis sed etiam ornamenta dignitatis meae* depends on *ad haec* and *reliqua* is the object of *addidistis* rather than that the object is *non modo adiumenta salutis sed etiam ornamenta digni-tatis meae reliqua* and *ad haec* is the prepositional phrase (both grammatically possible). While such a structure creates a slightly awkward break between *meae* and *reliqua*, it highlights the importance of the first decree and marks the further arrangements as additional. Thus, Cicero presents even the initial decree of recall not only as support for his well-being, but also as a demonstration of respect.

vos idem: emphasizes that the senators are also responsible for the further decrees.

decrevistis: introduces the list of elements of the decrees, reported in indirect speech. The report is not a verbatim summary (at any rate the text has been adapted to the situation and the personal pronouns have been adjusted), but the substance could be inspired by the actual decrees.

rem: an unspecific description of Cicero's recall and the arrangements for it.

impediret…impedisset: indicates the prohibition and the repercussions, should someone obstruct proceedings (Cic. *Sest.* 129: *vel quod est postridie decretum in curia populi ipsius Romani, et eorum qui ex municipiis convenerant admonitu, ne quis de caelo servaret, ne quis moram ullam adferret; si quis aliter fecisset, eum plane eversorem rei publicae fore idque senatum gravissime latu-rum, et ut statim de eius facto referretur; Pis.* 35: *de me senatus ita decrevit Cn. Pompeio auctore et eius sententiae principe, ut, si quis impedisset reditum meum, in hostium numerum putaretur*), including by *obnuntiatio* or *intercessio* (Ryan 1998, 33). – Some manuscripts have *id impedisset* after *rem impediret*: while it is possible to take up a masculine or feminine noun by a neuter demonstrative pronoun in a generic reference (K.-St. I 61–2), this is less likely in the case of a general term such as *res*. Thus, it is more plausible to supply *rem* again, which does not need to be expressed.

qui impedisset, vos: *vos* (found in some manuscripts) is the subject of the first accusative and infinitive construction and needed for clarity (Boll 2019, 202). According to the transmitted text the object of *vos graviter molesteque laturos* has to be developed from the context; the following clause specifies the resulting assessment with regard to the individual concerned (*illum*) and then the measures to be taken (*ut…referretur*). – Boll (2019, 201–2) suggests reading <*si*> *quis impedisset* (cf. Cic. *Pis.* 35), on the basis that *aegre/moleste/graviter ferre* is not attested with a person as the object in classical Latin. This change does not seem necessary, since the action can be regarded as the object and *qui* as introducing a relative clause with a conditional connotation (K.-St. II 309).

contra…facturum: this tricolon listing the items someone causing obstruction would act against agrees with how Cicero reports the substance of the decree elsewhere (Cic. *Sest.* 129; *Pis.* 35), though presumably with is own emphasis: he again aligns his fate with the welfare of the Republic, presents the *boni* as on his side, in contrast to his opponents, and claims that support for him ensures the welfare of the Republic and consensus among all (right-minded) citizens.

calumniarentur: according to this sketch the Senate decrees said that Cicero was to return in any case even if there were delaying tactics by false accusations. If these delays concern the ratification of the recall by the popular assembly, the basis for the envisaged alternative process would be that the procedure triggering Cicero's departure was not regarded as legally valid; then a law for recall would not be needed and the authority of the Senate would be sufficient (Cic. *Sest.* 73). According to the detailed report in *Pro Sestio*, the Senate decrees said that they should be ratified within the next five comitial days and that, if not, Cicero was to return all the same (Cic. *Sest.* 129). In fact, the law for Cicero's recall (the preferred measure) was passed by the popular assembly on 4 August 57 BCE (see Introduction, section 2). If a measure to prevent potential interventions for delay was included in the Senate decree, it must have been a plausible expectation that such techniques of obstruction might be attempted (on such tactics, see De Libero 1992, 28). – The unspecific subject in the third person plural refers to Cicero's opponents, while it avoids specific accusations.

quid? ... quid? ... quid denique ... ?: this anaphoric, asyndetic and climactic tricolon of questions punctuates the enumeration and highlights the individual items (*OLD* s.v. *quis*[1] 12).

ut: the *ut*-clauses following *quid?* still depend on initial *decrevistis* and *iussistis.*

agerentur gratiae: according to Cicero's comments elsewhere, at a Senate meeting in May 57 BCE people from municipal towns all over Italy were called to Rome (Cic. *RS* 24 and n.), and it was decreed in July 57 BCE that thanks should be paid to those who had come (Cic. *Sest.* 129: *decrevit eodem tempore senatus ut iis qui ex tota Italia salutis meae causa convenerant agerentur gratiae*).

qui e municipiis venissent: the antecedent, the demonstrative pronoun on which the relative clause depends (*eis*), has been omitted, which is rare in such constructions in the classical period (K.-St. II 282).

municipiis: *municipia* were established in Italy from the fourth century BCE; these settlements in areas conquered by the Romans were attached to the Roman Republic by being obliged to carry out certain duties and receiving some of the rights of Roman citizens, but retained a level of independence (of varying degrees and evolving over time). *Lex Iulia de civitate Latinis (et sociis) danda* (90 BCE; *LPPR*, pp. 338–9) and *Lex Plautia Papiria de civitate sociis danda* (89 BCE; *LPPR*, pp. 340–1) gave all confederate communities in Italy south of the Po Roman citizenship and turned them into *municipia* (see Cicero, *Comm. pet.* 30; on *municipium* and *cives sine suffragio*, see Humbert 1978; see also Cic. *RS* 31 n.). Thus, this word can then function as a general term for settlements in Italy.

ad illam diem: i.e. 4 August 57 BCE, the day on which the bill for Cicero's recall was to be voted on by the People (see Introduction, section 2). – *ad illam diem* (on the construction, see K.-St. I 521) is followed by *ille dies* in the next sentence: although there is some variety in texts from the classical period (and in their medieval manuscripts), the word tends to be feminine when it refers to a specific date or appointed day and masculine when it means 'day' generally.

res cum redissent: indicates that the same issues would be resumed then. Although the sense agrees with what is said in *Pro Sestio* and the wording is partially similar (Cic. *Sest.* 129: *ut idem ad res redeuntes ut venirent rogarentur*), the construction is different (see also Boll 2019, 203); therefore, it is unlikely that *ad* (before *res*) has dropped out, as Guerriero (1955, 45) suggests. The pluperfect probably indicates that a renewed look at the matters is arranged before people return.

pari studio: claims that people were asked to show the same eagerness in coming to vote for Cicero's recall in August 57 BCE that they demonstrated in supporting him previously, especially by attending a *contio* on the recent Senate decrees about Cicero in July 57 BCE.

quid denique: *denique* marks the concluding climax of the enumeration by moving to the decisive day in August 57 BCE, when the vote on Cicero's recall took place. A change in structure indicates the transition from the summary of the Senate decrees to the description of the day for which the People were called, by an evaluation of this day: this is no longer a phrase depending on *decrevistis* and *iussistis*, but rather a separate exclamatory question. – The main clause consists of this exclamatory question (*quid* connected with a noun: *quid…ille dies*) and does not have a finite verb; the noun (*dies*) is defined by a series of clauses (*quem…quo die…quo die*). The actions on that day constitute a further step: therefore, the nominative as transmitted in some manuscripts, which turns the clause into a separate phrase, is preferable to the (equally transmitted) ablative (favoured by Boll 2019, 203–4).

ille dies: still 4 August 57 BCE.

P. Lentulus: P. Cornelius Lentulus Spinther, one of the consuls of 57 BCE (Cic. *RS* 5 n.). – Here the consul Lentulus is presented as bringing the proposal to the *comitia* (also Cic. *Dom.* 75; *Pis.* 35), while Cassius Dio reverses the roles of the two consuls in the Senate and has both consuls engage with the *comitia* (Cass. Dio 39.8.2; see Cic. *RS* 26 n.). Q. Caecilius Metellus Nepos, who would have been the leading consul in August (see Cic. *RS* 26; *RQ* 11 nn.), might have given up his right to preside (Ryan 1998, 32 n. 135).

fratrique meo: Cicero's brother Quintus Tullius Cicero (Cic. *RS* 1 n.).

liberisque nostris: probably Cicero's children and those of his brother (Cic. *RS* 1 n.).

natalem: Cicero describes the return as a 'rebirth' and increases its relevance by extending the impact to relatives (see Introduction, section 3.4).

non modo ad nostram verum etiam ad sempiterni memoriam temporis: Cicero enhances the praise of the consul and the significance of the deed by claiming that it will always be remembered, in addition to the grateful recollection of himself and his family in their lifetime (cf. Cic. *RS* 3). – Like the possessive pronoun *nostram* replacing a subjective genitive, *sempiterni…temporis* indicates the agent who will remember, emphasizing the long time throughout which the memory will last (cf. Cic. *Sest.* 129: *ad memoriam posteri temporis sempiternam*).

quo die: refers to *ille dies, quem* and provides another feature of the day; the clause moves on from a characterization of the day to a description of the action on that day.

comitiis centuriatis: since the *comitia centuriata* (voting assembly) approved the decision on Cicero's recall, the same *comitia*, Cicero claims, that had elected him consul also ratified this law. Later Cicero highlights that the restitution of his house happened *comitiis centuriatis, omnium aetatum ordinumque suffragiis* (Cic. *Har. resp.* 11). The law on Cicero's recall is the only known law from the period 70 to 49 BCE passed by this voting assembly. The seleced procedure is justified by the fact that only the *comitia centuriata* were entitled to make decisions about the life or exile of citizens (Taylor 1966, 103–4; cf. Cic. *Sest.* 65; 73; *Rep.* 2.61). – Cicero goes on to contrast his return with those of ex-consuls exiled earlier, who were recalled by tribunician bills (Cic. *RS* 38; *RQ* 10; Cic. *Dom.* 87). For exiles in the past Cicero notes that they were found guilty by the *comitia centuriata* and were recalled 'by the same People', without clarifying whether this was done by another decision in the *comitia centuriata* (Cic. *Dom.* 86: *at vero, ut annales populi Romani et monumenta vetustatis loquuntur, Kaeso ille Quinctius et M. Furius Camillus et C. Servilius Ahala, cum essent optime de re publica meriti, tamen populi incitati vim iracundiamque subierunt, damnatique comitiis centuriatis cum in exsilium profugissent, rursus ab eodem populo placato sunt in suam pristinam dignitatem restituti.*).

iusta: the *comitia centuriata* are presented as traditional, valued, and lawful, probably in contrast to the *comitia curiata*, which only had residual function in Cicero's time (Taylor 1966, 3), and the *comitia tributa*, which might be regarded as less significant, as they mainly elected junior magistrates (Taylor 1966, 6, 59; for a contrast between the different types of *comitia*, see Cic. *Leg agr.* 2.27; on the different types of *comitia* and the *comitia centuriata*, see, e.g., Botsford 1909, 168–261; Taylor 1966; Stuart Staveley 1972, 121–32; Lintott 1999a, 40–64). – The phrasing emphasizes that the ancestors valued the *comitia centuriata* particularly (*maxime*) and made sure to have their lawfulness recognized (cf. Cic. *Div.* 1.103: *praerogativam etiam maiores omen iustorum comitiorum esse voluerunt.*). When the vote on Cicero's behalf takes place in *comitia* characterized in such a way, it gains further significance and validity.

arcessivit: the subject is still Lentulus: as the consul in charge, he arranged for the *comitia* to take place and to vote on the bill for Cicero's recall.

ut ... comprobarent: in Cicero's presentation, recalling him, who had to leave Rome because of activities during his consulship, means approving these and thus his consulship. Such approval is particularly meaningful if it comes from the same body who elected Cicero to the consulship; then it implies that their expectations have been fulfilled and he enjoys continued support.

eaedem centuriae: the centuries voting for Cicero's recall and those having voted for him to become consul might not literally be the same, or the individuals representing them might not be exactly the same. The focus is on the identity of the body (Cic. *RQ* 17): both votes were passed successfully by the centuriate assembly representing the People. In both cases Cicero claims that the vote was basically unanimous (Cic. *Leg. agr.* 2.4; *Pis.* 3; *Dom.* 142).

quae me consulem fecerant: on Cicero's presentation of his election to the consulship, see, e.g., Cic. *Leg. agr.* 2.4; 2.7; *Pis.* 3; *Off.* 2.59; *Vat.* 6.

28 quo die: Madvig (1873, 213) suggested changing *quo die* to *eo die* (adopted by Peterson 1911; supported by Boll 2019, 203) or deleting the expression. Yet the anaphoric repetition of a relative pronoun introducing another clause is effective. The character of the sentence here switches to a question, achieved by the subsequent phrase *quis civis*, while the connecting relative links the clause to the preceding ones. Therefore, the transmitted text should be kept (e.g. Maslowski 1981).

fas: while *fas* here has a weakened sense (*OLD* s.v. *fas* 3 'That which is morally right, fitting, or proper'), the original meaning (*OLD* s.v. *fas* 1 'That which is right or permissible by divine law') assimilates Cicero's recall and the processes leading up to it to something governed by divine law.

aut aetate aut valetudine esset: elsewhere too Cicero claims that nobody felt that age or illness was a sufficient reason for preventing them from attending and voting, thus demonstrating the general eagerness to support him (Cic. *Sest.* 112; *Pis.* 36).

se: emphasizes the personal involvement of each *civis*, though not grammatically required (omitted in some manuscripts).

sententiam ferre: while *sententiam ferre* is often a *terminus technicus* for expressing an opinion in the Senate, it can be applied to 'a vote or opinion given in any assembly' (*OLD* s.v. *sententia* 4a; e.g. Cic. *Balb.* 34): here it refers to the votes of the People at the *comitia centuriata*.

quando ... vidistis: two questions introduced by *quando* (the first consisting of two anaphoric parts and the second including an asyndetic tricolon) illustrate the extraordinary glamour of the occasion, achieved by the attendance of a large number of people and the presence of individuals of high rank.

tantam frequentiam: Cicero asserts that the centuriate assembly voting for his recall was one of the largest the senators had ever seen, thus appealing to their direct experience of the occasion. While Cicero repeats this claim in other speeches (Cic. *Dom.* 75; *Pis.* 36; *Att.* 4.1.4), it cannot be verified from other sources. – For important *contiones* too Cicero claims for argumentative reasons that they are particularly well attended (e.g. Cic. *Sest.* 107; *Phil.* 4.1; 6.18).

in campo: i.e. in the Campus Martius (*LTUR* I 220–4), where voting took place (Mommsen, *StR* III 380, 382–3).

tantum splendorem: *splendor* (*OLD* s.v. *splendor* 5) is also attributed to this meeting elsewhere (Cic. *Dom.* 75; *Pis.* 36).

Italiae totius ordinumque omnium: Cicero highlights that people from all over Italy and from all classes attended (Cic. *Dom.* 75; 90; *Att.* 4.1.4), according to the summons of the Senate (Cic. *RS* 27), with the two groups overlapping. Cicero has mentioned that all of Italy had come together (Cic. *RS* 25; 26), but he has not stressed so explicitly that all classes were represented (cf. T 4), which demonstrates that the Senate's decision was supported by the People as a whole.

illa dignitate rogatores, diribitores custodesque: as Cicero explains elsewhere, senators (*illa dignitate*) took on the role of voting officials in this case (Cic. *Pis.* 36: *hoc certe video, quod indicant tabulae publicae, vos rogatores, vos diribitores, vos custodes fuisse tabellarum, et, quod in honoribus vestrorum propinquorum non facitis vel aetatis excusatione vel honoris, id in salute mea nullo rogante vos vestra sponte fecistis.*). – On the voting procedures and the roles of these officials, see Mommsen, *StR* III 403–8. Mommsen implies that all three terms could refer to the same function. Cicero, however, seems to regard them as separate entities and thereby indicates the substantial involvement of the nobility and the care taken to ensure proper voting.

rogatores: supervisors of the voting.

diribitores: distributors and counters of voting tablets.

custodesque: those taking charge of the vessel with the voting tablets, the counting, and the entering of the results (Cic. *RS* 17).

P. Lentuli beneficio: in drawing the conclusion from the general approval (*itaque*), Cicero emphasizes that Lentulus' initiative provoked his honourable return.

non reducti…reportati: because he was fully restored with everyone's agreement, Cicero says metaphorically that he was not just recalled and came back, but was carried back (Cic. *RS* 34; 39) and returned with the honours of a triumphator. Thus, indirectly, Cicero enjoyed the triumph he was never granted as a result of his lack of military successes (Cic. *Pis.* 35: *eisque verbis ea de me senatus auctoritas declarata est, ut nemini sit triumphus honorificentius quam mihi salus restitutioque perscripta*). – Lange (1875, 19), who believes that the speeches of thanks were written prior to Cicero reaching Rome, refers this description not to Cicero's return and instead to the *comitia* in July 57 BCE; for that stage it would be an odd metaphorical expression. Weiske (1807, 272) wonders why *reducti* is chosen as the contrast to *reportati* rather than *revocati* or *restituti*. A word of this kind might create a greater opposition between recalling and bringing back. But *reducere* probably has the neutral sense of 'to bring home (from captivity, exile, etc.)' (*OLD* s.v. *reduco* 1b) rather than 'to escort home (as a mark of honour)' (*OLD* s.v. *reduco* 1c).

sicut non nulli clarissimi cives: Cicero does not provide examples; these men might include the ex-consuls who also had to leave Rome and are mentioned for comparison elsewhere in this pair of speeches (Cic. *RS* 37–8; *RQ* 6–7; 9–11).

equis insignibus et curru aurato: a triumphator rode on a gilded chariot (e.g. Liv. 10.7.10; Flor. 1.5.6), and the horses drawing the chariot were decorated (e.g. Ov. *Fast.* 5.51–2; *Trist.* 4.2.19–22). Therefore, *insignis* probably describes the impressive appearance of such horses (*OLD* s.v. *insignis* 3 'Remarkable in appearance, outstanding'; Verg. *Aen.* 4.134–5: *ostroque insignis et auro / stat sonipes*; 5.310: *primus equum phaleris insignem victor habeto*). In Suetonius the collocation is applied to a special horse (Suet. *Iul.* 61.1); on several occasions in Tacitus it indicates particularly splendid animals (Tac. *Hist.* 1.88.3; 2.89.1; *Ann.* 3.45.2). Caesar, for his triumph, was granted white horses (Cass. Dio 43.14.3); these then seem to have become common (e.g. Tib. 1.7.5–8; Ov. *Ars am.* 1.213–16). If *insignis* was meant to signify 'white' or 'with white patches' (Paul. Fest., p. 114 M. = 101 L.: *insignes appellantur boves, qui in femine et in pede album habent, quasi insigniti.*; *OLD* s.v. *insignis* 1b), the word would be used anachronistically (affecting the discussion of the oration's authenticity); moreover, in later references in Latin to white horses at triumphs the word *insignis* does not appear. Thus, this meaning is unlikely here.

29 Cn. Pompeium: the next item is Cicero's gratitude to Cn. Pompeius Magnus (on Pompey and the relations with Cicero in this period, see Cic. *RS* 4 n.; Introduction, section 2). There is no explicit transition to the new topic, rather a vague chronological link, as Pompey spoke at the meetings about Cicero's recall in July 57 BCE; this leads to a summary record of Pompey's activities in support of Cicero. – In the corresponding section in the speech to the People (Cic. *RQ* 16) the praise for Pompey is more prominent and elaborate, assigns a leading role to him, and focuses on his interactions with the People (e.g. Mack 1937, 40–2; Wuilleumier 1952, 24; Boll 2019, 46, 207–8).

qui … elaboravit: almost the entire paragraph is taken up by a series of six *qui*-clauses (some with several predicates) describing Pompey's actions on Cicero's behalf. The first three *qui*-clauses report verbal interactions with others whom Pompey tried to persuade to adopt a supportive attitude towards Cicero and the corresponding action, the fourth alludes to his engagement with other magistrates, the fifth describes initiatives taken in the colony of Capua, and the sixth refers to Pompey's influence on his followers. – According to the transmission, the verbs of the first four clauses are in the subjunctive and the verbs in the last two are in the indicative. Editors usually follow Lambinus and turn the last three verbs (in the last two clauses) into subjunctives, which is an easy change palaeographically (supported by Boll 2019, 211). These three verbs, however, focus on actions of Pompey rather than on his initiating procedures by influencing others; therefore, it is not impossible that this switch is mirrored linguistically and the indicative emphasizes the factual nature of these deeds. The indicative appears in relative clauses describing T. Annius Milo and P. Sestius in what follows (Cic. *RS* 30).

qui ... dixerit: Cicero frequently mentions interventions by Pompey in the Senate and before the People on his behalf, including the decisive ones in July 57 BCE (Cic. *RS* 31; *RQ* 16; *Sest.* 107; 129; *Har. resp.* 46; *Dom.* 30; *Prov. cons.* 43; *Pis.* 34; 80; *Mil.* 39; Cass. Dio 39.8.2–3; Plut. *Cic.* 33.3).

non solum apud vos ... sed etiam apud universum populum: one reason given for Cicero's gratitude is that Pompey spoke both before the unanimous Senate and before the People: he thereby spread Cicero's preferred interpretation of the situation before both bodies and aligned them in the support for Cicero.

vos, qui omnes idem sentiebatis: Cicero states unanimity among the senators and with Pompey (i.e. with regard to Cicero's situation), indicating unity among this body and positing flatteringly that they did not need a reminder from Pompey and he was rather expressing the general feeling.

universum populum/salutem populi Romani: conceptually, the entire People Pompey addresses (*universum populum*) and the well-being of the Roman People discussed (*salutem populi Romani*) concern the same group. Thus, *populus* would not need to be repeated and could be replaced by an implied or expressed pronoun. Instead, Cicero juxtaposes the terms without indicating identity: this structure enables him to employ the full phrase *salutem populi Romani* in connection with his own role and to stress that the entire Roman People was reminded of Cicero's position by Pompey. – *universus populus* literally denotes the Roman People in their entirety, though with emphasis on the concept (in contrast to the Senate) rather than the physical presence. This emphasis might imply that the Roman People is to be brought to the same unanimity as observed in the Senate.

salutem populi Romani et conservatam per me et coniunctam esse cum mea: Cicero attributes views and expressions to Pompey (also Cic. *RQ* 16) with which he elsewhere describes his position himself (e.g. Cic. *Pis.* 77). That the well-being of the Roman People was preserved by Cicero alludes to his combating the Catilinarian Conspiracy, which he characterizes as preserving the Republic (Cic. *RS* 8 n.). That the Republic's and Cicero's welfare are linked and that they both left and returned together are frequent motifs in Cicero's speeches after his return (see Introduction, section 3.4). – For a concise and pointed expression (contrast Cic. *RQ* 16), *salus* is the reference point in both parts (*cum mea* [i.e. *salute*]); this yields the phrase *salutem conservare* rather than the more common *rem publicam conservare*.

causam meam ... imperitos edocuerit: a double accusative of matter and person (K.-St. I 297–8; Pinkster 2015, 164–5).

prudentibus commendarit, imperitos edocuerit: Cicero does not reveal whether the two groups in this pair match the different audiences mentioned

(Senate and People; thus Kaster 2009, 314–15) or whether they cut across them. Thus, the description remains neutral and will not offend anyone; at the same time, it is indicated that there were people with different levels of experience and understanding and that Pompey's speeches were adjusted to motivate all of them in the appropriate form.

improbos...bonos: for this pair, too, Cicero does not specify how these two groups relate to the pairs of groups already mentioned (or identify anyone belonging to these groups); again he highlights that Pompey had an influence on both in the required way. Implicitly, the presence of *improbi* and *boni* in the Republic is acknowledged (on *boni* and *improbi* as political opposites, see also Cic. *RS* 20 n.).

auctoritate: Cicero emphasizes Pompey's personal authority (*OLD* s.v. *auctoritas* 12) rather than an official position of power, as Pompey did not hold a magistracy in that year (Cic. *Dom.* 30; *Pis.* 8).

pro me tamquam pro fratre aut pro parente: the comparison highlights Pompey's effort and personal engagement in that he acted for Cicero, another citizen, as if he was a close relative (Raccanelli 2012, 69–84; cf. similarly on P. Cornelius Lentulus Spinther and Cn. Plancius: Cic. *RS* 8; 35).

non solum hortatus sit, verum etiam obsecrarit: Cicero frequently stresses that in the decisive speech Pompey addressed the People as a suppliant (Cic. *RS* 31; *RQ* 16; *Har. resp.* 46; *Pis.* 80; *Sest.* 107), in addition to exploiting his *auctoritas* at other times. In such an approach speakers present themselves as inferiors asking for the goodwill of the audience; it is a self-humbling gesture usually reserved for close friends or relatives (as highlighted by the comparison), which again shows the respect Pompey paid to Cicero (Kaster 2006, 333–4, on Cic. *Sest.* 107; 2009, 314–15).

cum...teneret: on the attacks against Pompey and his subsequent avoidance of public appearances, see Cic. *RS* 4 n.

metum dimicationis et sanguinis: the genitives express the notion of 'bloody fighting' in hendiadys (for *metum dimicationis*, see Cic. *RS* 33).

domo se teneret: *se tenere* is construed with an instrumental ablative indicating the location (K.-St. I 352; Pinkster 2015, 803–4, 824–5; cf. Cic. *Dom.* 6: *domo me tenui*) rather than a locative (Cic. *Sest.* 26: *se domi continebat*; *Brut.* 330: *nos...domi teneamus*).

iam...referrent: Cicero claims that Pompey entreated the Tribunes of the People of 58 BCE to put forward a bill on Cicero and arrange for discussion in the Senate. Elsewhere Cicero says that Pompey held himself back and encouraged the consuls of 58 BCE to take the lead (Cic. *Sest.* 41; *Pis.* 77). Yet in the speech of thanks Pompey's support for Cicero is to be highlighted. – The general comment does not make it clear to what extent Pompey's intervention is linked to the promulgation of a bill by eight Tribunes of the People on 29 October 58 BCE (see Cic. *RS* 4 n.; Introduction, section 2). Some scholars posit a connection: on the basis of this passage Gelzer (1939, 921) assumes Pompey's approval; F. Miltner (*RE* XXI 2 [1952], 2134) states that Pompey was behind the move of the Tribunes; and Boll (2019, 209–10) believes that Pompey supported or even initiated the proposal of the eight Tribunes (see also Spielvogel 1993, 74).

a superioribus tribunis: i.e. the Tribunes of the People of the preceding year (58 BCE), identified from the perspective of the time at which this speech is given (cf. Cic. *RQ* 11).

promulgarent et referrent: technical terms for putting forward a bill and arranging for discussion in the Senate (*OLD* s.v. *promulgo*; *refero* 7).

in colonia nuper constituta: this colony must be the one at Capua, founded in 59 BCE; the consul L. Calpurnius Piso Caesoninus was *duumvir* there in 58 BCE (Cic. *RS* 17 and n.).

cum ipse gereret magistratum: Cn. Pompeius Magnus was *duumvir* in Capua in 58 or, more likely, in 57 BCE (e.g. Nisbet 1961, 89, on Cic. *Pis.* 25): the activities described seem to refer to the period shortly before Cicero's recall and would have been difficult to accomplish if Pompey had held the office of *duumvir* at the same time as Piso.

nemo erat emptus intercessor: implies a contrast with Rome and alludes to the Tribune of the People Aelius Ligus, who was allegedly 'bought' by Clodius to interpose a veto when L. Ninnius Quadratus proposed the recall of Cicero on 1 June 58 BCE (Cic. *RS* 3 n.).

privilegi: Cicero's description of *Lex Clodia de exilio Ciceronis*. A *privilegium* is a legal arrangement in favour of or against an individual (Gell. *NA* 10.20.1–6). According to Cicero (Cic. *Dom.* 43; *Sest.* 65; *Prov. cons.* 45; *Pis.* 30; *Leg.* 3.44; also *Leg.* 3.11) the *leges sacratae* and the Twelve Tables did not permit such laws. Cicero, therefore, regards *Lex Clodia de exilio Ciceronis* as unconstitutional and often calls it *privilegium* or *proscriptio* (see Cic. *RS* 4; 8 nn.; Introduction, section 2). Here he attributes such a view to Pompey and the local Senate of Capua, which strengthens this negative interpretation, which is also emphasized by highlighting the measure's *vis* and *crudelitas*.

auctoritate...consignavit: apparently the assessment of Clodius' law concerning Cicero was shown by a decree of the local Senate in Capua (Cic. *Mil.* 39; *Pis.* 25) and a public recording of this view initiated by Pompey.

auctoritate honestissimorum hominum: a decree of the local Senate described by avoiding *termini technici* common for political processes in Rome. *auctoritas* can refer to decrees of bodies other than the Senate in Rome (*OLD* s.v. *auctoritas* 4). The characterization *honestissimorum* highlights the standing and worth of the men involved; such a characterization increases the value of the resolution and complements the claim that there was no *emptus intercessor*.

publicis litteris: *litterae* may denote 'an official paper, document, record, or sim.' (*OLD* s.v. *littera* 6a) or 'A letter (personal or official), missive, dispatch' (*OLD* s.v. *littera* 7a). Here it is likely to refer to public records of the decree rather than to official letters.

consignavit: indicates official documentation and thus long-term demonstration.

princepsque: with reference to time rather than to standing. – It is implied that Pompey was not only the first to believe that the whole of Italy should be invoked, but also the first to take action to realize it. Cicero frequently mentions that Pompey travelled through Italy to drum up support for him (Cic. *RS* 31; *Dom.* 30; *Prov. cons.* 43; *Har. resp.* 46; *Pis.* 80; *Mil.* 39; see also Cic. *RQ* 10 n.). Asconius (Ascon. ad Cic. *Pis.* [p. 3.20–3 C.]: *de se autem optime meritos Placentinos ait, quod illi quoque honoratissima decreta erga Ciceronem fecerunt certaveruntque in ea re cum tota Italia, cum de reditu eius actum est.*) mentions that the people of Placentia passed decrees honouring Cicero, thereby vying with all of Italy in the context of Cicero's recall. There is no further evidence as to which other peoples or towns followed the example set by Pompey in Capua in demonstrating their views. Nisbet (1961, 89, on Cic. *Pis.* 25) notes that '[t]he resolution at Capua was the first of many throughout Italy', without providing details.

Italiae totius: another reference to the whole of Italy engaging with Cicero's case (Cic. *RS* 24; 25; 26; 28; 39; *RQ* 1; 10; 16; *Dom.* 5; *Sest.* 72).

semper amicissimus...amicos: Pompey is singled out as *semper amicissimus*, implying a continuous close relationship with Cicero; this quality is demonstrated by Pompey's initiative to turn his associates also into *amici* of Cicero (on Pompey's *amici*, see Rollinger 2019). In other speeches delivered after his return Cicero also stresses the friendship between himself and Pompey (Cic. *Sest.* 15; 133; *Pis.* 76), though initially, when Clodius had taken action against Cicero, Pompey did not support Cicero (Cic. *Att.* 3.15.4 [17 Aug. 58 BCE]; *Q Fr.* 1.4.4 [Aug. 58 BCE]; Plut. *Cic.* 31.2–3; on the relationship between the two men, see Cic. *RS* 4 n.; Introduction, section 2).

suos necessarios: Pompey's close associates may include his father-in-law C. Iulius Caesar (Cic. *Prov. cons.* 43) or veterans settled in colonies, which might explain Pompey's activities throughout Italy (Spielvogel 1993, 76; Boll 2019, 212).

30 quibus autem officiis...quid: the renewed references to T. Annius Milo and P. Sestius are marked by a rhetorical question each, indicating the greatness of their achievements that can hardly be matched by gratitude or appropriate words.

T. Anni...de P. Sestio: towards the end of the section on voicing gratitude to individuals, mostly magistrates, Cicero comes back to T. Annius Milo and P. Sestius, Tribunes of the People in 57 BCE, with a brief expression of thanks, as their activities have been described in greater detail at the start (Cic. *RS* 19; 20 nn.). This structure enables Cicero to highlight their engagement and the resulting gratitude on his part (Cic. *RS* 18–31 n.), just before he says that he cannot thank everyone individually on that occasion (Cic. *RS* 30–1).

remunerabor: the emphasis in this renewed mention of Milo is on the difficulty of rendering thanks adequately for his great deeds. This aspect is already included in the introduction to the first mention of Milo (Cic. *RS* 19); this choice of verb underscores the aspect of gratitude.

cuius … salutis meae: this clause sketches Milo's deeds for Cicero by describing his general attitude, concern, and support rather than by listing individual actions.

omnis ratio, cogitatio, totus denique tribunatus: in this tricolon the first two items describe the underlying mental activity; the final one, set off by *denique* and another word expressing totality, indicates how this reasoning determined Milo's actions during his tribunate. The abstract noun for the office illustrates how the entire tribunate was allegedly focused on Cicero's well-being (for a similar claim about Sestius, see Cic. *Sest.* 14: *quoniam tribunatus totus P. Sesti nihil aliud nisi meum nomen causamque sustinuit*). As Cicero returned to Rome in August 57 BCE, this cannot be literally true, as Milo's tribunate continued after that; even for the preceding period a sole focus on Cicero is probably an exaggeration: such a description rhetorically presents Milo's efforts for Cicero as extensive.

constans, perpetua, fortis, invicta: this tetracolon of adjectives emphasizes Milo's perseverance and strength in his support for Cicero.

corporis vulneribus: for P. Sestius the distinctive feature of his support is highlighted again (complementing *animi dolore*): he was wounded and even risked his life in confronting Clodius and his supporters (Cic. *RS* 7; 20 and nn.).

vobis…, patres conscripti: Cicero returns to talking about his rendering thanks to the senators individually (*singulis*) and collectively (*universis*). After having spent the last few paragraphs talking about individuals, mainly magistrates, Cicero hastens to add that he is equally grateful to all the senators, but is not able to thank all of them individually in this context, and to explain that on this occasion he is only thanking by name the magistrates and one private individual (Cic. *RS* 30–1). – *vero* emphasizes the focus on the senators (*OLD* s.v *uero*[1] 5).

singulis et egi et agam gratias: Cicero asserts that he has thanked and will thank senators individually: in this speech he thanked them as a group at the beginning (Cic. *RS* 1–5). – If the claim is taken literally, it may include gratitude rendered through letters prior to Cicero's arrival back in Rome (e.g. Cic. *Fam.* 5.4.1 [Jan. 57 BCE], to the consul Q. Caecilius Metellus Nepos: *litterae Quinti fratris et T. Pomponi, necessarii mei, tantum spei dederant, ut in te non minus auxili quam in tuo conlega mihi constitutum fuerit. itaque ad te litteras statim misi, per quas, ut fortuna postulabat, et gratias tibi egi et de reliquo tempore auxilium petii.*). The thanks in the future could be in further letters or at meetings in person; there is no evidence of other speeches by Cicero in which individuals might have been thanked. – *et… et* emphasizes that Cicero has started rendering thanks to individuals and will continue to do so; this continuity refers to the activity and does not imply that the same individuals will be thanked twice.

initio: this word (in this reading) is not another chronological marker continuing the notion of past and future adumbrated in the previous clause. Instead, it is a chronological and local indication with reference to this speech and refers to its beginning (Cic. *RS* 1–5).

quantum potui: more explicitly than at the start of the speech Cicero reiterates that he is doing his best, but that it is basically impossible to find suitable words to express appropriately his gratitude for the huge favours received from the Senate (Cic. *RS* 1; see also Cic. *RS* 24).

ornate: Cicero maintains that he is not able to render due thanks in an appropriately elaborate style. Such a claim does not invalidate the thanks rendered, but rather highlights that the favours granted are enormous and merit an elaborate expression of thanks.

praecipua merita multorum: without mentioning names or details, Cicero thanks and flatters the senators: everyone in the audience can assume that they are included in the 'many' individuals.

quae sileri nullo modo possunt: emphasizes again that the favours received are so outstanding that they should not be passed over. Cicero thereby takes care to make it clear that he does not pass over anything because he does not value it, but rather because it is simply not possible to mention everything in this speech.

huius temporis ac timoris mei: Karsten (1879, 409) suggested deleting *ac timoris*, arguing that it does not fit the context and the resulting phrase could be seen as parallel to *non est mei temporis iniurias meminisse* (Cic. *RS* 23; see n.). Even if these words were deleted, the two phrases would be different as a result of *huius* vs *mei*. Therefore, a more plausible interpretation is to keep the transmitted text and assume a neutral meaning of *temporis* (*OLD* s.v. *tempus*[1] 10). In contrast to avoiding talking about injuries received, in omitting the expression of thanks there is an additional motive for Cicero: the fear of passing over anyone (see also Boll 2019, 213–14).

beneficia in me singulorum: a prepositional phrase forms the attribute of a noun (similarly *eorum erga me merita*); such a construction is not infrequent in connection with these prepositions (K.-St. I 213–14; Pinkster 2015, 1044–5).

difficile est non aliquem, nefas quemquam praeterire: describes the dilemma arising if one attempted to mention everybody: it would be easy to pass over someone, but an offence to do so (Cic. *Planc.* 74 [T 2]). – The strong word *nefas* denoting an offence against divine or moral law emphatically expresses how severe a fault forgetting someone would be. – Of the two negative phrases appropriately the first has *aliquem* and the second *quemquam*: in such negative clauses *aliquis* has a qualitative sense and indicates 'someone worth mentioning'/'someone of importance', whereas *quisquam* has the general sense of 'anyone'/'even a single person' (K.-St. I 640–1; also Pinkster 2015, 1165–9).

deorum <in> numero: lit. 'in the category of gods': the phrase indicates that all the senators (highlighted by the preceding address) will have to be regarded as gods, but does not set up a direct comparison (Cic. *RS* 1; Cole 2013, 69). – In view of the fact that *deorum numero* is generally construed with *in* (without *in* only at Caes. *B Gall.* 6.21), Boll (2019, 214) mentions Kayser's (1862, 366) conjecture *deorum <in> numero* (Kayser prints *deorum in numero* without commenting on the constitution of the text) and opts for *<in> deorum numero* (referring to Cic. *Leg. agr.* 2.95: *in deorum immortalium numero*). Adding *in* seems necessary for creating a standard expression; the position of the preposition between *deorum* and *numero* gives a better explanation for the loss of the word through haplography (for *deorum in numero*, see Cic. *Nat. D.* 1.118; *Rep.* 2.17).

sed … recolenda: assigning the senators a status like that of gods provides the basis for the next step in Cicero's argument by way of comparison: one does not always pay respect to the same gods, but to different ones on different occasions; Cicero will act similarly with reference to the senators; thus, there will be time over the course of the rest of his life to recognize everyone.

in hominibus de me divinitus meritis: picks up the comparison of the Senate with divinities, with a general hyperbolic statement (enhancing the mention of *merita* and *beneficia*). – Markland (1745, 248–9) notes that the appropriate word would be *divine* rather than *divinitus*. Yet *divinitus* not only means 'By divine agency or inspiration' (*OLD* s.v. *diuinitus* 1), but also 'In a godlike manner, with supreme excellence, divinely' (*OLD* s.v. *diuinitus* 2). – The collocation *divinitus merita* is only attested again in Augustine (August. *C. Iulianum* 4.3.28).

omnis erit aetas: i.e. Cicero's entire life or, rather, what is left of it. – The expression governs a prepositional phrase headed by *ad*; *esse*, therefore, has the meaning '(indicating availability for a purpose)' (*OLD* s.v. *sum*[1] 3b).

praedicanda atque recolenda: this doublet indicates that, just as for the comparable situation of the gods, Cicero will offer praise and 'worship' to the senators on different occasions.

31 hodierno … die: i.e. 5 September 57 BCE, the day on which this speech was delivered (see *RS*, Introduction).

nominatim: after having expressed his gratitude to everyone and explained that he will not be able to thank everyone individually, Cicero can reveal the selection of people mentioned by name in this speech: magistrates and a single private individual.

a me: a prepositional phrase instead of a dative to avoid ambiguity (K.-St. I 730).

magistratibus: in this speech Cicero thanks magistrates of 57 BCE: the consuls P. Cornelius Lentulus Spinther (esp. Cic. *RS* 5; 8–9; 27–8) and Q. Caecilius Metellus Nepos (esp. Cic. *RS* 5; 9; 25–6), the praetors (esp. Cic. *RS* 21–3), and the Tribunes of the People (esp. Cic. *RS* 19–20; 30).

de privatis uni: i.e. Cn. Pompeius Magnus, without an official magistracy in Rome in 57 BCE (Cic. *RS* 29).

qui...reddidistis: a *qui*-clause with three asyndetically linked predicates summarizes what Pompey is being thanked for, taking up preceding descriptions of his actions and corresponding expressions of gratitude (Cic. *RS* 4; 29 nn.). Here (contrast Cic. *RS* 29 and n.) the subjunctive probably expresses the reason why Cicero feels that the private individual Pompey should be added to the list of people thanked specifically (K.-St. II 291–3).

municipia coloniasque adisset: elaborates on the earlier statement that Pompey encouraged the whole of Italy to contribute to Cicero's recall (Cic. *RS* 29 [and n.]).

municipia coloniasque: in the late Republic *municipia* (Cic. *RS* 27 n.) and *coloniae* (settlements founded by the Romans) are frequently mentioned side by side (e.g. Cic. *Phil.* 2.76; 3.13; 5.37; 8.4; *Lex agraria* of 111 BCE, *cap.* 31 [*FIRA* I², no. 8, p. 110 = *Roman Statutes*, no. 2, pp. 116–17]). In Cicero's time the terminology reflected a historical distinction on the basis of the origin of these settlements in Italy; in practical and administrative terms there was no longer a real difference (on the terms for settlements of Roman citizens, see Bruna 1972, 235–66). The collocation then emphasizes general coverage.

populum Romanum supplex obsecrasset: on this initiative of Pompey, see Cic. *RS* 29 and n.

sententiam dixisset: Pompey is said to have put forward the key motions for Cicero's recall in July 57 BCE (Cic. *Dom.* 30; *Prov. cons.* 43; *Sest.* 129; *Pis.* 35; *Mil.* 39). – According to *Pro Sestio* Pompey delivered the *sententia* from a written script. Giving the *sententia* from a script was less unusual than doing so for an entire speech (as Cicero presumably did for the present speech: Cic. *Planc.* 74 [T 2] and n.); such a procedure makes the occasion and the particular wording of the *sententia* appear more important and indicates that the measures were planned.

quam vos secuti: Cicero stresses that the Senate endorsed Pompey's motion (Mitchell 1991, 156 n. 41), thereby adding praise for the Senate to that for Pompey and justifying his gratitude to both Pompey and the Senate. – The case of the relative pronoun is determined by the participle *secuti*; the main verb of the clause has a separate object.

dignitatem meam: the nature and the importance of the Senate decree are highlighted by the claim that it restored Cicero's former standing, something more significant than being recalled physically (Cic. *RS* 1).

vos...defendistis: with another emphatic *vos* Cicero elaborates on the consistent support of the senators whatever his situation (*me florentem* vs *laborantem*).

semper ornastis: the demonstration of appreciation is most likely to refer to the honours awarded to Cicero after crushing the Catilinarian Conspiracy (Cic. *Cat.* 3.15; *Pis.* 6; *Sest.* 121; Plut. *Cic.* 23.6). The addition of *semper* creates the impression of recurring and constant support from the Senate, while no specifics are identified.

mutatione vestis et prope luctu vestro, quoad licuit: the senators are said to have changed into mourning clothes in order to demonstrate their sympathy in reaction to Clodius' actions against Cicero (Cic. *RS* 12 n.); further, they are said to have 'almost' shown mournful feelings to the extent to which it was allowed. The addition of *prope* presumably indicates that they almost felt personal grief and were on their way to mourning Cicero like a dead relative when they were interrupted.

quoad licuit: the senators' demonstrations of sympathy were limited by the consuls' edicts, further described in the following sentence, where this phrase is repeated.

nostra... nudarunt: Cicero goes on to juxtapose the behaviour of senators on behalf of themselves and the reaction of the Senate on Cicero's account. With *senatores* in the plural, continued by *senatus*, the statement probably refers to the Senate as a group and remains in the political realm: the Senate has not even changed clothing when it was in danger, but did so on this occasion to show solidarity with the individual Cicero (see also Savels 1828, xiii). The comparison insinuates that the senators regarded Cicero's fate as particularly serious and therefore decided to indicate their assessment publicly (Cic. *RS* 12 n.). – Markland (1745, 249–59) considered the statement incorrect because Cicero and other senators changed their clothing in personal dangers. Cicero did so before leaving Rome, as he admits later (Cic. *Att.* 3.15.5 [17 Aug. 58 BCE]); as this action refers to the same context, it does not invalidate the comparison. References to other senators not wearing their usual dress relate to their appearances at trials (e.g. Cic. *Mur.* 85; *Sull.* 88), not to the political situation. The introduction *nostra memoria* qualifies the statement as a time-limited assessment and does not assign universal truth to it (cf. Cic. *RS* 38; *RQ* 7). Kaster (2009, 312) sees the comment as referring to an earlier practice of senators not putting on mourning clothes when on trial, which had become expected by the mid-first century; then the comparison would yield a less effective contrast. – Weiske (1807, 274) interprets *in suis...periculis* as equivalent to *in suorum...periculis*, referring to relatives of the senators. While a possessive pronoun can be used instead of the genitive of the personal pronoun (K.-St. I 599; Pinkster 2015, 977–8), as in the immediately following phrase *in meo periculo*, it would be unusual and confusing for the possessive pronoun to replace nominal *sui*.

in meo periculo... mea pericula: the statement of Cicero's precarious state changes from a description of the circumstances to an object affected by the actions of others.

quoad licuit per eorum edicta: edicts of the consuls L. Calpurnius Piso Caesoninus and A. Gabinius (Cic. *RS* 4 n.) ordering the senators to remove their mourning clothes (Cic. *RS* 12; 16 nn.).

nudarunt: the metaphor (appropriate to the context of clothing) emphasizes the complete absence of support: according to Cicero, the consuls not only did not protect him, as he suggests would have been their duty, but also prevented the Senate's intervention (Cic. *RS* 10; *Dom.* 55).

2.3. Cicero's departure (32–5)

In the final part (Cic. *RS* 32–5) of the main section (Cic. *RS* 3–35) Cicero moves away from voicing thanks and returns to a description and explanation of his movements. He thereby takes up the sketch of his recall at the beginning of the main section (Cic. *RS* 3–7) and completes the survey with his departure. After he has pointed out his successful recall and described his opponents and his supporters, the decision to depart can be presented emphatically: Cicero did not leave because he was isolated and there was no hope of winning and rehabilitation; rather, he realized the upheaval in the Republic and the lack of functioning structures; thus, in order to avoid violence and bloodshed and not to affect other people besides himself, he preferred to withdraw from Rome. This decision places him in the position of a superior and independent states-man rather than of a victim forced to leave (Mack 1937, 37–40 on Cic. *RS* 32–4 vs *RQ* 13–14). Similar descriptions of the situation in 58 BCE and of Cicero's decision to sacrifice himself for the sake of the Republic recur in other speeches (Cic. *Sest.* 47–9; *Dom.* 95–9; see Introduction, section 3.4). In this passage the individual Cn. Plancius is singled out for an expression of gratitude: he hosted Cicero during his absence; his intervention is, therefore, closely linked to Cicero's movements (Cic. *RS* 35).

32 quibus ego rebus obiectis: a transition from the adverse situation in spring 58 BCE just sketched (Cic. *RS* 31) to Cicero's thoughts and actions (*ego*) in consequence.

ego . . . multa mecum ipse reputavi: emphasizes the fact that Cicero took the decision to leave Rome after careful consideration of the situation and his options.

privato . . . consul: a contrast and parallelism between Cicero's current pos-ition and his role when confronting Catiline in his consular year (Cic. *RS* 34; *Sest.* 47): as a private person, Cicero now has to face a similar confrontation.

cum eodem exercitu: means literally that the followers of Catiline have resurfaced and Cicero would have to fight against them again. Later Cicero states more clearly that Catiline's troops are being recalled (Cic. *RS* 33 [and n.]; *RQ* 13). Irrespective of the accuracy of the claim, such a description assimilates Clodius and his followers to Catiline and his followers amid strong implied criticism and suggests that they are similar as regards their attitude to and actions against the Republic and Cicero (for comparisons, see Cic. *Dom.* 60–1; *Har. resp.* 5; *Sest.* 42; *Pis.* 15–16).

non armis sed vestra auctoritate: Cicero frequently emphasizes that he combated the Catilinarian Conspiracy as a 'general in a toga' without civil war rather than with the force of arms (Cic. *Cat.* 2.28; 3.15; 3.23; 4.5). Elsewhere, he tends to single out his own role; yet in a speech of thanks to the Senate he highlights its involvement: the Senate passed a *senatus consultum ultimum* in October 63 BCE (Sall. *Cat.* 29.2–3) and a decree to punish the captured conspirators with the death penalty on 5 December 63 BCE (Cic. *Cat.* 4; Sall. *Cat.* 50.3–53.1; 55). Stressing that he acted on the Senate's authority justifies Cicero's measures at the time and thus invalidates the criticism that triggered the backlash leading to his departure from Rome.

dixerat in contione: on this *contio* of one of the consuls of 58 BCE, see Cic. *RS* 12 (and n.); *Dom.* 55; *Planc.* 87.

consul: i.e. A. Gabinius, consul in 58 BCE (Cic. *RS* 4 n.).

se clivi Capitolini … repetiturum: for this threat, see Cic. *RS* 12 and n.

nominatim … relegabantur: implies that the consul not only threatened to take action against the knights generally, but also punished some individually by summoning them to court or banishing them (Cic. *RS* 12 n.). The plural and the imperfect tense suggest a frequent occurrence affecting a number of people; here and elsewhere Cicero keeps the allegation generic without providing details (Cic. *Dom.* 55; *Sest.* 35; *Pis.* 23). An example of those affected is L. Aelius Lamia (Cic. *RS* 12 n.); his is the only known case (Boll 2019, 219). As Cicero highlights Lamia's fate as unprecedented (Cic. *Fam.* 11.16.2), Goldmann (2012, 30 n. 154) concludes that further relegations are unlikely.

aditus … sublati: a zeugmatic expression: access is removed because the entrance is blocked by guards and, literally, the steps leading up to the entrance have been demolished. Emphasizing that even the steps were destroyed highlights the determination to prevent access.

aditus templorum: Cicero describes in greater detail elsewhere that Clodius had armed men stationed in the Forum, weapons brought to the Temple of Castor, and the steps of the temple removed, allegedly to establish a reign by violence and to prevent the ordinary procedures of assemblies and voting (Cic. *Dom.* 5; 54; 110; *Sest.* 34; 85; *Pis.* 11; 23; *Parad.* 4.30). The plural is probably rhetorical (Boll 2019, 219). 'Demolition', equally emphatically, only applies to part of the temple building. Shackleton Bailey (1991, 21 n. 80) suggests that access to temples was barred to prevent prayers on Cicero's behalf: such an intention is not mentioned elsewhere.

praesidiis et manu: this collocation does not seem to be attested elsewhere: *manu* could mean 'by force' (*OLD* s.v. *manus*[1] 8b) or complement *praesidiis* (*OLD* s.v. *praesidium* 4) as a term also denoting a 'troop' (*OLD* s.v. *manus*[1] 22). Juxtaposition and context suggest the former, adding the aspect of violence, so that the phrase is equivalent to 'guards resorting to violence'.

alter consul: i.e. L. Calpurnius Piso Caesoninus, the other consul of 58 BCE (Cic. *RS* 3; 4; 10; 16–18 [and nn.]), in relation to *consul* in the preceding sentence.

me et rem publicam: another parallelization of Cicero and the Republic (see Introduction, section 3.4).

hostibus rei publicae proderet: the direct object *me et rem publicam* has to be supplied from the preceding phrase. That these *hostes* are then also in opposition to Cicero is implied; focusing on *res publica* presents these men as public enemies and thus as a great and general danger, whom the consul should have confronted, rather than entering into any pacts with them. – Mack (1937, 34, 38) interprets this passage as saying that Piso had even got in touch with external enemies to destroy Cicero. Yet in Cicero's terminology *hostes rei publicae* usually denotes opponents opposed to a Republican system of the sort that Cicero defends (here P. Clodius Pulcher and his followers) rather than external enemies.

pactionibus se suorum praemiorum obligarat: probably refers to the law on the consular provinces characterized by Cicero as an arrangement (*pactionibus* rhetorical plural) granting lucrative provinces to the consuls in return for supporting or not obstructing the activities of Clodius and his followers (Cic. *RS* 4 n.; for *pactio* in this sense, see Cic. *Sest.* 69: *cum consules provinciarum pactione libertatem omnem perdidissent*). In the transmitted version of the text (*eos* instead of *se*) the perspective is odd: then, the emphasis would be on the consul's role and on the fact that by agreeing to this pact he almost forced the *hostes* to do something against Cicero and the Republic (Maslowski 1981, in app. ad loc., interprets *eos* as *hostes rei p.*). Since the *pactiones* are offering an advantage to the consul, this interpretation seems implausible. Thus, it seems best to follow Peterson (1911) in adopting Halm's conjecture *se* for *eos* and refer the remark to the consul (see also Boll 2019, 220). Luterbacher (1912, 346) criticizes this text and suggests *pactionibus se iis* (with *iis* denoting *hostibus rei publicae*), but *iis* can be inferred. Weiske (1807, 275) proposed changing the punctuation and placing a comma after *alter*, so that *pactionibus ... obligarat* would refer to P. Clodius Pulcher. This is an ingenious way of making the sentence more straightforward with little change; still, the last agent mentioned is one of the consuls; the only natural way in which *alter* can be understood is as referring to the other consul (in contrast to following *alius*). – *suorum praemiorum* is most likely a kind of *gen. appositivus* (K.-St. I 418–19; Pinkster 2015, 1023–5), and *suorum* replaces a *gen. obiectivus*.

alius: an allusion to C. Iulius Caesar (*RE* Iulius 131; cos. 59 BCE [*MRR* II 187–8]; see, e.g., Klass 1939; Nicholson 1992, 47–51; Boll 2019, 21–6), without mention of the name, probably to tone down Cicero's disappointment at his behaviour (Kaster 2006, 150, on Cic. *Sest.* 16). In the corresponding speech to the People Caesar is not referred to (Mack 1937, 38; Klass 1939, 86–7; MacKendrick 1995, 138), which avoids any assessment of his position. Here there is subdued criticism by means of the unnecessary pointer to Caesar's long *imperium* and the reminder of his silence (Klass 1939, 86–7; Boll 2019, 221). – Caesar initially was not interested in Cicero's immediate recall; when Clodius' activities began to affect the Julian laws and Pompey strongly advocated the recall, Caesar became a supporter of this policy. – Following on from his consulship in 59 BCE, Caesar was awarded a proconsular *imperium* in Gaul for five years. He set off from Rome in spring 58 BCE, when he learned that the Helvetii were planning to march through the Roman province (Caes. *B Gall.* 1.7.1); he did not go into the province until Cicero had left Rome (see Introduction, section 2), giving him the option to take up the offer (Cic. *Prov. cons.* 42) to join him as one of his staff (Tatum 1999, 154). Initially Caesar had one Roman legion at his disposal in Gaul (Caes. *B Gall.* 1.7.2; 1.8.1); soon after his arrival, when the Helvetii asked for permission to march through the province, in order to gain time, he told them that he would consider their request and they could return for the Ides of April (Caes. *B Gall.* 1.7.5). In the meantime he strengthened his fortifications (Caes. *B Gall.* 1.8.1–2); then he went back to Italy to acquire another five legions (Caes. *B Gall.* 1.10.3). Thus, it is likely to be true that just before Cicero's departure from Rome Caesar was located outside the city gates with *imperium* (the *contio* Caesar spoke at in spring 58 BCE was held outside the *pomerium*: Cic. *RS* 13 n.). That a large army was waiting outside the city gates is probably an exaggeration: Caesar seems to have had access to armed forces in northern Italy and Gaul, but nowhere else is it stated that troops were located just outside Rome. Caesar's *imperium* for a period described as *in multos annos* consists of five years: five years is longer than the standard single propraetorian and proconsular year as apparently stipulated by *Lex Cornelia de provinciis ordinandis* (81 BCE; *LPRR*, p. 353) (on Caesar's military position in spring 58 BCE, see Cic. *Sest.* 40; 41; 52; Suet. *Iul.* 23.1; Plut. *Caes.* 14.10; 14.16–17; Cass. Dio 38.17.1–4). – The phrase *ad portas* might recall the use of this expression with reference to Hannibal and thus contribute to indicating danger (for the phrase *ad portas* applied to Hannibal's position and then in a proverbial way, see Otto 1890, 158–9, s.v. *Hannibal* 2; Liv. 21.16.1–2; 23.16.2–4; Cic. *Phil.* 1.11; *Fin.* 4.22).

tacuisse…scio: signals awareness of Caesar's ambiguous position: Cicero rejects the rumour that Caesar was his enemy (Cic. *Sest.* 41), but accepts that Caesar never denied this description, which Clodius applied to him (Cic. *Sest.* 39; 71; see Klass 1939, 82–3; Spielvogel 1993, 76).

33 duae partes: the two *partes* in the Republic are distinguished by their attitude to Cicero: this again assimilates Cicero's fate to the situation of the Republic (see Introduction, section 3.4). – The adherents of the two *partes* are not defined; they must be Cicero's enemies and his supporters, acting aggressively and timidly, respectively (Cic. *RS* 23).

putarentur…putabatur…videbantur: Cicero stops short of claiming that these two *partes* exist and instead cautiously presents the description as a general view.

me deposcere: the first group 'demanded Cicero for punishment' (*OLD* s.v. *deposco* 2; see Cic. *Sest.* 46).

propter suspicionem caedis: the second group allegedly felt that supporting Cicero openly might cause a bloodbath; this implies that they too regard Cicero's fate as impacting public life and acknowledge the existence of different opinions.

qui ... minuerunt: the blame for a climate of fear of fighting and slaughter is placed upon Cicero's opponents: that they did not deny any rumours implies that they had the alleged plans or at least were keen to create and maintain a sense of fear based on rumours. – Boll (2019, 223) refers the comment to Caesar, Pompey, and Crassus, who did not intervene: there is no indication of an allusion particularly to these men; Clodius and his followers are more likely to be the main focus.

ii hoc: Halm's conjecture (1856, 844 in app.) *ii* for *in* (Halm has *hoc* in the text), adopted by Shackleton Bailey (1991, 227), removes an awkward construction of *in hoc* (transmitted in some manuscripts; kept, e.g., by Peterson 1911; Maslowski 1981); at the same time it creates an effective emphasis on the party described by *qui ... videbantur* and helps to structure the sentence. One could leave out *in/ii* (as in other manuscripts; favoured by Boll 2019, 223), but the presence of *in* suggests that it might have replaced another word (for the juxtaposition of two demonstrative pronouns, see, e.g., Cic. *Cat.* 2.20; for *augere* with the ablative, see K.-St. I 385–6).

dimicationis metum: picks up *suspicionem caedis*, emphasizing the way in which the confrontation will take place (*dimicatio*) rather than its potential outcome (*caedes*). For the phrase, see Cic. *RS* 29.

numquam ... minuerunt: negated *minuerunt* corresponds to *auxerunt* with enhanced emphasis.

infitiando ... curamque: alludes to a line from tragedy quoted by Cicero in *In Pisonem* (Cic. *Pis.* 82: *numquam istam imminuam curam infitiando tibi*), spoken by Thyestes to Atreus in Accius' *Atreus* (Acc. *Trag.* 234 R.[3]) according to Asconius (Ascon. ad Cic. *Pis.* 82 [p. 16 C.]), used similarly elsewhere (Cic. *Sest.* 8: *numquam illum illo summo timore ac periculo civitatis neque communem metum omnium nec propriam non nullorum de ipso suspicionem aut infitiando tollere aut dissimulando sedare voluisse*).

suspicionem: picks up *suspicionem caedis* from the preceding sentence.

qua re cum viderem ... defuit: Cicero provides a detailed description of the political situation in 58 BCE (*qua re* indicating that it follows on from the preceding sketch) as a basis for outlining and justifying his reaction: he first states that in these circumstances he would have been able to and courageous enough to fight to defend himself; he goes on to explain that he decided not to do so for the sake of the community. Since Cicero left before the law confirming his exiled status was officially passed (see Introduction, section 2), it is important for him to present a rationale so that he does not appear like a coward or deserter.

senatum ducibus orbatum: apart from the fact that Cicero does not regard the consuls of 58 BCE as proper consuls (Cic. *RS* 4), the phrase suggests that in Cicero's view the Senate does not have ex-consuls taking action as leaders (Cic. *Sest.* 35). Cicero voices similar laments for the period of the fight against Mark Antony (e.g. Cic. *Phil.* 8.20–32; *Fam.* 10.28.3).

me a magistratibus…derelictum: Cicero claims that the magistrates did not support him, which takes different forms (*partim…partim…partim*): *oppugnatum* might refer to P. Clodius Pulcher because of his open opposition in putting forward bills against Cicero (see Introduction, section 2), *proditum* to the consuls, who, in Cicero's presentation, entered an alliance with Clodius by the arrangement on the consular provinces (Cic. *RS* 4 n.), and *derelictum* to others, thought to be supportive, but then not standing up for Cicero (Cic. *RS* 23 [and n.]; *RQ* 21). Similar sequences appear elsewhere with reference to the consuls (Cic. *RS* 10 n.).

servos simulatione collegiorum…conscriptos: *collegia* or 'clubs' deemed to be a threat to public order were outlawed by a decree of the Senate in 64 BCE (Ascon. ad Cic. *Pis.* 8 [p. 7.9–11 C.]), though apparently not entirely suppressed; they were revived and new ones permitted as a result of a law of Clodius early in 58 BCE (*Lex Clodia de collegiis*: *LPPR*, p. 393; on the law and Clodius' use of *collegia*, see Nowak 1973, 112–17; Lintott 1999b, 77–83, 193; Tatum 1999, 117–19). Cicero frequently alleges that the formation and restoration of clubs by Clodius and his supporters was a means to set up paramilitary gangs of people from low social classes (Cic. *RQ* 13; *Dom.* 5; 54; 129; *Sest.* 34; 55; *Pis.* 9; 11; 23), though in the speech to the People the description is more neutral and there is no mention of *collegia* or *servi* (Cic. *RQ* 13). Applying the language of military recruitment to the setting up of *collegia* highlights the potential danger emanating from them and creates a tension between the alleged social status of the members and the implied military organization (Nisbet 1961, 70, on Cic. *Pis.* 11).

nominatim: Courtney (1960, 96–7; *contra* Boll 2019, 225) argues that *nominatim* is a scribal error triggered by the word's occurrence in *RS* 31 and 32 and its similarity in certain scripts to *vicatim*, which he regards as the correct reading, since the *collegia compitalicia* were organized by *vici* (Cic. *Sest.* 34). Yet *nominatim* can be explained as indicating that slaves were recruited individually: such a detail demonstrates the well-organized operation of extensive recruitment. Boll (2019, 225) suggests the sense 'expressly, specifically' for *nominatim* (*OLD* s.v. *nominatim* 2). In the context of referring to individuals *nominatim* is more likely to have the standard meaning 'by naming specifically, by name' (*OLD* s.v. *nominatim* 1).

copias…revocatas: Cicero claims that Catiline's 'troops' were recalled with almost the same leaders (Cic. *RQ* 13; *Dom.* 58; *Dom.* 61; 92; *Pis.* 11; 16; 23; *Sest.* 42; *Parad.* 4.27). In *Pro Sestio* he speaks of a *novus dux* (Cic. *Sest.* 42), which must mean that Clodius replaced Catiline. Here he says *paene isdem ducibus* in the plural, which is most naturally understood in the sense that some leaders are the same and others have changed; the generic expression leaves identities open. As with respect to the activities led by Catiline, Cicero claims that these troops are intent on *caedes* and *incendia* (Cic. *Cat.* 2.6; 2.10): this description presents devastation as their sole aim (Cic. *RS* 7) and increases the impression of their destructive potential. – These men are most likely to have been a mixture of supporters of Catiline and new recruits (Lintott 1999b, 77), though Nicholson (1992, 28–9) regards the allegations as 'empty rhetorical invective', and Tatum (1999, 144–5), after reviewing the evidence and various views, concludes: 'The matter can now be settled. Clodius was not the commander in chief of the *veteres Catilinae milites*' (145). In terms of historical individuals, only L. Sergius (*RE* Sergius 15; Nowak 1973, 109) is known as a Catilinarian (Cic. *Dom.* 13) and then a follower of Clodius (Cic. *Dom.* 14; 21; 89).

Catilinae: in the speeches about his absence from Rome Cicero often compares Clodius and Catiline and suggests that Clodius thinks and behaves in a similar way (e.g. Cic. *Dom.* 72; 75; *Pis.* 15; 16; *Har. resp.* 5).

equites...permotos: this tricolon gives three examples of people in fear, starting with a social group, followed by places outside Rome metonymically representing the inhabitants, and then a summarizing 'all' encompassing everyone inside and outside Rome. *permotos* agrees with the nearest noun (K.-St. I 49; Pinkster 2015, 1267–8), and *metu* governs all three genitives, one item referring to each example. – The last item, the fear of *caedes*, picks up the preceding discussion, while the other two add new dimensions: in this speech Cicero has not yet mentioned *proscriptio* of knights (Cic. *Dom.* 55; *Planc.* 87), though he has talked of trials and relegation in response to their behaviour in 63 BCE (Cic. *RS* 12; 32 and nn.). The fear of devastation in the *municipia* expands the destructive scenario beyond Rome (on *municipia*, see Cic. *RS* 27 n.).

potui, potui, patres conscripti: the repetition of the verb followed by an address to the audience underlines that Cicero could have defended himself if he had decided to do so (on the indicative, see K.-St. I 170–1). The contrast introduced by the subsequent sentence (*sed videbam...*) juxtaposes what he realized and therefore did instead. Whether defence would have been possible remains open, and how this would have done is never specified. – The verb appears twice in one manuscript; in the others only once. The repetition fits the tone of the sentence, and one instance could have been lost in some manuscripts due to haplography. Such a development might be more plausible than assuming dittography where the verb is found twice (thus Boll 2019, 226).

multis auctoribus fortissimis viris: that Cicero could have defended himself by resorting to arms is made plausible by the claim that many courageous people recommended this course of action, suggesting a large number of supporters (Cic. *Dom.* 63). Plutarch reports that friends of Cicero advised leaving Rome (Plut. *Cic.* 31.5).

ille animus idem meus vobis non incognitus: i.e. the same courage that Cicero showed as consul in 63 BCE when confronting the Catilinarian Conspiracy and thus well demonstrated to the senators (e.g. Cic. *Cat.* 3.28).

sed videbam: corresponds to *qua re cum viderem* at the start of the previous sentence and presents the insights on the situation that prompted Cicero not to defend himself.

si vicissem…esse pereundum: if Cicero had decided to fight, the outcome would have been either his victory or his defeat: in both cases the result would not have resolved the situation; instead fighting would have continued, including supporters on either side (Cic. *RQ* 13; *Dom.* 63; 96).

praesentem adversarium: i.e. P. Clodius Pulcher. – Only here in the two speeches of thanks does Cicero call Clodius *adversarius*; more frequently he uses *hostis* (Cic. *RS* 19 n.).

multis bonis: again in a political sense (Cic. *RS* 12 n.), indicating citizens supporting Cicero and the Republic in his interpretation.

et pro me et mecum, etiam post me: inserting a comma after *mecum*, as Shackleton Bailey (1987, 272) suggests, clarifies the structure (cf. Cic. *Har. resp.* 21: *respondebis et pro te et pro conlegis tuis, etiam pro pontificum conlegio*) and makes further changes unnecessary (Karsten 1879, 409–10: *multis bonis propter me, et mecum et etiam post me, esse pereundum…poenas iudicio posteritatis reservari*). The phrase stresses that many would have perished on account of Cicero, both at the time and subsequently: the construction places the focus on the fate of the many others; repeated *me* emphasizes that Cicero would be the reason for the projected developments.

tribuniciique…reservari: *-que* does not link this infinitive construction directly with the preceding one, as if both were connected with *si victus essem* (though the sequence depending on *videbam* continues). Instead, *-que* introduces a new aspect consisting of two phrases in adversative asyndeton; this section takes up the contrast between *si vicissem* and *si victus essem* by sketching the consequences of one of the parties being killed from a temporal point of view.

tribuniciique sanguinis ultores esse praesentis: Cicero envisages that, if he had been victorious and the Tribune of the People P. Clodius Pulcher killed, there would have been avengers straight away. In this more conciliatory context he leaves it open who these might have been (Cic. *Planc.* 88), while elsewhere he indicates that they would be the consuls (Cic. *Dom.* 91; *Sest.* 43). – Condom (1995, 52 n. 121) identifies the Tribune of the People alluded to as P. Sestius, but the context suggests an opponent of Cicero, who must be P. Clodius Pulcher. – In connection with envisaged fighting *sanguis* means 'blood shed in violence' (*OLD* s.v. *sanguis* 2).

meae mortis poenas iudicio et posteritati reservari: by contrast, if Cicero had died, his death would only be followed up in the future. *iudicio et posteritati* is a hendiadys (replacing a noun governing the genitive of another: K.-St. II 26–7), indicating that posterity will make an (appropriate) judgement on the matter. The choice of words in the two juxtaposed phrases (contrasting revenge with punishment) suggests that Cicero's death would be unjustified and demand punishment. – Shackleton Bailey (1991, 227) proposes changing *et* to *aut*, interpreting *iudicio* and *posteritati* as two different alternatives, i.e. a trial in the immediate future or appreciation by posterity. Such a text would disrupt the temporal contrast between the two parts.

34 nolui … -que … malui: *-que* links two strong statements of Cicero's intention, making it clear that his decision was a deliberate choice and taken in the interest of the community (see Introduction, section 3.4).

consul … privatus: again (Cic. *RS* 32) a contrast and parallel between Cicero as consul in 63 BCE and his current status (in relation to the common and his private well-being): Cicero claims that he did not wish to use arms to defend himself because he managed to protect the common welfare as consul without arms (*sine ferro* and *armis* correspond to each other with variation; *consul communem … meam privatus* forms a chiasmus). Although the two situations are different, Cicero's argument is based upon inferring a certain tradition for himself.

sine ferro defendissem: in the *Catilinarian Orations* Cicero frequently stresses that he successfully fought and defeated the Catilinarian Conspiracy like a military leader, yet without using weapons (Cic. *Cat.* 2.28; 3.15; 3.23; 4.5).

bonos … viros: assuming impact on *boni viri* (Cic. *RS* 12 n.) stresses the relevance of Cicero's fate and behaviour.

lugere … meas fortunas quam suis desperare: verbs of sentiment may be used transitively with the accusative; *desperare* only takes the dative in reflexive phrases (K.-St. I 260–2; Pinkster 2015, 893–4). – On the notion of Cicero sacrificing himself on behalf of the Republic, see Cic. *RQ* 1 n.; Introduction, section 3.4.

fortunas: refers to the (negative) fortune of individuals (*OLD* s.v. *fortuna* 8). The personalized expression emphasizes again that Cicero sacrifices himself selflessly to safeguard others.

ac si … essem interfectus, … videbatur: a counterfactual conditional construction, with the verb in the main clause in the indicative marking the reality of the expectation of future developments (K.-St. II 401–3; Pinkster 2015, 660).

mihi turpe: if Cicero alone was killed, it would be disgraceful for him, demonstrating that he had not managed to avoid it by the appropriate action, but it would not affect the Republic directly.

cum multis: constrasts with *solus* in the preceding *si*-clause; *essem interfectus* has to be supplied again. – For the thought, see Cic. *RS* 33.

rei publicae funestum: the death of many people would be grievous for the Republic because it is implied that *boni* supporting the Republic would be victims.

quod si … multassem: while Cicero has claimed up to this point that he was prepared to sacrifice himself for the sake of the common welfare, he now adds that he would not want to undergo permanent suffering, and, if there had not been any hope of change, he would have killed himself. This would have resolved the immediate issue of the conflict between Cicero and his opponents, because it would have removed him from the scene; in addition, it would have avoided any future suffering for him, but also cut off the possibility of becoming active for the Republic again. While Cicero still has it appear as if he chose the best option for the community, the notion of his own convenience is added. In a letter to Atticus written on the journey from Rome Cicero mentions thoughts of suicide (Cic. *Att.* 3.3 [March 58 BCE]). Considering suicide is in line with Stoic doctrines, which approved of suicide in certain circumstances (see also Cic. *RS* 14 n.; on attitudes to suicide in the ancient world, see, e.g., van Hooff 1990; Hill 2004; on views expressed in Cicero's works, reproducing those of different schools of philosophy, see Hill 2004, 31–71).

aerumnam: one of Cicero's periphrases for his absence from Rome (see Introduction, section 3.4): its connotations allude to the associated emotional strain, as appropriare in this context of the potential negative consequences.

arbitrarer: the imperfect subjunctive implies that this part of the conditional construction also applies to the present, i.e. that Cicero is still (not) of this opinion.

morte me ipse potius … multassem: *ipse*, agreeing with the subject (rather than the object), emphasizes that Cicero would have taken action himself if he subscribed to the view that the situation would last forever (for the construction, cf. Cic. *Scaur.* 3).

sed … reportavit: another statement by which Cicero creates a parallel between himself and the Republic (see Introduction, section 3.4), here in the strong form that their absence and presence match: for the time of his departure he posits that the Republic had been banished, i.e. no longer existed properly in Rome due to the political conditions, and that he should not be present in such a system; when the Republic was 'called back', i.e. proper political procedures were re-established, the Republic brought Cicero back along with it (Cic. *RQ* 14; *Dom.* 141; on *reportare*, see Cic. *RS* 28 n.). The verb *revocare* combines the concepts of 'calling home from exile' (metaphorically applied to the Republic) and 'restoring' (*OLD* s.v. *reuoco* 3b, 12). – Cicero does not give reasons why he believed that he would not be away forever; he might have assumed that a change of magistrates in the following year or politicians such as Pompey changing their minds would open up opportunities for his recall. Or he might claim retrospectively, after he was recalled successfully, that he expected such a development.

ex hac urbe: i.e. Rome.

neque … et: links (K.-St. II 48) the two consequences of Cicero's recognition that his own movement and that of the Republic would be aligned, with each of them subject in one of the parts (*ego … illa*, expressed for emphasis and clarity), illustrating departure and return respectively.

remanendum: some manuscripts have (*esse*) *amplius* after this word, which Boll (2019, 229) accepts into the text. However, *non amplius* is not common in Cicero (K.-St. II 461), and the phrase looks like a clarification, perhaps developed from *non diutius* in the *cum*-clause, which reduces the effect of single *remanendum* as a marker of Cicero immediately following the Republic.

mecum … afuerunt: a sequence of seven items, all introduced by anaphoric *mecum*, illustrates the circumstances during Cicero's absence in his view; in his terminology these are signs of the absence of the Republic, here linked with Cicero's absence. The first five items identify key features and players of the political system, the sixth (emphasized by *etiam*) refers to food supply (affected by the absence of an orderly political system), and the list ends with a generalizing element (*omnes*) encompassing secular and religious aspects (suggesting a lack of proper behaviour and perhaps implying an allusion to the arrangements concerning Cicero's house). While the claim of the complete absence of all these features is an exaggeration, the tenor agrees with what Cicero sketches elsewhere (Cic. *Dom.* 17; *Pis.* 32).

leges: the idea of laws being 'away' illustrates that they (or at least some of them) were ignored and society was no longer guided by an established law and order system.

quaestiones: to illustrate that the judicial system was no longer working properly, Cicero mentions the absence of standing commissions dealing with serious public crimes rather than generally *iudicia* (a slightly different, tendentious description at Cic. *Sest.* 85: *non modo nulla nova quaestio, sed etiam vetera iudicia sublata*). This nuance puts the focus on court cases that might affect former or aspiring magistrates; thus, it may imply a lack of control of political misbehaviour.

iura magistratuum: ignoring the rights of magistrates (e.g. *ius agendi cum senatu* or *ius agendi cum populo*: see Kunkel/Wittmann 1995, 242–6, 246–9) prevents them from carrying out their offices properly.

senatus auctoritas: Cicero has indicated that the Senate did not have leaders at the time (Cic. *RS* 33) and says elsewhere that it was ignored by the consuls and hindered in its accustomed activities (Cic. *RS* 31; *Sest.* 42; 44).

libertas: indicates the absence of political freedom in a non-violent and lawful society, which Cicero sees as a characteristic feature of the Roman People.

frugum ubertas: the time of Cicero's recall and return to Rome saw variations in the price of grain. These even led to demonstrations because of a lack of food, apparently soon after Cicero's return (Cic. *Dom.* 6; 10–12; 14–18). In other contexts Cicero refers to a Senate speech he delivered two days after this one, when the price of grain had risen to a high level; in that speech he puts forward the motion that Pompey be asked to take charge of supplies (Cic. *Att.* 4.1.6–7; *Dom.* 7–9; see *RQ*, Introduction). Cn. Pompeius Magnus was eventually given a special command to ensure a sufficient supply (Liv. *Epit.* 104; Plut. *Pomp.* 49.6–9, Cass. Dio 39.9.2–3; 39.24.1–2). In the speeches of thanks Cicero suggests that the price of grain fell in response to his return (Cic. *RQ* 18), though the presentation is vague and leaves it open whether this happened in response to the decision to recall him or to his return or just roughly around this time. In *De domo sua* Cicero says that the price first came down after the decree on his recall and went up again at the time of his return (Cic. *Dom.* 14–15; 17). Thus, it seems that Cicero gives a tendentious presentation without observing strict chronology rather than that this is an inaccurate or ill-informed account; this detail is thus not an argument against the speeches' authenticity (as put forward by Markland 1745, 251–4).

deorum et hominum sanctitates omnes et religiones: the application of *sanctitates* and *religiones* to gods and men simultaneously is probably meant to indicate that any regard for others and the associated behaviour has gone. In this context, the words could describe a revered quality or, more likely, high regard and the corresponding duties and attitude.

si ... abessent, ... lugerem ... desiderarem ...; sin ... revocarentur, intellegebam: in these two conditional constructions (constrasting with each other) all the verbs are in the imperfect: although these thoughts refer to the time when Cicero was about to leave or was away from Rome, they are thus presented as expressions of a timeless, general point of view. The indicative in the final main clause (in contrast to the preceding subjunctives) might indicate that Cicero was expecting (as a fact) that these items would be recalled and he would return with them.

vestras fortunas ... meas: *fortunas* has to be supplied to *meas*, where it has a positive meaning, in contrast to the negative meaning in the first phrase.

revocarentur: picks up the verb used with respect to the Republic a few lines earlier. Even for the Republic the metaphorical application of 'calling home from exile' is somewhat stretched; for the items listed here it is even more difficult: the word expresses the notion of restoration, while adding the idea that the items did not return by chance, but rather as a reaction to people actively wanting them restored; and it creates a parallel with Cicero's own movement.

cum illis: refers to the items listed in the preceding *mecum* sequence: Cicero now links his return with that of these items rather than with that of the Republic; as signs of a functioning Republic, they represent it. There is a shift in agency: it is said that the items were away with Cicero, and he returned with them, while the Republic brought him back; such an activity is perhaps to be reserved for the Republic. In any case, the idea of a close relationship between Cicero, the Republic, and characteristics of the Republic is maintained.

35 cuius mei sensus: i.e. Cicero's expectation that he and the items listed in the previous paragraph (Cic. *RS* 34) would return.

hic idem: emphasizes the identity of the person (Cn. Plancius) who is both *testis* and *custos*. – The first *qui*-clause describes Plancius' important function for Cicero; the second *qui*-clause after the mention of the name provides details of how he carried it out.

custos capitis: this description of Plancius' role for Cicero presents him as a kind of lifesaver, as an essential guardian of his survival (*OLD* s.v. *caput* 4).

Cn. Plancius: during Cicero's exile Cn. Plancius (*RE* Plancius 4) was in Thessalonica (modern Thessaloniki), as quaestor of the governor of Macedonia in 58 BCE (*MRR* II 197; see Nicholson 1992, 73–4; Goldmann 2012, 118–19). Cicero stayed in Thessalonica until almost the end of 58 BCE and was hosted and supported by Plancius (e.g. Cic. *Planc.* 1–4; 25–6; 61; 68–9; 71–4; 77–80; 98–102; *Att.* 3.14.2; 3.22.1; *Fam.* 14.1.3; Schol. Bob., arg. ad Cic. *Planc.* [pp. 152.31–3.7 Stangl]; Hieron. *Ab Abr.* 1956 = 61 BCE [p. 154d Helm]). Because of his outstanding efforts and care for Cicero, Plancius is singled out for special thanks and mentioned outside the sequence of officials active for Cicero's recall (Cic. *RS* 18–31 n.). These thanks are also included in the speech *Pro Plancio* (esp. Cic. *Planc.* 74 [T 2]; 78), which Cicero delivered as Plancius' defence when the latter was charged with misconduct in the election campaign for the aedileship of 54 BCE (*TLRR* 293).

omnibus provincialibus ornamentis commodisque depositis: in the speech *Pro Plancio* too Cicero indicates that Plancius did away with the role of quaestor (on the insignia of a quaestor, see Mommsen, *StR* II 519–20) and only cared for Cicero (Cic. *Planc.* 61; 100). When Cicero says that Plancius 'devoted his entire quaestorship' (*OLD* s.v. *colloco* 12) to efforts on Cicero's behalf (similarly about other magistrates: Cic. *RS* 8; 30), this must mean hyperbolically that, during a substantial part of the quaestorship, Plancius chose to support Cicero, while he did not regard the ordinary tasks of a quaestor as a priority and even abandoned the advantages of this position for Cicero's sake.

sustentando et conservando: combines the concept of practical support and the broader sense of defending Cicero.

qui si ... fuisset: a hypothetical thought experiment for describing the relationship between Cicero and Plancius based on the fact that Plancius was actually quaestor

quaestor imperatori: quaestors typically did not serve an *imperator*, but rather the governor of a province. Such a description of the governor of a province enables wordplay on *imperium* in the subsequent clause. Quaestors in provinces fulfilled administrative and finance functions in addition to supporting the governors in their juridical and administrative work (Kunkel/Wittmann 1995, 527–8). – Cicero frequently expresses the idea of a close connection between a senior magistrate and a quaestor resembling that between parents and children (Cic. *RS* 21; *Planc.* 28; *Div. Caec.* 46; 60; 61; 62; *Fam.* 2.17.6; 13.10.1; 13.10.4; Mommsen, *StR* II 563–4; Moreau 1989b). – Markland (1745, 254–9) notes that Cicero was not *imperator*, but rather governor of a province, though not by the time of the oration. The reference to *imperator*, however, is not linked to Cicero's position, but rather part of a generic consideration.

in fili loco: the collocation of *in loco* + genitive has the sense of 'in place of' (K.-St. I 349); combined with *esse* it indicates 'be regarded as' when the item in the prepositional phrase does not denote what something actually is, but how it should be seen (K.-St. I 18–19).

nunc certe: contrasts the hypothetical thought experiment with the true situation (*OLD* s.v. *nunc* 11).

in parentis: suppl. *loco* from the preceding phrase.

quaestor ... doloris mei: while, according to Cicero, a quaestor typically has the role of a son towards a senior magistrate, Plancius was like a father to Cicero (see also Raccanelli 2012, 65–8): Plancius looked after him with great care and devotion when Cicero was not in a position of power, but rather in a sorrowful state. This situation is expressed by denoting the quaestor's field of activity by an abstract term (rather than a superior they would serve) in a poignant juxta-position of the standard area of a quaestor's responsibility and the task in this case (see similarly Cic. *Sest.* 8: *quaestor hic C. Antoni, conlegae mei, iudices, fuit sorte, sed societate consiliorum meus.*). To enable this wordplay, the text should not be changed (Boll 2019, 233); Peterson (1911), for instance, reads *consors* (criticized by Luterbacher 1912, 346).

3. Conclusion (36–9): Cicero's promise to the Republic

The conclusion of the speech (Cic. *RS* 36–9) consists of a statement of Cicero's continued commitment to the Republic and his readiness to be active for the community again (cf. Cic. *Fam.* 1.9.4 [T 3]). He stresses that he now owes the Republic a lot and it is, therefore, appropriate for him to act on its behalf (after he had done so in the past when the Republic owed something to him). He emphasizes that material items may have been taken away from him, but that he never lost his moral and intellectual qualities, so that he can start again where he left off or even be more motivated because of the confidence shown in him (cf. Cic. *RQ* 18–25). Such a description creates the impression of a man who has worked selflessly for the Republic and will do so again, since his strength of mind has not been affected by absence from Rome; on the contrary, the nature of the recall and the widespread appreciation confirm his attitude. This support distinguishes Cicero's return from that of other exiled ex-consuls, who had large families interceding on their behalf, whereas Cicero only had two relatives taking action for him in his absence (Cic. *RS* 37–8); these ex-consuls were called back on the basis of the interventions of their large and influential families, but not by the Senate (cf. Cic. *RQ* 6–7; 9), while Cicero was recalled by a decree of the Senate (cf. Cic. *RQ* 10–11). Cicero's sketch of the respective situations, combined with an expression of gratitude for the efforts of his brother and his son-in-law (cf. Cic. *RQ* 7–8), demonstrates the unanimity between Cicero and the Senate. This impression is more prominent in the speech in the Senate, where Cicero, while placing himself in a sequence with these three precedecessors, distinguishes his fate favourably from theirs; in the speech before the People all these men are presented more positively, Marius in particular (Mack 1937, 30–2 on Cic. *RS* 38 vs *RQ* 9–11).

In the speech to the People Cicero announces his future actions for the Republic more firmly and confidently, which would be less appropriate in front of the Senate (Boll 2019, 47–8). Thus, without appearing too pompous or arrogant, Cicero, in the course of this speech, has changed his portrayal from that of an individual grateful for this restoration to someone suited to regaining a position as a key element of the Republic, as acknowledged by all. Such a closure gives an emphatic ending to a kind of inaugural speech and provides Cicero with the appropriate basis for resuming his former position. The same aim and attitude are expressed in the speech given before the People, where Cicero highlights his own position and adds his personal relationship to them (Mack 1937, 44–8 on Cic. *RS* 36–9 vs *RQ* 18–25).

36 quapropter, patres conscripti: the start of the concluding section is marked by a conjunction signalling a summative assessment and an address to the senators.

in rem publicam…cum re publica restitutus: Cicero repeats his central claim that his own fate and that of the Republic work in parallel and they both have returned (see Introduction, section 3.4). For a pointed expression, he uses *res publica* in two senses: *res publica* as defining a country by its political system and *res publica* as a well-run, properly functioning political system. When Cicero, therefore, claims that he was restored to the Republic and with the Republic (*OLD* s.v. *restituo* 6b), this does not contradict earlier statements that both he and the Republic had been away (see also Hodgson 2017, 147).

in ea defendenda: *in* with the ablative of the gerund or gerundive describes the concomitant means or circumstances and can be equivalent to a present participle (K.-St. I 753). – *ea* refers to *res publica*.

imminuam: both *imminuam* and *minuam* are transmitted, and both verbs are grammatically correct and make sense. Boll (2019, 234) may be right in arguing for the compound *imminuam* to balance *adaugebo*. And compounds are often simplified in the manuscript tradition.

de libertate: Cicero confirms that the experience of his enforced absence from Rome has not made him more timid or less engaged in political affairs than he was in the past; on the contrary, now that he and the Republic are back, he will speak out even more (*OLD* s.v. *libertas* 7). In the speech to the People, the statement on *libertas* is even stronger, and this quality is promised to be used more specifically in support of the Republic (Cic. *RQ* 24).

etenim…nam…nam: the series of causal clauses gives two reasons for Cicero's increased efforts for the Republic after his return in the shape of rhetorical questions; the third clause provides further detail on the positive statement implied in the second question.

tum ... nunc: again a juxtaposition of what Cicero did as consul and what he is doing now: Cicero saved the Republic in the past, when it owed him something; now when he owes it a lot as a result of having been reinstated, he cannot do anything other than continue his support. The argument is not entirely logical, since in the former case the Republic could only owe Cicero something after the event, and in the latter case he has just claimed that he was recalled by the Senate and the efforts of individuals and that the Republic was away with him. Irrespective of this, the reciprocal relationship (underlined by the wording) and Cicero's debt to the Republic are to be stressed as a justification for his present attitude.

quid est ... videatis: Cicero presents it as implausible that his absence could have weakened his spirit by claiming that it demonstrated not a crime but instead confirmed two favours done by him to the Republic (Cic. *RQ* 19). In that context his absence is described as *calamitas* (see Cic. *RS* 20 n.; Introduction, section 3.4).

cuius: grammatically refers to the person 'I' implied in *animum meum* (K.-St. I 30–1).

duorum: preferable to *divinorum* (both transmitted): Cicero presumably would not go so far as to state that his achievements are 'divine'; he rather alludes to two of them, emphasized if *et ... et* is read in the next sentence, as transmitted in the same manuscripts (Klotz 1913, 489; Maslowski 1980, 411; Boll 2019, 234–5).

videatis: the subjunctive in the relative clause indicates a causal connotation (K.-St. II 292).

nam: this sentence explains how *calamitas* (subject) followed on from Cicero's deeds for the Republic.

importata ... suscepta: outlines two reasons for *calamitas*, i.e. Cicero's great deeds for the Republic with their contexts or aims (see, e.g., Cic. *RQ* 1; *Dom.* 76; 99; *Sest.* 49; *Pis.* 78; Introduction, section 3.4): (1) *calamitas* happened as a result of Cicero's initiatives against Catiline; the vague phrasing indicates that it was brought upon him externally, while it does not make anyone responsible. (2) Cicero accepted *calamitas* when he left Rome voluntarily to avoid harm to the Republic.

quia defenderam: i.e. in 63 BCE during the Catilinarian Conspiracy.

ne ... vocaretur: Cicero claims that the reason for his decision to leave was that he did not wish the Republic, which he had saved, to suffer just because of him, the previous saviour (*per eundem me*). Thus, he presents himself as the constant selfless benefactor and servant of the Republic, which justifies his resuming his service for the Republic after his return.

37 pro me non ...: Cicero continues with the discussion of his return: to illustrate its special features, he moves on (without any marked transition) to comparing and contrasting his situation with those of three earlier ex-consuls who went into exile for political reasons: P. Popilius Laenas, Q. Caecilius Metellus Numidicus, and C. Marius. To some extent Cicero places himself in the tradition of these famous earlier exiles; at the same time he stresses the difference, noting that he was not able to rely on the support of many influential relatives, and he implies that he surpasses the others owing to his devotion to the *res publica*, his non-violent behaviour, his honourable return, and the wide-spread support for his recall (Gnauk 1936, 40–3; Grasmück 1977, 168; Bücher 2006, 246–9; Kelly 2006, 153–4). These predecessors also appear in the speech of thanks delivered to the People (Cic. *RQ* 6–7; 9–11); there they are given a more prominent position earlier in the speech, their achievements are alluded to, and Marius is discussed in a detailed and emotive way (Thompson 1978, 101–3). Here the presentation of Metellus is more extensive than that of Popilius, and Metellus is also mentioned (Cic. *RS* 25) earlier in the speech (Boll 2019, 236). – The difference in Cicero's situation from those of the other exiled men is stressed with regard to the nature of the laws concerning them in *De domo sua* (Cic. *Dom.* 82). In that speech Cicero adds a few further examples (Cic. *Dom.* 86) before discussing P. Popilius Laenas and Q. Caecilius Metellus Numidicus (Cic. *Dom.* 87): these other men had been found guilty by the *comitia centuriata*, and Cicero highlights that he, in contrast, had never been brought to trial (see Introduction, section 2). The present speech is concerned with the modalities of return and thus does not feature these examples.

Publio Popilio: P. Popilius Laenas (*RE* Popilius 28; cos. 132 BCE [*MRR* I 497–8]), when consul in 132 BCE, took action against the followers of the dead Ti. Sempronius Gracchus. Therefore, he went into exile in 123 BCE to avoid a trial as a result of C. Sempronius Gracchus' measures (*Lex Sempronia de P. Popillio Laenate*: *LPPR*, p. 309); after Gracchus' death, in 121 or 120 BCE (*MRR* I 524 with n. 3), he was recalled by the Tribune of the People L. Calpurnius Bestia (*Lex Calpurnia de P. Popillio Laenate revocando*: *LPPR*, p. 317; dated to 120 [?] BCE) and was thus the first Roman to be recalled from exile (Cic. *RS* 38; *RQ* 9; 11; *Dom.* 82; 87; *Clu.* 95; *Brut.* 95; 128; *Rep.* 1.5–6; *Leg.* 3.26; Schol. Bob. ad Cic. *RQ* 6 [p. 111.18 Stangl]; ad Cic. *De aere alieno Milonis* F 23 [p. 174.14–15 Stangl]; Plut. *C. Gracch.* 4.1–2; see Gruen 1968, 80–4; Nicholson 1992, 32–4; Pina Polo 1996, 108; Kelly 2006, 71–6; van der Blom 2010, 195–203 [on Numidicus and Popilius as exempla for Cicero]).

adulescentes filii: singled out separately from the large number of Popilius' relatives, also in the speech to the People (*RQ* 6); the activity of a son in *adulescentia* is also mentioned for Metellus Numidicus. Apart from the fact that such activity would be expected of a dutiful son, perhaps there is an implied contrast with Cicero (Weiske 1807, 235), as at the time of his absence from Rome his son (Cic. *RS* 1 n.) was too young to take any action (Cic. *RQ* 8). – A son Gaius is mentioned in Cicero's *Brutus* (Cic. *Brut.* 95); no other individuals are securely attested as sons of Popilius.

propinquorum multitudo: also referred in the speech to the People (Cic. *RQ* 6; on the terms for relatives, see Cic. *RS* 17; *RQ* 6 nn.), equally without any details about their identity; the emphasis is on their large number. – The group may have included women, if the attested speech *In Po{m}pil<l>ium et matronas* by C. Sempronius Gracchus (Fest., p. 136.16–19 L. [*ORF*⁴ 48 F 38]) is directed against women asking for Popilius' return (Kelly 2006, 73–4).

populum Romanum ... populo Romano: the activities of relatives are said to have been directed towards the People (Cic. *RQ* 6), and there is no particular mention of the Senate (Boll 2019, 46). In the subsequent comparison of the return of these earlier men with that of Cicero, his recall by the Senate is highlighted as a contrast.

est deprecata: expresses a strong entreaty (*OLD* s.v. *deprecor* 3; Cic. *RS* 31; *RQ* 6–7; 9; 16; 18).

Q. Metello: Q. Caecilius Metellus Numidicus (cos. 109, censor 102 BCE [*MRR* I 545, 567]; see Cic. *RS* 25 n.).

spectata iam adulescentia filius: indicates that the son was a young man at the time when his father was exiled (*c.* 100 BCE), but had already emerged into public life so that he and his qualities had become recognized (*OLD* s.v. *spectatus* 2 '(of persons, their lives, etc.) of observed merit or worth, distinguished'). The phrase corresponds to *iam spectata aetate* in the speech to the People (Cic. *RQ* 6).

filius: Q. Caecilius Metellus Pius (*RE* Caecilius 98; cos. 80 BCE [*MRR* II 4]; see van Ooteghem 1967, 178–216). He fought with his father in Numidia as a young man and received the cognomen Pius because of his constant attempts to have his father recalled (Cic. *Arch.* 6; Vell. Pat. 2.15.3–4; Val. Max. 5.2.7; *Vir. ill.* 63.1; Ampel. 18.14; App. *B Civ.* 1.33).

L. et C. Metelli consulares: L. Caecilius Metellus Diadematus (*RE* Caecilius 93; cos. 117 BCE [*MRR* I 528]; see van Ooteghem 1967, 93–7) and C. Caecilius Metellus Caprarius (*RE* Caecilius 84; cos. 113, censor 102 BCE [*MRR* I 535, 567]; see van Ooteghem 1967, 102–5), described in greater detail in the speech to the People (Cic. *RQ* 6); they were cousins of Q. Caecilius Metellus Numidicus.

eorum liberi: the sons of C. Caecilius Metellus Caprarius were Q. Caecilius Metellus Creticus (*RE* Caecilius 87; cos. 69 BCE [*MRR* II 131]; see van Ooteghem 1967, 220–39), L. Caecilius Metellus (*RE* Caecilius 74; cos. 68 BCE [*MRR* II 137]; see van Ooteghem 1967, 240–4), M. Caecilius Metellus (*RE* Caecilius 78; praet. 69 BCE [*MRR* II 131–2]; see van Ooteghem 1967, 244) and (probably) C. Caecilius Metellus (*RE* Caecilius 71). – Q. Caecilius Metellus Celer (tr. pl. 90 [*MRR* II 26]; *RE* Caecilius 85) may have been a son of L. Caecilius Metellus Diadematus.

Q. Metellus Nepos: Q. Caecilius Metellus Nepos (*RE* Caecilius 95; cos. 98 BCE [*MRR* I 4]; see van Ooteghem 1967, 217–19), a son of Q. Caecilius Metellus Baliaricus (*RE* Caecilius 82; cos. 123 BCE [*MRR* I 512–13]), a grandson of Q. Caecilius Metellus Macedonicus (*RE* Caecilius 94; cos. 143 BCE [*MRR*

I 471–2]), and a nephew of L. Caecilius Metellus Diadematus and C. Caecilius Metellus Caprarius; his father was a cousin of Q. Caecilius Metellus Numidicus.

qui tum consulatum petebat: in 99 BCE Q. Caecilius Metellus Nepos was a candidate for the consulship of 98 BCE (Cic. *RQ* 6).

Luculli: L. Licinius Lucullus (*RE* Licinius 103; praet. 104 BCE [*MRR* I 559]) was married to Caecilia Metella (*RE* Caecilius 132), a daughter of L. Caecilius Metellus Calvus (*RE* Caecilius 83) and a sister of Q. Caecilius Metellus Numidicus; the couple's sons were L. Licinius Lucullus (*RE* Licinius 104; cos. 74 BCE [*MRR* II 100–1]; *ORF*⁴ 90; see van Ooteghem 1959) and M. Licinius Lucullus, called M. Terentius Varro Lucullus after adoption (*RE* Licinius 109; cos. 73 BCE [*MRR* II 109]; *ORF*⁴ 91).

Servilii: C. Servilius Vatia (*RE* Servilius 91; praet. or promag. before 100 BCE [*MRR* II 465]) was married to Caecilia Metella (*RE* Caecilius 130), a daughter of Q. Caecilius Metellus Macedonicus (*RE* Caecilius 94; cos. 143 BCE [*MRR* I 471–2]), a sister of L. Caecilius Metellus Diadematus and C. Caecilius Metellus Caprarius and a cousin of Q. Caecilius Metellus Numidicus; the couple's son was P. Servilius Vatia Isauricus (*RE* Servilius 93; cos. 79 BCE [*MRR* II 82]; see Cic *RS* 25 n.).

Scipiones: P. Cornelius Scipio Nasica Serapio (*RE* Cornelius 355; cos. 111 BCE [*MRR* I 540]) was married to Caecilia Metella (*RE* Caecilius 131), another daughter of Q. Caecilius Metellus Macedonicus and a sister of L. Caecilius Metellus Diadematus and C. Caecilius Metellus Caprarius and a cousin of Q. Caecilius Metellus Numidicus; the couple's son was P. Cornelius Scipio Nasica (*RE* Cornelius 351; praet. 93 BCE [*MRR* II 14]).

Metellarum filii: the preceding names in the plural could be understood as actual plurals, each of them referring to a father and their male offspring with the same *nomen* (with the father married to a Metella). Then *Metellarum filii* (with Manilius' generally accepted conjecture *Metellarum* for *Metellorum*; see Cic. *RQ* 6: *Metelli aut Metellarum liberi*, where *Metellarum* is transmitted in some manuscripts) would highlight that *Luculli*, *Servilii*, and *Scipiones* include *Metellarum filii*. In view of the sentence structure and the description of the same men in the speech to the People (Cic. *RQ* 6), the plurals are probably generic plurals (K.-St. I 72), and *Metellarum filii* is an explanatory apposition specifying that the examples given belong to this category. The emphasis is on support from members of the same *gens* and thus on the sons rather than the fathers.

sordidati: i.e. in mourning clothes (Cic. *RS* 12 n.).

supplicaverunt: i.e. for the return of Q. Caecilius Metellus Numidicus.

frater: Cicero's brother Quintus (Cic. *RS* 1 n.). – In contrast to the many relatives supporting the men from the past just mentioned, Cicero claims that he had only his brother to assist him (*unus*). He then adds his son-in-law as a second supporter (Cic. *RS* 38: *alter*), though his brother remains the only blood relative. The efforts of this single close relative are highlighted when he is said to fulfil the functions of different types of direct relatives and his thoughts and actions are described in detail (see also Raccanelli 2012, 84–90; Boll 2019, 239). There is even more emphasis on the brother's activities in the speech to the People (Boll 2019, 49), in line with the more personal tone in that speech (Cic. *RQ* 7–8; on the brother's activities and his role for Cicero, see also Cic. *RQ* 5; *Dom.* 59; *Sest.* 68; 76; 145; *Q Fr.* 1.3.3 [13 June 58 BCE]; *Att.* 4.1.8 [Sept. 57 BCE]; Plut. *Pomp.* 49.3).

qui…inventus est: the single person supporting Cicero not only fulfilled the role of a brother (by his attitude, rather than just the relationship), but also of a son and father by his care and concern (Cic. *Q Fr.* 1.3.3 [13 June 58 BCE]: *cum enim te desidero, fratrem solum desidero? ego vero suavitate fratrem prope aequalem, obsequio filium, consilio parentem. quid mihi sine te umquam aut tibi sine me iucundum fuit?*). – In the sequence of characteristics defining the three types of relationship (*pietate…consiliis…amore*) the first and the last words (in the singular) describe an attitude and the middle one indicates an activity (stemming from a similar underlying attitude). The nuances match the various familial relationships.

squalore et lacrimis et cotidianis precibus: by both his appearance and his activities Cicero's brother is said to have aroused sympathy for Cicero. The less detailed version in the speech to the People only has *fletu* (Cic. *RQ* 8).

desiderium mei nominis renovari: 'name' here stands for the person (*OLD* s.v. *nomen* 17). *renovari* suggests that *desiderium* existed before and was interrupted or reduced: the attitude towards Cicero thereby appears consistent and varying in intensity, but not in substance. This does not undermine the influence of Cicero's brother in rekindling this feeling, while indicating the underlying goodwill among the population.

rerum gestarum memoriam usurpari: it might be more natural to speak of (*OLD* s.v. *usurpo* 5b) deeds than of their memory. Thus, the expression seems to merge two ideas: to remember the deeds and to maintain memory of them by talking about them. The briefer version in the speech to the People has a less complex construction with the verb *renovare* only and a focus on the person of Cicero (Cic. *RQ* 8: *desiderium mei memoriamque renovaret*). – The unspecific positive term *res gestae* might include another allusion to Cicero's actions in the face of the Catilinarian Conspiracy (Boll 2019, 238).

coegit: this strong verb describes Cicero's brother's intervention as effective, although there is only one person interceding. Because of the lack of an object (for *cogo* with passive accusative and infinitive construction, see K.-St. I 694–5), the emphasis is on the attitude towards Cicero the brother created, and there is no indication of exerting pressure on anyone in particular. Only in the next sentence reporting Quintus' alleged thoughts is the audience given as the object of his activity; when the same notion is repeated before the People, they are the addressed audience from whom action is expected (Cic. *RQ* 8).

nisi me per vos reciperasset: the word order *me per vos* found in some manuscripts is preferable to the alternative reading *per vos me*; the emphasis should be on *me* (Klotz 1913, 490; Boll 2019, 239).

eandem subire fortunam atque idem sibi domicilium et vitae et mortis deposcere{t}: in both the speech to the Senate and that to the People Cicero claims that his brother decided to have the same fortune as Cicero (either follow him away from Rome or die) if Cicero was not restored. The version before the People is more explicit and uses a less audacious metaphor (Cic. *RQ* 8).

tamen: Shackleton Bailey (1987, 272; 1991, 227), following Lambinus and Orelli (cf. Halm 1956, 845), suggests deleting *tamen*, arguing that Cicero's brother's resolve would not make him any less ready to intervene on Cicero's behalf. The transmitted text may stand if the underlying meaning is that Cicero's brother had made a decision how to resolve the situation for himself if unsuccessful, but nevertheless continued to be active in public in the interest of his brother and was not afraid of circumstances that might suggest a negative outcome.

magnitudinem negoti: i.e. the task of having Cicero recalled. Presenting the task as a huge challenge enhances the efforts made and the eventual success.

solitudinem suam: after Cicero's departure his brother was the only adult male member of the immediate family in Rome; their grandfather, father, uncle, and cousin were already dead at that time. What is highlighted is probably not that Quintus 'had lost Cicero' (Shackleton Bailey 1991, 23 n. 89), but that he is alone in his efforts to support Cicero (*unus*) in contrast to the situation of earlier ex-consuls (Boll 2019, 240).

vim inimicorum ac tela: could be metaphorical or indicate that violence against Cicero's brother was going on or to be expected (Cic. *Dom.* 59). He was attacked amid the disturbances connected with the attempted vote on Cicero's recall by the People on 23 January 57 BCE (Cic. *Sest.* 76; Plut. *Cic.* 33.2; see Cic. *RS* 6 n.). – The *inimici* are probably Cicero's and, by extension, those of his brother, i.e. presumably Clodius and his followers (Cic. *RS* 38 and n.).

38 alter: the second person supporting Cicero besides his brother was his son-in-law C. Calpurnius Piso Frugi.

propugnator... et defensor: these terms, with their military connotations (*OLD* s.v. *propugnator* 1; *defensor* 2b), describe a determined champion (*OLD* s.v. *propugnator* 2) and supporter (*OLD* s.v. *defensor* 3). For the combination, see Cic. *Sest.* 144: *video P. Sestium, meae salutis, vestrae auctoritatis, publicae causae defensorem, propugnatorem, actorem, reum.*

summa virtute et pietate: Piso is given a similar positive characterization in the speech before the People (Cic. *RQ* 7 [and n.]). – *pietas*, applied to the relationship with the generation of parents (*OLD* s.v. *pietas* 3a; see Cic. *RS* 37), here refers to the attitude towards the father-in-law rather than towards parents. – The descriptive ablatives are combined with a personal name without a supporting apposition like *vir* or *homo* (K.-St. I 226–7; Lebreton 1901, 83–4).

C. Piso gener: C. Calpurnius Piso Frugi (Cic. *RS* 15 n.), Cicero's son-in-law (married to Cicero's daughter Tullia: see Cic. *RS* 1 n.); he was quaestor of Pontus and Bithynia in 58 BCE (though he did not go to the province) and died in 57 BCE before Cicero's return. – Cicero frequently mentions Piso's qualities and his outstanding devotion to his case as well as the rough treatment he suffered from the consul Piso in return (Cic. *RS* 17 [and n.]; *RQ* 7; *Sest.* 54; 68; *Pis.* 12–13; *Fam.* 14.1.4; 14.2.1–2; 14.3.3; 14.4.4).

minas inimicorum meorum: for the son-in-law Cicero makes it clear that the enemies he faced are those of Cicero (cf. Cic. *RS* 37 and n.). He does not specify what the threats of his so-called enemies against his son-in-law might consist of.

adfinis mei, propinqui sui, consulis: L. Calpurnius Piso Caesoninus, consul in 58 BCE, was a kinsman of Piso Frugi and related to Cicero through Piso Frugi's marriage with Cicero's daughter (Cic. *RS* 15 n.). The different types of kinship are indicated by the appropriate terms (Cic. *RS* 17; *RQ* 6 nn.). – When Piso is said to have ignored the enmity of his kinsman, he is presented as having actively and openly adopted a position of support for Cicero and not being moved by the fact that this stance put him at odds with the consul.

Pontum et Bithyniam quaestor...neglexit: when he was quaestor in 58 BCE (*MRR* II 197), Piso did not go to the province of Pontus and Bithynia, as he was supposed to do, and instead stayed in Rome in order to be in a better position to support Cicero. The most obvious statement that Piso did not take up the role in the province is this passage. – The combination of the predicate *neglexit* with the objects *minas, inimicitias,* and *Pontum et Bithyniam* is zeugmatic: in the last case Piso forgoes a material item (for *provinciam neglegere*, see Cic. *Cat.* 4.23; *Phil.* 3.26; *Fam.* 15.4.13); in the first two cases he ignores the negative attitude of others towards him.

prae mea salute: *prae* indicates a circumstance or reason affecting one's actions (K.-St. I 513; *OLD* s.v. *prae*² 5).

nihil...fugisset: Cicero adds as a further point: not only were there fewer relatives interceding for him than for the men mentioned; additionally, those men were recalled not by Senate decrees but rather by tribunician bills (by L. Calpurnius Bestia [tr. pl. 121 or 120 BCE; *MRR* I 524 with n. 3] and Q. Calidius [tr. pl. 98 BCE; *MRR* II 5] respectively) after the death of their enemies (Cic. *Dom.* 87; *Planc.* 69; *Brut.* 128; *Vir. ill.* 62.3). That Cicero mentions this contrast and the intervention by the Senate on his behalf (Cic. *RQ* 9–10; see Ryan 1998, 30) makes his recall appear more noteworthy and demonstrates the recognition Cicero gained from the Senate. – *rogatio* literally refers to a proposal and does not indicate whether it was approved (which was the case in these instances). This wording emphasizes that the initiatives came from Tribunes of the People.

interfectis inimiciis: the 'enemy' of P. Popilius Laenas was C. Sempronius Gracchus (Cic. *RS* 37 n.), that of Q. Caecilius Metellus Numidicus was L. Appuleius Saturninus (Cic. *RS* 25 n.).

cum alter eorum senatui paruisset, alter vim caedemque fugisset: this comment refers to P. Popilius Laenas (Cic. *RS* 37 n.) and Q. Caecilius Metellus Numidicus (Cic. *RS* 25 n.) respectively, though it is not obvious what is alluded to and in which order the two men are mentioned. Perhaps Numidicus' bearing the consequences of observing the Senate decree and the approval of the law and Popilius' confrontation with the Gracchi are meant. According to Boll (2019, 241) Popilius only went into exile when he was forced after having been officially banished, and Metellus fled the bloody violence of his own accord before having been officially banished: there is no clear evidence to corroborate this assumption.

nam: provides a reason for an unexpressed point that could be put forward as an objection: 'so that you do not claim that the situation is different with respect to the third ex-consul: for…' and thus marks a transition (K.-St. II 117–18; *OLD* s.v. *nam* 4; cf. Cic. *RS* 13).

C. quidem Marius: C. Marius (*c.* 157–86 BCE; *RE* Marius 14 [Suppl. 6]; cos. 107, 104, 103, 102, 101, 100, 86 BCE [*MRR* I 550, 558, 562, 567, 570–1, 574; II 53]; born in Arpinum like Cicero). – When P. Cornelius Sulla was consul in 88 BCE, the Tribune of the People P. Sulpicius and Marius prepared new legislation, including a transfer of the supreme command in the war against Mithridates VI to Marius, and started riots in Rome; in reponse Sulla led his army against Rome and had his opponents declared enemies and some killed, while Marius escaped. In 87 BCE, when Sulla was fighting Mithridates in the east and the conflict between different factions in Rome escalated, Marius returned to Rome with the support of L. Cornelius Cinna. Marius and Cinna usurped control in Rome and had many of their political opponents declared political enemies, proscribed, and killed (e.g. Cic. *RQ* 7; 9–11; 19–21; *Planc.* 26; *Sest.* 50; *Pis.* 43; *Div.* 2.140; *Fin.* 2.105; *Parad.* 2.16; Plut. *Mar.* 35–43; App. *B Civ.* 1.55–75; Schol. Bob. ad Cic. *RS* 38 [p. 109.28–32 Stangl]; see Carney 1961; Nicholson 1992, 32–4). Marius is included in this sequence of politicians who were expelled and returned, although he was not an exile in the traditional sense, as he left Rome as a result of the fighting against Sulla, when he had been declared a *hostis* (called *fuga* at Cic. *De or.* 3.8), and later returned to Rome by armed force. That is probably the reason why Cicero does not create as close a parallel with Marius as with the other exiles, though elsewhere the great deeds of both men from the same town are put in parallel (e.g. Cic. *Leg.* 2.6) and Marius is even presented as predicting Cicero's return in an envisaged dream (Cic. *Div.* 1.59). – In the speech to the Senate Marius is introduced in a more restrained manner than in that to the People (Mack 1937, 26–7; Grasmück 1977, 168 n. 40; Claassen 1999, 159–60; Kelly 2006, 152–3; van der Blom 2010, 206; Boll 2019, 51–2; on Cicero's presentation of Marius as an exemplum for himself, see van der Blom 2010, 203–8; on Cicero's portrayal of Marius, see Gnauk 1936, esp. 38–46; Carney 1960).

hac hominum memoria: the demonstrative pronoun indicates that not the whole memory of men, i.e. the entire history, is meant (Cic. *RS* 10 n.), but rather 'living memory', 'present memory' (as in *hoc tempus* = 'the present', 'our time'), i.e. the tangible memory connected to present-day men, as is more explicit in the speech before the People (Cic. *RQ* 7). – The selection of examples focuses on instances closer in time to the present and does not exclude the possibility of further cases in the distant past.

tertius ante me: Cicero establishes the following sequence of ex-consuls: (1) Popilius, (2) Metellus, (3) Marius, (4) Cicero (Cic. *RQ* 7).

consularis: all four men left Rome after their respective consulships (Cic. *RQ* 7).

tempestate civili: a euphemistic reference to civil war (*OLD* s.v. *tempestas* 4).

a senatu non est restitutus: like the other two examples, and in contrast to Cicero, Marius was not recalled by the Senate (Cic. *RQ* 9–10).

reditu suo senatum cunctum paene delevit: in contrast to Cicero (and also to the other two examples), Marius is said to have even attacked the Senate due to political differences (for the phrase, see Cic. *Sest.* 17). This refers to the fact that a number of senators were among those killed by Marius upon his return in 87 BCE (Plut. *Mar.* 43–4). The description is vaguer and milder in the speech to the People (Mack 1937, 31 n. 73), where *oppresso senatu* is used and the reference to arms is general (Cic. *RQ* 10; see *RQ* 7; 20–1; *De or.* 3.8; *Rep.* 1.6).

nulla…exstiterunt: the list with the fourfold repetition of *nullus/nulla* highlights emphatically widespread support (in two pairs: magistrates and People of Rome; Italy and municipal towns), which was not the case for the other three ex-consuls, but applied to Cicero (Cic. *RQ* 18; *Pis.* 51–2). – Riggsby points out that emphasis on the unanimity shown upon Cicero's return argumentatively contributes to playing down the developments prompting him to leave (Riggsby 2002, 184: 'But unanimity may have a particular point here. If virtually everyone were on Cicero's side (only Clodius and a few close relatives and allies are admitted as exceptions), then he could not "really" have been exiled in the first place; there would have been no one to support it.').

de illis: summarizing all three men given as precedents.

magistratuum consensio: as Cicero has said (Cic. *RS* 3–4), apart from a few exceptions (ignored here), all magistrates of different ranks supported his recall in 57 BCE.

populi Romani convocatio: a reference to the fact that the Senate called everyone to Rome (see Cic. *RS* 24 n.; Introduction, section 2), with emphasis on the involvement of the Roman People as a political body rather than the geographical spread. When the purpose of the meeting is *ad rem publicam defendendam*, Cicero's return is again presented as beneficial for the Republic (see Introduction, section 3.4).

Italiae motus: refers to the demonstrations of support (*OLD* s.v. *motus* 9c) shown to Cicero on his way back and by those who had come to Rome (Cic. *RS* 39 n.).

decreta municipiorum et coloniarum: Cicero implies that there was not only a decree of the Senate in Rome recalling him, but also others in his support across the settlements of Italy (Cic. *RS* 29; *RQ* 10 nn.). – In the speech to the People the same points are made with similar words, but in chiastic order as it were: *Italia* linked with *decreta* and *municipia et coloniae* with *motus* (Cic. *RQ* 10). – On the terminology for municipal towns and colonies, see Cic. *RS* 27; 31 nn.

39 cum . . . reportarit: another fourfold sequence illustrating the unanimous support for Cicero's return, partially overlapping with the list in the previous sentence (Cic. *RS* 38).

vestra auctoritas arcessierit: highlights the Senate's responsibility for Cicero's return (in initial position) and prepares for the emphatic final address to the senators. – *auctoritas* probably indicates the Senate's authority (*OLD* s.v. *auctoritas* 6c) rather than an informal resolution of the Senate (*OLD* s.v. *auctoritas* 4).

populus Romanus vocarit: presumably a reference to the vote on the law for Cicero's restoration (see Cic. *RS* 27–8 nn.; Introduction, section 2) rather than to demonstrations in his support upon his return.

res publica implorarit: a metaphorical description of the personified Republic, implying that the political system desired Cicero's return and could not function without him. The image might appear as a slight contradiction of the concept presented elsewhere that Cicero and the *res publica* left and came back together (Boll 2019, 244). Yet it may be seen as defining a country by its political system and referring to its remnants rather than a well-run functioning institution in Cicero's interpretation (see Cic. *RS* 36 and n.).

Italia cuncta: an exaggerated indication of universal support, both political-ly and geographically, experienced particularly on Cicero's journey from Brundisium to Rome. – *Italia* is again personified and metonymically refers to the inhabitants (Cic. *RS* 24 n.). – Boll (2019, 244) refers the comment to the Senate's request in May 57 BCE that all citizens of Italy should come to Rome to vote on Cicero's recall. But *paene suis umeris reportarit* suggests more concrete support at a later stage.

paene suis umeris reportarit: *paene* is frequently used in this speech to qualify hyperbolic statements. Here, because of the word order, it almost cer-tainly refers to *suis umeris reportarit* rather than to *Italia cuncta* (K.-St. II 613–14); a qualification of *cuncta* would not suit the context (on *reportare*, see Cic. *RS* 28 n.). Despite the qualification Cicero's return is described in hyperbolic fashion almost like a divine event (Cole 2013, 65–6). – Cicero claims support from all of Italy elsewhere, but does not go as far as saying that it carried him on its shoulders. This metaphor and the associated activity are attributed to Clodius as an announcement made during Cicero's absence and referring to himself (Cic. *Dom.* 40: *quod si fieret, dicebas te tuis umeris me custodem urbis in urbem relaturum*). In Cicero's presentation of his return (see also Cic. *Att.* 4.1.4; *Dom.* 75–6; *Sest.* 131; *Pis.* 51–2) it is not Clodius but Italy who carried him back. – This feature of Cicero's return was taken up in the later ancient reception (Macrob. *Sat.* 2.3.5; Ps.-Sall. *Inv. Cic.* 7; Sen. *Contr.* 7.2.5; Plut. *Cic.* 33.7–8). Glucker (1988) suggests that the motif there might ultimately come from Cicero's *De temporibus suis*, but this assumption cannot be verified.

non committam: *non committo* is followed by a consecutive *ut*-clause, negated by *ut...non* (K.-St. II 234; Lebreton 1901, 128 n. 3); for the same construction, see Cic. *RQ* 20.

ut...amiserim: the speech ends with an address to the senators and an emphatic declaration of Cicero's continual efforts for the Republic by means of qualities he never lost, additionally motivated by gratitude for the restoration of items he had lost (for similar thoughts, see Cic. *RQ* 19; *Att.* 3.5; *Parad.* 4.29; C. Aurelius Cotta at Sall. *Hist.* 2.47.1 M. = 2.43.1 R.).

cum ea mihi sint restituta quae in potestate mea non fuerunt...praesertim cum illa amissa reciperarim: refers to external features not connected with an individual's character and dependent on physical proximity, such as the company of relatives, social standing, and material possessions (e.g. Cic. *RS* 1). That these have been returned to Cicero as a consequence of his recall increases his motivation to use his own qualities for the benefit of the Republic and thus implies both gratitude and the advantage the audience gains from their actions.

quae ipse praestare possim...virtutem et fidem numquam amiserim: contrasts with external goods and describes innate qualities and characteristics, such as *virtus* and *fides*; Cicero claims that he never lost these and that they are under his control and can be deployed for public benefit (*OLD* s.v. *praesto*[2] 9). Such a statement provides a confident closure to the speech, implying that Cicero maintained his strength and loyalty to the Republic during his absence, though in letters from that period he appears despondent (see Introduction, section 3.4).

M. Tulli Ciceronis post reditum ad Quirites oratio

Introduction

While Cicero mentions the speech of thanks to the Senate (Cic. *RS*) in two of his letters and the speech *Pro Plancio* (T 1–3), he does not refer to a speech of thanks before the People (Cic. *RQ*) elsewhere. Other ancient sources record that Cicero delivered speeches of thanks to both the Senate and the People

(T 4–7); at least some of them could have inferred such a scenario from the existence of the two speeches. Only the testimony of Cassius Dio (T 7) links the speech to the People to a specific context of delivery created for Cicero by the consuls of that year (even Markland regarded Cassius Dio's remark as unambiguous, though he felt justified in ignoring it [1745, 265]: '...the Testimony of *Dio*...proves, that if Cicero *spake* to the *Senate*, he did the same to the *People*: tho' I am very well satisfied that he neither *wrote* nor *spake* either of these Orations'). All these sources imply that the speech to the People was delivered soon after the speech of thanks in the Senate (5 September 57 BCE; see *RS*, Introduction); a precise date for the speech to the People is not given.

As a result of the nature of the available evidence, scholars have discussed potential dates, the character of the speech, and whether or not it was delivered (on the uncertainties, see, e.g., Wuilleumier 1952, 20 and n. 9). A date of delivery close to that of the speech in the Senate is usually assumed (dates proposed: De Benedetti 1929, 782; Guerriero 1936, 161, 162, 165; Gelzer 1939, 926; Klass 1939, 86; Caprioli 1966, 67; Desideri 1966, 14; Cipriani 1975, 337; Grasmück 1977, 167 n. 24; Mitchell 1991, 157 n. 45; Morstein-Marx 2004, 25 with n. 92; Kelly 2006, 154: same day [5 Sept.]; also considered by Nicholson 1992, 127; Bücher 2006, 243 with n. 70: day after the delivery of the Senate speech; Watts 1923, 44; Condom 1995, 12, 59: 'two days later'; Lenaghan 1969, 18: 'shortly thereafter'; MacKendrick 1995, 136: '7 Sept. 57 [probably]'; Marinone 2004, 111, 112: shortly after the speech in the Senate, perhaps on the same day; Boll 2019, 6 with n. 35: shortly after the speech in the Senate, perhaps two days later; Grillo 2015, 4, 7: 7 September; for an overview of dates and options proposed, see Marinone 2004, 112; Raccanelli 2012, 7–8 n. 2). As has been pointed out (Nicholson 1992, 127; see also Citroni Marchetti 2000, 170 n. 39), the sequence of the speeches could be the other way round (with the speech to the People given on 4 September, before that in the Senate; see Lucas 1837, 8–9: on the day of Cicero's arrival in Rome before the speech to the Senate on the following day), in line with their position in the manuscripts. The conventional arrangement in modern editions, implying assumptions on the order of delivery, is based on the fact that in other extant pairs of Senate and *contio* speeches the Senate speech usually comes first. Pina Polo (1996, 103) suggests that Cicero choose the date of delivery carefully, waiting until the *Ludi Romani* (5–19 September) to have a good audience: it is doubtful, though, how much control Cicero would have had over the choice of date, when he was not in a position to call a *contio* himself in that year.

In a letter to Atticus Cicero mentions a speech he gave to the People a couple of days after his appearance in the Senate, when he spoke about the grain supply (Cic. *Att.* 4.1.6; see Introduction, section 2). While it is generally assumed that this speech to the People concerned the grain supply and is different from the speech of thanks upon Cicero's return (e.g. Gelzer 1939, 926, 928; Crawford 1984, 134–5, no. 40–1; Nicholson 1992, 126–8; Marinone 2004, 112), Kaster

(2006, 8 n. 16; App. n. 27; already suggested by Savels 1828, vii, xxix–xxx, assuming that the first section got lost; Rauschen 1886, 10 and n. 28 [pp. 31–5], discerning a parallel with *Leg. agr.* 2 in that an expression of thanks is followed by a discussion of a substantive issue) argues that the speech mentioned in this letter is the extant speech of thanks to the People (then dated to 7 September 57 BCE), since the details provided in the letter 'combine to suggest that all the participants viewed the occasion as having a symbolic importance it would have lacked had C. addressed the people in assembly two days earlier—an address (the common view requires us to suppose) that C. did not bother to mention in the same letter' (see also Kaster 2006, 365, on Cic. *Sest.* 129: 'C. elsewhere says that Appius Pulcher, as praetor, and two tribunes (Atilius Serranus and Numerius Rufus, ...) were the only magistrates not to join in promulgating the law for C.'s recall (*Pis.* 35, ...), as they were the only magistrates not to join in inviting him to address the people after his return, in the *contio* that survives as *Red. pop.* (*Att.* 4.1(73).7, cf. App. 1).').

It seems indeed odd that in this letter (Cic. *Att.* 4.1.6) Cicero does not mention what would be an earlier speech to the People within a sequence that appears to be a chronological record of his public appearances after his return. Yet the narrative is not a neutral description, but rather focused on the public appreciation Cicero experienced on those occasions; thus, mention of the speech of thanks to the People would interrupt the climactic arrangement in that letter. Further, it would be equally strange if Cicero delivered a version of the extant speech of thanks to the People after the Senate decree on the grain supply and did not even refer to this recent development, while in the present speech he seems to suggest that there is an abundance of grain (Cic. *RQ* 18; see Cic. *RS* 34 n.; Hiebel [2009, 450] apparently assumes that Cicero talked about the decreed arrangements for the grain supply and thanked the People for his return from exile in a single speech). Therefore, it has been suggested (Fuhrmann 1978, 151; 1992, 95; Nicholson 1992, 127–8; Lintott 2008, 9, 13–14, 15 [*contra* Seager 2009, 226, saying that Lintott's argument only demonstrates that the speech was not delivered on 7 September]; reported by Raccanelli 2012, 7–8 n. 2) that the speech to the People was never delivered and instead was merely written up and circulated as a complement to the speech to the Senate. This possibility cannot be excluded, although the motivations for such a procedure are difficult to determine. In any case it is unlikely that the preserved speech is the same as the one mentioned in the letter.

Another difficulty consists in the fact that Cicero, talking about his appearance in the Senate in connection with the discussion on the grain supply in *De domo sua*, says that he was summoned to deliver thanks, when he delivered thanks in the first speech to the Senate and the subsequent speech in the Senate was provoked by the matter of the grain supply. Yet the statement in *De domo sua* could mean delivering thanks and demonstrating gratitude anew by supporting the population in a difficult situation (Cic. *Dom.* 7: *an ego, cum*

P. Lentulus consul optime de me ac de re publica meritus, cum Q. Metellus, qui cum meus inimicus esset, frater tuus, et dissensioni nostrae et precibus tuis salutem ac dignitatem meam praetulisset, me arcesserent in senatum, cum tanta multitudo civium tam recenti officio suo me ad referendam gratiam nominatim vocaret, non venirem, cum praesertim te iam illinc cum tua fugitivorum manu discessisse constaret?). Then this remark would not exclude the possibility of earlier speeches of thanks to the Senate and the People.

The scholiast identifies (Schol. Bob., arg. ad Cic. *Planc.* [T 5]) the context for the speech to the People as a *contio* (while the other Latin sources speak of *populus*), which would be the expected venue for such an oration. A *contio*, usually held in the Forum, is an informal meeting of the People at which magistrates and other politicians deliver speeches to inform the People of bills for laws, discussions in the Senate, the current political situation, or particular plans agreed in the Senate, while no votes are taken. As only magistrates could call a *contio* and then either speak themselves or ask others to do so, someone would have had to call this *contio* for Cicero (as he reports for the *contio* taking place after the Senate decree on the grain supply: Cic. *Att.* 4.1.6), perhaps the consul P. Cornelius Lentulus Spinther, as he is highlighted as one of Cicero's main supporters (see Cic. *RS* 5 n.; Introduction, section 3.3), as Cassius Dio implies (T 7).

Thus, on balance, unless one doubts the reliability of the various sources, it is likely that the speech to the People was delivered at a *contio* called by one of the magistrates of the year, that it is not identical with the later speech on the grain supply and that it is not mentioned in the letter to Atticus because this text does not give a mere chronological list.

Generically, like the speech in the Senate, because of its audience and venue, the extant speech could be defined as 'political' in the broadest sense (see Introduction, section 3.2). Yet, as no specific political aim is pursued, and the speech focuses on Cicero and on thanks to the People and other supporters, as well as on some criticism of those who had provoked Cicero's departure or did not work towards his recall, it is largely epideictic in nature. This character was noted by the scholiast, who remarks that it covers the entire *genus demonstrativum* by including praise and blame (Schol. Bob., arg. ad Cic. *RQ* [T 4]).

In content the speech covers roughly the same ground as the speech in the Senate, while the presentation is adjusted to the different audience. This speech is shorter and less detailed, especially as regards the presentation of individuals, and includes less polemic. Instead, the expression of thanks is elaborate and emphatic; Cicero emphasizes his debt to the People and the great joy they have brought to him. He confirms that he will never stop repaying this debt; as he implies that he has been recalled because of his importance for the Republic, he can draw the conclusion that he will work tirelessly for the Republic to show his gratitude and that he has been justly recalled. Thus, as in the speech delivered in the Senate, Cicero combines the expression of thanks with preparations for resuming his position as a respected and influential ex-consul in the community. Yet here a connection with the audience is achieved on an emotional level rather than by logical argument; this might also be a reason why the polemic is reduced in line with the aim of not confronting the opponents but rather of arousing the People's sympathies for Cicero.

Outline of structure and contents

1. <u>Introduction (1–5):</u> Cicero's expression of thanks
2. <u>Main section (6–17):</u> Review of Cicero's (departure and) recall
    2.1. Comparison between Cicero and earlier ex-consuls (6–11)
        2.1.1. Ex-consuls of the past returned to Rome (6–7)
        2.1.2. Cicero's situation (7–11)
    2.2. Details of Cicero's recall (11–17)
        2.2.1. Initiatives of new consuls of 57 BCE (11–12)
        2.2.2. Activities of opponents and their consequences (13–14)
        2.2.3. Support from senators and the population (15–17)
3. <u>Conclusion (18–25):</u> Cicero's gratitude and promise to the Republic

Like the speech of thanks given in the Senate, due to its particular nature, this speech does not display an obvious structure as outlined in rhetorical handbooks. Individual sections and transitions between them are even less clearly indicated than in the Senate speech; different aspects of a single theme, namely Cicero's departure and recall, as well as his reaction to this situation, are presented throughout the oration with associative rather than marked logical transitions (Wuilleumier 1925, 25: 'Ainsi la composition se fonde moins sur un ordre logique ou chronologique que sur des antithèses sentimentales.'). Still, sections highlighting different aspects can be identified, as in the outline above (on the structure of this speech, see Weiske 1807, 229–30; Masoero 1905, 11–12; Mack 1937, 19–20; Wuilleumier 1952, 25, 71; Paratte 1963, 10; Fuhrmann 1978, 155; Thompson 1978, 121; Shackleton Bailey 1991, 25; Nicholson 1992, 114–21; Condom 1995, 60–1; MacKendrick 1995, 136–8).

The oration starts with an elaborate expression of thanks emphasizing the great service the People have done to Cicero by recalling him and the great joy he experienced on being re-established in his previous position and reunited with family members (Cic. *RQ* 1–5): this is a version of *captatio benevolentiae* adapted to the situation; it demonstrates the important role of the audience in Cicero's recall and the close relationship between the two parties.

On this basis most of the speech is concerned with a review of Cicero's recall (Cic. *RQ* 6–17), the action the audience was involved in, and its effects. In contrast to the speech in the Senate (Cic. *RS* 32–5), Cicero's departure is only briefly alluded to in flashbacks. The main section stresses Cicero's unique position as an ex-consul away from Rome in that he did not have a large family back home to plead for him (Cic. *RQ* 6–11): this reminds the audience of Cicero's position as a *homo novus* and 'one of them' (cf. Cic. *Leg. agr.* 2), which improves the rapport between them and provides the basis for the claim that Cicero was recalled because of his own worth and his importance for the Republic. The widespread support for this measure is highlighted (Cic. *RQ* 11–12; 15–17), while opposition, overcome eventually, is acknowledged briefly (Cic. *RQ* 13–14).

In the conclusion (Cic. *RQ* 18–25), in light of the details referred to, Cicero can again express his gratitude elaborately and emphatically and proclaim that he will never be found wanting in demonstrating it. In his definition his gratitude and his superiority to his opponents will be shown by constant activity for the welfare of the Republic; on this basis he can combine the final expression of thanks with the promise to employ his undented strength of mind for the benefit of the Republic. Such a statement provides the starting point for resuming a position as an influential ex-consul.

Notes

1. Introduction (1–5): Cicero's expression of thanks

The introduction of this speech (Cic. *RQ* 1–5) opens with a long and complex sentence (Cic. *RQ* 1), stressing that by his departure Cicero undertook a sacrifice on behalf of the community and that his recall confirmed that it was accepted and valued by all. Thus, in contrast to the speech given in the Senate, Cicero starts with a confident statement of his own role (which follows later in the Senate speech) and then proceeds to voice his gratitude (for a comparison with the *exordium* of the Senate speech, see Loutsch 1994, 494–5; on this *exordium*, see also Raccanelli 2012, 29–46). Although Cicero's recall is based on a vote in the popular assembly, as an ex-consul, he might see himself in a leading position in relation the People and regard it as opportune to underline his role as 'a consul for the People', as in his inaugural speech as consul (Cic. *Leg. agr.* 2).

When Cicero moves on to expressing gratitude (Cic. *RQ* 2–4), he emphasizes the great effect of the People's intervention on him (highlighting their *beneficium*), for the reason that one enjoys everything more when it is returned after one has had to go without it for a while; therefore, the favour they conferred upon him is presented as a divinely occasioned rebirth (Cole 2013, 64). This technique was already noted by the scholiast (Schol. Bob. ad Cic. *RQ* 2 [p. 110.29–31 Stangl]: *concepte posita sententia. etenim cum manet inlibata felicitas, minor est gratulantium fructus; cum vero ab dolore intercedentis iniuriae ad prosperitatem fortunae revocatur, pressiore iudicio sensus felicitatis accipitur.*; ad Cic. *RQ* 4 [pp. 110.34–11.8 Stangl]: ἀπὸ τοῦ ὁμοίου... *et supra copiose et hic abundantissime dilatavit sententiam, volens ostendere plus esse gratulationis mala depulisse quam fortunae incommoda numquam sentire potuisse: quippe sensus incommodorum commendabilia facit illa quae prospera sunt. qualis sententia Vergiliana est* [Verg. *Aen.* 1.203]: *'forsan et haec olim meminisse iuvabit.' verum Plato in* Πολιτείᾳ [Pl. *Resp.* 583c10–d1] *his, ut opinor, verbis eandem conceptionem sententiae posuit:* 'ἆρ' οὐ μνηονεύεις τοὺς τῶν καμνόντων λόγους, οὓς λέγουσιν, ὅτε ἂν κάμνωσιν, ὡς οὐδὲν ἄρ' ἐστιν ἥδιον <τοῦ ὑγιαίνειν, ἀλλὰ σφ>ᾶς ἐλελήθει πρὶν κάμνειν ἥδιστον ὄν'; *et Isocrates* [Isoc. *Demon.* 35]: '<κα>ὶ γὰρ τ<ῆς> ὑγι<είας> πλείσ<την ἐπιμέλει>αν ἔχομεν, ὅτα<ν τὰς λύπας τὰς ἐκ τῆς ἀρρω>στία<ς ἀναμνησθῶμεν>.').

In the opening of the speech given in the Senate Cicero also expresses thanks because items such as his family or his standing have been returned to him; here this notion is more elaborate, emotional, and emphatic because of this additional twist and the order and selection of items: the sequence starts with the mention of his children, followed by his brother, and it not only includes items indicating social and political position, but also relationships to a wider range of closely connected people (*amicitiae, consuetudines, vicinitates, clientelae*) as well as the attractions of city life (*ludi denique et dies festi*), which might be what is regarded as important to the audience (Loutsch 1994, 494–5). That Cicero is so grateful and happy about having received back these features shows that they are dear and important to him and thus how highly he values his country when he made the sacrifice for its sake by leaving those behind (Cic. *Dom.* 98).

Cicero connects the idea of his deserved return and his sacrifice for the community with the notion of a successful prayer and devotion to the gods (Cic. *RQ* 1). As has been noted (Heibges 1969, 834), only very few of Cicero's speeches start with a religious appeal (Cic. *Mur.* 1; *Rab. perd.* 5); in those cases what Cicero utters is a kind of prayer to the gods. Here the motif is adapted: the gods are presented as having granted what he asked for in the past and thus confirming and elevating Cicero's sacrifice. With such a beginning Cicero introduces himself both as a grateful beneficiary of support received (in line with values such as *pietas, officium*, and *gratia*: see Raccanelli 2012, 43) and as a leading statesman taking care of the Republic's welfare in a selfless way. The allusion to the rite of *devotio* and the appeal to the gods endow the opening of the speech with a religious tone (Raccanelli 2012, 40). Thus, Cicero's departure appears as a personal decision of a responsible politician, and any thought of a juridical controversy is removed (Raccanelli 2012, 37–8).

Cicero concludes this part of the argument with the comment starting the speech given in the Senate (Cic. *RS* 1), namely that there is no adequate eloquence to render thanks appropriately for such an enormous favour (Cic. *RQ* 5). In this position the statement is more straightforward, as Cicero has already explained how great these favours are; he combines this description with further expressions of thanks, highlighting the role of the People.

The style of this section is more effusive and emotional than the corresponding section in the speech in the Senate (Mack 1937, 99–106).

1 quod...laetor: the long opening sentence (on its structure, see Wimmel 1973; Dyck 2004, 307–8) has the oration start with an emphatic statement of Cicero's interpretation of the situation: by leaving Rome he sacrificed himself for the Republic; his absence was intended to draw the hatred of malicious citizens against him rather than the community. His recall confirms his community spirit and that he does not deserve eternal punishment, and it demonstrates that his prayer to the gods was fulfilled, which shows divine support for his activities. By undertaking this self-sacrifice Cicero has continued his selfless work for the Republic already demonstrated in his consulship. The thought underlying this sentence is expressed more explicitly in the speech *De domo sua* (Cic. *Dom.* 145:...*meque atque meum caput ea condicione devovi ut, si et eo ipso tempore et ante in consulatu meo commodis meis omnibus, emolumentis, praemiis praetermissis cura, cogitatione, vigiliis omnibus nihil nisi de salute meorum civium laborassem, tum mihi re publica aliquando restituta liceret frui, sin autem mea consilia patriae non profuissent, ut perpetuum dolorem avolsus a meis sustinerem, hanc ego devotionem capitis mei, cum ero in meas sedis restitutus, tum denique convictam esse et commissam putabo.*) and explained by the scholiast (Schol. Bob. ad Cic. *RQ* 1 [p. 110.15–19 Stangl]: *sponsionem quandam votorum suorum perquam oratorie facit in exordio, ut non humanitus modo, verum etiam divinitus de restitutione sua iudicatum intellegi velit, quandoquidem sic eum constet omnia in praeteritum pro patriae incolumitate sensisse, ut numquam de suo periculo laboraret, cum exilium non meruerit aeternum, sed mature in patriam et decretis senatus et consensus populi restitutus sit.*). – The sentence begins with an indication of what Cicero prayed for (*quod precatus...sum*) at a certain time (*eo tempore cum...devovi*). The content of the prayer follows in a double *ut*-clause (*ut...defigeretur*) presenting two options, each with a subordinate *si/sin*-clause; in the first case *ut* is placed at the beginning, and the second *ut* follows after the *sin*-clause; in the second *ut*-clause the subject is expressed by a *quod*-clause taken up by *id*. The second part of the sentence draws the conclusion, with the main verb of the main clause placed at the very end (*laetor*); this verb governs an accusative and infinitive construction (*eius devotionis me esse convictum*). That the second alternative outlined in the first part of the sentence (*sin...*) was realized means a general recognition of Cicero's attitude to the Republic, as summarized in a *si*-clause (with subordinate *ut*-clause) preceding the final statement.

quod precatus...sum: a similar beginning is only found in Cicero's speech *Pro Murena* (Cic. *Mur.* 1).

precatus...sum: the wide hyperbaton between the different parts of the predicate emphasizes the verb and the mention of the gods sandwiched in between (K.-St. II 603).

a Iove Optimo Maximo ceterisque dis immortalibus: highlights Jupiter and ensures that no divinity is passed over. – When Cicero gives a list of gods involved in his fate in *De domo sua*, he again starts with Jupiter (Cic. *Dom.* 144–5; in general, see Cic. *Verr.* 2.5.184–8).

Quirites: the usual address of the People in *contio* speeches. It is the official designation of the Roman People in their role as Roman citizens; the term unites members of the audience by their essential function in the present situation (Léovant-Cirefice 2000).

eo tempore cum: in spring 58 BCE, when Cicero decided to leave Rome.

me fortunasque meas: in this collocation *fortunae* probably refers to the possessions Cicero is leaving behind rather than his fortune (*OLD* s.v. *fortuna* 12 vs 8).

pro vestra incolumitate otio concordiaque: Cicero's act of sacrificing himself, a single individual, is to prevent civil war and to ensure safety, tranquillity (*OLD* s.v. *otium* 4), and concord (*OLD* s.v. *concordia* 2) for all (Cic. *Dom.* 30; 63; 68; 96; *Sest.* 43–9). – Cicero proclaims similar ideals as items that are *popularis* and that he will support as consul in his inaugural speeches in his consular year of 63 BCE (Cic. *Leg. agr.* 1.23; 2.102; 3.4).

devovi … devotionis: the best-known version of Roman *devotio* is a military general laying down his life in an act of self-sacrifice as a means to ensure victory and survival for his army (Liv. 8.9.4–10; 10.28.12–18); this ritual is associated particularly with P. Decius Mus (340 BCE) and also with his son (295 BCE) and less securely with his grandson (279 BCE). Cicero applies the concept metaphorically to his departure from Rome (on Cicero's assimilation of the motif, see Dyck 2004; La Farina 2008). As Dyck (2004, 311–12) points out, the parallel does not fit completely, since Cicero is neither a general nor does he die; Dyck suggests interpreting the transfer along the lines of the idea of *dux togatus* developed in the *Catilinarian Orations*, where Cicero presents his efforts for the community as those of an especially considerate leader who avoids fighting and bloodshed (Cic. *Cat.* 3.15; 3.23; 4.5; see also Raccanelli 2012, 39; Farina 2008, esp. 339). Dyck further observes that the metaphor is only applied in the speeches delivered immediately after Cicero's return (for the motif of self-sacrifice for the Republic, supported by gods, in parallel to the *devotio* of Decius, see Cic. *Dom.* 64; 144–7; *Sest.* 42–9). – There is no other evidence that Cicero ever made such a vow. Bellardi (1975, 130 n. 1) suggests that it was made when Cicero offered the statue of Minerva on the Capitol in March 58 BCE (see Introduction, section 2).

ut … ut: introduce subordinate clauses depending on *precatus … sum*, reporting the content of the prayer in past sequence of tenses.

meas rationes: i.e. considerations for Cicero's own welfare expressed more neutrally (*OLD* s.v. *ratio* 8), creating a contrast with the following *salus*.

vestrae saluti: throughout the two speeches delivered upon his return Cicero's concern is with his own *salus* (sometimes linked to the *salus* of the community). At the beginning of this speech he twice stresses that he acted in the interest of *vestra salus*, which makes him appear unselfish from the start (supported by *pro vestra incolumitate otio concordiaque*).

sempiternam poenam: if Cicero had put concern for his own welfare above that of the People, 'everlasting punishment' (presumably, in this context, absence from Rome without recall) would be justified.

et ... et: links what Cicero did on behalf of the Republic as consul and what he did by leaving Rome; this puts the two actions in parallel as two interventions for the welfare of Rome (see Introduction, section 3.4).

ea quae ante gesseram: i.e. as consul in 63 BCE, alluding in particular to Cicero's dealing with the Catilinarian Conspiracy, though with a vague expression avoiding mention of activities that ultimately provoked his departure from Rome.

illam miseram profectionem: Cicero never describes his absence as 'exile'; *profectio* is one of his preferred euphemistic terms (see Introduction, section 3.4). The qualifying adjective stresses the aspect of sacrifice rather than Cicero's state of mind.

quod odium ... id: the noun qualified by the relative clause is included in the relative clause (K.-St. II 309–10); it forms the object of the superordinate clause and is taken up by *id* after the relative clause.

scelerati homines et audaces: frequent adjectives to designate political opponents challenging the traditional Republic in Cicero's works, describing these people as morally depraved, here probably alluding to P. Clodius Pulcher and his followers (Wirszubski 1961, 14; see Cic. *RS* 12, 19 nn.).

in rem publicam et in omnes bonos: taken up chiastically by *in optimo quoque et universa civitate* in the following clause. This presentation emphasizes that Cicero offers himself as the sole target (*in me uno potius*) for ill-feeling affecting all right-minded citizens. Such a focus implies that the current conflict is not a personal opposition between Cicero and P. Clodius Pulcher, but rather a fundamental opposition between all responsible people in the Republic, including Cicero, and a group of criminals.

conceptum ... continerent: a combination of a past participle with verbs such as *habeo* or *teneo* emphasizes the ongoing state resulting from a completed action (K.-St. I 763–4; Pinkster 2015, 478–9), here indicating that these individuals have been full of hatred for some time.

iam diu: i.e. at least since 63 BCE.

in me uno ... defigeretur: emphasizes again that Cicero sacrifices himself for the Republic. – This conclusion from the second *si/sin*-clause is not exactly parallel to the first one (one might expect: 'then it is not actually a punishment, but rather a sacrifice and should only be short-lived'). Instead, the focus is on the sacrifice and the preparation of the subsequent final conclusion, implying that Cicero's concerns for the community are the reasons for the *odium* and also for his departure and recall.

defigeretur: the transmitted verb (*deficeret*) has often been questioned and emended (e.g. *defigerent*: Lambinus, supported by Busche 1917, 1357; *defigeretur*: Wimmel 1973, esp. 111). Courtney (1960, 95) defends transmitted *deficeret* and the resulting zeugma, referring to an example in Curtius Rufus (Curt. 4.4.17: *duo milia in quibus occidendis defecerat rabies crucibus adfixi*): yet the notion that the hatred 'tires itself out' on Cicero does not fit the overall argument. Thus, Wimmel's conjecture *defigeretur* offers an appropriate sense with only slight changes, emphasizing that the hatred should be transferred from everyone to Cicero alone (*OLD* s.v. *defigo* 3; see, e.g., Cic. *Phil.* 7.5).

hoc si animo in vos liberosque vestros fuissem, ut…: takes up *sin…suscepissem* with a focus on the people affected, to prepare for the conclusion.

ut…teneret: this clause claims that the reason for Cicero's recall is the People's pity for him and their desire to have him back, as a response to the way in which Cicero has selflessly served the community. This phrasing puts the People indirectly in the position of the agent, which prepares for Cicero's expression of thanks and reduces the self-congratulatory elements.

memoria mei misericordiaque desideriumque: this phrase has been transmitted in various versions, with and without -*que* after *misericordia* and *desiderium*. The most straightforward interpretation is as a tripartite sequence where the items could be linked in various ways. The sequence with -*que* added twice is parallel to the immediately preceding *vos patresque conscriptos Italiamque universam* and therefore preferable. Müller (1885, 447) and Peterson (1911) opt for *memoria mei misericordia desideriumque*, on the model of a similar structure earlier in the sentence (*pro vestra incolumitate otio concordiaque*). The addition of <*et*> or <*ac*> before *desiderium* (instead of adding -*que*) is a greater change and may put unnecessary additional stress on the final item. Aiming to create regular *clausulae*, Bornecque (1909, 45 n. 2) suggests *misericordiaque desiderium*; as he points out, *memoria mei misericordiaque* are then no longer linked to *desiderium* but rather have to be understood as ablatives (in an alliterative pair); this expression would function as the reason for *desiderium*. Such a construction is rather complex; and as *memoria* and *desiderium* appear in parallel later in the speech (Cic. *RQ* 8), this is likely to be the case here too (*OLD* s.v. *teneo* 10).

eius devotionis me esse convictum…beneficio divino immortalique vestro: Cicero's return is presented as both the result of a successful prayer to the gods and the realization of his attitude by human actors, though he does not clearly define or distinguish between the two. In the final statement, Cicero provides a list of divine and human actors on the same level; he even describes the contribution of the audience as *beneficio divino immortalique vestro* and thus blurs the boundaries further (Thompson 1978, 61–2; Riggsby 2002, 188–9; Cole 2013, 69).

devotionis…esse convictum: the noun *devotionis* takes up the verb *devovi*. – The collocation is a standard phrase (*OLD* s.v. *convinco* 2b '~*incere deuotionis* (of a god) to find against, in respect of payment made in expectation of the granting of a request', 4c '*deuotionem ~incere*, (of a god) to reject a payment made in expectation of the granting of a request (in effect, to grant the request)'), similarly used of Cicero's leaving of Rome in *De domo sua* (Cic. *Dom.* 145: *hanc ego devotionem capitis mei, cum ero in meas sedis restitutus, tum denique convictam esse et commissam putabo*), effectively meaning that the gods have accepted the sacrifice (Schol. Bob. ad Cic. *RQ* 1 [p. 110.25–6 Stangl]: *vetuste locutus est. 'voti' enim 'convictos' dicimus eos qui ad effectum perveniant eorum quae sibi evenire semper optaverint. convictum ergo se dicit.*). The expression is similar to the structure *voti damnatus* (Liv. 7.28.4; Nep. *Timol.* 5.3) or *voti reus* (Verg. *Aen.* 5.237). – The verb *convinco* has judicial associations reinforced by the complement *iudicio*. Thus, the wording makes the recall appear like a legally confirmed procedure. While Cicero stresses that he was never convicted and therefore the exile was unjustified (see Introduction, section 3.4), he thereby implies that his recall is officially sanctioned by human and divine entities; even though he does not directly assimilate it to formal legal proceedings, this presentation strengthens his status upon his return.

testimonio senatus: further on in the speech Cicero stresses the unanimity of the Senate concerning his recall and its attempts to get it actioned in contrast to the ways in which previous ex-consuls returned (Cic. *RQ* 10).

consensu Italiae: for the support of 'all of Italy', see, e.g., Cic. *RS* 24–5; 39.

confessione inimicorum: implies that *inimici* (of Cicero and/or the Republic) have accepted Cicero's recall as justified. These *inimici* are not identified, and the plural avoids a focus on individuals. Later, Cicero suggests that there are still different groups of his *inimici*, describing their attitude, but again not identifying individuals (Cic. *RQ* 21–2). – Weiske (1807, 232) sees the comment here as a rhetorical statement referring to the consul Q. Caecilius Metellus Nepos. Elsewhere, Cicero states that Nepos was originally an enemy and later supported his recall (Cic. *RS* 5 n.). While this statement could, therefore, be applied to Nepos, it is questionable whether in this context Cicero would have defined him as *inimicus*; later, he calls him an *inimicus*, while he mentions his support at the same time (Cic. *RQ* 10).

2 <namque,> Quirites: at this point an address to *Quirites* (or letters suggesting an abbreviation of the word) is transmitted, but it is generally felt that a logical connection with the preceding sentence is needed; thus, scholars have added a conjunction or changed the transmitted word into a conjunction. Madvig's (1873, 214) *qua re* (widely adopted), instead of *Quirites*, stays close to the transmitted letters. Courtney (1989, 48) suggests reading *quia* (instead of *Quirites*), taking up the sense of Peterson's (1911) <*namque*> (criticized by Luterbacher 1912, 346) with a word closer to the transmission (Shackleton Bailey's [1991, 227] *etenim* expresses the same idea, but is far from the transmission), arguing that a conjunction indicating a causal relationship is needed rather than one expressing the sense of 'therefore'; he admits that this emendation creates a very long sentence, but adduces a parallel in *De domo sua* (Cic. *Dom.* 144–5). Indeed, a causal connection is preferable; yet to make a sentence already rather long even longer by a conjecture is not ideal. Thus, on balance, Peterson's <*namque*> might be best; such a word could have got lost before *Quirites*, which should be kept: although the address *Quirites* does not occur too frequently in this speech, it is regularly inserted for emphasis and focus. Here, after the initial long sentence, it helps to clarify the structure, mark the next logical step, and highlight the impact of the favour bestowed by the audience.

etsi...caruissem: highlights that, although a course of life with obstacles might not initially seem desirable, it can bring particular appreciation of benefits and of oneself (cf. Cic. *Dom.* 86). – After warding off the Catilinarian Conspiracy Cicero claims that valued items such as possessions, family, the city, and the political system have been regained (Cic. *Cat.* 3.1).

homini...mihi: the first part of the sentence is phrased as a general statement; the second part refers to Cicero.

prospera, aequabilis perpetuaque fortuna: a series of three adjectives indicates continuous good fortune.

secundo...cursu: is a term originally applied to favourable sailing conditions (*OLD* s.v. *secundus*[1] A1; cf. Caes. *B Civ.* 3.47.3); here it is used in transferred sense and applied to prosperous and favourable conditions for the course of one's life (*OLD* s.v. *secundus*[1] A4b). The nautical metaphor is continued in *tranquilla et placata*, as these adjectives can be applied to the sea and have a transferred sense.

sine ulla offensione: sandwiched between *secundo...cursu* emphasizes the notion of happy and effortless proceeding without any obstacles or mishaps (*OLD* s.v. *offensio* 2).

omnia: refers unspecifically to Cicero's circumstances and his life's experiences.

incredibili quadam et paene divina...laetitiae voluptate caruissem: at the end of the previous paragraph Cicero expresses his joy (*laetor*) in connection with *beneficio divino immortalique vestro* (Cic. *RQ* 1). Now Cicero's joy is described as *incredibili quadam et paene divina*. While it may seem an exaggeration to characterize one's joy as 'almost divine', it can be regarded as a transferred expression serving to illustrate the greatness of the *beneficium* received (given as the reason for this feeling) and thus an element of showing gratitude. The wide hyperbaton between the noun phrase and the complementing adjectives highlights the phrase; the inserted relative clause stresses the People's activity enabling this joy. – Ammianus Marcellinus (15.5.23: *et quamquam ut bestiarii obiceremur intractabilibus feris, perpendentes tamen hoc bonum habere tristia accidentia, quod in locum suum secunda substituunt, mirabamur illam sententiam Tullianam ex internis veritatis ipsius promulgatam, quae est talis: 'et*

*quamquam optatissimum est perpetuo fortunam quam florentissimam perma-
nere, illa tamen aequalitas vitae non tantum habet sensum, quantum cum ex
miseris et perditis rebus ad meliorem statum fortuna revocatur.*') takes up this
notion, attributing it to Cicero; he does not give a reference and uses his own
phrasing, but he might be referring to this passage (Wuilleumier 1952, 73 n. 1).

qua nunc vestro beneficio fruor: of the two ablatives in this relative clause,
qua (referring to *laetitiae voluptate*) is the direct complement to *fruor* (Pinkster
2015, 115–16). *vestro beneficio* provides an *ablativus causae*, giving the reason for
the emotion (K.-St. I 394–7; Pinkster 2015, 89–90).

laetitiae voluptate: the transmitted construction is a noun defined by a *gene-
tivus appositivus* or *explicativus* (K.-St. I 418–19; Pinkster 2015, 1023–5). Because
of the slightly unusual nature of the expression, Markland (1745, 266) suggested
reading *laetitia et voluptate* (cf. Cic. *Sull.* 91), but it is not sufficiently odd to
justify such changes.

quid dulcius: the neuter (also Cic. *RQ* 3) conveys a generalizing sense (K.-St.
I 61–2).

hominum generi: continues the generic sense of *homini* in the preceding
sentence. The variation in the wording including *genus* suits a context dealing
with nature and progeny.

ab natura: the preposition *ab* added to the agent in a passive construction
personifies the agent, which is common for *natura* (Lebreton 1901, 410–11;
Masoero 1905, 14).

sui cuique liberi: *quisque* with the reflexive possessive pronoun applies the
statement to all people individually (K.-St. I 644–5; Lebreton 1901, 118; Pinkster
2015, 1067; see Cic. *RQ* 3). The expression refers to the individuals implied in
hominum generi.

mihi: the general statement is exemplified in Cicero's situation by a statement about his children (Cic. *RS* 1 n.).

propter indulgentiam meam: indicates Cicero's great fondness for his children (*OLD* s.v. *indulgentia* 2; cf. Cic. *De or.* 2.168), while the corresponding item
propter excellens eorum ingenium justifies his great love.

eorum: a rare construction of a pronoun in a prepositional phrase referring
to the (unexpressed) subject of the sentence (K.-St. I 601; Lebreton 1901, 113,
142): it is needed to balance *meam* and to make the reference clear.

vita…mea cariores: takes up and enhances *quid dulcius*, indicating the
extraordinary importance of and love for Cicero's children.

tanta voluptate…quanta: the sentence elaborates on the idea that joy is
increased if one has been without certain people, things, or experiences. The
notion is repeated with reference to further items in what follows; both the joy
and the absence are expressed by different expressions in each case. – The
transmitted ablative (of attendant circumstances) is unproblematic (adopted
by Shackleton Bailey 1991, 227); thus, there is no need to change to a dative, as
in the text given by the scholiast (Schol. Bob. ad Cic. *RQ* 2 [p. 110.27–8 Stangl]).

suscepti: lit. 'taken up', refers to the Roman practice of acknowledging children: fathers signify their intention to rear newborns and not to expose them by taking them in their arms (*OLD* s.v. *suscipio* 4a).

3 nihil…iucundius: corresponds to *quid dulcius* (Cic. *RQ* 2); in both cases the phrasing is generic (*hominum generi* and *cuiquam*), while the statement is focused on Cicero. – The term *iucundus* is applied to human beings (*OLD* s.v. *iucundus* 2; cf. Cic. *Att.* 16.16A.7: *mihi nemo amicior nec iucundior nec carior Attico*). On the neuter form, see Cic. *RQ* 2 n.

meus frater: after having talked about his children (Cic. *RQ* 2), Cicero moves on to his brother (Cic. *RS* 1 n.): again, the impact of the reunion on the intensity of their relationship is noted.

id: refers to the statement of the preceding sentence and is the object of *sentiebam*. – The verbs in the *cum*-clauses (*fruebar* and *carebar*) are used without an expressed object (Lebreton 1901, 166), and a complement (a reference to Cicero's brother) has to be supplied (from *illi* and *eum*).

vos me illi et mihi eum reddidistis: the added pronoun *vos* increases the element of the audience's agency, implying gratitude for their role in enabling the reunion. In contrast to that with the children, with reference to the brother Cicero expresses their being reunited reciprocally (*me illi et mihi eum*), with the two individuals listed in parallel and the cases arranged chiastically.

res familiaris sua quemque: after the importance of being reunited with family members has been described (Cic. *RQ* 2–3), a material item, the restoration of possessions, is added. The initial term chosen (*res familiaris*, taken up by *fortunae*) provides a connection.

reliquae meae fortunae reciperatae: in contrast to the reunion with individuals, in the case of *fortunae* it is possible not to recover all of it. Thus, the qualification *reliquae* must indicate that Cicero has not (yet) recovered all his *fortunae*: at the time of this speech Cicero still had to argue (*De domo sua*; 29 Sept. 57 BCE) for the return of his house and was concerned about his property (Cic. *Att.* 4.1.3; 4.1.7 [Sept. 57 BCE]; 4.2 [Oct. 57 BCE]), though the Senate decree prompting Cicero's return stipulated the full restoration of Cicero's dignity (Cic. *Sest.* 129). In line with the argument in the preceding instances Cicero still claims that the recovered fortune (though incomplete) affords more delight than access to all his possessions in the past.

tum incolumes adferebant: this reading of *codd. rec.* gives a plausible text (other readings are grammatically problematic): it yields an adjective balancing *reciperatae*, expressing the expected contrast. Zielinski (1904, 205) and Bornecque (1909, 46 n. 3) approve of this reading for rhythmical reasons. Changes are not necessary: Sydow (1937, 227) suggested reading *quam tum incolumitate <adfectae> adferebant*; Markland (1745, 266–9) proposed *incolumi*. – The addition of *reliquae* makes the construction less straightforward, since in the second part *meae fortunae* (without *reliquae*) has to be supplied.

amicitiae, consuetudines, vicinitates, clientelae, ludi denique et dies festi:
the next (multipart) item that can be enjoyed more after absence concerns
social relationships: an asyndetic list of four terms describing different forms of
close connections with others is followed by a two-part item (added by *denique*)
indicating social events.

consuetudines: close connections with no particular emphasis on social
status or location (*OLD* s.v. *consuetudo* 5).

vicinitates: in a list describing different types of relationships between
people, the word not only indicates physical proximity between neighbours
(*OLD* s.v. *uicinitas* 1), but also the corresponding interactions and attitudes.

clientelae: in parallel with the other terms, probably used in an abstract
(*OLD* s.v. *clientela* 1) rather thaa concrete sense (*OLD* s.v. *clientela* 2).

ludi...et dies festi: *ludi* refers to the major festivals in honour of various
gods (such as *Ludi Romani* or *Ludi Apollinares*), which, in addition to religious
ceremonies, included dramatic performances and games in the circus; *dies festi*
denotes holidays, which do not need to include organized performances. –
Cicero highlights elements of Roman life that are regarded as important to the
People; he lists *ludi* and *dies festi* among the advantages of living in Rome in
another speech to the People (Cic. *Leg. agr.* 2.71). About himself Cicero says
elsewhere, in different argumentative contexts, that he is not too interested in
ludi and prefers to spend free time otherwise occupied (Cic. *Fam.* 7.1; *Arch.* 13;
Planc. 66; *Att.* 4.8.2).

4 iam vero: marks the addition of a further point in the series of elements
lost and recovered (*OLD* s.v. *iam* 8; see Cic. *RS* 22).

honos, dignitas, locus, ordo, beneficia vestra: this asyndetic list of five items
illustrates political and social standing in the community (Kranz 1964, 54). The
first four terms describe an esteemed position based on public office and social
status, with different nuances. The final item is summative and establishes a link
to the audience by defining them as responsible for such a standing (with
implied thanks) by electing individuals to political offices.

beneficia vestra: does not primarily refer to Cicero's recall, as frequently in
these speeches (e.g. Cic. *RS* 1; 24; *RQ* 1; 2), but rather to election to public office
(e.g. Cic. *Verr.* 2.5.175; *Leg. Man.* 68; 69; 71; *Leg. agr.* 2.1–2; 2.5; 2.26; *Mur.* 90:
Dom. 98; see Cic. *RS* 2 n.; Kranz 1964, 50–1).

clarissima visa sunt...inlustriora videntur...obscurata: an extended
metaphor of light illustrates the greatness of these benefits and the fact that
they are shining even more brightly after having been 'obscured' (not lost)
during Cicero's absence.

ipsa autem patria: adds the last substantive item in the list (*OLD* s.v. *autem* 3),
highlighted by *ipsa*: *patria* is the basis for and encompasses the items mentioned up to this point.

patria: is the subject of the *quid*-clauses, fronted to highlight it as the next item and the topic of the sentence.

di immortales: the only exclamation of this kind in the speech to the People (cf. Cic. *RS* 9): it highlights the emotional value of *patria*.

caritatis...voluptatis: define two emotions towards *patria* (*OLD* s.v. *habeo* 14).

quae...maiestas: a series of nine anaphoric exclamations (no complete sentences), exemplifying the pleasures of *patria* through positive characteristics; the subsequent clause adds that after his absence from Rome Cicero can enjoy these even more than he did previously (Grasmück 1978, 122). The first five elements indicate various aspects of the beauty and the fertility of Italy, the sixth refers to Rome (*urbs* in contrast to *oppida* all over Italy), and the last three denote abstract items relating to the character and behaviour of the citizens and the political system. *cives* and *res publica* are not limited geographically; but their placement after zooming in on Rome insinuates a focus on this city. The sequence ends with an item explicitly linked to the audience, which singles them out as an important element of what makes Rome and the Republic desirable.

species Italiae: starts off the series with a general reference to appearance (*OLD* s.v. *species* 3b).

celebritas oppidorum: i.e. towns full of people and thus busy activity (*OLD* s.v. *celebritas* 1).

forma regionum: probably takes up distributively *species Italiae* and applies the notion to individual regions.

agri...fruges: most of the land in Italy was fertile (on Italy's fertility in literature, see, e.g., Verg. *G.* 2.173–6).

humanitas civium: the civil and humane character and behaviour of the inhabitants (*OLD* s.v. *humanitas* 3).

rei publicae dignitas: highlights not just the fact that the Republic exists, but also its esteemed position.

vestra maiestas: the political majesty and authority of the Roman People embodied in the *contio* addressed (*OLD* s.v. *maiestas* 2).

quibus...omnibus...rebus: *quibus* is a connecting relative, and *omnibus... rebus* refers to the preceding list of items.

antea: the time before Cicero's absence from Rome. It is not taken up by a straightforward contrast ('now'), but rather by a simile (introduced by *sed*) that exemplifies the intensified feelings after a period during which particular benefits were missed.

sic...ut nemo magis: the second half of this comparison is not a complete sentence: a form of *fruor* (corresponding to *fruebar*) has to be supplied. By claiming that nobody appreciated these items more than he did in the past, Cicero is at pains to stress that, even before being absent, he valued the benefits conferred by the Roman state and the Roman People.

tamquam bona valetudo: Cicero illustrates the regaining of all social, political, and communal values with the feelings experienced after recovering from illness.

quam qui: short for *quam iis qui* (parallel to preceding *iis qui*).

haec omnia: takes up *omnibus...rebus*.

desiderata: is not qualified by a temporal adverb like *adsidue percepta*, but implies a temporary lack in the past (*OLD* s.v. *desidero* 4).

5 quorsum...quorsum: after Cicero has talked about the (selfless) motivations for his departure and the (overwhelming) pleasures of the return owing to favours conferred by the People (Cic. *RQ* 1–4), he emphatically (with repeated *quorsum*) calls himself to order and asks himself to provide a reason for such a start. This question highlights the subsequent remark about the difficulty of adequately rendering thanks for this enormous favour, a concept opening the speech in the Senate (Cic. *RS* 1).

ut...possit: the answer consists of a final *ut*-clause without an expressed main clause (to be inferred from the preceding question).

ut intellegere possitis: Cicero explicitly states that he has arranged the speech in this way so that the audience can understand the point he is about to indicate: this comment is not patronizing because the preceding question suggests that the procedure may not be immediately obvious.

neminem: when Cicero makes a similar statement in the speech in the Senate, it is phrased in abstract form about rhetorical ability (Cic. *RS* 1 [and n.]). In line with the more personal approach in the speech to the People, the concept here is expressed with reference to the qualities of individuals. In both cases Cicero highlights that the potential lack of adequate thanks is not due to his own shortcomings or limited effort, but to the fact that it is impossible for anyone to deliver an appropriate speech in view of the magnitude of the favours received. – *eloquentia* corresponds to *dicendi copia* and *genere dicendi* to *genus orationis* (in *RS* 1).

vestram: Shackleton Bailey (1991, 227) suggests deleting this word. While it is indeed superfluous as the agent is identified in the subsequent relative clause, it can be regarded as an emphatic addition; it then has to be interpreted as a transferred epithet, qualifying *beneficiorum* (K.-St. I 220–1; Pinkster 2015, 1051–3), corresponding to *magnitudini vestrorum beneficiorum* (Cic. *RS* 1).

quam: according to the text as transmitted in the main manuscripts the relative pronoun refers to *magnitudinem multitudinemque*, agreeing with the nearest noun (K.-St. I 57–9) or with both words understood as forming a single expression. With the reading in later manuscripts (*quae*), adopted by Peterson (1911), it relates to preceding *beneficiorum*. While the latter might be more logical, the emphasis is on *magnitudinem multitudinemque* (also governing *vestram*).

in me fratremque meum et liberos nostros: as in the speech to the Senate, Cicero describes the favours received as not just applying to him, but also to his brother and their children (Cic. *RS* 1). Here the sequence of connectors is more straightforward (Cic. *RS* 1 n.).

non modo augere aut ornare oratione, sed enumerare aut consequi: corresponds to *non dicam complecti orando, sed percensere numerando* in the speech in the Senate (Cic. *RS* 1). The construction here is slightly easier, as it has two parallel infinitives for each part, rather than an infinitive complemented by a gerund. The construction *non modo..., sed* adds a second term 'correcting' a first one; in this case there is a reductive movement, as the second indicates a simpler version (K.-St. II 60).

a parentibus... debeamus: Cicero proceeds to illustrate the greatness of the favours experienced by providing a list of items naturally received in small and/ or undistinguished fashion initially and now returned bigger, greater, and more valuable. Similar points are made at the beginning of the speech in the Senate (Cic. *RS* 2), though with less emotive detail (Cic. *RS* 2 n.).

a parentibus... consularis: Cicero contrasts his being born to his parents as a young child in an insignificant position with his being born to the People as an ex-consul, thus presenting his return to Rome as a 'rebirth' and as a reassumption of his previous standing. The parenthetical comment *id quod necesse erat* indicates that the statement about the original birth sketches the natural course of events and is not intended to diminish the achievement of the parents. – The scholiast already notes that this presentation is determined by the aim to have a positive effect on the audience by demonstrating their great deeds for him (Schol. Bob. ad Cic. *RQ* 5 [p. 111.11–16 Stangl]: *popularis magis quam pressa et gravis haec sententia videtur, sed facit ad aures volgi: ut, cum parentes procreaverint hominem, ipsi provexisse et quodammodo gradibus honorum conroborasse videantur senatoriam dignitatem. et hoc totum facit... cum populi gratia conferendo beneficia divina, ut eo libentius dicentem populus audiat plus a populo consecutum quam aput ipsos deos inmortales habuerit optatum.*; see also Raccanelli 2012, 95). – The difference between the two kinds of 'births' is supported by the verbs chosen, as *natus* is more easily used in transferred sense.

illi... reddidistis: with regard to Cicero's brother (Cic. *RS* 1 n.) the contrast is that, when the parents (*illi*) gave him to Cicero, it was not known how he would turn out, but when the People (*vos*) returned him to Cicero, his good qualities had been proved and recognized. In the doublet *spectatum et incredibili pietate cognitum* the first part expresses general worth and the second highlights a characteristic essential for the support shown to Cicero. This presentation implies praise for both the People and his brother's activities on Cicero's behalf (Cic. *RS* 37 n.).

incognitum: an adjective governing an indirect question (K.-St. II 487–8).

pietate: while *pietas* among humans (*OLD* s.v. *pietas* 3) often refers to the relationship between parents and children (Cic. *RS* 37), here it describes the feelings between brothers (e.g. Hor. *Epist.* 1.14.6–8).

rem publicam...accepi: after the two personal points about the birth of Cicero and his brother, a political item is added. – The time at which Cicero received the Republic (i.e. in order to do something effective for it) must refer to his consulship in 63 BCE (Masoero 1905, 17; Bellardi 1975, 132 n. 2; Hodgson 2017, 143), and the description of its state indicates the situation at the start of the year (cf. Cic. *Leg. agr.* 2.8) before Cicero brings everything back to order (in his view). The wording (rather than *civitas* or *patria*) emphasizes the political organization to which these activities apply.

illis...temporibus: Shackleton Bailey (1991, 27) translates *illis* twice, as a complement to *temporibus* and with the force of *ab illis* ('From them in those days I received back a Commonwealth which was almost lost: from you I have received back a Commonwealth which in the judgment of all its citizens was once saved by a single man.'). It is true that, in order to parallel the preceding two sentences, the expression of an agent in both parts of the clause would be expected; because of the parallelism, however, such an expression would have to come at the beginning of the sentence; *illis* without the preposition *ab* and in this position must go with *temporibus*. Perhaps the agent is left out to enable fronted emphasis on *res publica* and because the identification of the agent from whom the Republic has been received is avoided. – The indication of time by a vague *illis... temporibus* avoids the specification of details.

eam quae...eam...quam: repeated *eam* (referring to *rem publicam*), each followed by a relative clause, underlines the particular appearance of the *res publica* in each case.

amissa est: the indicative presents the description as a fact; the perfect tense is used in place of a pluperfect, indicating the reference to the past, but not specifying the chronological sequence (K.-St. I 129–30).

reciperavi: Cicero claims that he received the Republic back in a state in which everyone acknowledged that he had 'preserved' it singlehandedly (his standard description: see Introduction, section 3.4), i.e. by successfully fighting the Catilinarian Conspiracy in his consular year of 63 BCE. The argument does not work on the basis of strict logic; what is implied is Cicero's achievements for the Republic (now recognized by everyone), his return on this basis, and the unexpressed assumption that he could again fulfil a political function in the Republic.

aliquando omnes...iudicaverunt: implies that the recall demonstrates that the view that the Republic was preserved by Cicero has now been generally accepted. The wording suggests a general view, now widely held, rather than a reference to official pronouncements of this assessment which could be inferred from Senate decrees passed after the successful quelling of the Catilinarian Conspiracy (Cic. *Cat.* 3.14; 3.15; 4.5; *Sull.* 85; *Pis.* 6).

unius opera: a reference to Cicero and his activities as consul (cf. Cic. *Pis.* 6: *sine ulla dubitatione iuravi rem publicam atque hanc urbem mea unius opera esse salvam*).

liberos: from politics Cicero returns to family matters, now to the next generation, his children (Cic. *RS* 1 n.). Here there is no contrast expressed in the sense that they have now been received as something better, but the fact that they were originally given by the gods and now returned by the People sufficiently enhances the intervention of the People. To create this juxtaposition Cicero describes the children as given by the gods, ignoring the parents, whom he has just mentioned in his own case: a similar structure here would mean that he initially gave the children to himself, which would be odd in this argumentative context.

multa praeterea: towards the end of the enumeration, Cicero adds a generic and all-encompassing item.

a dis immortalibus optata: describes elements of life that individuals wish for themselves and regard as granted by divine intervention. When it is then stated that 'all divine gifts' can only be enjoyed because of the People's intervention (leading to Cicero's return), this does not put the People in a position of gods, but rather indicates that they have created circumstances in which gifts given by the gods can be enjoyed.

nisi vestra voluntas fuisset: a positive and untechnical description of the People's support for Cicero's return (cf. Cic. *RQ* 6). The People passed the law on Cicero's recall on 4 August 57 BCE (Cic. *Att.* 4.1.4; see Introduction, section 2).

vestros...honores: political offices gained through election by the People.

denique: signals the final item of the sequence (*OLD* s.v. *denique* 3).

quos eramus gradatim singulos adsecuti: refers to the *cursus honorum* in which the individual offices would be gained in a prescribed sequence.

universos: marks the contrast with winning offices sequentially (for the structure, see Cic. *RS* 2). Obviously, Cicero did not have all the offices again after returning to Rome; yet, as he was recalled as an ex-consul, it was thus acknowledged that he had successfully gone through the *cursus honorum* and was an ex-magistrate for all other magistracies too. – The presentation (*vestros...a vobis*) emphasizes that Cicero was elected by the People to all these offices and has now been restored to the position of an ex-magistrate also by them (Thompson 1978, 62).

ut: that Cicero posits that he has essentially been restored to his former position leads him to conclude that he now owes the Roman People everything he previously received from different entities. This is not strictly logical and is meant to highlight the key role of the Roman People (cf. Cic. *RS* 1–2).

quantum...ipsis: this anaphoric and asyndetic tricolon summarizes the items identified in the preceding list, for which these three entitites have been made responsible.

hoc tempore: refers to the present of Cicero's return and contrasts with *antea*.

universum: repeats the notion of *universos* and stresses again (now in generalized form) that everything won at different times from different entities has now been regained all at once (agreeing with *quantum...tantum*).

cuncto populo Romano: since the individuals present at a public meeting were seen as representing the Roman People, this point of view implies that on some level the audience is identical with *cunctus populus Romanus* and also with *vobis* and *vobismet ipsis*. The abstract term in the generalizing final phrase emphasizes the People's role as one of the major bodies in the Roman Republic and thus in Cicero's recall by virtue of passing the relevant law.

2. Main section (6–17): Review of Cicero's (departure and) recall

The main section (Cic. *RQ* 6–17) of this speech provides a review of the circumstances of Cicero's recall. There are some flashbacks to the time of his departure and his motivations for it, but this period is not discussed separately as it is in the speech given in the Senate (Cic. *RS* 32–5).

Cicero starts with a comparison (Cic. *RQ* 6–11), recalling the fate of ex-consuls of the past who also had to leave Rome (Cic. *RQ* 6–7): on the one hand, this makes his situation less unique when it is shown that he is not the only senior politician experiencing such a fate; on the other hand, the argument continues by distinguishing his circumstances from those of the others, outlining that he had less support from relatives or arms and that he was recalled by the Senate (Cic. *RQ* 7–11). Such a juxaposition establishes Cicero's value for the Republic before details of his recall are discussed in the second part of the section (Cic. *RQ* 11–17). There Cicero highlights at the beginning (Cic. *RQ* 11–12) and at the end (Cic. *RQ* 15–17) the assistance received from the consuls of 57 BCE, other senators, and the population more widely, while he acknowledges in between that there has been opposition (Cic. *RQ* 13–14). Overall, Cicero demonstrates again the widespread support for his restoration and the important role in the Republic assigned to him.

2.1. Comparison between Cicero and earlier ex-consuls (6–11)

The first part (Cic. *RQ* 6–11) of the main section (Cic. *RQ* 6–17) describes Cicero's situation (Cic. *RQ* 7–11) in comparison with those of previous ex-consuls who had to leave Rome (Cic. *RQ* 6–7): in their cases a large number of relatives or amount of arms succeeded in prompting their recall, while Cicero merely had himself, his brother, and his son-in-law; at the same time Cicero singles out the fact that he is the only one to have been recalled by the Senate (cf. Cic. *RS* 37–8).

Placed in a separate section early in the speech, the juxtaposition between Cicero and the other ex-consuls is more explicit and prominent than in the speech in the Senate (Mack 1937, 106–9). Although the predecessors are presented more positively here (Mack 1937, 30–2 on Cic. *RS* 38 vs *RQ* 9–11), such a comparison still illustrates the particular worth attributed to Cicero: he was seen as sufficiently important for the Senate to take action on his behalf and was recalled because of his personality and achievements (Schol. Bob. ad Cic. *RQ* 6 [p. 111.18–20 Stangl]: ... *conparatione facta reditus sui cum P. Popilio, qui C. Graccho cesserat, et cum Q. Metello, cui Apuleius Saturninus causa exilii* *fuerat, ostendit se maiorem glo<riam consecutum>.*). While these arguments do not directly concern the relationship between Cicero and the People, they enhance the value of their deed and the resulting gratitude, as it is insinuated that they have contributed to the recall of such a respected individual.

2.1.1. Ex-consuls of the past returned to Rome (6–7)

This subsection (Cic. *RQ* 6–7) compares Cicero's fate with that of three ex-consuls of the past who had to leave Rome and then came back: Cicero stresses that P. Popilius Laenas and Q. Caecilius Metellus Numidicus had a number of relatives petitioning the Roman People on their behalf (Cic. *RQ* 6; cf. Cic. *RS* 37) and that C. Marius recalled himself with arms (Cic. *RQ* 7; cf. Cic. *RS* 38). This description prepares for the conclusion that Cicero's return is outstanding.

6 nam: this section elaborates on the greatness of the favour received from the People.

in ipso beneficio vestro tanta magnitudo: while Cicero says *vestram magnitudinem multitudinemque beneficiorum* in the previous paragraph (Cic. *RQ* 5), here he talks about a single (highlighted) favour: his recall. The preceding plural can be seen as an introduction to a list of aspects that combine to make up the key favour. – Elsewhere too Cicero mentions gratitude for *beneficia* received from the People, where the term refers to elections (esp. Cic. *Leg. agr.* 2.1–2; 2.4), or applies the word in a broader sense, including elections (Cic. *Phil.* 4.16; on this topos, see Dyck 2004, 305, who does not seem to distinguish between different nuances of *beneficium*).

eam: this reading of some manuscripts (vs *iam*) provides the object of *complecti oratione*, referring to *magnitudo* (Cic. *RQ* 5 n.), and is thus preferable (supported by Busche 1917, 1355).

complecti oratione: takes up *non modo augere aut ornare oratione, sed enumerare aut consequi* (Cic. *RQ* 5), using a verb from the comparable phrase in the speech given in the Senate (Cic. *RS* 1: *non dicam complecti orando, sed percensere numerando*). The phrase continues the concept that the favour received is too great to be acknowledged adequately in a speech.

in studiis vestris tanta animorum declarata est voluntas: again (Cic. *RQ* 5 n.) refers to the People's support for Cicero's return. The indirect and paraphrastic expression puts emphasis on the People's attitude and presents their action as a visible declaration of their views.

calamitatem: on this term, see Cic. *RS* 20 n.; Introduction, section 3.4.

dignitatem auxisse: takes up the previously outlined idea (Cic. *RQ* 2–5) that, as a result of his departure and subsequent return, Cicero received everything back as something greater and better: while his standing has been resumed and not actually changed, the initiatives to recall him have demonstrated the People's concern and respect for him, which equals a perceived enhancement of his position. A visible effect is independent of the possibility of offering appropriate thanks.

videamini: means 'you are seen' (e.g. Shackleton Bailey 1991, 27) and continues the emphasis on the visibility (*declarata est*) of the People's attitude, their actions, and the result (rather than 'you seem': e.g. Kasten 1977, 47).

non enim ...: as in the speech in the Senate (Cic. *RS* 37–8), Cicero compares his situation with those of other Roman ex-consuls exiled in the past.

pro P. Popili: suppl. *reditu*. – The first example is P. Popilius Laenas (Cic. *RS* 37 n.).

adulescentes filii: on these individuals, see Cic. *RS* 37 n.

multi ... cognati atque adfines: distinguishes between blood relations (*OLD* s.v. *cognatus*[1] 1) and in-laws (*OLD* s.v. *affinis*[1] 2). The phrase corresponds to *propinquorum multitudo* (*OLD* s.v. *propinquus* 4) in the Senate speech (Cic. *RS* 37), which seems to encompass both groups, while elsewhere *propinquus* denotes a blood relationship (Cic. *RS* 38: *adfinis mei, propinqui sui, consulis*).

Q. Metello: the second example is Q. Caecilius Metellus Numidicus (Cic. *RS* 25; 37 nn.).

iam spectata aetate filius: on Q. Caecilius Metellus Pius, see Cic. *RS* 37 n.

Lucius Diadematus consularis, summa auctoritate vir, ... C. Metellus censorius: in contrast to the speech given in the Senate, Cicero offers identifying information on L. Caecilius Metellus Diadematus and C. Caecilius Metellus Caprarius (Cic. *RS* 37 n.) by providing an additional *cognomen* for L. Metellus and a higher, distinguishing office for C. Metellus.

eorum liberi: on the offspring of these Metelli, see Cic. *RS* 37 n.

Q. Metellus Nepos: on Q. Caecilius Metellus Nepos, see Cic. *RS* 37 n.

sororum filii: an explanatory addition in comparison with the speech in the Senate: it clarifies that *Luculli, Servilii*, and *Scipiones* included sons of sisters of the Metelli mentioned (Cic. *RS* 37 n.).

permulti ..., Metelli aut Metellarum liberi: *Metelli aut Metellarum liberi* is a parenthetical exemplification of *permulti*. *Metellarum liberi* corresponds to *Metellarum filii* in the speech given in the Senate (Cic. *RS* 37) and takes up *sororum filii*. The entire phrase indicates support by men from the same *gens*, who are related through the paternal or the maternal line.

vobis ac patribus vestris: corresponds to *populo Romano* in the speech in the Senate (Cic. *RS* 37). – The relatives interceding on behalf of Q. Caecilius Metellus Numidicus would have approached *patribus vestris* at an occasion more than a generation ago. *vobis* is perhaps added in a generic sense to create the notion of a permanent *populus Romanus*, now represented by these Romans. Mention of the current Romans facilitates the comparison with Cicero in the present.

quod si ... potuerunt: such a concluding sentence is only added in the speech to the People. In Metellus Numidicus' case, if his great deeds should not have been a sufficient motivation, the pleading of the relatives could have motivated the Roman People. The comment avoids the impression that the standing and achievements of Metellus Numidicus were not relevant, while it highlights that the interventions were still an important motivating factor.

ipsius: i.e. Q. Caecilius Metellus Numidicus, the last exiled person mentioned.

summa dignitas maximaeque res gestae: Q. Caecilius Metellus Numidicus was an ex-consul and ex-censor, a leading optimate politician, and a successful general in the war against Jugurtha (Cic. *RS* 25 n.).

fili...lacrimae: a summarizing list of the different people supporting Metellus Numidicus coupled with words illustrating their feelings and actions to evoke pity. While each of these words is particularly appropriate for the people to whom it is linked, altogether they describe the attitude and the resulting behaviour for the entire group. – The noun attached to the son is the only one in this sequence describing feelings rather than behaviour demonstrating feelings: *pietas* is the appropriate term for the relationship of a son to his father and might allude to the cognomen Pius given to this Metellus because of the support shown for his father (Cic. *RS* 37 n.).

fili...propinquorum: the son as the closest relative is mentioned separately; the others are subsumed under a general *propinqui*. – The young men and the older men added are not further individuals, but rather denote the same group of *propinqui* divided up from a different perspective.

adulescentium...maiorum natu: according to the preceding description, Metellus Numidicus' supporters included ex-consuls and ex-censors as well as younger men who had not yet reached a senior public office.

squalor: i.e. mourning dress as a sign of mourning (Cic. *RS* 12 n.).

7 C. Mari: as in the speech given in the Senate, the third example of an ex-consul leaving Rome is Marius (Cic. *RS* 38 n.); Cicero comes back to him later in this speech (Cic. *RQ* 19–20). Before the People Cicero provides a more positive and more extended portrayal of Marius, highlighting his bad treatment and toning down the disastrous effects of his actions for the Republic. Still, Cicero presents his own actions as superior (Carney 1960, 114–15).

illos veteres clarissimos consulares: i.e. P. Popilius Laenas and Q. Caecilius Metellus Numidicus (Cic. *RS* 37; *RQ* 6).

hac vestra patrumque memoria: this collocation refers to the memory of the present Romans and their fathers, i.e. the living memory of the current generation; it corresponds to *hac hominum memoria* in the Senate speech (Cic. *RS* 38 and n.; see Cic. *RS* 10 n.), expressing the concept in a more personal way.

tertius ante me: as in the Senate speech (Cic. *RS* 38), Cicero establishes the following sequence: (1) Popilius, (2) Metellus, (3) Marius, (4) Cicero.

indignissimam fortunam praestantissima sua gloria: in contrast to the neutral description in the speech given in the Senate, Cicero characterizes

Marius' fortune as *indignissimam fortunam* and contrasts it with *praestantissi-ma sua gloria* (a kind of ablative absolute: K.-St. I 779–80).

ratio: i.e. the method by which the return was realized.

deprecatione: i.e. pleas and entreaties by relatives as described for the other two ex-consuls (Cic. *RQ* 6).

in discessu civium: a paraphrase for civil unrest: *discessus* seems to be used in a metaphorical sense developed from its original meaning of separating, i.e. different groups of citizens moving in different directions in their views and then clashing with each other. Such a transferred sense is more common for *discessio*. – Divisions among the citizenry are mentioned as an attendant circumstance, but not connected with Marius' (violent) activities (see also Carney 1960, 117).

exercitu se armisque revocavit: in line with Marius' positive presentation, Cicero presents his return with violence (Cic. *RS* 38 n.) as an act of 'recalling himself', though he notes the application of weapons and force (Cic. *RQ* 10; 20–1). The expression that Marius 'recalled himself' is an effective twist of what normally happens and gives a positive spin to the events.

2.1.2. Cicero's situation (7–11)

This subsection (Cic. *RQ* 7–11) sketches Cicero's situation in comparison with that of earlier ex-consuls described in the preceding subsection (Cic. *RQ* 6–7): in contrast to these men, Cicero was not able to rely on the force of arms or a large number of relatives pleading for him. He had just his brother and his son-in-law; yet others have supported him, and he was recalled by a decree of the Senate (cf. Cic. *RS* 37–8). Thus, according to Cicero, he was restored just because of himself and regarded as worthy of the Senate's attention. By pointing out the lack of relatives Cicero can highlight the role of the People in his recall and the greatness of the favour received from them (Mack 1937, 23–4).

7 at: contrasts the conditions of Cicero's recall with those of the three ex-consuls of the past (Cic. *RQ* 6–7). – Cicero characterizes his situation with three attributive phrases: the first two are adjectives/participles agreeing with *me* and refer to the absence of relatives (as in the case of P. Popilius Laenas and Q. Caecilius Metellus Numidicus); the third is a kind of ablative of quality (K.-St. I 454–6; Pinkster 2015, 782–3) and indicates the absence of the opportunity for applying armed force and unrest (as in the case of Marius).

me nudum a propinquis, nulla cognatione munitum: indicates the absence of relatives generally and blood relations specifically (*OLD* s.v. *propinquus* 4; *cognatio* 1; on the terms, see also Cic. *RS* 17; *RQ* 6 nn.) in Cicero's case (Cic. *RS* 37; *RQ* 6) by military imagery (cf. Cic. *RQ* 16).

nudum a propinquis: *nudus* with *a* + ablative is the common construction with reference to people (K.-St. I 374).

nullo armorum ac tumultus metu: does not indicate fear of *arma* and *tumultus* on Cicero's part, but rather the threat to others caused by the ability to employ these (*OLD* s.v. *metus* 5), implying that there was no force and violence in Cicero's case.

C. Pisonis, generi mei: Cicero gives fewer details about the intervention of his son-in-law C. Calpurnius Piso Frugi (Cic. *RS* 1; 15; 38 nn.) than in the speech in the Senate: he leaves out the conflict with the consul Piso and the neglect of his duties as quaestor: perhaps these aspects concerning magistrates are deemed not to be of interest to the People. According to Mack (1937, 24–5), Piso's intervention is described more briefly so as to emphasize that it was the People who called Cicero back without being influenced by any relatives (as in the case of earlier ex-consuls).

pietas atque: one manuscript has *satque*, and the rest of the transmission has *auctoritas atque* (approved by Busche 1917, 1355; adopted by Wolf 1801, 95; Weiske 1807, 236, Peterson 1911; Maslowski 1981; criticized by Luterbacher 1912, 346–7). Ernesti proposed reading *pietas atque* (supported by Courtney 1989, 49; adopted by Shackleton Bailey 1991, 227) on the basis of the speech in the Senate (Cic. *RS* 38 [and n.]). What suggests *pietas* is not only the parallel, but also the fact that the context points to an attitude or behaviour under the individual's control. *divina pietas* occurs once elsewhere in Cicero, in an ironic context (Cic. *Phil.* 13.43); *divina auctoritas* is not attested in Cicero's works. Sydow's (1941, 171–2) proposal to read *alacritas* adds a novel notion with little support from the transmission.

fratrisque: on Cicero's brother and his interventions for Cicero, see Cic. *RS* 1; 37 nn.

miserrimi atque optimi: this collocation both expresses Cicero's pity for his brother, for whom he has caused such an unhappy and awkward situation, and his respect and appreciation for him.

cotidianae lacrimae sordesque lugubres: corresponds to *squalore et lacrimis et cotidianis precibus* in the Senate speech (Cic. *RS* 37). The phrase here (cf. Cic. *Dom.* 59: *mea filia, cuius fletus adsiduus sordesque lugubres*) emphasizes the mournful appearance through the clothing (*squalore* follows in the next sentence) and the pitiful activity (*cotidianae lacrimae*, taken up by *suo fletu*).

a vobis deprecatae sunt: this main verb governs *me* at the start of the sentence, fronted to mark the contrast and the transition. This construction is repeated later (Cic. *RQ* 16; cf. Cic. *Fam.* 4.7.6), while elsewhere the verb is used with a prepositional phrase introduced by *pro* (Cic. *RS* 37; *RQ* 6).

8 frater: Cicero continues with further details about his brother's intervention (Cic. *RS* 37). The focus zooms in on the brother (*unus*); the role of the son-in-law is momentarily ignored. Towards the end of the paragraph a comment is added to explain why Cicero's other relatives (his wife and children) were less prominent. – As Mack (1937, 25) notes, in this speech Cicero does not

use the verb *coegit* (Cic. *RS* 37) to indicate the effect of the brother's intervention on the People, assigning a more active role to them; and the relationship to
the brother is described more emotionally.

qui: introduces a consecutive relative clause in the subjunctive (K.-St. II
303–4; Lebreton 1901, 315).

suo squalore: on this feature, see Cic. *RQ* 7 n.

vestros oculos…renovaret: while *desiderium* and *memoria* are also mentioned in the Senate speech (Cic. *RS* 37), that oration places the emphasis on
Cicero's (political) deeds and his position rather than on his person; the verb
renovare again implies that an existing attitude only has to be reactivated (Cic.
RS 37 n.). The concept of *oculos inflectere* appears only here: it shows the immediate effect of his brother's intervention.

qui statuerat…fortunam: the same statement by Cicero's brother is reported in the speech given in the Senate (Cic. *RS* 37), yet in a less emphatic and less
emotionally moving way (Mack 1937, 25). – There the condition for determining whether to take action is phrased with reference to him (the brother receiving Cicero back), whereas here it is expressed as depending on the audience
(the audience giving Cicero back to his brother). – The *qui*-clause provides
additional factual information (in Cicero's view); therefore, the mood changes
to the indicative.

sibi: the reflexive pronoun occurs in a clause in indirect speech and refers to
the subject of the superordinate clause (K.-St. I 607–8; Pinkster 2015, 1124–5).

fortunam: tanto: Courtney (1960, 95) calls to mind Halm's (1856, 850) conjecture *fortunam; <nam>*. While it is true that the following sentence provides
an explanation, the *asyndeton causale sive explicativum* is a well-recognized
rhetorical feature (K.-St. II 158).

ut negaret…seiunctum: *domicilio* and *sepulcro* are *ablativi respectus*,
indicating the aspect to which the separation (from Cicero) refers. – For the
construction *non modo…sed ne…quidem*, see K.-St. II 62–3.

pro me praesente: i.e. when Cicero was still in Rome (contrasts with *pro
eodem absente*).

senatus hominumque praeterea viginti milia vestem mutaverunt: in the
Senate speech too Cicero notes that the Senate and other people changed into
mourning clothes to demonstrate their sympathy with Cicero (Cic. *RS* 12
[and n.]).

unius…unus: i.e. Cicero's brother (cf. *frater erat unus*). – The brother is said
to have been the only one to demonstrate support in Cicero's absence: this is
probably not meant as a criticism of others who had previously shown sympathy, but rather to highlight how little help from relatives Cicero was able to
receive in contrast to other men in exile (cf. Cic. *RQ* 7).

squalorem sordesque: repeats the preceding sketch (Cic. *RQ* 7–8).

vidistis: describing Cicero's brother's activities as something the audience
could see presents it as a fact and engages them in the presentation.

hic qui quidem in foro posset esse: this clarification forestalls the potential impression that Cicero might ignore other members of his family or that they were not sympathetic: he goes on to outline that his wife and children were also dressed in mourning and full of grief, but did not appear in public like his brother, an established ex-magistrate. – The relative clause introduced by *qui quidem* has the subjunctive because of a consecutive connotation (K.-St. II 303) and indicates a restriction (K.-St. II 307–8; *OLD* s.v. *quidem* 1d).

mihi pietate…fuit frater: repeats the idea voiced in the speech given in the Senate that his brother fulfilled the function of son, parent, and brother for Cicero (Cic. *RS* 37). Here the qualification for parent is *beneficio* (rather than *consiliis*), which puts more emphasis on supportive kindness rather than on caring thought and advice. Kranz (1964, 15–16) explains the comparison by the fact that providing *beneficia* is a characteristic feature of parents.

coniugis…pueriles: after having talked about his brother, Cicero turns to describing the reactions of his wife Terentia, his daughter Tullia, and his young son Marcus; he thereby explains (*nam*) why, although these family members were also responding to Cicero's absence, his brother was the only one to be seen in public and potentially having an effect. In the Senate speech Cicero's joy at being reunited with his children is mentioned (Cic. *RS* 1), but there is no description of their grief during his absence, which might be added here for its emotional effect (Mack 1937, 25–6). – Cicero gives a rhetorical sequence of items for the three family members, with varying descriptions of increasing length, ending with the emotionally most moving, as in the presentation of family members in law court speeches (e.g. Cic. *Brut.* 90; Val. Max. 8.1.abs.2; Liv. *Epit.* 49.19). The variations in nuances are in line with the differences in gender, age, and standing (on their feelings and treatment during Cicero's absence, see, e.g., Cic. *Dom.* 59; *Prov. cons.* 3; *Sest.* 54; 145; Cael. 50; Mil. 87; *Fam.* 14.2.2 [5 Oct. 58 BCE]).

coniugis: Terentia (*c.* 98 BCE – 6 CE), Cicero's (first) wife from *c.* 80/77 until their divorce in 47/46 BCE (*RE* Terentius 95). During Cicero's exile, despite not always being well, Terentia tried to support Cicero morally and financially (Cic. *Fam.* 14.3.2–3; 14.4.3; *Att.* 3.19.2; on the women around Cicero, see Treggiari 2007; on Terentia's situation during and after Cicero's exile, see Treggiari 2007, 56–73).

squalor et luctus: the description of the pitiable situation of Cicero's wife combines references to mourning clothes (as the outward sign of one's attitude) and feelings.

optimae filiae: Cicero's daughter Tullia (79–45 BCE; see Cic. *RS* 1 n.). – Her excellent character and the continuity of her grief are highlighted.

filique parvi: Cicero's young son Marcus (b. 65 BCE; see Cic. *RS* 1 n.). – The sketch of a young boy shedding tears yearning for his father is an emotionally moving picture. – *lacrimae…pueriles*, in theory, could refer to the son or to both children, since the adjective can be applied to boys or to children generally. As the young age is only highlighted for the son (*parvi*), and the daughter, who was already married, was probably beyond the age that could be described as *puerilis*, the phrase must refer to the son.

aut itineribus necessariis aut magnam partem tectis ac tenebris continebantur: in contrast to his brother's feelings and activities, Cicero says, the grief of his wife and children was hardly visible, as it was only shown inside the home or on necessary errands: such a description implies both that Cicero's family did not go out deliberately to make an ostentatious show of their emotions in order to influence public mood and that, as a result of their social position, his wife and children had less opportunity to act in public. Treggiari (2007, 60), however, states: 'This was all very proper as a statement to the assembly [Cic. *RQ* 8]. But Terentia and Tullia did not spend all their time shut up in their shady houses. They put on their black clothes and left their hair dishevelled in order to show themselves outside in the classic form of protest, and they visited the houses of others in order to work for Cicero's return.' There is no clear evidence for this behaviour: while Cicero's letters from exile to his family (esp. Cic. *Fam.* 14.1–4) indicate that Terentia was suffering from ill health during his absence and was running the family's affairs, there is only one allusion to his wife and children wearing mourning dress; yet this is a desciption of how Cicero pictures them (Cic. *Fam.* 14.3.2). In any case the family's activities are not of a kind to influence the People, though the presentation is still more emphatic than in the Senate speech; the key point is that Cicero was recalled on his own account and by the intervention of a limited number of relatives. – Weiske (1807, 237) refers *itinera* to travels to *praedia* to look after them; this would be a specific application of a general term, though perhaps in line with the fact that Cicero's wife looked after the family's financial and property affairs in his absence, even using her own assets (e.g. Cic. *Fam.* 14.1.5; 14.2.3). Yet that such journeys were particularly connected with a demonstration of grief is unlikely.

tectis ac tenebris: the alliterative pair emphasizes that the grief was felt in private and hardly visible. *OLD* lists the passage as an example of *tenebrae* in the meaning '(as typical of squalid or disreputable buildings, etc.); (quasi-concr.) a dark corner, den, or sim.' (*OLD* s.v. *tenebrae* 1c). It is unlikely that Cicero would have presented the home of his family in that way. More plausibly, *tenebrae* entails a metaphorical connotation and underlines that the grief happened in private and unobserved (*OLD* s.v. *tenebrae* 4 'A condition in which one (a thing) is unknown or unobserved, obscurity, concealment').

qua re: introduces the conclusion that the People's favour is particularly great in Cicero's case, as it focused on Cicero and happened without the involvement of a large number of relatives.

hoc…quod: *hoc* (ablative) is elaborated on by the *quod*-clause (K.-St. II 270–1).

multitudini propinquorum: contrasts with the situation described for P. Popilius Laenas and Q. Caecilius Metellus Numidicus, for whom *(per)multi* relatives are said to have interceded (Cic. *RQ* 6), which does not apply to Cicero (Cic. *RQ* 7).

sed nobismet ipsis nos reddidistis: almost the same phrase appears in the speech given in the Senate (Cic. *RS* 1: *qui denique nosmet ipsos nobis reddidistis*). In that passage the emphasis is on the accusative, with the item set off in a list of other objects in the same case; here the focus is on the dative, forming a contrast with *multitudini propinquorum*. Markland (1745, 270–1) comments that, unusually, the meaning of this phrase is 'to restore me for my own sake' rather than 'to myself'. Yet the construction suggests interpreting both datives as indirect objects: because there was not a large number of relatives pleading for him, Cicero is not returned to them but rather to himself.

9 quem ad modum ... sic: this comparative structure has the connotation of contrast (K.-St. II 451; *OLD* s.v. *sic* 7c; *ita* 4): Cicero does not have numerous relatives pleading for him; instead, he enjoys the support of a large number of people not related to him (based on his *virtus* and thus on his own worth and activity).

propinqui, quos ego parare non potui: does not mean that Cicero does not have any close family (they have just been mentioned), but rather that, as a *homo novus*, he does not have a large number of high-profile adult male relatives who could plead for him in public (on the relationship expressed by *propinquus*, see Cic. *RS* 17; *RQ* 6; 7 and nn.), as applies to exiled ex-consuls of the past (Cic. *RQ* 6).

calamitatem: on this term, see Cic. *RS* 20 n.; Introduction, section 3.4.

illud quod ... debuit: Cicero claims that any support he received was a consequence of his *virtus*. What the relative clause describes in the abstract (neuter) is then exemplified by a list of the kinds of supporters Cicero's *virtus* provoked.

adiutores, auctores hortatoresque: this tricolon of terms indicating various nuances of encouragement is organized according to an increasing measure of activity.

ita multi: used in place of *tot*, probably to facilitate comparison with (*per*)*multi*/*multitudo* mentioned in relation to the relatives of others (Cic. *RQ* 6; 8).

superiores omnes: could mean 'above-mentioned' (*OLD* s.v. *superior* 3) or 'living earlier' (*OLD* s.v. *superior* 4). Since Cicero establishes a temporal sequence of these ex-consuls and himself (Cic. *RS* 38; *RQ* 7), and *superior* in the sense of 'above-mentioned' seems to be more common in connection with things, the sense 'earlier' is more plausible (cf. Cic. *RQ* 10).

hac dignitate copiaque: the large number of supporters of high rank asserted here contributes to underlining Cicero's own standing.

numquam ... facta est: the asyndetic and anaphoric tricolon emphasizes a situation that did not apply to the three previous ex-consuls in implicit contrast to what happened to Cicero: their fate was not discussed in the Senate. The same point is made in a less rhetorically emphatic way in the speech delivered in the Senate (Cic. *RS* 38). – All three men are given honorary epithets differing from their preceding characterization (Cic. *RS* 37; *RQ* 6): *nobilissimus* and *clarissimus* are switched around between Popilius and Metellus, and there is an additional attribute for each of them (*fortissimus* and *constantissimus*). Marius, who has not received a specific epithet previously, is described as *custode civitatis atque imperi vestri*: his achievements for the community and the audience are thereby singled out (probably an allusion to Marius' victories over external enemies such as Jugurtha or the Cimbri and Teutones). *de P. Popilio, clarissimo ac fortissimo viro* could refer to Popilius' courageous intervention against the followers of the dead Ti. Sempronius Gracchus (*fortis/fortissimus* also at Cic. *Dom.* 82; 87), and *de Q. Metello, nobilissimo et constantissimo cive* could indicate that Metellus did not bow to the demands of the Tribune of the People L. Appuleius Saturninus. While C. Marius is highlighted as the People's hero and the preserver of the Republic, the connotations evoked by the descriptions of the other two men might go against what one would expect in a speech to the People; yet they are sufficiently generic to be understood also as general praise.

P. Popilio: see Cic. *RS* 37; *RQ* 6 nn.

Q. Metello: see Cic. *RS* 25; 37; *RQ* 6 nn.

C. Mario: see Cic. *RS* 38; *RQ* 7 nn.

in senatu mentio facta est: an emphasis on the agreement of the senators might be seen to reduce the role of the People in Cicero's recall, for which he is expressing gratitude in this speech. This is not the perspective applied: a contrast is created between earlier exiles who did not enjoy widespread support from the establishment and cooperation with the Senate and Cicero, who was supported by and recognized the senators; this presentaton confirms Cicero's credentials as a unifying figure who entertains good relationships with both the Senate and the People.

10 tribuniciis...rogationibus: Popilius and Numidicus were recalled as a result of activities of Tribunes of the People (Cic. *RS* 38 n.).

superiores illi: a vague reference to all three earlier exiled ex-consuls or only the two earliest (on *superiores*, see Cic. *RQ* 9 n.). *nulla auctoritate senatus* applies to all of them, but *tribuniciis...rogationibus* only to the first two.

auctoritate senatus: here probably denotes an informal decree (*OLD* s.v. *auctoritas* 4), indicating the lack of active involvement of the Senate (for other meanings of *auctoritas senatus*, see Cic. *RS* 4; 6; 16; 39; *RQ* 18 nn.).

oppresso senatu: a vague description of Marius' confrontation of senators upon his return. The sketch in the speech given in the Senate is more explicit (Cic. *RS* 38 and n.).

nec rerum gestarum memoria in reditu C. Mari sed exercitus atque arma valuerunt: this impersonal phrasing leaves it open who was responsible for the fighting on Marius' return (cf. Cic. *RQ* 7). The contrast highlights the violence on Marius' return, while the memory of his achievements, which are not questioned, is said not to have played a role (in contrast to Cicero's recall).

at de me…perfecit: the way in which the earlier ex-consuls, C. Marius in particular, were recalled is contrasted (*at*) with the circumstances in Cicero's case (*de me*); therefore, the reference to Cicero is fronted; a connection is created by the repetition of the same verb (*valuerunt…valeret*). The mention of Cicero is followed by two asyndetically linked main clauses (*semper senatus flagitavit…frequentia atque auctoritate perfecit*), each determining an *ut*-clause preceding them. Grammatically, the unexpressed subject of both *ut*-clauses could be *rerum gestarum memoria*, to be inferred from the preceding sentence (so Markland 1745, 269–70 [while assuming that *ut res perficeretur* is meant for the second *ut*-clause]; apparently Shackleton Bailey 1991, 29), or it could be *senatus*, with the subject of the main clause valid also for the subordinate clauses, or it could be *rerum gestarum memoria* in the first *ut*-clause and *senatus* in the second (so apparently Masoero 1905, 21; Kasten 1977, 49/51). If the reading *proficeret* is kept, the final option is most plausible and logical; in the required sense this verb seems mainly connected with personal agents (*OLD* s.v. *proficio* 1). The paraphrastic construction (*ut…proficeret…perfecit*) emphasizes the difficulties in getting to this result and the means by which it was eventually achieved (without mentioning the recall explicitly).

semper senatus flagitavit: emphasizes the Senate's continued appreciation of Cicero by the constant demonstration of its willingness to honour Cicero. The concept is expressed less emphatically and less directly than in the speech to the Senate (Cic. *RS* 3 and n.).

cum primum licuit: alludes to the fact that, as a result of interventions and obstructions by P. Clodius Pulcher, the consuls of the previous year, and the Tribunes of the People, the Senate was not in a position to pass a fully ratified decree in 58 BCE. Even at the beginning of 57 BCE there were difficulties because of the opposition of individuals (see Cic. *RS* 4; 8 nn.; Introduction, section 2). Yet, as Cicero stresses, the Senate passed a decree as soon as possible (in July 57 BCE). – *cum primum* is construed with an indicative of *perfectum historicum* in a narrative (K.-St. II 353).

frequentia atque auctoritate: Shackleton Bailey (1991, 29 n. 9) assumes that '[t]he word *auctoritate* probably refers to the vetoed decree mentioned in *Red. sen.* 3'. Yet the emphasis is on the Senate's effect and the speech continues with aspects of the recall; thus, the expression must refer to the eventual successful Senate decree passed with the votes of a large number of senators. Hence *auctoritas* is unlikely to indicate an informal decree of the Senate (*OLD* s.v. *auctoritas* 4) and more likely to describe its authoritative position (*OLD* s.v. *auctoritas* 6). *frequentia* recalls that, according to Cicero, the Senate meeting voting almost unanimously for Cicero's recall in July 57 BCE was well attended (Cic. *RS* 25–6 [and n.]; *RQ* 15; *Sest.* 129; see Introduction, section 2).

nullus…revocavit: Cicero juxtaposes the attitude and behaviour of all of Italy with respect to his return and that of the other ex-consuls.

in eorum reditu: i.e. as regards the return of the three earlier ex-consuls.

motus municipiorum et colononiarum: support for Cicero from towns all over Italy (on *municipia* and *coloniae*, see Cic. *RS* 27; 31 nn.; on *motus*, see Cic. *RS* 38 n.) was prompted by Senate decrees in July 57 BCE and shown upon Cicero's return (Cic. *RS* 24; 38 [and nn.]; see Introduction, section 2).

me in patriam ter suis decretis Italia cuncta revocavit: in contrast to the lack of involvement of *municipia* and *coloniae* for other exiles, Cicero claims to have received approval of his recall from communities outside Rome There were indeed expressions of support from municipal towns in Cicero's favour which could be interpreted in an exaggerated manner as approval from all of Italy. The term *decretum* is broader than, e.g., *senatus consultum* and thus can be applied to bodies other than the Roman Senate (*OLD* s.v. *decretum* 3b). Elsewhere the emphasis is on the widespread support by all groups of people and communities throughout Rome and Italy (e.g. Cic. *RS* 25; 38; 39; *RQ* 11; 16; 18). A triple repetition is only mentioned here, and the precise reference is unclear. According to MacKendrick (1995, 139; similarly Bücher 2006, 247 n. 82) 'the three motions on Cicero's behalf are (1) that of Capua, inspired by Pompey as magistrate of the colony; (2) that of the knights, especially the tax-collectors (cf. *Dom.* 74); and (3) the 4 August vote of the *centuriata*' (Fuhrmann [1978, 483, n. 42] also refers the third time to the vote on 4 August). All these are collective expressions of support for Cicero by groups in Rome or else-where in Italy (see also Cic. *RS* 29 [and n.]; 31; *Dom.* 30; 73–5; *Har.* 46; *Pis.* 41; 80; 128; Ascon. ad Cic. *Pis.* [p. 3.20–3 C.]), but they do not amount to all of Italy recalling Cicero three times, which suggests a repeated action of the same collective body. Weiske (1807, 238) assumes that the remark refers to citizens being called to *comitia* to vote on a proposed bill for Cicero's recall three times (October 58, January 57, August 57 BCE): in the first two cases, however, the initiative did not get as far as the *comitia*, and no *decreta* were passed.

illi…esset: Cicero proceeds to compare the return of the three other ex-consuls (*illi*) and himself (*ego*) as regards their respective relationships to their enemies: for Cicero the circumstances were harder, because his enemies were still alive when he returned; at the same time this makes his return impressive, as it happened in spite of them.

inimicis interfectis, magna civium caede facta: P. Popilius Laenas returned to Rome after the death of C. Sempronius Gracchus (Cic. *RS* 37 n.) and Q. Caecilius Metellus Numidicus after the death of L. Appuleius Saturninus (Cic. *RS* 25 n.); when C. Marius came back to Rome after Sulla's withdrawal, he and L. Cornelius Cinna had many of their political enemies killed (Cic. *RS* 9; 38 nn.). Thus, the first phrase primarily refers to the two earlier ex-consuls and the second phrase to Marius. – The detail is also given in the Senate speech (Cic.

RS 38), but as a circumstantial element characterizing the return of these men and not as a basis for a contrast with Cicero.

iis ... amandatus esset: for himself, Cicero lists three groups of enemies who are still around, though, for different reasons, without being actively in opposition: the consuls of 58 BCE, one of the consuls of 57 BCE, and the Tribune of the People of 58 BCE, P. Clodius Pulcher. – These men are not named but rather identified by descriptions: this method enables the orator to mention selected features and to suggest that the audience knows about the circumstances (Uría 2006, 14, 18–19).

iis ... obtinentibus: i.e. the consuls of 58 BCE, L. Calpurnius Piso Caesoninus and A. Gabinius, who were assigned lucrative provinces by P. Clodius Pulcher and took up their governorships after the end of their consular year (Cic. *RS* 4 n.). These consuls were not directly responsible for 'driving away' Cicero; but as they did not stop the activities of the Tribune of the People P. Clodius Pulcher, Cicero can present them as responsible. The seemingly neutral description of them currently governing provinces alludes obliquely to what Cicero brands as a 'pact' elsewhere, as they were allegedly offered these provinces in return for not opposing Clodius' plans.

inimico: i.e. Q. Caecilius Metellus Nepos, one of the consuls of 57 BCE, originally an enemy of Cicero and later one of his supporters (Cic. *RS* 5 n.).

optimo viro et mitissimo: although Metellus Nepos is introduced as an *inimicus*, he is immediately characterized positively in recognition of the fact that he moved to Cicero's side (cf. Cic. *RQ* 15).

altero <cum> consule referente: *altero ... consule* denotes P. Cornelius Lentulus Spinther, the other consul of 57 BCE (Cic. *RS* 5 n.). – Scholars often add *<consule>* (before *altero* with Madvig [1884, 138] or before *referente* with Mommsen [ap. Orellium]), but this supplement leads to a clumsy construction, and the mere statement that Cicero's enemy was consul is not very emphatic (not added by Shackleton Bailey 1991, 227). In the version adopted here (a development of Luterbacher's [1912, 347] suggestion: *<consule cum> altero consule referente*), the loss of the word could be explained easily, there is a single ablative absolute construction, *altero* has a reference point in the preceding mention of the other consul (though without identification of his status), and it is clear that both consuls are involved in working towards Cicero's recall (Cic. *RQ* 15; on the consuls' roles in proposing the decisive decrees, see Cic. *RS* 26 n.).

is inimicus qui: a further *inimicus*, P. Clodius Pulcher, also called *inimicus* elsewhere in this pair of speeches (Cic. *RS* 4 n.). – Weiske (1807, 238) and Masoero (1905, 22) refer the remark to Sex. Atilius Serranus (Gavianus) (Cic. *RS* 5; *RQ* 12 nn.); but the description only fits a more powerful and influential opponent.

communibus hostibus: the change of wording from *inimicus* to *hostis* and the addition of *communis* indicates that the people activated by Cicero's *inimicus* are no longer to be presented as Cicero's personal enemies. In the context they are most likely to be Catilinarians, political enemies of the Republic and thus of all (good) citizens in Cicero's view. According to Cicero, P. Clodius Pulcher supported them in their quest to take revenge (Cic. *RS* 4; 26). – Grammatically, an adjective is used in place of a genitive (K.-St. I 212–13), i.e. instead of *communitatis hostibus*.

spiritu...esset: this metaphorical expression must mean that the enemy (P. Clodius Pulcher) is alive physically by fulfilling vital bodily functions, but in fact is dead, i.e. no longer of relevance and able to take decisive action (*OLD* s.v. *amando* 'To send away, relegate'; on the substantival use of the participle *mortuus*, see Pinkster 2015, 954). There is no qualification of the metaphor, which makes the statement forceful and determined.

11 numquam...cohortatus: Cicero points out that for the other exiled ex-consuls no consul took the initiative to rouse the Senate or the People. That this happened in Cicero's case (as is implied) demonstrates the recognition he enjoys. – The speech to the Senate (Cic. *RS* 38) does not include references to particular consuls (MacKendrick 1995, 138). The comment that Metellus was not recalled by Marius leads to a connection between two of the examples. The addition of the consuls of the following year acting in the same way implies that the lack of recall has to do with the situation rather than personal enmity.

<P.> Popilio: see Cic. *RS* 37; *RQ* 6 nn. – The abbreviated praenomen is generally added to create consistency with the references to the other men named in this sentence.

L. Opimius: was consul in 121 BCE (*RE* Opimius 4; *MRR* I 520–1) and, on the basis of a *senatus consultum ultimum*, responsible for the death of C. Sempronius Gracchus (for which he was taken to court the following year: *TLRR* 27), after which P. Popilius Laenas returned to Rome (e.g. Cic. *Sest.* 140; *Planc.* 70; 88). Since L. Opimius was the consul dealing with C. Sempronius Gracchus, enabling the return of P. Popilius Laenas, the other consul of that year (Q. Fabius Maximus Allobrogicus) is ignored. L. Opimius confronted C. Sempronius Gracchus on the basis of a *senatus consultum ultimum*, but the Senate was not involved in the return of P. Popilius Laenas.

Q. Metello: see Cic. *RS* 25; 37; *RQ* 6 nn.

C. Marius: see Cic. *RS* 38; *RQ* 7 nn.

qui erat inimicus: Marius initially supported the Tribune of the People L. Appuleius Saturninus (Cic. *RS* 25 n.) and was in opposition to the conservative politics of Metellus, who did not follow Saturninus' request for the ratification of his land law. Marius was the dominant consul in 100 BCE; therefore, the second consul (L. Valerius Flaccus) is not mentioned.

M. Antonius: consul in 99 BCE, after C. Marius' sixth consulship (cos. 107, 104, 103, 102, 101, 100, 86 BCE). M. Antonius (*RE* Antonius 28; cos. 99 censor 97 BCE [*MRR* II 1; 6–7]) was killed in the civil war by the faction of C. Marius and L. Cornelius Cinna in 87 BCE (b. 143 BCE). He was a great and learned orator

(*ORF*⁴ 65; e.g. Cic. *De or.* 3.32; *Brut.* 139–42) and is one of the main interlocutors in Cicero's *De oratore*.

cum A. Albino: Shackleton Bailey (1985, 141–2) suggests that Cicero might have said <*neque solus neque*> *cum A. Albino*. But such a change, not suggested by the transmission, does not seem necessary: Cicero implies that both consuls of the year acted unanimously, while he places the emphasis on M. Antonius.

A. Albino: A. Postumius Albinus was the second consul of 99 BCE (*RE* Postumius 33; *MRR* II 1). In Cicero's *Brutus* he is praised for his elegant Latin diction (Cic. *Brut.* 135).

senatum aut populum: the juxtaposition of the two entities with *aut* (rather than *senatus populusque Romanus*) presents them as two separate and independently acting bodies, indicating that no action was taken in relation to either of them (on the wording, see Mommsen, *StR* III 1257–8 n. 4).

2.2. Details of Cicero's recall (11–17)

In the second part (Cic. *RQ* 11–17) of the main section (Cic. *RQ* 6–17) Cicero continues to give a self-centred review of the political events of the recent past (cf. Cic. *RQ* 7–11), providing details on his recall and mentioning both support and opposition. Leading on from the point at the end of the preceding section that ex-consuls of the past were not recalled by the intervention of the Senate or the People prompted by the consuls (Cic. *RQ* 11), Cicero turns to outlining the consuls' activities in his case (Cic. *RQ* 11–12): while the consuls of 58 BCE were passive, the consuls of 57 BCE became active on Cicero's behalf directly upon entering office. To explain why these initiatives were not immediately successful, Cicero adds a sketch of the views and actions of opponents, including a flashback to the time when he left Rome (Cic. *RQ* 13–14): this part serves to stress his avoidance of violence and his close connection with the Republic. Afterwards Cicero continues to talk about supporters, starting again from the consuls and then adding other senators and the general population (Cic. *RQ* 15–17). With the opposition dealt with in the middle (as in the speech in the Senate), and in a way that highlights Cicero's positive characteristics, the impression conveyed is that Cicero enjoys widespread support, he has done great deeds for the Republic, his fate is closely linked to that of the Republic, and his return will contribute to everyone's welfare. While Cicero reports activities in the Senate, he makes sure to stress their positive effects for the People and their contribution.

2.2.1. Initiatives of new consuls of 57 BCE (11–12)

Following on from the statement that, in contrast to ex-consuls of the past, Cicero was recalled by the Senate and the People (Cic. *RQ* 7–11), this subsection (Cic. *RQ* 11–12) proceeds to provide details of the process, starting with the crucial developments in January 57 BCE (cf. Cic. *RS* 5; 8–9): after new consuls had come into office, especially P. Cornelius Lentulus Spinther, there were renewed and energetic attempts to recall Cicero. They were not immediately successful because of the opposition of a Tribune of the People, but Cicero stresses that, as a result, the attitude of the Senate became clear and the issue was referred to the People for a vote, as he makes sure to keep the audience involved.

11 at pro me: Cicero contrasts (*at*) the lack of consular interventions for the earlier ex-consuls (Cic. *RQ* 11) with the activities of the consuls for him (*pro me*). This juxtaposition provides a transition to a review of the events eventually leading to his recall.

superiores: i.e. the consuls of the previous year (58 BCE; see Cic. *RS* 29 n.), L. Calpurnius Piso Caesoninus and A. Gabinius.

ut referrent flagitati sunt: a passive version of *flagitare* combined with the person addressed in the accusative (in the active) and the thing asked for expressed by a subordinate clause (K.-St. I 300; *OLD* s.v. *flagito* 2b '(w. acc. of person foll. by *ut*)'). – On *referre* as a technical term, see Cic. *RS* 3 n. – The emphasis on constant (*semper*) initiatives to get Cicero's case resolved implies that, if the consuls had behaved differently, he would have been recalled in the preceding year.

gratiae causa: ironically gives a potential (respectable) reason for the consuls' reluctance detailed in the subsequent subordinate clause (*OLD* s.v. *gratia* 3). The true reason in Cicero's view follows in the next sentence. – Such personal considerations are not mentioned in the speech in the Senate (Mack 1937, 33–4; Boll 2019, 49).

alter: i.e. L. Calpurnius Piso Caesoninus (Cic. *RS* 4 n.).

adfinis: the consul L. Calpurnius Piso Caesoninus was a distant relation of Cicero's son-in-law; Cicero highlights this connection for the sake of the argument (Cic. *RS* 15 n.).

alterius: i.e. A. Gabinius (Cic. *RS* 4 n.).

causam capitis: Cicero ironically claims that Gabinius might be concerned about being seen to be obliged to him after Cicero defended him on a capital charge (referring to life and death or citizen rights). – *TLRR* lists a trial as 'uncertain' on the basis of this passage (*TLRR* 380); there is no other extant evidence. Therefore, Markland (1745, 273–6) assumes that the author of this (in his view, spurious) speech made an error concerning the dates (see Introduction, section 3.1). Guerriero (1936) highlights the oddity that there is no other reference to such a trial and concludes that, in combination with the fact that this speech is not mentioned in the letter to Atticus about Cicero's activities in the days after his return (Cic. *Att.* 4.1), these points again raise doubts concerning the oration's authenticity. Gruen (1974, 527) regards the comment as a 'red herring', pointing out that it is the only reference to such a trial and there is no other evidence for a trial of Gabinius prior to 57 BCE; he agrees with the possibility raised by Guerriero that the passage might be a later insertion. On that assumption the entire sentence *sed veriti… receperam* would have to be deleted; this would remove the explicit expression of a contrast and a poignant ironic comment. Thus, it is more likely that the text is genuine and refers to a case about which nothing else is known; if it was an obscure case, the irony of the remark would be even sharper. – In 54 BCE (after the date of this speech) Gabinius was prosecuted under *Lex Cornelia de maiestate,* when Cicero appeared as a witness (*TLRR* 296), and under *Lex Iulia de repetundis,* when he was defended by Cicero (*TLRR* 303; see Crawford 1984, 188–97, nos. 64 and 65).

provinciarum foedere inretiti: an allusion to the law put forward by P. Clodius Pulcher that assigned the provinces of Macedonia and Syria (originally Cilicia) to the consuls L. Calpurnius Piso Caesoninus Piso and A. Gabinius (Cic. *RS* 4 n.). Their conduct in this matter is characterized negatively by means of a metaphor describing them as entangled in a pact. – The transmission of the verb (*OLD* s.v. *irretio* b) is corrupt: this is not surprising for a less common verb used in an unusual metaphor. Cratander's restoration is plausible and stays close to the transmitted text.

totum illum annum: i.e. the year of their consulship, 58 BCE. – Whether the grief of the Senate, the *boni,* and Italy refers to the laws concerning Cicero and his withdrawal from Rome is not said explicitly, and that it lasted for the entire year (or rather the rest of the year from Cicero's departure onwards) may be an exaggeration. What Cicero wishes to emphasize is that these (bribed) consuls did not change their mind and retained their hostile and unsympathetic view until the end of the year despite the public pressure from various groups.

querelas senatus, luctum bonorum, Italiae gemitum: an asyndetic tricolon with three different words for grief applied to three different entities: it illustrates that the main political body, the right-minded people (*boni* again in a political sense: Cic. *RS* 12 n.), and the entire country felt aggrieved and thus indicates the extent of the feeling. – The word applied to the Senate most obviously denotes voicing grief, as the consuls would be most likely to hear protests from this body.

pertulerunt: this verb (*OLD* s.v. *perfero* 8) gives an ironic aspect to the consuls' inaction by suggesting that they had to 'endure' the demonstration of grief.

Kalendis… Ianuariis: i.e. 1 January 57 BCE, when the new consuls P. Cornelius Lentulus Spinther and Q. Caecilius Metellus Nepos (Cic. *RS* 5 n.) came into office.

orba res publica: a metaphorical description of the loss of proper guardians for the Republic. According to Cicero such a situation applies to 58 BCE, when the consuls did not act as their office required (Cic. *RS* 4 and n.).

consulis fidem tamquam legitimi tutoris: the Republic, having been bereft of guardians in 58 BCE, as Cicero claims, turns to the new consul at the start of the new year, hoping that he would again fulfil such a role. The addition of *legitimi* indicates the official position of such a person and the associated duties (*OLD* s.v. *legitimus* 2).

P. Lentulus consul: the focus is initially on P. Cornelius Lentulus Spinther (rather than on both consuls) because he is Cicero's key advocate and not a former enemy (Cic. *RS* 5 n.). – That Lentulus is said to have put forward the motions on 1 January 57 BCE suggests that he was the leading consul in that month (Cic. *RS* 26 n.). – On the activities on 1 January 57 BCE, see Cic. *Dom.* 68–9; *Pis.* 34; *Sest.* 72.

parens, deus, salus nostrae vitae, fortunae, memoriae, nominis: as in the Senate speech, the emphatic description of the salutary role of Lentulus (with asyndetic sequences) shows his enormous effect on Cicero's well-being (Cic. *RS* 8 [and n.]). In comparison with the Senate speech, the addition of *salus* (*OLD* s.v. *salus* 6) governing the genitives makes the expression less bold.

de sollemni deorum religione: religious matters dealt with at the start of year include determining the date of the Latin Festival (*Feriae Latinae*) on Mount Alba, as its date changed from year to year and was fixed each year by the consuls upon entering office (e.g. Cic. *Fam.* 8.6.3 [Feb. 50 BCE]). Senate decrees referring to these matters could be characterized as *sollemnia* (Liv. 9.8.1). – The combination of *sollemnis* and *religio* (without *deorum*) only occurs once elsewhere in Cicero's speeches (Cic. *Mil.* 73: *eum cuius supplicio senatus sollemnis religiones expiandas saepe censuit*). – Luterbacher (1912, 347) suggests reading *deum* to avoid the sequence *-rum re*, but this is not a sufficient reason to change the text.

nihil humanarum rerum … prius: at the first meeting of the Senate chaired by the new consuls on 1 January political issues would only be taken up after religious matters had been dealt with (Mommsen, *StR* I 617; III 941; see, e.g., Gell. *NA* 14.7.9; Liv. 6.1.9; 22.9.7; 22.11.1; 37.1.1). – Cicero's claims that the consul felt that Cicero's situation should be the first issue relating to human affairs to be dealt with shows the importance attached to this issue (Cic. *RS* 8).

agendum: a *terminus technicus* for transacting business in the Senate (*OLD* s.v. *ago* 38); in this sense the verb can be construed both with an accusative object in the active voice, turning into a subject in the passive voice, and with a prepositional phrase introduced by *de*, the latter used especially with reference to people (e.g. Liv. 37.1.1).

12 eo die: i.e. on 1 January 57 BCE.

tribunus plebis: the Tribune of the People is not named (Cic. *RS* 3 n.); the parallel report in Cicero's *Pro Sestio* shows that he is Sex. Atilius Serranus (Gavianus) (Cic. *RS* 5 n.), who asked for an adjournment at this Senate meeting. Thus, by making use of the Tribunes' right to intercede against Senate decrees (see Cic. *RS* 3 n.; on this case, see De Libero 1992, 34), though not directly, he prevented a decree in Cicero's favour (Cic. *Sest.* 74). Soon after the Tribunes of the People for 57 BCE had come into office on 10 December 58 BCE, Atilius had withdrawn his name from an initial joint proposal of the Tribunes of the People in Cicero's favour as a result of bribery (Cic. *Sest.* 72; for criticism of the Tribune's behaviour, see Cic. *Sest.* 94; *Pis.* 35; Ascon. ad Cic. *Pis.* 35 [p. 11.15–18 C.]; Schol. Bob. ad Cic. *Mil.* 39 [p. 122.29–30 Stangl]; on Atilius being controlled by Clodius, see Kunkel/Wittmann 1995, 661–2). Atilius tried to employ the same method of asking for an adjournment at a meeting of 1 October 57 BCE dealing with Cicero's house (Cic. *Att.* 4.2.4). This time the Senate decree was passed on the following day (Cic. *Att.* 4.2.5). – The description 'Gavianus' only occurs in one passage in *Pro Sestio* (Cic. *Sest.* 74). Kaster (2006, 280, on Cic. *Sest.* 72) points out that there 'it is surely meant insultingly', continuing the mockery of the man's adoption from the family of the Gavii into that of the Atilii (Cic. *Sest.* 72); thus, it is uncertain whether this element was an official part of the name.

quem . . . ornaram: elsewhere Cicero speaks of the close, almost familial relationship between quaestors and their superiors (Cic. *RS* 35 n.); whether, beyond that, Cicero, as consul in 63 BCE, organized any particular benefits for Atilius is not known. The fact that Cicero mentions this aspect insinuates that Atilius should have acted gratefully in return.

et cunctus ordo et multi . . . summi viri: *multi . . . summi viri* are part of *cunctus ordo* (the Senate); they are mentioned separately to indicate that the initiative was not only carried by everyone, but even supported by many of the most senior senators (in the *et . . . et* construction the second item is an intensification of the first; K.-St. II 34). The intervention of the senators is described dramatically in *Pro Sestio* (Cic. *Sest.* 74: *clamor senatus, querelae, preces*). – *multi* qualifies *summi viri*, while the numeral and the adjective are not linked by a conjunction, perhaps because of the word order with hyperbaton (K.-St. I 240–1).

Cn. Oppius: Cn. Oppius Cornicinus (*RE* Oppius 28; see Nicholson 1992, 77), a senator in 57 BCE (*MRR* II 494) and Atilius' father-in-law, entreated him to change his mind on both occasions of his opposition in the Senate (Cic. *Sest.* 74; *Att.* 4.2.4).

ad pedes flens iaceret: a dramatic description of Oppius' intervention (cf. similarly Cic. *Sest.* 74; *Att.* 4.2.4). – Such a scene, not mentioned in the speech given in the Senate (Lintott 2008, 10), can be exploited for emotional effect (see also Mack 1937, 36).

noctem: the sentence as transmitted in the majority of manuscripts (*noctemque*) is ungrammatical. This is why A. Klotz (1915, ed.; 1919; followed by Shackleton Bailey 1991, 228 and Maslowski 1981) posits a *lacuna* (Klotz: e.g. <*respondere dubitasset*>) before *noctemque*. An easier correction is Courtney's suggestion (1989, 49) that the reading *noctem* in one manuscript should be selected. While Courtney notes that Maslowski (1980, 411–12) points out correctly that the omission is due to the rearrangement of part of this sentence in that manuscript, his suggestion remains the easiest resolution to what seems to be scribal confusion. No logical element is missing, and the description in *Pro Sestio* (Cic. *Sest.* 74) does not have any additional points.

{**deliberatio**}: picks up *ad deliberandum*; the addition of a noun makes the structure clearer and the irony more emphatic. Shackleton Bailey (1985, 142; 1991, 228) suggests deleting this word and (1985, 142) notes his 'misgivings about a deliberation spent in repaying or enlarging a bribe'; besides, the collocation *deliberationem consumere* seems not to be attested elsewhere. Thus, it looks as if the noun has entered the text in an attempt at clarification (maybe influenced by the report at Cic. *Sest.* 74) and should be deleted (*quae* before {*deliberatio*} then refers to *noctem*)

non in reddenda … sed … in augenda mercede: according to Cicero's report some believed that the Tribune of the People might use the night to return the money by which he had been bribed, so as to be free to vote in favour of Cicero on the following day; instead, it turned out that the time was used to increase the reward for his opposition. Here Cicero leaves it open by how much the reward was increased; in *Pro Sestio* he asserts that it was doubled (Cic. *Sest.* 74).

ut patefactum est: i.e. what the Tribune of the People did during the night became clear or could be inferred afterwards, when he still did not support Cicero. Presumably he then vetoed the decree outright (Kunkel/Wittmann 1995, 606; Kaster 2006, 285, on Cic. *Sest.* 74). – The transitive verb *patefacere* is used absolutely here (Lebreton 1901, 162).

postea: i.e. after the meeting of the Senate in early January 57 BCE.

res acta est in senatu alia nulla, cum variis rationibus impediretur: as becomes clear from the more specific description of the situation of the Senate in *Pro Sestio* (Cic. *Sest.* 74–5: *consecuti dies pauci omnino Ianuario mense per quos senatum haberi liceret; sed tamen actum nihil nisi de me. cum omni mora, ludificatione, calumnia senatus auctoritas impediretur, venit tandem concilio de me agendi dies, viii Kal. Febr. princeps rogationis, vir mihi amicissimus, Q. Fabricius, templum aliquanto ante lucem occupavit.*), Cicero claims that at its meetings the Senate dealt with no other matter than Cicero's case despite the fact that its deliberations were obstructed. The *cum*-clause (*cum causale* according to Masoero 1905, 24) illustrates why the Senate was limited in what it could achieve in this period.

<s>ed: this sentence does not provide an addition, but rather a contrast to the preceding point; therefore, Halm's emendation of the transmitted text (*et*) is the best option (accepted in Maslowski 1981). Peterson (1911) opts for the asyndeton of the later manuscripts: this gives the same sense, but fails to explain how *et* entered the text.

voluntate … perspecta senatus: while it was not possible to pass a Senate decree in Cicero's favour at the meeting at the beginning of January 57 BCE, the fact that it had been proposed, discussed. and almost voted through and that Cicero's fate continued to be a concern demonstrated the Senate's supportive attitude towards Cicero. The expression *voluntas senatus* is rare in Cicero's speeches (Cic. *Verr.* 2.2.95; *Sest.* 87; on this term, see Bonnefound-Coudry 1989, 683). – Transmitted *perfecta* is generally changed to *perspecta*, following

Angelius, as the collocation *voluntatem perficere* is not attested in classical Latin.

tamen: highlights that despite the obstructions to the workings of the Senate and its inability to make decisions, its views had become obvious.

causa ad vos...deferebatur: while the Senate's activities were stalled, an attempt was made to make progress with Cicero's case by presenting it to the People: on 23 January 57 BCE the Tribune of the People Q. Fabricius (*RE* Fabricius 7; *MRR* II 202), together with colleagues, proposed Cicero's recall to an assembly of the People (*vos*); the attempt was obstructed by P. Clodius Pulcher's gangs (Cic. *RS* 6; 22 nn.).

deferebatur: the transfer of the matter to the People is expressed by a non-technical term (*OLD* s.v. *defero* 10).

2.2.2. Activities of opponents and their consequences (13–14)

This subsection (Cic. *RQ* 13–14) outlines how Cicero's opponents reacted in light of renewed initiatives for Cicero's recall from magistrates and in the Senate (Cic. *RQ* 11–12) and how Cicero's decision to leave Rome contrasts with their behaviour and the underlying attitude. While the description of the opponents' actions mainly refers to January 57 BCE (cf. Cic *RS* 6–7), the subsection includes a flashback to the time of Cicero's departure (cf. Cic. *RS* 32–4): Cicero claims that, when he saw an armed conflict being prepared and the Republic no longer functioning, he did not wish to trigger fighting on account of his well-being and therefore withdrew, while he was ready to return along with the Republic when it was restored. The passage thus elaborates on Cicero's self-sacrifice for the Republic (suppressing any potential personal reasons) and on his superiority to his opponents; his close connection with the Republic justifies his recall and the audience's involvement. In presenting the justification in a comparison with his enemies, Cicero can highlight his attitude by contrast, even though the discussion thus is not entirely coherent in logical and chronological terms, as details from 58 and 57 BCE are merged (Mack 1937, 37–40 and note on Cic. *RS* 32–5).

13 hic tantum interfuit: this summarizing sentence provides a transition to the juxtaposition of the opponent's activities to prevent Cicero's recall and his behaviour when leaving Rome the previous year (cf. Cic. *RS* 6). *at inimici mei* at the start of the next paragraph (Cic. *RQ* 14) marks the return to the discussion of the events in January 57 BCE and continues the point preceding the comparison that the decision on Cicero's fate was transferred to the People (Cic. *RQ* 12).

ego: introduces the first half of the comparison of *inter me et inimicos meos*, continued by the contrast *at inimici mei* (Cic. *RQ* 14).

cum...perirent: before the main clause introduced by fronted and high-lighted *ego* is continued, the dangerous situation of the Republic is described by nine inserted asyndetic *cum*-clauses. Such a structure (cf. Cic. *RQ* 14) creates dramatic suspense, which reaches its climax in the revelation of Cicero's selfless decision at the end of the long sentence. – The *cum*-clauses seem to be envisaged as grammatically parallel, although they are not entirely parallel in presentation, as some describe Cicero's perception of the situation with verbs in the first person and others sketch activities in the third person, though with vocabulary determined by Cicero's assessment. Therefore, it might be better to interpret *cum* vaguely as temporal-causal rather than as straightforwardly concessive (thus Masoero 1905, 24).

cum ... vidissem: on the recruitment of fighters, see Cic. *RS* 33 and n. – The term *homines* (rather than *servi*) is more open and thus more appropriate before the People.

in tribunali Aurelio: the *tribunal Aurelium* (named after an Aurelius) only appears here and in three other passages about the same process of recruitment by P. Clodius Pulcher (Cic. *Sest.* 34; *Dom.* 54; *Pis.* 11). In two other passages Cicero refers to *gradus Aurelii* (Cic. *Clu.* 93; *Flacc.* 66), which might be connected. There are no mentions of this tribunal after Cicero; presumably it fell out of use or was removed. A tribunal is usually a wooden platform (though this one might have been made of stone) in the Forum used for magisterial functions. The location of the *tribunal Aurelium* and details about this structure are unknown (*LTUR* V 86–7).

conscribi centuriarique: the doublet (in contrast to Cic. *RS* 33) makes the process seem even more like proper military recruitment.

veteres ad spem caedis Catilinae copias esse revocatas: the recall of Catiline's forces corresponds to another item in the equivalent description in the Senate speech (Cic. *RS* 33 [and n.]). Here, however, it is toned down: there is no mention of 'all' the troops, of the leaders, or of arson.

cum viderem ... salutis meae: alludes to people from Cicero's own 'party', which must include his peers in the Senate and perhaps especially other ex-consuls: Cicero insinuates that these people, from whom one might have expected support, abandoned him or worked actively against him for personal reasons (Cic. *RS* 23 n.; on *invidia* as a motivation, see Cic. *RQ* 21). The two types of reaction correspond to the two reasons given in the two *quod*-clauses. In either case, these people are presented as weak, egoistic, and disloyal (cf. Cic. *Q Fr.* 1.4.1).

ex ea parte ... cuius partis: the term *pars* indicates a group of people with similar views, not a 'political party' in the narrow sense. – The word governing the relative clause is repeated in the relative clause (K.-St. II 283–4).

numerabamur: Cicero does not claim that he was the leader or the most enthusiastic member of this 'party', only that he was regarded as such (*OLD* s.v. *numero*[1] 8).

duo consules: i.e. L. Calpurnius Piso Caesoninus and A. Gabinius, the consuls of 58 BCE (Cic. *RS* 4 n.).

empti pactione provinciarum: Cicero claims elsewhere in this pair of speeches given after his return that the assignment of provinces to the consuls was a bribe and they 'sold' his well-being and the welfare of the Republic in return for lucrative provinces (Cic. *RS* 3; 10; *RQ* 21); here the emphasis is on their weak and egoistic behaviour when they are said to have been 'bought' by the pact on the provinces (on the arrangements for the provinces of these consuls, see Cic. *RS* 4 n.).

auctores: this addition (as a predicative expression) implies that the consuls did not just tolerate the activities of the *inimici*, but actively supported them (*OLD* s.v. *auctor* 5).

inimicis rei publicae: presumably refers to P. Clodius Pulcher and his followers and denotes the same people as *domesticis hostibus* in the next clause. The perspective activated thereby elevates the conflict involving Cicero from a personal one to a matter affecting the Republic and makes the behaviour of the consuls appear outrageous if, for personal reasons, they hand themselves over to the power of people opposing the very institution they are tasked with looking after.

egestatem, avaritiam, libidines suas: this tricolon identifies the (negative and egoistic) motivations for the consuls' collusion with Cicero's opponents (in Cicero's view). The first two items refer to their need and desire for money: first, as a description of their poverty and financial need, and, then, as a characteristic of theirs. The third item extends the focus and claims unspecifically that they thereby intend to satisfy their lusts (Cic. *RS* 10; 11; 14–15 [and nn.]; *Sest.* 18; *Pis.* 12–13; 86).

<me>: the addition of an object (Naugerius) is necessary, as it cannot be inferred from the context.

constrictum...dedissent: indicates metaphorically the removal of opportunities for any initiatives on the part of Cicero and the lack of attempts by the consuls to confront his enemies (Cic. *RS* 17 n.).

domesticis hostibus: the term appears in the singular for Clodius in the speech in the Senate (Cic. *RS* 19 and n.). The plural makes the comment more open, but presumably focuses again mainly on Clodius.

cum...vetarentur: the Senate and the knights put on mourning clothes on Cicero's behalf; this move was opposed by the consuls of 58 BCE (Cic. *RS* 12 n.). – In the speech to the People the detail is added that the senators and knights aim to plead with the People in mourning dress: thus, their action is linked to the audience, and the opposition of the consuls indirectly affects them too.

edictis atque imperiis: this collocation also appears in the speech to the Senate, where the consul L. Calpurnius Piso Caesoninus is identified as responsible for these interdictions (Cic. *RS* 16 [and n.]). In this speech, which lacks the invective dimenson (Cic. *RS* 10–18), agents responsible for the ban on wearing mourning clothes are not given.

cum ... sancirentur: alleges that not only arrangements about the provinces, but also other treaties were confirmed on the basis of Cicero's removal. The repetition *omnium ... omnia ... omnibus* implies that everything was affected. While the arrangements cannot literally have been confirmed 'by Cicero's blood', the phrase illustrates emphatically the political trafficking; it also insinuates a fight affecting life or death, which provides a transition to the theme of the following clause.

reconciliationes gratiarum: the reading in the main manuscripts (*reconciliatione*) gives a harsh second ablative in addition to *sanguine meo*, and the reading in others (*reconciliationes*) results in a third nominative after *pactiones* and *foedera*, without another repetition of *cum* or a copulative conjunction. Therefore, emendation seems advisable; a number of suggestions have been made (e.g. Mommsen [ap. Halm 1856, 853]: <de> *reconciliatione*; Maslowski 1980, 412–13: <in> *reconciliatione* [approved by Lebek 1984, 6–7], referring to Cic. *Pis.* 28). Keeping *reconciliationes* in the plural to match *gratiarum* seems preferable, and a prepositional phrase in between two other ablative phrases would be awkward. Thus, inserting the conjunction *ac*, which could easily have been omitted after *foedera*, gives a smoother enumerative sequence (R. Klotz; Madvig 1884, 138). Repeated *cum* then separates treaties on provinces from any other arrangements. *reconciliationes gratiarum* describes the restoration of goodwill.

cum omnes boni ... perirent: while in the Senate speech Cicero envisages that many *boni* might die with him if he entered an armed fight against his opponents (Cic. *RS* 33), he says here that all *boni* were prepared to die with or for Cicero. This statement enhances the potential support for Cicero in terms of numbers and readiness for personal sacrifice on his behalf and makes his decision not to opt for armed conflict appear even more selfless and full of concern for the community.

armis decertare pro mea salute nolui: Cicero ends the section on himself with the emphatic statement that, in contrast to the violence planned or carried out by his opponents, he decided not to raise arms, thereby avoiding trouble for the Republic (see Introduction, sections 2 and 3.4). As he has just stated that the magistrates at the time neglected their care for the Republic (Cic. *RQ* 11; 13), he creates another contrast and presents himself as the true guardian of the Republic. The result of both winning and losing (each involving numerous victims) is briefly described as grievous for the Republic, whereas the Senate speech has a distinction between the two options (Cic. *RS* 33).

14 at inimici mei: adds the second part of the contrast announced by *tantum interfuit inter me et inimicos meos* after the description of the situation applying to *ego* (Cic. *RQ* 13).

mense Ianuario cum de me ageretur: Cicero's case was first discussed in the Senate on 1 January 57 BCE; on 23 January 57 BCE the Tribune of the

People Q. Fabricius, together with colleagues, was about to propose Cicero's recall to an assembly of the People when the attempt was obstructed by P. Clodius Pulcher's gangs with violence (see Cic. *RS* 6; 22; *RQ* 12 nn.; Introduction, section 2).

corporibus civium trucidatis flumine sanguinis meum reditum intercludendum: this vivid image is an intensification of the corresponding passage in the Senate speech (Cic. *RS* 6). Shackleton Bailey (1985, 142) suggests adding <*et*> between the two ablatives, as he regards them as coordinate; this is not necessary when they are seen to fulfil different functions: *corporibus civium trucidatis* is an ablative absolute, and the action described creates the precondition; *flumine sanguinis* is an ablative of instrument with *intercludendum*.

itaque: introduces the consequences from the political situation described, namely that no proper 'Republic' existed in Rome. As a result (*ut*), the need arose to restore both Cicero and the Republic. Cicero thereby develops the frequent theme of the identity of or a close relationship between himself and the Republic (see Introduction, section 3.4). Here he introduces it as the view of the audience, which creates a contrast between the opinions of the audience, regarded as his supporters (*putaretis*), and his opponents (*putaverunt*).

dum...absum...habuistis: a *dum*-clause with present indicative usually describes an ongoing situation during which an action described in the main clause happens (K.-St. II 374–5; Pinkster 2015, 615–16). Here, while Cicero's absence and the bad state of the Republic are contemporaneous, the realization that action is needed happens at a point in time during Cicero's absence.

eam rem publicam habuistis ut: during Cicero's absence a *res publica* both existed and had to be restored. This is not a contradiction because of the qualifications: the *res publica* that continued to exist was not a proper one and of such a kind (*eam*) that people felt that both Cicero and the (true) *res publica* needed to be restored.

ego autem...putavi: Cicero contrasts what has just been attributed to the audience with his own view, a stronger version of their position, and combines this juxtaposition with a detailed description: while the audience is said to have believed that the true *res publica* needed to be restored while a semblance of it remained, Cicero claims that the situation equalled the complete absence of a *res publica*. – Grammatically (as in Cic. *RQ* 13), *ego* (fronted to emphasize the contrast and the transition to a different agent) looks forward to the main verb and the rest of the main clause at the end of the sentence; sandwiched in between are a multipart relative clause and a multipart *cum*-clause: the relative clause provides generic and abstract sketches; the *cum*-clause gives illustrative examples.

in qua civitate: the word governing the relative clause is included in the relative clause: i.e. the phrase is short for *in ea civitate in qua* (K.-St. II 309–11).

nihil valeret senatus: in 58 BCE the consuls did not respect the Senate appropriately in Cicero's view (Cic. *RS* 4; 12 n.).

omnis esset impunitas, nulla iudicia, vis et ferrum in foro versaretur: the suspension of proper legal proceedings is also mentioned in the Senate speech, but in less vivid form (Cic. *RS* 6; 34 and nn.). – Grammatically, *essent* (plural) has to be supplied to *nulla iudicia*; the third phrase has a different verb. This verb is in the singular, agreeing with the nearest noun (Lebreton 1901, 6–7), while the phrase *vis et ferrum* could also be regarded as a single entity (K.-St. I 49; Pinkster 2015, 1254–5).

cum privati … tuerentur: Cicero makes the same comment with reference to Cn. Pompeius Magnus in the speech in the Senate (Cic. *RS* 4 [and n.]). In this oration the situation is assigned to unspecific plural *privati*: such a description applies to Pompey, who was without an office at the time. The plural is probably rhetorical, and only Pompey is meant. The generic phrasing is perhaps chosen so as not to affect Pompey's popularity with the People by attributing behaviour to him that could be regarded as unheroic.

<se>: in the speech in the Senate the object of *tueri* is *vitam suam*. Here, without any addition, there would not be any object; the loss of *se* is more likely than that of a longer phrase. The original position of the lost object cannot be determined with certainty. Halm's placing is generally adopted.

tribuni plebis … vulnerarentur: although the expression is in the plural (in line with the generic phrasing in the previous phrase), the reference must be to P. Sestius, a Tribune of the People in 57 BCE, almost killed in the tumults in early 57 BCE (Cic. *RS* 7 n.).

vobis inspectantibus: emphasizes that the terrible events happened in full view of the Roman People: such an appeal to the role of the audience as eyewitnesses confirms that these events happened, as they took place while Cicero was away, and highlights the shamelessness of the perpetrators. When describing the same situation in similar terms to the Senate, Cicero also stresses the fact that the audience will have seen these events (Cic. *RS* 7).

ad … iretur: for attacks on houses of magistrates, see Cic. *RS* 7 n.

consulis fasces frangerentur: for possible identifications of this incident, see Cic. *RS* 7 n.

templa incenderentur: on this incident (again with a rhetorical plural), see Cic. *RS* 7 n.

rem publicam esse nullam: gives the conclusion from the preceding description: because of these circumstances there was no proper *res publica* in Cicero's view, i.e. an appropriately functioning political system.

neque … reduceret: as a consequence (*itaque*) of the description of the political situation Cicero states emphatically that his location should match that of the Republic (another identification of Cicero and the Republic: see Introduction, section 3.4) and that therefore he could not stay after the Republic had been removed and that he would return once it had been re-established (Cic. *RS* 34 and n.). In contrast to the speech in the Senate Cicero does not claim that the Republic brought him back with itself, but rather presents this scenario as an expectation for the future at the time of his departure. Such an expression makes the assertion less bold. The metaphor is slightly more complex than that in the speech in the Senate: there the Republic is expelled and then returns; here the Republic is expelled, then restored, and leads Cicero back with itself. The latter seems to be a mixture of the absence of an untouched Republic and a reduction of its functions *in situ*, with the consequent restoration.

reduceret: an imperfect subjunctive replaces a (periphrastic) future in this subordinate clause (K.-St. II 180; Lebreton 1901, 191; see Masoero 1905, 26).

2.2.3. Support from senators and the population (15–17)

After the comparison of the attitude and behaviour of Cicero and those of his opponents and a description of the consequences for the *res publica* of the activities of the latter during his absence (Cic. *RQ* 13–14), in this subsection (Cic. *RQ* 15–17) Cicero returns to activities in support of him (Cic. *RQ* 11–12). He highlights again the initiatives of the consul P. Cornelius Lentulus Spinther and then widens the focus to include other men active on his behalf. Some of these are mentioned by name: T. Annius Milo, P. Sestius (Cic. *RQ* 15), Cn. Pompeius Magnus (Cic. *RQ* 16), P. Servilius Vatia Isauricus, and L. Gellius (Cic. *RQ* 17). L. Gellius is an addition in comparison with the speech given in the Senate (MacKendrick 1995, 138; Lintott 2008, 10); the other men are also mentioned in the section on supporters there (Cic. *RS* 18–31). The corresponding passage here is shorter, and fewer individuals are singled out by name: with all the supporters being senators, it is probably more important to name them in the speech in the Senate. Accordingly, the emphasis here is on the People, the municipal towns, and colonies, as well as all of Italy, and on the fact that some of these senators gave speeches about Cicero before the People, which shows that the senators were not isolated in their opinion, but demonstrated an attitude shared by all. Cicero indirectly reminds the audience that he preserved the Republic when consul and that the People have now put him back in this position, which implies both that they have done the right thing and that Cicero will continue to work for their welfare.

15 an ego ... dubitarem: again fronted *ego* followed by descriptive subordinate clauses and the main clause towards the end of the sentence (Cic. *RS* 32; *RQ* 13; 14). As in the previous sentence (Cic. *RQ* 14), Cicero does not present the situation as realized from the perspective of the current year 57 BCE, but as a certainty to be expected from the perspective of 58 BCE. The rhetorical question is chosen for the sake of variation and amounts to a statement (again based on a lack of doubt). – Letters written to friends and family from exile in 58 BCE do not display the same confidence, but rather show worry and despair as well as appeals for further support (e.g. Cic. *Att.* 3.12 [17 July 58 BCE]; 3.22 [27 Nov. 58 BCE]), though Cicero expresses some hope after the election of the magistrates for 57 BCE (*Q Fr.* 1.4.3 [Aug. 58 BCE]).

P. Lentulum: P. Cornelius Lentulus Spinther, one of the consuls of 57 BCE (Cic. *RS* 5 n.).

proximo anno: i.e. 57 BCE, in a narrative referring to 58 BCE, when Cicero left Rome and was away from the city.

qui...fuisset: the subjunctive in the relative clause indicates a causal connotation (K.-St. II 292–4).

illis ipsis rei publicae periculosissmis temporibus: Lentulus was a curule aedile in 63 BCE (*MRR* II 167), when Cicero was consul and confronted with the Catilinarian Conspiracy (Sall. *Cat.* 47.4). – The difficult situation in 63 BCE is indicated by a vague allusion avoiding the mention of any details.

aedilis curulis: on the role of curule aediles, see Kunkel/Wittmann 1995, 477–81.

me consule...meorum: the ablative absolute refers to a person also mentioned elsewhere in the clause; this is an easier construction than attaching a participial construction to a possessive pronoun in the genitive (K.-St. I 787).

omnium...socius: Cicero claims that Lentulus, as curule aedile in 63 BCE, was on his side in the fight against Catiline and thus shared all his plans as well as the dangers incurred on that account. Cicero thus indicates a long-standing association between the two men, without providing a detailed exposition. Apart from the fact that one of the captured conspirators was entrusted to his custody (Sall. *Cat.* 47.4), there does not seem to be any other evidence on particular activities of Lentulus in connection with the Catilinarian Conspiracy.

is: the consul P. Cornelius Lentulus Spinther.

consularibus vulneribus consulari medicina: Cicero employs the same medical metaphor in the speech in the Senate (Cic. *RS* 9) to indicate how the wound inflicted upon him by the consuls of 58 BCE (by not opposing the Tribune of the People P. Clodius Pulcher) was healed by the consuls of 57 BCE, when he was recalled.

hoc duce: again the consul P. Cornelius Lentulus Spinther.

collega...eius: the other consul of 57 BCE, Q. Caecilius Metellus Nepos (Cic. *RS* 5 n.). His support for Cicero is appreciated, but described in more subdued terms, since he used to be an enemy of Cicero and only later became active on his behalf (Cic. *RS* 25; 26 nn.).

clementissimo atque optimo viro: for this characterization of Metellus, see Cic. *RQ* 10 n.

primo non adversante, post etiam adiuvante: again without identifying specific occasions (see Introduction, section 2), Cicero indicates that, when Metellus entered office on 1 January 57 BCE, he dropped his hostility, did not obstruct the activities of Lentulus, and later even supported them (Cic. *Sest.* 72), when he was involved in the bill for Cicero's recall (Cic. *RS* 26 and n.).

reliqui magistratus paene omnes: of the other magistrates in office in 57 BCE all supported Cicero except for the praetor Ap. Claudius Pulcher and the

Tribunes of the People Sex. Atilius Serranus (Gavianus) and Q. Numerius Rufus (Cic. *RS* 5 n.).

excellenti animo…divino studio exstiterunt: this clause includes two groups of ablatives without prepositions: the first group (*excellenti animo… copiis*) provides the basis for the praise bestowed, and the second group (*praestanti…studio*) denotes the attitude by which the men excelled. – The men are singled out for their outstanding initiatives on behalf of Cicero (cf. Cic. *RS* 19 on Milo, 20 on Sestius, 30 on both).

excellenti animo, virtute, auctoritate, praesidio, copiis: this series of five asyndetic ablatives indicates how Milo and Sestius provided outstanding support to Cicero. The first two describe their character, and the last two denote the features at their disposal to deploy for Cicero's benefit; the item in the middle is transitional, referring to their standing enabling them to command such resources.

T. Annius: T. Annius Milo (Papianus), a Tribune of the People in 57 BCE (Cic. *RS* 19 n.).

P. Sestius: P. Sestius, a Tribune of the People in 57 BCE (Cic. *RS* 7; 20 nn.).

eodemque…commendavit: after the digression on Milo and Sestius as examples of other magistrates taking action for him, Cicero moves on to the crucial official step of the Senate decree on Lentulus' initiative (Cic. *RS* 26; *RQ* 10).

eodemque P. Lentulo auctore et pariter referente collega: in July 57 BCE the consuls put forward a proposal for a Senate decree on Cicero's recall (for details and their respective roles, see Cic. *RS* 26 n.).

frequentissimus senatus: on the implications of this phrase, see Cic. *RS* 25 n.; on the numbers involved, see Cic. *RS* 26 n.

uno dissentiente: i.e. P. Clodius Pulcher (Cic. *RS* 26 n.).

nullo intercedente: no Tribunes of the People obstructed the passing of this decree of the Senate (on the tribunician right of intercession, see Cic. *RS* 3 n.).

dignitatem meam quibus potuit verbis amplissimis ornavit: more detail on the content of this laudatory Senate decree is provided in the speech in the Senate (Cic. *RS* 26). The result of the praise, a confirmation of Cicero's *dignitas*, is most important for re-establishing his status.

salutem…commendavit: also mentioned as an element of the Senate decree in another speech (Cic. *Planc.* 78). Here, *vobis* is added, for the explicit participation of the audience. The reference to settlements outside Rome is in line with Cicero's constant emphasis on the involvement of the whole of Italy and the relevance of his fate for everyone (Cic. *RS* 24 n.).

municipiis, coloniis: on these two types of settlement, see Cic. *RS* 27; 31 nn.

16 ita: probably expresses a comparison rather than a consequence: as *semper* indicates, this sentence describes an ongoing pattern of behaviour during Cicero's absence similar to what has just been outlined.

me nudum a propinquis, nulla cognatione munitum: the phrase is repeated from an earlier passage (Cic. *RQ* 7 [and n.]). It emphasizes that, in contrast to established noblemen with vast family connections, Cicero had no family pleading for him (Cic. *RS* 37–8; *RQ* 6–9); instead, magistrates and official bodies interceded for him.

consules, praetores, tribuni plebis, senatus, Italia cuncta: this asyndetic list of groups of people pleading for Cicero starts with three terms for magistrates, including the holders of the highest annual offices and those most likely to influence the People, then adds the Senate as a whole, thus involving most of the nobility and specifying the body that complements the meeting of the People (on the Senate's support for Cicero, see, e.g., Cic. *RS* 12; 31; *RQ* 8; 13; *Dom.* 5), and finally extends to the population of all of Italy: the statement thereby amounts to a claim of universal support politically and geographically. Cicero does not reveal when these people and institutions would have been active and ignores that, for instance, some Tribunes of the People were hostile to him (Cic. *Pis.* 35).

a vobis deprecata est: the phrasing creates the impression that the final decision lies with the People and that others try to influence their action.

denique...fuerunt: denotes a further step in the activities in favour of Cicero: speeches made by senior politicians to the People after the passing of the Senate decree (Cic. *RS* 26 and n.).

omnes...sunt ornati: a paraphrase for senior magistrates emphasizing that they owe their position to being elected by the People, as Cicero does elsewhere for himself (e.g. Cic. *Leg. agr.* 2.3–5). – In the phrase *vestris maximis beneficiis honoribusque* the first item *beneficiis* refers to the benefit from the People that consists in election to public office (Cic. *RQ* 4 n.), which is specified by the second item (*OLD* s.v. *honor*[1] 5).

producti ad vos: a technical term for bringing speakers before a meeting of the People (Cic. *RS* 13 n.). Again, the audience is singled out as the body in charge of the decision while senior politicians make efforts to influence it.

ab eodem: must refer to the consul P. Cornelius Lentulus Spinther in view of the context and other evidence (Cic. *RS* 26 n.).

ad me conservandum: a paraphrase for recalling Cicero, presenting this process as an honourable and important action (see Cic. *RS* 8; Introduction, section 3.4).

auctores, testes, laudatores: while it would have been sufficient to ask the People to confirm the law on Cicero's recall, the speakers use the opportunity, according to Cicero, to attest and praise his achievements (indicated by an asyndetic tricolon). This functions as impressive proof of the esteem in which Cicero is held and as an indirect argument for the necessity of his recall. By referring to statements of others, Cicero can introduce the view without voicing it himself and point to available evidence of its general acceptance (though MacKendrick [1995, 139] notes that 'Cicero boasts like a general of his deeds of derring-do'). – While the three nouns can have a variety of nuances, they also occur in connection with court cases. Thus, the phrasing may imply that these men provide testimony to Cicero's good character as for a person accused.

princeps...princeps: the first instance, especially in a construction with *ad* and the gerundive, predominantly denotes a temporal sequence (*OLD* s.v. *princeps*[1] 1), though it implies connotations of leadership (*OLD* s.v. *princeps*[1] 2) and standing (*OLD* s.v. *princeps*[1] 5); the latter meaning becomes dominant when the word is repeated at the end of the sentence in a different construction (cf. Cic. *RS* 4; 5).

ad cohortandos vos et ad rogandos: *cohortandos* takes up *cohortati sunt* from the previous sentence as the description of what these speakers did; *rogandos* looks forward to the repeated *rogari/rogavit* with reference to Pompey's speech.

Cn. Pompeius: Cn. Pompeius Magnus (Cic. *RS* 4 n.), one of the speakers.

vir omnium...princeps: recalls the praise of Pompey in the speech given in the Senate (Cic. *RS* 5). The phrase *omnium qui sunt, fuerunt, erunt* (cf. Cic. *Fam.* 11.21.1) expresses the idea of *omnium gentium, omnium saeculorum, omnis memoriae* in a more straightforward way. *virtute, gloria, rebus gestis* is replaced by *virtute, sapientia, gloria*: it makes sense for *gloria*, as a result of the other qualities, to be mentioned at the end. Replacing *rebus gestis* by *sapientia* shifts the emphasis from achievements to intellectual insight, the basis for the assessment of the situation. – Pompey is described at greater length and more hyperbolically than in the speech in the Senate. Moreover, the content of the speech is reproduced, and only for him. This focus takes account of the views of the People and the political necessities (Mack 1937, 40–2 on Cic. *RS* 29 vs *RQ* 16).

qui mihi unus...dignitatem: juxtaposes Pompey's intervention for the entire *res publica* (*universae rei publicae*) with that for the private individual Cicero (*uni privato amico*). This again puts the two in parallel (see Introduction, section 3.4) and indicates that Pompey values Cicero highly. – The addition of *privato amico* suggests a close relationship between Cicero and Pompey (on the relationship between the two men, see Cic. *RS* 4; 29 nn.).

salutem, otium, dignitatem: this list of what Pompey is said to arrange for the Republic recalls the famous phrase *cum dignitate otium* from the speech *Pro Sestio*, where it is described as the goal of *optimates* and political leaders (Cic. *Sest.* 98). Applied to the Republic, these features amount to a functioning, peaceful, and respected political system.

quem ad modum accepi: Cicero takes care to clarify that his comments are based on what he has been told, having been away at the time of the delivery of Pompey's speech.

tripertita: Cicero claims that Pompey's speech consisted of three parts, described in what follows (*primum...tum...deinde*). This structure does not refer to parts as defined in the rhetorical tradition, but rather to the topics covered. The first topic seems to be discussed in greatest detail (itself consisting of three items), as the second and third parts are defined as *in perorando* and *ad extremum* respectively. The third item of the first part is an appeal to the audience to support Cicero, as a conclusion from the description of his activities for the Republic as indicated by the first two items; it is intensified at the end when Pompey reminds the audience that all major bodies are appealing to them and eventually does the same himself.

docuit... coniunxit: what is put in Pompey's mouth, as in the speech to the Senate (Cic. *RS* 29 [and n.]), is what Cicero claims frequently: that he saved the Republic and that his well-being and that of the Republic are aligned (see Introduction, section 3.4).

causamque... hortatusque: a construction with three items linked by repeated *-que* is rare in classical Latin, but attested elsewhere in Cicero (e.g. Cic. *Rosc. Am.* 131; *Verr.* 2.2.35; *De or.* 1.14; 1.120; *Fam.* 13.11.1; *Div.* 1.7; *Fin.* 5.42; K.-St. II 29–30).

auctoritatem senatus, statum civitatis, fortunas civis bene meriti: the People are asked to defend the authority (in a generic sense) of the Senate (rather than their own); the effect for themselves is implied in *statum civitatis* (on these items, see Cic. *RS* 20 n.). By ratifying what the Senate suggested, the People would uphold and respect its authority in contrast to the consuls of 58 BCE, who ignored the wishes of the Senate; they would thereby contribute to ensuring the proper operation of the Republic. – Mack (1937, 40 with n. 89) observes that there is no mention in the Senate speech that Cicero's return should support the authority of the Senate. Here Cicero describes Pompey's intentions in his own words; this functions as an element in encouraging the People to participate in maintaining a working and peaceful political system.

{me}: is generally deleted, though Peterson (1911) retains it and Sydow (1941, 77) argues for reading <pro> me. *me* can be explained as having developed from an unclear spelling of the preceding *tum* and would disturb the sense: *rogari* does not need a complement; in fact, if it was construed with the equivalent of a double accusative (in the active), the various bodies would be said to ask the People for Cicero (*OLD* s.v. *rogo* 2b), while they entreat them to support his recall (*OLD* s.v. *rogo* 2c), as indicated by the complement *pro mea... salute* in the next phrase.

in perorando... ad extremum: while *peroro* usually refers to delivering the final speech or the final part of an oration (*OLD* s.v. *peroro* 2), here it is followed by *ad extremum*: the emotional section at the very end of the speech is distinguished from the overall argument in the final part.

posuit: in a report about a speech means 'To state in speech or writing, specify, put down' (*OLD* s.v. *pono* 18).

rogari a senatu, rogari ab equitibus Romanis, rogari ab Italia cuncta: takes up (with variation) the general statement made before the section on Pompey, namely that all kinds of groups entreated the People (Cic. *RQ* 16). Here, there is no reference to individual magistrates; instead, *equites* are added. By claiming that the Senate, the knights, and all of Italy (i.e. the population outside Rome) address themselves to the People, a wide range of agents is covered in terms of both social class and geographical spread. That the Senate asks the People can be linked to the fact that they would like the recent Senate decree on Cicero's recall to be turned into a law and are organizing *contiones* for the People to vote on it (Cic. *RS* 26; *Sest.* 107–8). The involvement of Italy could allude to decrees in Cicero's favour made by individual places (Cic. *RQ* 10 n.) or all of them having been called together in Rome for the vote (Cic. *RS* 24 n.). Support of the knights, who put on mourning dress after Cicero left Rome (e.g. Cic. *RS* 12 and n.), is mentioned elsewhere (Cic. *Sest.* 87), while particular interaction with the People is not reported.

ipse … pro mea vos salute non rogavit solum verum etiam obsecravit: *ipse* contrasts Pompey's *rogare* at the very end of his speech with *rogare* by other bodies reported in what precedes. The doublet and the intricate word order stress the emphatic nature of Pompey's appeal (on the character of Pompey's speech, see Cic. *RS* 29 n.).

17 huic … homini: this term for Cn. Pompeius Magnus initially appears like a standard resumption, where the name is replaced by a description of the role or position. The continuation of the sentence expressing the great debt to a human being and using the term *fas* (even though applied in a weakened sense: *OLD* s.v. *fas* 3) endows it with a specific meaning: it implies that Pompey, though a human being, acts in a way that makes Cicero feel obliged to him almost as to a divine being (which is also highlighted by the address to the audience).

huius consilia: still those of Pompey, included in the speech just reported (Cic. *RQ* 16).

P. Lentuli: P. Cornelius Lentulus Spinther, one of the consuls of 57 BCE (Cic. *RS* 5 n.).

sententiam: while *sententia* can mean 'opinion' (*OLD* s.v. *sententia* 1), here it seems to be distinguished from Pompey's *consilia* not only by the different agent, but also in quality as a formal statement and is thus likely to denote a statement in the Senate (*OLD* s.v. *sententia* 3), although a presiding consul does not usually present a motion (Cic. *RQ* 18 n.); the word then probably indicates the consul's initiative in relation to the proposal to be voted on.

senatus auctoritatem: could indicate the Senate's authority or an informal decree (*OLD* s.v. *auctoritas* 4, 6). The Senate passed full decrees on Cicero's recall (Cic. *RS* 25–7; *Dom.* 14; *Sest.* 129), which were then ratified and turned into law by a vote of the People (Cic. *RS* 27–8; *Att.* 4.1.4). Thus, the emphasis is perhaps on the role of the Senate as a model and the weight of the Senate's authority in favour of Cicero.

secuti: Cicero claims that the People were motivated by three elements, not only Pompey's speech, but also the influence of the consul and the Senate; such a description suggests the unanimity of the major bodies in the Republic (Thompson 1978, 62).

in eo...loco in quo...fueram...reposuistis: the metaphor of place highlights that the process of recall means regaining a position. – The People can be said to restore Cicero to his former position, although they are not re-electing him, because, by another vote of the People, Cicero resumes his status as a (respected) ex-consul on the basis of an earlier election by the People. – In the speech given in the Senate Cicero presents the second vote as a confirmation of his consulship, thus focusing on the approval of his actions as consul (which follows here as the view of senators) rather than on the status achieved thanks to the People (Cic. *RS* 27).

<me>: the addition of this object is needed. Most editors, taking up Halm's suggestion, insert it after *secuti*. Only Klotz (1915, ed.; 1919) and Courtney (1989, 49), following Renaissance editors, place it after *eo*. The latter position results in a more sophisticated word order; it is in line with a structure such as *pro mea vos salute* in the previous paragraph (Cic. *RQ* 16). Where the word was placed originally cannot be determined.

vestris beneficiis: i.e. election to public offices by the People (Cic. *RQ* 4 n.).

isdem centuriis: i.e. votes of the centuries in the *comitia centuriata*: the *comitia centuriata* elected magistrates, and the law on Cicero's recall was approved by them (Cic. *RS* 27 n.).

eodem tempore: must refer to the *contio* organized by the consul at which several respected men spoke (Cic. *RQ* 16).

audistis...dicere...dixisset...dixerunt...audistis...dixit: the overview of men who spoke to the People is expressed with alternation and repetition of the two verbs *dicere* and *audire*, which demonstrates the interactive process between the two sides.

eodem ex loco: i.e. from the Rostra in the Forum, the venue for speeches to the People, from which, it must be inferred, Pompey's speech (Cic. *RQ* 16) and those of the other men were given.

summos viros...omnes praetorios: the groups listed as having spoken are not all mutually exclusive, but rather overlapping. The first three items underline the high standing and political influence of these men; the last two indicate their senior political roles. While all former consuls are also former praetors if they have gone through the regular *cursus honorum*, someone who had reached the consulship would not normally be called *praetorius*; thus, the last two items must refer to different groups exemplifying the influential men listed previously. In contrast to the generic terms these last two items are specified by *omnes*: this could mean that all former consuls and praetors still around spoke, that all men who spoke were former consuls or praetors, or that all former consuls and praetors who spoke said the same thing. The phrasing leaves the precise situation open and thus makes support for Cicero appear widespread.

eadem dicere, ut omnium testimonio per me unum rem publicam con-servatam esse constaret: the same thing (another form of *isdem*) that all these speakers said is indicated by what became clear from their speeches: the testimony of all (presumably all those who spoke) confirms that Cicero saved the Republic, again expressed with Cicero's preferred phrase (see Introduction, section 3.4). The phrasing makes it almost seem like a trial in which one view is confirmed by overwhelming evidence. No details or proofs are given; the great number of men coming forward on behalf of Cicero is intended to make the assessment plausible.

P. Servilius: P. Servilius Vatia Isauricus (cos. 79 BCE; see Cic. *RS* 25 n.).

gravissimus vir et ornatissimus civis: for *gravissimus* as an honorific attribute for P. Servilius Vatia Isauricus (Cic. *RS* 25 n.), see Cic. *Flacc.* 5, F 8 C.; *Har. resp.* 2.

opera mea…traditam: a consequence of Cicero's having preserved the Republic is that it can be handed over unharmed to other magistrates. The first to voice this further step is said to have been Servilius, while it is stressed again that it was a general opinion and that others then stated the same.

deinceps: the adverb has attributive function with *magistratibus* (K.-St. I 218; Pinkster 2015, 1047) and indicates the magistrates of the following year (*OLD* s.v. *deinceps²* 2).

sed: does not introduce a contrast, but another item strengthening a point just made (*OLD* s.v. *sed¹* 3).

eo tempore: must indicate the same *contio* (Cic. *RQ* 16–17): another speaker is singled out because their testimony provides strong confirmation of Cicero's role as benefactor for the Republic.

auctoritatem: in the sense of 'authoritative view' or 'weighty opinion' (*OLD* s.v. *auctoritas* 9).

testimonium: adds that the weighty statement was corroborated by testimony (by reference to the speaker's own experience). The word implies both the general concept of evidence and the notion that it attests to someone's merits (*OLD* s.v. *testimonium* 2, 3).

L. Gelli: L. Gellius (cos. 72, censor 70, BCE; *RE* Gellius 17; *ORF*⁴ 101) was a legate under Cn. Pompeius Magnus in the war against the pirates in 67 BCE and possibly the following years with a naval command (*MRR* II 148; App. *Mithr.* 95; Flor. 1.41.9: *Gellius Tusco mari inpositus*). In 63 BCE he supported a harsh verdict on the Catilinarian conspirators (Cic. *Att.* 12.21.1) and was one of those men who suggested honouring Cicero (Cic. *Pis.* 6; Gell. *NA* 5.6.15). It used to be thought that L. Gellius bore the cognomen Poplicola, but it is now clear that it was first held by his adoptive son (for the reasons, see Badian 1988, 8 and n. 11).

classem: scholars are divided as to whether *classis* means 'class' (going back to Paulus Manutius) or 'fleet' (going back to Ferratius) (*OLD* s.v. *classis* 1, 3). The latter would refer the incident to Gellius' activity as a naval legate and commander of the fleet during the war with the pirates. The former would mean that at an election Gellius was a supervisor for one class of the centuriate assembly in charge of overseeing the elections and noted some irregularities concerning that class. While the distribution into *classes* was relevant for the voting sequence and procedure even in the late Republic (e.g. Cic. *Phil.* 2.82), control seems to have been operated per voting *centuria* or ballot box or recording board (Cic. *RS* 17 n.). Moreover, the mention of Gellius' own *classis* (*suam classem*) and his own danger (*magno cum suo periculo*) suggests an attack on a *classis* he was responsible for, presumably some kind of subversion (*OLD* s.v. *attempto* 3 'Try to seduce, make an attempt on', suggested for this passage; MacKendrick 1995, 137: 'L. Gellius... testified that subversion had been at work in the fleet, and that only Cicero saved the situation—and the Republic'). Thus, on the basis of his personal experience as a naval legate Gellius is said to agree that Cicero, as consul, brought order back to the Republic, which was on the verge of disappearing.

paene sensit: this verb rather than another verb expressing cognitive processes underlines Gellius' personal feelings: amid great danger to himself Gellius experienced an attempt to persuade his fleet to defect from him.

in contione vestrum: apparently the same *contio* in 57 BCE at which the various speakers just mentioned (Cic. *RQ* 16–17) appeared (*eo tempore*, taking up *eodem tempore*), perhaps added to indicate that a testimonium was brought before the eyes of the audience. – A genitive of the personal pronoun replaces a possessive pronoun (K.-St. I 598; Lebreton 1901, 96; Pinkster 2015, 977).

si ego...non fuissem: places more emphasis on the negation than *nisi fuissem*, highlighting the crucial importance of Cicero's consulship (K.-St. II 411).

cum fui: i.e. when Cicero was consul in 63 BCE. – The clause is in the indicative although it is part of a passage in indirect speech because the temporal indication is presented as a fact (K.-St. II 542; Pinkster 2015, 669–70).

rem publicam funditus interituram fuisse: in a hypothetical conditional construction (in indirect speech: K.-St. II 405–7) this negative development prevented by Cicero's consulship amounts to the same as his 'saving the Republic' asserted by others (see Introduction, section 3.4).

3. Conclusion (18–25): Cicero's gratitude and promise to the Republic

The conclusion (Cic. *RQ* 18–25) of this speech outlines the consequences Cicero draws from having been recalled with widespread support among the population: he will venerate like gods those who helped him, and he will tirelessly work for the Republic (see also Cic. *Dom.* 71; Grasmück 1978, 116). He starts off with a brief recapitulation of the main figures who worked towards his recall; in return, he offers a solemn promise about his future contributions for the Republic (Cic. *RQ* 18; see Mack 1937, 42–3 and note on Cic. *RS* 18–31).

By another reference to the fate of C. Marius (Cic. *RQ* 19–21; cf. *RQ* 7), Cicero explains that one may lose material and physical items, but that a virtuous man will never lose courage and strength of mind; thus, when previous standing has been regained, it is imperative to be active for the Republic. Cicero will not spend effort on taking vengeance on his enemies, but rather focus on politics and prove any enemies wrong by acting as an outstanding citizen (Cic. *RQ* 21). More important than satisfying hatred and revenge is showing gratitude, which should never be omitted (Cic. *RQ* 22–3): demonstrating his gratitude to the People is what Cicero will, therefore, concentrate on; this can be achieved by his engagement for the Republic as a way of proving himself worthy of being recalled by all for the sake of the Republic (Cic. *RQ* 24–5).

Thus, the speech ends with another proclamation of Cicero's gratitude, but also with a reminder of his role in the Republic, which he is able and determined to fulfil: this approach provides a basis for resuming his role as a senior statesman. The conclusion of the speech in the Senate (Cic. *RS* 36–9) features some of these ideas (gratitude, connection with the Republic, no loss of strength of mind, determination to serve the Republic) expressed less elaborately and less personally. Before the People, acknowledging the debt to them and demonstrating how it will be paid to their advantage are key elements of the argument (Mack 1937, 44–8 on Cic. *RS* 36–9 vs *RQ* 18–25).

18 en: draws attention to Cicero's solemn promise at the end of the sentence (*OLD* s.v. *en* 2).

ego: fronted *ego* indicates the return to Cicero and helps to structure the long sentence, as it indicates that a predicate in the first person will follow after the inserted description.

tot testimoniis...comprobantibus: the extended sequence of asyndetic ablatives summarizes the circumstances and initiatives for Cicero's restoration (*restitutus*); the participial construction forms the basis of Cicero's promise to the People (*pollicebor*) at the end (for a comparable sequence, see Cic. *RQ* 1). – Lange (1875, 25) notes that all items in the enumeration refer to passages earlier in the speech, apart from *dis...comprobantibus*; he therefore assumes a lacuna before this section in which the issue of grain was mentioned. Although a preceding discussion of all issues is what might be expected, one could argue that the speech so far (after the opening) has focused on the activities of human agents and that the intervention of the gods is here added as a final climactic item (set off by *denique*).

tot testimoniis: i.e. the supportive public statements recalled in the preceding paragraphs (Cic. *RQ* 16–17).

Quirites: after two addresses to the People in the introduction (Cic. *RQ* 1; 2) and one each in the sections on Cicero's brother (Cic. *RQ* 8) and on Pompey (Cic. *RQ* 17), the conclusion features five addresses (Cic. *RQ* 18 [2x]; 21; 22; 25), which indicates the heightened emotional temperature towards the end of the speech.

hac auctoritate senatus: because of the demonstrative pronoun, *auctoritas* probably denotes the Senate decree on Cicero's recall (Cic. *RS* 25–7 nn.), although it was a formal Senate decree (*OLD* s.v. *auctoritas* 4); before the People the wording might indicate that the content of the Senate's decree still needed to be ratified by their vote. The connotation of the Senate's authority may also be implied (*OLD* s.v. *auctoritas* 6; see Cic. *RS* 4; 6; 16, 39; *RQ* 10 nn.).

tanta consensione Italiae: Cicero claims once again that his recall was approved by the whole of Italy (e.g. Cic. *RQ* 1; 10; 16).

tanto studio bonorum omnium: in Cicero's terminology *boni* (Cic. *RS* 12 n.) are the right-minded people acting in the interest of the Republic (*OLD* s.v. *studium* 5).

causam agente P. Lentulo: instead of *causam* (Halm's conjecture), most manuscripts have *cum* while some do not have anything in this place. *cum* does not make sense and can be interpreted either as traces of an original word or of something that has wrongly entered the text. Most modern editors accept the deletion (with the assumption of the absolute use of *ago*). Luterbacher (1912, 347) suggested reading <*vobis*>*cum*: while including the People in the list might be plausible, the addition would change the emphasis and insert a mention of the People in the description of the activities of the Senate and the magistrates. Courtney (1989, 49–50) recalls Klotz' proposal to read *consule* (originally abbreviated), arguing that it creates a balance with *ceteris magistratibus* and parallels the wording in a letter by Cicero to Lentulus of 54 BCE (Cic. *Fam.* 1.9.16: *duce senatu, comitante Italia, promulgantibus omnibus <paene magistratibus>, te ferente* [Lehmann : *referente* Ω] *consule, comitiis centuriatis, cunctis ordinibus hominibus incumbentibus*). In the letter the information that Lentulus was consul at the time might be necessary; in the speech it is not required, although it provides an explicit point of reference for *ceteris magistratibus*. This version could emphasize that Lentulus took the initiative and came forward with a *sententia* (Cic. *RQ* 17) while he was consul (presiding magistrates typically opened discussions in the Senate with a report, potentially indicating their views; but, unless it was a routine matter, when the report essentially included the possible courses of action, they did not put forward motions to be voted on; this was left to the *sententiae* of other senators, who could refer to the presiding magistrate's report and on whose statements the magistrate could comment: see Kunkel/Wittman 1995, 311–18). An abbreviated *consule* could equally be a gloss on Lentulus' role that entered the text, which would favour the deletion of the word. In comparison with the other descriptions, mere *agente P. Lentulo* is unspecific, especially at the point where the list seems to move from indicating general consent to particular actions. Thus, Halm's conjecture *causam* looks like the most plausible restoration.

P. Lentulo: P. Cornelius Lentulus Spinther, one of the consuls of 57 BCE (Cic. *RS* 5 n.).

consentientibus...magistratibus: Cicero notes that the consul Lentulus took the lead in arranging Cicero's recall (though he acknowledges the involvement of both consuls elsewhere: Cic. *RS* 26 n.) and was supported by other office holders (Cic. *RS* 26; *RQ* 15; 16), though he stops short of saying 'all' (Cic. *RS* 5; *RQ* 15 nn.). Thus, Cicero gives the consul his due, but makes it clear that there was general agreement.

deprecante Cn. Pompeio: refers to Pompey's entreaties of the People just described (Cic. *RQ* 16–17); the verb (Cic. *RS* 37 n.) again stresses that Pompey approaches the People as a suppliant rather than from a position of superiority.

omnibus hominibus faventibus: includes the groups and individuals mentioned earlier in this list and widens the perspective to all humans, to demonstrate universal support (Cicero's opponents being ignored, as often).

dis...comprobantibus: the series of human agents is concluded climactically with a mention of the gods. – Cicero also asserts in *De domo sua* that the gods showed their approval of his return by a fall in the price of grain (here with an emphatic asyndetic tricolon, *ubertate, copia, vilitate*) when the decision was made (although there he acknowledges that the price later rose again and takes account of other explanations: Cic. *Dom.* 14–15; see Cic. *RS* 34 n.; Introduction, section 2). Such an interpretation enables Cicero to present his return as supported by the gods (Heibges 1969, 845).

mihi, meis, rei publicae restitutus: a concise expression (with another asyndetic tricolon) of the notion (Cic. *RS* 1; 8) that Cicero's restoration is not only beneficial to himself, but also to his family and the entire Republic (on the parallel with the Republic, see Introduction, section 3.4).

pollicebor: introduces a solemn promise consisting of two parts (*primum... deinde*). The preparation *tantum vobis quantum facere possum* followed by an address to the audience identifies it as a major promise. It consists in demonstrating great gratitude to the two entities who have helped Cicero to come back: the People and the Republic (highlighted in this speech). Still, the initiatives of the magistrates and of groups all over Italy are mentioned in the lead-up to the promise.

qua...futurum: to express his immense gratitude and reverence, Cicero announces that he will regard and honour the Roman People like immortal gods for the rest of his life (Cic. *RQ* 25). – Markland (1745, 280–2) criticizes (*contra* Savels 1828, xxvii–xxviii) that this passage goes beyond a section in another speech where the Roman People are described as close to the gods (Cic. *Rab. perd.* 5: *vos, Quirites, quorum potestas proxime ad deorum immortalium numen accedit, oro atque obsecro*), as it presents them as equal to the gods. Cole (2013, 69–70) concludes that 'Cicero would actually hold the same esteem for the Roman gods and the Roman people is of course preposterous'. The text does not say that the Roman People are like gods, but rather is an emphatic expression of great appreciation: Cicero will regard and honour the People like gods because of their 'divine' favours for him. Thus, the notion might be hyperbolic, but it is not problematic (for other comparisons between human beings and gods in Cicero's speeches, see Cic. *Sest.* 143; *Planc.* 29; *Clu.* 195; *Mur.* 2; *Leg. agr.* 2.95; for consul Lentulus described as a 'god', see Cic. *RS* 8 and n.).

qua…pietate…soleant: the introduction of the relative clause equals *ea pietate qua* (taken up by *eadem* afterwards); the verb is in the subjunctive because the relative clause has a consecutive connotation (K.-St. II 296).

sanctissimi homines: what Cicero promises is not any kind of *pietas*, but a *pietas* comparable to that of *sanctissimi homines*, which suggests the utmost dutiful observance. *sanctus* fits into the religious context, although it is used in a moral sense (*OLD* s.v. *sanctus* 4).

fore…futurum: *esse* has to supplied to *futurum* (developed from *fore* = *futurum esse*). Because of the preceding adjectives *futurum esse* is presumably used in the second half of the clause.

numenque vestrum aeque…ac deorum immortalium: *ac* functions as a comparative particle after *aeque* (K.-St. II 18–19), and *numen* has to be supplied again with the genitive *deorum immortalium*.

quoniam…reduxit: another version of the notion that Cicero and the Republic were away together and came back together (see Introduction, section 3.4), here in the form that the Republic brought Cicero back to the community (realizing Cicero's expectation: Cic. *RQ* 14). The destination is given as *in civitatem* rather than using *res publica* in different senses in the same sentence (Cic. *RS* 36: *quoniam in rem publicam sum pariter cum re publica restitutus*).

nullo…defuturum: in return for the Republic having brought him back, so as to repay his gratitude and debt, Cicero announces that he will never fail it, i.e. will continuously work to support a functioning Republic (cf. Cic. *RS* 36) by resuming political activity.

nullo…loco: that there will be no circumstances that could prevent Cicero from working for the Republic emphasizes his determination (*OLD* s.v. *locus* 22).

19 quod si…permanebit: to confirm that he will be able to realize his promise and to show his mental strength, Cicero rejects the potential view that his attitude may have changed or have been weakened by his absence because such personal characteristics cannot be taken away from a *vir fortis* (a characterization thus implicitly applied to Cicero). As Cicero phrases the possible change as the potential opinion of someone and then classifies it as incorrect, he avoids a positive boastful statement and provides a superficial reason for the comment. – Cicero's dejected letters sent to friends and family paint a different picture of his strength of mind during his absence (e.g. Cic. *Att.* 3.5 [10 April 58 BCE]; 3.9 [13

June 58 BCE]; *Fam.* 14.4 [29 April 58 BCE]); such elements of potential weakness are ignored in the public speeches delivered after Cicero's return. – The characterization *vir fortis* (enhanced as *fortissimum virum*) applied also to Marius immediately afterwards (Raccanelli 2012, 107 n. 9) implies a parallel between the two men.

voluntate…virtute…animo: the three items not affected (polysyndetic tricolon) cover inclination, valour to take action, and strength of mind.

quod potuit…quod…non potest: a parallelism in structure and a contrast in sense between what Cicero's opponents were able to take away from him and what remains with a *vir fortis.*

vis et iniuria et sceleratorum hominum furor: phrased as a generic statement (another polysyndetic tricolon), yet referring to P. Clodius Pulcher and his followers. The list includes both their mode of action (characterized as violent and unjust) and their mindset. – *iniuria* might imply both that Cicero left Rome without a trial and that the allegations against him were wrong.

furor: a characteristic frequently attributed to Cicero's 'enemies' (on *furor* in a political context, see Achard 1981, 239–47; Taldone 1993, 8–16).

eripuit, abstulit, dissipavit: an asyndetic tricolon of verbs illustrating the process of removing eagerly and abusing someone else's possessions. The final verb in the sequence (*OLD* s.v. *dissipo* 3) insinuates that Cicero's opponents did not even take his possessions to enjoy them and instead destroyed them. – The reference must be to the confiscation and partial destruction of Cicero's property (Cic. *RS* 18 n.).

quod viro forti adimi non potest: i.e. non-material goods such as attitude and strength of mind.

id et manet et permanebit: adopting this reading of one manuscript is the easiest solution to the nonsensical *ideo manet et permanebit* of most manuscripts (Maslowski 1980, 413). Two related verbs linked by *et…et* provide a suitably weighty ending; *id* emphatically resumes the *quod*-clause. Other scholars have suggested different solutions: e.g. *id omne* (Peterson 1911), *id adeo* (Busche 1917, 1357), or *id <est> et* (Sydow 1941, 172). Bellardi (1975, 49) argues for *id mihi*, a reading found in one manuscript. Yet the double *et* makes sense as a pronounced link between the two verbs in different tenses; not including a personal pronoun retains the generic character of the statement.

vidi ego: introduces another comparison between Cicero and C. Marius, based on Cicero's own observations. Earlier in this speech Marius is one of the ex-consuls compared to Cicero because they all had to leave Rome (Cic. *RQ* 7). This additional section on Marius focuses on the attitude and state of mind in such a situation. Such a parallel with Marius, a hero respected by the People, enhances Cicero's position.

municipem meum, C. Marium: both Cicero and C. Marius were born in Arpinum (Cic. *Sest.* 50; on C. Marius, see Cic. *RS* 38 n.).

quoniam ... belligerandum fuit: the inserted clause provides the basis for the comparison by stating that both Marius and Cicero had to fight not only against their political opponents, but also against *fortuna* according to *quasi aliqua fatali necessitate*. The course of events is thereby characterized as inevitably predetermined (*OLD* s.v. *necessitas* 2), while the agency determining the course of events is distinguished from one's personal fate. Adding an abstract *fortuna* as an opponent to the identified enemies makes the struggle sound greater without the addition of any details.

nobis: i.e. Marius and Cicero, enhancing the parallel between the two men.

iis qui haec delere voluissent: i.e. political enemies. – *haec* refers to the existing political system in Rome and does not have an expressed antecedent.

belligerandum: the verb is relatively rare in the classical period. For the transferred sense of 'de hominibus contra res pugnantibus' *TLL* (*TLL* II.1815.14–16, s.v. *belligero*) only provides one further example (Plaut. *Truc.* 183: *qui cum geniis suis belligerant*).

eum ... vidi: takes up *vidi ego fortissimum virum, municipem meum, C. Marium* from the start of the sentence after the parenthesis.

tamen: indicates a contrast between the adverse fate Marius had to contend with and his unbroken spirit; it illustrates that strength of spirit cannot be taken away from a *vir fortis* (like Marius and Cicero).

summa senectute: 'very old' from a Roman point of view: when Cicero will have encountered Marius in the early 80s BCE, he would have been around 70 years of age (born *c.* 157 BCE). Velleius Paterculus gives Marius' age as 70 at the time of the flight from Rome (Vell. Pat. 2.19.2), and Plutarch makes him over 70 by the time he reaches Africa (Plut. *Mar.* 41.4). The stress on his old age (also at Cic. *Sest.* 50) enables an effective intensification of Marius' unbroken spirit in the face of adversity.

non modo non ... renovato: the juxtaposition of a negative and a positive description highlights the admirable achievement: Marius' spirit is not only not weakened, but even stronger.

magnitudinem calamitatis: a vague description of Marius' difficult situation (with some details given in the next paragraph); it contributes to underlining Marius' achievements in maintaining great strength of mind. – *calamitas* is also one of the terms Cicero uses for his absence from Rome (see Cic. *RS* 20 n.; Introduction, section 3.4).

20 quem: still C. Marius.

audivi: while the previous paragraph deals with what Cicero saw (Cic. *RQ* 19), this paragraph adds what he heard from Marius: Marius' strength of spirit was visible; what he said confirms the underlying attitude. – Carney (1960, 112) infers from this passage that 'Cicero heard the story of his flight and exile from Marius' own lips', but the reference might also refer to a single memorable statement or a brief summary.

tum…cum…cum…cum…cum…cum: the time at which Marius was in an unfortunate situation is illustrated by a sequence of five *cum*-clauses describing aspects of the circumstances during his absence from Rome (K.-St. II 344).

tum se fuisse miserum: Hotman and Markland added a negation to this phrase (*tum se <non> fuisse*), which was condemned by Halm (1856, 855 in app.). Shackleton Bailey (1979, 263) revived the idea, placing the negation in a different position (*<non> tum se fuisse*). Maslowski (1981) then adopted this reading (approved by Lebek 1984, 7). While it might initially sound odd to have Marius admit that he was *miser*, the argument is based on a distinction between inner attitude (strength of mind never lost) and external circumstances: Marius was *miser* (referring to outward conditions) for a while (*tum*) due to the conditions; these contrast (*vero*) with the recovery of his standing (*reciperata…sua dignitate*); with his social position regained, he is determined to demonstrate his constant strength of mind.

cum careret patria: a paraphrase for exile emphasizing the loss of 'home' rather than the political framework (for the expression, see, e.g., Cic. *Sest.* 145; *Lig.* 11; *Fam.* 4.7.4; 4.9.3; 4.9.4; *Att.* 3.26.1).

obsidione: presumably referring to Marius' decisive victories over the Germanic tribes of the Cimbri and Teutones in 102 and 101 BCE. They were not actually besieging Rome, but they had been moving towards it, and a siege was feared. – The addition, highlighting Marius' achievements for the community, makes his forced absence from Rome appear even more outrageous (just as in Cicero's case).

sua bona possideri ab inimicis ac diripi: when Marius and others were declared public enemies, their property was confiscated (App. *B Civ.* 1.60). – In a report of what Marius said, *inimici* gives his assessment and denotes Marius' political enemies, particularly L. Cornelius Sulla and his followers.

audiret…videret: Marius could only learn by reports what happened to his property while he was away. By contrast, he could see his son, who was with him, and the effect of the situation on him (on *calamitas*, see Cic. *RQ* 19 n.).

adulescentem filium: C. Marius' son, also called C. Marius (*RE* Marius 15; b. 109 BCE; cos. 82 BCE [*MRR* II 65–6]), accompanied his father on his flight to Africa in 88 BCE and returned to Rome with him in 87 BCE (e.g. Vell. Pat. 2.19.1; 2.20.5; Liv. *Epit.* 77; Plut. *Mar.* 35.6–7; 40.5–7).

in paludibus demersus: other sources confirm that Marius hid in the marshes around Minturnae after he left Rome (e.g. Cic. *Sest.* 50; *Pis.* 43; Vell. Pat. 2.19.2:; Plut. *Mar.* 37.5–38.2).

concursu ac misericordia Minturnensium: according to the (not entirely consistent) reports in other sources Marius was dragged out of the marshes by locals; thereupon, the people of Minturnae first decided to kill him, but then changed their minds and helped him to travel away from Italy (e.g. Cic. *Sest.* 50; *Planc.* 26; Vell. Pat. 2.19.2–4; Liv. *Epit.* 77; Plut. *Mar.* 38.1–39.3). The vague description here is a statement about the inhabitants of the town and presumably refers primarily to their collective decision not to kill Marius (the next stage of the flight follows in the next *cum*-clause). The phrase *concursu ac misericordia* indicates the activity (coming together for joint action) and the motivating feelings.

Minturnensium: Minturnae (modern Minturno) is a town about 100 miles from Rome, surrounded by marshes (*paludes Minturnenses*). The place was originally a town of the Aurunci; a Roman colony was established there in 295 BCE.

corpus ac vitam: indicates that both the physical body and the soul/spirit, amounting to 'life', were saved (*OLD* s.v. *vita* 4).

parva navicula pervectus in Africam: from Minturnae Marius travelled to Numidia in North Africa in a ship provided by the people of Minturnae (Cic. *Sest.* 50; *Planc.* 26; *Pis.* 43; Vell. Pat. 2.19.4; Liv. *Epit.* 77.; Plut. *Mar.* 40). – *navicula* is the only diminutive form found in this speech (see Introduction, section 3.5), emphasized by *parva*, in a section allegedly reporting what Marius said. It highlights the precariousness of the voyage across the Mediterranean.

regna: Marius settled the affairs of Numidia after the Jugurthine War in 105 BCE, when parts of Jugurtha's kingdom were granted to Bocchus, king of Mauretania and father-in-law of Jugurtha, and to Gauda, a grandson of Masinissa and half-brother of Jugurtha (*CAH* IX^2 30).

ad eos: the people defined by the preceding relative clause, i.e. leading men in Africa, to whom Marius had first assigned kingdoms and who later received him when he came as a fugitive.

inops supplexque: such a characterization of Marius in a dependent role vividly contrasts with the fact that previously Marius had been in a position of superior power in relation to these people. – *supplex* and *supplicare* are used of people intervening on behalf of men in exile elsewhere in these speeches (Cic. *RS* 12; 31; 37; *RQ* 6; 13); here it does not necessarily imply that Marius adopted the position of a suppliant towards these foreign rulers (on suppliant gestures, see Cic. *RS* 17 n.), but rather that he was in need of and asking for help.

reciperata vero sua dignitate: turns from the description of Marius' situation during his absence from Rome to the circumstances upon his return. The wording emphasizes the recovery of his previous dignified position and standing (the only item temporarily lacking) and suggests that this will also be possible for Cicero.

non commissurum ut: for this construction, see Cic. *RS* 39 and n.

cum ea quae amiserat sibi restituta essent: in the light of the information in the previous clause and the subsequent contrast, this item must refer to the loss of Marius' material possessions and standing, which were won back upon his return.

virtutem animi: according to himself, Marius never lost his strength of mind. – While in the comparable statement on Cicero, *virtus* and *animus* are separate, parallel items (Cic. *RQ* 19; see also *RS* 39), here one of them defines the other: thus the focus is placed on the quality of *virtus* with respect to mental strength (for the phrase, see Sall. *Cat.* 53.1).

non haberet: an emphatic declaration (double negation: *non commissurum ut…non haberet*) that Marius will continue to display his strength of mind, which he never lost, now that he has regained his position and material possessions.

sed hoc inter me atque illum interest: *sed* marks the transition from a section parallelizing the fates of Marius and Cicero (as they both retained their strength of mind and regained their standing) to a section contrasting their behaviour upon their return, with Marius providing a foil against which Cicero can stand out as a positive figure (see Cic. *RS* 6; *RQ* 13). – *hoc* looks forward to the subsequent *quod*-clause; *me atque illum* are exemplified in the *quod*-clause in chiastic order.

qua re … ea ipsa re: *re* (the noun governing the relative clause) is given both in the relative clause and then in the main clause (highlighted by *ea ipsa*); the word is followed by an identification of what *res* denotes in this context.

inimicos suos ultus est: when Marius returned to Rome in 87 BCE, he and L. Cornelius Cinna brought Rome under their control and killed many political opponents (Cic. *RS* 38 n.).

armis… <verbis>: according to Cicero, upon their return to Rome, both Marius and Cicero continued to work in the way in which they had before in line with their respective strengths: Marius uses *arma* and Cicero *verba*. Beyond their personal habits and abilities, Cicero explains the two procedures with reference to the different circumstances: one art is appropriate for war, the other for peace. He thereby implies that there was a civil war when Marius returned, while there is no armed conflict in his case. Moreover (as Cicero goes on to say), Marius made taking revenge on his enemies his main goal, while Cicero's concern is the *res publica*, and he only attends to the issue of his enemies to the extent allowed by the *res publica* (Cic. *RQ* 21 n.). Cicero does not criticize Marius explicitly, but he characterizes him as acting emotionally (Cic. *RQ* 21: *animo irato*).

qua consuevi: *ea re* has to be supplied as the antecedent for the relative clause (developed from *qua re … ea ipsa re*).

<verbis>: a complement marking a contrast to *armis* is needed: most manuscripts have nothing at this point; some manuscripts have *pietate*; scholars have made a variety of suggestions. As a contrast to *armis*, *verbis* is preferable (Sydow 1937, 227). Sydow places the inserted word after *consuevi*. Maslowski (1980, 413–14) notes that the position after *utar* is more emphatic; this arrangement creates a smoother parallel structure in both parts of the sentence. – Bornecque (1909, 56 n. 3) supports Lambinus' conjecture *utar <lenitate>* for rhythmical reasons. Lebek (1984, 7) believes that no supplement is necessary since Cicero elaborates on his principles in what follows. This applies to content, but the rhetorical structure requires a complement to *armis*, and the reference point of *huic* (*arti*) would be vague if none was mentioned.

21 quamquam … cogitabo: in addition to the fact that Marius and Cicero employ different types of activity (Cic. *RQ* 20), a difference in aim and extent, highlighting Cicero's intentions, is stated: Cicero announces his focus on the welfare of the *res publica*, so that personal matters will be overruled by the needs of the *res publica* (Cic. *RQ* 23 n.) while he here claims that Marius was angrily focused on vengeance on his enemies (cf. Cic. *Tusc.* 5.56; Carney 1960, 116).

quamquam: introduces a main clause (*OLD* s.v. *quamquam* 3).

de ipsis inimicis: Zielinski (1904, 205) suggested reading *amicis* (instead of *inimicis*) to create an antithesis; this reading was adopted by Peterson (1911) and Klotz (1915, ed.; 1919). Mack (1937, 45–6) argues for reading *de ipsis* (in the sense of *inimicis*). What is at issue is the way in which Marius and Cicero respectively deal with their enemies; the discussion of *inimici* continues in what follows. The repetition of *inimicis* emphasizes the contrast between the behaviour of the two men; in the collocation *ipsis inimicis* the pronoun emphasizes the continuing focus on *inimici*.

permittit: Shackleton Bailey (1991, 228) suggests changing the transmitted present tense to a future tense (*permittet*). Although the statement refers to the future, the present tense is possible in such subordinate clauses (K.-St. I 144–6).

denique: introduces a further point in the discussion on how to deal with enemies and how to behave after the return (*OLD* s.v. *denique* 2).

quattuor … hominum genera: Cicero claims that he has been wronged by four different types of people: he does not name representatives of any group or give an indication of the size of each or their whereabouts. Instead, he identifies them by their attitude and behaviour: in all cases their hostility towards Cicero is implicitly or explicitly linked with their attitude to the Republic, so that the conflict between them and Cicero is again presented as something fundamental beyond the personal (see Introduction, section 3.4). – Earlier in this speech Cicero mentions two groups among his peers as well as the consuls of 58 BCE as people not supporting him: the envious and the timid, who then turned into betrayers or deserters (Cic. *RQ* 13). In *Pro Sestio* Cicero gives six types of people opposing him (Cic. *Sest.* 46: *cum alii me suspicione periculi sui non defenderent, alii vetere odio bonorum incitarentur, alii inviderent, alii obstare sibi me arbitrarentur, alii ulcisci dolorem aliquem suum vellent, alii rem ipsam publicam atque hunc bonorum statum otiumque odissent et ob hasce causas tot tamque varias me unum deposcerent*). – A comparable list of different types of Catilinarians is included in one of Cicero's speeches about Catiline (Cic. *Cat.* 2.17–23; MacKendrick 1995, 138). Both examples of such lists appear in speeches to the People (Thompson 1978, 114–15).

unum: the first group (suppl. *genus*) is said to be enemies of Cicero motivated by hatred of the *res publica*; therefore, they are annoyed at Cicero preserving it (another opportunity for him to mention this achievement, i.e. combating the Catilinarian Conspiracy; see Introduction, section 3.4) and thus opposed to him. These people could include followers of Catiline. The description has them appear as dangerous and irresponsible citizens.

alterum: the second group are those who feigned friendship with Cicero and then betrayed him (Cic. *RS* 23 n.). A motivation is not given. These people are to be characterized as opportunists who sought Cicero's friendship when he had political power, but turned away when his position changed.

tertium: the third group is defined as those who were not as successful in their political careers as Cicero (a further opportunity to allude to his successes), allegedly due to laziness, and thus were envious of the renown and standing Cicero achieved (for *invidia* as a motivation for actions against Cicero, see Cic. *RQ* 13; *Sest.* 46).

eadem: is generic and does not have an explicit point of reference; it probably denotes high political offices and standing.

quartum: the fourth group is given the most detailed description, covering what they should have done and what they did do. These people must be the consuls of 58 BCE, L. Calpurnius Piso Caesoninus and A. Gabinius (Cic. *RS* 4 n.): they are said not to have cared for the welfare of the Republic, which includes or is parallel with Cicero's fate. Cicero claims frequently that, as a result of Clodius' law assigning lucrative provinces to the consuls, they gave up their freedom of action and then did not carry out or support initiatives on Cicero's behalf (Cic. *RS* 4 n.).

custodes rei publicae: previously, consuls have been characterized as *tutores* for the *res publica* (Cic. *RS* 4; *RQ* 11); Marius is identifed as a *custos*, though without explicit reference to his consulship (Cic. *RQ* 9). *custodes* here probably indicates that consuls should be guardians of the Republic (*OLD* s.v. *custos* 1), but that these men carried out their role irresponsibly for their own benefit, thus causing damage to an entity belonging to all citizens.

deb{u}erent: is Ernesti's conjecture for transmitted *debuerunt* (resulting in a concessive *cum*-clause). – One might have expected *debuissent* in a strict sequence of tenses. The imperfect subjunctive presents the failure to live up to expectations from the perspective of the present; this use of tenses is frequent in concessive *cum*-clauses in Cicero's writings (K.-St. II 189–90).

salutem meam, statum civitatis, dignitatem eius imperi: the asyndetic tricolon lists the items the consuls have 'sold', neglecting their expected duty of care for these matters (for the wording, see Cic. *RQ* 16). The sequence starts with the impact on Cicero as the individual victim and is then extended to the Republic as a whole and the office of consul.

sic ulciscar … provocatus: Cicero announces that he will take revenge on all four groups in different ways, depending on the way in which they have wronged and provoked him. When he proceeds to detail his revenge plans, it becomes clear that there is no contradiction with the statement of limited revenge in line with the *res publica* at the start of the paragraph: what is defined as revenge is mainly excellent service for the Republic; these groups of people are opposed to Cicero because of what he did for the Republic, and he will therefore annoy them by continuing in this vein. – Grasmück (1978, 115) suggests that Cicero was not in a sufficiently powerful position to carry out proper revenge and therefore declared a (limited) renouncement of revenge. While this may be true, Cicero presents what he does as a carefully considered plan that sets him off positively.

facinora <eor>um singula: this emendation proposed by Halm (1856, 856) seems the easiest restitution of the transmitted text (*facinora singula* needs a reference point). Another reference to *genera*, as considered by Sydow (1941, 169: *facinorum <genera> singula*), would be a greater change and is not required, since this expression is not to indicate a list of different *genera* of deeds, but rather to create a link between the different kinds of enemies and their respective deeds.

malos civis … repetenda: each item in the list of actions of 'revenge' on the four groups consists of a repetition of their defining characteristics (in the accusative as objects of *ulciscar*; sometimes with different wording) followed by a gerund or gerundive identifying Cicero's action in response.

malos civis rem publicam bene gerendo: the 'revenge' on the first group. Initially they are characterized as opposed to the Republic and motivated by *odio rei publicae*; now they are more explicitly described as *malos cives*. Cicero will annoy them by conducting public affairs well, though without specifying how he envisages doing so. Cicero did not hold the position of a magistrate at the time, but as a senior senator and ex-consul he could exert influence in the Senate. Luterbacher's (1912, 347) suggestion of adopting the variant *regendo* yields a less idiomatic expression.

perfidos amicos nihil credendo atque omnia cavendo: Cicero will deal with the second group by being cautious, so that these people will not have the chance to betray him again. *nihil* and *omnia* stress the absolute and all-encompassing nature of this method (for *cavere* with accusative object, see *OLD* s.v. *caueo* 2).

invidos virtuti et gloriae serviendo: the third group, envious of Cicero's *laus* and *dignitas*, will be confronted by Cicero demonstrating *virtus* and thus acquiring further *gloria*. Thus, basically, he will do more of the same, which will annoy the others and also distinguish him from them. By introducing *virtus* Cicero makes it clear that there is a solid basis for his glory (due to a quality presumably lacking in his enemies).

mercatores provinciarum: the fourth group, the consuls of the previous year, are characterized negatively again (e.g. Cic. *RS* 10). For them an act of revenge targeted directly at what they have done is envisaged: they will be called back from their provinces and asked to account for their administration (see Cic. *Prov. cons.*, focusing on their recall and misbehaviour in the provinces; on the allocation, see Cic. *RS* 4 n.). This does not abolish the criticized arrangement (which would be impossible); on the assumption that it was attractive to them because they expected to enrich themselves, the request for a potentially short-ened tenure and detailed accounts makes realizing their plans without any repercussions more difficult.

22 quamquam mihi, Quirites: with another address to the audience Cicero confirms emphatically that, in spite of the plans for limited revenge he has out-lined (Cic. *RQ* 21), rendering thanks to the People is more important to him (for *quamquam* introducing a main clause, see Cic. *RQ* 21 n.). By this move Cicero returns to the motivation for this speech, while the contrast with potential revenge increases the impression of the extent and seriousness of his gratitude.

inimicorum iniurias crudelitatemque: at the start of the section on *inimici* Cicero describes their actions against him as *me . . . violarunt* without providing details (Cic. *RQ* 21). Here, in a contrast with the favour received from the People, Cicero brands his enemies' behaviour as *iniuriae* and *crudelitas*. This collocation still does not specify any actions, but marks the behaviour as unacceptable for the dual reason that these individuals do not follow fair pro-cesses, thus comitting an injustice, and operate violence. – Elsewere *iniuria* characterizes the situation according to which Cicero had to leave Rome with-out a trial as a result of Clodius' activities (Cic. *RS* 23; *RQ* 19; *Dom.* 64; 65).

etenim . . . exaequari: Cicero claims that the reason (*etenim*) for his being more concerned about demonstrating gratitude than carrying out revenge is the greater difficulty of the former: people one might want to take revenge on are qualified as *improbi*, and it is fairly easy to be superior to them, whereas people who have been supportive are regarded as *boni*, and it is more difficult to be equal to them. This argument is somewhat indirect: being equal means of the same moral worth and thus rendering thanks as appropriate (on the terms *boni* and *improbi* in a political context, see Cic. *RS* 12; 20 nn.).

superiorem esse contra improbos: *contra* probably means 'in relation to' (*OLD* s.v. *contra* B 23c; K.-St. I 541), but retains an element of its basic meaning of 'against'.

tum etiam: introduces an additional point in the argument (*OLD* s.v. *tum* 9).

referre quod debeas: a comparison between opponents (*male meritis*) and supporters (*optime meritis*, highlighted by a superlative) by means of a financial metaphor: one owes repayments (of different kinds) to those who have wronged one and those who have supported one; it is more urgent to repay the latter, i.e. to show gratitude than take revenge (generic second person singular).

23 odium . . . definire: continues the argument by illustrating the different conditions for the development of feelings of hatred and gratitude over time:

hatred may subside or be abandoned for various reasons; by contrast, it would not be right to forget and not to honour good deeds under any circumstances.

vel: as a disjunctive particle structures a list of four potential alternative situations (K.-St. II 108–9) in which acts of revenge motivated by hatred might not be carried out. The first two refer to external forces, to circumstances in which someone may forgo such acts; the last two describe developments whereby acting out the hatred becomes unfeasible for the individual concerned.

precibus mitigari: hatred (and acts of revenge prompted thereby) might be softened in response to entreaties from the object of hatred or others aiming to prevent acts of retaliation.

temporibus rei publicae communique utilitate deponi: hatred is less important than the situation of the Republic: if taking revenge interfered with the welfare of the Republic, one might abandon such acts. Such considerations only apply to hatred with a political dimension: this is presupposed because of the connection with Cicero's circumstances.

difficultate ulciscendi teneri: if it is difficult to take revenge, hatred might be repressed and acts of vengeance avoided (*OLD* s.v. *teneo* 19b).

vetustate sedari: feelings of hatred may become less strong over time, so that they will no longer prompt acts of revenge (*OLD* s.v. *uetustas* 4). Thus, an act of revenge may never be undertaken if none was carried out immediately, or further acts at a later stage might not occur.

bene meritos…definire: complementing the options for hatred, this sentence surveys the same four potential developments (now linked by *nec/neque*) with respect to gratitude: then these reasons or excuses are not valid, and gratitude will always have to be felt and demonstrated.

bene meritos ne colas nec exorari fas est neque id rei publicae remittere utcumque necesse est: the text of this clause is corrupt; restoration is difficult and controversial. The content must be that, in contrast to what is said about hatred, one should not let oneself be dissuaded from showing gratitude or be less diligent in that because of the situation of the Republic. To express that, this version of the text, with relatively few changes to what is transmitted, makes sense. In this reading, as each phrase seems to have its own predicate, *necesse est* is probably the main verb in *neque id…necesse est*, and *utcumque* functions as an indefinite adverb (rather than as a conjunction introducing a clause *utcumque necesse est* with the infinitive *remittere* still governed by *fas est*). The clause *bene meritos ne colas* (*OLD* s.v. *colo*[1] 6d; Cic. *RQ* 24) depends on *exorari* (itself depending on *fas est*). – Shackleton Bailey (1979, 263) argues that Cicero could not have said something like this because for him the Republic always came first (he therefore suggests: <*nisi*> *utique* instead of *utcumque*). While the Republic is important to Cicero, here there is a contrast with hatred: gratitude is so essential that it has to be maintained irrespective of the state of the Republic. In Cicero's case, as it turns out, there will not be a contradiction: his showing of gratitude consists in work for the Republic's sake. Further changes, such as those suggested by Jeep (1862, 5–7), do not seem necessary (*odium vel precibus mitigari potest—vel difficultate ulciscendi leniri vel vetustate sedari: ut bene meritos colas nec exorari fas est neque id rei publicae rependere verum neque necesse est*).

id: takes up the clause *bene meritos ne colas.*

remittere: is Garatoni's emendation for transmitted *repetere,* providing the expected sense (*OLD* s.v. *remitto* 10).

neque... definire: the last two points on gratitude are expressed straightforwardly: there can be no excuse of difficulty or length of time; gratitude will always have to exist.

tempore et die: *et* links a general term and a specific one of the same type (K.-St. II 24–5), emphasizing the setting of a precise time limit.

postremo: introduces an additional point to the comparison: if one is relaxed in pursuing revenge, one earns praise; if one is slow in repaying gratitude, one is cricitized (*necesse est* presents this as the appropriate consequence). While the comparison so far has been abstract and neutral, the second part in this juxtaposition inserts a reference to the *beneficia* Cicero received from the People (*beneficia* presumably primarily denoting Cicero's recall rather than his election to office: see Cic. *RQ* 4 n.). This addition makes it explicit that the general considerations apply to Cicero: he will feel obliged to demonstrate his gratitude and not to be deterred from this purpose.

bono rumore certe utitur: while the transmission is corrupt, it is obvious that an expression of praise is required. For the wording, various suggestions have been made (e.g. Sydow 1944, 186: *in eo rum<or populi summis laudibus> aperte utitur*; Shackleton Bailey 1979, 263: *is fere semper laudatur*). Maslowski's (1980, 414) version is perhaps the most economical and relates well to the transmission (adopted by Condom 1995, 76). The phrasing is infrequent, but not unparalleled (for *bonus rumor,* see Cic. *Leg.* 1.50; for *uti* with such a complement, see Cic. *Scaur.* 43; *Mur.* 14).

ingratus... impius: a person who is slow to show gratitude for huge favours is said to be not only *ingratus,* but even *impius.* This assessment does not need to allude to the fact that Cicero previously presented the People as gods for him (Cic. *RQ* 18; 25); it describes the moral duty towards one's benefactors (*OLD* s.v. *impius* 1).

{atque... dissolvit.}: this generic statement, not found in all manuscripts, appears in similar form elsewhere in Cicero (Cic. *Planc.* 68 [with comments at Gell. *NA* 1.4]; *Off.* 2.69). It is probably an interpolation and should be deleted (thus most modern editions and approved by Busche 1917, 1357, regarded as 'perhaps spurious' by MacKendrick 1995, 142). The point made in the following sentence (Cic. *RQ* 24) follows better from the notion in the preceding sentence that it is imperative to show gratitude under all circumstances. – In a play on words this phrase states: if one still has the money owed, one has not repaid the debt: if one has paid the money, one no longer has it. On the contrary, gratitude

is both 'had' (felt) and 'paid' back at the same time with the two states continuing. – The expression *in officio persolvendo* provides the point of reference
(*OLD* s.v. *in* 41); it is parallel to *pecunia debita*, where *in* has to be supplied. *et* is
used instead of *ac* for comparison after an expression of dissimilarity (K.-St. II
6–7): it compares *in officio persolvendo* with *pecunia debita* ('*scil.* atque in pecunia debita': Maslowski 1981, in app.).

24 quapropter…defuturam: following on from the justification for the
obligation to show gratitude to the People for their favour to him, for that reason (*quapropter*) Cicero announces his determination to fulfil that obligation. – A
similar phrase is found in a panegyrical expression of gratitude by Claudius
Mamertinus in the fourth century CE (Cic. *RS* 1 n.) at the end of a speech
(Mamertinus, *Pan. Lat.* 3(11).32.2–3: *omne negotium, omne otium meum in
ornandis rebus tuis celebrandisque ponetur; neque solum a vivente me ac vigente
grati animi benivolentia declarabitur, sed etiam cum me anima defecerit monumenta tui in me beneficii permanebunt.* [3] *in referenda autem gratia, sanctis-
sime imperator, hoc tibi polliceor semperque praestabo, mihi neque in suggerendis
consiliis veritatem neque in adeundis, si res poposcerit, periculis animum
neque in sententia simpliciter ferenda fidem neque in hominum voluntatibus
pro re publica teque laedendis libertatem neque in laboribus perferendis
industriam neque in augendis imperii tui commodis grati animi benivolentiam defuturam, idque omni vitae mea tempore summis opibus enisurum
elaboraturum effecturum ut honores in me tui non, quia necesse fuerit, ad
quemcumque delati, sed, quia ita oportuerit, recte positi et ratione conlocati
esse videantur.*).
    colam: for the meaning, see Cic. *RQ* 23 n.
    benivolentia sempiterna: if Cicero shows 'goodwill, benevolence, friendli-
ness' (*OLD* s.v. *beneuolentia*), it is emphasized that he will always think of the
favours received with a positive attitude.
    <nec eam>…permanebunt: this clause (with the text plausibly restored)
adds a further, stronger point to highlight the great deeds of the People on
Cicero's behalf and the resulting gratitude: not only will he always remember
these favours, but they will even continue to be remembered after his death on
account of memorials. This is probably not a reference to physical monuments,
but rather suggests that the deeds of the People for Cicero will always be known
and remembered, perhaps promoted by writings of Cicero or actions demonstrating his gratitude (*OLD* s.v. *monumentum* 3).
    <…eam>: may refer grammatically to *memoria* or *benivolentia*. Since this
clause is about memory and memorials of deeds, the reference point must be
memoria.
    cum anima exspirabo mea: a vivid metaphor presenting both life and
memory as items that one might 'breathe out' upon death. Cicero asserts that
'breathing out his life' will not mean that the memory of the People's great beneficial deeds will be lost. – *anima*, originally referring to the air breathed and

then to life depending on it, is the appropriate term in this metaphor (*OLD* s.v. *anima* 1, 3).

cum me vita <defecerit>: a verb is needed to complement the *cum*-clause; *deficio*, as suggested by Halm (1856, 857) and Madvig (1873, 214), on the basis of Mamertinus (*cum me anima defecerit*), is a possible solution (*OLD* s.v. *deficio* A 1). *vita* (Madvig) rather than *anima* (Halm) avoids repetition of words from the previous clause.

hoc vobis repromitto semperque praestabo…defuturam: Cicero utters another solemn promise (Cic. *RQ* 18) of what he will do to show his gratitude. – *hoc* looks forward to the promise, following in an accusative plus infinitive construction (*mihi neque…defuturam*).

neque…: details of Cicero's promise are given in a series of six items linked by *neque/nec*; they each consist of a a prepositional gerundive phrase describing an activity (taking up the introductory generic *in referenda…gratia*) and an accusative (subjects of *defuturam* in the accusative and infinitive construction) indicating the quality needed. The activities do not include immediate favours for the People in return for their support; instead, they concern mainly the role of a responsible senator active in the public interest to support what is positive and to ward off what is negative, enhancing living conditions and recalling Cicero's presentation of himself as 'a consul for the People' in his inaugural speech as consul (Cic. *Leg. agr.* 2). Such plans will benefit the People indirectly (only the final item mentions Cicero's gratitude and obligation to the People) and again link Cicero's fate and position closely with the welfare of the Republic (see Introduction, section 3.4).

in periculis a re publica propulsandis animum: Bornecque (1909, 59 n. 2) proposes interchanging the places of *periculis* and *propulsandis*, to end the phrase with *periculis animum*, on the model of the imitation by Mamertinus, to create a more common *clausula*. Likewise, Bornecque (1909, 59 n. 3) suggests reversing *voluntatibus* and *laedendis*, although in this case Mamertinus has the same word order as the Ciceronian manuscripts. The structure of the sentence and the transmission do not suggest changes.

in sententia simpliciter ferenda: Jeep (1862, 7) argues that *referenda* in one manuscript is a corruption of the original reading *sententia simpliciter e re p. ferenda* and the addition of *e re publica* would balance this phrase with *de/a/pro re publica* in the parallel phrases. While the point about parallelism is valid, *sententiam ferre* is a technical term for voicing one's verdict (*OLD* s.v. *fero* 27a) and thus does not require any further supplement (*OLD* s.v. *simpliciter* 4), in contrast to the other points for which the reference to the Republic is less straightforward; *res publica* is not mentioned in all phrases as the final two are general; and the error *referenda* could also have developed through confusion with *in referenda autem gratia* just before this clause.

in hominum voluntatibus pro re publica laedendis: implies that Cicero will not be afraid to oppose the wishes of others if these are detrimental to the Republic.

in perferendo labore industriam: to avoid an unusal *clausula*, Bornecque (1909, 59 n. 4) suggests reading *in laboribus perferendis industriam* (after the model of Mamertinus). The transmitted singular expresses the idea generically and is appropriate.

benivolentiam: Cicero again stresses his goodwill, but does not specify which *commoda* his activities might apply to.

25 haec cura: refers summatively back to the activities mentioned in what precedes (Cic. *RQ* 24) and looks forward to the subsequent *ut*-clause.

sempiterna: again an emphasis on the everlasting nature of Cicero's gratitude and the resulting activities (Cic. *RQ* 24).

deorum immortalium vim et numen: takes up the idea expressed earlier that the People will be like gods to Cicero (Cic. *RQ* 18). Added *vis* underlines not only the revered position, but also the associated power connected with it (*OLD* s.v. *uis* 12).

tum posteris vestris cunctisque gentibus: Cicero extends (*cum... tum*) the intended impact of his aim to show gratitude and work for the Republic chronologically and geographically: he wishes to appear worthy of what the People/ the community did for him not only in the immediate context, but also in such a way that it will be known and recognized in future and abroad.

quae suam dignitatem non posse se tenere, nisi me reciperasset: a final statement of the parallel fate of Cicero and the Republic (see Introduction, section 3.4), presented not as Cicero's view, but as that of the entire community (*cunctis suffragiis iudicavit*). Emphasizing the *dignitas* (here of the personified Republic, not of Cicero [Cic. *RS* 1; 5; 26; 27; 31; *RQ* 4; 6; 15]) stresses the positive effect of Cicero's return for the Republic.

cunctis suffragiis: i.e. the unanimous vote by the People for Cicero's recall when the relevant bill was approved on 4 August 57 BCE (see Introduction, section 2; for the phrase, see, e.g., Cic. *Off.* 2.59). Cicero says on numerous occasions that the assembly to vote on his recall was well attended and everyone felt obliged to vote for his *salus* (e.g. Cic. *RS* 27–8; *Dom.* 75; 90). He does not say explicitly elsewhere that it was a unanimous vote; this is stated by Plutarch (Plut. *Cic.* 33.5). – Cicero thus ends on a note of unanimity (the view of everyone and agreeing with Cicero's opinion), their shared concern for the Republic, and his importance in this context.

[M. Tulli Ciceronis] Oratio pridie quam in exilium iret

Introduction

This speech, rightly regarded as spurious by scholars (see Introduction, section 4), is envisaged as delivered by Cicero just before leaving Rome in spring

58 BCE. The title suggests that his departure is a given and he is making a kind of farewell speech; large parts of the speech, however, consist of an appeal to the audience for help to enable Cicero to stay in Rome, while the inevitability of departure is gradually becoming more and more accepted. It is uncertain whether the title goes back to the author of the speech; it might be an addition by a later editor. The title is the only element to provide the precise timing of the occasion of the speech, the eve of Cicero's departure. The text of the speech merely sets it at a point fairly close to Cicero's departure without indicating the exact timing and circumstances of the intervention. The phrase in the main version of the title *pridie quam in exilium iret* (with variations in some manuscripts) also appears in the work of the late antique writer Iulius Obsequens, though applied to a different activity of Cicero (Obs. 68: *turbinis vi simulacrum, quod M. Cicero ante cellam Minervae pridie, quam plebiscito in exilium iret, posuerat, dissipatum membris pronum iacuit, fractis humeris bracchiis capite: dirum ipsi Ciceroni portendit* [plebiscito *huc transp.* Scheffer: post Cicero *codd.*].); whether there is any connection cannot be established.

The assumed occasion for the speech is apparently a meeting of the People, including knights. While the beginning of the speech does not identify the audience, there are addresses to *Quirites* in the middle (*Exil.* 11; 12) and to *equites Romani* towards the end (*Exil.* 29; 30), and *contio* is mentioned as the framework (*Exil.* 19). In historical terms, it is unlikely that one of the magistrates of that year would have called a *contio* to give Cicero the opportunity to deliver such a speech; further, addresses to *equites* in *contiones* are not attested elsewhere, since *contiones* are meant to be given to the *populus Romanus* and specific groups are not normally singled out (*equites* may be addressed in law court speeches, as they are among the judges: see, e.g., Cic. *Sest.* 25; 26). In the additional manuscript signalled by De Marco (1957) the speech is defined as *ad equites* (1957, 187 n. 1; Keeline [2018, 168] talks of 'a speech supposedly delivered to the Roman *equites*'); the title in one manuscript is given as *in senatu*, which does not match the text (Corbeill 2020, 28). The addition of addresses to *equites* to a speech that in the main seems to be intended as a speech to the People could be triggered by the known good relationship between Cicero and the *equites* and by their support for him during his consulship and just before his departure from Rome.

As for the creation of such a scenario, it is sometimes thought that the writer might have been inspired by narratives about this period such as that in Plutarch's biography of Cicero (as a detailed report about Cicero's withdrawal from Rome does not appear in Cicero's own writings), where it is reported that, before he left Rome, Cicero put on mourning clothes and made suppliant entreaties to the People and that a large number of knights also changed their dress, escorted him, and joined his supplications (Plut. *Cic.* 30.6–1.1). These, however, seem to be informal and individual suppliant entreaties, while this piece is designed as a one-off full-scale speech. Still, the assumption that the speech was created on the basis of historical information might support the general theory that the speech was written as an item in the context of the imperial declamation schools, where it was common to create speeches that historical figures could have made in particular situations they were known to have encountered (see examples in Seneca the Elder).

The speech alludes to the presentation of Cicero's absence from Rome and of the events leading up to it in Ciceronian works from the period after his consulship (e.g. Cicero fought Catiline without weapons for the benefit of all: *Exil.* 3, 8, 14; Cicero was not given a trial and a chance of defence: *Exil.* 17–18; Cicero avoids fighting and sacrifices himself by leaving: *Exil.* 20–1). These items seem to have been put together to emphasize individual points throughout the speech, rather than to create a complete logical sequence, and are not always in line with the impression they are meant to create in Cicero's genuine works. For instance, the imminent absence from Rome is referred to as 'exile' (e.g. *Exil.* 29; 30), a term not used by the historical Cicero after his return (see Introduction, section 3.4); and the reminder of the great deeds for Rome and the appeal for help to avoid the 'exile' are not consistent. Therefore, this speech seems to have been composed by someone familiar with the history of the period and Cicero's writings, but not observing the distinction between different types of texts within Cicero's oeuvre and the aim of Cicero's presentation of himself. The result could perhaps be described as a combination of Cicero's public and private persona, as it emerges from speeches and letters respectively, which date to different times in his life.

Stylistically, the speech is characterized by an abundance of rhetorical figures (mostly the same as in Cicero's speeches, but in greater density): there is extensive use of elements such as parallelism, chiasmus, juxtaposition, contrast, alliteration, anaphora, asyndeton, hyperbaton (see Corbeill 2020, 31–3), and tricolon (e.g. Corbeill 2020, 18, 33). Doublets are frequent, i.e. two nouns or verbs linked by a copulative conjunction, expressing similar or related notions, to make the expression weightier and to cover more connotations. A substantial number of these collocations are not attested in the works of the historical Cicero and are rare or unique. In talking about himself, the speaker switches between personal phrases in the first person (singular and also plural) and impersonal statements in the third person, sometimes quite suddenly and within a single long sentence; while reasons cannot always be discerned, there seems to be a tendency to present more general descriptions of behaviour and situations as they appear to the audience in the third person and specific activities like speaking, leading, or leaving Rome in the first person. It has been suggested that this form of expression could be a way for the author to assert non-identity (Corbeill 2020, 29–30): while such an interpretation is possible on a metaliterary level, in rhetorical terms the method might simply be a ploy for the speaker to align himself with the audience, so as to engage them and make the plea more effective. While the genuine Cicero does not often talk about

himself in the third person using his name except for certain more formal contexts and in references to official documents (see *Exil.* 6 n.), he sometimes refers
to himself as *is* or *civis* in the third person in the genuine speeches delivered
after his return to Rome (Cic. *RS* 7 [and n.]; 8; 16; *RQ* 16) when he adopts someone else's perspective or creates a contrast with the activities of others.
That P. Clodius Pulcher is not mentioned by name in the spurious speech
(noted by Corbeill 2020, 30–1) is in line with the practice of the genuine Cicero
in the speeches delivered straight after his return to Rome (Cic. *RS* 3 n.).

The train of thought is marked by conjunctions indicating logical connections,
but the transitions between points tend to be vague. Beyond a repeated general
appeal for compassion and assistance, the speech does not display a clear
argumentative structure: the discussion seems to vacillate between a plea to
enable the speaker to remain in Rome (*Exil.* 3; 4–6; 8; 14; 16; 24–6; 29), the fear
of death (*Exil.* 6; 7; 23), and the acceptance of the impending exile (*Exil.* 7; 13;
19; 20–1; 23; 27; 30), which becomes more prominent towards the end. The presentation of several alternatives indicates that various scenarios are being
considered.

According to the assumed context, the speaker purports to be 'Cicero', but
obviously is not the historical Cicero. Since this speaker assumes the same name
as the person he impersonates, distinguishing between the two can be difficult
and confusing to indicate. Thus, in the absence of a better method, comments
concerning the writer/speaker of this oration will refer to 'Cicero'; statements
concerning the experience of the historical Cicero will be attributed to Cicero.
Admittedly, there will be some cases that might be assigned to either category,
but this principle should help to retain awareness of the basic distinction.

Outline of structure and contents

1. Introduction (1–6): Appeal for support in return for previous services
2. Main section (6–23): Analysis of the situation: 'Cicero', an innocent man,
   after great services to the Republic, is thrust out of the community
   2.1. Unjustified reasons for opposition to 'Cicero' (6–8)
   2.2. Need to retain 'Cicero' as a well-proven guardian (9–10)
   2.3. Need to defend innocent people (11–12)
   2.4. Particularly bad situation for 'Cicero' (13–16)
   2.5. No opportunity for defence for 'Cicero' (17–19)
   2.6. 'Cicero's' sacrifice for the community (20–2)
   2.7. Appeal to protect 'Cicero's' family (23)
3. Conclusion (24–30): Final appeal for support
   3.1. To the gods (24–5)
   3.2. To the human audience (26–8)
   3.3. To the knights (29–30)

The speech basically is a sustained plea for support justified by reminders of 'Cicero's' past services for the Republic, his innocence, and unjust treatment, and explained by the assumption that he should receive assistance in return for services rendered to the community. Therefore, while an introductory part (*Exil.* 1–6) and an emphatic and emotional conclusion (*Exil.* 24–30) can be distinguished, the speech as a whole is not characterized by a logical and argumentative sequence moving towards a clear persuasive goal, and there is no explicit statement of the aim or context. Instead, appeals to assist 'Cicero' are repeated throughout with varying focus, linked to various explanatory statements such as about 'Cicero's' unfair treatment by his opponents, his virtuous nature, his previous behaviour, or the general reciprocity of favours.

Notes

1. Introduction (1–6): Appeal for support in return for previous services

The introduction of this speech (*Exil.* 1–6) does not explicitly identify the speaker or the audience or the purpose of the speech; these become obvious over the course of it. With a number of general statements on giving and receiving favours, on the need for gratitude, and on reciprocal action, 'Cicero' reminds the audience that he has delivered great and important services and they now have a duty to repay these by supporting him, indicating that they may enjoy further benefits from his presence in future. It is not specified how the audience should assist 'Cicero' and what the intended outcome would be; the envisaged situation and comments later in the speech indicate that the goal is to enable 'Cicero' to stay in Rome.

   1 si quando…providere: the speech starts with the premise that threats from enemies are always to be expected and, if the audience would like to be in a position to ward them off, they should support 'Cicero' now because of his track record. 'Cicero' is not mentioned by name but rather identified by his previous services for the audience indicated allusively by a vivid metaphorical description (i.e. successful confrontation of the Catilinarian Conspiracy). The need to protect 'Cicero' is thus presented as advantageous to the audience.

   si quando…: Gamberale (1998, 57) notes that there are only two Ciceronian speeches without an address to the audience (group or individual) at the beginning and that both begin with a *si*-clause (Cic. *Balb.* 1; *Caec.* 1). In both speeches an address follows soon after the first paragraph (Cic. *Balb.* 2: *iudices*; *Caec.* 3: *recuperatores*), and the performance situation identifies the audience. Here the first address to the audience is only inserted almost halfway through the speech (*Exil.* 11); *di immortales* are invoked a little earlier (*Exil.* 9). – On the style of *Exil.* 1, including a variety of rhetorical figures and the appropriation of Ciceronian techniques, see Gamberale 1998, 56–9.

inimicorum...inimicorum: these *inimici* are not defined. In view of the allusions to Cicero's efforts against the Catilinarian Conspiracy, the first mention of *inimici* probably refers to individuals opposed to Cicero and equally to a stable Republic; thus, the audience can be motivated, as they will benefit from action against these. The second reference more clearly refers to the current situation and thus must denote P. Clodius Pulcher and his followers confronting Cicero at the time when he was about to leave Rome in 58 BCE (see Introduction, section 2). – Cicero's opponents are typically called *inimici* in this speech (*Exil.* 12; 14; 15; 16; 23; 26; 30); *hostes* is only used in the last paragraph (*Exil.* 30). – Throughout the speech names of contemporary individuals (apart from Cicero) are not used (see *Exil.*, Introduction). In the speeches Cicero delivered after his return he discusses the consuls of 58 BCE in an invective section (Cic. *RS* 10–18), but does not name P. Clodius Pulcher or any other opponents (Cic. *RS* 3; 16 nn.).

inimicorum impetum propulsare ac propellere: the collocation *impetum/ impetus propulsare* also appears in Cicero's genuine speeches (Cic. *Prov. cons.* 41; *Mur.* 2), while *propellere* is rare and the doublet *propulsare ac propellere* is not attested elsewhere (Gamberale 1998, 57; Corbeill 2020, 24).

defendite: the call to action is directed towards an audience not identified by an address or a reference to the venue. Overall, the speech has four addresses to the audience: two addresses to *Quirites* almost at the mid-point (*Exil.* 11; 12) and two to *equites Romani* towards the end (*Exil.* 29, 30). Even though Cicero sometimes addresses both a larger group and individuals from this group in the same speech (e.g. Cic. *Cat.* 1: Senate and Catiline), there are no examples of *equites Romani* addressed as a separate group in speeches delivered to the People. Apparently, it is envisaged that 'Cicero' is speaking to a *contio* attended also by *equites Romani* (see *Exil.*, Introduction).

unum, qui...mei capitis periculo non dubitavi: the identification of Cicero starts with a generic *unum* (contrasting with juxtaposed *universi*) and then changes to the first person singular, making the reference to the speaker obvious (for similar switches, see, e.g., *Exil.* 6; 8). The structure *is/ ego qui...* to describe what Cicero has done without identifying him by name or his role appears a number of times in this speech (e.g. *Exil.* 1; 2; 3; 14; 18; 26; 30).

mei capitis periculo: claims that Cicero did not hesitate to risk his own life to save everybody else, i.e. in combating the Catilinarian Conspiracy. In talking about his efforts to contain the Catilinarian Conspiracy the historical Cicero alludes to the situation's potential danger to himself (e.g. Cic. *Cat.* 2.3; 2.13; 3.1; 4.1; 4.9), but does not give details or stress it as the key component. Elsewhere it is reported that the conspirators planned an assassination attempt on Cicero (Sall. *Cat.* 27.4–28.3) and that he appeared with a breastplate beneath his toga on the day of the consular elections in 63 BCE to demonstrate the potential danger for the consul (Cic. *Mur.* 52; Plut. *Cic.* 14.7–8).

ne omnes ardore flammae occideretis: a metaphorical description of Cicero's achievement in protecting everyone from the threat posed by the Catilinarian Conspiracy in his consular year of 63 BCE. – *ardore flammae* is probably a vivid indication of great danger (*OLD* s.v. *ardor* 7; *flamma* 3; for the metaphor of fire applied to the Catilinarian Conspiracy, see Cic. *Sull.* 53; *Exil.* 6; 8; 9; 14) rather than an allusion to the conspirators' plans for an arson attack on the city of Rome (Cic. *Cat.* 1.3; 1.6; 1.9; 2.6; 2.10; 3.8; 3.10; 3.14; 4.4; *Sull.* 53; Sall. *Cat.* 24.4; 27.2; 32.1–2; 43.2; 48.4).

quem virtutis gloria cum summa laude ad caelum extulit: a vague reference to Cicero's success in dealing with the Catilinarian Conspiracy and the acknowledgement subsequently received, including a Senate decree on a festival of thanksgiving and the award of the title *pater patriae* (Cic. *Cat.* 3.15; *Pis.* 6; *Sest.* 121; Plut. *Cic.* 23.6). While emphasis is on the glory earned, it is stressed that the success is based on *virtus*; the corresponding behaviour is continually associated with Cicero in this speech (*Exil.* 2; 3; 6; 7; 12; 13; 14; 16; 18). The complement *cum summa laude* highlights the reward for the great deeds based on virtue.

invidia: in the *Catilinarian Orations* Cicero voices the apprehension that his actions against Catiline could lead to *invidia* (Cic. *Cat.* 1.23; 1.29; 2.15; 3.3; 3.29). Here it is implied that these fears have become true, identifying *invidia* as the motivation of his opponents (*Exil.* 1; 6–7; 16; 28). – *invidia* is also given as a motivation for some people opposing or not supporting Cicero in the speeches delivered after his return (Cic. *RQ* 13; 21).

oppressum deprimit: in this speech compounds of *premere* describe the opposition against Cicero and its effect on him (e.g. *Exil.* 7; 13; 23). – This phrase seems to be a unique collocation; it increases the contrast with the preceding status of *ad caelum extulit*.

supplicium: used as a generic term for 'punishment' alluding to the need for Cicero to leave Rome, although it is not a formal punishment at this stage (see Introduction, section 2). The same word, with its connotation of 'death penalty', is applied to the punishment of the captured Catilinarian conspirators elsewhere (e.g. Sall. *Cat.* 50.4; 55.1; 55.6; 57.1).

si … duxit: one reason why the audience should assist 'Cicero' (operating on a personal level) is that he values the audience's children highly (as shown by combating the Catilinarian Conspiracy and ensuring stable political circumstances) and that, therefore, if they enjoy their children, they should ensure 'Cicero's' continued presence in gratitude and to enable further support. – In the speeches given after his return Cicero talks about his feelings for his own children (Cic. *RS* 1; 27; *RQ* 2; 5; 8); it is not mentioned elsewhere that Cicero intervened in the Catilinarian Conspiracy out of concern for the People's children.

liberum conceptam dulcedinem animo inclusam continetis: of the two participles, *inclusam* is linked to *continetis: habere* or *tenere* combined with a past participle emphasizes the resulting status more than a standard perfect tense (K.-St. I 763–4; Pinkster 2015, 478–81). *conceptam* goes with *liberum…dulcedinem*; the participle presumably underlines that a feeling of *dulcedo* has been experienced (*OLD* s.v. *concipio* 6). This is then stored in the mind (*OLD* s.v. *includo* 3c; e.g. Cic. *Ac.* 1.11). *animo* is a summarizing singular referring to several people (K.-St. I 78–9).

nolite…velle carere: if the negative imperative of *velle* is expressed by *noli/nolite* plus infinitive, this leads to a pleonastic expression (K.-St. II 569); *velle* can then govern another infinitive (Cic. *Dom.* 146; *Balb.* 64; *Cael.* 79; *Mur.* 50; see also Gamberale 1998, 58; Corbeill 2020, 24). *carere* expresses 'Cicero's' impending absence from Rome from the point of view of the audience.

eo: denotes the speaker 'Cicero' and is further defined by the subsequent relative clause.

vestram procreationem: *procreatio* here denotes the result of the act of procreation (*TLL* X.2.1549.61–2, s.v. *procreatio*: 'II *metonymice significatur id*: A *quod procreatur*: 1 *de liberis*', where this passage and a few late antique examples are listed).

duxit: is the reading found in one corrected manuscript, while De Marco (1967, 39; 1991, 13) prints *dixit*, the reading exhibited by the other manuscripts. *dixit* implies a reference to an occasion on which Cicero uttered such a statement: this would make the proclamation more emphatic, while the author of this speech tends to avoid such specifics; there is no evidence of such a comment in extant sources.

2 est enim…retribuere: 'Cicero' explains (*enim*) why he almost requests support from the audience: it is implied that they are obliged to return the favours provided. – The phrase has a proverbial quality and could be a variation on the saying 'as you sow, so shall you reap' (Otto 1890, 221, s.v. *metere*).

liberale officium: in this context the adjective primarily emphasizes the nature of the deed (*OLD* s.v. *liberalis*[1] 2), while there might be the additional notion of 'generosity' (*OLD* s.v. *liberalis*[1] 5).

conducit: used as an impersonal verb governing an infinitive (*OLD* s.v. *conduco* 6).

in loco: stresses not only that a favour should be repaid, but also at the right moment (*OLD* s.v. *locus* 21b), implying that this is the case now that 'Cicero' needs assistance.

illic enim…hic: another explanatory sentence (*enim*) juxtaposes the characteristics acknowledged in conferring (*illic*) and rewarding favours (*hic*): it is appropriate for those who have received favours to remember them and show their gratitude.

itaque: introduces a conclusion to the argument up to this point: because of his interventions to maintain the liberty of the audience 'Cicero' deserves particular gratitude (and action in return).

si omnibus…servitutis: implies that Catiline's activities put liberty at risk and might have meant the introduction of servitude (unthinkable for those used to liberty like the Romans) and that 'Cicero's' actions (*is…qui*) have averted that threat. – The notion of the importance of liberty and its role for the Roman People is less prominent in Cicero's *Catilinarian Orations*, but is a feature of his *Philippics* against Marc Antony (e.g. Cic. *Phil.* 3.29; 6.19).

is vestris animis acceptissimus: for the phrase, see Liv. 1.15.8: *multitudini tamen gratior fuit quam patribus, longe ante alios acceptissimus militum animis* (*OLD* s.v. *acceptus* 1a).

a vestro corpore iugum acerbissimum reppulit servitutis: the vivid metaphorical description makes the threat appear as a physical risk and thus the salvation more impressive and worthy of gratitude. – Structurally, a plural (*animis*) is again followed by a summarizing singular (*Exil.* 1 n.).

3 et: adds another aspect justifying why 'Cicero' can expect support from the audience in return for preserving their liberty.

maiores vestri: appeals to the precedent of the *maiores* are common in Cicero's speeches (on the role of the *maiores* in Cicero's works, see Roloff 1938).

eos imperatores: a general statement on successful Roman generals of the past without any specific examples.

militum virtute hostium fregerunt furorem: characterizes the Romans and their opponents in a way that presents the Roman victory as the result of a superiority of character.

iucundissimo fructu libertatis reconciliato: in continuation of the ideas in the preceding sentence it is implied that the wars for which generals were honoured led to reclaiming liberty, which was under threat from the enemy (*OLD* s.v. *reconcilio* 2).

non solum statuis…decorarunt: one might think that statues are longer-lasting than triumphs. In this juxtaposition there may be an allusion to comments on the potential decay of statues in *Philippic* 9, though these are made in a different argumentative context (Cic. *Phil.* 9.14), and a reference to the notion that a triumph will be recorded and enter collective memory.

tum: marks the start of the main clause after the *si*-clause (*OLD* s.v. *tum* 5).

eum consulem, qui…vindicavit: a version of Cicero's claim that, in confronting the Catilinarian Conspiracy in his consular year of 63 BCE, he saved the Republic without war and bloodshed (e.g. Cic. *Cat.* 3.23). The emphasis is less on the figure of *dux togatus* (Cic. *Cat.* 2.28; 3.23) than on Cicero's *eximia animi virtus* (Cic. *RQ* 20). His *eximia animi virtus* contrasts with *militum praesenti fortitudine*, probably a variation of *militum virtute* assigned to ealier generations. – Here it is indicated for the first time that the vague references to 'Cicero's' achievements refer to his consulship.

hostilem civium mentem: after *inimici* at the start of the speech (*Exil.* 1 [and n.]), here *hostilis* denotes internal political enemies. In contrast to what is sometimes claimed in Cicero's genuine speeches, namely that people hostile to the Republic can no longer be regarded as citizens (e.g. Cic. *Phil.* 5.21; 5.25; 6.16), the citizen status of these hostile people is acknowledged; they are rather said to show hostile intentions as citizens.

senatus auctoritate: indicates that in taking action against Catiline Cicero acted on the basis of Senate decrees. Authorization by the Senate is the crucial element in Cicero's justification (see also Keeline 2018, 168) and something he was eager to obtain as the *Catilinarian Orations* show: while there was no proper trial for the captured Catilinarian conspirators, Cicero made sure that he acted on the basis of the will of the Senate (for later references to the involvement of the Senate, see, e.g., Cic. *Dom.* 94; 114; *Sest.* 53; *Phil.* 4.15); he therefore initiated another Senate decree on the punishment of the Catilinarian conspirators (Cic. *Cat.* 4) rather than just relying on the earlier *senatus consultum ultimum.*

existimate: 'Cicero' asks the audience to be of the opinion that he should be retained rather than requesting action. It might be slightly odd to ask for the adoption of an opinion, but the request is thus more indirect and easier to realize (for such a structure, see Cic. *Font.* 42; cf. Corbeill 2020, 24).

in civitate: *civitas* occurs frequently in this speech (even more often than in the speeches delivered after Cicero's return). Gamberale (1979, 87–8, on *Exil.* 8) notes that *civitas* here basically means *urbs.* While the word implies a local sense, it has a wider and stronger meaning in that it indicates the community of citizens and a functioning state. These broader aspects are relevant in the context of Cicero potentially being separated from *civitas* or him having preserved *civitas.*

4 si quae … universos: another direct appeal to the audience to assist 'Cicero': 'Cicero' first generically implies an individual beneficiary's obligation to gratitude towards the benefactor; then he infers from the fact that he has conferred favours upon everyone the justification for asking the audience for assistance.

beneficia … solent … esse fructuosa: states even more strongly that conferring favours is not necessarily an altruistic act, but is often advantageous for the benefactor.

iure et merito: emphasizes that the request and the expectation are justified. – *iure et merito* is not attested elsewhere until the fourth century CE, but *iure meritoque* occasionally appears earlier (Sen. *Clem.* 1.12.1; Val. Max. 1.6.ext.3; Curt. 10.9.3), and *iure ac merito* or *merito ac iure* is found in Cicero's writings (Cic. *Dom.* 3; *Cat.* 3.14) and in those of other authors (e.g. Iuv. 2.34).

salutis: *salus* is a frequent term for Cicero's situation in the speeches delivered after his return (see Cic. *RS* 3 and n.; Introduction, section 3.4).

nam neque … resisti: gives the reason (*nam*) why it is appropriate for an individual to ask for repayment from all after conferring favours upon the entire community, as these required more effort.

verius: employed as an evaluative term (*OLD* s.v. *uerus*[1] 9).

propterea quod in unius periculo...in rei publicae insidiis: an adversative asyndeton juxtaposing actions for an individual or for the entire Republic in need.

in rei publicae insidiis: the phrasing insinuates that these opponents are rightly confronted as they are attacking the Republic and do so in a devious way (for the phrase, see Cic. *Sull.* 14; 45).

quo firmius est quod oppugnatur: i.e. the Republic or parts of it.

inimici: on the use of this word, see *Exil.* 1 n.

magna sollicitudine, industria, virtute: an asyndetic tricolon indicating the qualities needed to resist political opponents, implicitly applied to the speaker 'Cicero'. This collocation does not seem to be attested elsewhere.

5 et: continues the argument of why more help as an expression of gratitude (*ad gratiam referendam*) can be expected from all: they have more resources at their disposal.

si...cupiant: on *si* in concessive sense, see K.-St. II 426–7.

eo plurimum prodest quo<d> firmioribus opibus est nixum: the subordinate clause explains why support by a large group is more effective; *eo* prepares the following cause. This construction requires *quo<d>* (*OLD* s.v. *quod* 2). The final letter could have easily been lost in the transmission process, especially since *eo...quo* (with comparatives) is also a standard phrase.

iure igitur...opitulari: provides a conclusion (*igitur*), recapitulating the preceding argument: saving the Republic is a greater deed than supporting an individual, and the audience as a group has access to more resources; thus, they are obliged and able to support 'Cicero'.

in patriam: choosing *patria* to denote the country (also at *Exil.* 6; 29) rather than *res publica* gives the appeal an emotional tone.

privata...defensione: the help offered to individuals, mentioned generally as a point of comparison so far, is defined as *defensio*, which might allude to advocacy, as the word can have a generic (*OLD* s.v. *defensio* 1) and a specific judicial meaning (*OLD* s.v. *defensio* 2). The adjective replaces a noun in the (objective) genitive (K.-St. I 212–13).

plus a vobis praesidii quam a ceteris opis: again justifies the request to the audience, since more protection can be expected from them than help from other (unspecified) individuals.

optestor: while so far imperatives and jussive subjunctives have been used, the request for help is now phrased as a proper appeal (*OLD* s.v. *obtestor* 2, in the variant spelling *optestor*; see also *Exil.* 9; 29).

6 non...tardiores: adds a further nuance: in response to the favours conferred by 'Cicero', the audience are obliged not just to assist him, but to do so promptly, to match his readiness in the past.

proferendum: is De Marco's (1967, 41; 1991, 14) emendation for transmitted *promerendum. proferendum* is palaeographically close and provides a plausible meaning, though the collocation is still unusual (*OLD* s.v. *profero* 2).

tardiores: ne … existemetis: the *ne*-clause does not provide a direct conclusion of the previous clause; therefore, it is better interpreted as a self-contained main clause rather than a subordinate clause depending on *non convenit … esse tardiores* (as indicated by the punctuation). *ne … existemetis* as a request might seem paradoxical, but it is simply a (negated) variation of preceding *existimate* (*Exil.* 3 [and n.]). This connection may explain the form: *ne* with present subjunctive, functioning as a negative imperative, is rare and does not occur in the works of the genuine Cicero with reference to a specific (not a generic) subject (K.-St. I 187–9). – De Marco (1991, 15) retains transmitted *tardiones*: such a word is not attested (perhaps a typographical error). Therefore, it is advisable to adopt the easy emendation *tardiores*, as other editors have done and De Marco (1967, 41) earlier.

ne … existimetis: 'Cicero' presupposes that his previous deeds should be extolled *laude atque honoribus* and concludes that his personal safety should also be ensured. The inference works, but the starting point about honours is an unproven assumption. It might be an allusion to honorific Senate decrees passed after Cicero's successful defeat of the Catilinarian Conspiracy (Cic. *Cat.* 3.15; *Pis.* 6; *Sest.* 121; Plut. *Cic.* 23). Since such rewards are presented as an obligation, it is left open whether anything has been awarded.

amplitudinem et gloriam … amplificare: for the combination of the two nouns, see Cic. *Verr.* 2.5.173; for *amplificare* (*OLD* s.v. *amplifico* 3), see Cic. *Dom.* 88; *Fin.* 5.72; *amplitudinem … amplificare* is a kind of *figura etymologica* (K.-St. I 279).

laude atque honoribus: similar expressions appear in the works of Cicero (*Planc.* 27; *Phil.* 4.4) and Lucretius (6.12), but these have the same number for both words rather than a combination of singular and plural.

2. Main section (6–23): Analysis of the situation: 'Cicero', an innocent man, after great services to the Republic, is thrust out of the community

The main section (*Exil.* 6–23) consists of reminders of 'Cicero's' past achievements, statements on the situation of the Republic, remarks on his decision to leave Rome, further comments on conferring and receiving favours, and a series of appeals. The various points are linked by association rather than by clear logical argumentative transitions. Still, there is a sense of progression: the section starts by highlighting that 'Cicero' is targeted because of his service for the Republic and not because of any crimes committed (*Exil.* 6–8); this assertion leads to the conclusion that he should be retained as an experienced guardian and so as not to set an odd precedent (*Exil.* 9–10). This view prompts a reminder of the principle that defending innocent people is always required and good for everyone involved (*Exil.* 11–12). Focusing again explicitly on the individual, 'Cicero' goes on to point out that he is suffering a great deal and in return for services for the community, ending with another emphatic appeal to the audience to support him in their own interests (*Exil.* 13–16). To make 'Cicero's' situation appear deserving of backing, it is then mentioned that he has not been given an opportunity to defend himself; this observation is balanced by an expression of the conviction that his virtue will proclaim his deeds and his opponents will suffer from the consciousness of their crimes (*Exil.* 17–19). At that point the impending departure seems to have become accepted as unavoidable; 'Cicero', therefore, announces that he will yield to the madness of a few to prevent civil war and bad fortune for the Republic (*Exil.* 20–2). As there is then less that can be done for 'Cicero', the appeals to assist him interspersed throughout this section change to a request to support his family and to remember his virtue in the final part (*Exil.* 23), creating an emphatic and emotional closure.

2.1. Unjustified reasons for opposition to 'Cicero' (6–8)

The first part (*Exil.* 6–8) of the main section (*Exil.* 6–23) emphasizes that 'Cicero' is in danger not because he has committed any wrongs, but rather because he has spent a virtuous and honest life and preserved the Republic. The renewed reminder of Cicero's achievements for the benefit of the audience leads to another emphatic appeal to stand by him, on the basis that they ought to pay back the favours received. Here it is indicated that the help the speaker is thinking of is interventions that would enable him to stay in the community.

6 etenim errat … malorum: the statement of what Cicero has done and has not done is made emphatic through a tricolon with triple anaphora of *quod* followed by four short clauses linked by anaphora of *non* and all including an antithesis (Gamberale 1979, 78–9).

etenim: introduces a corroboration of the preceding claim that Cicero deserves support for his great services to the community by emphasizing that this is what he has done, rather than any crime (*OLD* s.v. *etenim*).

errat si qui …: a generic statement.

M. Tullium: while *M. Tullius* is apparently the form of M. Tullius Cicero's name used for formal addresses in the Senate by other members (e.g. Cic. *Att.* 7.3.5) and in official statements about him (e.g. Cic. *Dom.* 44), Cicero usually calls himself *M. Cicero* when talking about himself in speeches apart from a few exceptions in specific contexts (esp. when he reports official documents about him or quotes others addressing him). This method and the preferred use of the *cognomen* can probably be explained by a desire to adopt naming conventions common for noblemen to mark social aspirations and increased standing (Adams 1978, esp. 157–9). The version of the name used here (*Tullius* and

M. Tullius also at *Exil.* 7; 8; 19; 27; 30) is attested in Cicero (*M. Tullius*: Cic. *Cat.* 1.27; *Tull.* 3; *Verr.* 2.4.79; *Dom.* 44; 47; 50; 85; 102; *Mil.* 94; *Tullius*: Cic. *Tull.* 4; *Div. Caec.* 51), Sallust (Sall. *Cat.* 51.35), and Pseudo-Sallust (Ps.-Sall. *Inv. in Cic.* 1), but would be a less common form in such a context in a Ciceronian speech (on the use of the third person in this speech, see Corbeill 2020, 29–30).

idcirco: looks forward to the causal *quod*-clauses.

in periculum capitis vocari: 'Cicero' claims that the current situation leaves him facing danger to his life, though not because of a misdeed (also *Exil.* 7). While in theory the death penalty was a consequence of a potential trial, in practice the danger was remote; typically, upper-class Romans went into exile before such a penalty was decreed (Polyb. 6.14.6–8; Kelly 2006, 17–19). Further, although the argument in this section is based on the notion of loss of life, *caput* might have the additional connotation of 'civil rights' (*OLD* s.v. *caput* 6a, though usually in other constructions), with the exile understood as a meta-phorical loss of life. – While the standard collocation for bringing to court is *in ius* or *in iudicium vocare* (*OLD* s.v. *uoco*[1] 4c), a comparable phrase *in discrimen capitis vocare* appears in Cicero's works (Cic. *Rab. perd.* 2; cf. Corbeill 2020, 24–5). Thus, the wording suggests a trial whose outcome could be 'death' for the defendant (for *periculum capitis*, see Cic. *Sest.* 98; *Mil.* 41; *Rab. perd.* 26).

quod…, quod…, quod…: three possible reasons for ordinary trials: any crime, high treason, or an unacceptable way of life (though the last could only trigger a court case if it led to obvious criminal acts).

deliquerit aliquid: for the construction of this verb with an accusative object (*OLD* s.v. *delinquo* 3), see, e.g., Cic. *Leg. agr.* 2.100; *Mur.* 57; *Sest.* 145; *Off.* 1.146.

patriam laeserit: emphasizes that it is wrong to believe that Cicero is accused of a crime against *patria* (*OLD* s.v. *laedo* 3c; for *laedere* with an abstract noun, such as *res publica*, see, e.g., Cic. *Sest.* 78; Sen. *Contr.* 10.5.14) and prepares the imminent contrast with his role as *pater patriae* (*Exil.* 8; on *patria*, see *Exil.* 5 n.).

non citatur…malorum: four contrasts listing what Cicero is and is not accused of (expressed with variation), loosely linked to the reasons of oppos-ition to the Republic and an inappropriately led life just mentioned.

non citatur reus…reus citatur: a double chiasmus contrasts a common reason for accusation and the unusual one in Cicero's case.

citatur reus: a *terminus technicus* for an accused person being formally sum-moned (*OLD* s.v. *cito*[2] 4a). The notion that Cicero is 'accused' is invalidated when 'Cicero' highlights positive features and claims that (paradoxically) he is accused of these (i.e. this is what criticism of previous deeds amounts to), rather than of a crime or an evil character trait. While the historical Cicero also notes in his speeches that his virtuous deeds in connection with combating the Catilinarian Conspiracy have caused the situation that forced him to leave Rome, he constantly stresses that there has not been a charge or trial, he has not been condemned in court, and thus has not been sent into 'exile' as a guilty person, rather than presenting the true reason in his view as a charge; for Cicero intends to highlight the unlawfulness of the process without any trial (see Introduction, sections 2 and 3.4; see esp. Cic. *Dom.* 26; 33; 62; 77; 83; 88; *Sest.* 53).

homo novus: the historical Cicero was aware that in Roman terminology he was a *homo novus* since his ancestors had not reached senior political offices in Rome (on ancient and modern definitions of *homo novus*, see Burckhardt 1990) and that he therefore faced particular obstacles (and advantages); he prominently expresses this view in his inaugural speech as consul to the People (Cic. *Leg. agr.* 2.1–10). He does not, however, voice the point directly that, because of his background, he suffers criticism for opposing noblemen (as Catiline and some of his followers belonged to the nobility). Cicero's status as a *homo novus* was raised against him by his rivals in the election campaign for the consulship of 63 BCE, when he was elected in preference to noblemen like Catiline (Asc. in Cic. *Tog. cand.* [pp. 93.24–4.3 C.]; Schol. Bob. ad Cic. *Sull.* 22 [p. 80.13–16 Stangl]; App. *B Civ.* 2.2.5). – The report of the charge (that a *homo novus* opposed noblemen) is mixed with the speaker's assessment of the activities of these noblemen as *perniciosus* (on the status of *homo novus* as a criterion, see also *Exil.* 28).

restinxerit: continues the fire imagery applied to the fight against the Catilinarian Conspiracy, although the object here is *furor* (*Exil.* 1; 8; 14; also Cic. *Sull.* 83).

furorem: in this speech *furor*, which occurs frequently (Keeline 2018, 168–9), is applied to the Catilinarian conspirators (*Exil.* 18; 19) and to the activities of P. Clodius Pulcher (*Exil.* 13; 14; 21; 24; 27). – On *furor* in political contexts, see Cic. *RQ* 19 n.

non obest … vita: one's character and way of life are not immediate legal or political items like the other points; this contrast fits if the marks of an honestly led life are seen as support of the Republic and opposition to people like Catiline.

non obest mihi: the description of *M. Tullius* in the third person changes to a first person narrative continued by *premor* (see *Exil.*, Introduction; *Exil.* 1 n.).

nocens et turpis, sed honestissime lautissimeque acta vita: *vita* is specified by adjectives in the first part and by a participle linked with adverbs in the second part. The positive statement has superlatives to enhance the good character of the individual being charged.

lautissimeque: this adverb in the superlative with the particle -*que* attached is not attested elsewhere (retained by De Marco 1967, 43). While both *laute* and *lautissime* occur (*OLD* s.v. *lautus* 2 'Having an air of respectability, substance, etc., well turned out, fine', b '(of conduct, etc.) splendid') in classical Latin, there is only one example of a combination with *vitam agere* or *vivere* (Nep. *Chabr.* 3.2: *vivebat laute*). The widely adopted emendation *laudatissimeque* results in an equally unattested word. Gamberale's (1979, 79–83) version *sanctissimeque* (adopted by De Marco 1991, 15) makes sense and has Ciceronian parallels (*OLD* s.v. *sancte* 3; cf. Cic. *Phil.* 9.15; *Balb.* 12; cf. Corbeill 2020, 24), but moves further away from the transmission and might introduce a *lectior facilior*. As *lautissimeque* is not impossible, the transmitted text can be retained.

bonorum: the standard word for people defending the Republic in Cicero's terminology (Cic. *RS* 12 n.). With reference to the political realm the contrast in Cicero's writings frequently is *improbi* rather than the straightforward opposite *mali* (Cic. *RS* 20 n.), though *malus* appears as well, often in connection with *improbus* (Achard 1981, 197–8). Actions displeasing *boni* are seen as a potentially valid reason for accusations.

invidia: see *Exil.* 1 n.

7 homines: on its own suggests a fresh generic statement, but the sentence seems to refer to the opponents mentioned in the previous sentence; one might, therefore, expect *isti homines* for clarity.

tot … comparatis: an ablative absolute, although the noun in the phrase also functions as the unexpressed subject (in the accusative) of the accusative and infinitive construction, which can happen for emphasis or ease of construction (K.-St. I 786–8).

tot et tam praeclaris testimoniis monimentisque virtutis: presumably refers metaphorically to testimonies generally, including items such as honorific Senate decrees; Cicero was not awarded any physical monuments. – These monuments are justified as testimonials of *virtus*; the vague and implicit statement is again a reference to Cicero's combating of the Catilinarian Conspiracy and the appreciation he won thereby (*Exil.* 1 n.). – *testimonia comparare* does not appear before Quintilan (Quint. *Inst.* 7.2.25); *monumenta comparare* is not attested elsewhere in classical Latin.

M. Tullio: on this version of Cicero's name, see *Exil.* 6 n.

dum sit incolumis: *dum* with subjunctive is used in a conditional sense (K.-St. II 446–8; Pinkster 2015, 652).

idcirco … iucunditatis: by taking action against 'Cicero', his opponents are said to want to deprive him of enjoying his rewards. This is described as taking away his life along with the consciousness of pleasantness. Earlier in the speech there is talk of not missing Cicero and of retaining Cicero in the community (*Exil.* 1; 3), and immediately afterwards it is mentioned that 'Cicero' will have to leave Rome; both points presuppose actions of his opponents that might or will lead to his exile. The possibility of death is another alternative for 'Cicero's' future and is considered at several points in this speech (e.g. *Exil.* 6; 21–2).

nonne igitur … tulerunt: 'Cicero' expresses the view (phrased as a question assuming a positive answer [*nonne*] and thus equalling a statement) that it is unfair that people are now envious and compete with him when they did not do so previously. These people are made up of two groups: the first consists of those who did not wish to enter a competition to demonstrate virtue; the second consists of those who previously bore it calmly that Cicero obtained offices. Each of them now reacts accordingly: the first group is becoming envious; the second wishes to compete.

qui virtute certare noluerunt: since elsewhere in this speech 'Cicero's' *virtus* in comparison to the behaviour of his opponents is highlighted (*Exil.* 1 n.), this might not just be a general statement, but also refer to the confrontation with the Catilinarian conspirators.

honoris: could look forward to *officiis* and have the same meaning of 'office' (*OLD* s.v. *honor*[1] 5) or refer to 'esteem' based also on the attainment of offices (*OLD* s.v. *honor*[1] 2). Both aspects might be implied; the aim of winning *honor* seems to be connected with obtaining *officium* (*OLD* s.v. *officium* 6).

qui officiis se superari animo aequissimo tulerunt: denotes individuals who did not obtain the offices Cicero did and initially bore that situation calmly. – Cicero was successful in the elections for the consulship of 63 BCE while Catiline was not (Ascon. ad Cic. *Tog. cand.* [p. 94 C.]; Sall. *Cat.* 23.5–24.1), but the latter can hardly be said to have borne the result *animo aequissimo* (on this election and Catiline's reaction, see Sall. *Cat.* 24.1–2), and he would no longer be in a position to enter a *contentio honoris* in 58 BCE. Thus, it is unclear who might be referred to; it is implied that several people belong to this category. – The phrase *officiis superare* is attested in Sallust, but in a different sense (Sall. *Iug.* 102.11).

si...animam: in contrast to how some people are envious of glory and suddenly start competing, 'Cicero' outlines how true glory can be achieved: by the path of *virtus*. – The imperative in the second person singular is generic and not addressed to any specific member of the audience (Pinkster 2015, 743); it gives the statement a gnomic quality.

noli abicere labores, perdere honorem: the sequence of thought suggests that the final infinitive phrase must express the consequence of not striving for *virtus* and not working hard: losing out on enjoying honour (which is subsequently elaborated). This idea is appropriately expressed by Orelli's reading *perdere* (*OLD* s.v. *perdo* 3) for transmitted *petere* (grammatically possible, but unsuitable in sense).

honorem...animam: a *correctio* exemplifies a series of items that might be lost in addition to honour if one does not pursue virtue and work hard. The list is arranged climactically, starting with external assets, moving to family, and concluding with the individual, focusing first on circumstances of life and then on life itself. – Of the items relating to the individual, the final point (highlighted by *ipsum denique*) describes the vital elements of life (*sanguis* and *anima*). The preceding alliterative pair *caput* and *corpus* could also indicate loss of life, with the final item focusing on what is essential to life. Alternatively, one might interpret *caput* as denoting the status and rights of a free citizen, although this meaning is more common in other types of constructions (*OLD* s.v. *caput* 6). The result for *corpus* might be the removal of the physical body from the centre of action, which means isolation and loss of opportunities for involvement (e.g. *Exil.* 22; also Cic. *RS* 5).

cedo…malorum: the first person verbs indicate that 'Cicero' returns to his own situation. His circumstances are not an exemplification of what has just been described, as he worked hard and achieved honour, but rather a kind of contrast: he has to leave and is about to lose all these values despite his achievements. This is the first mention in this speech of his impending departure from Rome and contrasts with the preceding appeals to the audience to agree to his staying in Rome (*Exil.* 1; 3). – The tricolon (building up to a climax and with items of increasing length) emphasizes that 'Cicero' is about to leave the *res publica* (mentioned in the first and last element, with the stronger compound verb at the end), unwillingly and unjustly, and thus will lose his status. In the speeches given after his return Cicero creates a parallel between himself and the *res publica* and often says that the two of them were away together (e.g. Cic. *RS* 36; see Introduction, section 3.4).

cedo…cedo…discedo: *cedere* and *discessus* are common euphemistic words to express Cicero's departure from Rome in the Ciceronian speeches connected with his return; in this speech the compounds *discedere* and *decedere* (*Exil.* 13) also appear (see Introduction, section 3.4). – The present tense refers to an action in the future; this use is common for verbs indicating movement in archaic Latin (K.-St. I 119).

invitus: is suitable to arouse pity among the audience prior to departure, but does not agree with the picture painted by the historical Cicero in the speeches given after his return, when he claims that he left willingly, avoiding conflict, in an act of self-sacrifice to ensure the welfare of the Republic (e.g. Cic. *RS* 32–4), a nuance that the statements on leaving in this speech also acquire on occasion (*Exil.* 13; 27). – The phrasing recalls famous lines in Vergil (Verg. *Aen.* 6.460: *invitus, regina, tuo de litore cessi.*) and Catullus (Cat. 66.39–40: *invita, o regina, tuo de vertice cessi, / invita*; cf. Keeline 2018, 169 n. 58; Corbeill 2020, 25). – Keeline (2018, 169) argues that the aspect of leaving unwillingly and yielding to the Tribune's madness is highlighted to combat the view that Cicero is taking to flight, as expressed in other sources (Ps.-Sall. *Inv. in Cic.* 5; Ps.-Cic. *Inv. in Sall.* 10; Cass. Dio 46.21.1–2). This is a possible reading, depending on assumptions about the date of composition and the purpose of this text.

de fortuna, de dignitate: indicates that Cicero leaves a well-established position (*OLD* s.v. *fortuna* 9; *dignitas* 4).

audacia: does not identify the deeds of the opponents, but rather disqualifies their behaviour as reckless (*Exil.* 27; on the political use of *audax*, see Cic. *RS* 19 n.).

malorum: on this term applied to political opponents in this speech, see *Exil.* 6 n.

8 liceat manere…debuistis: after 'Cicero' seemed to accept the fact that he will have to leave and give way to his opponents' power (*Exil.* 7), in this paragraph, without any transition, he turns to expressing his wish to stay (on the style, see Gamberale 1998, 59–61). This emphatic plea consists of three asyndetic and anaphoric sentences, each starting with *liceat*: the first expresses the notion of staying, the second of being in the community one has served, the third of being safe in appreciation of his having saved the community by his earlier sacrifice. A final pair of sentences justify the request with a reminder of Cicero's services for the Republic and thereby the audience's obligation to honour and repay these. – The wish to be safe might be realized more easily by 'Cicero' leaving Rome; in this context it seems to be a plea to confront his opponents and keep him safe in the city.

si non illum M. Tullium…Tulli: the clause literally asks that, if it is not possible for the renowned M. Tullius to stay, at least his *reliquiae* may. This word, often used for the remains of a dead person, might suggest the request that at least the ashes or the shade should be able to remain. As the continuation of the sentence indicates a focus on ways to stay in Rome as a living individual (rather than on death and burial), what is meant is presumably remaining in the city, even if only in a reduced capacity, having lost the public role and the accompanying appreciation: living in Rome as an ordinary person is envisaged as being half-dead, but better than leaving. – On the versions of Cicero's name used in this speech, see *Exil.* 6 n.

defensorem omnium: one might have expected something like *defensorum omnium bonorum* (at least in Cicero's genuine writings) as *omnium* on its own literally includes the enemies. This wording may stress the universality of the services provided by Cicero. – For Cicero characterized as *defensor*, see Cic. *Dom.* 7: *me…, custodem defensoremque Capitoli templorumque omnium* (Corbeill 2020, 25).

patrem patriae: after the suppression of the Catilinarian Conspiracy the Senate passed decrees calling for a festival of thanksgiving and awarding Cicero the title of *pater patriae* (Cic. *Cat.* 3.15; *Pis.* 6; *Sest.* 121; Plut. *Cic.* 23.6).

ex parricidarum faucibus: the vivid metaphor emphasizes the severity of the threat and the effect of Cicero's deed of salvation for the Republic. – Political opponents confronting the Republic (i.e. Catiline and the Catilinarian conspirators) are metaphorically called parricides because they are attacking the fatherland (e.g. Cic. *Cat.* 1.17; 1.29). – The choice of words leads to a slightly mixed metaphor (not attested elsewhere): one would assume that parricides kill rather than swallow, as suggested by saving the city from their 'throats' or 'gullets'. The expression is probably meant to illustrate the threat of the opponents destroying and absorbing everything and, by contrast, Cicero's great and courageous deed of salvation.

tecta…civitatem: in this tricolon two items referring to buildings (of humans and gods) are followed by a third item referring to the population. – In ring composition, the final point picks up *in conspectu civium* in the first phrase of this *liceat*-clause.

hominum: Gamberale's (1979, 83–7) conjecture (adopted by De Marco 1991, 15) *hominum* for transmitted *omnium* (retained by De Marco 1967, 45) gives a neater contrast between *tecta hominum* and *fana deorum*. *omnium* could have arisen not just from the similarity of the writing, but also from *defensorem omnium* just above; confusions between forms of *omnis* and *homo* are frequent.

<expertem>: a term to govern *periculi* is needed. This conjecture by Halm (cf. Baiter 1856, 1414 in app.; adopted by De Marco 1967, 45; 1991, 16) makes good sense; the loss of this word in the vicinity of *periculi* can be explained.

ex hac flamma evolare: i.e. to avoid the current danger for 'Cicero', with *flamma* used metaphorically (*OLD* s.v. *flamma* 3c '(fig.) a highly dangerous situation'; see Cic. *Brut.* 90; for the collocation, see Cic. *Verr.* 2.1.70; 2.1.82; cf. Gamberale 1998, 60; Corbeill 2020, 26).

illud impium incendium perditorum hominum: *illud…incendium* (another fire metaphor; see *Exil.* 1 n.) contrasts with *ex hac flamma* and refers to the past, namely the destructive activities of the Catilinarian conspirators, denoting either literally planned arson attacks on the city of Rome (*Exil.* 1 n.) or, more likely, metaphorically the strength and violence of the opposition (*OLD* s.v. *incendium* 3 '(in fig. context): a (of outbreaks of hostility, violence, or sim.)'). The two adjectives (*impium, perditorum*) emphatically describe the character of the opponents.

lacrimis potius meis quam vestro sanguine restingui malui: referring to the opposition to the Catilinarian conspirators. In the metaphorical expression connected with *incendium* the two ways of action are expressed by different types of fluids to extinguish the fire. Like the historical Cicero (esp. Cic. *Cat.* 2.28; 3.23), 'Cicero' stresses that the conspirators were overwhelmed non-violently, without a civil war and the loss of the lives of ordinary Roman citizens. Instead, the revolt was contained by his labours (for the expressions, see Cic. *Font.* 47; *Dom.* 144; cf. Gamberale 1998, 60–1; Corbeill 2020, 25).

meis…malui: another switch from a description of Cicero in the third person to the first person (see *Exil.*, Introduction; *Exil.* 1 n.).

neque enim…debuistis: the sentences specify the request and outline (*enim*) why it is justified (somewhat elliptically): Cicero is not asking to be 'born' and thus be brought to life. Instead, he has given (i.e. risked) his life for the Roman citizens and thus saved their lives from the threat caused by the Catilinarian conspirators. Therefore, the audience should remember his sacrifice and not forget to return the favour by giving him back the life he has risked for them, i.e. by allowing him to lead the rest of his life in the community in an appropriate fashion.

non debetis…quod debuistis: the same verb in different tenses and different senses indicates that the audience should now pay off the debt incurred in the past. The perfect denotes the result of an action in the past and can therefore be translated as a present (K.-St. I 125–6).

{istis}: deletion is advisable, as the pronoun does not have a clear reference point.

2.2. Need to retain 'Cicero' as a well-proven guardian (9–10)

The second part (*Exil.* 9–10) of the main section (*Exil.* 6–23) starts with another reminder of 'Cicero's' salutary deeds for the community, more specific than previous ones, with a clear reference to the (Catilinarian) conspiracy (*Exil.* 10; 14; 29). Thus, it is argued, it would be unthinkable that 'Cicero' is rejected by those he has helped, and it is pointed out that the impression that citizens are not supported against injustice will set a bad precedent. 'Cicero' tries to bring home the notion that the audience would act in an unjustifiable and irresponsible way if they did not take steps to assist him.

9 vos, vos optestor, di immortales: an emphatic appeal to the immortal gods (see Gamberale 1998, 64–5), reminding them of their assistance in suppressing the Catilinarian Conspiracy (on *optestor*, see *Exil.* 5). In the *Catilinarian Orations* the perspective varies as to whether the success is due to Cicero's activity or to divine inspiration (e.g. Cic. *Cat.* 3.17–18).

qui meae menti lumina praetulistis: this metaphorical paraphrase implies that the gods led Cicero along, which serves as an indirect justification of his actions during the Catilinarian Conspiracy (cf. Cic. *Sull.* 40 [paragraph including an address to the gods]; Val. Max. 3.2.2; cf. Gamberale 1998, 64–5; Corbeill 2020, 25).

consensum … coniurationis: in this collocation *consensus* could have a general meaning (*OLD* s.v. *consensus* 1a 'Agreement in opinion or sentiment, consent, unanimity') or already a negative sense (*OLD* s.v. *consensus* 1b 'a subversive or factious agreement, conspiracy, collusion'); it is described as consisting in the *coniuratio* (*gen. appositivus*: K.-St. I 418–19; Pinkster 2015, 1023–5).

arcemque urbis: literally refers to the Capitol in Rome (*OLD* s.v. *arx* 1b) and could indicate an attack against this part of the city; or the Capitol could be mentioned as *pars pro toto* as the most iconic and significant part of the city, denoting an attack in Rome. Plans for an attack on the Capitol by the Catilinarian conspirators are not mentioned in Cicero or Sallust, while an intended arson attack in the city is referred to (*Exil.* 1 n.).

incendio ac flamma liberavi: another doublet; it could indicate literally a planned arson attack or use the fire imagery metaphorically for violent uproar (*Exil.* 1 n.). The phrasing recalls the Senate decree thanking Cicero for defeating the Catilinarian Conspiracy as quoted by him before the People (Cic. *Cat.* 3.15: *quod urbem incendiis, caede cives, Italiam bello liberassem*; cf. Corbeill 2020, 25).

liberavi liberosque: De Marco (1967, 45; 1991, 16) assumes a lacuna after *liberavi*. This is not required grammatically: without a lacuna there is a *cum*-clause with three predicates, all linked by *-que* (rarer than connected by *et*, but not impossible: K.-St. II 29–30). The third item is considerably longer and more vague, but can still be regarded as an element of Cicero's salutary activities on the advice of the gods; the final and most emotional point is expressed most vividly and elaborately.

liberosque vestros...abstrahi: implies that the Catilinarian conspirators would even have brutally snatched away children and killed them if Cicero had not intervened. Such plans are not mentioned in Cicero or Sallust, but could be envisaged here as a major threat (cf. *Exil.* 1). – It would be most natural to refer *vestros* to the gods addressed at the beginning of the sentence, but the reference must be to the children of the citizens in the audience (De Marco 1967, 44 n. 2 [p. 64]).

non igitur potest fieri...: it is reiterated that Roman citizens who have bene-fited from Cicero's efforts should take care of him; otherwise, because their behaviour sends a signal about their appreciation of Cicero, not even clients outside Rome would receive him and thus his life would be put in jeopardy. – In the transmitted version this sentence is a negative statement. The first word has often been changed to *num*, which turns the sentence into a question. This sentence is followed by a series of questions (initially introduced by question words); thus, the change would extend this sequence. However, the subsequent questions (forming a tricolon) seem to be of a different nature, contrasting the situation of citizens and of others, and to take the statement in this sentence as a starting point: here it is strongly denied (with *non* in an emphatic position) that Cicero could be received by clients if he is thrown out by his fellow citizens; the subsequent questions elaborate on the potential consequences of such an action. Moreover, the link to the preceding sentence by *igitur* (*OLD* s.v. *igitur* 3) indicates that such a scenario is an emphatic inference on that basis rather than a question of whether it might be the case.

a clientibus: the reference must be to people potentially receiving Cicero outside Rome; thus, these cannot be personal clients, but must rather be groups of people outside Rome with close links to people in Rome (*OLD* s.v. *cliens* 2).

cum...instituant: an indirect accusation of those who should be supporting Cicero to remain in Rome, but, in 'Cicero's' view, are not doing so. The notion of *instituant* is appropriate because Cicero is about to be thrown out, and it opens up the opportunity to change behaviour before the action is completed. – The subject of the *cum*-clause is an unexpressed *ei* defined by the relative clause.

socii...eripiatur: this section exemplifies the repercussions for the percep-tion of Rome if it is seen as not offering protection to its own citizens. This concept is developed through a series of contrasts between outside and inside with variation in terminology and perspective (*socii...custodi*; *reliquis... civibus*; *extraneis...domesticis*). – While the expulsion of worthy citizens is described generally, the features highlighted indicate an indirect reference to Cicero, and the characterizations, though generic, serve again to point out implicitly his actions of protection and salvation for Rome.

socii... sit: in view of the parallelism with the other statements in this sequence, this comment probably identifies Cicero as the *custos* (of the city of Rome) (*Exil.* 8), who is denied access to the city of Rome and its institutions. As a result, Rome will become a less desirable safe haven for allies.

fugient: this reading (found in one manuscript), yielding a future tense, is preferable in view of the tenses in the subsequent questions parallel to this one.

quo modo... incolumitatis: as a contrast to *civibus*, *reliquis* must refer to allies and others who are not citizens: like the previous sentence, this one indicates that, if Cicero's example demonstrates that there is no support and safety even for Roman citizens, Rome will no longer be an attractive place of refuge for anyone.

pax... eripiatur: the final item is not marked as a question by a question word, but in view of the parallelism in structure and sense, it must be another one. The person concerned (i.e. Cicero) is defined as *providenti* (*OLD* s.v. *prouideo* 4; picking up *custodi*), emphasizing his taking care of the public (*publice*) in the face of the Catilinarian Conspiracy. As the climactic endpoint of the sequence, *pax et concordia* is the most comprehensive and most political item; the lack is described with respect to both the citizens generally and Cicero specifically. The connection of *pax et concordia* with *insidere* is unusual (not attested with *pax* in Cicero); the phrase implies that *pax et concordia* should be inherent features of a functioning community.

10 nam... vestros: after alluding to the threat of the Catilinarian Conspiracy (*Exil.* 8–9), 'Cicero' calls himself back from elaborating on it further, in a kind of *praeteritio*. The reason given is concern for the feelings of the audience, which broadens the perspective away from the focus on 'Cicero'. – This question, introduced by *nam* to indicate its force (*OLD* s.v. *nam* 7), is followed by four further ones, again dealing with the consequences (for 'Cicero' and the audience) if the audience does not offer protection to 'Cicero'.

improborum: opponents of the *boni* (Cic. *RS* 12; 20 nn.), as often in the works of the historical Cicero, here denoting the Catilinarian conspirators.

redintegratione: a fairly rare word and mostly attested in late antique texts (but see *Rhet. Her.* 4.38). The reading *redintegratione... vulnerem* (rather than *redintegratio... vulneret*) is preferable in parallel to *renovem oratione* and to avoid an odd personification.

illius coniurationis: i.e. the Catilinarian Conspiracy in 63 BCE (*Exil.* 9).

animos vulnerem vestros: a metaphorical expression illustrating that recalling bad experiences can create mental wounds (cf. Cic. *Cat.* 1.17). – *vestros* addresses the citizens in the audience (*Exil.* 9 n.)

auxilium... deseratis: a warning to the audience that they will not be in a good position (in future) to ask for help from external nations if they do not value their own citizens (as others will see that actions of support are not appreciated).

sociorum . . . praesidium: vice versa, 'Cicero' wonders whether he should appeal to allies if he is not receiving protection from his fellow citizens. In contrast to the preceding comment on the allies (*Exil.* 9), this is a consideration of the impact on 'Cicero's' own fate. – *subsidium* and *praesidium* at the end of each clause create a sound effect based on two words with similar nuances.

quam colere gentem non institui: 'Cicero' implies that he has started to cultivate good relations with all communities and that it should, therefore, be fine for any to receive him once he has left Rome; still, he shows himself worried about the view of him that will prevail (essentially his own assessment or that of others) and the corresponding reaction. – *gens* is a wider and more generic term than *socii* (*Exil.* 9 n.).

utrum custos . . . erunt omnia: if other nations regard Cicero as a *custos* and *conservator* (as he sees himself), it will be embarrassing for the Romans, as they are not treating him accordingly and others show themselves to be wiser. If other nations regard him as a *proditor* and *oppugnator* (as his opponents do), the people currently powerful at Rome will have successfully spread their version, with all hope for assistance for 'Cicero' cut off.

praecisa erunt omnia: the reference point of *omnia* is not defined; it generically encompasses all options if 'Cicero' (in his view) is cast out from Rome unfairly and in disrespect of his achievements, and nobody is willing to receive him.

itaque . . . exitio: *quod* (taken up by *id*) is not defined; it must refer to combating the Catilinarian Conspiracy and the memory of this event: it is claimed that 'Cicero' anticipated that containing the Catilinarian Conspiracy and its recollection would create joy, while in fact this has caused disaster. – That he anticipated pleasure from dealing with the Catilinarian Conspiracy is not mentioned by the historical Cicero in surviving utterances from before or during the campaign. In retrospect, when trying to persuade L. Lucceius to write a historiographical monograph about the event, he claims that reading about his experiences would cause pleasure (Cic. *Fam.* 5.12.4–5 [April 55 BCE]). – The verb *exstitit* (highlighting the development) can be employed like an intensified *esse* and take a final dative (for *esse* with dative, see K.-St. I 342–3; Pinkster 2015, 778–80; for *exitio esse*, see, e.g., Cic. *Mur.* 56; *Q Fr* 1.4.4).

2.3. Need to defend innocent people (11–12)

The third part (*Exil.* 11–12) of the main section (*Exil.* 6–23) appeals to the audience's concern for their own well-being: it points out that it is advantageous for oneself to fight for the innocent and to oppose the guilty, and it states that it is difficult to confront potential enemies on one's own. Thus, the section again asks the audience for help by making them consider the consequences for themselves (cf. *Exil.* 1; 16).

11 si . . . coniuncta: a multipart *si*-clause leads to the conclusion that people should act in situations that are difficult for others in the same way in which

they would in their own difficulties, that it is useful for them to back the innocent and fight the guilty, and that their own fortune is linked to the situation of
the good and the bad. This thought experiment implies that 'Cicero' belongs to
the category of the innocent and thus should be supported for his own sake and
for the benefit of those assisting him. – The first two verbs are in the imperfect
subjunctive, and the third is in the present subjunctive followed by an adhorta-
tive present subjunctive in the main clause, which gives a mixture of counterfactual and potential presentation in this conditional sequence (K.-St. II
398–401; Pinkster 2015, 655–7).

Quirites: the first address to the audience in this speech (see *Exil.*,
Introduction; *Exil.* 1 n.).

haberemus: this verb and the following ones display a generic first person
plural: the speaker appeals to shared views and general ways of behaviour.

nobis utilissimum esse arbitraremur: the motivation given for the actions
towards the innocent and the guilty is the advantage for oneself rather than any
moral values.

si cum … putemus coniuncta: as a further motive it is outlined that one's
own circumstances are connected with the situation of very good and very bad
men. This is expressed by intertwined contrasts: the bad fortune of good men
will affect well-being, and the good fortune of bad men will lead to dangers.

frequentes: while the presentation in the *si*-clause might have suggested the
conclusion that people should become active individually for their own benefit,
the consequence drawn is that they should act *frequentes*. The focus on collective intervention can be explained in a context in which repercussions for
everyone are envisaged. Moreover, it makes the implied application to the present situation more straightforward, as 'Cicero' tries to persuade the community to act on his behalf.

**partim innocentia freti, partim nobilitate nixi, partim potentia ac multitu-
dine amicorum fulti:** a list (with asyndeton and anaphora) of three potential
reasons why people might think that they could easily confront enemies if
necessary and therefore do not do anything until it is too late: they believe that
they are innocent and therefore cannot be attacked (assuming that everyone is
following the laws and the rules), or they think that a high social position renders one unassailable, or they rely on a large number of powerful friends
(assuming that nobody would dare to attack them or that any attack could
easily be fought off).

potentia ac multitudine: a rare collocation (cf. Vell. Pat. 2.20.2).

cum … existimemus: this kind of temporal clause (with attraction of mood)
explains the action in the main clause by the simultaneous action in the subordinate clause (K.-St. II 330–1; Pinkster 2015, 611–12).

adversariorum vim ac factionem: suggests an allusion to a group of opponents with a shared attitude (*factio*) and using force (*vis*), such as Catiline or
P. Clodius Pulcher and their supporters. The construction of two object nouns

linked by a coordinating conjunction places more emphasis on each of them than a single object defined by a genitive attribute; what is envisaged as being thrust back must still be *vis* operated by *factio*. The collocation *vim ac factionem* does not seem to be attested elsewhere. – *adversariorum* is another term for 'opponents' in addition to *inimici* and *hostes* (*Exil.* 1 n.).

simili periculo: *simili* does not have an explicit point of comparison. The context suggests that, although one thought that one would be unaffected, one suddenly finds oneself in a difficult situation like others (*aliorum*; cf. *in ceterorum periculis*), of whose fate one is reminded: one then complains about the situation. This reaction does not have an effect at this stage; one should have taken action earlier.

in nostro eventu: a general term (*OLD* s.v. *euentus* 3) taking up *in nostris difficultatibus, nostram salutem*, and *nostra pericula*. When applied to the 'fate' of individuals (often implying 'death'), *eventus* can be linked with a possessive expression (e.g. Cic. *Amic.* 14; Liv. 8.10.1).

iure id nobis accidere nequiquam queramur: if one does not take action to counter threats at an early stage, the only option is to complain later; complaining at this point and about a justified development will not have any effect, and one will suffer because of the preceding lack of action (on evaluative *iure*, see Pinkster 2015, 928–9).

12 quis est enim…: this sentence gives Cicero's situation as an example (*OLD* s.v. *enim* 3d), illustrating the preceding general claim (*Exil.* 11): it describes the expected feelings of others who see Cicero suffer fom the onslaught of his opponents.

Quirites: another address to the audience shortly after the previous one (*Exil.* 11). There will be no further addresses to *Quirites* (see *Exil.*, Introduction; *Exil.* 1 n.).

inimicorum: on this term, see *Exil.* 1 n.

nostrorum: the first person plural must refer to 'Cicero' (on this use of the plural, see K.-St. I 87–8; Pinkster 2015, 1119–20; see *Exil.* 13), contrasting with a preceding true plural for argumentative purposes (*Exil.* 11).

cum…recognoscat: on this kind of temporal *cum* (with attraction of mood), see *Exil.* 11 n.

vim ac violentiam: an alliterative hendiadys describing the activities of Cicero's opponents: they are not using physical violence against Cicero at present, but their general behaviour is presented as violent opposition. – The collocation *vis ac violentia* is rare (cf. Varro, *Ling.* 5.70).

nostrum periculosissimum casum: an emphatic description of Cicero's situation with an adjective in the superlative; it picks up preceding generic *in ceterorum periculis* (*Exil.* 11).

qui non sibi…fortunis: because it has been stated that others will be affected by the bad fate of innocent men (*Exil.* 11), it is inferred that seeing the force of

Cicero's opponents and his precarious situation will make everyone less confident (for the phrase, see Sall. *Cat.* 31.3). – The situation of individuals is expressed by a direct reference to themselves and an abstract one to their fate (*OLD* s.v. *fortuna* 8).

quo enim...praesidio: explains (*enim*) that people will be worried when they cannot see any sufficiently safe protection for themselves after what one would usually regard as protection has failed in Cicero's case in the face of violent and unjustified attacks.

virtutis gloria...oppugnent: a list of three items (in the form of questions) that might offer protection, but have not in Cicero's case (outlined in *at*-clauses following each question).

virtutis gloria: could be a potential protection, since opponents would not dare to attack a well-known and virtuous person. In Cicero's case, it is said, this quality opposes him, obviously not *virtutis gloria* directly, but rather its consequences: it is implied that envy of Cicero's virtuous achievements provokes the activities of opponents (Cic. *RQ* 21; *Exil.* 7). – *virtutis* is probably a *genitivus appositivus* indicating that *gloria* consists in or is built on *virtus* (K.-St. I 418–19).

multitudine amicorum: a large number of friends might offer protection: because of them nobody would dare to attack, or the friends could fight back quickly and efficiently (*Exil.* 11). 'Cicero' stops short of saying that Cicero does not have many friends or that these are not willing to take action; rather, he states generally that friends do not offer sufficient protection if they are powerless (without providing details).

at parum est fortes esse amicos: this emendation of the corrupt transmitted text suggested by Baiter (1856, 1415 in app.) stays close to the transmitted words and makes sense in the context.

paucitate imicorum: contrasts with *multitudine amicorum*. Usually it would be assumed that a small number of enemies reduces the risk of attacks and that the number of enemies can be kept low if one makes sure not to do any injustice to anyone. 'Cicero' notes that this strategy fails if there are enough people who become enemies of their own accord (*voluntarii inimici*), even if they have not suffered any injustice, just because they do not like one's achievements. Thus, the final item overlaps with the consequences of the first item, *virtutis gloria*. It is stressed again that influencing the situation is beyond one's control (*in aliorum voluntate*).

facias...tuis...te: a switch to a generic second person singular (K.-St. I 653–4).

tuis praemiis: this ablative gives achievements and acknowledgement as a reason (K.-St. I 395–6; Pinkster 2015, 903–4) for opposition. Such an *ablativus causae* with *oppugnare* is unusual; more commonly the verb governs an ablative of manner or instrument.

2.4. Particularly bad situation for 'Cicero' (13–16)

The fourth part (*Exil.* 13–16) of the main section (*Exil.* 6–23) continues to out-line Cicero's appalling and desperate situation, stressing the features making it particularly bad for him: the consequences of his service for the Republic affect his family, and there is no fair hearing, so that he is suffering abuse, but has little opportunity to defend himself. This description again leads to the extended conclusion that these circumstances should move people to help and that con-taining the enemies might be in the audience's interest. Thus, the sequence ends with an emotionally moving appeal to support Cicero as an innocent man against his opponents and the repeated reminder that this would be for the benefit of the audience's own safety.

13 atque adeo: adds another point emphatically (*OLD* s.v. *atque* 4).

cum...tum vero: contrasts the consequences for everyone with those for Cicero, highlighting the particular severity in his case (on *tum vero*, see Cic. *RS* 25 n.).

haec omnia: i.e. the fact that there is no protection from enemies who arise of their own accord and are provoked by good deeds (*Exil.* 12).

nobis: refers to 'Cicero' in contrast to *omnibus* (*Exil.* 12 n.).

quorum...versantur: the particularly bad effect on 'Cicero' results from the fact that both his great deeds and his sacrifices for the *res publica* affect his family. *officia in rem publicam recentissima* must be the actions against the Catilinarian Conspiracy; one might just wonder whether these could still be called *recentissima* at the envisaged date of this speech in spring 58 BCE (though what must be the same year of 63 BCE is defined as *paulo ante* in *Exil.* 14); this dating may be intended to indicate the connection between the actions against Catiline and the current situation. Cicero's initiatives against Catiline did not have an immediate negative effect on his family; yet they exposed him, trig-gered resentment, and are thus the starting point for the subsequent fallout. *incommoda ob rem publicam frequentissima* could refer to the impending absence from Rome (which Cicero describes in letters as affecting his family: e.g. Cic. *Fam.* 14.1; 14.2; 14.3; 14.4); yet this is a one-off event and still in the future at this point. If the qualification is justified to some extent (and not just an exaggeration), it may allude to previous dangerous situations, such as when Cicero appeared with a breastplate in the Forum on the day of the elections to the consulship in 63 BCE (Plut. *Cic.* 14.7–8) and was the object of an assassin-ation attempt by Catiline and his supporters (Sall. *Cat.* 27.3–28.4). While these incidents still do not concern other members of Cicero's family directly, the threat to Cicero exemplified by them might be said to affect them. – *versari in* most frequently indicates a location (Cic. *RS* 13; *RQ* 14), but a transfer to people also occurs in Cicero's writings (for phrasing coming close to the construction here, see Cic. *De or.* 1.39; *Tusc.* 5.43).

nunc: introduces a new scenario in which the negative consequences outlined so far would not apply (*OLD* s.v. *nunc* 9c).

si...praebebuntur: describes conditions for a fair and equal contest. The vocabulary does not refer specifically to a trial in a court, but a discussion before an unbiased jury is envisaged.

eadem condicio...aequi auditores...aures...vacuae: three conditions ensuring an objective and lawful contest and verdict. The sequence moves from the description of the circumstances via the characteristics of the jury to the body part essential for the task, representing the jury's activity and attitude.

qui sunt...pervenient: sketches the consequences of a fair hearing for those who have obtained *honores* and those who are still hoping to.

qui sunt assecuti summum gradum honoris: i.e. those who have reached the consulship, i.e. the highest point in the *cursus honorum* (*OLD* s.v. *gradus* 8; *honor*[1] 5; see Cic. *Planc.* 60: *honorum gradus*).

qui sperant: i.e. those who are still hoping to obtain high offices (*assequi summum gradum honoris* to be supplied).

ad laudem nobilitatis: *laus* must mean 'esteem' or 'reputation' rather than 'praise' (*OLD* s.v. *laus*[1] 2); the genitive defines what it consists in (*gen. appositivus*; K.-St. I 418–19; Pinkster 2015, 1023–5). *nobilitas*, as something to be obtained, denotes distinction based on one's standing (*OLD* s.v. *nobilitas* 2).

quam ob rem...casus: as the previous sentence outlines that one would not have anything to fear or would not suffer any disadvantage if conditions were fair, 'Cicero' expresses the view that for that reason (*quam ob rem*) he does not want the People to be drawn into what is happening now, when Cicero is about to be 'punished' without proper justification or the opportunity to defend himself by what is therefore a 'deceitful punishment' in his view (*supplicii...ad fraudem*) and would mean a return to his previous state of misfortune (*OLD* s.v. *casus* 5), when he was first attacked and retaliation came to be expected. This situation is presented as having repercussions for the audience, since it affects trust in the justice system and 'Cicero's' availability for protecting the People.

me duce: as in the *Catilinarian Orations*, where Cicero highlights that he acts as *dux togatus* and that under his leadership the People were saved without bloodshed (Cic. *Cat.* 2.28; 3.23), 'Cicero' presents himself as a *dux* who is trying to prevent the People from falling victim to devious machinations.

nunc igitur: marks the transition to the conclusion, i.e. alternatives for a resolution (*OLD* s.v. *nunc* 10).

si...consuevi: a series of three *si*-clauses describes different ways in which 'Cicero's' confrontation with opponents could take place. The first two envisage a juxtaposition of words or deeds respectively; the third climactically outlines violent opposition. The reaction is marked by a decreasing level of opposition and thus of success: 'Cicero' would engage in a contest of words and is confident that he would win, on the basis of *innocentiae virtus*; in a contest of deeds he

suggests (cautiously) that parity could be achieved; if his opponents use violence, he will not start a fight, but withdraw as a sacrifice for the community in
line with his custom. – As an anticipated victory in a contest of words is linked
to *innocentiae virtus* rather than oratorical ability, moral behaviour is established as a criterion for all confrontations, while the structure of the sentence
avoids specifying the character of the deeds to be juxtaposed.

conferamus aequitatem: the plural denotes 'Cicero' and any opponent(s). –
The expression probably indicates that in this comparison a level playing field
and parity between both parties will be achieved (as an intermediate step
between victory and withdrawal).

opprimimur, decedam: although both verbs refer to 'Cicero', there is a
change from the first person plural to the first person singular (on *decedere*, see
Exil. 7 n.; Introduction, section 3.4). The switch might strengthen the key mes-
sage and imply that the onslaught of violence affects everyone and is confronted
by Cicero sacrificing himself.

pro omnibus unus: a rhetorical version of the frequent emphasis (in this
speech and in the genuine speeches) on Cicero sacrificing himself on behalf of
the community by leaving Rome (see Introduction, section 3.4; see Ps.-Cic. *Inv.
in Sall.* 10: *furori tribuni plebis cessi; utilius duxi quamvis fortunam unus experiri
quam universo populo Romano civilis essem dissensionis causa.*; cf. Corbeill
2020, 25).

tribunicio furori: while this speech talks generically of 'opponents' without
naming them, expressions mentioning a Tribune of the People (*Exil.* 14; 17; 24;
see Ps.-Cic. *Inv. in Sall.* 10) are the most explicit about the nature of the opposition, referring to P. Clodius Pulcher, Tribune of the People in 58 BCE. In all
phrases about a Tribune of the People the identification is combined with a
description of a negative form of behaviour or character trait. Here *furor* (cf.
Cic. *RS* 11) suggests irrational and unjustified conduct (Cic. *RQ* 19 n.). When
Cicero is said to avoid the conflict with such a person, he appears even more
generous and superior.

quoniam … consuevi: that Cicero got used to bearing hardship on behalf of
everybody (*pro cunctis* taking up *pro omnibus*) is an effective argument, but
probably an exaggeration, referring primarily to the preceding confrontation
with Catiline. It is in line, though, with the genuine Cicero's later generaliza-
tions, when he claims in *Philippic Two* that he has been fighting against political
enemies for twenty years (Cic. *Phil.* 2.1).

14 iis hominibus: the argument is based on an appeal to Roman tradition; as
elsewhere in this speech (*Exil.* 3), the description remains generic and no
examples are given. The conclusion is that, if the People have shown support for
dutiful men in the past, they should do this again in Cicero's case, as he took
care of honouring the gods and the well-being of the audience.

quorum animus ... defunctus est: *animus* stands for the person, emphasizing the mindset (*OLD* s.v. *animus* 2a). – The collocation *religione defungi* is not attested elsewhere.

religione pietatis: *religio* is defined by a genitive and underlines the display of *pietas* (*OLD* s.v. *religio* 10), here apparently applying to gods and humans. – While the words *religio* and *pietas* are frequent in Cicero's writings, this collocation is not attested there and only occurs (rarely) in medieval and early modern Latin.

numen deorum consecratum: *numen deorum* emphasizes the divinity of the gods (*OLD* s.v. *numen* 4b; for the combination, see Cic. *Scaur.* 17; *Phil.* 13.22; *Nat. D.* 2.7). – The collocation *numen consecratum* is not attested elsewhere in classical Latin and only a few times in later Latin.

sartum ac tectum: if *sartum ac tectum* is used in a literal sense, *aedes* or *templum* would be expected as a complement (*OLD* s.v. *sartus, sarctus*; cf., e.g., Cic. *Verr.* 2.1.131: *quaesivit quis aedem Castoris sartam tectam deberet tradere.*). Here *sartum ac tectum* is more likely to be applied in a metaphorical sense (cf. Cic. *Fam.* 13.50.2: ... *ut M'. Curium 'sartum et tectum', ut aiunt, ab omnique incommodo, detrimento, molestia sincerum integrumque conserves*).

ab omni periculo: is the reading of most manuscripts, while one has *ab omni piaculo*. If *numen deorum consecratum* refers to a concept of divinity rather than concrete temples, *piaculo* might be seen as providing a suitable sense. Yet *ab omni periculo* is preferable: it is more open as regards any kind of threat, and 'Cicero' highlights the idea of safety and security also in relation to his achievements on behalf of the People.

conservavi: 'Cicero' appears as a person who has preserved the gods' divinity and thus complied with *religio pietatis*.

vos: the subject of the *ut*-clause, expressed and fronted for emphasis (of the effect of 'Cicero's' activities on the audience). – The word balances *numen deorum consecratum* and adds the impact of Cicero's activities on human beings.

traheretis: *fortuna* almost has the sense of *vita*, with the added notion of destiny (*OLD* s.v. *traho* 17; *fortuna* 8). *trahere* enhances the alliteration in *tutam ac tranquillam*. The phrase *fortunam trahere* does not seem to be attested elsewhere.

mea perfeci vigilantia: 'Cicero' claims to have ensured a quiet life for the People by his vigilance: this does not mean literally that he continuously watched over them, rather that he was alert, and so noticed and foresaw dangers for the Republic and then thwarted these.

nam ... calamitatem: provides the reason (*nam*) why the audience should support 'Cicero': despite his acknowledged achievements he is subject to maltreatment.

me, quem ... honorem: a tricolon describing Cicero's previous honoured status. The first two items are abstract and describe this result as an achievement of Cicero and the circumstances; the third adds the honour shown to Cicero by the People as a confirmation.

paulo ante: i.e. in Cicero's consular year of 63 BCE (*Exil.* 13 n.), when he successfully combated the Catilinarian Conspiracy and was honoured for it (Cic. *Cat.* 3.15; *Pis.* 6; *Sest.* 121; Plut. *Cic.* 23.6).

fortuna erexerat ad gloriam: *fortuna* is repeated from the previous sentence, but here has a different sense (*OLD* s.v. *fortuna* 2).

erexerat... contulit... tribuit... depellit: the chronological sequence of these items is indicated by the change of tense: the events in the relative clauses refer to the past (and that *fortuna* had raised Cicero to glory is the precondition for the honours received); this is contrasted, by emphasizing that this fate is befalling the same person (*eundem*), with the current situation, when Ciceo is thrust into calamity by a Tribune of the People.

<cui> virtus contulit laudem: since the relative pronoun is required in a different case for the final two items, its insertion in that case (as supplied by Baiter 1856, 1416) helps to clarify the structure. While in a sequence of relative clauses requiring relative pronouns in different cases the pronoun is not always repeated in the new case, this usually does not happen in such a sequence of cases (K.-St. II 323–4). – The phrase again highlights Cicero's achievements as consul and the acknowledgement received in response.

populus tribuit honorem: the People are said to have honoured Cicero after the successful quelling of the Catilinarian Conspiracy (Plut. *Cic.* 22.5–8). – If this speech is envisaged as being given to an assembly of the People (see *Exil.*, Introduction; *Exil.* 1 n.), the audience is the same as *populus*. The impersonal phrasing emphasizes the effect rather than the contribution of the audience.

eundem: picks up the object *me*; after the insertion of the relative clauses, it is repeated for clarity. The addition enhances the contrast that the person who was honoured recently now experiences disaster.

tribuni furor exagitatus: i.e. the activities of P. Clodius Pulcher (*Exil.* 13 n.). – The collocation *furor exagitatus* does not seem to be attested elsewhere.

ad calamitatem: the unspecific term *calamitas* is used several times in this section (*Exil.* 14–16) for 'Cicero's' current predicament; it implies the anticipation of the fact that he will have to leave Rome, but is not restricted to his absence. In the speeches of the historical Cicero connected with his return the word appears as a paraphrase for his absence from Rome (see Introduction, section 3.4).

animadvertistis: appeals to what the audience witnessed, to allude to evidence and stress that the statement is not a mere claim.

illam conspirationem... incendii: the containment of the Catilinarian Conspiracy is again described by fire imagery (*Exil.* 1 n.). Here the underlying imagery suggests that the conspiracy was like a glowing fire about to be kindled, but was extinguished so quickly (thanks to Cicero's decisive action) that not even a proper spark emerged. – The term *conspiratio* does not appear with reference to the Catilinarian Conspiracy in Cicero's *Catilinarian Speeches* or the genuine speeches given after his return to Rome.

vos quoque: it is not an immediate logical conclusion that, as the audience has seen how the conspiracy was contained, they too should oppose the Tribune of the People. The underlying reasoning is: 'Cicero' ensured that the lives of the People were not affected by the conspiracy; therefore, they should now embark on a similar act of safeguarding.

tribuniciam...temeritatem: a paraphrase of the Tribune of the People's actions and their character, highlighting *temeritas*: this definition is less accusatory than, e.g., violence, but still describes the person as an irresponsible and irrational individual. – The collocation does not seem to be attested elsewhere.

sedate: might continue the fire imagery in its literal meaning, but bears a transferred sense in connection with *temeritatem* (*OLD* s.v. *sedo* 1, 2).

qui nunc se mihi inimicum ostendit: i.e. the current opposition of P. Clodius Pulcher towards 'Cicero'. – The relative pronoun *qui* refers to *tribunus* implied in *tribuniciam* (K.-St. I 30; Pinkster 2015, 1298–9).

se prius esse vestrum professus est inimicum: 'Cicero' claims that P. Clodius Pulcher was previously hostile towards the People, while he now is an opponent of 'Cicero'; this chronological link connects the two groups in being affected by this man (marked by the contrast of *nunc* with *prius* and *mihi* with *vestrum*). Such an attitude on the part of Clodius may be inferred from the fact that he started his public career in the traditional way of a nobleman, though an active demonstration of hostility to the People does not seem to be attested elsewhere.

ne...praecavete: an emphatic appeal to the audience to avoid potential consequences for them, implying that *crudelitas* and *calamitas* affecting Cicero might hit them, and on a larger scale, if they do not take action (*OLD* s.v. *praecaueo* 2). – The two nouns introduce one part of the clause each, are then further described by a participial construction focused on Cicero, and finally complemented by verbs indicating growing.

rei crudelitas: a vague expression for cruel actions of Cicero's opponents against him and potentially other Romans.

experta in me: the deponent is used in a passive sense (*OLD* s.v. *experior* 5). That *crudelitas* has been experienced against Cicero is a concise way of saying that the audience has seen cruelty against Cicero and therefore should be motivated to take steps to avoid suffering from it as well, especially after it might have grown.

remorata longius: it is implied that *calamitas* has been held up by its focus on 'Cicero': this is another incentive for the audience to take action to prevent this situation spreading further.

serpat ac progrediatur: indicates by a metaphorical and more concrete verb that *calamitas* might grow slowly and develop into something more substantial (*OLD* s.v. *serpo* 3; *progredior* 3).

15 vel…vel: from encouraging the audience to take precautions in their own interest 'Cicero' again moves to appealing to their sympathy by highlighting his own fate: 'Cicero' considers that he might be the only one or the first person to undergo such a calamity. While the second alternative implies that other people might suffer a similar fate in the future, the main point is that his situation should move everyone.

delectus: transmitted *defectus* is generally changed to *delectus* (though De Marco [1967, 51; 1991, 19] retains *defectus*). *delectus* gives a balanced parallel to *evocatus* in a sentence built on parallelism and contrast. The construction of *deficere* that would have to be assumed is primarily attested in military contexts (*OLD* s.v. *deficio* 10b '(w. *ad*) to go over (to the enemy's side)'); while such a meaning might be applied metaphorically, it would suggest activity on the part of Cicero rather than him being affected by the circumstances. Thus, the small change to the transmission seems advisable.

omnium animos iure debeo commovere: 'Cicero' states that his plight is such that he can justifiably command sympathy from everyone; consequently, there is a good reason for asking for pity.

omnia sunt immutata: the point of comparison must be the time period before *calamitas* and *periculum* struck. Now it is not even possible to point out *iniuria, calamitas*, and *rei indignitas*. For each item a different metaphorical expression is chosen, for variation and emphasis: overall, the three elements needed to communicate (*manus, lingua, animus*) the injustices (expressed with different nuances) are described as being held back by force. – The expressions *iniuria* and *rei indignitas* give an assessment of the situation; *calamitas* is more generic (*Exil.* 14 n.).

lingua inciditur: a rare collocation (in the classical period only at Cic. *De or.* 3.4; cf. Corbeill 2020, 25). The phrase combines the notion of literally cutting the tongue and metaphorically interrupting speech (*OLD* s.v. *incido*² 4c, 6).

ad deplorandam calamitatem: for the phrase, see Cic. *Div. Caec.* 21; *Phil.* 11.6; Liv. 26.32.8; 43.7.7 (cf. Corbeill 2020, 27).

animus praecluditur: apparently a transferred use of 'to stifle (an utterance)' (*OLD* s.v. *praecludo* 3b). The collocation does not seem to be attested elsewhere. As in the case of the body parts, the phrase illustrates the suppression of the demonstration of the unworthy situation in public.

humilitatem generis: i.e. the fact that Cicero was a *homo novus* (*Exil.* 6 n.). – The expression is attested a few times elsewhere (e.g. Sall. *Iug.* 73.4; Suet. *Vesp.* 4.5), especially in later Latin, but not in Cicero's genuine writings.

nobis: first person plural, while all other statements referring to 'Cicero' in this paragraph are in the first person singular or in impersonal form. Keeline (2018, 168) suggests that this form may be intended to include 'the imaginary corona'. Such an expression may indeed be an element of encouraging the goodwill of the audience (including others from non-noble backgrounds). In the first instance, however, because of the context, the comment will refer to the speaker.

qui...laudes: the relative clauses refer to an unexpressed *ei*, the subject of the main clause. – These people are unnamed opponents of 'Cicero' (taken up by *illorum*), and the description of their activities is vague. The point must be that they reproach Cicero with being a newcomer and then themselves introduce novelties and do not value the traditions and achievements of the ancestors (*OLD* s.v. *obtero* 3; cf. Cic. *Verr.* 2.5.2; Nep. *Timol.* 1.5).

novam rationem suscitant: *suscitare* literally refers to rousing something already there, yet in a dormant state (*OLD* s.v. *suscito* 4), while *nova ratio* denotes something novel: these people generate something new (potentially out of some existing basis), not honouring the traditional value system.

sed quid ego plura...loquar: a kind of *praeteritio*, as 'Cicero' says that he is breaking off before elaborating on his opponents' actions against him and the audience. Here the device does not mean that a few details or examples are presented all the same; instead, the following sentence reiterates that it is not necessary to say anything since the misdeeds are so obvious. – *sed quid ego* is a common Ciceronian formula of transition, especially in the speeches.

illorum: opponents of Cicero just characterized, perhaps including the Tribune of the People P. Clodius Pulcher and his followers.

in vos scelerate...factis: contrasts with *in me maledictis* (presumably the reproaches mentioned in the previous sentence) and does not have a precise reference point; perhaps these are not specific crimes against the People, but rather attacks on the Republic affecting the lives and livelihood of everyone. – The expression *scelerate factum* occurs in Pseudo-Quintilian (Ps.-Quint. *Decl.* 257.1) and Augustine (August. *De civ. D.* 2.27), but not in Cicero's genuine writings.

quorum...negare: illustrates why 'Cicero' does not need to talk about the misdeeds of his opponents (*me tacente*): they are obvious anyway.

improbitas...coarguitur turpitudine vitae: *improbi* contrasts with *boni* in works of the historical Cicero, merging political and moral elements (Cic. *RS* 20 n.). Here the emphasis is on the moral aspect if this characteristic becomes apparent through *turpitudo vitae*.

inimicos praedicare: *inimicos* is a qualification from the point of view of the *improbi* and refers to 'Cicero' and others on his side; it also operates as a contrast with the *amici* of the *improbi*. The moral depravity of these *improbi* is so obvious that there is no need for their opponents to spread the information.

de...negare: the criminal character of these people is claimed to be so evident that not even their friends or they themselves can deny it. – The construction of *negare* with *de* may have been chosen in parallel with *praedicare de* in the preceding clause (*OLD* s.v. *nego* 1d; cf. Cic. *Rosc. Am.* 82; *De or.* 2.105; 2.106).

scelere: probably referring to a general disposition of character (*OLD* s.v. *scelus* 2e; cf. Cic. *RS* 3; 17) rather than a specific criminal act.

16 vos ego appello: breaking off the discussion on the character of the *inimici*, 'Cicero' returns to addressing the audience with a highlighted *vos*. When 'Cicero' claims that the audience has great power over him, they are probably envisaged as members of the popular assembly voting in elections and on laws.

apud vos loquor . . . quos habui . . . testes: a close familiarity of the audience with his character is given as the motivation for 'Cicero' addressing himself to them.

calamitate: a vague term for 'Cicero's' situation (see *Exil.* 14 n.; Introduction, section 3.4).

innocentiae et virtutis: a reminder of 'Cicero's' great qualities (*Exil.* 1; 6; 12; 13; 14; 23; 28), which should ensure that he does not face any accusations or repercussions. – For the collocation, cf. Cic. *Verr.* 2.1.56; Sall. *Iug.* 85.4.

testes: to strengthen the claim to *innocentia* and *virtus*, the audience is reminded that they have been witnesses to the display of these characteristics. The occasions on which these qualities have become apparent are not defined; a reference to Cicero's dealing with the Catilinarian Conspiracy is presumably implied again.

igitur . . . indigne: De Marco (1967, 51; 1991, 19) punctuates the sentence as a rhetorical question designed to provoke the answer 'This should not happen'. The statement seems more forceful as a resumption of the argument after the inserted appeal to the audience (*OLD* s.v. *igitur* 5). Now the situation and the impact of 'Cicero's' opponents' activities on him are described in the third person with emphasis on his qualities and position. – The sentence starts with an emphatic description of being expelled (fronted *ex civitate* followed by two strong verbs); then the laudatory mention of the worthiness of this citizen for the Republic is enhanced by *consularis homo*; it concludes with two contrasting participles, the first continuing the positive presentation, the second highlighting the appalling behaviour now encountered. – In Cicero's genuine speeches *igitur* usually occurs in second position; its appearance in first position is rare.

non minimis facultatibus usus quondam amicorum: contrasts the past (*quondam*), when the *civis* had ample support of friends, with what is happening now (*nunc*), when he is attacked by others. Such assistance from friends is the standard description of the position of a politician and nobleman; it does not take into account that 'Cicero's' status as *homo novus* has just been alluded to (*Exil.* 6; 15) and that the historical Cicero stresses that he relied on himself and that his success in obtaining magistracies was not due to the support of others (as allegedly in the case of some noblemen: Cic. *Leg. Agr.* 2.1–10; *Pis.* 2). Orelli's supplement (*amicorum <multorum praesidio munitus>*) gives more emphasis to Cicero's own faculties, but still retains the claim that Cicero used to be supported by many friends. As there is no linguistic reason for additions and the change does not fully resolve the tension, it is better avoided.

partim ab invidis, partim ab inimicis: suggests that *invidi* and *inimici* are two groups, though there is likely to be overlap (*Exil.* 1 n.): *inimici* can be opposed to Cicero for any reason, and *invidi* confront him because they are jealous of his achievements (*Exil.* 1; 6; 7; 28).

circumventus indigne: *circumventus* implies prosecution (*OLD* s.v. *circum-uenio* 6). This connotation adds a further nuance and might contradict 'Cicero's' criticism that he was never given a fair trial (e.g. *Exil.* 13; see Introduction, section 3.4); perhaps the allusion is not to a proper trial, but to the behaviour of the opponents, which approximates an unfair prosecution, a point reinforced by the adverb. – The collocation is not attested elsewhere in classical Latin.

in periculo capitis: on the alleged danger to life for 'Cicero', see *Exil.* 1; 6; 7 and nn.

retinebitis: Gamberale (1997, 332–4) suggests reading <*non*> *retinebitis*. This would be necessary if the sentence is not understood ironically. But *credo* (*OLD* s.v. *credo* 8c) and highlighted *vos* suggest that the main clause is an ironic comment.

qui...fecistis in patriam: the relative clause characterizing the audience states that they do not enjoy such a standing and have not achieved as much for the country (as 'Cicero'); the implied consequence is that, therefore, if he loses his liberty, they will do so as well. This description of the audience goes against the principle of flattering them and establishing their goodwill (e.g. Cic. *Inv. rhet.* 1.22; *De or.* 2.115). The nuance is probably triggered by the aim of highlighting Cicero's importance and thus encouraging actions on his behalf in the audience's own interest.

tanta...auctoritate...tantorum officiorum: sets up an implicit comparison with the achievements of the *civis*. – The reading *tanta...auctoritate* (instead of *tantum*) is preferable in view of the parallel with *tantorum officiorum*.

in uno...multorum...ad omnium perniciem: states emphatically (*mihi credite*) that in this case the fate of a single person will have a noticeable and stronger effect on that of all if the community does not save the individual and thus contain the negative developments (see *Exil.* 14).

incommodum confirmatum: *incommodum* appears as another vague term of the current predicament like *calamitas* (*Exil.* 14 n.). *confirmatum* is probably predicative (*OLD* s.v. *confirmatus* 3) and indicates that the situation of 'Cicero' will be a disaster for the audience if it is confirmed and not prevented. Expressing strengthening vs weakening by two different compounds of *firmare* highlights the contrasting developments and the respective outcomes.

proinde...fortunis: the conclusion (*proinde*) of the description of the situation and the link between 'Cicero's' circumstances and those of all is that they either need to help the individual so that his sad fate does not affect the *salus communis* or can expect the same bad fortune for themselves (*hoc idem... incommodum* picking up *hoc in uno incommodum*). While the presentation of this alternative is rhetorically focused on the consequences for the audience as a motivation, it is a strong appeal to action on 'Cicero's' behalf.

2.5. No opportunity for defence for 'Cicero' (17–19)

The fifth part (*Exil.* 17–19) of the main section (*Exil.* 6–23) starts with a new point without a marked transition: it highlights that 'Cicero' has not been given a chance to justify himself, while even criminals are given such an opportunity. In addition, he stresses that he has not committed any crime, but rather crushed the madness of wicked people. 'Cicero' accepts that there will be no chance for him to speak, trusting in the fact that his deeds will be memorized by the People. His opponents, however, if they punish him for the treatment of the Catilinarian conspirators, whom he characterizes as morally inferior individuals, will pay the penalty to him and the People after his expulsion by being tormented by their conscience. 'Cicero' does not commment on the actual criticism that the Catilinarians were assigned the death penalty without trial (see Introduction, section 2).

17 nemo…addiceretur: claims that even the worst criminal is properly convicted in a trial before being punished, to build up a contrast to 'Cicero' (*ego*).

nemo tam perdita…qui: for the construction, see Cic. *Rab. perd.* 23 (cf. Gamberale 1997, 38; Corbeill 2020, 25).

tam perdita auctoritate, tam facinerosa inventus est vita: the person introduced as a foil is described highly negatively in terms of standing and morals. – For adjectival *perditus* here *OLD* gives the meaning 'No longer in one's possession, lost' (*OLD* s.v. *perditus*[1] 5), but the word could have the more common sense 'Morally depraved (often w. implication of wild behaviour), abandoned' (*OLD* s.v. *perditus*[1] 4). Being of 'depraved worthiness' amounts to having no worthiness at all.

de scelere fateretur: for *fateor* combined with *de* (*OLD* s.v. *fateor* 1c), cf., e.g., Cic. *Inv. rhet.* 2.77; Liv. 24.5.10, Tac. *Dial.* 7.1; *Ann.* 15.56.2.

supplicio addiceretur: a strong expression for punishment (*OLD* s.v. *addico* 7).

ego: contrasts the standard proceedings in court cases with what is happening to 'Cicero', who is not given a chance to state his case.

repente: makes it appear as if the backlash from the Tribune of the People happened suddenly. The decisive action in early 58 BCE may have come about soon after the magistrates for the year entered office, but opposition to Cicero's way of dealing with the Catilinarian Conspiracy could be sensed earlier, at least since the time when he was not allowed to deliver the customary oration when stepping down from office as consul at the end of 63 BCE (Cic. *Fam.* 5.2.6–8; *Pis.* 6; 35; *Sull.* 33–4; Plut. *Cic.* 23.1–2; Cass. Dio 37.38.1–2).

vi tribunicia: again a reference to P. Clodius Pulcher without naming him (on such expressions, see *Exil.* 13 n.).

non modo loquendi...sed ne consistendi quidem...habeo potestatem: identifies what is not granted to 'Cicero'.

loquendi libere in iudicio: denotes a defence in a law court; the addition of the adverb *libere* implies a trial with a fair hearing.

sed ne consistendi quidem in civitate: could denote the opportunity to stay within the community, taking the impending departure from Rome as a fact (*OLD* s.v. *consisto* 8; cf., e.g., Cic. *Flacc.* 77: *praesertim cum ille cui dies dicta est praetor postea factus sit et consul, ille qui diem dixit non potuerit privatus in civitate consistere*). It could also mean a public speech in a *contio* (although abstract *civitate* is slightly odd) before the People (*OLD* s.v. *consisto* 6; cf., e.g., Cic. *Leg. Agr.* 1.25: *ne mihi non liceat contra vos in contione consistere*), as the subsequent phrase apud *vos loqui non licebit* may indicate (*Exil.* 18 [and n.]), or emphasize that there was not even a chance for justification before the People in a kind of informal law court (*OLD* s.v. *consisto* 6c). While the current speech is envisaged as an address to the People (see *Exil.*, Introduction) and 'Cicero' thus has the opportunity to speak to them, the last two alternatives would stress that he did not have the chance when the allegations were first raised. The juxtaposition with *loquendi libere in iudicio* suggests that the second item also refers to a context of self-defence (though a less formal one).

eicior...scelere: a consequence of the lack of a trial and the chance of justification is that 'Cicero' feels that he is thrown out without all the elements of a trial (listed in an asyndetic and anaphoric sequence), on top of the fact that there is not even a crime (in 'Cicero's' interpretation).

eicior: the verb *eicere*, here applied to 'Cicero' having to leave Rom, is used (in some contexts) in the *Catilinarian Orations* of the historical Cicero for Catiline leaving Rome (Cic. *Cat.* 2.1; 2.12; 2.13; 2.14; 3.3).

sine crimine: since the climax in this list of items not valid for 'Cicero' is that he has not even committed a crime (*sine...scelere*), *crimen* must refer to the charge.

sed sine etiam scelere: initial *non solum* points forward to a second part introduced by *sed etiam*: it makes sense to single out the last item *scelere* (as the transmission suggests, though other options have been considered by scholars): this is the fundamental fact to prompt a court case, while the other items are circumstantial elements of the legal process. – The word order is unusual (instead of *sed etiam sine*); it might have been caused by a scribal error in the manuscripts or the insertion of a previously omitted word in the wrong place.

18 hostibus...non licebit: 'Cicero's' situation is contrasted with that of enemies in a war: although enemies are at war and oppose each other in arms, they are said to have the opportunity to talk and debate (i.e. to resolve the conflict), while this procedure will be denied to the citizen Cicero, who has contributed to safeguarding the community, in peace. – The future tenses in the section referring to 'Cicero' imply a connotation of potentiality (K.-St. I 142–3). – The description of the enemies in war consists of a threefold relative clause (*qui…oppugnant*); the main clause is made emphatic by the anaphora of *licet* in two short asyndetic phrases. In the part about 'Cicero', the phrase *loqui non licebit* (specified by *apud vos*) repeats in chiasmus *licet loqui* (without the second verb *disputare*); likewise, *in pace, civi* corresponds in chiasmus to *hostibus, in bello* (both followed by descriptive relative clauses).

qui dissident voluntate: *voluntate* is probably an ablative of respect (K.-St. I 392–3; Pinkster 2015, 914–15) and indicates the area in which the two parties differ, in their 'inclination' (*OLD* s.v. *uoluntas* 7): this contrasts with 'Cicero's' situation, as he has to fight against citizens after he has done something for the benefit of all citizens. Alternatively, since *voluntate* can mean 'voluntarily' (*OLD* s.v. *uoluntas* 1b), the phrase could say that enemies going to war have decided that they wish to be at variance with each other, in contrast to 'Cicero' who, in this presentation, has been forced into the current situation.

vitam cotidie oppugnant: enemies attack the lives of people involved in the fighting literally at each battle and metaphorically on a daily basis because the constant threat remains. – *vitam* must be a generic singular when a contest involving groups is envisaged. The collocation *vitam oppugnare* does not seem to be attested elsewhere.

in ipsa acie cum proeliantur: in view of its tense and mood, the *cum*-clause is most likely temporal, specifying the time of the action in the main clause (K.-St. II 333–4). Then, if the description is to be understood literally, fighters are envisaged as having the opportunity to stop in the middle of a battle and resolve the issue by talking to each other. – *ipsa* emphasizes the scenario that these conversations can happen in the middle of a battle (*OLD* s.v. *ipse* 9; K.-St. I 628–9).

licet loqui, licet disputare: the doublet (with anaphora and asyndeton) consists of a more general and a more specific verb for speaking, indicating an argument for one's case, thus suggesting that these people have the chance not only to say something, but also to represent their case.

qui perditorum hominum fregi furorem: another reference to Cicero's crushing of the Catilinarian Conspiracy, with the frequent negative characterization of the Catilinarians (*Exil.* 6; 8). – Earlier in this speech the expression *frangere furorem* is applied to military commanders (*Exil.* 3; for this phrase, see Cic. *Pis.* 32; *Vat.* 6; *Mil.* 34; *Phil.* 10.21; *Q Fr.* 2.14.2; cf. Corbeill 2020, 27). The similarity of phrasing might suggest comparability of the two actions, in the sense of the *dux togatus* of the historical Cicero (*Exil.* 13 n.).

pro fortunis meis: if a defence situation is assumed, *pro* is best interpreted as indicating the object being defended and *fortuna* as referring to 'Cicero's' fate (*OLD* s.v. *pro*[1] 4; *fortuna* 8). If the emphasis is on 'Cicero's' status in relation to those of the other groups in the comparison, the phrase might indicate that

'Cicero' is not given the opportunity appropriate to his standing (*OLD* s.v. *pro*[1] 14; *fortuna* 11). In the context of threats the first option is more likely.

servi . . . conservavi: a second comparison, this time with slaves: it is claimed that slaves caught trying to kill others often state their case before the intended victims (just before being punished), while 'Cicero', an ex-consul, cannot even speak before those he preserved. By an emphatic contrast this scenario enhances the notion of 'Cicero' being treated unfairly, not even given the rights that (guilty) slaves have. The two situations, however, are not fully comparable: the slaves are confronted with the immediate objects of their planned misdeeds, while the People may have benefited indirectly from Cicero's interventions. Moreover, slaves would not be given a proper trial and would hardly have the chance to 'argue' (as the verb *disputare* suggests) before being punished.

apud eos non loquar quos conservavi?: takes up the question *apud vos loqui non licebit?* (see note on future tense above). The parallel and the description confirm that the envisaged addressees are the People, whom Cicero kept unharmed by fighting against Catiline and thus preserving the Republic in his view (on the wording, see Cic. *RS* 8 n.; Introduction, section 3.4).

tacebo: after complaining that there will not be a chance to speak and defend himself, 'Cicero' yields and announces that he will be silent, if this is what the conditions impose, as his virtue will plead his cause anyway. The demonstration of virtue is a confident statement that his good deeds and character will be obvious even against the odds. Then a speech would not be necessary; yet the previous complaint still stands as a criticism of procedure.

tacebo, inquam, animo aequo: the repetition of *tacebo* and the expansion (taken up by *me tacente*) demonstrate 'Cicero's' relaxed attitude and the extent to which he relies on his virtue. The decision to be silent is illustrated by *mutam fugam* (*Exil.* 19).

agit meam causam: this phrase, a *terminus technicus* for proceedings in court (*OLD* s.v. *ago* 41c; *causa* 3a), describes metaphorically *virtus* taking over the role of the defence in the absence of other options.

19 itaque: introduces the consequences of being silent for 'Cicero' (*OLD* s.v. *itaque* 1).

ut: introduces a concessive *ut*-clause, as subsequent *tamen* shows (K.-St. II 251).

in contione mea: such phrases consisting of *contio* and a possessive within a speech to the People often refer to a *contio* called by the person thus identified (Cic. *Leg. agr.* 3.1–2). In 58 BCE (the envisaged date of this speech) Cicero would not have had a role enabling him to call a *contio*; he would have to rely on other people giving him the opportunity to speak in *contiones* called by them (see *Exil.*, Introduction). In other contexts the phrase can denote a *contio* speech delivered by the person indicated by the pronoun (e.g. Cic. *Fam.* 9.14[= *Att.* 14.17A].7: *legi enim contionem tuam*). Thus, the emphasis here is probably on the speech rather than the occasion; the expression amounts to a *praeteritio* in mock modesty: although 'Cicero' will not talk about his achievements in this speech, they will still be left in people's minds.

nihil ponam de meis rebus gestis: *ponere* denotes making an utterance (*OLD* s.v. *pono* 18).

in animis et memoria vestra: this reading is the most plausible and follows the text in some manuscripts. *vestra* then is an attribute going with both nouns and agreeing with the nearest (K.-St. I 54; Pinkster 2015, 1273–7). *relinquam* does not have an expressed object (the alternative reading *memoriam* would require an additional genitive attribute); instead, the object has to be supplied from *de meis rebus gestis* in the preceding clause: the People will be aware of Cicero's deeds and remember them.

largiter relinquam: the collocation *largiter relinquere* does not seem to be attested elsewhere (and *largiter* does not occur in Cicero's genuine works). – *relinquam* is most likely future (rather than present subjunctive). *largiter* expresses vividly that the memory of the deeds will be all over the minds of the audience and will have great impact.

isti ... possint: adds the consequences even of a 'silent flight' for the others, which will provide some satisfaction for 'Cicero'.

isti: a derogatory reference to the opponents (K.-St. I 621–2). Their identities are not defined; presumably P. Clodius Pulcher and his supporters are again alluded to.

hanc meam mutam fugam: if 'Cicero' is envisaged as delivering this speech prior to his departure, his withdrawal has not been *muta* so far; what is probably meant is the lack of a proper defence (*Exil.* 17–18). – *fuga* is a negative term for Cicero's withdrawal, which is not found in the genuine speeches given after his return.

meam ... fugam ferre possint: the phrase *fugam ferre* also occurs in Cicero's genuine writings (Cic. *Att.* 7.2.8). The twist here is that others are said to have to find a way to bear the consequencs of 'Cicero's' *fuga*.

etenim: the surprising statement that 'Cicero's' opponents might have problems bearing his flight is explained by their self-reproaches and expectation of danger.

si ... repetunt: a report of the view of the opponents that some of the Catilinarian conspirators are demanding satisfaction (*OLD* s.v. *repeto* 8b); obviously, this would have to be enforced by others sympathizing with Catiline, since these conspirators were dead (*mortui*) by the envisaged time of this speech. – While it is plausible that the view reported is the opinion of the opponents (*ut isti existimant*), the wording is that of 'Cicero', giving all individuals a negative characterization and picking up details found in Cicero's *Catilinarian Orations*, though with adjustments and additions (Cic. *Cat.* 3.16: *quem quidem ego cum ex urbe pellebam, hoc providebam animo, Quirites, remoto Catilina non mihi esse P. Lentuli somnum nec L. Cassi adipes nec C. Cethegi furiosam* *temeritatem pertimescendam.*; cf. Corbeill 2020, 25). The construction (as in Cic. *Cat.* 3.16), with the names of the men in the genitive depending on key features, emphasizes these negative characteristics.

isti... istis: again 'Cicero's' current opponents.

Lentuli mortui sordes: P. Cornelius Lentulus Sura (*RE* Cornelius 240; praet. 74, cos. 71, praet. II 63 BCE [*MRR* II 102, 121, 166]), one of the chief figures in the Catilinarian Conspiracy (*MRR* II 166). – *sordes* must refer to character (*OLD* s.v. *sordes* 5 'Moral turpitude, baseness') and thus is a more generic description than *somnum* in Cicero's *Catilinarian Orations* (Cic. *Cat.* 3.16).

Catilinae notissimus furor: L. Sergius Catilina (Cic. *RS* 10 n.; on *furor* attributed to Catiline in Cicero's *Catilinarian Orations*, see, e.g., Cic. *Cat.* 1.1; 1.2; 1.15; 1.22; 2.1; on *furor*, see *Exil.* 6 n.). – *notissimus* presents Catiline's *furor* as a fact that the audience is aware of, probably implying negative fame (*OLD* s.v. *notus* 7).

amentia Cethegi: C. Cornelius Cethegus (Cic. *RS* 10 n.). – *amentia* indicates a different aspect of not being fully in rational control of one's mind from that of *furiosa temeritas* in Cicero's *Catilinarian Orations* (Cic. *Cat.* 3.16; see Sall. *Cat.* 43.4–4).

luxuries ac stupra Cassi: L. Cassius Longinus (*RE* Cassius 64; praet. 66 BCE [*MRR* II 152]) was a follower of Catiline in 63 BCE (Sall. *Cat.* 17.3); he was not among the captured conspirators, but his punishment was demanded at the same meeting of the Senate (Sall. *Cat.* 50.4). – While *luxuries* could be regarded as a precondition for *adipes* mentioned by Cicero (Cic. *Cat.* 3.16); *stupra* is an additional item. Both points are generic elements of abuse and invective alleged without any specific evidence.

profecto... poenas: the argument is somewhat condensed: if the opponents believe that retribution is demanded for people punished and treated unfairly (like those conspirators), the same will apply to them if they make Cicero withdraw from Rome without justification. Thus, they will have to worry about potential repercussions constantly, but 'Cicero' will not seek retribution, and they will rather pay the penalty as a result of the force of their conscience (see Cic. *Cat.* 3.13).

eiecto Tullio: on the verb *eicere* for 'Cicero's' departure from Rome, see *Exil.* 17 n. – Cicero is referred to by one part of his name, in an ablative absolute and a sentence without a focus on his personality; therefore, no changes are required (on naming conventions for Cicero, see *Exil.* 6 n.).

non meis insidiis, quae nullae a me parantur: again a pronounced statement of the fact that 'Cicero' acts fairly and without any deceit.

suorum conscientia scelerum cruciati: the collocation *cruciatur conscientia* is otherwise only attested a few times from Calpurnius Flaccus (Calpurnius Flaccus, *Declamationum excerpta* 49) in the early second century CE onwards.

mihi absenti et populo Romano: again turns the confrontaton from a personal one to a conflict involving the audience and the entire Roman People. The argument presupposes that the People have also been affected by Cicero having been forced to leave Rome without a trial and therefore Cicero's opponents will pay retribution to them too.

2.6. 'Cicero's' sacrifice for the community (20–2)

In the penultimate part (*Exil.* 20–2) of the main section (*Exil.* 6–23) 'Cicero' announces that he will yield to the mad behaviour of a few individuals for the sake of the welfare of the community, thus preventing civil war and fulfilling his civic duties. He proclaims that exile or death for the sake of the community is not miserable or disgraceful; he just feels sad at the state of the Republic. Thus, 'Cicero' admits defeat, but still makes it appear as a heroic act when the superior person gives way to avoid worse consequences, and his opponents will not be able to influence his concern for the Republic or the glory already won.

20 quas ob res: introduces the conclusion that 'Cicero' will leave Rome for the benefit of the community. It is not a direct inference from a point made immediately previously, but a more indirect consequence of the argument in the last section: 'Cicero' accepts the situation; but at least he acts as the morally superior and more generous individual, and the authors will experience punishment for this deed.

amentiae cupiditatique paucorum omnium salutis causa: an emphatic juxtaposition of *pauci* and *omnes*, highlighting 'Cicero's' sacrifice for the community when faced with a few madmen. – The statement might provoke the question why 'Cicero' yields if his opponents are just a few: the underlying notion seems to be that they are sufficiently powerful and determined because of their characteristics (*Exil.* 27) and that his withdrawal is the best way to save everyone. One might also ask why 'Cicero' complained about the lack of opportunities for defence if he is to give in anyway: even in the case of a quiet withdrawal it has to be pointed out that the process does not follow proper procedure. – *amentiae* picks up *furor* (*Exil.* 13; 14) to describe the irrational behaviour of the opponents (again unnamed) and a characteristic just ascribed to Cethegus (*Exil.* 19); *cupiditati* might imply (in hindsight) that they are keen on 'Cicero's' possessions.

decedam: on this verb, see *Exil.* 13 n.

neque in eum locum <rem> deducam aut progredi patiar: this section has suffered different types of corruption in the various manuscripts; when <rem> is added to create a standard idiom and the readings for individual words from different manuscripts are put together, a plausible text can be constituted (*OLD* s.v. *deduco* 12b). – The doublet *in eum locum…deducam aut progredi patiar* emphasizes that Cicero will not be the cause of the consequences described in the *ut*-clause (for *neque…aut*, see *OLD* s.v. *neque* 7).

ut…fiat: *vos* and *civium* refer to the same group of people: a personal expression addressed to the audience is followed by a description of their status in the third person; this enables both engaging the audience and introducing the vocabulary of civil war. – The two prepositional phrases with *inter* highlight that members of the same group are fighting against each other (for the expression, see Sall. *Hist.* 1.55.19 M. = 1.49.19 R.: *manus conserentis inter se Romanos exercitus*).

multoque potius ipse … quam … dimicetis: stresses again the frequent notion of Cicero's sacrifice on behalf of the community (see the contrast between *unum me* and *vos*; see Cic. *RQ* 1 n.), with an emphasis not just on leaving, but on missing *patria* and children (Keeline 2018, 170). Gratitude for being reunited with these occurs in the speeches delivered after Cicero's return (Cic. *RS* 1; *RQ* 4; 5; on Cicero's children Tullia and Marcus, see Cic. *RS* 1 n.). – The phrase recalls a statement expressing the contrary in a letter from Cicero to Atticus (Cic. *Att.* 3.26.1: *mihi in animo est legum lationem exspectare et, si obtrectabitur, utar auctoritate senatus et potius vita quam patria carebo.*; on the expression, see Cic. *RQ* 20 n.). – The subjunctive in the comparative clause signals a rejection of that alternative option (K.-St. II 300; Pinkster 2015, 665).

de fortunis vestris reique publicae: both *vestris* and *rei … publicae* qualify *fortunis*: the possessive relationship is expressed by a possessive in relation to a personal pronoun and by a genitive attribute for an ordinary noun. The phrase assumes that any fight will affect not only the audience, but also the Republic, perhaps as it is seen as a conflict about power relations and organization of the Republic.

sic … procreatum: explains (*enim*) the decision to sacrifice himself as in line with 'Cicero's' general attitude: he has always been of the opinion that he was born not for himself, but for the Republic, and thus has acted selflessly and in the public interest (for the phrase, see Cic. *Phil.* 14.25; cf. Corbeill 2020, 25).

ab initio: while *initium* can mean 'birth', in line with common uses of *ab initio*, the phrase here means 'since the beginning of being involved in politics' (*OLD* s.v. *initium* 1).

animatus: on this expression, see *OLD* s.v. *animatus* 2 (cf. *Exil.* 29).

quam rei publicae: could be dative with *procreatum* or genitive with *causa* supplied from *mea causa* in the preceding clause (*causa* with possessive: K.-St. I 422–3). In view of the parallelism (with *variatio*) apparently aimed for, the latter is more plausible.

21 quod … calamitatem: could be a relative clause defining *illud* or a causal *quod*-clause with *illud* as the implied subject. The structure of the sentence suggests the former: the relative clause defines the effect of the situation referred to by *illud*. The subsequent infinitives indicate what the matter consists in.

ad universorum struitur calamitatem: implies activities designed not only for the extinction of an individual (i.e. 'Cicero'), but to everyone's disadvantage. This comment is another item that gives 'Cicero's' predicament general relevance, so that the matter seems worthy of the audience's attention.

conqueri…non licere: a list of verbs illustrating various ways of speaking reveals what the complaint is about: no opportunity to state one's case in any way is provided. The list starts with verbs indicating lament, followed by phrases suggesting a context of justifying and refuting allegations, potentially at a trial. The statement illustrates that proper legal processes are not in place; in the context it alludes again to the situation that Cicero was not taken to court and not given the chance to present his case (*Exil.* 17–18). – The collocation *suspicionem demovere* does not seem to be attested elsewhere.

ore oppresso cervices esse praebendas: summarizes drastically the consequences of the described lack of opportunity to speak: no plea or justification is possible (*ore oppresso*); punishment follows straight away (*cervices esse praebendas*). The expression is vivid and metaphorical: Cicero's mouth has not literally been shut, and he is not literally running the risk of being beheaded immediately. It is a dramatic description of the situation that there is no chance of voicing one's point of view and one has to succumb to the force of one's opponents. – The form *ore oppresso* is only attested here. For *cervices praebere*, see Sen. *Contr.* 9.2.8; *Suas.* 6.17 (on Cicero's death).

quae tamen…introducta: again the consequences for the Republic are put above the experiences of the individual: it is claimed that the fact that 'Cicero' has to undergo such a sitution is not as bad as the fact that this is happening in the Republic. *calamitosa…mihi…perniciosa…in rem publicam* picks up *ad unius perniciem…universorum…calamitatem*, with the qualities of *pernicies* and *calamitas* chiastically placed and each applied to both the single individual and the community across the two sentences.

omnia: summarizes what was outlined in what precedes.

quam ob rem…libidinosus: the wording and the impersonal phrasing (*statutum est atque decretum*) make the statement appear like an official decree; for, while *statuo* and *decerno* may mean 'to decide' generally, these verbs are frequently employed in connection with decisions by political and judicial bodies. Thus, 'Cicero' presents the intention to bear everything that *furor libidinosus* will demand as if it was an official decision, while it describes the consequences 'Cicero' has drawn for himself from the current conditions (*OLD* s.v. *tempus*[1] 12; cf., e.g., Cic. *Verr.* 2.5.2; *Phil.* 5.38). – Personified *furor*, the qualifying attribute, and the verb *volet* highlight the arbitrariness, unconsidered actions, and madness of the opponents. Since *furor* has been introduced as a characteristic of the Tribune of the People (*Exil.* 13; 14; see *Exil.* 6 n.), it is implied that P. Clodius Pulcher is again one of the opponents behind these measures, although the phrasing is abstract.

vim…condono: a series of short sentences outlines potential activities of the opponents and 'Cicero's' reaction. The conclusion in each case is that 'Cicero' is ready to do whatever is required despite the negative consequences for himself and the inappropriateness of the request, in line with his aim to preserve the Republic and deflect harm from the citizens.

vim: P. Clodius Pulcher and his followers are not known to have used violent force against Cicero to make him leave Rome, but they operated with violence in Rome and used force against people supporting Cicero (see Introduction, section 2).

praesto sum: 'Cicero's' reaction to the intention to use force: he is ready to accept it.

eicere: on this verb for Cicero's leaving Rome, see *Exil.* 17 n.

exeo: the reaction to being thrown out is that 'Cicero' leaves (again avoiding conflict).

indicta causa volunt abire: suggests again that there will be no trial and no official occasion for 'Cicero' to justify himself in response to the charges. Associations of a trial are triggered by the technical wording (*OLD* s.v. *indictus* 1b; cf., e.g., Cic. *Verr.* 1.13: *absentes rei facti indicta causa damnati et eiecti*). – The first three actions described consist of repeated *volunt* with an infinitive each and no object expressed (forms of *ego* to be supplied). As *indicta causa* usually refers to the defendant, it is most likely that this point is a specification of preceding *eicere*, adding the fact that no hearing will take place beforehand; the construction changes from simple infinitive constructions (with the opponents as logical subjects) to an accusative and infinitive (with *me* supplied).

aliud quippiam conantur: after the list of three specific actions, this generalizing phrase catches everything else the opponents might plan; this corresponds to an equally general reaction of acceptance (*agant*). – For the combination of *aliud* and *quispiam*, cf., e.g., Cic. *Nat. D.* 3.87; *Tusc.* 3.19.

nihil . . . condono: 'Cicero' elaborates that he is prepared to undergo anything and will not regard it as harsh for him if it is done for the benefit of the Republic. The reason (*enim*) is the feeling that he has not been defeated, but rather is handing himself over voluntarily to safeguard the citizens (*vobis*, referring to the People envisaged as forming the audience: see *Exil.*, Introduction; *Exil.* 1 n.). Thus, this is an interpretation of the situation, while it is stated as a fact and thus appears as the only version. – If one read *concedo* in the first half, this could be interpreted as almost synonymous in sense with *condono*, here construed with dative (*OLD* s.v. *condono* 5; *concedo* 4). Yet, apart from the fact that *cedo* is a more common verb in Cicero's speeches given after his return (see *Exil.* 7 n.; Introduction, section 3.4), though in a slightly different sense, 'Cicero' is not handing himself over to his enemies (*illis*), but yielding to them by leaving (*cedo*; *OLD* s.v. *cedo*[1] 10), which, in his view, means that he sacrifices himself (*me condono*) for the People, who remain unharmed (*incolumibus vobis*) by avoiding civil war. Thus, the reading *cedo* is more plausible.

22 neque . . . consolationem: outlines, in a further expansion of the reasoning (*enim*) of the previous sentence (*Exil.* 21), the two possible ways of yielding to *furor* (*neque . . . mors . . . neque exilium*) and an assessment of them: neither death nor exile is a negative experience if there is a positive motivation. – This tactic aligns with the strategy found in the speeches delivered after Cicero's return to argue away his 'exile' or at least its potential appearance as a negative event (see Introduction, section 3.4).

mors … capitur: since this a general observation on the value of sacrifices on behalf of the Republic, it does not reveal whether the danger of death is envisaged as a real consequence for 'Cicero' at this stage (see *Exil.* 6; 7). – The phrase *mortem capere* is rare (but see Ps.-Quint. *Decl.* 3.8); it is a development of other uses of *capere*, and it creates assonance with the verb used in the parallel relative clause (*suscipitur*).

exilium: the historical Cicero does not use *exilium* for his period of absence from Rome in the speeches delivered after his return (see Introduction, section 3.4), though he discusses the term's meaning and assessment. In *De domo sua* he denies that *turpis* is an appropriate description of exile unless it is a punishment for a misdeed (Cic. *Dom.* 72). – The characterization of *exilium* (*turpe*) is different in quality from that of preceding *mors* (*miseranda*), and the reason why the assumed negative assessment does not apply is also suitably different: *mors* can be regarded positively when it occurs in connection with a deed for the Republic, *exilium* when it is based on *virtus* (implicitly assigned to 'Cicero').

cum … consolationem: in addition to the positive aspects of *mors* and *exilium* in the right circumstances, there is a further positive point in that these situations are *poenae*, but include some consolation, which is outlined in what follows.

nam … removebunt: this sentence explains (*nam*) why the punishments *mors* and *exilium* have some consolation: they only affect physical aspects, but not (in the case of *mors*) one's long-lasting reputation or (in the case of *exilium*) the mind's focus on the *res publica*. – Grammatically, it would be most straightforward to infer *hae poenae* as the subject for the four verbs in this sentence, since no subject is expressed and this was the last plural noun mentioned. The resulting sense, however, is odd: *hae poenae* consist of *mors* and *exilium*, and here there is one clause about each with these items being mentioned as instruments of action. Therefore, an unspecified group of opponents have to be assumed as the agents.

non adiment gloriam <im>mortalem: it is claimed that death will take away life only, but not immortal, i.e. everlasting glory (*OLD* s.v. *immortalis* 2c), presumably based on previous achievements and/or a heroic death. The stucture of the argument requires the reading <*im*>*mortalem*, as generally emended; the two letters could easily have fallen out after *gloriam*: the contrast is between the end of one's physical life and glory continuing after death.

corpus non animum a re publica removebunt: as *mors* affects only life, *exilium* affects only the body: exile cannot make individuals stop thinking about the Republic. The notion that the mind is still with the Republic might be prompted by the frequent concept in Cicero's speeches delivered after his return that the Republic left with him and they both returned together (e.g. Cic. *RS* 34; 36; *RQ* 14; 18; *Dom.* 87; see Introduction, section 3.4). It is slightly at odds with this concept, though, when it seems to presuppose that the Republic remains where it is and the body is separated from it.

nam . . . existimabo: from the general exposition this sentence returns to 'Cicero', applying the considerations to his situation: he will always feel removed merely physically from the People and the Republic, but will not lose touch or feel thrust out by them. Such a statement basically denies the background to 'Cicero's' absence from Rome and implies that other individuals are responsible for 'Cicero's' departure, not the People in the audience (*vobis*).

haec semper futura mea: in this reading of the majority of manuscripts it is unclear whether the phrase is another main clause (with *erunt* to be supplied) or an accusative and infinitive construction depending on *cogitabo* (with *esse* to be supplied). In view of the flow of the sentence, the latter is more likely: then, *me-que* connects the two first-person verbs *cogitabo* and *existimabo*, each supplemented by an accusative and infinitive construction without *esse* in chiastic sequence (for such an order, see, e.g., *Exil.* 6; 18). In any case *futura* is to be understood as a noun qualified by *mea*. While the noun *futurum* in the plural denoting future events is well attested (*OLD* s.v. *futurum* 2 '(pl.) Future events, the future'), the connection with a possessive in the sense of 'future events affecting me' or 'my future' is odd (i.e. that 'Cicero' will always think that his future will be that only his body is removed from Rome). Therefore, various emendations have been suggested: Gamberale's (1997, 334–5) proposal *futura mea <mens>*, however, would result in an awkward impersonal main clause in the middle of the sentence.

repudiatum: De Marco (1991, 22) prints *repudiantum* without a note in the apparatus; this is likely to be a printing error (*repudiatum* in De Marco 1967, 57).

2.7. Appeal to protect 'Cicero's' family (23)

The final part (*Exil.* 23) of the main section (*Exil.* 6–23) seems to accept that the fate awaiting 'Cicero' is unchangeable, so that his thoughts turn to what will happen to his family left behind. Therefore, the focus of the appeal shifts: 'Cicero' now asks the audience to care for his children and his whole family. They should protect them from his opponents, remembering his virtuous and selfless deeds rather than his current bad fortune. Thus, the plea is linked to a reminder of Cicero's great services for the Republic as well as his exemplary honest and fair behaviour; this justifies the request along with contributing to the desired portrayal of 'Cicero'.

23 vobis universis: the most likely and most emphatic reading, when the speaker returns to addressing the audience and asking them for support, is to combine the two words found in one branch of the transmission each (for the phrase, see, e.g., Cic. *De or.* 1.225; *Parad.* 5.41).

peto postuloque, si ... si ... uti: 'Cicero' explicitly asks for something in return from the People for a behaviour that is phrased as a condition, but meant as a statement of fact.

si ... tutatus: a description of what 'Cicero' did for the community while he was allowed to stay (*Exil.* 26); the wording is obviously determined by the current situation. The *si*-clause consists of four parts: two short elements indicate what Cicero did not do to anyone (*nemini*) and two longer elements (introduced with repeated *si*) outline what Cicero did for the citizenry (*omnibus ... plurimosque*). 'Cicero' claims that he has never been a threat to anyone or caused trouble for innocent people (what his enemies are doing to him according to him); instead, he has provided help and protection for all and defended many.

dum in civitate manere licitum est: i.e. before 'Cicero' (suppl. *mihi*) was forced to leave Rome, as he is about to do.

sum tutatus: as this item seems to be different from the preceding activity, it probably refers to serving as a lawyer (*OLD* s.v. *tutor*² 2).

uti ... neve ... utique: a series of requests (governed by *peto postuloque*): a two-part positive one relating to 'Cicero's' children, a negative one concerning his family as a whole, and another positive one about 'Cicero' himself.

liberos meos: Cicero's children Tullia and Marcus (Cic. *RS* 1 n.).

in vestram fidem recipiatis: as someone needs to look after his children in his absence, 'Cicero' asks for the guardianship of the audience for his children as their wards (*OLD* s.v. *fides*¹ 1).

eosque defendatis: *eos* refers to *liberos meos*; the phrase exemplifies the role of the audience as guardians.

longius in familiam nostram progredi: this appeal extends beyond the children to 'Cicero's' family as a whole (perhaps envisaged as including his wife and his brother as well as the entire household): it is assumed that his opponents (*inimicos meos*) have started taking action against the family by forcing 'Cicero' to leave Rome and should be prevented from any further steps against members of the family.

sive hinc abiero sive hic ero oppressus: indicates the expectation that 'Cicero' will not be successful against his opponents: he will either have to leave Rome (*hinc*) or be overwhelmed in Rome (*hic*).

ea maneat opinio et existimatio, quae virtute parta, non quae infelicitate inlata est: while 'Cicero' is aware that there is little chance of prevailing against his opponents, he encourages the audience to preserve his memory in the right (positive) way. The contrasting and asyndetic parts of the relative clause emphasize that the view of 'Cicero' that should remain should be based on the achievements he won through his character and abilities (*virtute*), presumably as a politician for the benefit of the Republic, rather than on his current misfortune (*infelicitate*). By characterizing the situation as *infelicitas* brought upon him, 'Cicero' has it appear as a mishap rather than a negative development for

which he might be responsible or that might be justified. Such a skewed presentation is similar to the strategies in the speeches delivered after Cicero's
return, in which his 'exile' is reinterpreted (see Introduction, section 3.4). –
opinio et existimatio is another of the frequent doublets in this speech; the
variant *existimationem opinionemque* is attested in Ambrose (Ambrosius, *Off.*
2.7.29).

3. Conclusion (24–30): Final appeal for support

The concluson to this speech (*Exil.* 24–30) consists of an emphatic appeal to the
gods (*Exil.* 24–5), the human audience generally (*Exil.* 26–8), and the knights
in particular (*Exil.* 29–30). The oration thus ends in an emotional way, with the
inclusion of the major players. While this section continues the request for
help, it also restates 'Cicero's' virtue, innocence, and previous services for the
Republic. Thus, on the one hand, the conclusion presents 'Cicero' as anticipating
his impending fate, but still asking for help as a suppliant; the appropriate emotional tone in a peroration is thereby created. On the other hand, this presentation leaves the audience with an image of a virtuous, innocent, selfless, and
community-minded Cicero who is superior to his opponents and therefore
yields graciously.

3.1. To the gods (24–5)

The conclusion (*Exil.* 24–30) starts (*Exil.* 24–5) with an emphatic appeal to the
gods of the Roman pantheon, the Capitoline Triad in particular, with numerous epithets and extensive descriptions of their functions, in a lofty, almost
poetic register. Such a presentation agrees with the rules for praise of gods in
the epideictic oratorical genre as outlined by Quintilian (Quint. *Inst.* 3.7.7–8).
As in the interaction with the human audience, 'Cicero' reminds the gods of his
salutary deeds for them; he asks them to bring help to him and the Republic in
return and to avoid him being driven off. Naturally, details of what the gods are
supposed to do remain vague.

    24 nunc ego te . . .: *nunc* marks the transition to a new aspect (*OLD* s.v. *nunc*
9c). Introductory *ego* is followed by a long list of gods with attached characterizations (*te . . . conlocatum*) and eventually the predicate *oro atque opsecro* (governing the names of gods in the accusative), which in turn introduces a series
of requests (as independent clauses in the imperative). – Similar appeals to the
gods (albeit with different descriptions) can be found in speeches given in
Cicero's consular year and in connection with his return to Rome (Gamberale
1997, 337; 1998, 61–3; Corbeill 2020, 25–6). Like the invocation here, the comparable passage at the end of *De domo sua* implies that the gods should support
Cicero because he saved them previously (Cic. *Dom.* 144–5). The invocation
here looks like an elaborate version of a type of address to the gods of which an

example survives in Livy (Liv. 6.16.2: *Iuppiter... optime maxime Iunoque regina ac Minerva ceterique di deaeque, qui Capitolium arcemque incolitis*; cf. also Cic. *Rab. perd.* 5; *Cat.* 1.33).

Iuppiter Optime Maxime: Jupiter is first addressed as Iuppiter Optimus Maximus (on this title of Jupiter and its implications, see Wissowa 1912, 125–9), as part of the Capitoline Triad, and then again as Iuppiter Stator. He is thus the only god to be mentioned twice, at the beginning and the end of the sequence. The descriptive relative clauses highlight the god's powerful dominion across the entire world as Iuppiter Optimus Maximus and his role as protector and supporter of the state as Iuppiter Stator, which enables the speaker to recall Cicero's successful quelling of the Catilinarian Conspiracy and to place him indirectly in the tradition of Romulus.

nutu ac dicione: since Homer's *Iliad* (e.g. Hom. *Il.* 1.511–30) Zeus' nodding is a symbol of his power (e.g. also Verg. *Aen.* 10.113–16). – The collocation *nutum dicionemque* appears in Cicero and Livy (Cic. *Quinct.* 94; Liv. 35.32.8), and *dicione nutuque* is found in Pliny (Plin. *Pan.* 4.4); the version *nutu ac dicione* seems only to be attested here.

sola terrarum: because of the plural verb, *sola* must be nominative plural of the noun *solum*. The phrase *sola terrarum* is not frequent, but attested elsewhere (Enn. *Ann.* 461 Skutsch; Cic. *Balb.* 13) and functions as an elevated periphrasis for *terrae*.

particeps conubii, socia regni: puts Juno on a par with Jupiter, as his wife and co-ruler. This emphasizes her official position rather than the way in which Jupiter is said to have treated Juno in some myths (on Juno, see Wissowa 1912, 181–91). – The collocation *particeps conubii* seems only to be attested here; the phrase *socium regni* appears in Augustine (Aug. *De civ. D.* 3.13).

Regina Iuno: the title *regina* is often used for Juno as a powerful member of the Capitoline Triad besides Iuppiter Optimus Maximus (Cic. *Dom.* 144; *Verr.* 2.5.184; *Scaur.* 47; on this title of Juno, see Wissowa 1912, 189 with n. 5). – The sequence *regina Iuno* is elsewhere only attested once (Liv. 5.22.4); usually it is *Iuno regina*.

Tritonia, armipotens Gorgophona Pallas Minerva: the third member of the Capitoline Triad, Minerva (Wissowa 1912, 253–6), is described by a series of known, but rare epithets.

Tritonia: the precise meaning of this epithet for Athena/Minerva is uncertain; in classical Latin *Tritonia* only appears in poetic texts (e.g. Verg. *Aen.* 2.171; 5.704; Ov. *Met.* 5.250; 5.270; 6.1; Val. Flacc. 7.442).

armipotens: allludes to the function of the goddess as a strategic actor in war, for instance supporting the Greeks in the Trojan War. *armipotens Minerva* is a rare collocation (Accius, *Trag.* 127 R.[2–3]; Maximian, *El.* 3.89–90).

Gorgophona: may allude to the fact that Athena assisted Perseus in cutting off the head of Medusa, one of the Gorgons ('Gorgon-slayer'); it could also mean 'fierce-eyed' (see *gorgōpis* at Soph. *Ai.* 450; Eur. *Hel.* 1316). The term

Gorgophona appears in Greek literature (Eur. *Ion* 1478); in Latin *Gorgophona* is only attested here.

Pallas Minerva: the combination *Pallas Minerva*, corresponding to the frequent title Pallas Athena (with the Greek name of the goddess), is only attested once elsewhere in classical Latin (Vitr. *De arch.* 4.8.4).

ceterique di deaeque immortales: after the gods of the Capitoline Triad have been singled out, the rest of the divine pantheon is added. Such formulae (*generalis invocatio*) are common in Roman religious language to put emphasis on particular gods and at the same time to make sure that none is left out (Wissowa 1912, 38; cf. Serv. ad Verg. *G.* 1.21; ad Verg. *Aen.* 8.103).

qui <in> excellenti tumulo civitatis sedem Capitoli in saxo incolitis constitutam: this clause includes a number of indications of place, and various interpretations are possible: the most plausible reading is the assumption of a wide hyperbaton between *sedem* and *constitutam* and interpreting *Capitoli in saxo*, sandwiched in between, as a description of place qualifying *constitutam*. *<in> excellenti tumulo civitatis* (with the text suggested by Baiter 1856, 1418 in app.), then, is an additional specification of *incolitis*. – The gods can be said to 'dwell' on the Capitoline Hill because of their temples, i.e. their 'homes' (*OLD* s.v. *sedes* 5a), located there. Since the *qui*-clause refers also to the divinities not mentioned by name (cf. Liv. 6.16.2), this description, strictly speaking, not only covers the Temple for the Capitoline Triad on the Capitoline Hill, but also other temples located there, presumably in the *area Capitolina* (*LTUR* I 114–17; see Serv. ad Verg. *Aen.* 2.319). The simultaneous definition of the location as *excellens tumulus civitatis* creates a strong link between the centre of the political organization and divine representation. – *excellens tumulus* is a rare phrase (see [Caes.] *B Hisp.* 24.3). *civitas* in the sense of 'city' (*OLD* s.v. *civitas* 3b) is attested from Seneca and Pliny the Younger onwards, though a connotation of 'community' (here taken up in the next phrase) is maintained. *Capitoli saxum* appears in Vergil (Verg. *Aen.* 9.448–9) and, as a quotation of that passage, in Seneca (Sen. *Ep.* 21.5); it is a rare collocation.

ut…civitatem: the gods' position on the Capitol means that they are able not only to see the entire community by looking out over the Forum, but also to protect it, presumably by watching developments from this point and providing a safe space of refuge if required. – *civitatem* has to be supplied in the first part and *cunctam* in the second; there is wordplay with a verb from the same stem in both parts.

a quorum…reppuli: as a further characterization of the gods appealed to (double *quorum*), 'Cicero' claims that he once saved their altars and temples from the impious attacks of citizens and from destructive fire (for the phrasing, see Cic. *Cat.* 1.24; *Dom.* 144; cf. Gamberale 1998, 63; Corbeill 2020, 26). This assertion must refer to combating the Catilinarian Conspiracy, as the conspirators allegedly planned an arson attack on Rome, though the temples on the

Capitol are not mentioned as specific targets elsewhere (Cic. *Cat.* 1.3; 1.6; 1.9; 2.6; 2.10; 3.8; 3.10; 3.14; 4.4; Sall. *Cat.* 24.4; 27.2; 32.1–2; 43.2; 48.4).

impiam civium manum: a characteristic of the people is transferred to the hand carrying out the deed (K.-St. I 220–1; Pinkster 2015, 1051–3; on the singular with reference to several people, see K.-St. I 85–6; more common in prose from the early imperial period onwards). Since what is envisaged is religious sacrilege, *impius* might be applied with reference to the relationship to gods. At the same time *impius* is one of the words applied in a moral-political sense to opponents of the Republic in contrast to *boni* (Cic. *RS* 12 n.), a connotation also evoked here (Hellegouarc'h 1972, 530–1; Achard 1981, 290–316).

meo periculo: implies that 'Cicero' saved the temples at the risk of his own life. It is true that Cicero was subject to an assassination attempt by the Catilinarian conspirators (Sall. *Cat.* 27.4–8.3), but there is no evidence of particular initiatives to protect buildings and any danger in connection with that.

ne inlustrissimum orbis terrarum monumentum cum principe omnium terrarum occideret civitate: *inlustrissimum orbis terrarum monumentum* (*inlustrissimum monumentum* seems only to be attested here) presumably refers to the Temple of Iuppiter Capitolinus on the Capitol (with the focus again moving from all the gods to Jupiter); if that important building was destroyed, it would mean the ruin of the entire Roman state, the foremost in the world. The parallel is indicated by the corresponding complements *orbis terrarum* and *omnium terrarum*. That keeping this monument is important to the welfare and survival of gods and humans enhances the value of Cicero's efforts in protecting it. – *civitas* described as *princeps* appears in Cicero's writings (Cic. *Mur.* 30), but in a different sense; the usage here and *princeps omnium terrarum* cannot be paralleled.

teque, Iuppiter Stator: in the second address to Jupiter in this sequence another function of this god and his role for the community are highlighted: this title identifies Jupiter as the 'stayer', as the god who upholds and keeps in check (Varro, *Div.*, F 137 *GRF*). In Cicero's time two temples in Rome were dedicated to Iuppiter Stator, one in the area of the Palatine Hill and another, later one near the Circus Flaminius (Wissowa 1912, 122–3; *LTUR* III 155–9; on the topographical implications of this description, see Wiseman 2004, 180–1).

quem vere…nominaverunt: a comment on this cult title for Jupiter referring the quality of *stator* to the *imperium* (*Romanum*). The mention of *maiores* gives credibility to the argument (*Exil.* 3 n.), and the appropriateness of the title will be proved shortly by Cicero's experiences (for the phrasing, see Cic. *Cat.* 1.33; cf. Corbeill 2020, 26).

cuius…muris: the meeting at which Cicero delivered a version of the *First Catilinarian Oration* was held in the older Temple of Iuppiter Stator linked to Romulus (Cic. *Cat.* 1.33). In the *Catilinarian Orations* Cicero initially presents himself as uncertain how to describe his intervention and its effect, but then states unequivocally that he threw Catiline out of Rome (Cic. *Cat.* 1.13; 1.20; 1.22–3; 2.1; 2.12; 2.13; 2.14; 3.3). In view of the fact that Catiline was still in the city of Rome at the time of the *First Catilinarian Oration* delivered in the Temple of Iuppiter Stator, the claim that there he was 'thrust back from the city walls' is not literally true. This statement metaphorically refers to Cicero safeguarding Rome from attacks, as Catiline left the city after the speech and Cicero asserts in the *Catilinarian Orations* that by removing Catiline he reduced the risk of an attack on Rome as planned by the conspirators (Cic. *Cat.* 1.3; 1.6; 1.9; 2.6; 3.8; 3.10; 4.4).

in templo: of the two temples dedicated to Iuppiter Stator in Rome only the older temple, referred to in Cicero's *Catilinarian Orations*, is taken account of.

a Romulo: ancient tradition connects the vow to build a temple and the subsequent founding of the original temple of Iuppiter Stator with Romulus and with the fight of the Romans against the Sabines (Liv. 1.12.3–7; Dion. Hal. *Ant. Rom.* 2.50.3; Plut. *Rom.* 18.6–7; Ov. *Fast.* 6.793–4; Flor. 1.1.13; *Vir. ill.* 2.8). The temple actually built and existing in Cicero's time was a structure dedicated by M. Atilius Regulus during the fight against the Samnites in 294 BCE (Liv. 10.36.11; 10.37.15). – Highlighting that Cicero carried out the deed to preserve the Republic in the temple allegedly built by the founder of Rome establishes an implicit parallel between the two men (cf. Cic. *Cat.* 1.33; 3.2).

victis Sabinis: according to tradition, the Sabines (a people in central Italy) already had contacts with Rome in the eighth century BCE; after the famous 'rape of the Sabine women' the Sabines and the Romans were gradually integrated. In historical times the Sabines received full Roman citizenship in 268 BCE.

in Palati radice: probably refers to the general area at the foot of the Palatine Hill (for the phrase, see Cic. *Div.* 1.101: *a Palati radice*, with commentary at Wiseman 2004, 169–70). – The exact location of the older temple of Iuppiter Stator is not entirely certain; it seems to have been on the Via sacra, on the elevated ground of the Velian Hill leading up to the Palatine Hill (*LTUR* III 156–7; Ov. *Fast.* 6.793–4; Plut. *Cic.* 16.3).

cum Victoriae: the transmission is divided between *Victoria* and *Victoriae*; both versions are found in editions. The former means that Romulus built the Temple of Iuppiter Stator with the support of Victoria (on Victoria as a goddess, see Wissowa 1912, 139–41), the latter that he also built a Temple of Victoria (*templo* to be supplied from *templum*). In the context of *victis Sabinis* it is more plausible that the latter is meant (Wiseman 2004, 180–1, seems to assume a reference to a temple also for the text *cum Victoria*). If this phrase indicates another temple, it might refer to the shrine of Vica Pota (*LTUR* V 148–9), identified with Victoria by Asconius (Ascon. ad Cic. *Pis.* 52 [p. 13.15 C.]), located at the foot of the Velian Hill (Liv. 2.7.12). A Temple of Victoria, dedicated in 294 BCE by the consul L. Postumius Megellus, was on the Palatine Hill (*LTUR* V 149–50).

oro atque opsecro: introduces the long invocation of the gods (on the spelling, see *Exil.* 5 n.).

ferte... resistitite... favete... subvenite... miseremini... nolite: in a series of six imperatives 'Cicero' asks the gods invoked for help, both for the Republic and for himself.

pariter rei publicae cunctaeque civitati meisque fortunis: this sequence of three terms could be read as a list of three items or a juxtaposition of two in which the first item is presented by a double expression. In view of the numerous doublets in this speech and the frequent parallelization of Cicero and the Republic in the speeches connected with his return (see Introduction, section 3.4), the latter is more likely. Also, the connection of three or more items with repeated *-que* is rare (K.-St. II 29–30), while the first two items could be seen as a hendiadys or the second of them as illustrating the first (K.-St. II 25–7). – 'Cicero' is identified by the periphrasis *meis fortunis* (rather than directly by a personal pronoun), which puts emphasis on the fate affecting him and thus the reason for the request.

resistite tribunicio furori: the unnamed Tribune of the People must be P. Clodius Pulcher in 58 BCE (see Introduction, section 2). *furor* is again employed to characterize him (*Exil.* 13 n.).

favete innocentiae, subvenite solitudini, miseremini senectutis: the gods are asked to support abstract qualities representing 'Cicero'. Such a description characterizes him indirectly and can evoke pity for a lonely old man, as 'Cicero' is envisaged to be if removed from Rome. – In 58 BCE Cicero was an ex-consul of 48 years of age. According to ancient sources men above the age of 45 or 46 could be called *seniores*, though not yet *senes* (Gell. *NA* 10.28; Censorinus, *DN* 14.2). – The phrase *subvenire solitudini* is only attested once elsewhere (Tac. *Ann.* 4.53.1), where it is used in a different sense.

nolite... templis: the final and longest item is based on reciprocal obligations: 'Cicero' is *supplex* towards the gods and saved them previously (as mentioned earlier in this invocation); therefore, he now deserves their support.

a vobis absterrere et excludere: if Cicero left Rome, he would not be 'shut out' from the gods, as he could still honour them wherever he was. The emphasis is on the physical separation from the temples, identified as the 'homes' of the gods and the places Cicero saved for them. – The combination of verbs does not seem to be attested elsewhere.

in suo magistratu: although this is a generic term for being in office, the reference point is the highest magistracy Cicero held, his consulship in 63 BCE, when he confronted the Catilinarian Conspiracy.

funestam facem a vestris reppulit templis: repeats *a quorum templis meo periculo funestam flammam reppuli*.

25 si... sic... ferte opem divinam: the address to the gods continues: if they have previously supported other politicians (tricolon with anaphoric and asyndetic *si*-clauses) who protected the Republic (C. Marius), warded off attacks from the gods' temples (P. Cornelius Scipio Africanus), or defeated external enemies (Cn. Pompeius Magnus), it is inferred (*sic*) that they should now (*nunc*) help Cicero (on the construction *si … sic*, see K.-St. I 387).

C. Mario: C. Marius (Cic. *RS* 38 n.). – On some of the men mentioned here adduced as points of comparison (cf. De Marco 1991, 23; Gamberale 1997; 1998, 63–4; Corbeill 2020, 26), see Cic. *Cat.* 4.21; *Rab. perd.* 31.

quod … caedem: this allusion to an action of C. Marius could refer to the confrontation with the Tribune of the People L. Appuleius Saturninus (*RE* Appuleius 29; tr. pl. 103, 100 BCE [*MRR* I 563, 575–6; II 1]) and his followers: these men had set up themselves on the Capitoline Hill; as a result of a *senatus consultum ultimum*, Marius, initially an ally of Saturninus and consul at the time, took action against them and shut off the water supply to force them to surrender. Marius then enclosed the men in the Senate house to deal with them in a legal manner later, but the People stormed the building and killed them (Liv. *Epit.* 69; *Vir. ill.* 73.9–12; App. *B Civ.* 1.32.143–5; Plut. *Mar.* 30; on the date of Saturninus' death, see *MRR* Suppl. 21–3). The characterization of the victims as *improbi cives* (on *improbus*, see Cic. *RS* 9 n.) assumes an 'optimate' perspective. – As in Cicero's genuine orations, C. Marius is presented positively in a speech apparently addressed to the People (on the audience, see *Exil.*, Introduction; on the portrayal of C. Marius, see Cic. *RS* 9; 38; *RQ* 7 and nn.). Accordingly, Saturninus is characterized as a rebellious opponent whom Marius justly confronts (e.g. Cic. *Cat.* 1.4; 1.29).

P. Scipioni: P. Cornelius Scipio Africanus (maior) (*RE* Cornelius 336; cos. 205, 194, censor 199 BCE [*MRR* I 301, 327, 342–3]) was a key figure in the Second Punic War (218–201 BCE) against the Carthaginian leader Hannibal and was responsible for the major defeat of Hannibal at the Battle of Zama in 202 BCE, which earned Scipio the *agnomen* Africanus and brought the Punic War to an end.

quod … templis: an exaggerated reference to the threat to Rome caused by Hannibal's military campaign: Hannibal managed to occupy substantial parts of southern Italy, but never to attack Rome. The scenario envisaged here might be developed from the proverbial phrase '*Hannibal ad portas*' (Cic. *RS* 32 n.). When Scipio started fighting in northern Africa, Hannibal was forced to leave Italy and return to Carthage.

Hannibalis furibundam mentem: a periphrasis for Hannibal with emphasis on his state of mind. – The characteristic of *furor* approximates Hannibal to the Tribune of the People P. Clodius Pulcher (*Exil.* 6 n.), which facilitates the parallelism with Cicero's situation. – For *furibunda mens*, see Cic. *Div.* 1.114.

Cn. Pompeio: Cn. Pompeius Magnus (Cic. *RS* 4 n.).

quod … pacatos: refers to Pompey's successful dealing with the piracy in the Mediterranean, his successful fighting against kings of the east, and the reorganization of several Roman provinces (e.g. Seager 2002, 43–62). – *hostes*

reddere pacatos is an unusual and elaborate way of saying that the threat emanating from these *hostes* has been eliminated: while *pacatus* can be applied to
people, in connection with the process of rendering something peaceful it is
more commonly applied to the area affected.

in meis calamitatibus...in meis miseriis: paraphrases for Cicero's current
situation, avoiding the appearance of guilt or punishment (see Introduction,
section 3.4).

**aliquam ferte opem divinam...divinum aliquod auxilium et numen
ostendite:** emphasizes that divine help is expected, which might be on a scale
different from human help. The qualification by *aliquam/aliquod* may enhance
or tone down the request (K.-St. I 634–5; Pinkster 2015, 1105): thus, there could
be a combination of mock modesty ('just a little help') and the hope of meaningful intervention ('substantial help'). – *numen* is 'shown' rather than 'brought':
it indicates divine interest, support, and protection, but is less concrete. – Gods
would not need to be asked for 'divine' help; yet *opem divinam* and *divinum...
auxilium* express this twice, presumably to emphasize the quality of the help
expected.

aliquam ferte opem divinam: takes up the earlier address to the gods in
intensified form: *ferte opem...meisque fortunis* (*Exil.* 24).

ut...ostendite: after 'Cicero' has mentioned prominent examples as reference points for the appeal for help, he recalls previous support to many in
dangerous situations; again it is inferred (*sic*) that help for Cicero now (*nunc*)
should, therefore, follow (construction changed to *ut...si*). This sentence
seems to be a second comparison focusing on *pericula* rather than great deeds;
then *multorum* is not an exaggerated repetition of the three examples given and
instead a reference to another group: the emphasis moves from individual support in return for great deeds to the large number of people helped in the past
(which would turn lack of help for Cicero into an unexplained exception).

3.2. To the human audience (26–8)

The second part (*Exil.* 26–8) of the conclusion (*Exil.* 24–30) moves the focus
from the gods to the human audience, while placing them close to the gods
(*Exil.* 26). This section is linked to the previous one, since 'Cicero' appeals to the
human audience also like a suppliant. Otherwise, this part is concrete, as appropriate, and functions as a summary of the main section: 'Cicero' repeats that he
has carried out great services for the community, that he is yielding generously
and sacrificing himself for the welfare of all, and that this move will not detract
from his virtue and the glory achieved by his actions, which is the defining
feature of his personality rather than any crime.

26 deinde vos, quorum...opsecro: 'Cicero' turns his pleas for help to the
human audience; in order to indicate that they are valued as much as the gods,
but in order not to offend the gods, they are addressed as almost as 'divine' as

the gods. This conceit and the corresponding phrasing appear in one of Cicero's genuine speeches (Cic. *Rab. perd.* 5; cf. Gamberale 1997, 337; Corbeill 2020, 26). – *oro atque opsecro* is also used in relation to the gods (*Exil.* 24 [and n.]).

quibus…sublevastis: 'Cicero' claims that he has already pleaded with audience members individually (*singillatim…singuli*), when they responded positively; therefore, the audience should now be doing the same as a group (*universi*). – Plutarch and Appian report that Cicero went about and entreated the People after the publication of P. Clodius Pulcher's first bill affecting Cicero (Plut. *Cic.* 30.6–31.1; App. *B. Civ.* 2.15).

supplex: another link to the description of Cicero's position in relation to the gods (*Exil.* 24).

ad pedes: based on the literal position of a *supplex*: addressees show their willingness to help by lifting up the suppliant lying at their feet (Cic. *RS* 17 n.).

conservatum: on the application of this verb to 'Cicero's' current situation, see Cic. *RS* 8; Introduction, section 3.4.

si…sufferre: 'Cicero's' achievements for the community are listed in a series of four *si*-clauses; on that basis the audience should feel obliged to support him now. This list (cf. *Exil.* 23) again begins with a statement of personal innocence, while the second (two-part) *si*-clause highlights the opposite, the speaker's own readiness to help. *si denique* marks a new start and adds two references to political achievements.

ut quisque…non dubitavi: could be referring to help generally or specifically to support as a lawyer in court cases. The mention of requests from others adds the dimension that 'Cicero' was always available, approachable, and ready to help.

quaecumque administravi, ex vestra auctoritate et patrum conscriptorum voluntate feci: stresses that everything 'Cicero' did in a political capacity was carried out in agreement with the People and the Senate (*OLD* s.v. *uoluntas* 3). While this statement shows concern for the views of fellow citizens and a willingness to cooperate, it implies a justification in view of the reproaches levelled against Cicero with respect to the Catilinarian conspirators by stressing that he did not act on his own, but was supported by the appropriate political bodies (see Cic. *RS* 32 n.; Introduction, section 2). – Such a statement also alludes to claims in Cicero's inaugural speeches as consul that he will work with both the Senate and the People and be a *consul popularis* (Cic. *Leg. agr.* 2.6–9).

administravi: used in a political context (*OLD* s.v. *administro* 4). The generic object *quaecumque* encompasses any political activity.

si malui…sufferre: indicates that, in his view, 'Cicero' is being forced into 'exile' (i.e. 'punished') by the activities of his opponents, not as a result of a proper trial: *legitimae auctoritati* refers to a verdict arrived in a proper process; *rei publicae* implies that it would be in the interest of the Republic and in line with its procedures. *cupiditas* ascribed to the opponents characterizes them as governed by personal motives rather than a sense of conviction or public responsibility. – The dative with *poenas sufferre* (cf. Plaut. *Cist.* 202) denotes the entity responsible for causing the suffering of punishment.

uti existimetis…convenire: the audience is not asked to do anything, but rather to believe that assisting Cicero is appropriate (cf. *Exil.* 3; 6). Agreement on Cicero's position and acknowledging the injustice of the measures against him are important steps. Not asking for action prepares the acceptance of reality in the next paragraph (*Exil.* 27). – The *uti*-clause adds a second request depending on *oro atque opsecro*, after the intervening *si*-clauses.

ex illo crudelissimo inimicorum impetu ereptum: a paraphrase for being saved from impending exile imposed by the opponents. What 'Cicero' is experiencing is not a physical onslaught; it is presented as an attack (from which Cicero needs to be snatched away to safety) for emphasis. *impetus* is described as *crudelissimus*, again not because of actual violence, but because (in 'Cicero's' view) it is unjustified as well as ungrateful in the light of his achievements for the community. Such a presentation makes helping Cicero seem more urgent and justified.

in antiquum statum dignitatis: reveals 'Cicero's' true concern: to be restored to his previous (*OLD* s.v. *antiquus* 3) respected position. That this aim was important for the historical Cicero becomes obvious from the speeches delivered after his return (see Cic. *Dom.* 9; 86; cf. Gamberale 1998, 65; Corbeill 2020, 26).

27 sed quoniam…magistratui: following on from the appeal to the audience to believe that he should be preserved and restored, 'Cicero' turns to a description of what he regards as the current reality (with the contrast marked by *sed*): he recognizes the desolate state of the Republic when neither he nor the audience are able to act freely and instead the Republic is suppressed by force. This is the basis for the statement of his decision to yield and to leave without waiting to see whether his appeal for help will have an effect.

quoniam…potestatem: in this analysis of the current state in 'Cicero's' view the first half selectively highlights what is not possible for Cicero and the audience respectively; the second half (introduced by *sed*) describes the situation generally, indicating the suppression of proper political activity illustrated with reference to a personified *res publica*.

mihi libere loquendi: in view of the fact that 'Cicero' is in the process of making a speech, the claim that he was not given the opportunity to speak freely might seem odd. The reference must be to the chance to confront his opponents and to speak either at a trial or in a more formal political setting without the risk of repercussions (*Exil.* 17).

vobis…iudicandi: the clarification (*omnino iudicandi*) strengthens the statement (so the text transmitted in the main manuscripts can be kept) and emphasizes that the audience does not have any opportunity to make a judgement. The specification that there is no opportunity of *clementer iudicare* might sound as if a biased judgement is not possible (so not necessarily something negative). Yet it is a paraphrase for finding 'Cicero' not guilty; thus, this description indicates a lack of freedom to demonstrate what is regarded as the appropriate assessment.

paucorum furore et audacia: identifies the reasons for the current lack of freedom. – *furor* is a quality assigned to the Tribune of the People as the main opponent (*Exil.* 13 [and n.]) and here applied to *pauci* (*Exil.* 20 [and n.]). *audacia* has been mentioned before (*Exil.* 7), but not as a prime characteristic or driver. It may be stressed to emphasize activities against standard constitutional procedures. – For the collocation, see Cic. *Cat.* 1.31.

sed oppressa est … potestatem: suggests that the Republic is in the grip of an armed gang and thus that Republican values and conventions are ignored (on Clodius' violent groups of followers, see Tatum 1999, 141–4). – The consequence of a loss of freedom and of enforcement by arms is a feeling of servility or a fear of impending slavery (i.e. the adjective replaces an objective genitive; K.-St. I 212–13). – The complete oppression of the Republic is expressed metaphorically by illustrating the effects on the personified Republic; therefore, it can be said not to be able to breathe (*OLD* s.v. *duco* 25a). The epithet *liberum* does not literally qualify the air or breath; it rather indicates the breath of a free person (attribute instead of *genitivus possessivus*; K.-St. I 210–11).

cedam … magistratui: as a consequence of acknowledging the existing lamentable situation, 'Cicero' no longer asks for help to avoid having to leave Rome, but states that he will leave, although he is morally in a superior position. – The notion is expressed by a series of three asyndetic phrases with contrasts. While the first two juxtapositions give his opponents in the plural, the third uses the singular and is more specific: the mention of a *furibundus magistratus* (a collocation only attested here) makes the allusion to the contrast between 'Cicero' and the Tribune of the People P. Clodius Pulcher obvious (on *furor* assigned to him, see *Exil.* 6; 13 nn.).

cedam: on this term for Cicero leaving Rome, see *Exil.* 7 n.; Introduction, section 3.4.

neque enim … libertatem: in order to justify his decision to leave and to stress that it will not detract from his standing, 'Cicero' gives a list of three politicians from earlier decades in the Roman Republic (in chronological order) who yielded to irrational political opponents and still retained their *virtus* (Q. Caecilius Metellus Numidicus, C. Aurelius Cotta, and C. Marius).

Q. Metellus: Q. Caecilius Metellus Numidicus (cos. 109, censor 102 BCE; see Cic. *RS* 25 n.).

cessit … cedendum putavit: for Metellus' and Cotta's departures from Rome the same verb is used that is frequently applied to Cicero's withdrawal (see Introduction, section 3.4).

L. Saturnino: L. Appuleius Saturninus (tr. pl. 103, 100 BCE; see Cic. *RS* 25 n.).

C. Cotta: C. Aurelius Cotta (*RE* Aurelius 96; cos. 75 BCE [*MRR* II 96]; *ORF*⁴ 80) was accused of the death of the previous year's Tribune of the People M. Livius Drusus in 90 BC under the *Lex Varia de maiestate* and had to go into exile (*TLLR* 105), although he defended himself with a speech written by L. Aelius Stilo Praeconinus (Cic. *De or.* 3.11; *Brut.* 205; 303; 305; App. *B Civ.* 1.37.167). Cotta returned to Rome after L. Cornelius Sulla's victory in 82 BCE (Cic. *Brut.* 311). – C. Aurelius Cotta is here presented as yielding to the Tribune under whose law he was tried, while the historical Cicero says that he was driven out of the country (Cic. *De or.* 3.11; *Brut.* 303).

Q. Vario tribuno plebis, inferiore genere orto: Q. Varius Severus Hybrida (*RE* Varius 7), sometimes called Sucronensis (because he came from Sucro in modern Spain), was a Tribune of the People in 90 BCE (*MRR* II 26–7), best known for the *Lex Varia de maiestate* he proposed (on this law and the trials held on this basis, see Gruen 1965a). This law ordered investigations of those individuals with whose support allies had taken up arms against the Roman People (Val. Max. 8.6.4; Ascon. ad Cic. *Scaur.* I.3 [p. 22.5–8 C.]; *Lex Varia de maiestate*: *LPPR*, pp. 339–40). On this basis many eminent men were taken to court (Cic. *Brut.* 304). In 89 BCE Q. Varius Hybrida himself was prosecuted under the same law, found guilty, and went into exile (Cic. *Brut.* 305; Val. Max. 8.6.4) (*TLRR* 109). Varius' obscure origin is only mentioned here and in Valerius Maximus, with a different nuance (Val. Max. 8.6.4: *propter obscurum ius civitatis Hybrida cognominatus*; see Gamberale 1979, 78 n. 2).

C. Marius: C. Marius (cos. 107, 104, 103, 102, 101, 100, 86 BCE; see Cic. *RS* 38 n.; *Exil.* 25 n.). – For Marius, the construction changes (an intertwined relative clause and indirect question), and his achievements are highlighted, while no opponents or specific actions are mentioned. Instead, 'Cicero' praises Marius for his deeds for the People, thereby involves the audience in the favours accrued through Marius, points to evidence for this assessment, and highlights *libertas*, a key quality for the Roman People (e.g. Cic. *Phil.* 3.29; 6.19).

neque M. Tullius...libertatem: 'Cicero' (on the version of the name, see *Exil.* 6 n.) presents himself as the fourth in this line (on such lists, see Cic. *RS* 38; *RQ* 7). The construction (with a new main clause) and the nuances are different (prepared by the presentation of Marius, already deviating from what precedes) with the emphasis on the relationship to the People. The description implies that by leaving Rome Cicero does not abandon the People; on the contrary, he confirms that his attitude has not changed and that he is leaving them their liberty as evidence of his mindset. There is some tension, since earlier in the paragraph the speaker claims that the Republic is oppressed and there is a lack of freedom. Thus, the two statements can only be reconciled if it assumed that 'Cicero' indicates that, by leaving, he prevents a civil war that might lead to the loss of freedom as a consequence. – The phrase *praecipuum...obsidem* seems only to be attested here; for *libertatem relinquere*, see Cic. *Prov. cons.* 39; Caes. *B Gall.* 7.77.14.

a vestra ... potestate: such a paraphrase probably means that 'Cicero' ensures the People's power by helping to guarantee their liberty.

28 quam ob rem ... privari: 'Cicero' draws a conclusion (*quam ob rem*) from the fact that the reputation of the historical exiles mentioned who bowed to illegal violence was not reduced: he adduces the gods and the audience as witnesses of the fact that he is not punished because of crimes, but out of envy of his *virtus* and his achievements; thus, his reputation could also be preserved.

testor deos deasque immortales vestrasque maxime mentes: three items are appealed to as witnesses: the first two form a closely linked pair; the third item switches from the divine (recalled from the previous section) to the human sphere. The gods, who give the status of witnesses greater weight, are addressed directly, the humans with reference to *mentes* (perhaps as *pars pro toto*); this phrasing may indicate that what the audience sees, feels, and thinks is most important.

non vitae..., non prae..., non propter...infamiam: a sequence of three (asyndetic and anaphoric) reasons that 'Cicero' rejects for his punishment. In contrast to the striving for parallelism elsewhere, each of these three items has a different construction and expresses different aspects of a morally degenerate life: *vitae turpitudine* describes a general characteristic of the way of life; it is exemplified by *prae magnitudine scelerum*, denoting particular crimes committed, and *propter reliquae aetatis infamiam*, referring to behaviour and consequent bad repute incurred through other actions in one's life.

poenas iure et lege persolvere: 'Cicero' adds that, on top of the odd reasons for his treatment, he is not punished according to proper legal procedure (esp. *Exil.* 13; 17; 21). – The collocation *iure et lege* is not frequent, but variations of it appear in Cicero's writings (Cic. *Dom.* 43: *iure legeque*; *Tim.* 41: *iure et lege*).

sed propter...gestarum: contrasting (*sed*) with the three non applicable reasons, a list of three relevant reasons follows (in anaphoric and asyndetic parallel constructions): *invidia* of the opponents with respect to 'Cicero's' virtue, the good reputation of his *ingenium*, which is *iucundissima* to him (some indirect self-glorification), and the great deeds he has achieved (which may indicate his success against Catiline or other successful political or juridical interventions). The good reputation and the achievements are to be regarded as reasons for the envy of the opponents. While previously there was a contrast mainly between 'Cicero's' virtue and the behaviour of his opponents (e.g. *Exil.* 1; 3; 6; 7; 13; 14; 16; 18; 23), here *ingenium* is added.

civitate privari: when Cicero leaves Rome, he is not deprived of his citizenship (*OLD* s.v. *ciuitas* 4), but rather of a functioning community (*OLD* s.v. *ciuitas* 1). – This verbal expression contrasts with *poenas...persolvere* and emphasizes again what the punishment consists in despite 'Cicero's' achievements. – The qualification *crudelissime* picks up *crudelissimo inimicorum impetu* (*Exil.* 26).

quodsi idem … mirandum: following on from the statement that he is being thrown out of the *civitas* unjustly, 'Cicero' mentions three other politicians (different from those in *Exil.* 27) who suffered the same (in another asyndetic and anaphoric tricolon): if these men were treated in such a way, it should not be regarded as surprising that he experiences the same.

Q. Caepioni: Q. Servilius Caepio (*RE* Servilius 49; cos. 106 BCE [*MRR* I 553]; *ORF*⁴ 62) was said not to have looked after the so-called *aurum Tolosanum*, booty gained in Tolosa (modern Toulouse) and lost in transit in 106 BCE, and suffered a major defeat in the fight against the tribes of the Cimbri and Teutones in 105 BCE, for which he was regarded as mainly responsible. After much criticism, in 103 BCE he was taken to court and found guilty (*TLRR* 65; 66); he ended up in exile in Smyrna (Cic. *Balb.* 28; Val. Max. 4.7.3). In Cicero Caepio is presented as a scapegoat (Cic. *Balb.* 28; *De or.* 1.181–2; 2.197; *Tusc.* 5.14; *Part.* 104–5).

Mancino: C. Hostilius Mancinus (*RE* Hostilius 18; cos. 137 BCE [*MRR* I 484]), when fighting the Numantians, was forced to agree a treaty with them. When the Senate did not wish to accept this treaty, it was agreed that Mancinus should be placed in front of their city gates, as this was regarded as a way to enable the Romans not to accept the treaty without violating any religious rules. The Numantians did not accept Mancinus, and he returned to Rome: then there was a controversy about whether he had lost his citizen rights; while the jurists provided different answers, the People declared that he had regained them because he had not been accepted by the enemy (Cic. *De or.* 1.181–2; 2.137–8). Here Mancinus seems to be presented as having been in 'exile' like the other men mentioned, although he did not experience proper 'exile'.

Rutilio: P. Rutilius Rufus (*RE* Rutilius 34; cos. 105 BCE [*MRR* I 555]; *ORF*⁴ 44) was active in Asia in the 90s BCE and introduced measures against the absuses of the tax collectors. Thus, upon his return, he was taken to court on a charge of extortion of money. He conducted himself honourably and did not adduce any support or have recourse to means to provoke pity. Despite his innocence, he was found guilty through the perjury of the judges, who supported the tax collectors, and went into exile in Asia (*TLRR* 94). The trial came to be seen as an example of a wrongful condemnation of a virtuous and innocent person (Cic. *Font.* 38; *Pis.* 95; *Rab. Post.* 27; *Scaur.* F d; *De or.* 1.228–31; *Brut.* 115; *Nat. D.* 3.80; Val. Max. 6.4.4; Vell. Pat. 2.13.2).

cum praesertim … consecutus: adds another reason why Cicero being expelled is not a surprise: in contrast to the examples just mentioned, Cicero is a *homo novus* (*Exil.* 6 n.) and gained his position not through the antiquity of his family, but rather as a result of his own activity, which again highlights his virtue. Accordingly, he is exposed to ill feeling in view of his achievements (for this concept, see Cic. *Leg. agr.* 2.5–6). – The collocation *antiquitas generis* is not frequent; it is attested twice in Cicero (Cic. *Clu.* 43; *Font.* 41).

summam laudem: 'Cicero' does not hesitate to claim that he obtained a respected position.

3.3. To the knights (29–30)

The final part (*Exil.* 29–30) of the conclusion (*Exil.* 24–30) singles out a particular group within the human audience, the knights, who have not been mentioned in this speech so far (see *Exil.*, Introduction). A section directed at them is presumably prompted by the fact that the historical Cicero is a knight by origin, that their presence, interpreted as support by Cicero, on the day on which the Catilinarian conspirators were condemned to death (Cic. *RS* 12; 32; *Sest.* 28; *Phil.* 2.16; *Att.* 2.1.7; Sall. *Cat.* 49.4) is frequently referred to, and that Plutarch mentions support from knights for Cicero's supplications to the People just before he left Rome in 58 BCE (Plut. *Cic.* 31.1) and Cassius Dio refers to their intercessions with the Senate (Cass. Dio 38.16.2–3).

This group is asked for support for 'Cicero' to remain in Rome (after he expressed his willingness to leave: *Exil.* 27–8); as befits the closing section of a peroration, the appeal is particularly emotional, mentioning 'Cicero's' impending separation from his children, wife, and home while stressing his innocence and service for the Republic. Although 'Cicero' initially requests efforts to retain him in the community, in the final paragraph he seems again to accept the inevitability of the departure and to ask for support in his yielding. This turn still has the speech conclude on the positive note of the virtue of 'Cicero' and makes him appear superior as he graciously and generously gives way.

29 nunc: introduces the final appeal to the audience. In this long sentence (*nunc…subire*) 'Cicero' combines flattery of the knights and reminders of his achievements for the knights and the *civitas* with the request not to be separated from his family.

equites Romani: the conclusion of the speech features two addresses to *equites Romani* (also *Exil.* 30), after two addresses to *Quirites* just before the middle (*Exil.* 11; 12). On the assumed audience, see *Exil.*, Introduction; *Exil.* 1 n.

optestor: used also in previous appeals (*Exil.* 5; 9), followed by *peto et rogo* (*Exil.* 30), a variation of *oro atque opsecro* (*Exil.* 24; 26) employed for the first two groups addressed in the peroration (on the spelling, see *Exil.* 5 n.).

quorum…hostes: a flattering mention of the achievements of the knights (alluding to military victories against external enemies). Of the two asyndetic and anaphoric relative clauses, the first praises the triumphant *virtus* of the knights, while the second describes the impact of their deeds on three groups.

nomen Romanum: a paraphrase for the Roman state or the Roman People putting emphasis on the concept of Rome and its importance (*OLD* s.v. *nomen* 19).

victoriam cum laude…coniunctam: the addition of *laus* to *victoria* suggests a victory in some way remarkable and praiseworthy. – The phrase *victoriam possidere* otherwise only appears rarely from late antiquity onwards.

cives…socii…hostes: three groups potentially affected by a war between Romans and foreign enemies and thus by the results achieved by the knights.

These three groups fall into two camps: the citizens and the allies experience positive emotions, and the enemies suffer.

ut ... ut: when the *ut*-clause follows, *ut* is repeated after the long inserted *si*-clauses illustrating 'Cicero's' deeds to clarify the construction.

si erga ... consuestis: in a series of three asyndetic and anaphoric clauses 'Cicero' lists what he has done for the knights, so as to prompt them to support him in return. These three items move from a general attitude to concrete actions for the Republic and thus indirectly benefiting the knights and then to specific support.

animatus: see *Exil.* 20 n.

si mea pericula ... propulsarem: again a reference to Cicero's intervention in the Catilinarian Conspiracy highlighting his personal initiative and the risk to himself (see *Exil.* 1 n.). – Previously, the emphasis was on the Republic; here it is on *patria* (see Cic. *Cat.* 1.17–19; 27–9), prepared for by the reminder of Cicero having been called *pater patriae* (*Exil.* 8).

dum ... propulsarem: in postclassical Latin *dum* in the sense of 'while' is also used with the imperfect subjunctive in narratives of past events (K.-St. II 377–8): this seems to be the case here.

timorem: implies that 'Cicero' intervened in the early stages, when the consequences of the actions of the Catilinarians were still a threat to be feared.

si aeque ... parentes consuestis: the transmitted text (*parentibus*) says that Cicero's care and concern for the children of the knights in the audience is equal to theirs for their parents. The text is grammatically sound and gives a possible sense (*prospicere* to be supplied with *consuestis* [a perfect in a present sense] from the first part of the clause), though the comparison is odd. Therefore, Gamberale (1997, 335–7) suggests changing *parentibus* to *parentes* (the assumed mistake in the manuscripts could be explained by an incorrect resolution of an abbreviated ending): then, the sentence means that Cicero looked after the audience's children in the same way as they do as parents, which is more straightforward and more plausible.

ut nunc ... subire: the *ut*-clause summarizes what Cicero asks the addressees to do, first in positive form (*ut ... velitis ... retinere*), followed by a parenthesis (*quae civitas ... restincta est*), and then in a negative version (*nec patiamini ... subire*).

nunc ... retinere: in the positive part, the main idea is *me ... in hac civitate retinere*; *me* is further described by participles and adjectives providing preconditions for the main verb: the audience should defend 'Cicero' (i.e. against the attacks of his opponents, who are trying to force him to leave Rome); then he will be unharmed and can remain in the city. If it is understood in this way, *defensum* can be kept (*contra* Baiter 1856, 1419).

vestris opibus: *ops* in the sense of 'aid' is usually singular (*OLD* s.v. *ops*[1] 5); thus, the plural suggests particular resources (*OLD* s.v. *ops*[1] 3). It remains open, however, what these may be and what kind of action should be taken.

quae civitas…restincta est: this parenthesis (with repetition of *civitas* within the relative clause) stresses implicitly why 'Cicero' should be retained in the community: only through his labour has the community been preserved. – The parenthesis consists of a relative clause with an inserted *cum*-clause, with *civitas* the subject in both. Literally, the metaphorical relative clause says that the *civitas* has been extinguished while affected by the fire of the *coniuratio*; what happened was that the *coniuratio* was extinguished to save the *civitas*. While transferred epithets are used elsewhere in this speech (e.g. *Exil.* 24), this transfer is somewhat stretched. Therefore, one may wonder whether *restincta* might be an incorrect reading (it could have entered the text as a contrast to *incensa*) and instead *restituta* should be read. *incensa* is employed metaphorically, indicating upheaval, not plans for burning the city (*OLD* s.v. *incendo* 5). – The qualifying ablative going with *restincta est* is the alliterative pair *luctu ac labore* in the transmitted text (retained by De Marco 1967, 63; 1991, 26). This phrase has often been changed to *ductu ac labore* (Cic. *Man.* 61: *rem optime ductu suo gerere? gessit.*), probably in view of Cicero's description of himself as *dux togatus* in the *Catilinarian Orations* (Cic. *Cat.* 2.28; 3.23). *ductu* is not used by Cicero in these contexts; alliteration is probably to be preferred, and the emphasis is on the sacrifices made for the benefit of the community. – While the Catilinarian Conspiracy is mostly referred to by paraphrases in this speech, here (as at *Exil.* 9; 10) it is explicitly identified as a conspiracy, with the expected negative characterization.

nec patiamini…subire: the negative part of the *ut*-clause paints a sad picture of loneliness and desperation for an exile with an emotional and personal dimension. It consists of three asyndetic and anaphoric descriptions of *me* followed by two asyndetic infinitives.

a meis liberis…proiectum: the separation caused by Cicero's departure from Rome is described more graphically and forcefully than previously.

a meis liberis: Cicero's children Tullia and Marcus (Cic. *RS* 1 n.).

a coniuge: Cicero's wife Terentia (Cic. *RQ* 8 n.).

ab aris focisque: a common paraphrase for 'home' (*OLD* s.v. *ara* 1d); the plural must be rhetorical.

proiectum: see also *proicitur…in exilium* (*Exil.* 30; *OLD* s.v. *proicio* 7b).

in exilio: the state expected for 'Cicero' he is trying to avoid is again defined as *exilium* (see *Exil.* 22 and n.), which is not the case in the speeches delivered after Cicero's return (see Introduction, section 3.4).

miserrimi mortalis casum: being in exile, away from family, home, and community, is described as 'the situation of the most wretched mortal', presumably equivalent to 'the most wretched situation of a mortal'.

30 proicitur Tullius in exilium: 'Cicero' is mentioned in the third person, referred to by only one part of the name (on the use of forms of Cicero's name, see *Exil.* 6 n.). – On *proicitur…in exilium*, see *Exil.* 29 n.

itaque nimirum: this sentence draws an ironic consequence from the fact that Cicero is sent away and illustrates how odd and unjustified it is: *itaque* marks the sentence as a consequence, and *nimirum* indicates the ironic tone, as usually the characteristics of the two parties given here would be reversed (*OLD* s.v. *itaque* 1; s.v. *nimirum*).

innocens…ab hoste: a tricolon of contrasts (depending on *proicitur*) between the positive characteristics of 'Cicero' and the negative ones of his opponents. That 'Cicero' is innocent and well disposed towards the community has been said before (*Exil.* 13; 16; 23; 24); the quality of *religiosus* has not been mentioned so far. Contrasting with *sceleratus*, the word probably focuses on scrupulous integrity (*OLD* s.v. *religiosus* 8). – *inimico* and *hoste* seem to be used almost synonymously (*Exil.* 1 n.).

o misera vitae ratio: an emotional exclamation on the changeable and thus distressing nature of life (*OLD* s.v. *ratio* 13c; *miser* 2), which remains pleasant as long as fortune wishes and can change at the whim of fate (*OLD* s.v. *libido* 2). The exclamation is made emphatic by the direct address to *vitae ratio*. The following *quae* probably refers to *vita*. – The phrase *residere in voluptate* seems only to be attested here; *fortunae…libido* occurs in Tacitus (Tac. *Hist.* 3.41.1).

egone…interfeci: a series of two twofold short questions and one answer for each pair, describing the same situation with different variations, ironically characterizes it as implausible that 'Cicero' is an *inimicus* or *hostis* when he killed *inimici* or *hostes*. The phrase partly adopts the opponent's perspective when it is asked whether 'Cicero' is an *inimicus* or *hostis*, but in the answers the definition of the victims as *inimici* or *hostes* is 'Cicero's' interpretation. On this basis, 'Cicero's' deeds are justified, and the application of the term *inimicus* or *hostis* to Cicero is rejected. – *sum* has to be supplied to *egone inimicus huic civitati* and *sum huic civitati* to *egone hostis*, to create complete sentences.

quid ita? quia…: in Cicero's works the rhetorical question *quid ita?* is often answered by a clause introduced by *quia* if it is intended to provoke the identification of a reason.

heu condicionem huius temporis: another emotional exclamation about the situation. It recalls the famous *o tempora, o mores* in Cicero's *First Catilinarian Oration* (Cic. *Cat.* 1.2; cf. Keeline 2018, 169; Corbeill 2020, 26). – The collocation *condicio temporis* is otherwise only attested in late antique authors.

antea…nunc…administrarunt: explains the preceding desperate exclamation about the state of things by the juxtapositon of an earlier and the current situation: activities leading to appreciation in the past are now regarded as the deeds of *scelerati ac parricidae*. These actions are referred to by *haec* without an explicit antecedent: in the context it must refer to eliminating people who are regarded as opponents of the Republic. An example of someone killing Roman citizens for the sake of the Republic might be P. Cornelius Scipo Nasica Serapio (cos. 138 BCE), who was instrumental in the opposition to Ti. Sempronius

Gracchus, which led to his death in 133 BCE. *scelerati ac parricidae* are strong terms not assigned to 'Cicero' in this speech so far. *parricida* might recall its application to followers of Catiline in Cicero's *Catilinarian Orations* (Cic. *Cat.* 2.7; 2.22) and carries an undertone of opposition to *patria*. *administrarunt* picks up *perfecerunt* with variation and is used in a generic sense (*OLD* s.v. *administro* 3). – Variations of the phrase *gloria ac laude* occur as *gloria laus* (Plaut. *Stich.* 281), *laudi gloriaeque* (Cic. *Prov. cons.* 27), and *laus et gloria* (e.g. Cic. *Cat.* 1.23; *Pis.* 41; 82; *Arch.* 28).

sint sane ... conservetis: in a sentence introduced by a concessive subjunctive emphasized by *sane* (K.-St. I 189–90; Pinkster 2015, 360–1), 'Cicero' concedes that his opponents will win. Accepting this, 'Cicero' implores the knights to save him as they had honoured him in the past.

si modo victoria appellanda est: if his opponents manage to drive Cicero out of Rome, it is a 'victory' for them; as it will bring grief to the community, 'Cicero' doubts whether it could be called a victory. This reasoning seems to assume that victory should be universally positive and beneficial, while there are Pyrrhic victories bringing grief to the winner. The focus presumably is on the fact that the conflict has a political dimension for the entire community, and success for individuals, which does not benefit the entire community, cannot be called victory. – A similar expression about the appropriateness of a term is applied to *exilium* and *calamitas* in Cicero's speech *De domo sua* (Cic. *Dom.* 76).

palmam: takes up the idea of *victoria* with a concrete expression (*OLD* s.v. *palma* 5).

ex innocentis cruore: might indicate literally that 'Cicero' envisages that his opponents may kill him in Rome for their complete victory or might be meant metaphorically, comparing exile to death (as these notions fluctuate throughout the speech). Painting the worst scenario is a good basis for the final appeal to help at the end of the speech. – Cicero again characterizes himself as innocent, as he frequently does in this speech, in particular in the final section (*Exil.* 28–30).

illud: looks forward to the *ut*-clause and provides a reference for *tantum*.

equites Romani: see *Exil.* 29 and n.

ut ... conservetis: the speech ends with an emphatic appeal to the knights to preserve 'Cicero' in a difficult and dangerous situation for him, while it is not specified what this would entail.

quem saepenumero vestra laude cohonestastis: Cicero was supported by the knights on 5 December 63 BCE, when the death penalty for the Catilinarian conspirators was decreed, as they lined Capitoline Hill on that day (Cic. *RS* 12; 32); he was later honoured as *pater patriae* by the Senate (*Exil.* 8 n.). After the publication of the first of P. Clodius Pulcher's laws that could be referred to Cicero in 58 BCE (see Introduction, section 2), the knights, like other groups in the population, put on mourning dress and pleaded with the consuls on Cicero's

behalf (Cic. *RS* 12 [and n.]; *Sest.* 26; Cass. Dio 38.16.2–4). While the historical
Cicero seems to have had a close and special relationship to the knights (Berry
2003), still, the claim that the knights frequently praised and honoured 'Cicero'
is probably an exaggeration. – The verb *cohonestare* also occurs in the writings
of the historical Cicero (e.g. Cic. *Quinct.* 50; *Fam.* 13.11.3).

in dubiis vitae periculis: indicates that at present 'Cicero's' life is in danger
and the outlook is not promising (*OLD* s.v. *dubius* 9; for the collocation, see
Lucr. 3.1076; Tertullian, *De res.* 21.4 [in different sense]). In connection with *ex
innocentis cruore*, this phrase again adumbrates the risk of death.

vestra virtute: when the knights are asked to preserve 'Cicero' by their virtue,
it is not clear what kind of actions are envisaged. If *virtus* refers to valour in
fighting (*OLD* s.v. *virtus* 1), a confrontation in arms could be meant. Or there
could be a reference to moral superiority in relation to the opponents (*OLD* s.v.
virtus 3).

Bibliography

Note: The names of ancient authors and the titles of their works are abbreviated according to the *Oxford Classical Dictionary*.
In cases of multiple references, Cicero's works precede those of other authors, and among Cicero's writings passages from the *Post reditum* speeches (*RS* and *RQ*) are given first. The abbreviated title is always added for clarity's sake. Cicero's correspondence is cited according to the vulgate numbering.
Works by modern authors are referred to in abbreviated form (name of author and year of publication); full references are given in the bibliography.
Standard reference works and collections not listed here (e.g. *CAH*, *CIL*, *LTUR*, *OLD*, *RE*, *TLL*) are abbreviated according to the *Oxford Classical Dictionary*.

1. Editions, commentaries, and translations of the three speeches

Baiter 1856: see Orelli/Baiter/Halm 1856.

Beck, C. D. (ed.): *M. Tullii Ciceronis Opera*, ad optimos libros recensuit, animadversionibus criticis instruxit, indices et lexicon Ciceronianum addidit, 4 vols., Leipzig 1795–1807.

Bellardi, G. (ed.): *Le orazioni di M. Tullio Cicerone. Volume terzo, dal 57 a 52 a.C.*, Torino 1975.

Boll, T.: *Ciceros Rede cum senatui gratias egit. Ein Kommentar*, Berlin/Boston 2019 (Göttinger Forum für die Altertumswissenschaft, Beihefte, Neue Folge, Band 10).

Bortone, G. (ed.): *M. T. Cicero, Oratio post reditum in senatu. Introduzione e note*, Napoli 1938.

Caprioli 1966: Desideri, S./Caprioli, G./Corsanego, C./Pasquale, M. (eds.): *Marco Tullio Cicerone. Le orazioni di ringraziamento al senato*, a cura di S. Desideri, *di ringraziamento al popolo*, a cura di G. Caprioli, *sulla propria casa*, a cura di C. Corsanego, *sul responso degli aruspici*, a cura di M. Pasquale, Milano 1966 (Centro di Studi Ciceroniani: Tutte le opere di Cicerone 7).

Condom, D. (ed. and trans.): *M. Tul·li Ciceró. Discursos. Vol. XI. Discurs de gratitud al senat, Discurs de gratitud al poble, Sobre la seva casa, Sobre la reposta dels harúspexs. Introducció, text revisat i traducció*, Barcelona 1995 (Fundació Bernat Metge, Escriptors LLatins, Text i traducció 293).

De Marco, M. (ed.): *Marco Tullio Cicerone: La consolazione, le orazioni spurie*, Milano 1967 (Centro di Studi Ciceroniani: Tutte le opere di Cicerone 33).

De Marco, M. (ed.): *[M. Tulli Ciceronis] Orationes spuriae. Pars prior. Oratio pridie quam in exilium iret, Quinta Catilinaria, Responsio Catiline*, Roma 1991.

Desideri 1966: Desideri, S./Caprioli, G./Corsanego, C./Pasquale, M. (eds.): *Marco Tullio Cicerone. Le orazioni di ringraziamento al senato*, a cura di S. Desideri, *di ringraziamento al popolo*, a cura di G. Caprioli, *sulla propria casa*, a cura di C. Corsanego, *sul responso degli aruspici*, a cura di M. Pasquale, Milano 1966 (Centro di Studi Ciceroniani: Tutte le opere di Cicerone 7).

Frenzel, F. C.: *Cicero's Rede an den Senat nach seiner Zurückkehr, mit einem Commentar versehen*. Eine Einladungsschrift auf das Frühlingsexamen, Soest 1801.

Fuhrmann, M. (trans.): *Marcus Tullius Cicero. Sämtliche Reden*. Eingeleitet, übersetzt und erläutert. *Band V. Rede für Sullla, Rede für den Dichter Archias, Rede für Flaccus, Danksagung an den Senat, Danksagung an das Volk, Rede über das eigene Haus, Rede für Sestius, Befragung des Zeugen Vatinius, Rede über das Gutachten der Opferschauer*, Zürich/Stuttgart 1978 (Bibliothek der Alten Welt. Römische Reihe); repr. in: *Marcus Tullius Cicero. Die politischen Reden. Band II. Lateinisch—deutsch*. Hg., übers. u. erl., München 1993 (Sammlung Tusculum).

Guerriero, E. (ed.): *M. Tullio Cicerone. L'orazione 'Post reditum in senatu'. Introduzione e Commento*, Milano 1955 (Scrittori Latini).

Guerriero, E. (ed.): *M. Tullio Cicerone. L'orazione "Post reditum ad Quirites„ con introduzione e commento*, Milano 1964 (Scrittori Latini).

Guillen, J. (ed.): *Oratio cum senatui gratias egit*. Recognovit, praefatione historica atque critica instruxit, Milano 1967 (M. Tulli Ciceronis opera omnia quae extant critico apparatu instructa).

Halm 1856: see Orelli/Baiter/Halm 1856.

Kasten, H. (ed. and trans.): *Cicero. Staatsreden. Zweiter Teil. Dankrede vor dem Senat, Dankrede vor dem Volke, Rede für sein Haus, Über die konsularischen Provinzen, Über die Gutachten der Haruspices, Gegen Piso*. Lateinisch und Deutsch, 3., unveränderte Auflage, Berlin 1977 (Schriften und Quellen der alten Welt) (orig. 1969).

Kayser, C. L. (ed.): *M. Tullii Ciceronis Opera quae supersunt omnia*. Ediderunt J. G. Baiter, C. L. Kayser. *Vol. IV. M. Tullii Ciceronis Orationes*. Recognovit C. L. Kayser. Editio stereotypa, Leipzig 1862.

Kayser, C. L. (ed.): *M. Tullii Ciceronis Opera quae supersunt omnia*. Ediderunt J. G. Baiter, C. L. Kayser. *Vol. XI. M. Tullii Ciceronis Orationum fragmenta et Orationes suppositiciae*. Edidit C. L. Kayser. *M. Tullii Ciceronis Ceterorum librorum fragmenta. Index nominum. Index librorum Tullianorum*. Composuit J. G. Baiter. Editio stereotypa, Leipzig 1869.

Klotz, A. (ed.): *M. Tulli Ciceronis scripta quae manserunt omnia. Fasc. 21. Orationes cum senatui gratias egit, cum populo gratias egit, de domo sua, de haruspicum responsis*, recognovit, Leipzig 1915.

Klotz, A./Schoell, F. (eds.): *M. Tulli Ciceronis scripta quae manserunt omnia. Volumen VII. Orationes cum senatui gratias egit, cum populo gratias egit, de domo, de haruspicum responsis, pro Sestio, in Vatinium, pro Caelio, de provinciis consularibus, pro Balbo, in Pisonem, pro Rabirio Postumo* recognovit A. Klotz. *Pro Scauro* recognovit F. Schoell, Leipzig 1919.

Long, G. (ed.): *M. Tullii Ciceronis orationes. With a Commentary. Vol. III*, London 1856 (Bibliotheca Classica).

Maslowski, T. (ed.): *M. Tulli Ciceronis scripta quae manserunt omnia. Fasc. 21. Orationes cum senatui gratias egit, cum populo gratias egit, de domo sua, de haruspicum responsis*, Leipzig 1981 [see reviews: W. D. Lebek, *Gnomon* 56, 1984, 4–8; H. Solin, *Arctos* 18, 1984, 178–9].

Masoero, G. B. (ed.): *M. Tullii Ciceronis Post Reditum ad Quirites oratio. Con introduzione e commento*, Torino/Roma/Milano/Firenze/Napoli 1905 (Biblioteca scolastica di scrittori latini, con Note).

Müller, C. F. W. (ed.): *M. Tulli Ciceronis scripta quae manserunt omnia. Partis II, Vol. II*, Leipzig 1885.

Müller, C. F. W. (ed.): *M. Tulli Ciceronis scripta quae manserunt omnia. Partis IV, Vol. III*, Leipzig 1890.

Orelli, I. C./Baiter, I. G./Halm, C. (eds.): *M. Tullii Ciceronis opera quae supersunt omnia ex recensione Io. Casp. Orellii. Edito altera emendatior. Opus morte Orellii interruptum continuaverunt I. G. Baiterus et Car. Halmius. Voluminis II. Pars II: M. Tullii Ciceronis Orationes.* Ad codices ex magna parte primum aut iterum collatos emendaverunt I. G. Baiterus et Car. Halmius. *Pars posterior*, Zürich 1856 [*M. Tullii Ciceronis Oratio cum senatui gratias egit*, rec. Car. Halmius, pp. 830–46; *M. Tullii Ciceronis quae fertur Oratio cum populo gratias egit*, rec. Car. Halmius, pp. 847–58; [*M. Tulli Ciceronis] Oratio pridie quam in exsilium iret*, rec. I. G. Baiterus, pp. 1412–20].

Peterson, G. (ed.): *M. Tulli Ciceronis orationes. Vol. V. Cum senatui gratias egit, Cum populo gratias egit, De domo sua, De haruspicum responso, Pro Sestio, In Vatinium, De provinciis consularibus, Pro Balbo*, recognovit brevique adnotatione critica instruxit, Oxford 1911 (repr.).

Shackleton Bailey, D. R. (trans.): *Cicero: Back from Exile: Six Speeches upon His Return. Translated with Introductions and Notes*, Chicago 1991 (American Philological Association Classical Resources Series 4) [see reviews: J. Webster, *BMCRev* 03.05.20, 1992; F. Hinard, *REG* 105, 1992, 284; D. H. Berry, *CR* 43, 1993, 174–5; D. Knecht, *AClass* 63, 1994, 388–9].

Wagner, H. (ed.): *M. Tulli Ciceronis Oratio post reditum in senatu.* Recensuit, scripturae varietatem adiecit, prolegomenis instruxit, annotationibus et superiorum interpretum et suis explanavit, defendit, Leipzig 1857.

Watts, N. H. (ed. and trans.): *Cicero. Pro Archia poeta—Post reditum in senatu—Post reditum at Quirites—De domo sua—De haruspicum responsis—Pro Plancio. With an English translation*, Cambridge (MA)/London 1923, repr. (LCL 158, Cicero XI) [see reviews: A. Klotz, *PhW* 44.43–4, 1924, 1059–60; W. Miller, *CPh* 20, 1925, 288; A. C. Clark, *CR* 38, 1924, 125–6].

Weiske, B. (ed.): *M. Tullii Ciceronis orationes XIII selectae, Pro Roscio Amerino, Pro lege Manilia etc. novis animadversionibus in usum scholarum illustratae*, Leipzig 1807.

Wolf, F. A. (ed.): *M. Tulli Ciceronis quae vulgo feruntur Orationes quattuor. I. Post reditum in senatu, II. Ad Quirites post reditum, III. Pro domo sua ad pontifices, IV. De haruspicum responsis*, recognovit animadversiones integras I. Marklandi et I. M. Gesneri suasque adiecit, Berlin 1801.

Wuilleumier, P. (ed. and trans.): *Cicéron. Discours. Tome XIII. Au sénat, Au peuple, Sur sa maison. Texte établi et traduit*, Paris 1952 (CUF).

2. Other works cited

Achard, G.: *Pratique rhétorique et idéologie politique dans les discours "optimates" de Cicéron*, Leiden 1981 (Mnemosyne Suppl. 68).

Adams, J. N.: 'Conventions of Naming in Cicero', *CQ* 28, 1978, 145–66.

Adams, J. N.: *The Latin Sexual Vocabulary*, London 1982.

von Albrecht, M.: 'Marcus Tullius Cicero. Sprache und Stil', *RE* Suppl. XIII, 1973, 1237–347.

von Albrecht, M.: *Cicero's Style. A Synopsis Followed by Selected Analytic Studies*, Leiden/
Boston 2003 (Mnemosyne 245).

Arena, V.: 'Roman Oratorical Invective', in: W. Dominik/J. Hall (eds.), *A Companion to
Roman Rhetoric*, Malden (MA)/Oxford/Chichester 2007, 149–60.

Astin, A. E.: 'Leges Aelia et Fufia', *Latomus* 23, 1964, 421–45.

Badian, E.: 'The Early Career of A. Gabinius (*cos.* 58 B.C.)', *Philologus* 103, 1959, 87–99.

Badian, E.: 'The Clever and the Wise. Two Roman *Cognomina* in Context', in: N. Horsfall
(ed.), *Vir bonus discendi peritus. Studies in Celebration of Otto Skutsch's Eightieth
Birthday*, London 1988 (BICS Suppl. 51), 6–12.

Balsdon, J. P. V. D.: 'Provinces under the Late Republic – II. Caesar's Gallic Command',
JRS 29, 1939, 167–83.

Balsdon, J. P. V. D.: 'Roman History, 58–56 B.C.: Three Ciceronian Problems', *JRS* 47,
1957, 15–20.

Bellemore, J.: 'Cicero's Retreat from Rome in Early 58 BC', *Antichthon* 42, 2008,
100–20.

Benner, H.: *Die Politik des P. Clodius Pulcher: Untersuchungen zur Denaturierung des
Clientelwesens in der ausgehenden römischen Republik*, Stuttgart 1987 (Historia
Einzelschriften 50).

Berry, D. H.: 'The Value of Prose Rhythm in Questions of Authenticity: The Case of *De
Optimo Genere Oratorum* Attributed to Cicero', *Papers of the Leeds International
Latin Seminar* 9, 1996, 47–74.

Berry, D. H.: '*Equester ordo tuus est*: Did Cicero Win His Cases because of His Support
for the *equites*?', *CQ* 53, 2003, 222–34.

Bleicken, J.: *Lex publica: Gesetz und Recht in der römischen Republik*, Berlin 1975.

Bleicken, J.: 'Das römische Volkstribunat: Versuch einer Analyse seiner politischen
Funktion in republikanischer Zeit', *Chiron* 11, 1981, 87–108.

van der Blom, H.: *Cicero's Role Models: The Political Strategy of a Newcomer*, Oxford 2010
(Oxford Classical Monographs).

van der Blom, H.: 'Character Attack and Invective Speech in the Roman Republic:
Cicero as Target', in: M. Icks/E. Shiraev (eds.), *Character Assassination throughout the
Ages*, New York 2014, 37–57.

Bonnefond-Coudry, M.: *Le Sénat de la République romaine de la guerre d'Hannibal à
Auguste: Pratiques délibératives et prise de décision*, Paris/Roma 1989 (BEFAR 273).

Bornecque, H.: 'Le *Post reditum ad Quirites*. Texte commenté au point de vue des
clausules métriques', in: *Philologie et linguistique. Mélanges offerts à Louis Havet par
ses anciens élèves et ses amis. A l'occasion du 60ᵉ Anniversaire de sa Naissance le
6 Janvier 1909*, Paris 1909, 39–61.

Botsford, G. W.: *The Roman Assemblies from their Origin to the End of the Republic*, New
York 1909 (repr. 1968).

Brennan, T. C.: *The Praetorship in the Roman Republic*, 2 vols., Oxford 2000.

Bruna, F. J.: *Lex Rubria: Caesars Regelung für die richterlichen Kompetenzen der
Munizipalmagistrate in Gallia Cisalpina. Text, Übersetzung und Kommentar mit
Einleitungen, historischen Anhängen und Indizes*, Leiden 1972 (Studia Gaiana V).

Brunt, P. A.: 'Iudicia sublata (58–57 B.C.)', *LCM* 6, 1981, 227–31.

Bücher, F.: *Verargumentierte Geschichte: Exempla Romana im politischen Diskurs der
späten römischen Republik*, Stuttgart 2006 (Hermes Einzelschriften 96).

Bücher, F./Walter, U.: 'Mit Manuskript in den Senat? Zu Cic. Planc. 74', *RhM* 149, 2006, 237–40.

Burckhardt, L. A.: 'The Political Elite of the Roman Republic: Comments on Recent Discussion of the Concepts *Nobilitas* and *Homo Novus*', *Historia* 39, 1990, 77–99.

Busche, K.: Review of '*M. Tulli Ciceronis Scripta quae manserunt omnia. Orationum fasciculi 21–27. 29* rec. A. Klotz et F. Schöll. Leipzig 1914–17, Teubner. Geh. 1 M. 40, 70 Pf., 70 Pf., 1 M 40, 1 M. 20, 60 Pf., 50 Pf., 1 M. 40; ed. minor, fasc. 27: 30Pf.' I, *BPhW* 37.44, 1917, 1353–61.

Carney T. F.: 'Cicero's Picture of Marius', *WS* 73, 1960, 83–122.

Carney, T. F.: 'The Flight and Exile of Marius', *G&R* 8, 1961, 98–121.

Christ, K.: *Pompeius: Der Feldherr Roms: Eine Biographie*, München 2004.

Christopherson, A. J.: '*Invidia Ciceronis*: Some Political Circumstances Involving Cicero's Exile and Return', in: R. I. Curtis (ed.), *Studia Pompeiana & Classica in Honor of Wilhelmina F. Jashemski. Volume II: Classica*, New Rochelle (NY) 1989, 33–57.

Cimma, M. R.: *Reges socii et amici populi Romani*, Milano 1976 (Università di Roma, Pubblicazioni dell'Istituto di diritto romano e dei diritti dell'oriente mediterraneo L).

Cipriani, G.: *Struttura retorica di dieci orazioni ciceroniane*, Catania 1975.

Citroni Marchetti, S.: *Amicizia e potere nelle lettere di Cicerone e nelle elegie ovidiane dall'esilio*, Firenze 2000 (Studi e testi 18).

Claassen, J.-M.: 'Cicero's Banishment: *Tempora et Mores*', *AC* 35, 1992, 19–47.

Claassen, J.-M.: *Displaced Persons: The Literature of Exile from Cicero to Boethius*, London 1999.

Clark, A. C. (ed.): *M. Tulli Ciceronis orationes. Vol. VI. Pro Tullio, Pro Fonteio, Pro Sulla, Pro Archia, Pro Plancio, Pro Scauro*. Recognovit brevique adnotatione critica instruxit, Oxford 1911.

Cohen, S. T.: 'Cicero's Roman Exile', in: J. F. Gaertner (ed.), *Writing Exile: The Discourse of Displacement in Greco-Roman Antiquity and Beyond*, Leiden/Boston 2007 (Mnemosyne Suppl. 283), 109–28.

Cole, S.: *Cicero and the Rise of Deification at Rome*, Cambridge 2013.

Colin, J.: 'Luxe oriental et parfums masculins dans la Rome alexandrine (d'après Cicéron et Lucrèce)', *RBPh* 33, 1955, 5–19.

Constans, L. A.: *Un Correspondant de Cicéron: Ap. Claudius Pulcher*, Paris 1921.

Corbeill, A.: *Controlling Laughter: Political Humor in the Late Roman Republic*, Princeton (NJ) 1996.

Corbeill, A.: 'Dining Deviants in Roman Political Invective', in: J. P. Hallett/M. B. Skinner (eds.), *Roman Sexualities*, Princeton (NJ) 1997, 99–128.

Corbeill, A.: 'Ciceronian Invective', in: J. M. May (ed.), *Brill's Companion to Cicero: Oratory and Rhetoric*, Leiden/Boston/Köln 2002, 197–217.

Corbeill, A.: 'The Republican Body', in: N. Rosenstein/R. Morstein-Marx (eds.), *A Companion to the Roman Republic*, Malden (MA)/Oxford/Chichester 2006, 439–56.

Corbeill, A.: 'How not to Write like Cicero: *Pridie quam in exilium iret oratio*', *Ciceroniana On Line* 4.1, 2020, 17–36.

Courtney, E.: 'Notes on Cicero', *CR* 10, 1960, 95–9.

Courtney, E.: 'Notes on Ciceronian Manuscripts and Textual Criticism', *BICS* 10, 1963, 13–16.

Courtney, E.: 'Notes on Cicero's *Post reditum* speeches', *RhM* 132, 1989, 47–53.

Craig, C.: 'Audience Expectations, Invective, and Proof', in: J. Powell/J. Paterson (eds.), *Cicero the Advocate*, Oxford 2004, 187–214.

Crawford, J. W.: *M. Tullius Cicero: The Lost and Unpublished Orations*, Göttingen 1984 (Hypomnemata 80).

De Benedetti, G.: 'L'esilio di Cicerone e la sua importanza storico-politica', *Historia* [Milano] 3, 1929, 331–63, 539–68, 761–89.

Degl'Innocenti Pierini, R. (ed.): *Marco Tullio Cicerone. Lettere dall'esilio, dalle Epistulae ad Atticum, ad Familiares, ad Quintum fratrem. Introduzione, testo, traduzione, commento*, Firenze 1996 (Il Nuovo Melograno XXX).

Degl'Innocenti Pierini, R.: 'Orgoglio di esule: Su due frammenti di un'epistola di Q. Cecilio Metello Numidico', *Maia* 52, 2000, 249–58.

Degl'Innocenti Pierini, R.: 'Scenografie per un ritorno: La (ri)costruzione del personaggio Cicerone nelle orazioni *post reditum*', in: G. Petrone/A. Casamento (eds.), *Lo spettacolo della giustizia: Le orazioni di Cicerone*, Palermo 2006 (Leucone 10), 119–37.

DeLacy, P.: 'Cicero's Invective Against Piso', *TAPhA* 72, 1941, 49–58.

De Libero, L.: *Obstruktion: Politische Praktiken im Senat und in der Volksversammlung der ausgehenden römischen Republik (70–49 v. Chr.)*, Stuttgart 1992 (Hermes Einzelschriften 59).

De Marco, F.: 'Un nuovo codice del "Cicero novus" di Leonardo Bruni Aretino', *Aevum* 31, 1957, 186–9.

Desideri, S.: 'Il retroscena dell'orazione *Post reditum in senatu*', *GIF* 16, 1963, 238–42.

Dickey, E.: *Latin Forms of Address: From Plautus to Apuleius*, Oxford 2002.

Dighton, A.: '*Mutatio vestis*: Clothing and Political Protest in the Late Roman Republic', *Phoenix* 71, 2017, 345–69.

Doblhofer, E.: *Exil und Emigration: Zum Erlebnis der Heimatferne in der römischen Literatur*, Darmstadt 1987 (Impulse der Forschung 51).

Driediger-Murphy, L. G.: *Roman Republican Augury: Freedom and Control*, Oxford 2019 (Oxford Classical Monographs).

Dyck, A. R.: 'Cicero's *devotio*: The Rôles of *dux* and Scape-Goat in His *Post reditum* Rhetoric', *HSPh* 102, 2004, 299–314.

Edmondson, J.: 'Public Dress and Social Control in Late Republican and Early Imperial Rome', in: J. Edmondson/A. Keith (eds.), *Roman Dress and the Fabrics of Roman Culture*, Toronto/Buffalo/London 2008, 21–46.

Edwards, C.: *The Politics of Immorality in Ancient Rome*, Cambridge 1993.

Elster, M.: *Die Gesetze der mittleren römischen Republik: Text und Kommentar*, Darmstadt 2003.

Englisch, B.: *L. Calpurnius Piso Caesoninus, ein Zeitgenosse Ciceros*, PhD diss. München 1979.

Epstein, D. F.: *Personal Enmity in Roman Politics 218–43 BC*, London/New York/Sydney 1987.

Erler, M.: 'Erstes Kapitel: Epikur', in: H. Flashar (ed.), *Die Philosophie der Antike. Band 4. Die Hellenistische Philosophie*. Von Michael Erler, Hellmut Flashar, Günter Gawlick, Woldemar Görler, Peter Steinmetz, Basel 1994 (Grundriss der Geschichte der Philosophie. Begründet von Friedrich Ueberweg. Völlig neubearbeitete Ausgabe), 29–202.

Erler, M./Schofield, M.: 'Epicurean ethics', in: K. Algra/J. Barnes/J. Mansfeld/M. Schofield (eds.), *The Cambridge History of Hellenistic Philosophy*, Cambridge 1999, 642–74.

Fantham, E.: *Comparative Studies in Republican Latin Imagery*, Toronto 1972 (Phoenix Suppl. X).

Fantham, E.: 'Meeting the People: The Orator and the Republican *Contio* at Rome', in: L. Calboli Montefusco (ed.), *Papers on Rhetoric III*, Bologna 2000 (Università degli Studi di Bologna, Dipartimento di filologia classica e medioevale 5), 95–112.

Ferrary, J.-L.: '*Princeps legis* et *adscriptores*: La Collégialité des magistrats romains dans la procédure de proposition des lois', *RPh* 70, 1996, 217–46.

Fezzi, L.: 'Lex Clodia de iure et tempore legum rogandarum', *SCO* 45, 1995 [1997], 297–328.

Fezzi, L.: 'La legislazione tribunizia di Publio Clodio Pulchro (58 a.C.) e la ricerca del consenso a Roma', *SCO* 47, 2001, 245–340.

Fezzi, L.: *Il tribuno Clodio*, Roma/Bari 2008 (Biblioteca Essenziale Laterza 79, Storia antica).

Flaig, E.: 'Den Konsens mit dem Volk herstellen. Überlegungen zu den *contiones*', in: M. Haake/A.-C. Harders (eds.), *Politische Kultur und soziale Struktur der Römischen Republik: Bilanzen und Perspektiven: Akten der internationalen Tagung anlässlich des 70. Todestages von Friedrich Münzer (Münster, 18.–20. Oktober 2012)*, Stuttgart 2017, 517–34.

Fogel, J.: *Cicero and the "Ancestral Constitution": A Study of Cicero's contio Speeches*, PhD diss. Columbia University, New York 1994.

Fuhrmann, M.: *Cicero and the Roman Republic*. Translated by W. E. Yuill, Oxford/Cambridge (MA) 1992 [translation of 1990 German edition].

Gamberale, L.: 'Pseudociceroniana (*exil.* 6; 8)', *Invigilata Lucernis* 1, 1979, 77–88.

Gamberale, L.: 'Dal falso al vero Cicerone: Note critiche all'orazione *Pridie quam in exilium iret* e alla *Pro Rabirio perduellionis reo*, 31', in: *MOYΣA: Scritti in onore di Giuseppe Morelli*, Bologna 1997, 331–43 (Edizioni e saggi universitari di filologia classica 5), 331–43.

Gamberale, L.: 'Dalla retorica al centone nell'*Oratio pridie quam in exilium iret*: Aspetti della fortuna di Cicerone fra III e IV secolo', in: *Cultura latina pagana fra terzo e quinto secolo dopo Cristo. Atti del Convegno, Mantova, 9–11 ottobre 1995*, Firenze 1998 (Academia Nazionale Virgiliana di Scienze, Lettere e Arte: Miscellanea 6), 53–75.

Garcea, A.: *Cicerone in esilio: L'epistolario e le passioni*, Hildesheim/Zürich/New York 2005 (Spudasmata 103).

Gelzer, M.: *Caesar, der Politiker und Staatsmann*, Wiesbaden 1960.

Gelzer, M.: *Cicero: Ein biographischer Versuch*, Wiesbaden 1969; 2., erweiterte Auflage mit einer forschungsgeschichtlichen Einleitung und einer Ergänzungsbibliographie v. W. Riess, Stuttgart 2014.

Gelzer, M.: *Pompeius: Lebensbild eines Römers. Neudruck der Ausgabe von 1984 mit einem Forschungsüberblick und einer Ergänzungsbibliographie von Elisabeth Herrmann-Otto*, Stuttgart 2006.

Gelzer, M./Kroll, W./Philippson, R./Büchner, K.: 'Tullius (29): M. Tullius Cicero', *RE* VII A 1, 1939, 827–1274.

Glucker, J.: 'As has been rightly said … by me', *LCM* 13, 1988, 6–9.

Goldmann, F.: *Die Statthalter der römischen Provinzen von 60 bis 50 vor Christus: Politisches Handeln in einem Jahrzehnt der Krise*, PhD diss. Göttingen 2012.

Gnauk, R.: *Die Bedeutung des Marius und Cato maior für Cicero*, Berlin 1936 (Historische Abhandlungen 6).

Grasmück, E. L.: 'Ciceros Verbannung aus Rom: Analyse eines politischen Details', in: A. Lippold/N. Himmelmann (eds.), *Bonner Festgabe: Johannes Straub zum 65. Geburtstag am 18. Oktober 1977 dargebracht von Kollegen und Schülern*, Bonn 1977 (Beihefte der Bonner Jahrbücher 39), 165–77.

Grasmück, E. L.: *Exilium: Untersuchungen zur Verbannung in der Antike*, Paderborn/ München/Wien/Zürich 1978 (Rechts- und Staatswissenschaftliche Veröffentlichungen der Görres-Gesellschaft, Neue Folge, Heft 30).

Greenidge, A. H. J.: *The Legal Procedure of Cicero's Time*, Oxford/London/New York 1901.

Grillo, L.: *Cicero's De Provinciis Consularibus Oratio: Introduction and Commentary*, Oxford 2015 (American Philological Association, Texts and Commentaries Series).

Grimal, P.: *Études de chronologie cicéronienne (années 58 et 57 av. J.-C.)*, Paris 1967 (Collection d'Études Anciennes).

Gruen, E. S.: 'The *Lex Varia*', *JRS* 55, 1965a, 59–73.

Gruen, E. S.: 'The Exile of Metellus Numidicus', *Latomus* 24, 1965b, 576–80.

Gruen, E. S.: *Roman Politics and the Criminal Courts, 149–78 B.C.*, Cambridge (MA) 1968.

Gruen, E. S.: *The Last Generation of the Roman Republic*, Berkeley/Los Angeles/London 1974.

Guerriero, E.: 'Di una supposta 'causa capitale' assunta da Cicerone in favore di Aulo Gabinio, e nuovi dubbi intorno all'autenticità del discorso 'Post reditum ad Quirites'', *MC* 6, 1936, 160–6.

Gurlitt, L.: 'Lex Clodia de exilio Ciceronis', *Philologus* 59, 1900, 578–83.

Halm, K.: 'Interpolationen in Ciceronischen Reden aus dem codex Parisinus Nro. 7794 nachgewiesen', *RhM* 9, 1854, 321–50, 638.

Harrison, S. J.: 'Cicero's 'De temporibus suis': The Evidence Reconsidered', *Hermes* 118, 1990, 455–63.

Haury, A.: *L'Ironie et l'humour chez Cicéron*, PhD diss. Paris, Leiden 1955.

Haye, T.: *Oratio: Mittelalterliche Redekunst in lateinischer Sprache*, Leiden/Boston/Köln 1999 (Mittellateinische Studien und Texte XXVII).

Heibges, U.: 'Religion and Rhetoric in Cicero's Speeches', *Latomus* 28, 1969, 833–49.

Heinze, R.: 'Auctoritas', *Hermes* 60, 1925, 348–66.

Hellegouarc'h, J.: *Le vocabulaire latin des relations et des partis politiques sous la république*, Paris 1963, 2ème tir. rev. et corr., Paris 1972.

Herescu, N. J.: 'Les Trois Exils de Cicéron', in: *Atti del I Congresso internazionale di studi ciceroniani. Roma. Aprile 1959. Volume I*, Roma 1961, 137–56.

Heskel, J.: 'Cicero as Evidence for Attitudes to Dress in the Late Republic', in: J. L. Sebesta/L. Bonfante (eds.), *The World of Roman Costume*, Madison 1994 (Wisconsin Studies in Classics), 133–45.

Hiebel, D.: *Rôles institutionnel et politique de la contio sous la République romaine (287–49 av. J.-C.)*, Paris 2009 (Romanité et Modernité du Droit).

Hill, T.: *Ambitiosa Mors: Suicide and Self in Roman Thought and Literature*, New York/ London 2004 (Studies in Classics 10).

Hodgson, L.: *Res Publica and the Roman Republic: 'Without Body or Form'*, Oxford 2017.

Hoffmann, W.: 'De fide et auctoritate orationis Ciceronianae quae inscribitur de haruspicum responso', in: *Programm des Victoria-Gymnasiums zu Burg (Nr. 187)*, Burg 1878, 3–20.

van Hooff, A. J. L.: *From Autothanasia to Suicide: Self-Killing in Classical Antiquity*, London/New York 1990.

Hughes, J. J.: 'Piso's Eyebrows', *Mnemosyne* 45, 1992, 234–37.

Humbert, M.: *Municipium et civitas sine suffragio: L'Organisation de la conquête jusqu'à la guerre sociale*, Roma 1978 (CEFR 36).

Hutchinson, G. O.: 'Rhythm, Style, and Meaning in Cicero's Prose', *CQ* 45, 1995, 485–99.

Hutchinson, G.: *Plutarch's Rhythmic Prose*, Oxford 2018.

Jeep, J.: 'Zu Ciceros Reden', *Jahrbücher für classische Philologie* 6 / *Jahnsche Jahrbücher für Philologie und Paedagogik* 81, 1860, 613–23.

Jeep, J.: 'Kritische Bemerkungen zu Ciceros Reden', in: *Zu der auf den 14. April angesetzten öffentlichen Prüfung der Schüler des Herzoglichen Gymnasiums in Wolfenbüttel ladet ehererbietigst ein Justus Jeep, Director und Professor: Kritische Bemerkungen zu Ciceros Reden: Schulnachrichten*, Wolfenbüttel 1862, 1–12.

Jeep, J.: 'Kritische Bemerkungen zu Ciceros Reden', in: *Zu der auf den 30. März angesetzten öffentlichen Prüfung der Schüler des Herzoglichen Gymnasiums in Wolfenbüttel ladet ehererbietigst ein Justus Jeep, Director und Professor: Kritische Bemerkungen zu Ciceros Reden: Schulnachrichten*, Wolfenbüttel 1863, 1–10.

Johannemann, R.: *Cicero und Pompeius in ihren wechselseitigen Beziehungen bis zum Jahre 51 vor Christi Geburt*, PhD diss. Münster, Emsdetten 1935.

Johnson, W. R.: *Luxuriance and Economy: Cicero and the Alien Style*, Berkeley/Los Angeles/London 1971 (University of California Publications: Classical Studies 6).

Karsten, H. T.: 'Cicero: Orationes post reditum tres', *Mnemosyne* 7, 1879, 399–410.

Kaser, M.: *Das römische Privatrecht. Erster Abschnitt: Das altrömische, das vorklassische und klassische Recht*, München 1955 (HbdA III.3.1).

Kaster, R. A.: *Marcus Tullius Cicero: Speech on Behalf of Publius Sestius: Translated with Introduction and Commentary*, Oxford 2006 (Clarendon Ancient History Series).

Kaster, R. A.: 'Some Passionate Performances in Late Republican Rome', in: R. K. Balot (ed.), *A Companion to Greek and Roman Political Thought*, Chichester 2009, 308–20.

Keeline, T. J.: *The Reception of Cicero in the Early Roman Empire: The Rhetorical Schoolroom and the Creation of a Cultural Legend*, Cambridge 2018.

Keeline, T./Kirby, T.: '*Auceps syllabarum*: A Digital Analysis of Latin Prose Rhythm', *JRS* 109, 2019, 161–204.

Kelly, G. P.: *A History of Exile in the Roman Republic*, Cambridge 2006.

Kennedy, G. A.: 'Cicero's Oratorical and Rhetorical Legacy', in: J. M. May (ed.), *Brill's Companion to Cicero. Oratory and Rhetoric*, Leiden/Boston/Köln 2002, 481–501.

Klass, J.: *Cicero und Caesar: Ein Beitrag zur Aufhellung ihrer gegenseitigen Beziehungen*, PhD diss. Gießen, Berlin 1939.

Klodt, C.: 'Prozessparteien und politische Gegner als *dramatis personae*: Charakterstilisierung in Ciceros Reden', in: B.-J. Schröder/J.-P. Schröder (eds.), *Studium declamatorium: Untersuchungen zu Schulübungen und Prunkreden von der Antike bis zur Neuzeit*, München/Leipzig 2003 (BzA 176), 35–101.

Klotz, A.: 'Zur Kritik einiger ciceronischer Reden (*pro Caelio* und *de domo*)', *RhM* 67, 1912, 358–90.

Klotz, A.: 'Zur Kritik einiger ciceronischer Reden. II. (*cum senatui gratias egit, cum populo gratias egit, de domo*)', *RhM* 68, 1913, 477–514.

Klotz, A.: 'Sprachliche Bemerkungen zu einigen Stellen in Ciceros Reden', *Glotta* 6, 1915, 212–23.

Koster, S.: *Die Invektive in der griechischen und römischen Literatur*, Meisenheim am Glan 1980 (Beiträge zur Klassischen Philologie 99).

Kranz, P.: *Beneficium im politischen Sprachgebrauch der ausgehenden Republik*, PhD diss. Münster 1964.

K.-St.: Kühner, R.: *Ausführliche Grammatik der lateinischen Sprache: Zweiter Teil: Satzlehre*, neu bearb. v. C. Stegmann, 2 vols., 2nd ed., Hannover 1914, 5th ed., Darmstadt 1976 mit Zusätzen und Berichtigungen v. A. Thierfelder (repr.).

Kumaniecki, K.: 'De numeris Tullianis et arte critica factitanda observationes aliquot', *Ciceroniana* 1, 1973, 69–82.

Kunkel, W./Wittmann, R.: *Staatsordnung und Staatspraxis der römischen Republik.* Von W. Kunkel †. *Zweiter Abschnitt. Die Magistratur.* Von W. Kunkel † und R. Wittmann, München 1995 (HbdA X.3.2.2).

La Bua, G.: *Cicero and Roman Education: The Reception of the Speeches and Ancient Scholarship*, Cambridge 2019.

La Farina, R.: 'L'esilio eroico, ovvero la *devotio* di Cicerone', in: G. Picone (ed.), *Clementia Caesaris: Modelli etici, parenesi e retorica dell'esilio*, Palermo 2008 (Letteratura classica 31), 327–43.

Lahmeyer, G.: *Orationis de haruspicum responso habitae originem Tullianum defendit*, Göttingen 1850.

Lange, M.: *De Ciceronis altera post reditum oratione commentatio*, PhD diss. Leipzig, Dresden 1875.

Laurand, L.: *Études sur le style des discours de Cicéron. Avec une esquisse de l'histoire du 'cursus'.* 4ᵉ édition, revue et corrigée, Paris 1936–8 (repr. Amsterdam 1965).

Lausberg, H.: *Handbook of Literary Rhetoric: A Foundation of Literary Study.* Foreword by G. A. Kennedy. Translated by M. T. Bliss, A. Jansen, D. E. Orton. Edited by D. E. Orton & D. Anderson, Leiden/Boston/Köln 1998 [translated from original German edition first published in 1960].

Lebreton, J.: *Études sur la langue et la grammaire de Cicéron*, Paris 1901.

Lehmann, C. A.: 'Quaestiones Tullianae. Pars IV', *Hermes* 15, 1880, 348–55.

Lenaghan, J. O.: *A Commentary on Cicero's Oration De haruspicum responso*, Den Haag/ Paris 1969 (Studies in Classical Literature).

Lentano, M.: 'Il dono e il debito: Verso un'antropologia del beneficio nella cultura romana', in: A. Haltenhoff/A. Heil/F.-H. Mutschler (eds.), *Römische Werte als Gegenstand der Altertumswissenschaft*, München/Leipzig 2005 (BzA 227), 125–42.

Leo, F.: Review of 'P. Cornelii Taciti dialogus de oratoribus, edited with prolegomena, critical apparatus, exegetical and critical notes, bibliography and indexes by Alfred Gudeman. Boston, Ginn and company, 1894. CXL, 447 S.', *GGA* 160.3, 1898, 169–88.

Leopold, H. M.: *De orationibus quatuor, quae iniuria Ciceroni vindicantur: Specimen litterarium inaugurale*, Leiden 1900.

Léovant-Cirefice, V.: 'Le Rôle de l'apostrophe aux *Quirites* dans les discours de Cicéron adressés au peuple', in: G. Achard/M. Ledentu (eds.), *Orateurs, auditeurs, lecteurs: à propos de l'éloquence romaine à la fin de la République et au début du Principat: Actes de la table-ronde du 31 janvier 2000*, Lyon/Paris 2000 (Collection du Centre d'Études et de Recherches sur l'Occident Romain, Nouvelle série no 21), 43–55 (56: discussion).

Lintott, A. W.: 'Clodius Pulcher: *Felix Catilina?*', *G&R* 14, 1967, 157–69.

Lintott, A.: *Imperium Romanum: Politics and Administration*, London/New York 1993.

Lintott, A.: *The Constitution of the Roman Republic*, Oxford 1999a.

Lintott, A.: *Violence in Republican Rome*, 2nd ed., Oxford 1999b.

Lintott, A.: *Cicero as Evidence. A Historian's Companion*, Oxford 2008.

Loutsch, C.: *L'Exorde dans les discours de Cicéron*, Bruxelles 1994 (Collection Latomus 224).

Lovano, M.: *The Age of Cinna: Crucible of Late Republican Rome*, Stuttgart 2002 (Historia Einzelschriften 158).

LPPR: Rotondi, G.: *Leges publicae populi Romani: Elenco cronologico con una introduzione sull'attività legislativa dei comizi romani: Estratto dalla Enciclopedia Giuridica Italiana*, Milano 1912 (repr. Hildesheim 1966: Mit Nachtrag aus G. Rotondi, Scritti Giuridici, I, Milano 1922).

Lucas, T.: 'Quaestiuncularum Tullianarum specimen', in: *Programm des Gymnasii zu Hirschberg 1837*, Hirschberg 1837, 3–12.

Luterbacher, F.: 'Ciceros Reden. 1910–1912', *Jahresberichte des Philologischen Vereins zu Berlin* 38, 1912, 333–68.

MacDowell, D. M.: 'Piso's Face', *CR* 14, 1964, 9–10.

MacGillivray, E. D.: 'The Popularity of Epicureanism in Late-Republic Roman Society', *Ancient World* 43, 2012, 151–72.

Mack, D.: *Senatsreden und Volksreden bei Cicero*, Würzburg 1937, repr. Hildesheim 1967 (Kieler Arbeiten zur klassischen Philologie 2); partly reprinted (III. Hauptteil, Kapitel 1, pp. 80–92) entitled: 'Der Stil der Ciceronischen Senatsreden und Volksreden', in: B. Kytzler (ed.), *Ciceros literarische Leistung*, Darmstadt 1973 (WdF CCXL), 210–24.

MacKendrick, P.: *The Speeches of Cicero: Context, Law, Rhetoric* (with the technical assistance of Emmett L. Bennett, jr.), London 1995.

Mackie, N.: '*Popularis* Ideology and Popular Politics at Rome in the First Century B.C.', *RhM* 135, 1992, 49–73.

Madvig I. N.: *Adversaria critica ad scriptores Graecos et Latinos: Vol. II: Emendationes Latinae*, Copenhagen 1873.

Madvig I. N.: *Adversariorum criticorum ad scriptores Graecos et Latinos Volumen tertium: Novae emendationes Graecas et Latinas continens*, Copenhagen 1884.

Mannsperger, M.: *Frisurenkunst und Kunstfrisur: Die Haarmode der römischen Kaiserinnen von Livia bis Sabina*, Bonn 1998.

Marinone, N.: *Cronologia ciceroniana*, Roma/Bologna 1997, Seconda edizione aggiornata e corretta con nuova versione interattiva in Cd Rom, a cura di E. Malaspina, Roma/Bologna 2004 (Collana di studi ciceroniani VI).

Markland, J.: *Remarks on the Epistles of Cicero to Brutus and of Brutus to Cicero: In a Letter to a Friend: With a Dissertation upon Four Orations ascribed to M. Tullius Cicero: viz. 1. Ad Quirites post reditum, 2. Post reditum in Senatu, 3. Pro Domo sua, ad Pontifices, 4. De Haruspicum responsis. To Which Are Added, Some Extracts of the Notes of Learned Men upon those Orations; And Observations on Them*, London 1745.

Maslowski, T.: 'Domus Milonis Oppugnata', *Eos* 64, 1976, 20–30.

Maslowski, T.: 'Notes on Cicero's Four *Post reditum* Orations', *AJPh* 101, 1980, 404–20.

Maslowski, T.: 'Some Remarks on London, British Library, MS Harley 4927', *RhM* 125, 1982, 141–61.

Maslowski, T./Rouse, R. H.: 'The Manuscript Tradition of Cicero's Post-Exile Orations. Part I: The Medieval History', *Philologus* 128, 1984, 60–124.

May, J. M.: 'The Rhetoric of Advocacy and Patron-Client Identification: Variation on a Theme', *AJPh* 102, 1981, 308–15.

May, J. M.: *Trials of Character: The Eloquence of Ciceronian Ethos*, Chapel Hill/London 1988.

May, J. M.: 'Cicero and the Beasts', *Syllecta Classica* 7, 1996, 143–53.

Meister, J. B.: 'Pisos Augenbrauen: Zur Lesbarkeit aristokratischer Körper in der späten römischen Republik', *Historia* 58, 2009, 71–95.

Mitchell, T. N.: *Cicero: The Ascending Years*, New Haven/London 1979.

Mitchell, T. N.: 'The *Leges Clodiae* and *obnuntatio*', *CQ* 36, 1986, 172–6.

Mitchell, T. N.: *Cicero: The Senior Statesman*, New Haven/London 1991.

Mommsen, *StR*: Mommsen, T.: *Römisches Staatsrecht*, 3 vols., Leipzig 1871–88 (Handbuch der römischen Alterthümer, Erster bis dritter Band) (repr.).

Moreau, P.: 'La lex Clodia sur le bannissement de Cicéron', *Athenaeum* 75, 1987, 465–92.

Moreau, P.: 'La *rogatio* des huit tribuns de 58 av. J.-C. et les clauses de *sanctio* reglementant l'abrogation des lois', *Athenaeum* 77, 1989a, 151–78.

Moreau, P.: 'La Relation de pseudo-filiation entre questeur et préteur: les vicissitudes d'un modèle politique romain tiré des relations de parenté', in: F. Thelamon (ed.), *Aux sources de la puissance: sociabilité et parenté: Actes du Colloque de Rouen, 12–13 novembre 1987*, Rouen 1989b (Publications de l'Université de Rouen 148), 37–46.

Morstein-Marx, R.: *Mass Oratory and Political Power in the Late Roman Republic*, Cambridge 2004.

Mouritsen, H.: *Plebs and Politics in the Late Roman Republic*, Cambridge 2001.

Mouritsen, H.: 'From Meeting to Text: The *Contio* in the Late Republic', in: C. Steel/H. van der Blom (eds.), *Community and Communication: Oratory and Politics in Republican Rome*, Oxford 2013, 63–82.

MRR 1: Broughton, T. R. S.: *The Magistrates of the Roman Republic. Vol. I. 509 B.C.–100 B.C.*, New York 1951 (Philological Monographs, Number XV, Vol. I).

MRR 2 Broughton, T. R. S.: *The Magistrates of the Roman Republic. Vol. II. 99 B.C.–31 B.C.*, New York 1952 (Philological Monographs, Number XV, Vol. II).

MRR 3: Broughton, T. R. S.: *The Magistrates of the Roman Republic. Vol. III. Supplement*, Atlanta (GA) 1986 (Philological Monographs, Number XV, Vol. III).

Müller, F.: Review of 'H. M. Leopold, *De orationibus quatuor, quae iniuria Ciceroni vindicantur. Specimen litterarium inaugurale*. Leyden 1900, S. C. van Doesburgh. 109 S. 8', *BPhW* 20.25, 1900, 777–81.

Naiden, F. S.: *Ancient Supplication*, Oxford 2006.

Narducci, E.: 'Perceptions of Exile in Cicero: The Philosophical Interpretation of a Real Experience', *AJPh* 118, 1997, 55–73; repr. as 'Percezioni dell'esilio in Cicerone. Esperienza vissuta e interpretazione filosofica', in: E. Narducci, *Cicero e i suoi interpreti: Studi sull'opera e la fortuna*, Pisa 2004 (Testi e studi di cultura classica 29), 95–113.

Nicholson, J.: *Cicero's Return from Exile: The Orations Post reditum*, New York/San Francisco/Bern/Baltimore/Frankfurt am Main/Berlin/Wien/Paris 1992 (Lang

Classical Studies 4) [see reviews: C. P. Craig, *CO* 72.2, 1995, 70–71; D. H. Berry, *CR* 45, 1995, 36–7; P. M. Martin, *Latomus* 55, 1996, 464–5].

Nicolet, C.: '«*Consul togatus*». Remarques sur le vocabulaire politique de Cicéron et de Tite-Live', *REL* 38, 1960, 236–63.

Nippel, W.: 'Publius Clodius Pulcher – «Der Achill der Straße»', in: K.-J. Hölkeskamp/E. Stein-Hölkeskamp (eds.), *Von Romulus zu Augustus: Große Gestalten der römischen Republik*, München 2000, 277–91.

Nisbet, R. G. (ed.): *M. Tulli Ciceronis De domo sua ad pontifices oratio*, Oxford 1939.

Nisbet, R. G. M. (ed.): *M. Tulli Ciceronis In L. Calpurnium Pisonem oratio. Edited with text, introduction, and commentary*, Oxford 1961 (repr.).

Nisbet, R. G. M.: 'Cola and Clausulae in Cicero's Speeches', in: E. M. Craik (ed.), '*Owls to Athens': Essays on Classical Subjects Presented to Sir Kenneth Dover*, Oxford 1990, 349–59, repr. in: R. G. M. Nisbet, *Collected Papers on Latin Literature*, ed. by S. J. Harrison, Oxford 1995, 312–24.

Novotný, N. F.: 'Rhythmické poznámky k Ciceronově řeči Cum senatui gratias egit', in: *Sborník Prací Filologickych Universitnímu Professoru F. Grohovi*, Prague 1925, 25–34.

Nowak, K.: *Der Einsatz privater Garden in der späten römischen Republik*, PhD diss. München 1973.

van Ooteghem, J.: *Lucius Licinius Lucullus*, Bruxelles 1959 (Académie Royale de Belgique, Classe des Lettres, Mémoires, Collection in-8°. Deuxième série, Tome LIII, fasc. 4).

van Ooteghem, J.: *Les Caecilii Metelli de la république*, Bruxelles 1967 (Académie Royale de Belgique, Classe des Lettres, Mémoires, Collection in-8°. Deuxième série, Tome LIX, fasc. I).

Opelt, I.: *Die lateinischen Schimpfwörter and verwandte sprachliche Erscheinungen: Eine Typologie*, Heidelberg 1965.

Otto, A.: *Die Sprichwörter und sprichwörtlichen Redensarten der Römer. Gesammelt und erklärt*, Leipzig 1890.

Paratte, V.: *Étude du discours de Cicéron, Ad Quirites post reditum*, Mémoire pour l'obtention de la licence des Lettres, Fribourg 1963.

Peck, A. G.: *Haec Patria Est: The Conceptualisation, Function and Nature of patria in the Roman World*, PhD diss. Warwick 2016.

Peirano, I.: *The Rhetoric of the Roman Fake: Latin Pseudepigrapha in Context*, Cambridge 2012.

Peterson, W.: 'Cicero's *Post reditum* and Other Speeches', *CQ* 4, 1910, 167–77.

Pina Polo, F.: *Las contiones civiles y militares en Roma*, Zaragoza 1989.

Pina Polo, F.: *Contra arma verbis: Der Redner vor dem Volk in der späten römischen Republik.* Aus dem Spanischen von Edda Liess, Stuttgart 1996 (Heidelberger Althistorische Beiträge und Epigraphische Studien 22).

Pina Polo, F.: '*Contio, auctoritas* and Freedom of Speech in Republican Rome', in: S. Benoist (ed.), *Rome, a City and Its Empire in Perspective: The Impact of the Roman World through Fergus Millar's Research/Rome, une cité impériale en jeu: L'impact du monde romain selon Fergus Millar*, Leiden/Boston 2012 (Impact of Empire 16), 45–58.

Pinkster, H.: *The Oxford Latin Syntax. Volume I: The Simple Clause*, Oxford 2015.

Pohl, H.: *Die römische Politik und die Piraterie im östlichen Mittelmeer vom 3. bis zum 1. Jh. v. Chr.*, Berlin 1993 (UaLG 42).

Powell, J. G. F.: 'Invective and the orator: Ciceronian Theory and Practice', in: J. Booth (ed.), *Cicero on the Attack. Invective and Subversion in the Orations and Beyond*, Swansea 2007, 1–23.

Primmer, A.: *Cicero numerosus: Studien zum antiken Prosarhythmus*, Graz/Wien/Köln 1968 (Österreichische Akademie der Wissenschaften, Philosophisch-Historische Klasse, Sitzungsberichte, 257. Band).

Raccanelli, R.: *Cicerone, Post reditum in Senatu e Ad Quirites: Come disegnare una mappa di relazioni*, Bologna 2012 (Testi e manuali per l'insegnamento universitario del latino, Nuova serie 125).

Rafferty, D.: *Provincial Allocations in Rome, 123–52 BCE*, Stuttgart 2019 (Historia Einzelschriften 254).

Rampulla, S.: 'Orizzonti incrociati: Il conflitto apparente fra rappresentazione stoica dell'esilio e *mos maiorum* in Cicerone e Seneca', in: G. Picone (ed.), *Clementia Caesaris: Modelli etici, parenesi e retorica dell'esilio*, Palermo 2008 (Letteratura classica 31), 307–25.

Ramsey, J. T.: 'The Date of the Consular Elections in 63 and the Inception of Catiline's Conspiracy', *HSPh* 110, 2019, 213–69.

Rauschen, G.: *Ephemerides Tullianae rerum inde ab exsilio Ciceronis (mart. LVIII a. Chr.) usque ad extremum annum LIV gestarum*, PhD diss. Bonn 1886.

Rawson, E.: *Cicero: A Portrait*, London 1975.

Renda, C.: '*Pisonis supercilium*: Tratti e ritratti nella Pro Sestio di Cicerone', *BStudLat* 32, 2002, 395–405.

Riggsby, A. M.: 'The *Post Reditum* Speeches', in: J. M. May (ed.), *Brill's Companion to Cicero: Oratory and Rhetoric*, Leiden/Boston/Köln 2002, 159–95.

Robb, M. A.: *Beyond Populares and Optimates: Political Language in the Late Republic*, Stuttgart 2010.

Robinson, A.: 'Cicero's References to His Banishment', *CW* 87.6, 1994, 475–80.

Rollinger, C.: 'Die kleinen Freunde des großen Pompeius: *Amicitiae* und Gefolge in der Späten Republik', in: G.-P. Schietinger (ed.), *Gnaeus Pompeius Magnus: Ausnahmekarrierist, Netzwerker und Machtstratege: Beiträge zur Heidelberger Pompeius-Tagung am 24. September 2014*, Rahden 2019 (Pharos 43), 93–137.

Roloff, H.: *Maiores bei Cicero*, PhD diss. Leipzig, Göttingen 1938.

Roman Statutes: Crawford, M. H. (ed.): *Roman Statutes*, 2 vols., London 1996 (BICS Suppl. 64).

Rouse, R. H./Reeve, M. D.: 'Cicero: Speeches', in: L. D. Reynolds (ed.), *Texts and Transmission: A Survey of the Latin Classics*, Oxford 1983, 54–98.

Rück, C.: 'De M. Tulli Ciceronis oratione de domo sua ad pontifices', in: *Programma Gymnasii Guilielmini Monacensis MDCCCLXXXI*, München 1881, 3–62.

Rundell, W. M. F.: 'Cicero and Clodius: The Question of Credibility', *Historia* 28, 1979, 301–28.

Ryan, F. X.: *Rank and Participation in the Republican Senate*, Stuttgart 1998.

Sanford, E. M.: 'The Career of Aulus Gabinius', *TAPhA* 70, 1939, 64–92.

Savels, I. A.: *Disputatio de vindicandis M. Tull. Ciceronis quinque orationibus, Post reditum in senatu, Ad Quirites post reditum, Pro domo sua ad pontifices, De haruspicum responsis, Pro M. Marcello*, Köln 1828.

Savels, I. A.: *M. Tull. Ciceronis oratio post reditum in senatu. Cum notis J. Marklandi, J. M. Gesneri, F. A. Wolfii, P. Manutii, Garatonii, aliorum edidit et ab iniectis suspicionibus defendit Jo. Aug. Savelius*, Köln 1830.

Schaum, L.: 'De consecratione domus Ciceronianae', in: *Programm des Großherzoglichen Gymnasiums zu Mainz. Schuljahr 1888–89*, Mainz 1889, 3–8.

Schofield, M.: 'Cicero's Definition of *Res Publica*', in: J. G. F. Powell (ed.), *Cicero the Philosopher: Twelve Papers*, Oxford 1995, 63–83.

Schönberger, J. K.: 'Mitteilungen: Zu Cicero', *Wochenschrift für Klassische Philologie* 30.50, 1913, 1381–3.

Schönberger, J. K.: 'Mitteilungen: Zu Ciceros Reden', *Wochenschrift für Klassische Philologie* 31.23, 1914, 645–6.

Seager, R.: 'Clodius, Pompeius and the Exile of Cicero', *Latomus* 24, 1965, 519–31.

Seager, R.: 'Cicero and the Word *popularis*', *CQ* 22, 1972, 328–38.

Seager, R.: *Pompey the Great: A Political Biography. Second Edition*, Oxford/Malden (MA) 2002.

Seager, R.: Review of Lintott 2008, *JRS* 99, 2009, 222–27.

Seager, R.: 'The (Re/De)Construction of Clodius in Cicero's Speeches', *CQ* 64, 2014, 226–40.

Sellars, J.: *Stoicism*, Chesham 2006 (Ancient Philosophies).

Shackleton Bailey, D. R.: 'Two Tribunes, 57 B.C.', *CR* 12, 1962, 195–6.

Shackleton Bailey, D. R.: *Cicero*, London 1971.

Shackleton Bailey, D. R.: 'On Cicero's Speeches', *HSPh* 83, 1979, 237–85.

Shackleton Bailey, D. R.: 'More on Cicero's Speeches (*Post reditum*)', *HSPh* 89, 1985, 141–51.

Shackleton Bailey, D. R.: 'On Cicero's Speeches (*Post reditum*)', *TAPhA* 117, 1987, 271–80.

Shackleton Bailey, D. R.: *Onomasticon to Cicero's Speeches. Second revised edition*, Stuttgart/Leipzig 1992.

Spielvogel, J.: *Amicitia und res publica: Ciceros Maxime während der innenpolitischen Auseinandersetzungen der Jahre 59–50 v. Chr.*, Stuttgart 1993.

Stabryla, S.: 'P. Clodius Pulcher: A Politician or a Terrorist?', in: J. Styka (ed.), *Violence and Aggression in the Ancient World*, Kraków 2006 (Classica Cracoviensia X), 203–15.

Starbatty, A.: *Aussehen ist Ansichtssache: Kleidung in der Kommunikation der römischen Antike*, München 2010 (Münchner Studien zur Alten Welt 7).

Steel, C.: *Reading Cicero: Genre and Performance in Late Republican Rome*, London 2005 (Duckworth Classical Essays).

Steel, C.: 'Name and Shame? Invective against Clodius and Others in the Post-Exile Speeches', in: J. Booth (ed.), *Cicero on the Attack. Invective and Subversion in the Orations and Beyond*, Swansea 2007, 105–28.

Stein, P.: *Die Senatssitzungen der Ciceronischen Zeit (68–43)*, PhD diss. Münster, Münster 1930.

Sternkopf, W.: 'Ueber die „Verbesserung" des Clodianischen Gesetzentwurfes de exilio Ciceronis', *Philologus* 59, 1900, 272–304.

Sternkopf, W.: 'Noch einmal die correctio der lex Clodia de exilio Ciceronis', *Philologus* 61, 1902, 42–70.

Sternkopf, W.: 'Jahresbericht über Ciceros Briefe 1901-1907', *Jahresbericht über die Fortschritte der klassischen Altertumswissenschaft*, Jg. 36, Bd. 139, 1908, 1–80.

Stock, G.: 'De recensenda Ciceronis oratione quam habuit cum senatui gratias egit', in: *Genethliacon Gottingense. Miscellanea philologica in honorem Seminarii regii philologici Gottingensis scripserumt philologi Gottingenses XXIV*, Halle 1888, 106–111.

Stroh, W.: '*De Domo Sua*: Legal Problem and Structure', in: J. Powell/J. Paterson (eds.), *Cicero the Advocate*, Oxford 2004, 313–70.

Stuart Staveley, E.: *Greek and Roman Voting and Elections*, London 1972 (Aspects of Greek and Roman Life).

Sumner, G. V.: 'Lex Aelia, Lex Fufia', *AJPh* 84, 1963, 337–58.

Swain, S: 'Bilingualism in Cicero? The Evidence of Code-Switching', in: J. N. Adams/ M. Janse/S. Swain (eds.), *Bilingualism in Ancient Society: Language Contact and the Written Text*, Oxford 2002, 128–67.

Sydow, R.: 'Kritische Beiträge zu Ciceros Reden', *Philologus* 92, 1937, 224–38.

Sydow, R.: 'Kritische Beiträge zu Ciceros vier Reden nach seiner Rückkehr', *RhM* 90, 1941, 77–79, 168–74.

Sydow, R.: 'Kritische Beiträge zu Cicero', *RhM* 92, 1944, 184–8, 353–65.

Taldone, A.: 'Su *insania* e *furor* in Cicerone', *BStudLat* 23, 1993, 3–19.

Tatum, W. J.: *The Patrician Tribune: Publius Clodius Pulcher*, Chapel Hill/London 1999 (Studies in the History of Greece and Rome).

Tatum, W. J.: 'The Late Republic: Autobiographies and Memoirs in the Age of the Civil Wars', in: G. Marasco (ed.), *Political Autobiographies and Memoirs in Antiquity: A Brill Companion*, Leiden 2011, 161–87.

Taylor, L. R.: *Party Politics in the Age of Caesar*, Berkeley/Los Angeles 1949 (Sather Classical Lectures 22).

Taylor, L. R.: *Roman Voting Assemblies: From the Hannibalic War to the Dictatorship of Caesar*, Ann Arbor 1966 (Jerome Lectures 8); repr. Ann Arbor 1990.

Taylor, L. R./Scott, R. T.: 'Seating Space in the Roman Senate and the *Senatores Pedarii*', *TAPhA* 100, 1969, 529–82.

Tempest, K.: *Cicero: Politics and Persuasion in Ancient Rome*, London 2011.

Thommen, L.: *Das Volkstribunat der späten römischen Republik*, Stuttgart 1989 (Historia Einzelschriften 59).

Thompson, C. E.: *To the Senate and to the People: Adaptation to the Senatorial and Popular Audiences in the Parallel Speeches of Cicero*, PhD diss. Ohio State University, Columbus 1978.

TLRR: Alexander, M. C.: *Trials in the Late Roman Republic, 149 BC to 50 BC*, Toronto/ Buffalo/London 1990 (Phoenix Suppl. XXVI).

Tondo, I.: 'Il volto criminale: La strategia del *corpore significare* nelle orazioni di Cicerone', *Pan* 21, 2003, 143–50.

Treggiari, S.: *Terentia, Tullia and Publilia: The Women of Cicero's Family*, London/New York 2007 (Women of the Ancient World).

Uría, J.: 'Personal Names and Invective in Cicero', in: J. Booth/R. Maltby (eds.), *What's in a Name? The Significance of Proper Names in Classical Latin Literature*, Swansea 2006, 13–31.

Venturini, C.: I '*privilegia*' da Cicerone ai romanisti', *Studia et Documenta Historiae et Iuris* 56, 1990, 155–96 (= *Processo penale e società politica nella Roma repubblicana*, Pisa 1996, 237–86, with Addenda, 286).

Verbeke, G.: 'Le Stoïcisme, une philosophie sans frontières', *ANRW* I 4, 1973, 3–42.

Vössing, K.: 'Mit Manuskript in den Senat! Zu Cic. Planc. 74', *RhM* 151, 2008, 143–50.

Weigel, R. D.: 'Meetings of the Roman Senate on the Capitoline', *AC* 55, 1986, 333–40.

Weinrib, E. J.: 'Obnuntiatio: Two Problems', *Zeitschrift der Savigny-Stiftung für Rechtsgeschichte, Romanistische Abteilung* 87, 1970, 395–425.

Williamson, C.: *The Laws of the Roman People: Public Law in the Expansion and Decline of the Roman Republic*, Ann Arbor 2005.

Wimmel, W.: 'Ciceros stellvertretendes Opfer: Zum Text der Oratio cum populo gratias egit, § 1', *Wiener Studien* N.F. 7, 1973, 105–12.

Wirszubski, C.: '*Audaces*: A Study in Political Phraseology', *JRS* 51, 1961, 12–22.

Wiseman, T. P.: 'Some Republican Senators and Their Tribes', *CQ* 14, 1964, 122–33.

Wiseman, T. P.: 'Where Was the *nova via*?', *PBSR* 72, 2004, 167–83.

Wissowa, G.: *Religion und Kultus der Römer*, München ²1912 (HbdA IV.5).

Zielinski, T.: *Das Clauselgesetz in Ciceros Reden: Grundzüge einer oratorischen Rhythmik*, Leipzig 1904 (Philologus Supplementband IX.4) [see review: A. C. Clark, *CR* 19, 1905, 164–72].

Major differences in the Latin text from the reference editions

Post reditum in senatu

This edition

Maslowski (1981)

4 quam meus inimicus promulgavit
9 quod ante in re publica {non} fuerat
13 non iuris <scientia> {studium}, non dicendi
 vi<s, non peri>tia rei militaris
33 ii hoc

cum meus inimicus promulgavit
quod ante in re publica non fuerat
non iuris <notitia> {studium}, non dicendi
 vi<s, non scien>tia rei militaris
in hoc

Post reditum ad Quirites

This edition

Maslowski (1981)

7 pietas atque
12 noctem
13 reconciliationes
20 tum se fuisse miserum
23 utcumque

auctoritas atque
* * * noctemque
<in> reconciliatione
<non> tum se fuisse miserum
† utrumcumque †

Pridie quam in exilium iret

This edition

De Marco (1991)

1 duxit
6 tardiores
6 lautissimeque
9 liberavi liberosque
15 delectus
22 repudiatum

dixit
tardiones
sanctissimeque
liberavi...liberosque
defectus
repudiantum

Index

This index provides references to pages of the Introduction and the Commentary for names of individuals and places as well as a selection of terms and concepts. For frequently mentioned items and individuals only the most relevant instances have been listed.